# LANGUAGE DEVELOPMENT

## THIRD EDITION

## ERIKA HOFF

*Florida Atlantic University*

**WADSWORTH**

**THOMSON LEARNING**

Australia • Canada • Mexico • Singapore • Spain
United Kingdom • United States

**WADSWORTH**

**THOMSON LEARNING**

Publisher: Vicki Knight
Assistant Editor: Jennifer Wilkinson
Editorial Assistant: Monica Sarmiento
Technology Project Manager: Darin Derstine
Marketing Manager: Dory Schaeffer
Marketing Assistant: Laurel Anderson
Advertising Project Manager: Brian Chaffee
Project Manager, Editorial Production: Catherine Morris
Art Director: Vernon Boes
Print/Media Buyer: Judy Inouye

Permissions Editor: Kiely Sexton
Production Service: Kelly Mabie, Graphic World Publishing Services
Text Designer: Lisa Henry
Photo Researcher: Kathleen Olson
Copy Editor: Jeanne Washington
Cover Designer: Irene Morris
Cover Image: Daly & Newton/Getty Images
Compositor: Graphic World, Inc.
Text and Cover Printer: Quebecor World/Kingsport

For more information about our products,
contact us at:
**Thomson Learning Academic Resource Center
1-800-423-0563**
For permission to use material from this text or product, submit a request online at **http://www.thomson-rights.com.**
Any additional questions about permissions can be submitted by email to
**thomsonrights@thomson.com.**

Library of Congress Control Number: 2004102961

ISBN 0-534-64170-9

**Thomson Wadsworth**
**10 Davis Drive**
**Belmont, CA 94002-3098**
**USA**

**Asia**
Thomson Learning
5 Shenton Way #01-01
UIC Building
Singapore 068808

**Australia/New Zealand**
Thomson Learning
102 Dodds Street
Southbank, Victoria 3006
Australia

**Canada**
Nelson
1120 Birchmount Road
Toronto, Ontario M1K 5G4
Canada

**Europe/Middle East/Africa**
Thomson Learning
High Holborn House
50/51 Bedford Row
London WC1R 4LR
United Kingdom

**Latin America**
Thomson Learning
Seneca, 53
Colonia Polanco
11560 Mexico D.F.
Mexico

**Spain/Portugal**
Paraninfo
Calle Magallanes, 25
28015 Madrid, Spain

To the children who are cited herein as sources of "personal data":

Mark, Alissa, Nicholas, Melanie, Alex, Julia, Kirsten, and Erik

At the dinner table—

Kirsten (aged 7 years): Are we having for dessert ice cream?

Author: Kirsten, *Are we having for dessert ice cream?* What kind of a sentence is that?

(A reflective pause)

Kirsten: You should write it down for your book.

# About the Author

**Erika Hoff** is Professor of Psychology at Florida Atlantic University. She has taught language development to undergraduate students for the past 20 years at the University of Wisconsin–Parkside and, since 1996, at Florida Atlantic University. She has held visiting scholar positions at Marquette University (Milwaukee), McGill University, and the National Institute of Child Health and Human Development. Dr. Hoff holds an M.S. in psychology from Rutgers–The State University of New Jersey (1976) and a Ph.D. in psychology from the University of Michigan (1981). She conducts research on the process of language development in typically developing monolingual and bilingual children and in children with language impairment. She has received funding for this research from the National Science Foundation, the National Institutes of Health, and the Spencer Foundation. Hoff's research has been published in *Child Development, Developmental Psychology, First Language, The Journal of Applied Psycholinguistics, The Journal of Child Language,* and the *Merrill-Palmer Quarterly*. She has contributed chapters to *Linguistic Disorders and Pathologies: An International Handbook* (1993), *The Handbook of Parenting* (2002), and the *Comprehensive Handbook of Psychology* (2003).

# BRIEF CONTENTS

CHAPTER

# Contents

CHAPTER

# PREFACE

To study language development is to consider the developing mind as it accomplishes one of its most astounding feats. I have tried, in this text, to introduce students to this field in a way that communicates both its content and its intellectual excitement. My aim in this book is to communicate the questions that are asked by researchers, the evidence that has been collected to address these questions, and the conclusions derived from this evidence that constitute our current state of knowledge. Understanding the questions is crucial, because if students do not understand the questions, they are not likely to be interested in the research findings that constitute the current answers. Also, in many areas of research, the questions are likely to outlive the tentative answers that the field can provide at this time. In discussing the theories that constitute the currently proposed answers, I have tried to present a balanced treatment that examines all sides of the arguments, even though this treatment is not strictly neutral. My goal is to help students understand the different theoretical points of view in the field and the evidence and reasoning that lead some to argue for and others to argue—with equal vigor—against each point of view. I also believe it is important for students to understand the research process. In presenting the findings in each area, I have tried to summarize the results from a comprehensive review of the literature and to show students where findings come from by presenting selected, illustrative studies in greater methodological detail.

This book was written for advanced undergraduate students. It does not assume that the reader has a background in any particular discipline; therefore, it can be used in courses taught in departments of psychology, linguistics, education, and communicative disorders. The text should also be suitable for graduate courses—to be used as a background and framework for readings from primary sources. The instructor's manual provides an outline of the central concepts in each chapter, questions to promote student discussion, suggested supplementary student activities, and a test bank of multiple-choice questions. Although this book does not assume any prior linguistic knowledge, it does not allow its readers to remain in that state. Some understanding of work in linguistics is necessary both to appreciate the magnitude of what every child accomplishes in acquiring language and to understand the research that asks how children manage this accomplishment. I have made every effort, however, not to intimidate the reader who is not linguistically inclined and to present the research in such a way that readers who miss the linguistic details can still appreciate the gist of what questions are being asked and why, and what conclusions the researchers are drawing. The central focus of this text is language development as a field of basic research, but applied issues are also considered. Chapter 1 provides an overview and history of the field and introduces the major questions about language development and the theoretical approaches to seeking answers that recur throughout the text. Chapter 2 considers the biological bases of language development, covering a wide range of topics, including the process of creolization, studies of brain injury and aphasia, the hypothesis of a critical period for language acquisition, studies of neurological correlates of language processing in intact children and adults, the genetics of language development, "wild children," the communication systems of other species, attempts to teach language to chimpanzees, and the evolution of the capacity for language in humans. Chapters 3 through 6 cover the major subcomponents of language development: Chapter 3 discusses phonological development; Chapter 4, lexical development; Chapter 5, the development of syntax and morphology; and Chapter 6, the development of communicative competence. Chapter 7 examines language development in special populations. These populations include children who are deaf, children who are blind, children with mental retardation, children with autism, and children with specific language impairment. Chapter 8 introduces the new and growing field of childhood bilingualism, and Chapter 9 discusses the language developments that occur during the school years, including the acquisition of literacy.

## NEW IN THE THIRD EDITION

Revisions made for the third edition have been shaped by feedback from users of the second edition and by developments in the field itself. The biggest changes from the second addition are substantial additions to the chapter on Childhood Bilingualism and the addition of a new chapter on Language in the School Years. All chapters have been updated to reflect the research published since the previous edition went to press.

## ACKNOWLEDGMENTS

It is a pleasure to publicly acknowledge those who contributed to this book's coming into being. I continue to owe a debt to Marilyn Shatz who first suggested (and persisted in suggesting) that I undertake the first edition. I would also like to thank my colleagues in the field who have used the earlier editions and whose enthusiasm for the book has encouraged me to create the third edition. Special thanks are due to Fred Genesee of McGill University and Peggy McCardle of the National Institute of Child Health and Human Development who arranged visiting appointments at their institutions during part of the time that I worked on this edition. I am grateful to many friends and colleagues who provided moral support, preprints of their work, and answers to specific questions. It has continued to be a personal and professional pleasure to work with my editor at Thomson Learning, Vicki Knight. I would also like to thank the many others at Thomson Learning who worked on producing this book.

This text is much better than it would have been otherwise because of the valuable comments provided by several reviewers. They are Eileen Abrahamsen, Old Dominion University; Farrell Ackerman, University of California–San Diego; Lynn Adams, Radford University; Michael Casby, Michigan State University; Jan Charles-Luce, University of Buffalo; Herbert Colston, University of Wisconsin–Parkside; Martha Dunkelberger, University of Houston; Joseph Galasso, California State University–Northridge; Jane Gaultney, University of North Carolina–Charlotte; Adele Goldberg, University of Illinois at Urbana; Carla Hudson, University of California–Berkeley; James Hunsicker, Southwestern Oklahoma State University; Laura Justice, University of Virginia–Charlottesville; Gretchen Kambe, University of Nevada–Las Vegas; Deborah Karres, San Francisco State University; Richard Meier, University of Texas–Austin; Lise Menn, University of Colorado–Boulder; David Minear, Iona College–New York; Betty Samraj, San Diego State University; Ann Tyler, University of Nevada–Reno; Rose-Marie Weber, SUNY–Albany; and Barbara Weitzner-Lin, Buffalo State College.

No child is safe from the pen and paper of an author looking for quotable examples of child language phenomena. Many of the quotations that are cited as personal data within the text come from my children, my nieces and nephews, and the children of friends. This book is dedicated to them.

*Erika Hoff*

# Introduction to the Study of Language Development

Somehow, in the span of just a few years, newborn infants who neither speak nor understand any language become young children who comment, question, and express their ideas in the language of their community. This change does not occur all at once. First, newborns' cries give way to coos and babbles. Then, infants who coo and babble start to show signs of comprehension such as turning when they hear their name. Infants then become toddlers who say *"bye-bye"* and *"all gone"* and start to label the people and objects in their environment. As their vocabularies continue to grow, children start to combine words. Children's first word combinations, such as *all gone juice* and *read me,* are short and are missing parts found in adults' sentences. Gradually children's immature sentences are replaced by longer and more adultlike sentences. As children learn to talk, their comprehension abilities also develop, typically in advance of their productive speech. As children master language, they also become masters at using language to serve their needs. One-year-olds who can only point and fuss to request something become 2-year-olds who say *"please";* later they become 4-year-olds capable of the linguistic and communicative sophistication of the child who excused himself from a boring experiment by saying, *"My mother says I have to go home now"* (Keller-Cohen, January 1978, personal communication).

This book is about these changes. It is about the *what* and *when* of language development—what changes take place and when they occur in the course of language development. It is also about the *how* and *why*. How do children learn to talk, and why is the development of language a universal feature of human development? In the following chapters, we will delve into these topics in detail. In this first chapter, we begin with an overview of the field we are about to study.

## LANGUAGE AND THE SCIENTIFIC STUDY OF LANGUAGE DEVELOPMENT

### A definition of language

Language is the systematic and conventional use of sounds (or signs or written symbols) for the purpose of communication or self-expression (Crystal, 1995). This definition is short and simple and, although true, it is misleading. It is difficult to capture the complexity of language in a short definition. The child who learns a language achieves the ability to recognize and produce a set of sounds and learns how these sounds can and cannot be combined into possible words. The child who learns English, for example, comes to know approximately 44 different consonants and vowels (Crystal, 1995) and that *pling* is a possible word but *gnilp* is not. By adulthood, the child who learns a language knows a vocabulary of tens of thousands of words. This vocabulary knowledge includes knowledge of each word's meaning and its possibilities for combination with other words. Adult speakers of English know, for example, that *give* and *donate* are synonyms, that *John gave a book to the library* and *John donated a book to the library* are perfectly fine sentences, that *John gave the library a book* is also fine, but that *John donated the library a book* is not. The child who learns a language also comes to know the multiple ways in which pieces of the language can and cannot be systematically combined to form words and sentences. *John kissed Mary* and *Mary kissed John* are both fine sentences, albeit with different meanings; *kissed* is made up of *kiss + ed,* and *Mary + ed John kiss* just does not work. The child who learns a language also comes to know how to combine sentences into larger units of discourse—to tell a story or have a conversation. As they learn a language, children learn to use that language to communicate in socially appropriate ways. They acquire the means to share their thoughts and feelings with others and the skill to do so differently with their peers and their grandparents. In a literate society, children also learn to use language in its written form. They master both a complex set of correspondences between written symbols and meanings and a literate style of language use.

Children develop these different sorts of language knowledge concurrently, and there are many mutual influences between developments in these different domains. It is useful, nonetheless, for researchers and for students of language development to make distinctions among the subcomponents of language. The sounds and sound system of a language constitute a language's **phonology.** The words and associated knowledge are the **lexicon.** The system for combining units of meaning (words and parts of words such as *–ed*) is **morphology;** the system for combining words into sentences is **syntax.** The knowledge that underlies successful and appropriate language use includes knowledge of **pragmatics** and **sociolinguistics.** Knowledge of reading and writing is referred to as **literacy.** We will define these components of linguistic knowledge further in later chapters. Readers with some background in language development or linguistics may be surprised not to find semantic development listed here. Semantics is the study of meaning, and certainly learning a language is learning a system for expressing meaning. Much of what is usually subsumed under the heading of semantic development is word meaning, which is discussed in this text in Chapter 4 on lexical development. The meanings expressed in word combinations are discussed in Chapter 5 on the development of language structure.

## A chronological overview of language development

In the chapters to follow, we will describe the course of language development in some detail and ask how children accomplish this remarkable feat. Here, as both overview and preview, we describe language development in broad outline. Figure 1.1 presents the major milestones of language develop-

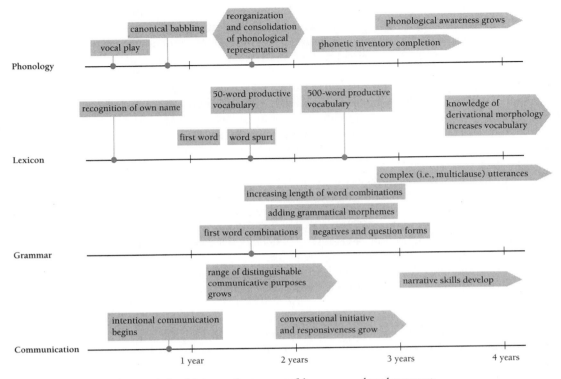

**Figure 1.1**   Major milestones of language development

ment on separate time lines for each language component. If you scan all four time lines from left to right, you can see that from birth to 1 year children change in the sounds they produce and in the communicativeness of their behavior. By 6 months children recognize their name and by 8 to 10 months children begin to understand a few words, but for most children there is very little productive speech before 1 year. We know from experimental studies, however, that these seemingly prelinguistic babies are learning about the sounds and even the grammatical properties of their language.

During the second year, the most obvious development is in the domain of vocabulary. Children typically begin this year by producing their first word, and by the end of the year they have a productive vocabulary of 300 words and are producing word combinations (Fenson et al., 1994). Their words do not sound quite adultlike. Both articulation abilities and underlying phonological representations undergo changes during this second year. Children are also becoming more communicative. Both the frequency and conversational relevance of their communicative acts increase.

During the third year of life, the most obvious development is children's increasing mastery of the grammar of their language. Typically, children start this year producing two- and three-word affirmative, declarative sentences that lack grammatical endings, such as plural markers and past tense markers, on nouns and verbs. By the end of the third year, children are producing full sentences, including questions and negated forms with most grammatical devices in place. Vocabulary continues to grow, articulation of sounds improves, and children begin to develop an awareness of the phonological properties of their language—as evidenced, for example, in their appreciation of rhymes. Children's conversational skills increase, and they begin to introduce short accounts of past events into their conversations.

The period from 3 to 4 is largely one of refining and further developing the skills that are already in place. The most obvious new development occurs in the area of grammar, where children start to produce complex, multiclause sentences. Because there is nothing completely missing from the linguistic competence of most 4-year-old children, it is commonly said that language acquisition is completed during the first 4 years of life. Although there is some truth to that statement, language skills continue to grow in every domain after the age of 4. Articulation, vocabulary, sentence structure, and communicative skills all develop. There are also major transitions involved as children move from a home to a school environment and learn new ways of using language; literacy development is further associated with changes in language knowledge. We will return to each of these developments in future chapters.

## Reasons for the scientific study of language development

***Language development as a basic research topic.*** A child who has acquired language has acquired an incredibly complex and powerful system. If we understood how children accomplish this task, we would know something substantial about how the human mind works. The modern field of language development emerged in the 1950s when it became clear that language acquisition would serve as a test for rival theories of how change in human behavior occurs (Gardner, 1985; Pinker, 1984). In the 1950s, two psychological theories were pitted against each other: behaviorism and cognitivism. According to **behaviorism,** change in behavior occurs in response to the consequences of prior behavior. Most readers are familiar with clear examples supporting this view. For instance, rats who initially do not press levers come to press levers after receiving food pellets for producing behaviors that increasingly approximate lever pressing. Radical behaviorism holds that all behavior can be accounted for in this way. A central tenet of behaviorism is the belief that it is not necessary to discern what goes on in the mind of the rat in order to explain the change in the rat's behavior; behavior can be fully accounted for in terms of things external to the mind.

**Cognitivism** asserts the opposite—that we cannot understand behavior without understanding what is going on inside the mind of the organism producing the behavior. From approximately 1930 to the early 1950s, behaviorism dominated American psychology. But in the 1950s, a "cognitive revolution" began (Gardner, 1985). Over the next 2 decades, behaviorism came to be seen as inadequate, and the focus of the search for explanations of human behavior shifted to internal mental processes. Studies of language played a crucial role in the cognitive revolution. The ability to speak and understand language is incredibly complex, and children acquire that ability without receiving positive reinforcement for successive approximations to grammatical sentences. Simple theories that may well explain why rats push levers, why dogs salivate at the sight of the people who feed them, and why humans get tense when they sit in the dentist's chair cannot explain how children learn to talk. When cognitivism displaced behaviorism, theoretical dispute concerning how to understand human behavior did not end. In fact, a new interdisciplinary field called **cognitive science** emerged from the cognitive revolution.

Cognitive scientists now agree that it is necessary to understand how the mind works in order to explain human behavior, but they do not agree on how the mind works. The study of language acquisition still plays a central role in the debate over how to characterize human cognition, for the same reason that language acquisition played a central role in the cognitive revolution. That is, it is so difficult to explain how language acquisition is possible that accounting for language acquisition is a test not likely to be passed by inaccurate cognitive theories. Language acquisition is the New York City of the field of cognitive science: if you can make it there, you can make it anywhere.

***Language development as an applied research topic.*** The goal for many researchers who study language development is perhaps less grandiose than discovering how the mind works, but it is more immediate. Success in modern industrialized society depends on having good verbal skills, and acquiring the verbal skills society requires is problematic for some children. For example, some minority children and some children from lower socioeconomic strata enter school with language skills that differ from those that mainstream, middle-class teachers expect, and they experience difficulty in school as a result. Thus, one area of research in language development focuses on understanding the nature of cultural differences in language use and on how teaching practices can be designed to best serve children with a variety of styles of language use. Acquiring adequate language skills is also problematic for children who have a variety of other conditions, including mental retardation, hearing impairment, or brain injury. Some children have difficulty acquiring language in the apparent absence of any other sort of impairment. A substantial body of research focuses on trying to understand the nature of the problems that underlie such children's difficulty and on finding techniques for helping these children acquire language skills.

For many children, language acquisition involves acquiring more than one language. In some cases, the language that children learn at home is not the language of their school, and thus they must learn a new language when they enter school. In other cases, children are exposed to and learn two or more languages from birth; in still other cases, children immigrate or are adopted into a new country with a new language. The social realities of many children's multilingual experience both raise interesting questions about how children achieve competence in more than one language and pose challenges for school systems charged with educating children from such backgrounds.

The areas of basic and applied research in the study of language development are not wholly separate. There are important points of contact. For example, basic research on the process of normal language development is used to develop interventions to help children who have difficulty acquiring language (Warren & Reichle, 1992), and research on the processes involved in reading has provided the basis for successful reading interventions (Bus & van Ijzendoorn, 1999; Ehri et al., 2001). Sometimes work on language disorders also informs basic research. For example, evidence that children with autism acquire language structure even though they have severe communicative deficiencies suggests that learning language involves more than learning how to fulfill a need to communicate (Tager-Flusberg, 1994). There are also important points of contact among the various disciplines that study language development. For example, anthropologists' descriptions of cultures in which no one talks to babies is relevant to the work of developmental psychologists who study how mother–infant interactions contribute to language development (Lieven, 1994).

## THE HISTORY OF THE STUDY OF LANGUAGE DEVELOPMENT

Although the modern study of language acquisition began in the 1960s, the linguistic capacity of children has been a source of fascination since ancient times. One can find examples in history of many of the motives that prompt current investigations of children's language.

## Big questions and studies of special cases

***The language in the brain.*** The first recorded language acquisition experiment was conducted by the ancient Egyptian king Psammetichus and described by the Greek historian Herodotus in the fourth century BC. The issue at hand concerned who among the peoples of the world represented the original human race. To resolve the issue, King Psammetichus ordered that two infants be raised in isolation by shepherds, who were never to speak in the children's presence. The idea behind this experiment was that the babies would start to speak on their own, and whatever language they spoke would be the language of the "original" people. According to Herodotus's account, one of the children said something like "becos" at the age of 2. *Becos,* as it turned out, was the Phyrgian word for bread. In the face of this evidence, King Psammetichus abandoned his claim that the Egyptians were the oldest race of humans and concluded that they were second oldest, after the Phyrgians.

Although the assumptions underlying that experiment seem slightly comical now, and the method of the experiment is certainly unethical, the idea of asking about the language the brain creates when it is not given an existing language to learn has not been discarded. Susan Goldin-Meadow has studied the gestural communication systems invented by children born deaf to hearing parents (Feldman, Goldin-Meadow, & Gleitman, 1978; Goldin-Meadow, 1997; Goldin-Meadow, 2003). Because the children's parents do not know any sign language (and have been instructed not to learn or use any sign language in these cases, in accordance with the oralist method of instruction for the deaf), these deaf children are just as isolated from a language model as were the infants in King Psammetichus's experiment. Children in these circumstances invent "signs" and combine them in two- and three-sign sequences, suggesting that putting symbols together to communicate is something that naturally emerges in the course of human development. In Chapter 7, we will come back to the specifics of these findings and what they suggest.

***"Wild children" and the nature of humankind.***   Occasionally there are children who are not only linguistic isolates but also social isolates, and these unfortunate children afford science the opportunity to ask an even broader question: What is the intrinsic nature of humankind? This question was hotly debated in the eighteenth century. On the one hand, there had been a long tradition of argument by philosophers such as Descartes (1662) that human nature (including having an immortal soul) was an innate endowment. On the other hand, the philosopher John Locke (1690) had argued that at birth the human mind was like a sheet of blank paper and that humans become what they become as a result of society's influence. What was needed to settle this question was a human raised outside of society. Such a human appeared in the winter of 1800.

That winter was an unusually cold one, and in January a young boy who had been living wild in the woods near Aveyron, France, approached a tanner's workshop on the edge of the forest (Lane, 1976). The child appeared to be about 12 years old. He was naked; he occasionally ran on all fours; he ate roots, acorns, and raw vegetables—but only after sniffing them first; and although he was capable of making sounds, he had no language. This "wild child" became the object of intense scientific interest because he provided an opportunity to examine the nature of the human species in its natural state. The young boy's muteness was problematic for theories of innate knowledge for two reasons: (1) Language was held to be one of the defining characteristics of humanity; and (2) his muteness made him a difficult subject to interview to determine whether he had an innate idea of God (Lane, 1976). However, the boy's muteness provided good support for the opposing idea that "man depends on society for all that he is and can be" (Lane, 1976, p. 5).

The wild boy of Aveyron, as he came to be called, was placed with young Dr. Jean-Marc Itard for training at the National Institute for Deaf-Mutes in Paris. The scientific community watched to see whether society could provide this child with the human characteristic of language. Although Dr. Itard was able to teach the boy some socially appropriate behaviors, the boy never learned more than a few words, and to this day we cannot be certain why. Perhaps the child was impaired from birth, perhaps the training methods employed were not the best, and perhaps the boy was too old to acquire language by the time his training began (Lane, 1976). Although the success that Itard achieved was quite limited, this scientific enterprise yielded practical dividends. Dr. Itard went on to use the training methods he had devised for the wild boy of Aveyron in teaching the deaf, and some of the techniques for teaching letters that Itard invented are used in Montessori classrooms today (Lane, 1976).

Over the course of history, there have been other "wild children" who were discovered mute at an age when children in normal environments have learned to talk (see Brown, 1958; Curtiss, 1989; Gleitman & Gleitman, 1991). The most famous modern case is that of a girl named "Genie," who became known to the public in 1970. She was 13 years old and had been kept locked in a room by her mentally ill father since the age of approximately 18 months. Her language remediation was somewhat more successful than the boy of Aveyron's, but Genie never acquired normal language (Curtiss, 1977; Rymer, 1993). To some, such cases suggest that there may be a critical period for some aspects of language acquisition, such that language acquisition begun after childhood is never quite as successful as language acquisition begun earlier. This is also a topic to which we will return in later chapters.

## Baby biographies

Another approach to investigating "the nature of humankind" is simply to observe what emerges in the course of normal development. In this vein, several investigators in the late 1800s and early 1900s kept diaries of their own children's development. The most famous of these "baby biographers" was Charles Darwin (better known for his theory of evolution), whose description of his son's communicative development (Darwin, 1877) follows the course illustrated in the child's speech excerpts presented in the chapter opening. Darwin's son said *"da"* at 5 months, and, before he was 1 year old, the young Darwin understood intonations, gestures, several words, and short sentences. At 1 year, the child communicated with gestures and invented his first word, *mum,* to mean food. Other well-known diaries include Clara and Wilhelm

Stern's *Die Kindersprache* (Stern & Stern, 1907) and Werner Leopold's (1939–1949) four-volume account of his daughter Hildegard's acquisition of English and German.

Diary studies are not entirely a thing of the past. Child language researchers often have children of their own, and some researchers have kept detailed records of their children's language development. Some of the data we will refer to in later chapters come from such diaries (for example, Bowerman, 1985, 1990; Dromi, 1987; Halliday, 1975; Mervis, Mervis, Johnson, & Bertrand, 1992; Robinson & Mervis, 1998; Sachs, 1983; Tomasello, 1992b). In addition, researchers have sometimes trained mothers to keep diaries so that the early language development of several children could be studied (for example, Bloom, 1993b; Gopnik & Meltzoff, 1987; Harris, Barrett, Jones, & Brookes, 1988; Nelson, 1973).

## Normative studies

In the period between the end of World War I and the 1950s, the goal of most research on language acquisition was to establish norms (Ingram, 1989). Toward that end, several large-scale studies were undertaken to provide data on when children articulate different sounds, the size of children's vocabularies at different ages, and the length of their sentences at different ages. Consonant with the behaviorist orientation of the times, the goal was not to ask theoretical questions about either the nature of humankind or the nature of language development but simply to describe what could be observed. These older studies are still valuable as descriptions of normative development (for example, McCarthy, 1930; Templin, 1957), and as new instruments for assessing children's language are developed, new normative studies continue to be conducted (e.g., Fenson et al., 1994).

## The Chomskyan revolution

In the 1960s, the study of children's language development changed radically. The catalyst for this change was the 1957 publication of a slim volume entitled *Syntactic Structures,* written by Noam Chomsky, then a young linguist at the Massachusetts Institute of Technology. That piece, along with Chomsky's subsequent prolific work, revolutionized the field of linguistics and, within a few years, the study of language development. Before Chomsky's work, linguists concentrated on describing the regularities of languages. Linguists could study their own language or, better yet, a little-known language, but the job was the same: to find the patterns in what speakers do. Chomsky caused a revolution by saying that what speakers do is not as interesting as the mental grammar that underlies what speakers do. Since Chomsky's writings, the work of linguists consists of trying to describe what is in the minds of speakers that explains how speakers do what they do.

That new goal of linguistics raised a question about children. If adults have a mental grammar that explains what they do when they talk, then children must have a mental grammar that explains what they do. Children's speech is different from adults' speech; therefore, children's mental grammars must be different. What are children's grammars like, and how do children eventually achieve adult grammars?

In 1962 Professor Roger Brown and his students at Harvard University began to study the grammatical development of two children given the pseudonyms Adam and Eve (Brown, 1973). Somewhat later a third child, Sarah, was added to the study. Every week for Sarah, and every 2 weeks for Adam and Eve, graduate students visited these children in their homes and tape-recorded their spontaneous speech. Transcripts of the children's speech were then analyzed with the goal of describing the grammatical knowledge that underlay the speech they produced. That project, begun by Brown, along with just a few other projects (Bloom, 1970; Braine, 1963; Miller & Ervin, 1964) marks the beginning of the Chomskyan era of studying children's language. The graduate students who met with Roger Brown to discuss the analyses of Adam's, Eve's, and Sarah's language—along with a few notable others who were not at Harvard that year—became the first generation of child language researchers. We will discuss some of these pioneering projects when we discuss grammatical development in Chapter 5.

Chomsky focused on grammar (the structure of language), and the first new wave of research on language development in the 1960s was on children's grammatical development. Later, in part following theoretical trends in linguistics, child language researchers shifted their focus more toward semantics and the acquisition of word meanings. In the later 1970s, the domain of language development was further expanded. Again following developments in linguistics, language use was added to the field of inquiry, and child language researchers began to study pragmatic and sociolinguistic development. In the 1980s and 1990s, linguistics and language development returned to focus on syntax, but the other questions about the lexicon and pragmatics have not been abandoned (or solved). The study of phonology and phonological development has continued throughout this period, somewhat outside the center ring of linguistic debate. (For fuller accounts of the history of child language research, see Golinkoff & Gordon, 1983; and Ingram, 1989.) Currently, the study of language development is a multifaceted field that includes a variety of very different research enterprises.

## The current study of language development

Current research on language development is guided by current views of what language is, and there are several such views. One can think of language development as the process of learning to communicate in the way that the

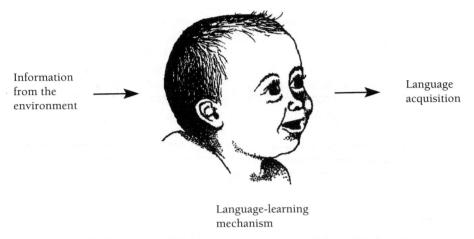

Information from the environment → [Language-learning mechanism] → Language acquisition

**Figure 1.2**   A model for studying the nature of the language-learning capacity

adults in one's social or cultural group do so. Language, in this view, is a social behavior, and language acquisition is really **language socialization.** The goals of language socialization research are to describe children's language use and their underlying understandings of language as a vehicle for social interaction at different ages and to identify the factors that influence that developmental course. This work includes, for example, studies of gender differences and cultural differences in styles of language use, and studies of how children recount stories, negotiate conflicts, and tell jokes (e.g., Slobin, Gerhardt, Kyratzis, & Guo, 1996). We will pursue these lines of work more fully in Chapter 6.

Language is also a complex system that maps sounds (for oral language) to meanings. If one thinks of language development as the acquisition of this system, the research question is, how does the child do it? That is, what is the mental capacity that underlies the human ability to learn to talk? This question can be conceptualized in the following manner: The human capacity for language is a device residing in the human brain that takes as its input certain information from the environment and produces as its output the ability to speak and understand a language. (This model is presented in Figure 1.2.) Everything that is part of adults' knowledge of language (i.e., the output of the device) must either be in the input, be in the internal device, or somehow result from the way the device operates on the input it receives. Noam Chomsky (1965) termed this capacity the *Language Acquisition Device (LAD)*. Not everyone uses this terminology, because it is associated with a particular,

Chomskyan, approach to the field, but everyone who is interested in how children acquire the language system is, in essence, asking the question: What is the nature of the human language acquisition capacity?

Researchers do not start out completely neutral with respect to an answer to this question. (Scientists must always start out with some ideas of how things work; the work of scientists is testing those ideas.) Current research on language development can be usefully organized in terms of four different approaches that researchers take—each motivated by a different premise regarding the nature of the LAD and the language development it produces. They are the biological, the linguistic, the social, and the domain-general cognitive approaches. We introduce them briefly here so that they are familiar when they come up in more detailed discussions of particular domains of language development.

The biological approach starts with the premise that the human capacity for language is best understood as a biological phenomenon and language development is best understood as a biological process. This premise then leads to research that investigates the degree to which language and language development share the hallmark features of other biological processes. Research in this vein looks for universal features of language development, for a hereditary basis to language ability, for evidence of a biologically based timetable for development, and more. In addition, biologically motivated research leads to the study of the structures and processes in the brain that underlie language development.

The linguistic approach to the study of language acquisition focuses on describing the nature of the child's innate linguistic knowledge. That is, this approach works from the premise that the LAD must contain some knowledge of the structure of language in order for language acquisition to be possible. That innate knowledge cannot be specific to any particular language; thus, it is **Universal Grammar** (UG). The linguistic approach seeks to describe UG and how it interacts with language experience to produce linguistic knowledge as a result.

The social approach rejects the premise that innate linguistic knowledge is necessary. It starts from the premises that language is essentially a social phenomenon and language development a social process, and seeks to describe the social processes that produce language acquisition. Research in this vein focuses on social aspects of interaction as the experience relevant to language acquisition and on the social–cognitive abilities of the child as the relevant learning capacities.

Another approach that seeks to do without innate linguistic knowledge is the domain-general cognitive approach. This approach starts from the premise that language acquisition is a learning problem no different from any other and that children solve it in the same way that they solve other learning problems. Research in this vein seeks an account of how language might be learned by the child's application of domain-general cognitive processes to the information available in input.

There is another bit of terminology to introduce with respect to characterizing approaches to the study of language development. A distinction has been made between the learnability approach and the developmental approach (see, for example, Bloom, 1991). The **learnability approach** focuses on explaining the fact that language is acquired (i.e., that language is learnable). The **developmental approach** focuses on explaining the course of language development. These approaches are not mutually exclusive, and few researchers focus on one goal and ignore the other. Rather, different lines of research may differ in emphasis.

## MAJOR ISSUES IN THE FIELD OF LANGUAGE DEVELOPMENT

Another way to organize current research and theory in the field of language development is in terms of the major issues that any account of language development must address. The major issues concern, among other things, the degree to which language is innate or learned from experience, the nature of the innate contributions and the learning processes, whether change over the course of development is continuous or discontinuous, and how the communicative functions of language are involved in the process of learning the language system. We elaborate these issues in the next sections.

*"The title of my science project is 'My Little Brother: Nature or Nurture.'"*

**Figure 1.3**   Source: © The New Yorker Collection, 2003 Michael Shaw from cartoonbank.com. All rights reserved.

## Nature or nurture?

Is the development of language in children the result of human's innate endowment (like the development of upright posture and bipedal locomotion), or is it the result of the circumstances in which children are nurtured (like the development of table manners or the ability to do calculus, both of which depend on particular experiences)? This is the **nature–nurture** debate, and it predates not only the modern study of language development but also the emergence of psychology as a discipline. This was the ongoing debate when the wild boy of Aveyron left the woods in 1800. The extreme experience-based position, known as **empiricism,** asserts that the mind at birth is like a blank slate; all knowledge and reason come from experience (Locke, 1690). The alternative view, known as **nativism,** asserts that knowledge cannot come from experience alone. The mind must have some preexisting structure in order to organize and interpret experience (Gleitman, 1995; see the works of Plato and Kant for the original arguments). This debate still rages among those who study language development.

***The nativist view.*** For proponents of nativism as an explanation of language development, there are three salient "facts" about language development: (1) Children acquire language rapidly, (2) children acquire language effortlessly, and (3) children acquire language without direct instruction. Rapid, effortless, untutored development seems more like maturation than like learning in the usual sense of the term. As Chomsky (1993) put it,

> Language learning is not really something that the child does; it is something that happens to the child placed in an appropriate environment, much as the child's body grows and matures in a predetermined way when provided with appropriate nutrition and environmental stimulation. (p. 519)

The modern-day descendant of the opposite, empiricist view is behaviorism. As mentioned earlier, behaviorism has not stood the test of time (or empirical evidence) as a theory of language acquisition. Behaviorist theories will be mentioned again in the following chapters, but primarily for historical completeness.

***The interactionist view.*** In current debate, the alternative to nativism is not pure empiricism but rather **interactionism** (Braine, 1994). Like nativists, interactionists acknowledge that there must be some innate characteristics of the mind that allow it to develop language based on experience. But the interactionist position places a greater burden of accounting for language development on the nature of children's language-learning experiences than the nativist position does. Research on the nature of the **language input** children receive and the relation of that input to the rate and course of development are relevant here (see, for example, Gallaway & Richards, 1994; Hoff-Ginsberg & Shatz, 1982; Morgan, 1990). The position known as **social interactionism** holds that a crucial aspect of language-learning experience is social interaction with another person. Interactionists contest the "facts" so salient to the nativists. As Catherine Snow has put it,

> We on the other side think that learning language is a long slog, which requires from the child a lot of work. And the child is working as hard as he can, fifteen, sixteen hours a day. We think it requires a relationship with an adult, and a whole set of cognitive abilities. (quoted in Rymer, 1993, p. 37)

Another term for this type of position is **constructivism.** Constructivism as a view of development was first argued with respect to cognitive development by Jean Piaget, and *constructivism* remains a term in current use. According to the constructivist view, language (or any form of knowledge) is constructed by the child using inborn mental equipment but operating on information provided by the environment. In 1975 Noam Chomsky and Jean Piaget debated their respective nativist and constructivist views of language development at the Abbaye de Royaumont near Paris. Nearly 200 years after the wild boy of Aveyron left his woods (and roughly 200 miles away), the debate about the essential nature of the human mind continued. In his foreword to the edited transcript of that debate, Howard Gardner (1980) summarized the two views:

> Piaget saw the human child—and his mind—as an active, constructive agent that slowly inches forward in a perpetual bootstrap operation, Chomsky viewed the mind as a set of essentially preprogrammed units, each equipped from the first to realize its full complement of rules and needing only the most modest environmental trigger to exhibit its intellectual wares. (p. xxiii)

More recently, the term **emergentism** has been used to label the view that knowledge can arise from the interaction of that which is given by biology and that which is given by the environment (MacWhinney, 1999). This new term tends to be used in the context of new models of learning that are termed *connectionist, parallel distributed processing,* or *neural network models* (Bates & Goodman, 1999). The advent of these new learning models has given new life and new form to the old nature–nurture debate. As Bates and Goodman (1999) have put it, "the debate today in the field of language development is not about nature versus nurture, but about the 'nature of nature'" (p. 33). That is, granting that there must be some innate characteristic of the human mind that allows language development, theorists still disagree about the nature of that which is innate.

## The nature of nature

There are different ways that something can be innate (Elman et al., 1996). The most strongly nativist view holds that knowledge itself is innate. A weaker form of innateness holds that the computational procedures for learning are innate and that knowledge results from the way in which those procedures operate on input. According to the innate knowledge view with respect to language acquisition, children have inborn knowledge of the general form of language, and it is this inborn, specifically linguistic knowledge that allows children to figure out a whole language in only a few years. Thus, this theoretical position holds that the internal contribution to language is **domain specific.** Various contrasting views differ from this position both in putting more burden on the input and learning procedures and also in questioning the domain specificity of the internal (i.e., innate) contribution to language acquisition.

***A language-specific module.*** Perhaps the first question to ask about the language-specific innateness view is, how could it be? To many, the notion that something as specific as knowledge of language is innate is bizarre. To others, postulating innateness amounts to giving up on explaining language development by turning the job over to the geneticists. However, the proposal that children have inborn knowledge of the general form of language may be more reasonable than it first appears. All languages of the world share many structural characteristics. These shared characteristics constitute the universal grammar of human language, of which each particular language is an example. (It's the different vocabularies that make languages other than our own incomprehensible.) Evolution seems to have equipped the human mind with other sorts of useful knowledge, such as the knowledge that the world is a three-dimensional place (our eyes alone cannot tell us this because our retinas are two-dimensional surfaces). Universal Grammar may similarly be an innate endowment. The view that the human ability to develop language is specific to language is part of a larger theory known as the **modularity** thesis (Fodor, 1983). According to this thesis, the innate human ability to develop language is a self-contained module in the mind, separate from other aspects of mental functioning. Chomsky (1991), in fact, referred to the human language capacity as a functionally separate "mental organ": "The mind, then, is not a system of general intelligence. . . . Rather, the mind has distinct subsystems, such as the language faculty, a cognitive system . . . " (pp. 50–51).

The issue of whether language acquisition is supported by a domain-specific mental module or by general cognitive processes is one question in a larger ongoing debate in cognitive psychology. The debate concerns whether cognition in general consists of the activity of a general-purpose set of reasoning abilities applied to different tasks, or whether there are many cognitive abilities that are specialized to handle different kinds of information (Hirschfeld & Gelman, 1994). The modularity thesis asserts that the mind is a bundle of many special-purpose modules—one for language, one for perception, one for understanding spatial location (map making)—and dismisses the concept of a "general ability to learn" (Barkow, Cosmides, & Tooby, 1992; Fodor, 1983; Pinker, 1994). Thus, the modularity issue is not specific to language development. Rather, it is an issue in cognitive psychology in which language plays a crucial, but not a singular, role. (For a discussion of modularity and nonmodularity in other domains, see Barkow et al., 1992; Cosmides, 1989; and Karmiloff-Smith, 1992.)

***Alternatives to language-specific innateness.***    The view that language acquisition results from the maturation of innately specified knowledge has the advantage of being a self-contained and, in principle, complete account. In contrast, the alternatives include a collection of ideas that are more difficult to summarize. Some early cognitive approaches to language development were based on Piagetian theory and sought to explain changes in children's language functioning in terms of stagelike developmental shifts in their nonlinguistic functioning. The shift from the sensorimotor intelligence of infancy to the preoperational intelligence of the toddler years was a particular focus of research (see, for example, Sinclair, 1969; and see Corrigan, 1979, for a review). However, that sort of across-the-board relation between cognitive development and language development was not supported by the evidence (Corrigan, 1979).

Subsequently, several studies have proposed how **domain-general** cognitive skills contribute to language acquisition. The kinds of cognitive skills suggested as contributing to language acquisition include the capacity for symbolic representation (Bates, Benigni, Bretherton, Camaioni, & Volterra, 1979), memory skills (Braine, 1988; Gathercole & Baddeley, 1990), skill in segmenting chunks of speech into their constituent parts (Bates, Bretherton, & Snyder, 1988), and a variety of processes that might be grouped under the heading of pattern analysis (Braine, 1988; Kelly & Martin, 1994; MacWhinney, 1987; Maratsos & Chalkley, 1980).

One kind of domain-general approach comes from the field of **connectionism.** Connectionism is a way of modeling how knowledge is represented in the brain, what thinking consists of, and how learning occurs. In very general terms, a connectionist model consists of a set of processing elements, called nodes, and the interconnections among those nodes. The nodes both collect input from the world or from other nodes and send activation out to other nodes. In a connectionist model, mental activity consists of activation spreading in a network of connected nodes, and knowledge is represented in the pattern of activation among the nodes (Elman, 2001). So, for example, thinking of a dog is a different pattern of activation than thinking of a cat. The former would involve activation of nodes pertaining to barking, among others; the latter would involve activation of nodes pertaining to meowing, among others. The particular pattern of activation that is present at any given time is a function of the current stimulus and the learner's past history of that stimulus. In the past, dogs and barking occurred together and cats and meowing occurred together, forging connections between the dog and barking nodes and the cat and meowing nodes.

Although connectionism is like behaviorism in that it depends heavily on the nature of the learner's experience and really only involves learning associations between things that are experienced together, it is a far more powerful learning mechanism than behaviorism. In behaviorism, the learner is learning what to do under what circumstances. Connectionism is a mechanism for extracting regularities from experience; that is, for acquiring knowledge that is not directly given in any single experience. Connectionist proposals have spurred new interest both in the nature of the input, because the regularities must be there to be extracted, and in the nature of the learning mechanisms available to the child. The next section reviews behavioral evidence regarding the nature of the child's learning mechanisms, which may also provide alternatives to language-specific innate knowledge as the explanation of language acquisition.

## What kind of learning mechanisms does the child have?

***Babies as statistical learners.*** A 1996 article in the prestigious journal *Science* described a study demonstrating that 8-month-old babies could learn something about the patterns in language (Saffran, Aslin, & Newport, 1996). The babies in this study listened for 2 minutes to a tape recording that presented four different "words" combined in random order in a single stream of sound. The words were, for example, *tupiro, golabu, bidaku,* and *padoti;* and thus the babies heard something like *tupirogolabubidakupadotibidakugolabubidakutupiro.* Next, the babies were presented with strings of the same "words" again on some trials, and on other trials they were presented with strings of "nonwords" made up of the same syllables combined in different orders. The result was that the babies listened longer to the nonwords than to the words. This finding is consistent with other research showing that babies of this age prefer novel stimuli to familiar stimuli.

The question is, how did the babies know the difference? The answer has to be that the babies noticed that in the first tape *tu* was always followed by *pi* and *pi* was always followed by *ro,* but the *ro* was followed by three different syllables, equally often. In the nonword tape, these transitional probabilities were different, even though the particular syllables presented as words and nonwords were the same (see also Aslin, Saffran, & Newport, 1998). In other words, the babies were doing what is called **statistical learning**— counting the frequency with which one stimulus is followed by another. This finding demonstrated that babies were more powerful learners than had previously been thought. Related findings support the notion that although these mechanisms are recruited for language acquisition, they are not language specific, because they can operate on nonspeech stimuli as well: 8-month-olds can learn the patterns in sequences of tones (Saffran, Johnson, Aslin, & Newport, 1999). Other research has pursued the question of just what statistical learning might explain. It turns out, for example, that statistical regularities are sufficient to allow 9-month-olds to distinguish possible from impossible phonological sequences (like the difference between *pling* and *gnilp*) (Saffran & Thiessen, 2003). Another line of relevant work investigates the degree to which input contains co-occurrence patterns that could reveal grammatical categories and structures to a statistical learner (Mintz, Newport, & Bever, 2002; Saffran, 2001).

***Babies as rule learners.***    Babies may be able to do more than mere statistical learning. In 1999 another article in *Science* claimed that 7-month-old infants were capable of learning rules (Marcus, Vijayan, Bandi Rao, & Vishton, 1999). The babies in this study also heard sequences of syllables for 2 minutes. For half the babies, the sequences followed an ABA pattern (e.g., *ga ti ga, li na li*), and for the other half, the sequences followed an ABB pattern (e.g., *ga ti ti, li na na*). Then the babies heard sequences of entirely new syllables that either matched the pattern they had heard or matched the other pattern. So, for example, the ABA sequence was *wo fe wo* and the ABB sequence was *wo fe fe*. When the babies were presented with the new syllable sequences, they were able to tell the difference between the pattern they had heard and the new pattern, even though they had never heard any of those sounds before.

This result demonstrated that babies can do more than learn the co-occurrence patterns among sounds they actually experience. Instead, babies can learn a pattern that must be described in terms of symbols (or variables) that stand for any sound. As Marcus and colleagues put it, the babies were learning algebraic **rules,** not just statistical regularities. The crucial difference is the fact that statistical regularities are regularities among stimuli actually experienced. In contrast, rules capture patterns among abstract variables that can refer to any stimuli, old or new. This issue has become central to the field of language acquisition. The mental ability to note co-occurrence patterns in input is essentially associative memory. Everyone agrees that children have associative memories and use them to acquire language. Learning vocabulary, for example, is almost entirely a process of rote memorization. The issue is whether language acquisition also depends on another mental ability: the ability to learn rules (Pinker, 1999). The issue of whether such **rule learning** is a necessary part of the language acquisition process is intimately connected to another hot debate: whether linguistic knowledge can be characterized as knowing statistics or knowing rules.

## What kind of knowledge does the child acquire?

Fundamental disagreement exists between two types of models of what it is to know a language and, therefore, how such knowledge can be acquired. According to traditional accounts in cognitive psychology, linguistic knowledge consists of a system of rules that operate over symbols. The symbols stand for abstract categories such as "Noun" and "Verb," for example. These categories are also called variables, because the actual word that is the Noun or Verb can vary, but the rule applies just the same. Knowledge has to be represented this way because knowing a language involves knowing how to do things with words you have never heard before, so long as you know to what category the word belongs. For example, you know how to form the past tense of *blick* even though you have never heard *blick* used before. What you know, according to the symbolic account, is a rule of the form "past tense → Verb + *ed*," and you can apply that rule to anything that you categorize as a Verb.

In contrast, according to connectionist views, linguistic processing in the adult does not require positing a symbolic rule system. Rather, processing is carried out by a network of elementary units (i.e., the nodes). The specifics of what results from processing depends on the input to the network and the nature of the connections among units in that network. By this account, learning consists of establishing and setting weights on the connections among units. As we just discussed, the process by which weights are set is fundamentally that of association (Plunkett, 1998). According to the connectionist view, you know how to form the past tense of *blick* by virtue of the strength of the associations you have formed between similar sounding verbs and their past tense forms (for example, *kick–kicked, lick–licked,* and so on).

Often, the kind of research that addresses the dispute between the symbol/rule approach and the connectionist approach consists of writing computer programs that instantiate a particular connectionist model. Researchers feed the computer the kind of language input children are likely to hear, and then see whether the computer can mimic the course of human language development. The most optimistic view of connectionism sees it as a possible alternative to the trade-off between finding the structure of language in the input or building the structure into the acquisition mechanism. Instead, structure emerges from the effect of input on the connectionist network (Plunkett, 1998). Connectionist models also seem closer to biology than symbolic models, because we know that the brain is a set of interconnected neurons. If cognitive processing could be modeled in a system that is closer to the "wetware" of the brain (an analogy to a computer's hardware), we could eliminate the problem of determining how the brain represents symbols and rules. (For a more thorough introduction to connectionism see, for example, Bechtel & Abrahamsen, 1991; Elman, 2001; Martindale, 1991).

Both the claim that connectionism can eliminate the need for rules and symbols and the view that connectionist models bring us closer to understanding how the brain accomplishes language have been challenged. According to Marcus (1998), the connectionist models that work do so because they actually contain within them nodes that stand for variables. That is, they use the machinery of connectionism to implement a symbolic processor. Other sorts of connectionist models eliminate rules and symbols, but those, according to Marcus, do not work. In fact, Marcus (1998) has argued that any model that eliminates symbols and rules must ultimately fail to account for what people know when they know a language. The analogy between connectionist models and the brain has been criticized as illusory (Fodor, 1997). Nodes are not neurons, and no one knows how the neurons in the human brain represent what humans know. For that reason connectionism does not bring us closer to knowing how the brain represents human linguistic knowledge (Fodor, 1997).

To return to Saffran and colleagues' findings, the connectionist view would be that because the babies heard *tupiro, bidaku,* and so on over and over again, they formed very strong connections between *tu* and *pi* and between *pi* and *ro,* but weaker connections between *ro* and *bi* because *bi* did not follow *ro* as frequently. After 2 minutes of listening, the connections forged would activate *pi* and then *ro* after hearing *tu,* whereas only a weaker activation of any particular syllable would result from hearing *ro.* In other words, a learning mechanism that does nothing more than count the frequency with which things appear together can end up telling words from nonwords because the previously heard words result in a different level of activation in a network than nonwords. Although no one doubts that the mind can do this, some seriously doubt that a mind that could only do this could ever acquire language. The alternative argument is that to do language, the mind needs symbolic processes, like algebraic rules. In essence, then, two different proposals try to explain how the mind represents the patterns it learns from experience: as connections among the stimuli actually experienced or as rules that operate over abstract categories.

## Continuity or discontinuity in development

It is obvious that children's language knowledge changes as they grow. The 1-year-old who knows five words becomes the 2-year-old who knows hundreds of words. If what 1-year-olds understand about their first five words is the same sort of understanding that 2-year-olds have of their larger vocabularies, then vocabulary development is continuous—the change involves acquiring more of the same kind of thing as was there at the beginning. If, on the other hand, the 1-year-old has a very limited understanding of his first words—he says *bye-bye* and *night-night* as part of social rituals and says *up* only when he wants to be picked up—but the 2-year-old knows his words refer to objects and events in the world, then knowledge has changed in kind, not just in amount. Changes in kind are discontinuities in development. We will review this issue as it plays out in language development in the chapters on phonological, lexical, and morphosyntactic development. Like the nature–nurture issue, the issue regarding continuity is not unique to the study of language development. Researchers who study cognitive development ask whether children's understandings of the world change qualitatively over the course of development. Readers who are familiar with the theory of Jean Piaget know one proposal regarding discontinuous or qualitative changes in development.

## The relation between communication and language

Children use the language they learn to communicate. In fact, one might say that the value of language to the human species is the communicative power it affords. Although no one doubts that language is useful for communication, there are differing views on how important communication is to language and to language acquisition. The two extreme positions are (1) **formalism,** the view that the nature of language and its acquisition have nothing to do with the fact that language is used to communicate, and (2) **functionalism,** the view that both language itself and the process of language acquisition are shaped and supported by the communicative functions language serves.

*Formalist views.* A clear and strong statement of the formalist position comes from Chomsky (1991):

> For unknown reasons, the human mind/brain developed the faculty of language, a computational-representation system. . . . [This system] can be used . . . in specific language functions such as communication; [but] *language is not intrinsically a system of communication* [italics added]. (pp. 50–51)

For the formalists, language is an autonomous, arbitrary system whose form is independent of its function. Another position asserts that language was shaped in the course of evolution by its communicative value, but that the nature of that form cannot be derived from the functions it serves (see Pinker & Bloom, 1990). From the point of view of language-learning children, this position asserts, as does the Chomskyan formalist view, that language is an external system that has to be figured out—or provided innately—and the use to which that system is put provides no clues to how the system is structured.

***Functionalist views.*** The contrary view is that language "is not an arbitrary and autonomous systei ı" (Budwig, 1995) but rather a system shaped by the communicative functions it serves. And, one view holds, because the form of language reflects the communicative functions to which it is put, children are led to discover the form of language in using the system to communicate. As MacWhinney, Bates, and Kliegl (1984) state, "The forms of natural languages are created, governed, constrained, acquired and used in the service of communicative functions" (p. 128).

A number of different functionalist views exist today, and some make stronger claims than others about the usefulness of communication to language acquisition. One claim is that the infant's social capacities are the source out of which language emerges (Snow, 1999). The key to language acquisition, according to this view, is very young children's understandings that other people are trying to communicate with them. A related claim states that the desire to communicate one's thoughts and feelings to others is the motivation for language acquisition (Bloom, 1991). According to both these views, communication explains the *why* of language development, but not necessarily the *how*. A stronger claim comes from Tomasello and colleagues (e.g., Tomasello, 1992a, 2000, 2001; Carpenter, Nagell, & Tomasello, 1998), who argue that communication also provides the *how* of language development. According to Tomasello,

> Children are not engaged in a reflective cognitive task in which they
> are attempting to make correct mappings of word to world based on
> adult input, but rather they are engaged in social interactions in
> which they are attempting to understand and interpret adult
> communicative intentions... children acquire linguistic symbols as a
> kind of by-product of social interaction with adults, in much the same
> way they learn many other cultural conventions. (2001, p. 135)

## METHODS OF RESEARCH IN LANGUAGE DEVELOPMENT

### Cross-cultural and cross-linguistic research

The modern study of language development began with investigations of the acquisition of English by middle-class American children. Initially this geographic focus was not seen as a terrible limitation because, the thinking went, the processes underlying language acquisition are universal, and thus discovering how children in Cambridge, Massachusetts, acquire language is the same as discovering how all children acquire language. Currently the study of language acquisition by children who live in other cultures and the study of the acquisition of languages other than English are considered crucial to discovering the universal processes of language acquisition. Two insights provide the motivation for cross-cultural and cross-linguistic research. One is the recognition of individual differences in language development and of the possibility of more than one route to language acquisition. This is true of different children within a single culture, but it may be especially true when describing language acquisition in cultures that provide children with different kinds of language-learning environments (Lieven, 1994; Tardif, Gelman, & Xu, 1999). Thus, researchers no longer assume that if you've seen one child acquire language, you've seen them all.

The second reason for cross-cultural and cross-linguistic research is the observation that different languages present children with different language-learning tasks. The human capacity to acquire language works equally well whether the task is to acquire English, Mandarin, Spanish, or Georgian (see, for example, Bowerman & Choi, 2001; Maratsos, 1998; Naigles & Terraza, 1998). If researchers study only the acquisition of English and construct a theory of language acquisition that accounts for the acquisition of English, their theory may not account for the acquisition of Georgian. And a theory of language acquisition that cannot account for the acquisition of all languages is obviously not the correct description of the human language-learning capacity. Currently cross-cultural and cross-linguistic work is very much in the mainstream of child language research.

## Research designs

In their search for answers to the question of how children learn to talk, child language researchers use the same kinds of research designs that other scientists use. They engage in longitudinal and cross-sectional observational studies to describe developmental changes in children's language, and they analyze those patterns of development for what they might reveal about the process underlying that development. They do correlational studies in which they look for relations between different aspects of language development or between language development and other aspects of development or experience. They do experiments in which they provide children with different kinds of exposure to language and then look for differences in what children have learned. Sometimes researchers use computer simulations to test whether a hypothesized model of language development could work in principle, and sometimes researchers do case studies of individuals whose unique circumstances or pattern of development promises to shed light on some issue. The focus of studies of children's language development can be language production, language comprehension, or both. Researchers interested in comprehension have been very inventive in designing ways to get small children to reveal what they think a word or a sentence means. We will discuss the particulars of different methods in later chapters when the research is discussed. But one aspect of methodology in child language research is so often employed and so specific to this field that it is worth discussing by itself. The analysis of samples of spontaneous speech is the method Roger Brown used in his pioneering study of Adam, Eve, and Sarah, and it is a method that is still widely used today.

## Assessment of productive language from speech samples

***Speech sample collection.***    Child language researchers can often be identified by the equipment they carry. Videotape or audiotape records of spontaneous speech samples are the standard database for assessing children's language development. Typically, the researcher picks a setting in which children are likely to talk—a mealtime or toy play, for example—and then records interactions in that setting. The recording can be done in the children's homes or in a laboratory playroom. The children can be talking to the researcher or to someone more familiar to them (usually their mother). The purpose of collecting such **speech samples** is to find out the nature of the language children produce. Thus, the speech sample collected should be representative of everything the children say. Achieving representativeness can be difficult because speech may be different in different contexts (Bacchini, Kuiken, & Schoonen, 1995; Hoff-Ginsberg, 1991). Another concern is that the act of recording will alter children's speech in some way. This is probably more of a problem for recording the speech of adults than that of children, because children tend to be less self-conscious than adults; however, researchers typically spend some "warm-up" time with their subjects before turning on the tape recorder. One research project attempted to secure more representative speech samples by putting little vests with radio-controlled microphones on children (Wells, 1985). The children wore the vests all day, although the microphone was turned on only intermittently.

How much speech needs to be recorded to estimate characteristics of a child's language? How frequently does speech need to be recorded to capture developmental changes? Generally, a speech sample of approximately 100 utterances is considered large enough to yield reliable estimates of grammatical properties of children's speech. If the focus of interest is some characteristic of language use not present in every utterance, then of course the sample would need to be larger. There are also no established guidelines for how often children need to be recorded (Bloom, 1991). Researchers select different intervals using the existing literature to make their best guess at what interval will reveal the sorts of developmental changes they are studying.

Sometimes the research focuses on a particular type of language use, such as storytelling. In this case, more directive techniques of elicited production can be used. As we shall see in Chapter 6, an enormous body of research on children's narrative development is based on studies using the same technique of asking children to tell a story using a book that has pictures but no words (Berman & Slobin, 1994).

***Speech sample transcription.***   The invention of audiotape and videotape recorders made it possible to collect a record of everything a child says, which made a central kind of language development research possible. However, there is a downside to tape-recording speech samples: the tapes have to be transcribed. Child language researchers are sometimes envious when they see their colleagues in other fields say good-bye to study participants and then turn to the participants' just-completed questionnaires to find numbers ready for analysis. When child language researchers say good-bye to the little participants in their studies, the task of data collection has only just begun.

The next step in data collection is transcription, which consists of writing down what was recorded. What makes that task difficult is that the children being recorded were not giving dictation but were engaging in conversation. In conversation, people do not speak in full sentences; they interrupt each other and even talk at the same time. Furthermore, especially if they are children, their pronunciation is less than clear, and their usage not quite adultlike. Creating a transcript that is a faithful record of what was on the tape is difficult and time-consuming. It requires training to be able to transcribe, and then it can take as long as 5 hours to transcribe each hour of recorded speech.

***Transcript coding and analysis.***   After the speech has been transcribed, the researcher has to code the transcripts. Coding varies, depending on what the researcher is studying. For example, if the research is attempting to chart the development of verb usage, then coding the transcripts might involve identifying every verb in the children's speech. If the purpose of the research is to study children's conversational skill, then coding the transcripts might involve categorizing every utterance the child produces as related or unrelated to what was said before. Ultimately, for researchers to conduct the kinds of analyses that get reported in journal articles, the codes have to be turned into numbers. For example, a researcher might analyze changes in the number of different verbs in children's spontaneous speech or changes in the proportion of children's utterances that are related to prior speech.

When this sort of research started in the 1960s, transcripts were handwritten documents with columns for different codes. Graduate students in child language logged many hours over these transcripts, identifying verbs or whatever the research called for and adding numbers in the code columns. The advent of computer programs for analyzing child language transcripts has considerably lightened that load. It still takes a human being to transcribe and code, but the transcription can be entered directly into a computer-based file, and the coding can be entered onto the transcript as well. Then, instead of the researcher counting all the codes, the computer can do it—and far more quickly and accurately. Probably the most widely used programs for transcript analysis are those associated with the Child Language Data Exchange System **(CHILDES)** (MacWhinney, 1991). Another is SALT (Systematic Analysis of Language Transcripts) (Miller & Chapman, 1985). SALT was developed specifically for researchers and clinicians in communicative disorders, but it is a flexible program that can be used for basic research as well. Another program, Logical International Phonetics Programs, or LIPP, allows the user to transcribe in the International Phonetic Alphabet and thus permits fine-grained phonetic analysis (Oller & Delgado, 1999).

## CHILDES—A data archive

Another benefit made possible by computer-based transcripts is widespread data sharing. Although researchers have always been able to share data with colleagues by photocopying their transcripts, sharing is easier when the transcripts are in computer-based files and when (as a necessary side effect of computerized transcription) the transcripts are in a standardized format. The CHILDES project has taken the concept of data sharing even further by establishing an archive. In the early 1980s, the MacArthur Foundation funded a project, led by Brian MacWhinney and Catherine Snow, to establish an archive for transcripts of children's speech. Roger Brown contributed his transcripts of Adam, Eve, and Sarah, and other researchers contributed transcripts they had collected. Since then, other researchers have added their transcripts so that the CHILDES database now has more than 100 corpora (i.e., speech samples) representing more than 20 different languages, including both monolingual and bilingual children. Researchers whose questions can be addressed by looking at speech samples in the CHILDES archive can go straight to the coding phase of research. A full description of the archive and the corpora themselves are available at the CHILDES Web site, which can be accessed at www.psy.cmu.edu. The Web site also contains online tutorials and a bibliography of references in the field of child language.

## Standardized tests and measures of language development

Sometimes researchers want to be able to describe a child's language in terms that compare that child's language to the language of other children of the same age. Child language researchers are typically interested in such measures primarily for the purpose of describing the children they are studying, much the way researchers in cognitive development sometimes want to describe their samples in terms of IQ or mental age. By far the biggest users of standardized measures are practitioners in communicative disorders, who use such measures for diagnosis and for treatment evaluation.

There are essentially two ways to assess how a child's language development compares with that of other same-age children. One is to collect a speech sample and code it using a coding system for which norms have been collected. For example, the mean length of a child's utterances (MLU) is a good index of a child's level of grammatical development, and data that provide norms for MLU have been collected (Leadholm & Miller, 1992; Miller & Chapman, 1981; see Chapter 5 for more on this topic). SALT will calculate MLU on an appropriately entered transcript and will indicate the child's level of grammatical development. Age-referenced norms for phonological features of children's speech are also available (Grunwell, 1981).

The second way of getting a norm-referenced measure of a child's language level is to employ one of the many existing standardized instruments. These instruments estimate the child's language proficiency either by asking caregivers to report their children's language comprehension or production or by having an examiner test the child. An example of a caregiver report instrument is the MacArthur Communicative Development Inventories (CDIs) (Fenson et al., 1994). There are two versions of the MacArthur CDI: one for infants between 8 and 16 months of age and one for 16- to 30-month-old toddlers. These inventories consist of checklists that caregivers fill out to report on the gestures, words, and word combinations that their children understand and produce. Data from nearly 2000 children have been collected using these inventories, providing a basis for evaluating an individual child's level of development. An example of an examiner-administered instrument is the Peabody Picture Vocabulary Test (PPVT), which is used to assess vocabulary knowledge in children from 3 years to adulthood. The examiner presents the child with a word (Can you find *boat?*) and asks the child to select from four pictures the one that corresponds to the word. An individual child's performance is compared to a larger reference group that provided norms for this test. There are also a wide variety of examiner-administered tests of school-aged children's oral language and reading proficiency.

## SOURCES FOR RESEARCH ON LANGUAGE DEVELOPMENT

### Journals

One way students new to language development can get an idea of the range of topics, issues, and research methods in the field is to scan journals that publish research on language development. The titles of the articles in these journals give an idea of the topics being studied. The list of journals that contain papers on language development is long and includes journals from a variety of disciplines. The major sources are listed in Box 1.1.

## Box 1.1   Major journals that publish research on language development

Developmental psychology journals:

*Child Development*

*Developmental Psychology*

*Infancy*

*Journal of Experimental Child Psychology*

*Merrill-Palmer Quarterly*

Cognitive psychology journals:

*Cognition*

*Cognitive Psychology*

Linguistics journals:

*Discourse Processes*

*Language*

*Lingua*

Psycholinguistics journals:

*Applied Psycholinguistics*

*Journal of Psycholinguistic Research*

Language development journals:

*First Language*

*Journal of Child Language*

*Language Acquisition*

Language disorders journals:

*American Journal of Speech-Language Pathology*

*Journal of Communication Disorders*

*Journal of Multilingual Communication Disorders*

*Journal of Speech, Language, and Hearing Research*

*Language, Speech, and Hearing Services in Schools*

Neuroscience journals:

*The Behavioral and Brain Sciences*
*Brain and Language*
*Developmental Neuropsychology*
*Cognitive Neuropsychology*

Second-language learning journals:

*Applied Linguistics*
*Language Learning*
*Second Language Research*
*Studies in Second Language Acquisition*

Other specialized journals:

*American Journal on Mental Retardation*
*Journal of Autism and Developmental Disorders*
*Bilingualism: Language and Cognition*
*The International Journal of Bilingualism*

## Indexes

If you already have a particular interest in some topic, or if you find an interesting topic by scanning the journals, you may want to find other articles on the same topic. Indexes can help you track down everything that has been written on a particular topic in language development. Just as the index in the back of this book allows you to find all the places in this book that a particular topic is mentioned, these indexes allow you to find all the places a particular topic is mentioned in the set of journals they scan. **Psychological Abstracts** is a service that covers more than 1300 different journals in psychology and related fields and provides an index to material in those sources. Since 1987, Psychological Abstracts has also covered books and book chapters. **Linguistics and Language Behavior Abstracts** provides an index to material in 1500 journals in language and language-related fields. Psychological Abstracts and Linguistics and Language Behavior Abstracts are available online; the online version of Psychological Abstracts is **PsycInfo.** To use these databases, all you have to do is type in the subject you are interested in (such as "lexical development" or "sign language"), and you will get a list of all the articles on that topic that appear in all the sources covered by that indexing service.

# ● SUMMARY

Language development is a multidisciplinary field that has as its central question, How is language acquired? Because language is highly complex yet universally acquired, the answer to this question has profound implications for understanding the essential nature of the human mind. Because language is a vehicle for social interaction and acquired in a social context, the answer to this question also may reveal how development is supported and shaped by the social environment. The study of language development also has practical importance for education, for the treatment of communicative disorders, and for second language instruction.

Acquiring a language includes learning the sounds and sound patterns of the language (phonological development), learning the vocabulary of the language (lexical development), learning the structure of the language (grammatical, or morphosyntactic, development), and learning how to use language to communicate (pragmatic and sociolinguistic development). The study of language development has a long history because questions about how children's language emerges have long been considered central to larger philosophical and scientific debates. These debates have concerned the intrinsic nature of humankind and the role of experience in shaping human nature.

The modern study of language development began in the 1960s following the Chomskyan revolution in linguistics. Chomsky argued that the study of language is the study of the mind. In turn, the study of language development captured the interest of researchers interested in the study of the developing mind.

Language development is a field divided on several fault lines. Some major points of disagreement are (1) whether language is largely innate in the child or learned from experience, (2) whether the mechanism that underlies language acquisition is specific to language or consists of general-purpose cognitive abilities applied to the task of learning language, and (3) whether the communicative functions that language serves (for children and adults) account for language acquisition, contribute to the process of acquisition, or are merely a benefit of language acquisition that must itself be explained in other terms. Child language researchers also debate whether the most useful approach to understanding language development is to focus on children and ask how they acquire language (the developmental approach) or to focus on language and ask how it is acquired by children (the learnability approach).

Language development researchers use a variety of research methods and designs. Central to a great deal of research is the collection of speech samples from children for the purpose of characterizing the children's productive language. Collecting speech samples involves recording children as they talk, and transcribing and coding the recorded speech. Computer programs help in that process. For some purposes, researchers may not need to collect new speech samples if their question can be addressed by examining the speech samples contained in the CHILDES archive. For descriptive and assessment purposes, a variety of norm-referenced tests and measures of language development are available. Because language development is a multidisciplinary field, articles and chapters on language development appear in widely diverse sources. Most of these are indexed in one of two computer-accessible databases: PsycInfo or Linguistics and Language Behavior Abstracts.

# ● KEY TERMS

behaviorism

cognitivism

cognitive science

nature–nurture

empiricism

nativism

interactionism

language input

social interactionism

constructivism

emergentism

domain-specific capacities

domain-general capacities

Universal Grammar

modularity

connectionism

statistical learning

rule learning

formalism

functionalism

developmental approach

learnability approach

speech samples

CHILDES

Psychological Abstracts/PsychInfo

Linguistics and Language Behavior Abstracts

## ● REVIEW QUESTIONS

1. Describe the role the study of language development plays in cognitive science and applied fields.
2. Learning a language involves learning in several separable domains. List and define these components of language knowledge.
3. What questions can be addressed by studying children who grow up without exposure to language?
4. What was the Chomskyan revolution, and why did it affect the study of language development?
5. Define and contrast the nativist and interactionist views of language development.
6. What is the modularity hypothesis with respect to language development? What is the alternative?
7. What is the crucial difference between statistical learning and rule learning as applied to language acquisition?

8. Define and contrast formalism and functionalism as theories of language development.
9. Define and contrast the developmental and learnability approaches to the study of language development.
10. What can be learned from studying language development in other cultures and other language groups that cannot be learned from studying the acquisition of one language in one culture?
11. Imagine you had to explain to your skeptical family (or roommate, or somebody) why you are taking a whole course just on language development. How would you justify spending this much time on such a narrow topic?

# Biological Bases of Language Development

Having outlined the basic facts and major issues with respect to language acquisition, we now turn our attention to the organism that accomplishes this feat. Clearly some unique property of humans explains why all humans talk, but dogs and gerbils never do so. In this chapter, we will look for that biologically given aspect of human nature. We will begin by reviewing evidence that language is not only a universal characteristic of humans, but also that it is a virtually inevitable feature of human society. Next we will turn to a discussion of the particular biological structures that underlie language, including the human vocal tract, but most crucially, the brain. After a discussion of the neurological bases of language, we will examine whether language development displays two hallmarks of biologically based abilities: a critical period for development and heritability. Having thus explored the biological bases of language in humans, we will turn to the question of whether language is *uniquely* human. We will look at the naturally occurring communication systems of other species and determine whether they have the characteristics of language, and we will look at the results of attempts to teach a human language to another species. Finally, we will ask where the human capacity for language came from in the evolutionary history of our species.

## LANGUAGE AS A HUMAN UNIVERSAL

Wherever there are humans, there is language. Just as fish swim and birds (with a few exceptions) fly, humans talk. That characteristic depends on the fact that all humans (barring impairment) are capable of learning language. But when we compare language in humans to flying in birds or swimming in fish, we really mean something more. We mean that language is not merely something that humans can do if exposed to the right conditions; rather, that language is something that humans cannot help doing.

### Language creation

In the normal course of events, each generation learns to speak the language it hears spoken by others, and thus the universality of language could reflect both the universal availability of models to learn from and the universal ability to learn. However, evidence suggests that language is more intrinsic to human nature than that. If there is no language model to learn from, it seems that humans create language.

***Pidgins.***    Sometimes historical circumstance throws together people who share no common language. To communicate in this situation, people invent a language that typically uses the lexical items from one or more of the contact languages but which has its own, very primitive grammar. Such languages are called **pidgins,** and they have arisen many times in history. For example, Hawaiian Pidgin English arose on the sugar cane plantations in Hawaii during the early part of this century when immigrant workers from Japan, Korea, and the Philippines came together; they shared no language with one another or with the English speakers for whom they worked (Bickerton, 1981, 1984). Another example is Russenorsk, which arose when Russian and Norwegian fishermen needed to communicate with each other (Todd, 1974). These are not isolated examples. More than 100 pidgin languages are currently in use (Romaine, 1988). Most pidgins are structurally simple, although if used over many generations, they do evolve, as do all languages (Aitchison, 1983; Sankoff & Laberge, 1973).

*Creoles.*     Children born into a community in which a pidgin language is the common means of communication acquire that pidgin as their native language. When children learn a pidgin, they add to it. They do not merely acquire the simple language they hear; rather, they create a new language that is grammatically more complex. Usually we think of children as acquiring language, rather than the other way around. A creole, in contrast, results when a language acquires children (Sankoff & Laberge, 1973). A **creole** is usually defined as a language that once was a pidgin but which subsequently became a native language for some speakers (Todd, 1974). Thus, "creolization" is a process that creates new languages. It is unknown how many of the world's languages originated in this way because the evidence is lost to prehistory, but there are signs that Swahili may be the result of contact between Arabic and Bantu languages (Todd, 1974).

The process of creolization does tell us something about the biological basis of language. First, creolization suggests that the existence of language in a community does not depend on someone importing a language for the community to learn. People can invent their own. (In pidgins, the vocabulary is borrowed from one of the contact languages, but the grammar is not, as the example in Box 2.1 shows.) Furthermore, when children acquire the language, they add some grammatical features that are universal characteristics of

---

**Box 2.1     Examples of utterances in Hawaiian Pidgin English**

1. Ifu laik meiki, mo beta make time, mani no kaen hapai.
   (If like make, more better die time, money no can carry.)
   "If you want to build (a temple), you should do it just before you die—you can't take it with you!"
2. Aena tu macha churen, samawl churen, haus mani pei.
   (And too much children, small children, house money pay.)
   "And I had many children, small children, and I had to pay the rent."

Source: From Bickerton, 1990.

human languages. Creoles that arose independently in different places nonetheless have similar characteristics. The shared features of independently arising creoles suggest that the human mind tends to construct only certain kinds of languages (Gee, 1993; and see Todd, 1974).

Not everyone agrees with the foregoing view of the origin of pidgins and creoles. Some argue that the similarities among creoles do not necessarily result from properties of the human mind but from the common uses to which all languages are put (Jourdan, 1991), or from the fact that many creoles have been influenced by the same language (Muysken, 1988; and see Todd, 1974). For example, many creoles show the influence of either English or Portuguese because of Britain's history as a colonial power and because the Portuguese historically were worldwide seafarers and traders. Furthermore, some argue that the creolization process does not depend on children acquiring a pidgin as their native tongue. It is difficult to settle arguments about the origin of creoles as long as the processes under dispute occurred a long time ago. What would really be informative would be to watch a pidgin develop into a creole.

***The development of Nicaraguan sign language.*** A new language creating much interest has been developing for the past 25 years in Nicaragua. The setting for this event is the public schools for the deaf that the government of Nicaragua opened in 1978, enabling deaf children in that country to come together for the first time. When they entered the school, these deaf children had no shared language. They did have their own idiosyncratic manual systems that they had developed for communicating with their families, but no way of communicating with each other. (The manual systems that children invent are termed *home sign*. In Chapter 7, we will discuss the nature of the home sign systems that children develop and how they, too, are evidence of the language-making capacity of the human mind.)

Once these children were in daily contact with each other in these newly established schools, a new language, Nicaraguan Sign Language (NSL) began to develop. Ann Senghas has studied changes in this evolving language (Senghas & Coppola, 2001) by comparing the signing of individuals who learned the language in its early years of evolution to the signing of individuals who have learned the language more recently. She has found changes in the direction of the language moving from a structurally simpler language to a structurally more complex language. She has also found that the differences in structural complexity appear primarily in the signing of those who begin to learn the language at an early age. It is as though older learners are less able to master precisely those complexities that characterize the more evolved form of the language.

For example, in developed sign languages, such as American Sign Language, the location in which a sign is produced (slightly to the left or right of the signer) modulates the meaning of the sign. So, if a speaker produces the sign for "cup" and the sign for "tall" in the same location, that indicates that "tall" modifies "cup." In its first version, NSL did not have these spatial modulations; 20 years later it did. In 1995, Senghas studied the signing of individuals who entered the school before and after 1983 and found differences between these two groups in their use of spatial modulations—the second group used them much more. Within that second group, however, it made a difference how old the individuals were when they were first exposed to NSL. The younger they were at first exposure, the more they use spatial modulations in their signing. These findings suggest that the changes that have occurred in NSL over time depend particularly on having young children acquiring the language, and thus the findings suggest that it is children, more than adults, who contain within them the engine that drives language creation.

## The common basis of language creation and acquisition

It has been argued that the capacity for language creation evidenced in phenomena such as creolization and the development of NSL is the same capacity that underlies language acquisition. One argument holds that the processes are both ones in which children take a little bit of material from what they experience, add to it their own internal knowledge of language, and produce a language system as a result. This is essentially the **language bioprogram hypothesis** proposed by the linguist Derek Bickerton (1981, 1984, 1988), who has argued that humans are endowed with an innate skeletal or "core" grammar that constitutes "part or all, of the human species–specific capacity for syntax" (Bickerton, 1984, p. 178). Normally, in the process of language acquisition, input in the target language causes the language-learning child to modify and add to this bioprogram. In the absence of a full-fledged target language, the bioprogram builds a language using the available input to fill out the core grammar. Evidence for Bickerton's proposal consists of his analysis of a few creole languages and his claim of similarities between creoles and child language. Both types of evidence have been called into question (for example, Aitchison, 1983; Corne, 1984; Goodman, 1984). However, the general idea that the same language-specific inborn ability underlies both language acquisition and language creation is quite consistent with the nativist approach to language acquisition (Pinker, 1994; Senghas & Coppola, 2001).

Critics, however, have proposed an alternative point of view. It is possible to accept the proposal that creolization, language creation, and language acquisition all reflect the same process without accepting the idea that this process is language specific. Bates (1984) argued that both language creation and language acquisition result from nonlinguistic cognitive mechanisms seeking a solution to communicating. Meier (1984) also argued that general cognitive mechanisms could underlie creolization and language acquisition. According to Meier, a process similar to creolization occurs when deaf children acquire sign language from parents who are not themselves native signers. Newport (1982) described differences in the linguistic competence of first- and second-generation signers that show structural additions similar to some of the changes that Senghas (1995) described. In particular, second-generation signers have analyzed the morphological structure of words that first-generation signers use only as frozen forms. However, Newport (1982) explains this change as a result of the way children analyze form-meaning relations in their input, which, in turn, is similar to the way children analyze patterns in other cognitive domains.

In sum, the evidence clearly argues that language is an intrinsic part of human nature. Humans are not just able to learn language; by nature, they create language. Furthermore, this capacity to create language seems to belong especially to children. There is disagreement, however, over the extent to which this capacity is unique to children and specific to language. We will leave these questions for the moment and turn to a description of the anatomical structures that serve this capacity—the vocal tract and, more importantly, the brain.

## THE HUMAN VOCAL TRACT AND LANGUAGE

The capacity to produce speech depends on the structure and the functioning of the human vocal tract, which is illustrated in Figure 2.1. Speech is produced when air from the lungs exits the larynx and is filtered by the vocal tract above the larynx. We can change the pitch of the sound we produce by tightening or loosening the vocal folds in the larynx. We can further change the sound that comes out of our mouths by changing the shape of the vocal tract above the larynx (or, technically speaking, the **supralaryngeal vocal tract**).

Although the structures in our vocal tract serve other purposes—biting, chewing, swallowing, taking in air—these structures have features that seem better suited for speaking than for their other functions. Human teeth are even and upright, which is not necessary for eating but is useful for producing certain sounds, such as [s] and [f]. The human lips and tongue also have properties that are useful for rapidly producing different sounds but are not particularly necessary for anything else (Aitchison, 1989). The most notably speech-specific feature of the human vocal tract is the position of the larynx. In humans, compared with other mammals, the larynx is low. Although this feature is good for producing speech sounds, it comes at a cost. Because our larynx is low, food from our mouths can fall into the trachea, and we run the risk of choking to death. Other animals have a higher larynx, and they can close off the passage for air into the lungs. Thus, other animals can breathe through their nose and drink at the same time; humans cannot. Changes in the shape of the mouth that go along with the lower larynx also account for the frequent human problem of overcrowded teeth and impacted wisdom teeth (Lieberman, 1991). These life-threatening disadvantages that come with a vocal tract that is good for speech suggest that speech must have been very useful to the first hominids who had it. It must have given them a survival advantage that more than compensated

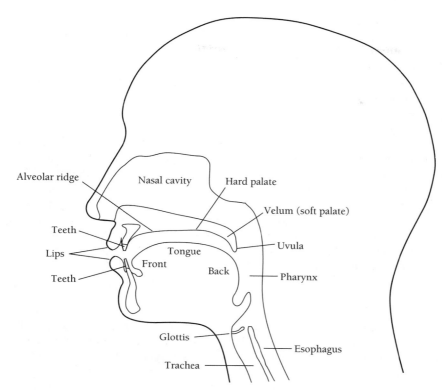

**Figure 2.1** The human vocal tract

for the risk of death from infected teeth and choking on food. It is possible to look at fossils to see when the hominid vocal tract first had a shape that would have supported modern speech. According to Philip Lieberman (1984, 1991), no hominid before Cro-Magnon was capable of producing the range of sounds in modern languages. Lieberman suggests that the advantage of having language may explain why the Cro-Magnon survived and its nonlinguistic contemporary, the Neanderthal, did not.

## THE HUMAN BRAIN AND LANGUAGE

A human vocal tract alone is not sufficient for language, and the existence of sign languages shows that it is not even necessary. Language requires a human brain. In this section, we describe what is known as the **functional architecture** of the brain—how the brain is organized to do what the brain does. To the untrained observer, the human brain appears to be an undifferentiated, wrinkly mass (see Figure 2.2). The only obvious structural feature is a fissure that divides the brain on its longer axis into two halves. Somewhere within this mass of tissue is the physical basis of the human capacity for language. **Neurolinguistics** is the study of the relation of the brain to language functioning. The goal of research in this field is to discover not only where language resides in the brain but also what it is about our brain that makes language possible.

One question that neurolinguistic investigations might answer is whether we have a "language organ" (to use Chomsky's term) that is in the brain but separate from the rest of it. This question is really the neuroanatomical version of the question of whether language is a separate, isolated ability or just one manifestation of humans' general cognitive capacity. Another question that studies of the brain might answer is whether language itself is one thing or many things. That is, are syntax, semantics, and pragmatics different competencies in the brain or only in the theories of the linguists who study language? Questions of what are separate competencies are addressed in neurolinguistics in part by examining whether these functions are carried out by different parts of the brain. To understand the research in this area, we need to begin with basic neuroanatomy.

## Some basic neuroanatomy

The appearance of the brain as an undifferentiated mass is misleading. The brain actually has different parts that perform different functions. When you look at an intact brain, what you see is the outer layer—the **cerebral cortex.** Hidden underneath the large cortex are the subcortical parts of the brain. Roughly speaking, the cortex controls higher mental functions, such as reasoning and planning, and **subcortical structures** control more primitive functions, such as eating and breathing. The cortex itself is divided into two cerebral hemispheres; in most individuals, the area of the cortex that sits over the ear (the temporal lobe) is larger in the left cerebral hemisphere than in the right (Geschwind & Levitsky, 1968). The left and right cerebral hemispheres are connected by a band of nerve fibers known as the **corpus callosum.** An interesting feature of the human nervous system, which will be important to understanding some of the research on the brain and language, is that each cerebral hemisphere is connected to the opposite side of the body. As a result of these **contralateral connections,** the right side of the brain controls the left side of the body, and vice versa. Also, information coming in to sense receptors (e.g., the ears, the skin) on the right side of the body goes directly to the left cerebral hemisphere, and vice versa. (There are also same-side or **ipsilateral connections,** but these are not as strong as the contralateral connections.) These, then, are the basic outlines of the organ that neurolinguists study: two cerebral hemispheres connected to the rest of the body by contralateral fibers, connected to each other by the corpus callosum, and sitting on top of subcortical structures. How can we find out what these different parts do?

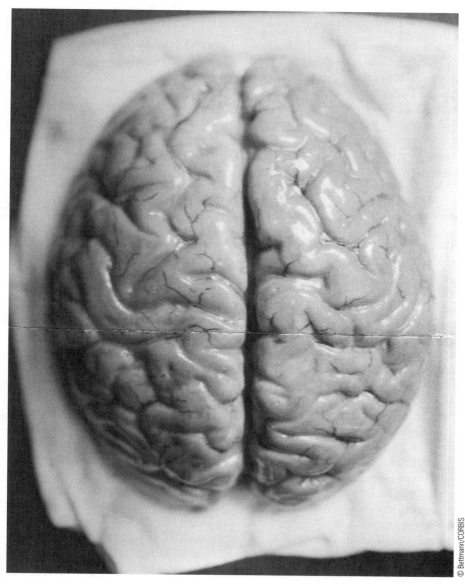

**Figure 2.2** The human brain viewed from above. The physical appearance of the human brain does not reveal what the brain does or how it does it. The field of neurolinguistics is devoted to the study of what structures in the brain are involved in language processing and language acquisition and how those structures serve their linguistic functions.

## Methods of neurolinguistic investigation

A relatively primitive but extremely useful way to examine what different parts of the brain do is to study patients who have suffered injuries to different parts of their brains and determine what functions are impaired as a result. This technique is known as the **lesion method**—lesions being localized areas of damaged brain tissue. The goal of the lesion method is to correlate bits of missing brain with bits of missing psychological functioning (Damasio, 1988). Some individuals have a severed corpus callosum but an otherwise undamaged brain. These patients are called **split-brain patients,** and studying them provides a unique window on how each hemisphere functions.

Other methods are used to study healthy, intact individuals. For example, **dichotic listening tasks** use the fact that the contralateral connections from the ears to the brain are stronger than the ipsilateral connections. Experimenters can present two stimuli simultaneously and ask which one is perceived. If the information presented to the left ear wins the competition to be processed, we can infer that the processing occurs in the right hemisphere. If the information presented to the right ear wins out, the processing must occur in the left hemisphere (Kimura, 1967). Another way to study the intact brain at work is to place electrodes on the scalp and monitor the electrical activity below the surface. These electrodes detect voltage fluctuations. The voltage fluctuations associated with the presentation of particular stimuli or the performance of particular tasks are known as event-related brain potentials (ERPs). The location of ERPs associated with different mental activities is taken as a clue to the area of the brain responsible for those activities (Caplan, 1987; Neville, 1995a).

In recent years, various **brain-imaging techniques** have been developed that enable researchers to monitor individuals as they perform different tasks (Saffran & Schwartz, 2003). For example, for positron emission tomography (PET scans), subjects inhale low-level radioactive gas or are injected with glucose that has been tagged with a radioactive substance; then computerized images can be obtained indicating which regions of the brain have the greatest blood flow or are using the most energy as individuals perform different tasks. Another brain-imaging technique, functional magnetic resonance imaging (fMRI), does not require the administration of a radioactive substance and can provide images of activity in the brain that result from patterns of blood flow and oxygen consumption.

Although the details of neurolinguistic research are technically difficult for those outside of neurology and the findings from this research are not wholly consistent, it is possible to draw some broad conclusions about the neurological representation of language in adults and to draw some tentative conclusion about areas of the brain used for language acquisition.

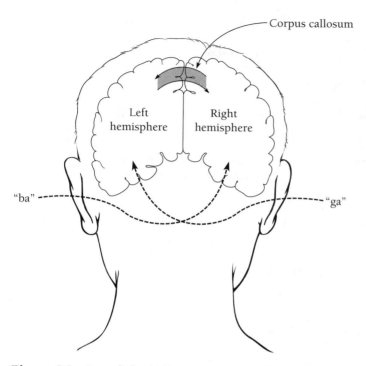

**Figure 2.3**   In a dichotic listening test, two different stimuli are presented simultaneously, one to each ear, and the listener is asked to report what was presented. Because the dominant neural connections are contralateral, information from the right ear reaches the left hemisphere before information from the left ear does, and vice versa. (The information presented to the left ear goes first to the right hemisphere and then must cross through the corpus callosum to reach the left hemisphere, and vice versa.) Thus if the listener reports hearing the stimulus presented to the right ear, the researcher infers that the left hemisphere is responsible for processing that stimulus. If the listener reports hearing the stimulus that was presented to the left ear, then the right hemisphere must be responsible for processing.

## Language as a left-hemisphere function

***Evidence from brain injury and aphasia.***   In 1861 the French physician Paul Broca reported to the Anthropological Society of Paris on a patient known as "Tan" because that single syllable was all he could say. Tan survived with this condition of near-total mutism for more than 20 years, although he also developed paralysis on the right side of his body in his later years. When

Broca examined Tan's brain in autopsy, he found a lesion on the left side caused by a fluid-filled cyst. Broca subsequently reported on many more cases in which patients had lost "the faculty of articulate language" (as Broca's words are often translated). All had left-hemisphere damage (see Caplan, 1987, for a full historical account).

The condition in which language functions are severely impaired is known as **aphasia.** Broca's basic observation that loss of language is typically a result of brain injury to the left but not the right hemisphere still stands today (Caplan, 1987; Goodglass, 1993; Saffran & Schwartz, 2003). Damage to the right cerebral hemisphere tends to cause different problems, particularly in processing visual-spatial information (Springer & Deutsch, 1981; Witelson, 1987). In broad terms, there seems to be a division of labor between the left and right hemispheres of the cerebral cortex: The left hemisphere is specialized for language (and some other things), and the right hemisphere is specialized for processing visual-spatial information. This state of affairs, in which one hemisphere is more important than the other for particular competencies, is known as **functional asymmetry.**

Although Broca concluded that "we speak with the left hemisphere," we can now modify that conclusion to say that the left hemisphere processes language—regardless of whether it is spoken or not. Bellugi, Poizner, and Klima (1989) studied deaf signers who had suffered strokes that damaged portions of either their left or their right hemisphere. The researchers found that left-hemisphere damage resulted in aphasia for signers just as it does for users of a spoken language. Furthermore, even though sign language uses a visual-spatial modality, signers with right-hemisphere damage were not aphasic. Thus, the left hemisphere is specialized for language, regardless of modality.

***Evidence from split-brain patients.***   Another source of evidence that language is a left-hemisphere function is found in individuals with a severed corpus callosum. The corpus callosum may be severed in a surgical procedure performed as a treatment for severe epilepsy that has not responded to other measures. Severing the connections between the two hemispheres seems to stop the spread of the electrical activity that accompanies seizures, reducing or eliminating the seizures (Gazzaniga, 1983). Patients who have had this surgery have an intact left hemisphere and an intact right hemisphere; thus, each hemisphere can still perform its normal functions. But because the corpus callosum is severed, there is no communication between the two hemispheres. These split-brain individuals have little difficulty functioning in daily life, but in experimental settings they provide researchers with the opportunity to study what each hemisphere does alone. Split-brain patients have been tested in experimental situations in which a picture is presented only in the left half of the visual field—that is, to the left of a center fixation point. Because the connections from the left half of each retina go to the right hemi-

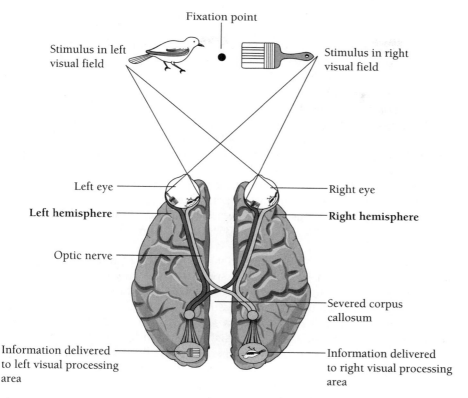

**Figure 2.4** Illustration of the information available to the left and right hemispheres of a split-brain patient

sphere, only the right hemisphere knows what is on the picture. The information available in this situation to each cerebral hemisphere of a split-brain patient is illustrated in Figure 2.4.

Split-brain patients in this situation typically cannot say what they saw. However, they are able to draw what they saw with their left hand (the one connected to the right hemisphere). Researchers believe that this inability of split-brain patients to indicate verbally what was presented to the left visual field means that the hemisphere that knows what's out there, the right hemisphere, cannot talk; and the left hemisphere, which can talk, doesn't know what's out there.

***Evidence from studies of undamaged adults.*** It is also possible to demonstrate that the left hemisphere is the locus of language activity in healthy, intact individuals. Imagine you are in an experiment in which you are wearing a headset, and syllables such as "ba" or "ga" are presented either to your left ear or to your right ear. Your task is to report what you hear. As you can probably imagine, this presents no problem. Now, what if the experimenter simultaneously presents "ba" to one ear and "ga" to the other? What would you hear? Doreen Kimura conducted this kind of dichotic listening experiment with adults and found a **right-ear advantage**—subjects reported more of the syllables that were presented to the right ear than to the left ear (Kimura, 1967).

This basic finding of a right-ear advantage for speech stimuli has been replicated many times (see Bryden & Allard, 1978; Springer & Deutsch, 1981), and it suggests that the part of the brain most directly connected to the right ear (the left hemisphere) is primarily responsible for processing speech stimuli (see Figure 2.3). Research using either scalp electrodes to measure ERPs or brain-imaging techniques to measure cortical activity has also found greater left-hemisphere activity associated with language processing (Ingvar & Schwartz, 1974; Mazziotta & Metter, 1988; Molfese, Freeman, & Palermo, 1975; Phelps & Mazziotta, 1985; Wood, Goff, & Day, 1971).

Why is the left hemisphere primarily responsible for processing language? It could be that the left hemisphere is specialized for language, per se; however, some research suggests other possibilities. Bever and Chiarello (1974) found that experienced musicians showed a right-ear (left-hemisphere) advantage for music, whereas naive listeners showed a left-ear (right-hemisphere) advantage for music. They suggested that trained musicians process music in a more analytical way than naive listeners do, and that analytical processing engages the left hemisphere. Another possibility is that the right hemisphere is better at processing novel stimuli, whereas the left is specialized for executing well-practiced routines (see Mills, Coffey-Corina, & Neville, 1997). Language, for adults, is a well-practiced routine. In either case, the findings suggest that the left hemisphere may be responsible for language because of how humans typically process language. Whatever it is about the organization of the left hemisphere, evidence from the study of the brain injuries associated with aphasia, from the study of split-brain patients, and from the study of functional asymmetries in intact adults all point to the conclusion that language is predominantly a left-hemisphere function.

## Language as not exclusively a left-hemisphere function

Sometimes damage to the left cerebral hemisphere does not result in aphasia, and sometimes damage to the right cerebral hemisphere does. This finding suggests that for some individuals, language may not be exclusively a left-hemisphere function. In some people, usually left-handed people, language is controlled by the right hemisphere. Also, the right hemisphere apparently shares language functions with the left hemisphere. It does so more for some individuals than for others, and (on average) more in women than in men.

***Right-hemisphere contributions to language.*** The right cerebral hemisphere makes some contribution to normal language functioning, even in individuals who show the typical left-hemisphere dominance for language. Evidence for this functioning is manifest in language impairments associated with right-hemisphere damage.

Right-hemisphere lesion patients sometimes produce abnormal intonation contour when they speak, and they may have difficulty recognizing the emotional tone of an utterance (Caplan, 1987). Right hemisphere–damaged patients have difficulty understanding jokes, understanding sarcasm, interpreting figurative language, and following indirect requests (Weylman, Brownell, & Gardner, 1988). These difficulties suggest that the right hemisphere may be involved in the pragmatic aspects of language use (Weylman et al., 1988), although not in the "core" psycholinguistic capacities (Caplan, 1987). Studies of ERPs in intact patients show that the right hemisphere is activated by semantic processing, whereas the left hemisphere is activated primarily by syntax processing (Neville, Nicol, Barss, Forster, & Garrett, 1991). In sum, studies of what the right hemisphere contributes to language when the left hemisphere is intact indicate that the right hemisphere is involved in semantics and pragmatics but that syntax is the province of the left hemisphere.

Another question about the linguistic functions of the right hemisphere concerns what the right hemisphere could do if it had to, as in cases of left-hemisphere damage. Again, the answer seems to be that the right hemisphere has some semantic and pragmatic competence, but limited syntactic (and phonological) abilities. This answer comes from studies of patients who have had their left hemispheres removed (because of severe pathology) and from studies of the language capacity of the right hemisphere in split-brain patients (Baynes & Gazzaniga, 1988; Dennis, 1980; Gazzaniga, 1983; Zaidel, 1985). This finding converges well with the findings from ERP studies that show more right-hemisphere involvement in language for individuals who learned language late (Neville, 1995a) and with the evidence that these late language learners are not quite as good at syntax as are those who learned language in infancy (Johnson & Newport, 1989; Newport, 1990). We will return to the question of the right hemisphere's capacity for language when we discuss the case of Genie—a child who acquired what language she did relatively late in life and who seems to have done so with her right hemisphere.

***Individual and sex-related differences.*** Everybody's brain is different. Although the standard description of the left hemisphere as the seat of language functions is true for most people (between 80 percent and 98 percent, depending on the source of the estimate), it is not true for everyone, and the degree of dominance is not always the same (Bryden, Hecaen, & DeAgostini, 1983; Caplan, 1987; Milner, 1974). People who are left-handed (but still left-hemisphere dominant) and even people who are right-handed but have left-handed family mem-

> **Box 2.2   Example of speech produced by a patient with Broca's aphasia**
>
> Yes . . . ah . . . Monday . . . er . . . Dad and Peter H . . . (his own name), and Dad . . . er . . . hospital . . . and ah . . . Wednesday . . . Wednesday, nine o'clock . . . and oh . . . Thursday . . . ten o'clock, ah doctors . . . two . . . an' doctors . . . and er . . . teeth . . . yah.

Source: From Goodglass, 1979, p. 256.

bers may show more bilateral participation in language (Caplan, 1987). Also, women show more bilateral participation in language than men do (McGlone, 1980). Even within the left hemisphere, there are individual differences in where language functions are represented, although the causes and consequences of individual differences in brain organization are open questions at this point (Goodglass, 1993).

## Other neurological divisions of labor

Language appears to be multifaceted, not only from the linguist's point of view, but also from the neurologist's. The "real estate" of the brain appears to be more finely zoned into areas of specialization than merely the distinction between the left and right hemisphere. One source of evidence for the multifaceted nature of language is the fact that there are many different types of aphasia. Some individuals with aphasia have difficulty producing speech, and the speech they do produce seems to lack grammatical structure. Instead, their speech tends to consist of short strings of content words—nouns and verbs—without grammatical morphemes. This syndrome is termed **Broca's aphasia.** Other individuals with aphasia have no trouble producing speech, but the speech they produce makes no sense. This syndrome is termed **Wernicke's aphasia.** When patients with Wernicke's aphasia speak, either they use words that are wrong for the meaning they are trying to express or they use made-up, meaningless words. The speech of Wernicke's aphasics has been described as "syntactically full but semantically empty" (Blumstein, 1988, p. 203). Examples of the speech of patients with Broca's and Wernicke's aphasia are presented in Boxes 2.2 and 2.3. When one function can be disrupted without affecting another, we say these two functions are dissociable. In fact, there are many more different types of aphasia than just these two. (For more detailed descriptions of aphasia in adults, see Blumstein, 1988; Caplan, 1987; Goodglass, 1993; Saffran & Schwartz, 2003.)

---

**Box 2.3   Example of speech produced by a patient with Wernicke's aphasia**

The patient is responding to the question, "How are you today?": "I feel very well. My hearing, writing been doing well. Things that I couldn't hear from. In other words, I used to be able to work cigarettes I didn't know how . . . Chesterfeela, for 20 years I can write it."

---

Source: From Goodglass, 1993, p. 86.

A great deal of research has been directed toward trying to relate the particular type of aphasia with the particular location of brain damage within the left hemisphere—to create a zoning map of the brain, in effect. Some findings suggest that the localization of function is fairly narrowly delineated. For example, Broca's aphasia is typically associated with damage to the front part of the left hemisphere, near the part of the cortex that controls movement: an area known as **Broca's area.** Wernicke's aphasia is typically associated with damage to a region more posterior than Broca's area, next to the primary auditory cortex: **Wernicke's area.** These areas are mapped in Figure 2.5. The association between the location of left-hemisphere damage and the particular sort of resulting language impairment inspired hypotheses that Broca's area was the seat of grammar and Wernicke's area the seat of meaning. Other sources of evidence on the localization of language functions are ERP and brain-imaging studies, and these also suggest that different parts of the left hemisphere carry out different linguistic jobs (Neville et al., 1991; Stromswold, Caplan, Alpert, & Rausch, 1996).

The enterprise of drawing a zoning map of the brain is a difficult one, however, and there is not even agreement on whether it can ultimately be successful. The patterns of symptoms seen in brain-damaged patients is actually messier than the foregoing description admits. Not only are there more than just two aphasic syndromes (Saffran & Schwartz, 2003), it is also the case that many patients are classified as "mixed" in the type of asphasia they present. Furthermore, the symptoms that brain-injured patients show are not reliably related to the site of their injury. Although it is clear from studies of brain-injured patients that language is not one unitary function carried out equally by all parts of the brain, it is not quite clear just how the task is divided into components and parceled out to different neural locations.

Another sort of correspondence between neurology and language processing that has been proposed is that two different and neurologically distinct

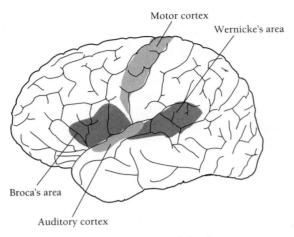

Motor cortex

Wernicke's area

Broca's area

Auditory cortex

**Figure 2.5** Language areas of the brain

mechanisms underlie language processing and language acquisition. As mentioned in Chapter 1, Pinker (1999) has argued that both an associative memory system and rule-based processes are the necessary ingredients for language. The associative memory system stores words; the rule-based processes take care of grammar. Neurological support for this dual-processes model comes from the study of patients who have particular deficits in either one system or the other. Both aphasic patients with word-finding difficulties and Alzheimer's patients with general memory impairments appear to have deficits in the associative memory system. In contrast, some aphasic patients and some patients with Parkinson's disease have specifically grammatical difficulties.

When these two different types of patients were given experimental tests in which they had to produce the past tense form of verbs, the two groups produced very different patterns of results. For the patients with associative memory difficulties, producing irregular past tense forms (e.g., *went*) was difficult; producing regular past tense forms was not. For the patients with grammatical difficulties, producing regular past tense forms (e.g., *walked*) was difficult; producing irregulars was not (Ullman et al., 1997). Thus, the evidence is consistent with the proposal that two separate neurological systems support language. Damage or degeneration in one (the associative memory system) affects lexical retrieval, including the ability to retrieve rote-learned forms such as irregular past tense forms. Damage or degeneration in the other (the rule-implementing system) affects the ability to produce grammatical speech, including the ability to generate rule-governed regular past tense forms.

## BRAIN DEVELOPMENT AND LANGUAGE DEVELOPMENT

Despite the qualifications required in describing the neurological basis of language, in most adults, language is controlled primarily by the left cerebral hemisphere, and the left hemisphere seems particularly specialized for grammar. We turn now to questions concerning how that adult organization is reached.

### The development of the left-hemisphere specialization for language

*The hypotheses.*    Traditionally, researchers have held two competing views on the development of the left-hemisphere specialization for language in the adult brain. One view, termed the **equipotentiality hypothesis,** holds that the left hemisphere is not specialized for language at birth. Rather, the left and right hemispheres have equal potential for acquiring language (Bishop, 1983, 1988; Lenneberg, 1967). This hypothesis has often been interpreted to mean that language is initially represented in both hemispheres and shifts to the left hemisphere only with maturation. Given that interpretation, one would expect that measures of dichotic listening performance, measures of brain activity during language processing, and the effects of brain injury on children should show a different and less-lateralized pattern than would the corresponding data from adults. However, it is also possible to interpret equipotentiality more narrowly—to mean that the right hemisphere has only the *potential* to serve language, not that it normally does serve language (Satz, Strauss, & Whitaker, 1990).

The opposite view regarding the ontogeny of cerebral lateralization is termed the **invariance hypothesis.** According to this view, the left hemisphere has the adult specialization for language from birth; nothing about lateralization changes with development. This view predicts that data from children—on lateralization of language processing and on effects of brain damage—should look much like the data from adults. (For fuller discussions of these two hypotheses, see Kinsbourne, 1993; Satz & Lewis, 1993; Satz et al., 1990; Witelson, 1987.) We turn now to the data that address these hypotheses.

*Evidence from processing studies with children.*    When researchers study the processing of speech stimuli in children, using the same methods to assess lateralization of function that are used with adults, they find evidence of left-hemisphere specialization beginning in infancy. For example, Molfese, Freeman, and Palermo (1975) presented spoken syllables, spoken words, and nonspeech sounds to three groups of children: infants under 10 months old, children between 4 and 11 years old, and adults. Using scalp electrodes, Molfese and associates recorded the left- and right-hemisphere electrophysiological activity associated with presentation of each kind of stimulus. As expected, they found that most of the participants showed greater left-hemisphere activity in response to the speech sounds and greater right-hemisphere activity in response to non-speech sounds. And, important for the developmental question, they found that the proportion of the children who showed this lateralization of speech sound processing remained constant from infancy to adulthood. This basic finding has been replicated many times (Molfese & Betz, 1988).

Asymmetries of function in children have also been found using dichotic listening tasks. Children as young as 2 years have shown a right-ear advantage for verbal stimuli, as adults do (Hiscock, 1988). Further investigations have tried to identify what it is about the speech stimuli that elicits left-hemisphere activity in infants. Using a dichotic listening procedure modified for use with infants, Best (1988) found a right-ear advantage for consonants but not for vowels. Best suggested that it is the rapidly changing acoustic properties of consonants—in contrast to the steady-state acoustic properties of vowels—that evoke the left-hemisphere response. This finding is consistent with the notion that the left-hemisphere specialization for language is really specialization for serial processing.

In sum, research on hemispheric differences in language processing in children suggests that the left hemisphere is specialized for language from as early an age as infants can be tested (including preterm infants). However, this is not to say that the infant brain is the same as the adult brain. It is not. In fact, the human brain does not reach its mature state until after the age of 15 (Neville, 1991); and although there is asymmetry from birth, the degree of that asymmetry changes with development (Witelson, 1987). Results such as those from Molfese and colleagues (1975) show constancy only in the proportion of participants who show left-hemisphere dominance for language. Results on the degree of dominance are a different and considerably more complicated matter. However, there is substantial evidence that the degree of lateralization of function increases with development, and we will come back to this fact shortly. First we review one other source of data used to address questions about the development of cerebral asymmetry.

***Evidence from childhood aphasia.***    There are fewer studies of childhood aphasia than of aphasia in adults, because the strokes and war-related gunshot injuries that are the primary cause of aphasia in adults affect children less frequently. Thus, the data on childhood aphasia are sketchier than the data on adulthood aphasia, and the picture that emerges is subject to different interpretations.

At one time it was thought that aphasia in children was equally likely to result from left- or right-hemisphere damage and that, unlike adults, children could recover completely from aphasia. If this were true, it would certainly support the equipotentiality theory, and a very famous argument to this effect was made by Eric Lenneberg in 1967. Although Lenneberg still deserves credit for being one of the first to see that biological data could inform studies of language development, more-recent data on childhood aphasia largely contradict the equipotentiality view.

In the first aphasia study to establish that language is a left-hemisphere function for children as well as for adults, Woods and Teuber (1978) looked at 65 children who suffered unilateral brain damage to either the left or the right hemisphere. They found that aphasia almost always followed left-hemisphere injury and rarely followed right-hemisphere injury, just as is the case for adults. Woods and Teuber argued that earlier reports of aphasia following right-hemisphere injury described cases that occurred before antibiotics were used, and that the aphasias that were observed following right-hemisphere injury were actually caused by bacterial infections that affected the whole brain. In the first research to question the notion that children fully recover from aphasia, Woods and Carey (1979) administered a battery of tests to adolescents and adults who had suffered from aphasia in childhood but who seemingly had recovered from their symptoms. These "recovered" individuals scored below normal controls on these tests, leading Woods and Carey to conclude that when left-hemisphere damage causes aphasia in childhood, it leaves "significant residual impairment" (p. 409). More-recent studies have confirmed this finding (Aram, Ekelman, Rose, & Whitaker, 1985; Vargha-Khadem, O'Gorman, & Watters, 1985). This newer aphasia evidence is generally interpreted as agreeing with the electrophysiological data and dichotic listening studies in suggesting left-hemisphere specialization for language from birth (for a contrary view, see Bishop, 1983, 1988).

Also like the processing data, however, the data on childhood aphasia suggest that the immature brain is not organized in quite the same way as the adult brain. Childhood aphasia differs from adulthood aphasia in several ways. The type of aphasia that children experience following left-hemisphere damage is different. Children are more likely to suffer nonfluent (Broca-type) aphasia, whereas Wernicke's aphasia is more common in adults. This difference suggests that within the left hemisphere, developmental changes affect the way language functions are organized (see also Satz & Lewis, 1993; Stiles & Thal, 1993). Also, recovery from aphasia is faster and more nearly complete in children than in adults; and for children, some evidence suggests that the earlier the damage occurs, the better the recovery (Vargha-Khadem et al., 1985).

***Evidence from brain injury prior to language.***     So far we have talked about the effects of left-hemisphere damage on children who have already acquired language. What happens when the left hemisphere is damaged prior to language acquisition? If the left hemisphere not only controls language processing but also is responsible for language acquisition, then left-hemisphere damage should severely impair the child's ability ever to acquire language.

Similarly, if the left hemisphere is solely responsible for language acquisition, then right-hemisphere damage should not affect language development.

Studies that have followed the language development of children who suffered brain damage either in utero or in the first few months of life find a different relation of injury site to language impairment than do studies of older children or adults. A crude summary of the very complicated findings in this field is as follows: brain damage in either the right or left hemisphere prior to language acquisition can cause language delay. The relation of injury site to delay is different for different components of language development and differs for expressive language and language comprehension. One thing that seems clear in the messy pattern of results is that the right hemisphere is more involved in language acquisition than it is in language functioning once language is acquired. That is, early right-hemisphere damage impairs language acquisition more than later right-hemisphere damage impairs language functioning.

In general, these brain-injured children catch up after their initial delays, and by age 5 to 7 years, children who experienced brain injury prior to language acquisition score within the normal range on standardized tests of language. Some effects of the early damage remain, however. When researchers study the effects of early brain damage, they typically identify a control group of children matched to the children with brain injury in terms of age, sex, and socioeconomic status. Although the children with early brain injury come to score within the normal range on standardized tests by the age of 5 to 7 years, they still do not score at the same level as the matched control children (Feldman, Holland, Kemp, & Janosky, 1992; Levy, Amir, & Shalev, 1992; Satz & Lewis, 1993; Stiles, Bates, Thal, Trauner, & Reilly, 1998).

In sum, data from the neurological study of language in children suggest a position somewhere between equipotentiality and invariance. On the side of invariance, the data from intact and brain-injured children suggest some cortical specialization present from birth. On the side of equipotentiality (if not true equipotentiality, at least more nearly equal potential of both hemispheres), the degree of asymmetry in brain function increases with development, and the ability of the right hemisphere to take over language functions for a damaged left hemisphere is greater in children than in adults. But why does the degree of asymmetry change, and why do children recover from aphasia better than adults do? We'll start with the question about developmental changes in the ability to recover from aphasia.

## Basic processes in neurological development

***Neural plasticity in childhood.***    That children recover language after left-hemisphere damage more rapidly and more fully than do adults suggests that something must be different in children's brains. Children's brains have more

**plasticity** than adults' brains do. Plasticity is the ability of parts of the brain to take over functions they ordinarily would not serve (Witelson, 1987). Brain tissue does not regenerate once it is damaged. Thus, when children with left-hemisphere damage recover language function, other areas of the brain must be taking over the functions previously carried out by the damaged portions of the left hemisphere. Although there is some plasticity in the adult brain, there is more in the child's.

The greater plasticity of the immature brain is the basis for children's better, if not perfect, recovery from aphasia. Evidence of subtle syntactic impairments even after recovery from childhood aphasia suggests that the right hemisphere is never quite as good as the left at some aspects of language. Although the plasticity of the immature brain allows one part to take over the work of another, there remain telltale signs that the right hemisphere is doing a job for which the left hemisphere is better suited. We have suggested to this point, then, that children recover better from left-hemisphere damage than adults do because the right hemisphere can take over, and we refer to this capacity as plasticity. But plasticity only labels the phenomenon; it doesn't explain it. We now turn to the question of what gives the immature brain its greater plasticity, and in so doing we start to find an explanation of why children have a greater capacity to recover from aphasia.

***Where does plasticity come from?***   The source of the great plasticity of the immature brain is likely the initial redundancy in the neural architecture. Beginning during the fetal period, the brain grows synaptic connections, reaching a peak between the ages of 2 and 5 years depending on the region of the brain. At this peak point, the brain has many more synaptic connections than it needs. Subsequent development consists primarily of losing connections (Huttenlocher, 1994; Bates, Thal, Finlay, & Clancy, 2001). As connections are lost, redundancy is lost, and thus particular functions come to be located in specifically dedicated areas rather than throughout the brain (Neville, 1995a).

For this sort of developmental process to work, there must be a way to ensure that only redundant connections, and not needed ones, are lost. This is accomplished by the activity of the young brain, which influences which connections are lost and which remain. A variety of evidence suggests that connections that are used become fixed or stabilized, whereas unused connections are eliminated. Unlike the early empiricists' notion of experience producing tracings on a blank slate, neurophysiological evidence shows that huge numbers of tracings are innately provided and that the absence of experience structures the brain by erasing some of them. (For fuller discussions, see Bertenthal & Campos, 1987; Greenough, Black, & Wallace, 1987; Huttenlocher, 1994; Neville, 1991; and Witelson, 1987.) Another metaphor used to describe the influence of experience on brain organization describes experience as a sculptor, shaping the brain by removing the portions it doesn't need (Kolb, 1989).

***Changes in functional asymmetry.***   This account of brain development as moving from an initial state of redundant capacity throughout the brain to one of nonredundant and hence localized function explains the difference between children and adults in recovery from aphasia. But it does not explain the developmental increase in asymmetry of function. In fact, if children use their right hemispheres for language, why is the right hemisphere's capacity for language ever lost? Shouldn't the bilateral activity associated with language in very young children preserve both hemispheres for language functions? The plasticity explanation explains only why an unused right hemisphere loses its language capacity; something else is needed to explain why the use of the right hemisphere for language declines.

Two proposals address what changes in children to account for the increasing lateralization of language functions to the left hemisphere. One holds that the brain changes; the other, that the children acquire grammar. The kind of brain change that would account for a shift of language to the left hemisphere is the maturation of those areas of the brain that serve language in the adult (see Satz, Strauss, & Whitaker, 1990). According to this account, the child initially uses both hemispheres more because the language centers in the left hemisphere aren't ready yet. (One would expect, then, that young children would be limited in their linguistic abilities, and indeed this seems to be the case.)

The second proposed explanation of increasing asymmetry of function holds that the brain doesn't change, but that children change the way they process language. As children come to process language in a way that makes use of what the left hemisphere has been ready to do all along, they use the left hemisphere more. According to this explanation, the increase in left-hemisphere specialization is a by-product or secondary manifestation of language development (see Witelson, 1977, 1987). Mills, Coffey, and Neville (1993, 1994) found a close correspondence between the acquisition of grammar in children and an increase in left-hemisphere language processing. Whether it is the acquisition of grammar that causes the shift to the left hemisphere or a change in the left hemisphere that causes the acquisition of grammar remains to be seen (Neville, 1995b).

Whatever the cause, under normal circumstances, a 2-year-old child has begun to acquire grammar and is predominantly using the left hemisphere to process language. Daily use of the left hemisphere for language appears to stabilize language in the left hemisphere and allows elimination of the redundant right-hemisphere capacity. If the left hemisphere is damaged early in life, the right hemisphere still has the capacity to take over language functions, but with age that capacity declines. Biology appears to set a timetable for removing connections that have not been used.

## THE CRITICAL PERIOD HYPOTHESIS

The notion that a biologically determined period exists during which language acquisition must occur, if it is to occur at all, is known as the **critical period hypothesis.** Nature provides many examples of biologically determined deadlines, the best known of which is probably the critical period for imprinting in birds. Some species of birds walk as soon as they hatch. Chicks and ducklings, for example, will follow the first moving thing they see, and then they will follow it forever. Normally, the first thing a baby sees when it hatches is its mother, with the result that chicks and ducklings then follow their mothers everywhere. When this occurs, the chicks and ducklings are said to be imprinted on their mother. Imprinting cannot happen any time; it must occur within a few hours after hatching. (This requirement is not always absolute, and the term **sensitive period** is sometimes substituted for critical period [Lieberman, 1993].)

There are well-documented human examples of critical periods as well. For example, some cells in the brain respond to input from both eyes in the normal adult, but if these cells fail to receive input from two eyes during the first year or two of life, they lose this capacity. Thus, the features common to all examples of critical or sensitive periods are these: some environmental input is necessary for normal development, but biology determines when the organism is responsive to that input. That period of responsivity is the critical period. If one were to design a study to test the critical period hypothesis, one would deprive children of exposure to language during the normal period of language development, provide the exposure later, and examine the language development that occurs. Of course, such an unethical experiment could never be done deliberately, but history has provided a few such cases.

### "Wild" children

Victor of Aveyron was such a case in which first exposure to language, so far as we know, came late. As mentioned in Chapter 1, Victor never acquired normal language. There are a few other cases of such wild children who also did not learn language under the circumstance of early deprivation and late first exposure, but it is difficult to learn much from such cases because they are so poorly documented. Furthermore, when such children fail to acquire language, we cannot be sure whether the failure was due to the late start or to some impairment the child might have had previously. Reviewing the evidence in 1967, Lenneberg came to the conclusion that "the only safe conclusions to be drawn from the multitude of reports is life in dark closets, wolves' dens, forests, or sadistic parents' backyards is not conducive to good health and normal development" (p. 142).

There is one success story among such children. In the 1930s, a 6-year-old child named Isabelle was discovered living hidden away in a dark room with only her deaf-mute mother for contact. After her discovery, Isabelle was trained intensively to speak, and she did learn to talk. Isabelle's success makes it clear that she was cognitively normal, but her deprivation was also less extreme than that of the other cases of wild children. Furthermore, we do not have the sort of psycholinguistic details about Isabelle we would like. Although at age 8 she was described as having "a normal IQ" and "not easily distinguished from ordinary children of her age" (Brown, 1958a, p. 192), no one administered the tests of linguistic competence that would allow detailed comparisons of her language competence with that of children with normal experience.

There is one modern case of a wild child who was discovered after linguistics and neurology were sufficiently advanced to allow us to ask questions that were not asked of the earlier cases.

## The case of Genie

In 1970 a woman who is known to most of the world only as "Genie's mother" was looking for the office of services for the blind in downtown Los Angeles. She was nearly blind, was seeking help for herself, and had only recently managed to escape virtual captivity by her mentally ill husband. By mistake, she entered the general social services office. She brought with her a 13-year-old daughter, Genie. The eligibility worker at the social services office noticed the small, frail-looking child with a strange gait and posture and called her supervisor, who, after questioning Genie's mother, called the police. The police took Genie into custody and admitted her into the hospital for severe malnutrition (Curtiss, 1977; Rymer, 1993).

The story of Genie's background that was eventually revealed was horrific. From the time Genie was 20 months old until her mother's escape when she was 13, Genie spent her time alone, strapped to a potty chair in a small bedroom. She was fed hurriedly, with minimal interaction and no talk. If Genie made any noise, her father would beat her with a large piece of wood he kept in the room for that purpose. Like the Wild Boy of Aveyron before her, Genie had no language when she was discovered. Also like Victor of Aveyron, Genie was immensely interesting to the scientific community. The story of Genie's life and treatment both before and after her discovery have been described by Curtiss (1977) and by Rymer (1993). We shall confine ourselves here to the investigation of Genie's language development, described by Susan Curtiss in her dissertation and subsequent papers (Curtiss, 1977, 1985, 1988, 1989).

Genie did not talk at all when she was first discovered. Four years later, she scored in the range of a normal 5-year-old on standardized vocabulary tests. She combined words into complex utterances, and she could express meanings. However, her language was far from normal. As the examples of Genie's speech in Box 2.4 show, her vocabulary and semantic skills far ex-

---

**Box 2.4    Examples of Genie's utterances**

Mama wash hair in sink.
At school scratch face.
I want Curtiss play piano.
Like go ride yellow school bus.
Father take piece wood. Hit. Cry.

---

Source: Curtiss, 1977.

ceeded her syntactic skills. Her grammar was deficient in both production and comprehension. In production, her utterances were telegraphic, lacking most grammatical morphemes. In comprehension tests, she failed to understand passive constructions and distinctions marked by tense, and she had other difficulties as well.

Another fact about Genie's language might be related to her grammatical limitations. Dichotic listening tests showed that language was a right-hemisphere activity for Genie. In fact, the nature of her grammatical limitations has been compared to the grammatical deficiencies of patients who have recovered language after surgical removal of the left hemisphere. One possible explanation of this phenomenon is that Genie was exposed to language too late for the normal process of acquisition of language as a left-hemisphere function. She acquired language with the right hemisphere, and—as we have seen in the aphasia data—the right hemisphere is not as good at language as the left. Genie's conversational competence was also extremely limited, and she often ignored the speech addressed to her. As Curtiss (1977) described it:

> Verbal interaction with Genie consists mainly of someone's asking Genie a question repeatedly until Genie answers, or of Genie's making a comment and someone else's responding to it in some way. . . . Except for those instances where Genie exerts control over the topic through repetition, verbal interaction with Genie is almost always controlled and/or "normalized" by the person talking to Genie, not by Genie. (p. 233)

Curtiss attributes this conversational incompetence to Genie's lack of early socializing experience.

The study of Genie is certainly more informative than earlier reports on isolated children. Evidence that language was a right-hemisphere function for Genie suggests that by age 13, a left hemisphere that has never been used for language has lost that capacity. However, interpretation of Genie's outcome is still hampered by the fact that we do not know with certainty that Genie was a normal child except for her experiences. Once, when Genie was seen by a doctor as an infant, she was diagnosed as mentally retarded. But there was never any follow-up to see whether that pediatrician's impression was correct, and even before Genie was totally isolated, she had something less than an ideal environment. Susan Curtiss, who worked most closely with Genie, vehemently disagrees with the possibility that Genie could be retarded (Rymer, 1993), but we simply do not know for sure.

## Late acquisition of American Sign Language

A better test of the critical period hypothesis is provided by individuals who have normal early experience except for being deprived of exposure to language. This is the circumstance of many children born deaf to hearing parents. These children have no language input at home because they cannot hear the language their family speaks, and their parents do not know sign language (and historically have been discouraged from learning it to communicate with their children, although this has changed in recent years). Many of these children are eventually exposed to sign language when they meet other deaf children, some of whom have deaf parents and have been exposed to sign language from infancy. Comparing the sign language acquisition of children who learned sign from infancy to that of children who were first exposed to it later in childhood or in adulthood provides a very nice test of the critical period hypothesis. If the young brain is better at language acquisition, deaf individuals who began to acquire sign as older children should be less proficient than those who acquired it in infancy.

Newport (1990) studied the sign language proficiency of deaf adults who ranged in age from 35 to 70, who used American Sign Language (ASL) in their everyday communication, and who had done so for more than 30 years. Some of these adults had acquired ASL as infants from their deaf parents. Some had first been exposed to ASL when they entered a school for the deaf between the age of 4 and 6; some had first been exposed only after the age of 12, when they entered the school as teenagers, or later, when they made friends with or married someone from that school. Newport administered a battery of comprehension and production tests to assess how well these deaf adults had mastered the grammar of ASL. She found that adults who were first exposed to ASL after early childhood—even after 30 years of using the language every day—did not perform as well as those who had been exposed as infants. Similarly, Mayberry and Eichen (1991) found that early learners of sign had an advantage over late learners in recalling and reproducing ASL sentences that were presented to them. This evidence suggests there is some benefit to being a young language learner.

## The evidence from second language acquisition

A far more frequently occurring test of the effect of age on language acquisition occurs in the realm of second language acquisition, and to the casual observer, the results are obvious. Children learn a new language readily, and soon after moving to a new language community they are indistinguishable from their native-born peers. Adults, in contrast, master a new language only with difficulty and never quite sound like native speakers. The gist of these everyday observations has been frequently supported by experimental tests: the younger one is when exposed to a second language, the better one's ultimate proficiency in that language. That fact does not necessarily support the critical period hypothesis, however. The hypothesis that biology sets a cutoff age after which language cannot be learned to native-like competence predicts an abrupt age-related change in the success of language learning that cannot be explained by other factors. As we shall see, the details of the findings regarding age and second language learning do not consistently support that strong hypothesis.

***Age effects on second language acquisition.*** Among adults who have emigrated to the United States from a non–English speaking country, their age of arrival in the United States predicts the degree to which they will have a foreign accent and their performance on grammatical judgment tasks. In both cases, the younger the immigrants were when they were first exposed to English, the more like native speakers they sound and perform.

In a study by Oyama (1976), the English speech of 60 Italian immigrants was tape-recorded, and two judges scored those records on a five-point scale ranging from no foreign accent to heavy foreign accent. Oyama then analyzed the influence of two variables: (1) the age of the immigrants at arrival in the United States and (2) the number of years living in the United States. Oyama found a strong effect of age at arrival, with young arrivals showing less accent than older ones. The number of years had no effect. Oyama (1978) similarly found strong age-of-arrival effects on second language users' ability to repeat English sentences presented to them under noisy conditions (i.e., static on the tape).

Other studies have similarly found that age of arrival affects the ability to speak a second language without an accent and that native-like performance depends on exposure beginning in early childhood (Flege, 1987; Flege & Fletcher, 1992). Sometimes the benefit of youth to acquiring unaccented speech in a second language is explained as the effect of age on acquiring a motor skill. Speech production involves moving the lips, tongue, and mouth in ways particular to each language, and that may be what is difficult for a late learner. However, there is more to knowing the sound system of a language than just the motor skill, and Oyama's (1978) finding of effects of age of arrival on comprehension suggests that not just the mouth, but also the brain, is involved in explaining age effects on the mastery of second language phonology.

A similar effect has been observed for measures of grammatical competence. Johnson and Newport (1989) presented grammatical and ungrammatical English sentences to Chinese and Korean natives who were living in the United States and who had learned English as a second language. As a group, they did less well on identifying the ungrammatical utterances than a comparison group of native English speakers. The interesting results with respect to the critical period hypothesis come from an analysis of subgroups of the second language speakers. Those who were between 3 and 7 years old when they arrived in the United States were not different from the native speakers of English. Those who were between 8 and 15 at arrival performed less well on the test than native speakers, but the younger they were at arrival, the more nearly they approximated native competence. Those who were 17 or older performed least well and did no better than those who were 30. As was the case for accent, differences were observed between those exposed as young children, under the age of 7, and those exposed as older, but still prepubescent, children. Additional evidence of age-of-arrival effects comes from Coppieters (1987), who found that native speakers outperformed adult second language learners on tests of grammatical competence—even when the second language learners worked as authors and professors, writing in their second language.

***Continuity or discontinuity in age-of-arrival effects.*** Although it is clear that the age at which one starts to learn a language is related to one's ultimate level of proficiency in that language, it is not clear that the cause of this relation is a change in the brain's specific capacity for language acquisition. The hypothesis that there is a biologically defined window during which language acquisition must occur predicts a discontinuity in the relation of age to ultimate proficiency. Proficiency should be good for those exposed during the critical period and less good for those exposed outside of the critical period. Some evidence suggests that, to the contrary, the function that relates age of first exposure to ultimate proficiency is a smooth one.

One study that found a continuous function mapping age of arrival to language competence used census data collected from 2 million immigrants, all of whom had been living in the United States for at least 10 years (Hakuta, Bialstok, & Wiley, 2003). The respondents reported how proficient they considered themselves to be in English, their age when they immigrated to the United States, and the level of education they had attained. The findings are presented in Figure 2.6 for native speakers of Chinese and Spanish. There is clear evidence that age of immigration makes a difference, but there is no clear evidence of a discontinuity. The observed effect of education level also argues against a biological account of proficiency differences. Although one potential criticism of these data is that the self-report measure was not very sensitive, it

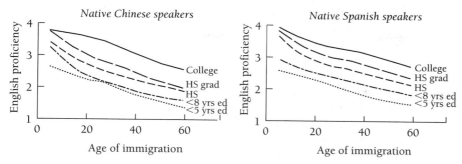

**Figure 2.6** The relation between age of immigration and English proficiency for native Chinese and Spanish speakers who emigrated to the United States
Source: From "Critical Evidence: A Test of the Critical-Period Hypothesis for Second-Language Acquisition." Psychological Science, 2003, 14, 31–38. Copyright 2003 American Psychological Association.

was sufficiently sensitive to reveal the age of immigration effect. More seriously, it has been suggested that Hakuta et al.'s (2003) data analytic techniques might have obscured evidence of a discontinuity in the age effect (Stevens, 2004). On the other hand, other studies have also found that even after puberty, younger is better with respect to second language acquisition and that some adults (approximately 5 to 25 percent, depending on the study) can achieve native-like proficiency in a second language. These other findings similarly suggest that a simple "puberty closes the window of opportunity" account of age effects on second language acquisition does not fully explain the data.

## Nonbiological influences on second language acquisition

Another argument against the critical period hypothesis is based on evidence that factors other than biological age contribute to the age-related decline in second language learning achievement. Typically, the input conditions for children and adults are different. Children attend school in the new language, whereas adults must do work that their limited language skills allow, thus limiting their exposure to the new language. Jia and Aaronson studied Chinese immigrants to the United States who were between 5 and 16 years old for their first year in their new country (Jia & Aaronson, 2003). They found that the children under age 2 were exposed to a richer English-language environment than the older children. These very young children watched more English-language television, were exposed to more English-language books, and had more English-speaking friends. The older children had richer Chinese language environments. Although all the children reported they were more comfortable using Chinese when they first arrived, by the end of the first year the younger children, but not the older, reported being more comfortable using English. The younger children also scored higher than the older children on tests of English proficiency. If young children, but not older children or adults, switch their dominant language when immigrating, then the studies that look for effects of age on language-learning ability by comparing younger and older arrivals have a problem.

To the extent that comparison of the language proficiency of young to adult learners of a second language is a comparison of language proficiency in speakers for whom that language is dominant to speakers for whom that language is not, the validity of that research is compromised. It may be that switching the dominant language is what causes the differences, not age per se. To investigate this **dominant language switch hypothesis,** Jia and Aaronson (2003) gave grammaticality judgment tasks in English and Chinese to native Chinese who had come to the United States between the ages of 1 and 38. Like Johnson and Newport, they found that younger arrivals performed better on the test of English grammar. They also found that the younger arrivals performed worse on the test of Chinese grammar. In fact, scores on the two tests were negatively related—the better a subject did on the English test, the worse he or she did on the Chinese test. This finding supports the hypothesis that better second language acquisition by younger children occurs at least in part because they switch to the second language as their dominant language.

Further support for the contention that the language-learning advantage of young children is not purely a reflection of a greater language-learning ability comes from a study of the acquisition of Dutch as a second language by English speakers who moved to the Netherlands (Snow & Hoefnagle-Höhle, 1978). The subjects ranged in age from 3 years to adult. Snow and Hoefnagel-Höhle tested their participants' mastery of Dutch using a variety of measures of pronunciation, vocabulary, grammar, and text comprehension, first 6 months after their arrival and then two more times at 4- to 5-month intervals. Contrary to the prediction of the critical period hypothesis, they found that the youngest children scored the lowest on every test and that the 12- to 15-year-olds showed the most rapid acquisition.

Also contrary to a biologically based account of the advantage of youth in second language acquisition, there is evidence that social psychological variables play a role in second language acquisition. Johnson and Newport found two such variables that affected the performance in English of their Korean and Chinese participants: self-consciousness and American identification. The participants who were less self-conscious about making errors and those who identified themselves as American showed greater mastery of English. Both the characteristics of not being self-conscious and of identifying with the new country are more likely to be true of children than adults, and thus these nonbiological factors may also contribute to the observed age difference in second language acquisition.

The data on second language acquisition suggest that if you give younger children and older children the same experience with a second language, the older children will learn more rapidly. However, in most immigrant situations, it is the younger children who actually learn more and ultimately achieve higher levels of proficiency. Some of the disadvantage that older learners have may be the result of general cognitive declines that come with age, including declines in memory, attention, and speed of processing. Some of the disadvantage of older learners is likely due to other, noncognitive factors including the conditions of input, their initial high level of proficiency in their native language, and their reluctance to switch cultural identities and language.

In sum, although it is widely believed that language acquisition is "a mysterious skill that seems to shut off automatically around the age of 12" (Osborne, 2003, p. 40), this view is simply not supported by the evidence. The evidence from Genie, from studies of sign language acquisition, and from recovery from aphasia show that children have an advantage over adults. However, that general conclusion leaves open many questions about the basis and the time of any critical period. Lenneberg (1967), who originally hypothesized the existence of a biologically based critical period for language acquisition, proposed puberty as the deadline. According to Bates (1993), however, the capacity for recovery from aphasia begins to decline after age 5. Newport's 1990 data on the acquisition of American Sign Language show a decline in ultimate achievement between those first exposed at 6 and those first exposed at 12, and another decline from 12 to adulthood. None of these sources of data supports the notion of puberty as a deadline or of an abrupt deadline at any age.

The largest source of data on the critical period hypothesis, which is also the source of most people's belief in it, is the observation of age-related differences in second language acquisition. What these data appear to show, however, is a continuous decline in ultimate language proficiency related to the age of first exposure—not an abrupt shutting-off of ability. Furthermore, some of the decline in language achievement may have nothing to do with language-learning ability. Rather, other sources of influence including conditions of exposure and willingness to identify with the new language group give children an advantage over adults. To the extent that the decline does reflect a decline in ability, it is not necessarily a language-specific ability. All sorts of general cognitive processes decline with age (Hakuta et al., 2003). Additionally, it has been proposed that one way in which children's cognitive abilities are limited relative to adults' may provide a language-learning advantage. Newport (1991) has argued that it is easier to figure out the structure of language if you analyze small chunks than if you analyze longer stretches of speech. Small chunks are all that children can extract from input and store in memory. Adults, in contrast, extract and store larger chunks, thereby giving themselves a more-difficult analytical task. Newport refers to this argument as the **"less is more" hypothesis.** This hypothesis has also received support from a computer simulation of language acquisition done within the connectionist approach, which found that the computer was more successful if fed shorter sequences as input (Elman, 1993, 2001), although that finding has been disputed (Rohde & Plaut, 1999).

One possible reconciliation of the data with respect to the critical or, more likely, sensitive period hypothesis is that there is a biological preparedness for language acquisition that is maximal in early childhood. Language acquisition also depends on other factors, including general cognitive processes and motivation. The benefit of these other factors typically decline more gradually than the biological advantage and are more variable after puberty. Thus, early childhood is the easiest time to acquire language, but it is doable after early childhood if other factors are maximally supportive.

## THE GENETIC BASIS OF LANGUAGE DEVELOPMENT

### The genetic basis of language universals

All normal children in anything remotely like a normal environment learn to talk. Furthermore, the course of language development is, in broad outline, constant across varying environments. The argument has been made that this invariance and robustness of language development reflects a genetic plan at work. Language development is to a large degree a maturational process according to this view—its course and timing determined by the unfolding of a genetic blueprint (Gilger, 1996; Gleitman, 1981).

On the other hand, it has been argued that the universal acquisition of language is the result of universal features of human environments. Although the circumstances under which children acquire language vary widely, all environments appear to provide two forms of support for the process of language acquisition. All environments show children that language is used to communicate with other people, and all environments provide children with samples of speech in a manner that allows children to figure out the relations between the sound and meaning (Crago, Allen, & Hough-Eyamie, 1997; Lieven, 1994). This is not to say that language acquisition does not also depend on biological properties of humans. Rather, the biologically provided language-acquisition device depends on finding a certain sort of environment—just as the biologically provided program for physical growth depends on nutrition.

### The heritability of individual differences

Just as the fact that all humans acquire language has been attributed to our shared genetic blueprint, the individual differences among children in their rate of language development have been attributed, to some degree, to genetic differences. The field that studies the genetic basis of individual differences in behavioral characteristics is behavior genetics, and the tools of behavior genetics have been used to study the contribution of heredity to variation in the pacing of language development. One such tool is the twin study. Roughly speaking, twin studies assess how similar monozygotic and dizygotic twins are. To the extent that some characteristic is genetically based, monozygotic twins, who are genetically identical, should be more similar to each other than dizygotic twins, who share on average only 50 percent of their genes. Comparing monozygotic to dizygotic twins provides a basis, then, for estimating how much of the variance in some characteristic is attributable to genetics.

Twin studies that have looked at children past the age of 3 years using standardized tests of children's verbal IQ, vocabulary, and reading ability find that about 50 percent of the variance among children on these measures can be attributed to genetics (Stromswold, 2001). For receptive and expressive language skills up to 24 months of age, heritability estimates range between 1 percent and 38 percent of the variance, depending on the measure (Reznick, Dorley, & Robinson, 1997). One aspect of the language measure that seems to make a difference is whether grammatical or lexical development is being assessed. One recent, large-scale twin study found that the heritability of grammatical development was 39 percent and the heritability of lexical development was 25 percent (Dale, Dionne, Eley, & Plomin, 2000).

Evidence of environmental effects on language development provides converging evidence for the greater heritability of grammatical than lexical development. Hoff-Ginsberg (1998) found grammar to be minimally susceptible to environmental influence and vocabulary development more so. The method of studying the influence of the environment was, in this case, to investigate the effects of family socioeconomic status (SES) and child birth order on language development. It is well established that children in higher SES families hear more speech than children in middle SES families (Hoff, Laursen, & Tardif, 2002), and it is reasonable to assume that firstborn children have more opportunity for one-to-one speech than later born children. Thus, these two variables serve as proxies for language experience. Vocabulary development was strongly affected by both birth order and family SES, with firstborn children and children from high SES families showing larger vocabularies; grammatical development was affected only by birth order, again, with firstborns showing more advanced language (Hoff-Ginsberg, 1998). It appears that grammatical development, more than lexical development, may be the result of the unfolding of a genetic blueprint; vocabulary development is more paced by environmental factors.

## The genetics of language impairment

Some children acquire language slowly and with difficulty. Signs that language impairment has a genetic basis have been suggested as another source of evidence for the genetic basis of language development. Children who are language impaired are far more likely than typically developing children to have family members who are also language impaired (Stromswold, 1998; Tomblin, 1989). Monozygotic twins are more likely to be concordant for language disorders than dizygotic twins (Eley et al., 1999). Adopted children with language-impaired biological relatives are more likely to be language impaired than adopted children with no language impairment among their biological relatives (Stromswold, 1998). Language impairment appears to be more heritable than individual differences in language development within the normal range (Eley et al., 1999). The evidence that language impairment has a genetic basis is strong, but it does not reveal what genetically based characteristic causes the impairment. Language impairment could be a result of subtle impairments in memory or pattern-learning abilities, and it could be that those more general abilities are genetically based (Leonard, 1996). This line of argument brings us back to the issue of domain specificity.

A very strong claim for both domain specificity and a genetic basis for language impairment was made by Gopnik (1990; Gopnik & Crago, 1991), who described a family in which 16 of 30 family members were seriously language impaired. Furthermore, the inheritance pattern in this family suggested that a single dominant gene was at work. Reports of this work in the popular press suggested that a gene for grammar was defective in this particular family. Since this original report came out, further study of this family has suggested that the truth is a little more complicated than that (Vargha-Khadem, Watkins, Alcock, Fletcher, & Passingham, 1995). While no one doubts that some genetic disorder affects language skills in this family, the disorder is far more pervasive than a defect in grammar. The story of a single gene that affects language and only language simply does not fit the facts of this family. Furthermore, the disorder present in this family is not like most cases of language impairment, and in most cases of language impairment, the data suggest that the cause is multiple genes, in interaction with the environment (Stromswold, 1998).

In sum, work on the genetics of language development makes a case that not only the universal course of language development, but also individual differences in the ease and speed of language development, have a genetic basis—both within the normal range of variation and in cases of atypical development. However, the work that establishes that something genetically based determines the pace of language development does not clearly reveal what that something is, nor how domain specific it is.

## LANGUAGE AND OTHER SPECIES

### The natural communication systems of other species

Other animals besides humans communicate with each other. If we want to know whether language is uniquely human, we need to ask whether these other communication systems should be counted as languages too. To answer that question, we need to describe the communication systems used by other species, and we need to define language. In describing the communication systems of other species, we will be selective rather than trying to survey the field. We will start with our closest relatives in the animal kingdom: primates. It is logical to think that the species most closely related to humans would be most likely to share the characteristic of having language. However, we will see that it is fairly easy to reject that possibility. We will then turn to research on more distant relations. Complex communication systems can be found among insects, and the development of song in some birds shares some features with language development in humans. However, we will see here, too, that fundamental features of human language are lacking in even the most sophisticated communication systems of other species.

***What constitutes a language?***   Human language is a vehicle for communication, but the fact that some activity is interpretable doesn't make it language. Crucial features of language are reference (symbols that stand for things) and syntax (a productive system for combining symbols to express new meanings). Another feature of human language is intentionality.

***Communication among primates.***   One of the more sophisticated communication systems among primates that has been studied is the call of the East African vervet monkey. These monkeys produce a distinct alarm call for each of three different predators; there is a "leopard" call, an "eagle" call, and a "snake" call. Vervet monkeys also respond differently to these distinct calls. They run into trees when they hear the "leopard" call, they look up or run into bushes when they hear the "eagle" call, and they stand on their hind legs and look around when they hear the snake call (Seyfarth & Cheney, 1993). Seyfarth and Cheney have argued that these calls are more than expressions of excitement; they also serve to denote things in the environment. In the absence of any decontextualized uses, though, we may not want to credit the monkeys with the capacity for reference. In terms of the other criteria for language, Seyfarth and Cheney do not argue for syntax, and they make it clear that there is no evidence that the monkeys produce their calls with the intent to modify the mental state of their listener. That intentionality is a crucial feature of truly communicative behavior.

Less is known about the naturally occurring communication system of our closer relatives among primates, although it is clear that chimpanzees do communicate via calls, facial expressions, and gestures (Goodall, 1986; Marler & Tenaza, 1977). Nobody has argued that there is a naturally occurring communication system in primates equivalent to a human language. The strongest argument made is for continuity. As anthropologist Richard Leakey put it, the continuity view holds that "spoken language [is] merely an extension and enhancement of cognitive capacities to be found among our ape relatives"

(Leakey & Lewin, 1992, p. 240). Empirical support for continuity of the learning mechanisms underlying language comes from evidence than tamarin monkeys show the capacity for the same sort of statistical learning that has been demonstrated by human infants (Hauser, Newport, & Aslin, 2001). Of course, just how far such a learning mechanism carries the child toward language is a matter of dispute. (For a further discussion of the continuity issue, see Aitchison, 1998.) A different perspective on the notion of what a complex system of communication requires comes from the study of communication systems in other species that are very distant relatives of humans. We tend not to talk about continuity with respect to birds or insects, yet when we look at birds and insects we find extremely complex communication systems.

***The birds and the bees.***    Bees do not communicate by making noises; they dance. After a bee finds a source of nectar, it returns to the hive and does a dance that communicates the location of the food source to the other bees. Different dances are used for nearby versus distant food sources; and if the source is distant, the dance also indicates the direction of the food source. Richer food sources cause the bee to dance longer and harder, which in turn more strongly arouses the other bees (Von Frisch, 1962). As effective and sophisticated as this system is, it fails to meet virtually every criterion for being a language. It does exceed the primate systems that have been documented as having some limited productivity. A bee can communicate a new message that has never been produced before (such as distant food at a 65-degree angle from the sun), but it can communicate only the location of food sources. Thus, it does not have the vast productivity that characterizes human language.

Some species of birds use their songs to communicate. The relevance of birdsong to language development is not so much in the properties of the song (but see Snowdon, 1993) but in how the song is acquired (Marler, 1970; Nottebohm, 1970). Not all birds are songbirds, and not all songbirds show the same developmental pattern. But in many species of songbirds, the development of the songs that males produce to attract mates and maintain territories requires exposure to adult birds who model the song (in contrast, for example, to chimpanzees who seem not to learn their gestures or calls from adults; Tomasello, Call, Nagell, Olguin, & Carpenter, 1994). The parallels between the acquisition of song in birds and language in humans are more specific than simply the requirement of an adult model. Both have early stages prior to the appearance of the adult form—babbling in humans and what is termed subsong in birds. Both birds and humans need to be able to hear their own early productions for normal development, although deafening after acquisition does not have the same deleterious effect as deafening before acquisition. For both birds and humans, there are sensitive periods during which the ability to learn is at its maximum. And finally, both the production of song and speech are lateralized in the left hemisphere of the brain.

In sum, research on the communication systems of other species has revealed more-complex communication systems in a number of species than many would have thought. And it is certainly true that the study of animal communication has contributed to defining the criterial attributes of human language; lists much longer than reference, syntax, and intentionality have been proposed (Hockett, 1960; and see Bradshaw, 1993). Some might claim that revising the definition of language while you are asking whether another species has it is not quite fair. It's something like raising the high jump bar as soon as someone gets close to clearing it. However, another way of looking at it is to say that the study of animal communication reveals, by way of contrast, what is unique about human language; and if there were nothing unique, comparison to animal systems would reveal that too. Raising the bar is precisely the way to find out whether one high jumper has an ability the others do not. If we set the bar at reference, syntax, and intentionality, only humans can clear it successfully.

So what light on the biological nature of the human capacity for language has been shed by this very brief foray into comparative psychology? Although not everyone would agree, a circumspect interpretation of the evidence leads to the conclusion that what humans do naturally is hugely different from anything our closest relatives seem to do. Richard Leakey, who is better known for his work on human origins, makes the contrary argument that "vervet 'language' is not so far removed from rudimentary human language" (Leakey & Lewin, 1992, p. 243). However, it is not at all clear just what this means, given that no normal human over the age of 3 years speaks anything that could be termed "rudimentary human language." Another implication can be found in the sophistication of bee dancing and the parallels between the development of birdsong and human language—that the complexity of a species' communication system is not a function of how close the species is to humans on the phylogenetic scale, nor is it a function of the species' general intellectual capacity. Rather, biology seems to separately equip species with communication systems that serve their needs. (For an account of how the developmental facts about birdsong are adaptive, see Nottebohm, 1970.) Whether that is the correct account of human language is an open question. We will address how our linguistic capacity might have been shaped by adaptation in the final section of this chapter. Before that, there is one more animal language topic to consider.

## The acquisition of human language by other species

Just because no other species has anything equal to human language doesn't mean another animal couldn't acquire language if it were exposed to language in the right sort of supportive environment. This is the logic behind a set of efforts, undertaken several times, to teach language to a member of another species. Like many other areas of language research, these animal language experiments have been the source of great controversy. Unlike many controversies, which are confined to academic circles, the animal language controversy plays out in newspapers, magazines, and television. In the following sections, we will review the history of attempts to teach language to apes. The ape experiments constitute the majority of animal language experiments, and they are the most nearly successful. The meaning of the carefully chosen words "nearly successful" should become apparent in the next few pages. (For discussion of the linguistic capacities of dolphins and parrots, see Kako, 1999; Premack, 1986; Roitblat, Herman, & Nachtigall, 1993.)

***Efforts to teach chimpanzees to speak.***   The first efforts to teach human language to a chimpanzee used spoken English as the target language. In the 1930s, the Kelloggs raised an infant chimp, Gua, in their home, along with their infant son Donald. The chimp wore diapers, slept in a crib, and was in every way treated like a human child. The result was that although Gua's motor development outpaced Donald's, only Donald learned to talk. In the 1940s and 1950s, another intrepid couple, the Hayeses, raised an infant chimp named Viki in their home, but, unlike the Kelloggs, the Hayeses actively tried to teach Viki to produce words. After 6 years Viki could approximate the sounds of "mama," "papa," "cup," and "up." These efforts to get a chimpanzee to talk were clearly failures, but it is not clear that these efforts were fair tests of the linguistic capacity of the species. Chimpanzees have a vocal tract that makes speech production essentially impossible. But the question of interest in these studies is not whether chimps have the articulatory apparatus for speech but whether they have the brain for language.

***Signing apes.***   The next efforts avoided the problem of speech and capitalized on chimpanzees' manual dexterity by employing American Sign Language as the target language. In 1966 Beatrice and Allan Gardner, faculty members at the University of Nevada in Reno, acquired a wild-born infant female chimp (Wallman, 1992). The chimp was named Washoe, after the county in Nevada where the Gardners lived. Washoe lived in a trailer in the Gardners' backyard, and she was cared for by the Gardners and by University of Nevada students. Everyone who interacted with Washoe was instructed to use only sign language, both with Washoe and among themselves in Washoe's presence. In addition, Washoe was actively taught signs by physically molding her hands into the proper shape and by drilling her and rewarding her for correct usage. After 4 years of this sort of language experience and language training, Washoe had learned to produce 132 signs and had been observed to produce many sign combinations. (At that point, Washoe grew rather large to handle in a trailer, and she was moved to the Institute for Primate Studies at the University of Oklahoma.) Washoe could correctly label a variety of objects and could sign MORE FRUIT, WASHOE SORRY, PLEASE TICKLE.

It seemed at the time that some great chasm had been bridged. Humans were not only talking to animals, animals were talking to humans. In 1972 Francine Patterson, a graduate student at Stanford, began a similar sign language project with a lowland gorilla named Koko. A *Nova* television program was made about these signing apes, and it is hard not to be amazed and impressed by the phenomenon of an animal producing a sign in a human language. Certainly the Gardners and Patterson were impressed. They have both claimed that their animals learned a human language. Patterson has claimed that Koko not only understands "everything that you say to her" (meaning in English), but she also communicates via her sign language skills "about the way animals view the world" (Patterson, 1985, p. 1, cited in Wallman, 1992). Patterson has also been very media savvy, and Koko has appeared on major network television programs and in *National Geographic* magazine. She has even graced the pages of the "Weekly Reader," a widely read newsletter for elementary school children. It is not surprising, then, that the belief that chimpanzees and gorillas can learn a human language is widespread.

However, careful analysis of just what the apes do suggests that the linguistic abilities of even our closest relatives are quite limited. During the 1970s, when stories of talking apes filled the airways and impressed enough psychologists to be reported in introductory textbooks, there were always some dissenting voices (see Seidenberg & Petitto, 1979). But the true unmasking of the supposed linguistic accomplishments of apes came in 1979 from a group of researchers who set out, as the Gardners did, to teach American Sign Language to a chimpanzee.

The chimpanzee that was the focus of this ASL project was named Nim Chimpsky, an allusion to well-known linguist Noam Chomsky. Project "Nim" was started by Herbert Terrace at Columbia University in New York City. (Terrace and Nim are pictured in Figure 2.7.) No backyards in Manhattan could accommodate a trailer, so Nim spent the first 21 months of his life raised in a private home, sleeping in a hammock in the dining room. For 2 years after that, he lived in splendor on the northern edge of New York City in a mansion that had been bequeathed to Columbia. As with Washoe, Nim's caretakers used sign language in interactions with him, and they also actively molded Nim's signs. Like Washoe, Nim learned more than 100 signs and produced many sign combinations. A sample of these is presented in Box 2.5.

Close examination both of Nim's "sentences" and of the circumstances under which they were produced revealed that Nim's language acquisition was very different from a human child's. The first problem with Nim's language can be seen simply by looking at the length and nature of the multisign utterances Nim produced. From the time that Nim started regularly producing sign combinations until his departure 2 years later, his mean length of utterances (MLUs) hovered between 1.1 and 1.6 signs. Unlike children, whose MLUs increase with development, Nim did not increase his mean utterance

Susan Kuklin, Photo Researchers, Inc.

**Figure 2.7** Chimpanzees have been successfully taught to use signs of American Sign Language to communicate with humans. However, the chimpanzees' accomplishments always fall short of full acquisition of the language. Just what the differences are between chimpanzee and human linguistic abilities and what they mean is a matter of considerable debate.

---

### Box 2.5    Examples of sign combinations produced by the chimpanzee Nim

| *2-sign combinations* | *3-sign combinations* | *4-sign combinations* |
|---|---|---|
| play me | play me Nim | eat drink eat drink |
| me Nim | eat me Nim | eat Nim eat Nim |
| tickle me | grape eat Nim | banana Nim banana Nim |
| more eat | me Nim eat | banana me eat banana |
| eat drink | finish hug Nim | play me Nim play |

Source: From Terrace, 1979.

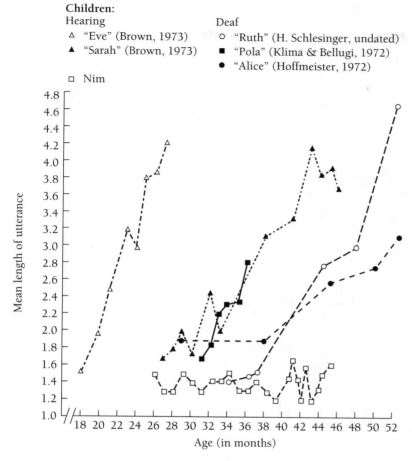

**Children:**

Hearing

△ "Eve" (Brown, 1973)

▲ "Sarah" (Brown, 1973)

□ Nim

Deaf

○ "Ruth" (H. Schlesinger, undated)

■ "Pola" (Klima & Bellugi, 1972)

● "Alice" (Hoffmeister, 1972)

**Figure 2.8** Age-related changes in mean utterance length for two hearing children, three deaf children (learning ASL), and one chimpanzee (also "learning" ASL)

Source: From *Nim* by Herbert S. Terrace. Copyright © 1979 by Herbert S. Terrace. Reprinted by permission of Alfred A. Knopf, a division of Random House, Inc.

length. To compare Nim's changes in MLU with those of hearing children acquiring English and deaf children acquiring ASL, see Figure 2.8. Also, even when Nim produced a long utterance—as he sometimes did—it was highly repetitive. Children's utterances get longer because children express more content in each utterance, but Nim's long utterances tended to say the same thing over and over. This can be seen in many of the four-sign combinations in Box 2.5 and is abundantly clear in Nim's longest-ever utterance, GIVE OR-

ANGE ME GIVE EAT ORANGE ME EAT ORANGE GIVE ME EAT ORANGE GIVE ME YOU.

The other problem with Nim's language is that he didn't produce his utterances by himself. Close inspection of the videotaped interaction between Nim and his teachers revealed that Nim's utterances were very dependent on his teachers' previous utterances. In fact, 90 percent of Nim's utterances were imitations, reductions, or expansions of prior utterances produced by his human interlocutor. The extent to which Nim's utterances depended on the teachers' signing is suggested by an interaction that happened to be captured in a sequence of still shots taken by an automatically advancing camera. In this sequence, Nim produced the multisign utterance ME HUG CAT. In the frame where Nim is signing ME, the teacher is signing YOU. In the frame where Nim is signing CAT, the teacher is signing WHO (Terrace, 1979; Terrace, Petitto, Sanders, & Bever, 1979). Thus, it appears that Nim produced the appearance of signing combinations with inadvertent support from his teachers.

Having found this problem with their own chimpanzee, Terrace and associates then analyzed the publicly available tapes of Washoe and Koko (one was a show produced for public television and the other a film produced by the Gardners), and they found the same phenomenon. The sign combinations Washoe produced were always preceded by a similar utterance or by a prompt from her teacher; all of Koko's signs were signed first by the teacher (Terrace et al., 1979).

The researchers who worked with Nim came to the conclusion that chimpanzees cannot acquire a human language. Syntax was not the only way in which the chimps' use of ASL differed from the language competence of children. Although Nim has 125 signs, he used only a few regularly, and these tended to occur only in particular contexts. Basically, Nim signed to request food and other objects. Also, Nim's conversational use of signing was inappropriate. Unlike children who master turn taking even before mastering language, Nim frequently signed while his teachers were signing. Although the limited use of signs might be attributed to chimps' limited range of interests, and although their lack of conversational skill might not be a fatal flaw, syntax and reference are criterial features of language. The analyses of Terrace and associates make it clear that Nim, Washoe, and Koko never achieved syntax. Laura Petitto, one of Nim's teachers, argued that chimps also lack reference. She wrote:

> For Nim, meaning seemed to have no role outside of the specific association between a form and its referent that had been explicitly taught to him. I had not succeeded in bringing him to the water fountain as Annie Sullivan had done for Helen Keller. For Nim, signs did not refer; he did not have words—signs, or names—for things. (1988, p. 189).

***Artificial language projects.*** Other attempts to teach language to chimpanzees have used experimenter-invented languages. David Premack taught the chimp Sarah a system that made use of metal chips on a magnetized board. Each chip had an arbitrary color, shape, and meaning, and there were rules for ordering the chips. After long and arduous training, Sarah learned to do things like request an apple by producing a sequence such as "Mary give apple Sarah" and to correctly respond to the instructions "Sarah insert banana pail apple dish" (meaning put the banana in the pail and the apple in the dish). Because Sarah was never exposed to full human language, it is not fair to judge her accomplishments against that criterion. However, it is clear that what she did accomplish is less than language, and Premack's more-recent work has focused on Sarah's and other chimps' cognitive, as opposed to linguistic, skills. At the Yerkes Regional Primate Center in Atlanta, Georgia, chimpanzees have been taught a language that uses a vocabulary of abstract symbols, called lexigrams, that can be combined according to a grammar that operates over semantically based categories. Lana, the first chimp taught this language (dubbed Yerkish), learned to produce and respond to sequences of symbols, but even her trainers made very limited claims for her accomplishments. What Lana learned was essentially a repertoire of rote-learned sequences associated with different situations and rewards (Savage-Rumbaugh et al., 1993; Wallman, 1992).

***Language in a bonobo.*** The next major development in the animal language controversy came when researchers at the Yerkes center began to work with a different species of chimpanzee—the bonobo. Bonobos seem more similar to humans than do the common chimpanzees that had been the subjects of previous experiments. For example, bonobos engage in upright posture more frequently, and they use eye contact, gesture, and vocalization in communication more frequently than common chimps do (Savage-Rumbaugh et al., 1993).

In 1981 Sue Savage-Rumbaugh began to teach the lexigrams of Yerkish to an adult bonobo chimpanzee named Matata. However, Matata was a complete failure at learning symbol use. The surprise development that reopened the debate about the linguistic capacity of apes came from Matata's son. While Matata was being trained, her infant son Kanzi was allowed to tag along; and without anybody paying any attention to him, Kanzi not only learned the lexigrams his mother failed to master, he also acquired some ability to understand spoken English.

Kanzi's accomplishments are the basis of claims made by Savage-Rumbaugh and her colleagues at Yerkes that chimpanzees—at least bonobos—are capable of both reference and syntax. In support of the claim for referentiality, Savage-Rumbaugh, McDonald, Sevcik, Hopkins, and Rupert (1986) cite Kanzi's performance on a vocabulary test and examples of his lexigram use in naturalistic exchanges. In the vocabulary test, Kanzi did a good job of matching lexigrams both to pictures of the objects that the lexigrams stand for and to spoken words. In interaction with his trainers, Kanzi used the lexigrams. Although Kanzi clearly could do some things with the lexigrams he knew, the question is how to characterize what he did and the nature of the underlying knowledge. To illustrate, Kanzi would use the lexigram for strawberry when he wanted to go to the place where strawberries are found, when he was asking for a strawberry to eat, and when shown a picture of strawberries. On the basis of this sort of variety in the contexts in which the lexigram strawberry was produced, Savage-Rumbaugh and associates argued that Kanzi used strawberry to refer. Seidenberg and Petitto (1987) disagreed, pointing out that outside the testing context, all Kanzi's uses of strawberry resulted in his getting to eat strawberries. According to Seidenberg and Petitto, lexigrams for Kanzi functioned as instruments for achieving goals rather than as symbols, and true language involves the use of symbols.

The argument that bonobos are capable of syntax rests on evidence from tests of Kanzi's comprehension of spoken English (Savage-Rumbaugh et al., 1993). In this case, Savage-Rumbaugh and colleagues explicitly compared Kanzi's comprehension abilities to those of a 2-year-old human child. Comprehension was tested by presenting the subject with commands, such as "Give Sue the bubbles," "Put the rubber band on the soap," "Go to the oven and get the tomato," and "Go get the carrot that's outdoors." Care was taken that many different objects were available so that correct responding depended on sentence understanding. Many of the sentences were presented in blind trials in which the researcher communicated to the subject from behind a one-way mirror and thus could not inadvertently cue the correct response. The results showed that Kanzi did about as well as the 2-year-old child, producing correct responses to the first presentation on 59 percent of trials, compared to the child's 54 percent correct.

Tapes of Kanzi's performance have been shown at academic conferences and on public television, and it is hard not to be impressed by the sight of a chimpanzee responding correctly to somewhat improbable commands. Again, however, the problem lies in what to make of this accomplishment. Kako (1999) argues that although Kanzi's comprehension abilities show understanding of some features of syntax, they fall short of demonstrating mastery of all the criterial features of syntax. Tomasello (1994) argues, even more strongly, that none of the sentences presented to Kanzi require much syntactic competence to figure out. The comparison with the 2-year-old child doesn't help this problem, because by many accounts, a 2-year-old child's syntactic knowledge is quite limited. Ultimately, the problem is that we know the child will go on to acquire language and would, if tested at maturity, do better than 54 percent correct. Kanzi was 8 years old when he was tested, and 59 percent correct is probably as high a score as he will ever achieve.

***Why can't chimpanzees acquire language?***    What do humans have in our brains that makes us the only linguistic species? What do chimpanzees lack that makes language unattainable for them? This is perhaps the most interesting thing to be learned from efforts to teach language to chimpanzees. Not unexpectedly, different and contradictory answers to this question have been proposed. However, there is one point of surprising agreement: The problem is not that chimpanzees lack intelligence. Both observations of chimps in the wild and laboratory experiments suggest to many observers that chimpanzees are highly intelligent. Although these impressions of chimpanzees' intellectual abilities do not constitute a detailed analysis of chimpanzee cognition, chimpanzees are clearly capable of learning concepts and of solving problems (see Petitto, 1988). As Seidenberg and Petitto (1987) put it, "Apes present a paradox: Why should an animal so demonstrably intelligent exhibit such dismal linguistic abilities?" (p. 284).

One possible explanation of why apes fail at language is that language is the expression of a domain-specific mental faculty that humans have and apes do not. But if humans' language-specific capacity is the capacity for syntax (the Universal Grammar argument and the bioprogram hypothesis would be versions of such a proposal), then we are still left with a paradox. The absence of innate Universal Grammar would prevent any other animal from fully acquiring a human language, but that absence wouldn't explain why chimpanzees, for example, don't do more with what they have. Premack (1986) argued that chimps have the conceptual ability to support a semantically based grammar of the sort often attributed to 2-year-old children. And some interpretations of Kanzi's accomplishments would grant him that level of linguistic achievement. So why don't bonobos in the wild have a communication system that makes use of a semantically based grammar?

One answer proposed by Savage-Rumbaugh and associates (1993) is that maybe they do. Maybe, their argument goes, if we looked more closely than anyone has so far at the naturally occurring communication system among bonobos, we would find something like a semantically based grammar. But the researchers also suggest that chimpanzees may be limited in language by their limited production abilities. Chimpanzees cannot produce the number of discriminably different sounds that humans can (nor can they produce the finely articulated gestures of fully competent signers). According to Savage-Rumbaugh and associates (1993), "Kanzi's ability to understand human speech suggests that, if apes could produce human-like sounds, they might well invent and utilize a language that would be similar to our own, although probably considerably simpler" (p. 107).

Seidenberg and Petitto (1987) offered a different explanation of what humans have that chimpanzees lack. Remember, Seidenberg and Petitto do not credit Kanzi with reference, and they claim that it is the inability to achieve that naming insight that accounts for chimpanzees' linguistic limitations. In this view, the human language-specific capacity is not just syntactic; it also includes reference. Chimps are incapable of either learning a human language or creating their own because they are incapable of understanding that things have names.

One final proposal is that what chimpanzees lack is culture. By culture, we don't mean museums and the ballet; rather, we use a very narrow definition: culture as socially transmitted behavior. It may seem odd to bring this up now, near the end of a chapter on the biological bases of language, but language in humans is also a cultural phenomenon. It is definitely a socially transmitted behavior. Human language acquisition depends on the human capacity to learn from other people. Even human language invention depends on more than one participant. As Shatz (1994b) pointed out, social isolates—such as Genie or Victor, the wild boy of Aveyron—did not invent languages, although linguistic isolates who have potential communicative partners do. A great deal of research suggests that the chimpanzee's ability to learn through interaction with others—that is, for the social transmission of behavior—is extremely limited (Tomasello et al., 1994; Wrangham, McGrew, de Waal, & Heltne, 1994). Chimpanzees certainly imitate behaviors they observe, and chimpanzees can learn from human instruction. What chimpanzees do not seem to do is figure things out in collaboration with others (chimpanzee or human). The reason they do not, according to Tomasello and associates (1994), is that they do not have the capacity for the sort of intersubjectivity that collaborative learning requires. That is, chimpanzees cannot conceive of another individual's thoughts about something else.

By this account, what keeps language out of the reach of chimpanzees is neither a lack of general intelligence nor the absence of a language-specific mental capacity; it is the lack of the social/cognitive ability to learn through interaction with others. By some accounts the crucial component of this social/cognitive ability to learn from others (and also the ability to teach, which chimpanzees also seem not to do) depends on the ability to attribute mental states to others. What chimpanzees may lack, then, is a theory of mind (Cheney, 1995; Worden, 1998). Having a theory of mind both allows and impels the child to read the communicative intentions of others, which, according to some, is the basis of language acquisition (Tomasello, 2003). Premack (1986) similarly argued that language is only one difference between humans and chimpanzees and concluded that language exists "as an instrument for consummating unique human social dispositions" (p. 155). At the risk of infinite regression, one can then ask where these unique human social dispositions come from. One suggestion, that experience may have a role, comes from the observation that the more linguistically successful apes were also ones with early experience being reared by humans. Perhaps something about human rearing encourages the social disposition that contributes to language development.

## THE ORIGIN OF THE HUMAN CAPACITY FOR LANGUAGE

If language is a biologically based characteristic of the human species, then it has an evolutionary history. Just as we can ask how the giraffe got its long neck and how humans came to walk on two feet, we can ask how humans came to have the capacity for language. As Cosmides and Tooby (1994) put it, "The human brain did not fall out of the sky, an inscrutable artifact of unknown origin, . . .[rather, it acquired its] particular functional organization through the process of evolution" (pp. 85–86). The idea that we can learn about aspects of human psychology and human development by considering their evolutionary origins is part of a relatively new approach known as **evolutionary psychology** (see Barkow, Cosmides, & Tooby, 1992; Bjorklund & Pelligrini, 2000; Geary & Bjorklund, 2000).

If we accept the central assertion of evolutionary psychology—that the brain, no less than the body, was shaped by evolution—then we could logically look to those disciplines that have figured out evolution for at least the outlines of an account of the origins of language. However, the disciplines that claim understanding of evolution are waging their own great debate (see Eldredge, 1995), and proposed accounts of the origin of language come from very different points of view. (Note that there is no scientific disagreement about whether evolution occurred, only about how it occurred.)

In the following section, we will briefly outline the positions that have been taken on the way the capacity for language evolved. As we will see, this last topic touches on two major issues that have appeared repeatedly in discussions of how children learn to talk. One is the issue of whether acquiring language is one thing that humans do with their general cognitive abilities or whether it reflects a domain-specific, modular ability. The other concerns the relation of language development to the social communicative functions that language serves.

## Language as an adaptation

The standard neo-Darwinian account of evolution explains species' features as adaptations to the circumstances in which they live and compete for survival. Thus, fish have streamlined bodies to more effectively move through the water, giraffes have long necks to reach leaves that other animals cannot, and so on. Evolution is not purposeful, but it selects features because they serve a useful purpose. Applied to the human capacity for language, the adaptationist view holds that humans have language because having it gave some of our hominid ancestors an advantage in survival and reproduction over those who did not have language. Thus, natural selection resulted in the evolution of the capacity for language. Two very different views of the human capacity for language (modular and nonmodular) share the view that language evolved as an adaptation to circumstances in which communication conferred a selective advantage. The issue among differing adaptationist accounts concerns just what resulted from this selection for the capacity to communicate.

***The modular view.*** According to one view, the nature of the human adaptation to circumstances in which communication conferred an advantage is a complex, special-purpose mechanism: a modular language faculty (Bloom, 1998; Pinker & Bloom, 1990). The notion that a special-purpose, complex mechanism was selected to serve its particular function is certainly in accord with the standard neo-Darwinian account of how other complex systems evolved. The eye evolved for vision, and the heart for pumping blood, so why not parts of the left cerebral hemisphere for language? This account of language as a special-purpose adaptation is also consistent with the evolutionary psychology approach, according to which all mental capacities are special-purpose faculties designed by evolution to serve specific functions. According to this view, the mind is not some generally useful, all-purpose tool. Rather, the mind is like a Swiss army knife with many different special-purpose tools. (For an argument as to why evolution would result in that sort of mental organization, see Barkow, Cosmides, & Tooby, 1992.)

***The nonmodular view.***    It is possible, however, to accept the insight from evolutionary psychology that human abilities have an evolutionary history without accepting that the result of evolution is necessarily a bundle of different special-purpose devices. Barring some huge mutation, evolution has to work with the material that is there. So even if language conferred an advantage on those who had it and they survived to pass on their genes in greater numbers because of it, language did not necessarily emerge from this evolutionary process as a domain-specific capacity. Instead, language may have been made possible by "quantitative changes in the size, power, and interactive potential of preexisting components" (Bates, Thal, & Marchman, 1991, p. 35). As Elizabeth Bates put it, language is "a new machine built out of old parts" (Bates et al., 1991, p. 35). This view finds no language module separate from the rest of the human brain. A compromise view, with relevance for the debate on the origins of language, suggests that the human language faculty can be thought of in a narrow sense—as just the abstract grammar and the computational system necessary to employ it, or in a broad sense—as also including the conceptual system that provides the meanings, the intentional system that underlies communication, and the sensory-motor system involved in perception and production. In this view, the evolutionary story and the uniqueness of language to humans could be different for the narrow sense and broad sense components of the language faculty (Hauser, Chomsky, & Fitch, 2002).

Although the differences among the foregoing views are substantial, these views share one premise: Whatever it is that underlies language, humans have that capacity because having language was advantageous on the savannah some 200,000 years ago (estimate from Corballis, 1992). Language is useful only to a species whose members are interested in communicating with one another. A system as complex as human language is more useful than calls and hoots only if the interacting members of the species are interested in exchanges of information more complex than food locations and predator warnings. The readily observable facts that humans are extremely interested in talking about other humans and that managing interpersonal relations is at the core of managing human society may be what gives human language its particular characteristics. Thus, both the nonmodular and modular adaptationist accounts of the origin of language assign a central role to the social nature of our hominid ancestors (Hurford, Studdert-Kennedy, & Knight, 1998). (For an argument on the way the demands of human communication require the structural complexity of human language, see Pinker & Bloom, 1990.)

## Nonadaptationist accounts of the origin of language

Adaptation isn't always the correct account of how things came to be the way they are. The fact that we use some part of our brain or our anatomy to serve a particular function doesn't mean that that physical structure was selected for, in evolution, to serve that function. Such a view has been dubbed "Panglossian," after Voltaire's fictional character Dr. Pangloss, according to whom "Everything is made for the best purpose. Our noses were made to carry spectacles, so we have spectacles" (quote from Eldredge, 1995). The adaptationist position that humans have language because language was selected for through evolutionary history has been criticized as Panglossian (Gould & Lewontin, 1979).

The alternative view claims that the capacity for language was selected for other purposes and then recruited for language—much the way our nose has other reasons for its shape, even though it is useful for supporting eyeglasses. A nonadaptationist account of the origin of the capacity for language would invoke other selection pressures that operated to increase the size and power of the brain (a generally better brain being a generally useful thing to have). Then, having gotten so much larger in the service of general improvement in its old functions, the brain was also able to perform new functions. This view of language as a by-product of design for other purposes has been suggested by Gould and Lewontin (1979). Interestingly, Chomsky suggested something similar. Although Chomsky certainly rejected the idea that language could be served by general cognitive capacities, he did suggest that language may well be the result of changes that occurred for other reasons:

> These skills may well have arisen concomitant to structural properties of the brain that developed for other reasons. Suppose there was selection for bigger brains, more cortical surface, hemispherical specialization for analytic processing, or many other structural properties that can be imagined. The brain that evolved might well have all sorts of special properties that are not individually selected; there would be no miracle in this, but only the normal workings of evolution. We have no idea, at present, how physical laws apply when 1010 neurons are placed in an object the size of a basketball, under the special conditions that arose during human evolution. (1982, p. 321)

# • SUMMARY

This chapter considered language development as a biological phenomenon. The reasons for characterizing language development as a feature of human biology and some of what we know about the biological bases of language development include the following:

1. Language is a universal characteristic of the human species. Not only do all human societies have language, but in situations where there is no target language to learn, humans in interaction will spontaneously create language.

2. The capacity for language is served by physical structures (in the vocal tract and in the brain) that seem, to a certain extent at least, to be specifically dedicated to their linguistic functions. In most mature adults, language functions are carried out primarily by the left cerebral hemisphere. The core feature of the left-hemisphere specialization for language appears to be its role in grammatical processing.

3. The brain appears to be biased from birth to represent language in the left hemisphere. In childhood, however, the mapping of language function to brain location is different and more diffuse than it is in adults.

4. The best-known "fact" about language development appears to have been greatly exaggerated. Children are better at learning language than adults, but the age-related decline in language-learning ability appears to be more continuous than abrupt. Also, the greater accomplishment of children than adults in second language acquisition is in part a reflection of different learning opportunities and different attitudes toward the new language. These data are not consistent with a critical period hypothesis according to which biology sets a deadline by which language must be acquired if it is to be acquired normally and completely.

5. In support of the biological bases of language development, there is good evidence of a genetic basis to both the species-universal and individual blueprints for development, particularly in the domain of grammatical development.

6. Finally, the human capacity for language is species-specific. The results of research on the naturally occurring communication systems of other animals and the results of experiments that have attempted to teach a human language to another primate suggest that language is uniquely human. Most interesting, the comparisons of the human's to the ape's capacity for language begin to provide a basis for hypotheses about the nature of the uniquely human characteristics that account for language.

# • KEY TERMS

pidgins

creoles

language bioprogram hypothesis

supralaryngeal vocal tract

functional architecture (of the brain)

neurolinguistics

cerebral cortex

subcortical (brain structures)

corpus callosum

contralateral connections

ipsilateral connections

lesion method

split-brain patients

dichotic listening tasks

brain-imaging techniques

aphasia

functional asymmetry

right-ear advantage

Broca's aphasia

Wernicke's aphasia

Broca's area

Wernicke's area

equipotentiality hypothesis

invariance hypothesis

plasticity

critical period hypothesis

sensitive period

dominant language switch hypothesis

"less is more" hypothesis

evolutionary psychology

## ● REVIEW QUESTIONS

1. How is the universality of language evidence for a biological basis to language? How is it not?

2. What does it mean to claim that the human vocal tract is specialized for language, and what evidence supports that claim?

3. Outline the evidence that language is a left-hemisphere function in adults.

4. What is the role of the right hemisphere in normal language functioning?

5. What is the evidence that the left hemisphere is specialized for language in children?

6. Children recover from aphasia more quickly and more completely than adults do. Why?

7. What is neural plasticity, and what causes its decline?

8. What is meant by the critical period hypothesis, and what is the evidence regarding this hypothesis?

9. What kind of evidence would support the notion that human language is genetically based? What do the data suggest?

10. What questions can be addressed by the study of animal communication systems and by the study of attempts to teach a human language to another primate? What answers does the evidence suggest?

11. What are the main points of disagreement among the several proposed accounts of the evolution of language?

# PHONOLOGICAL DEVELOPMENT: LEARNING THE SOUNDS OF LANGUAGE

## PHONOLOGICAL KNOWLEDGE IN ADULTS

Spoken languages are systems that express meaning through sound. In this chapter, we will focus on the sound component of language and on how children come to learn the sound system of the language they acquire. Before we consider the developmental account, however, we begin by describing the end state of the process of phonological development: what competent speaker/hearers know about the sound systems of their languages.

### The sounds of language

***What are speech sounds?***  Speech sounds are the acoustic signals languages use to express meaning. Of all the possible noises humans can produce, some 200 are used in language, and no single language makes use of all 200. For example, English uses 45 different sounds. If you have studied a foreign language, you are probably painfully aware that other languages use sounds English does not, such as the vowel in the French word *tu* (which means "you") or the middle consonant in the German word *sprechen,* as in *Sprechen sie deutsch?* (which means, "Do you speak German?"). The Zulu language has 12 different clicks (for example, the sound spelled *tsk-tsk*) in its sound inventory (Ruhlen, 1976). Just as some French vowels, German consonants, and Zulu clicks sound exotic to English-trained ears and are often difficult for English speakers to produce, some sounds of English are unfamiliar and difficult for speakers of other languages. Likewise, native speakers of French who learn English often have trouble pronouncing the English *h* sound, and native German speakers have trouble with the English *th* and *w*. The difficulty these speakers have with the unfamiliar sounds is one of the things that leads to their having an accent.

***How do speech sounds represent meaning?***  The phonological differences among languages are not just in what sounds are used but also in how the sounds are used. In some languages, the tone with which a word is produced is part of how the word is pronounced. A word can be produced with a high tone (like the high note of a song), low (like the low note of a song), rising, or falling, and the same sound uttered in different tones can be different words. To complicate matters, high and low are relative—just as one can talk about the high and low notes in a soprano's aria. For example, in Mandarin, /bā/ produced with a tone that neither rises nor falls means "eight," and /bā/ produced with a rising tone means "to pull" (Li & Thompson, 1977). (The brackets or slashes before and after a sound indicate that the sound is written in phonetic transcription, which will be explained later in this chapter.) Sometimes different languages include the same sounds but use them differently with respect to conveying meaning. For example, in English, the sound represented by the letter *p* can take two different forms depending on where it is in a word. When you say the word *pill,* the *p* sound is accompanied by a burst of air coming out of your mouth. (The technical term for this is *aspiration,* and it is represented in phonetic transcription as [pʰ].) When you say the word *spill,* the *p* sound has no burst of air. (It is unaspirated and represented in phonetic transcription as [p].) You may have difficulty hearing this difference, but you can see it. Hold a piece of paper a few inches away from your lips, and say the two words. You will see the piece of paper move more when you say pill. Although English has both an aspirated and unaspirated *p,* the form *p* takes depends on the sound that precedes it, and English speakers automatically produce the correct form. There is never a case in which two words differ only in the use of [p] or [pʰ]. Because aspiration is never the basis for a contrast between two words, aspiration is not a **distinctive feature** in English; it does not carry meaning.

Thai, the language spoken in Thailand, also has an aspirated and an unaspirated *p,* but the kind of *p* used makes a difference in meaning. In Thai, the word pronounced [paa] means "forest," and the word pronounced with an aspirated *p* [pʰaa] means "to split." Aspiration is a distinctive feature in Thai, and Thai speakers have control over the production of aspiration in a way English speakers do not. The proper technical way to describe this similarity and difference between English and Thai is to say that both languages have [p] and [pʰ] as phones, but only in Thai are [p] and [pʰ] different phonemes. **Phones** are the different sounds a language uses; **phonemes** are the meaningfully different sounds in a given language. **Allophones** are phones that do not differentiate meaning; in English, [p] and [pʰ] are allophones of the phoneme [p]. The purpose of introducing this little linguistics lesson here is to make the point that one task for the language-learning child is to figure out which sounds of the language signal meaning distinctions and which do not. Another task is to figure out the system of allophonic variation, such as when to use [p] and when to use [pʰ] for English learners.

## The phonological structure of words

Words are made up of smaller units, and adults know this. Adults can count the number of syllables in a word. Adults can recognize that *dreary* rhymes with *weary* and *napping* rhymes with *tapping,* showing appreciation for the level of structure that divides a syllable into its onset (*n* in *nap*) and rime (*ap* in *nap*). Adults make speech errors in which phonemes are moved from one word to another in a sentence, thus providing evidence that at some level of mental representation a word is composed of separable phonemes. (These errors are called spoonerisms after William Archibald Spooner of New College Oxford, 1844–1930, who had the unfortunate affliction of frequently producing such errors, as when he lifted his glass to toast his dear old queen and instead offered a tribute to the queer old dean.) Shortly, we will see that adults even mentally represent the phonetic features of which phonemes are composed.

## Phonotactics

Competent speakers also know how the sounds of their language can combine to form words. For example, if you came across the words *kpakali* or *zloty,* you would not have to look them up in a dictionary to know that they are not English words. In English, words cannot begin with the sequences *kp* or *zl*. In other languages they can, however. In many West African languages, *kp* is not only permitted, but frequent. In Polish, *zl* is a permissible combination. In fact, *kpakali* is the word for a three-legged stool in the West African language Mende (O'Grady, Dobrovolsky, & Aronoff, 1989), and *zloty* is a Polish word that refers to a unit of currency (Fromkin & Rodman, 1988). This knowledge of constraints on the sequencing of sounds is termed **phonotactic** knowledge.

## Phonological rules

Say the words *bugs* and *bikes* aloud, and pay close attention to the final sound in each word. (Putting your fingers on your throat will help you become aware of the difference between the two final sounds.) You will notice that the final sound in bugs is actually /z/, and the final sound in bikes is /s/. The difference between the /z/ and /s/ is that your vocal folds (popularly referred to as vocal cords) vibrate as you produce /z/ but not as you produce /s/. That is why your throat feels different to the touch as you produce the two sounds. This feature of sound production is called **voicing.** The /z/ sound is voiced; /s/ is voiceless. The standard account of this process is to say that the reason you produced two different sounds at the ends of *bugs* and *bikes* is that you were following a phonological rule of English— not that you have just memorized the different plural forms of *bug* and *bike*. If you were asked for the plural form of a made-up word, such as *wug,* you would know to say *wug* /z/. What you know is that the plural of a word is formed by adding one of the sounds represented by the letter *s,* and that the way *s* is pronounced depends on the sound that precedes it. You are consciously aware of the first bit of knowledge, but you are not aware of the second. Stated in phonological terms, the second bit of knowledge is a rule that *s* is pronounced /s/ after all voiceless consonants and pronounced /z/ after all voiced sounds. In fact, this regularity is one example of a larger regularity in English. When two consonants are together in a word, they match in terms of voicing. The rule is called voicing assimilation. So you have words with /k/ and /s/ next to each other in the middle of the word, such as *biscuit* and *trickster,* and words with /g/ and /z/ next to each other, such as the gangster nickname *Bugsy.* But it is rare to have a voiced and a voiceless consonant together, except in a compound word such as *dovetail* (Gleitman, Cassidy, Massey, & Schmidt, 1995).

It is interesting that children know this phonological property of English at an early age. In a very famous experiment, Jean Berko (1958) presented children with novel words like *wug* and *rick* and found that, by the age of 4, children were able to correctly indicate that the plural of *wug* was wu/z/ and that the past tense of *rick* was rick/t/. (Following /k/ with /t/ rather than with /d/ is another example of voicing assimilation. In contrast, the past tense of *rig* is rig/d/.) Children have been observed to obey this rule even when they get the rest of the word wrong. For example, children commonly have trouble producing the word *spaghetti,* and they frequently transform the first syllable from *spa* to *pas.* Often when they do this—although not always—the *s* gets pronounced /z/, so the resulting word is *pazghetti.* Thus, the word is not quite right, but voicing assimilation is observed. There is a competing connectionist account of these regularities that does not involve positing rules that speakers know, and we will discuss this account in the section on theory at the end of the chapter. There is no disagreement, however, that speakers behave in the systematic fashion just described.

To summarize, when adults know a language, they know, among other things, what sounds their language uses, what sound distinctions signal meaning distinctions, and what sound sequences are possible. More importantly, adults know about the structure of the sound system underlying these surface properties of the language. In discussing phonological development, we will be asking when children acquire this knowledge that adult speakers have and how they acquire it. We will begin to answer the question of when children acquire phonological knowledge by describing the course of phonological development for both perception and production. Because phonological development begins well before children start to talk, we will first describe infants' perceptual and productive abilities. Phonological development continues after speech begins, and therefore our description of phonological development will continue past infancy into the second and third years of life, when children are producing words and rudimentary sentences. In an attempt to answer the question of how children acquire the phonology of their language, we will describe what we know about the various factors that influence the course of phonological development. A recurring question concerns how much of the course of development is maturational and how much is influenced by children's experience with language. Finally, we will consider models that have been proposed to account for the process of phonological development. Before we can pursue these topics, however, we need to lay some groundwork for talking about speech sounds.

## DESCRIBING SPEECH SOUNDS

### Phonetics

As should be obvious by now, the letters of the alphabet are not adequate for describing speech sounds. (Remember, the letter *s* can be pronounced [z] or [s].) What we need is an alphabet in which each symbol can be pronounced only one way and every sound has its own symbol. The phonetic alphabet is just such a system. When a word is spelled in the phonetic alphabet, everyone who knows that alphabet can figure out how the word is pronounced, even if they do not know the language and have never heard the word before. When a word is being spelled phonetically, the standard is to enclose it in brackets. Therefore, the English word *pill* is represented as [pʰɪl] and *spill* is [spɪl].

### Phonemics

Often in describing how words sound, it is sufficient to indicate just the sounds that are phonemes. So in English, for example, information about aspiration could be left out. The standard way to indicate the use of phonemic transcription is to use slashes. So the English word *pill* is represented as /pɪl/, and *spill* as /spɪl/. Table 3.1 presents the phonemic symbols for the sounds of the standard variety of American English. (There are differences among dialects in how particular sounds are produced. This is discussed further in Chapter 9.)

**Table 3.1  Phonemic symbols for the sounds of American English**

| Consonants | | | | | | Vowels | | | |
|---|---|---|---|---|---|---|---|---|---|
| /p/ | pill | /t/ | toe | /g/ | gill | /i/ | beet | /ɪ/ | bit |
| /b/ | bill | /d/ | doe | /ŋ/ | ring | /e/ | bait | /ɛ/ | bet |
| /m/ | mill | /n/ | no | /h/ | hot | /u/ | boot | /ʊ/ | foot |
| /f/ | fine | /s/ | sink | /ʔ/ | uh-oh | /o/ | boat | /ɔ/ | caught |
| /v/ | vine | /z/ | zinc | /l/ | low | /æ/ | bat | /a/ | pot |
| /θ/ | thigh | /č/ | choke | /r/ | row | /ʌ/ | but | /ə/ | sofa |
| /ð/ | thy | /ǰ/ | joke | /y/ | you | /aɪ/ | bite | /au/ | out |
| /š/ | shoe | /k/ | kill | /w/ | win | /ɔɪ/ | boy | | |
| /ž/ | treasure | | | | | | | | |

## Phonetic features

Speech sounds can be described in terms of their physical properties, such as frequency and amplitude, just as other acoustic signals can. Speech sounds can also be described in terms of how they are produced. Research on phonological development makes reference to both sorts of descriptions, but it relies more on the latter, known as **articulatory phonetics.** Using articulatory phonetics, it is possible to describe the 40-plus sounds of English (and also the roughly 200 sounds of all languages) as combinations of a smaller number of features of the articulatory mechanism that produces those sounds. These features are called **phonetic features.** For example, /z/ and /s/ differ in terms of voicing but are the same in terms of every other feature. As you produce /z/ and /s/, you can feel that your teeth, lips, and tongue stay in about the same place; the main thing that changes is what you do with your vocal cords. Many other pairs of consonants differ only in voicing, such as /d/ and /t/ and /g/ and /k/. (The fact that different speech sounds can be made without changing the position of the lips limits how useful lip reading can be.) Voicing is not the only feature that differentiates speech sounds. Because we will need to talk about the relations among different sounds in order to talk about children's phonological development, we need, at this point, to present additional information about phonetic features.

A basic distinction among speech sounds is the difference between consonants and vowels. When you produce a consonant, the flow of air from your lungs through your mouth is obstructed somewhere along the line. In contrast, when you produce a vowel, the airflow is unobstructed. (That's why you can sing a vowel for as long as your breath lasts.) There are also distinctions among sounds within the class of consonants and within the class of vowels that can be described in terms of how the sounds are produced. (We will focus here on the consonants of English, although this method of description also applies to vowels and to all languages.)

Consonants differ both in where the vocal tract is closed (this feature is called **place of articulation**) and in how the vocal tract is closed (this feature is called **manner of articulation**). So, for example, in producing consonants like /b/ and /d/, the airflow is completely stopped for a moment, and these consonants are called **stops.** In contrast, in producing /f/ and /s/, the airflow is not completely stopped; these are called **fricatives.** Although /b/ and /d/ share the property of being stops, they differ in where the airflow is stopped. To make /b/ you put your two lips together; /b/ is called a bilabial (i.e., two lips) stop. To make /d/, you stop the airflow by placing your tongue against the ridge behind your front teeth. This ridge is called the alveolar ridge, and /d/ is called an alveolar stop. Similarly adding place features to our description of /f/ and /s/, we would say that /f/ is a labiodental (lip and teeth) fricative, and /s/ is an alveolar fricative. All the consonants of English can be

**Table 3.2   Classification of the consonant phonemes of American English**

| | PLACE OF ARTICULATION | | | | | | |
| --- | --- | --- | --- | --- | --- | --- | --- |
| | *Bilabial* | *Labiodental* | *Interdental* | *Alveolar* | *Palatal* | *Velar* | *Glottal* |
| *Manner of Articulation* | | | | | | | |
| *Stop* (oral) | | | | | | | |
| voiceless unaspirated | p | | | t | | k | ? |
| voiced | b | | | d | | g | |
| *Nasal (stop)* | m | | | n | | ŋ | |
| *Fricative* | | | | | | | |
| voiceless | | f | θ | s | š | | |
| voiced | | v | ð | z | ž | | |
| *Affricate* | | | | | | | |
| voiceless | | | | | č | | |
| voiced | | | | | ǰ | | |
| *Glide* | | | | | | | |
| voiceless | | | | | | ʍ | h |
| voiced | | | | | y | w | |
| *Liquid* | | | | lr | | | |

classified by how and where the airflow is obstructed. This system of classification is presented in Table 3.2.

We should understand one last distinction among consonants before we talk about children's phonological development: the now familiar distinction between voiced and voiceless sounds. As you can see in Table 3.2, two different consonants such as /b/ and /p/ sometimes have the same manner and place of articulation. The difference between them is in voicing. Voicing refers to the time the vocal cords start vibrating relative to the release of air. The consonant /p/ is called voiceless because the vocal cords do not start to vibrate until after the lips have released air, whereas in producing the voiced sound

/b/, the vocal cords start vibrating before air is released. Knowing that a system underlies the way speech sounds differ from one another is necessary for understanding phonological rules such as the voicing rule described earlier, and it will be important later in describing the systematic nature of children's early attempts at word production.

There is more to describing the sound of a language than simply describing the properties of individual sound segments (such as /p/, /ɪ/, /l/) and how these segments are sequenced in words. Languages also have stress patterns (most obvious in the rhythm of poetry) and prosodic qualities (like the melody in music). Later, we discuss infants' sensitivity to and control over these properties of speech, but the focus of this chapter is on the development of segmental phonology. (Readers interested in a more thorough introduction to metrical and prosodic phonology as applied to child language should see Demuth, 1993, 1996; Dresher, 1996; Kehoe & Stoel-Gammon, 2001; Selkirk, 1996; Vihman, 1996; and references therein.)

## PRELINGUISTIC SPEECH SOUND DEVELOPMENT

Although children do not produce speech until they are approximately 1 year old, the development of the ability to produce speech sounds begins in early infancy, and important developments in speech sound production occur throughout the first year of life. The next sections will describe the changes that occur during this period of prespeech vocal development, using Stark's (1986) five-stage division of this period.

## Stages of prespeech vocal development

***Reflexive crying and vegetative sounds.***   Newborns cry. They also burp, sneeze, and make a few other sounds that accompany the biological functions of breathing, sucking, and so on. In crying and in making these **vegetative sounds,** an infant's vocal cords vibrate, and the airflow through the vocal apparatus is stopped and started. Thus, even these unpromising sounds include some features that will later be used to produce speech sounds.

***Cooing and laughter.***   At around 6 to 8 weeks of age, infants start **cooing.** Coos are sounds that babies make when they appear to be happy and contented. Social interaction in particular seems to elicit cooing. The first coos that infants make sound like one long vowel. Infants continue to produce cooing noises for many more months, and the quality of these coos changes with age. One change is the variety of different vowel-like sounds that infants start to produce. Also, instead of producing a single sound, infants produce a series of different vowel-like sounds strung together but separated by intakes of breath. Although these infants are not talking yet, more features of speech sounds are present in these vocalizations than there were in earlier ones. Babies produce their first laughter around the age of 16 weeks.

***Vocal play.*** The period between 16 weeks and 30 weeks has been called the period of **vocal play** (Stark, 1986), or the **expansion stage** (Oller, 1980). During this stage, the variety of different consonant-like and vowel-like sounds that infants produce increases. Infants seem to gain increasing control over the production of their growing repertoires of sounds, and they combine their different sounds into increasingly long and complex series. The long series of sounds that infants produce by the end of this expansion stage has been called **marginal babbling.** Other noises that infants produce during this period include squeals, growls, and a variety of "friction noises." Because infants produce a wide variety of sounds that are not in the language spoken by adults around them, it was thought at one time that infants start out producing all the sounds in all the world's languages (Jakobson, 1941/1968). However, that turns out not to be true. In fact, the infant's repertoire is initially quite limited. In the first couple of months, the only recognizable speech sounds that infants produce are vowel-like. The first recognizable consonant-like sounds are heard at around 2 to 3 months of age, and they tend to be the ones produced in the back of the mouth (velars), such as [g] and [k]. (So babies really do say "goo goo," although the vowel sound is not quite that distinct.) Around 6 months of age, infants start to produce consonant-like sounds articulated in the front of the mouth, such as [m], [n], [p], [b], and [d], and may stop producing the back sounds for a while (Ingram, 1989; McCarthy, 1954).

***Reduplicated babbling.*** Sometime around 6 to 9 months of age, the quality of infants' vocalizations changes, and the infants start to babble. Technically speaking, what emerges is **canonical babbling** (Oller, 1986; Oller & Lynch, 1992). Canonical babbling is distinguished from the vocalizations that precede it by the presence of true syllables, and these syllables are typically produced in reduplicated series of the same consonant and vowel combination, such as [dada] or [nʌnʌnʌ]. Babies don't necessarily produce this reduplicated babbling, as it is sometimes called, in order to communicate (Stark, 1986). Babies will sit in their cribs or car seats and babble and show no evidence that they expect any reply at all. The appearance of canonical babbling is a major landmark in the infant's prespeech development. All babies babble, and they begin to babble somewhere between 6 and 9 months of age. However, deaf infants rarely produce canonical babbling (Oller & Eilers, 1988; Oller, Eilers, Bull, & Carney, 1985). Deaf infants do produce sounds, and the sounds they produce are not noticeably different from the sounds hearing infants produce up to this point. Canonical babbling is the first development that distinguishes the vocal development of hearing children from that of deaf children.

| Box 3.1 | Milestones of prespeech vocal development | |
|---|---|---|

*Approximate age in weeks*

| | | |
|---|---|---|
| 0 | BIRTH | reflexive crying and vegetative sounds |
| 4 | | |
| 8 | | cooing |
| 12 | | |
| 16 | | laughter; vocal play begins |
| 20 | | |
| 24 | | |
| 28 | | |
| 32 | | |
| 36 | | reduplicated (canonical) babbling |
| 40 | | |
| 44 | | |
| 48 | | nonreduplicated babbling |
| 52 | FIRST WORD | |

Source: Based on Stark, 1986.

***Nonreduplicated babbling.*** The appearance of canonical babbling is followed by a period of **nonreduplicated,** or **variegated, babbling.** During this period, the range of consonants and vowels infants produce expands further. Also, infants combine different consonant + vowel and consonant + vowel + consonant syllables into series, unlike the repetitive series that characterized the first canonical babbling. **Prosody**—the intonation contour of speech—becomes particularly noticeable at the stage of variegated babbling. Once prosody is added to the string of nonreduplicated babbles produced at this stage, infants sound as though they are speaking, until you listen closely and realize that the infant is producing the melody of language without the words. These wordless sentences are often referred to as **jargon.** Some infants produce much more jargon than others do, and some infants spend much longer in this stage than others do. Dore (1975) refers to children who produce a great deal of jargon and who do so for a long time as "intonation babies." In contrast, he refers to children who produce relatively little jargon and who move quickly on to learning the words to the tune as "word babies." An average time frame for children's prespeech vocal development is shown in Box 3.1.

## Influence of the target language on babbling

This course of prespeech vocal development appears to be universal, and even the particular sounds babies produce are similar across environments. However, beginning as early as 6 months, the sounds that babies produce are somewhat influenced by the language that they hear. This phenomenon is known as **babbling drift** (Brown, 1958a). Two techniques have been used to demonstrate this. One technique is to use the judgments of competent speakers to determine whether they can tell the differences among the babblings of babies who are acquiring different languages. This technique can tell you that differences in the babblings depend on the target language, but it cannot tell you how they are different. The other technique is to record babblings of children who are acquiring different languages and analyze them for the presence and frequency of features in the respective adult languages. This technique can potentially tell you not only whether babbling differs depending on target language but also how it differs.

Using the first technique, de Boysson-Bardies, Sagart, and Durand (1984) found that French speakers could tell the difference between French babies' babbling and Arabic or Chinese babies' babbling. The researchers tape-recorded French babies, Arabic babies, and Chinese babies who were 6 months, 8 months, and 10 months old. Fifteen-second segments of babbling were isolated from these recordings. Then the recordings were presented to French speakers in pairs of either French and Arabic babies' babbling or French and Chinese babies' babbling. The French speakers were asked to judge which sample of each pair came from a French baby. French speakers were able to make that judgment at better-than-chance levels on the basis of the recordings of 8-month-olds. (They were correct about 70 percent of the time.) Trained phoneticians, who presumably are better at noticing differences between sounds, were able to make the discrimination from recordings of 6-month-olds. Interestingly, the recordings of the 10-month-olds were harder to tell apart. De Boysson-Bardies and colleagues concluded that this difficulty arises because in the more advanced babbling of the 10-month-olds, the consonant sounds are more noticeable. Thus, the prosodic characteristics that differentiate the babbling of children acquiring different languages were less noticeable to the listeners. The researchers suggest, as have others (Crystal, 1986), that children learn to produce the melody of their language before they learn to produce their language's particular sounds, and it is easier to notice the melody in 8-month-old babies' babbles than in the babbles of 10-month-old babies.

Using the second technique of analyzing the sounds in babies' babbling, researchers working in different countries have found that the particular vowels and consonants in babbling also depend on characteristics of the language spoken by others in the infants' environments. This can be observed in babies as young as 9 months of age (de Boysson-Bardies, Halle, Sagart, & Durand, 1989; de Boysson-Bardies et al., 1992). For example, analysis of adults' productions of words infants are likely to hear showed that Japanese and French words contain more nasal sounds than Swedish and English words do, and analysis of the babies' babbling showed that Japanese and French babies use more nasal sounds in their babbling than Swedish and English babies do. De Boysson-Bardies and colleagues (1992) also consider it relevant that children start showing signs of understanding some words around the time when their babbling starts to show an influence of the sounds in the target language. The researchers conclude that babies pay attention to sounds that refer to things in their environment and that the sounds babies notice influence the sounds they produce. It should be pointed out, however, that these ambient language effects are subtle, and that for the most part babies from different language environments sound very much alike (Oller, 2000; Oller & Eilers, 1998).

## Speech sounds at the end of the babbling stage

By the end of the babbling stage, children have made great progress from their first vowels to an increasingly large repertoire of consonants and then to knowing something about the prosody and sound patterns of their target language. However, phonological development is far from complete at the end of the babbling period. Just 11 different consonants, /h, w, j, p, b, m, t, d, n, k, g/, account for about 90 percent of the consonant sounds produced by 12-month-olds who are acquiring American English, and children exposed to other languages have similar—although not identical—sound repertoires (Locke & Pearson, 1992). Children acquiring English rarely form consonant clusters, such as /kl/ or /pr/. Also, some vowels are more likely to be produced than others. The vowels /ʌ/, /ə/, and /æ/ are more frequent than /i/ or /u/ (Vihman, 1988). Another difference between the sounds children produce at this stage and the words in the target language is the number of syllables. Children's vocalizations at this point are most frequently single syllables, with some two-syllable productions.

## The transition from babbling to words

For many children, there is a transitional phase between babbling and the appearance of the first word. During this transitional period, children produce their own invented words. These invented words are sound sequences children use with consistent meanings but that bear no discernible resemblance to the sound of any word in the target language. Several researchers have discussed these transitional forms and have given them various labels, including **protowords** (Bates, 1976), sensorimotor morphemes (Carter, 1978), quasiwords (Stoel-Gammon & Cooper, 1984), and phonetically consistent forms

(Dore, Franklin, Miller, & Ramer, 1976). These transitional forms often express broad meanings, and their use tends either to be tightly bound to particular contexts or to serve particular functions. Sometimes, but certainly not always, the source of the child's invented "word" can be traced, such as a child's approximation of *yum yum* as a label for food.

Sometimes a particular gesture is part of these transitional forms. For example, pointing gestures often accompany a sound that has the general meaning "I want" or "give me." Sometimes the whole "word" is nonverbal. For example, "one 11-month-old child who observed adults blowing gently on the mobile above his crib apparently associated that gesture with the affective meaning 'delight' or 'wonder' and began using it to express that meaning; for example, he began blowing softly as he approached a Christmas tree" (Vihman, 1988a, p. 90). To this point, we have described the course of vocal development over roughly the first year of a child's life. At the end of their first year, children typically have not really begun to talk, but much of what they will need to produce the words of their language is in place. That is, prior to the beginning of speech, children have developed the ability to produce many of the sounds speech requires.

## Processes underlying infants' development of speech sounds

Three factors contribute to changes we see in infants' vocalizations over the first year of life: the physical growth of the vocal tract, the development of the brain and other neurological structures responsible for vocalization, and experience (Stark, 1986).

***Physical growth and development.*** The newborn infant's vocal tract is not only smaller than the adult's, it is also shaped differently. For example, the tongue fills the entire mouth, severely limiting its range of motion. Growth of the facial skeleton during the period of vocal play gives the tongue more room and probably contributes to the increased variety of sounds infants can make at this time. Also during this period, the muscles of the vocal tract are maturing, and the sensory receptors in the vocal tract are changing. These changes also may contribute to an increase in the infant's control over sound production. Some have suggested that the vocal play of this stage is the result of the infant's exploring what this apparatus can do and exercising it.

***Nervous system maturation.*** The cries and many of the vegetative sounds newborns make are controlled by very primitive structures in the brain stem. The fact that later neurological developments in higher brain structures happen at the same age as some developments in vocalization suggests that nervous system maturation is responsible for changes in infant vocalization. In particular, the onset of cooing at 6 to 8 weeks of age coincides with the beginning of functioning of some areas of the limbic system. This coincidence suggests a causal connection because the limbic area of the brain is associated with the expression of emotion in both humans and lower animals, and cooing tends to accompany a particular emotional state: contentedness. Further maturation of the limbic system may underlie the development of laughter at around 16 weeks. The maturation of still higher levels of the brain—areas of the motor cortex—may be required for the onset of canonical babbling at 6 to 9 months.

***Experience.*** Two sorts of experience also play roles in shaping the course of prespeech phonological development. One experience is hearing the speech adults produce. Evidence that the ambient language influences prespeech vocal development consists of findings (discussed earlier) that both the speech segments (the phones) and the prosodic character of late babbling differ among babies, depending on the language they hear, and both have features of the target language. The other experience that contributes to prespeech vocal development is infants' experience hearing their own vocal output. Kuhl and Meltzoff (1997) argue that "infants learn speech by listening to ambient language and attempting to produce sound patterns that match what they hear" (p. 33). In vocal play infants seem to be discovering the correspondence between what they do with their vocal apparatus and the sounds that come out (Kuhl & Meltzoff, 1988). The absence of auditory feedback may explain why deaf infants produce less elaborate vocal play than hearing infants do and may help explain why deaf infants reach the stage of canonical babbling much later than hearing infants, if at all (Oller & Eilers, 1988).

## PRELINGUISTIC SPEECH PERCEPTION

### Human language and human perception

For languages to express different meanings with different sound sequences, the human users of those languages not only must be able to produce the different sounds, they also must be able to perceive those differences. For example, for a language such as English to encode different meanings with the words *pill* and *bill,* humans must be able to hear the difference between /p/ and /b/. For students of language development, this fact raises the following question: Does learning English involve learning to hear the difference between /p/ and /b/, or can babies already hear that difference, and then use that ability in acquiring English? Infants must have some capacity to make discriminations among speech sounds or they would never be able to get started on the language acquisition process. However, some learning must also be involved, because adults who are learning a second language often have difficulty with sound discriminations their native language does not require.

Finding out just what the perceptual abilities of the infant are and how those perceptual abilities are affected by exposure to a particular language has been the focus of more than 30 years of research on infant speech perception. The next sections review that research, beginning with the most basic question of what infants can hear.

## Infants' hearing

Making discriminations among sounds in the ambient language depends, of course, on being able to hear the speech others produce. At one time, it was thought that babies were blind and deaf at birth and that basic sensory abilities matured only later. We now know that this is incorrect. Infants' hearing is not quite as sensitive as adults', but it is certainly adequate for hearing speech from the time infants are born (Kuhl, 1987). In fact, the auditory system is functioning in the fetus even before birth. The fetus will move in utero in response to external sound (Kuhl, 1987). (Some pregnant women report that their babies were particularly active during concerts the women attended, although if this were the only evidence, we might be suspicious that internal responses in the mothers were the cause of the fetal activity.)

Fetuses seem not only to hear but to remember what they hear. One group of researchers played recordings of their mothers' and a stranger's voice to 38-week-old fetuses (i.e., fetuses 2 weeks before they were due to be born), using a loudspeaker placed 10 cm away from the mothers' abdomens. The fetuses' heart rates went up in response to their mothers' voices and down in response to a stranger's voice, demonstrating that the fetuses made a discrimination (Kisilevsky et al., 2003). (Each mother's voice was the stranger's voice to a different fetus, so the effect was not specific to one individual's voice.) A preference for their mothers' voice was also shown in newborns who were less than 24 hours old (DeCasper and Fifer, 1980). (We will get to the methodological question of how infants demonstrate their preferences in the next section.) In another experiment, DeCasper and Spence (1986) demonstrated that newborns can indicate that they remember what they heard before birth. DeCasper and Spence had pregnant women read a particular passage aloud every day during the last 6 weeks of their pregnancy. When the babies were tested a few days after birth, these babies showed a preference for hearing that familiar passage over hearing a novel passage. A control group of newborns, whose mothers had not read either passage before their birth, responded equally to both passages.

The foregoing evidence makes it clear that babies hear speech before birth and that they remember something about what they hear. Having established that infants can hear speech, we can move to the question of what speech sounds infants can discriminate.

## Studying infants' perception

Finding out what babies can discriminate is a tricky business; we obviously cannot just ask them. However, child language researchers have been very inventive in designing experimental procedures that reveal when babies perceive two sounds as different from each other. The two most widely used procedures are the high-amplitude sucking technique and the head-turn technique.

*The high-amplitude sucking (HAS) technique.* The **high-amplitude sucking,** or HAS, **technique** makes use of three characteristics of babies: (1) babies like to hear sounds, (2) babies lose interest in a sound when it is presented repeatedly, and (3) babies who have lost interest in a previously repeated sound will become interested if a new sound is presented. Thus, to find out whether babies can tell the difference between two sounds, researchers present one sound until the baby loses interest, and then they present another. If the baby shows renewed interest, the researchers infer that the baby can tell that a new sound has been presented. In the HAS procedure, interest is measured by the baby's willingness to "work" to hear the sound played over a speaker. The work babies do consists of sucking on a nipple attached to a device that measures the pressure produced by the sucking. Every time the baby sucks with sufficient vigor, a sound is presented. After a while, the baby's rate of sucking declines; this apparent loss of interest is referred to as **habituation.** Once the infant demonstrates habituation to the first sound, a new speech sound is played over the speaker, and the baby typically starts sucking more rapidly. This renewed interested is referred to as **dishabituation.** The sucking rate after the shift is compared with the sucking rate of a control group of babies who continue to hear the same sound. If the post-shift sucking rate is higher for babies who heard a new stimulus than for the control babies, we conclude that babies can tell the difference. Figure 3.1 shows a baby whose sucking rate is being tested. An example of the kind of data produced by this procedure is illustrated in Figure 3.2.

One potential drawback to the HAS procedure is the fact that if the baby does not increase his or her sucking rate, the researchers can't know whether the baby was unable to make the discrimination or was just uninterested in the new sound, uninterested in the whole procedure, crying, sleeping, or doing other things that babies are wont to do. For this reason, a number of babies are usually tested, and the average sucking rate of babies who hear a new sound is compared with the average sucking rate of babies who hear the same sound continuously. Another problem with HAS is age constraints: It doesn't work very well with babies older than 4 months. Older babies get restless in the infant seat and tend not to be as interested in sucking on a nipple (Kuhl, 1987).

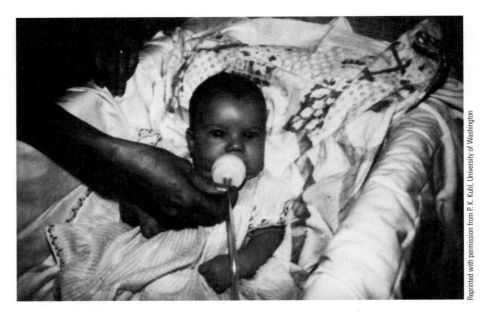

**Figure 3.1**   The high-amplitude sucking procedure

*The head-turn technique.*   The second procedure for testing speech sound discrimination in infants is the **head-turn technique,** which is pictured in Figure 3.3. It is typically used with babies between 5 and 12 months old. This procedure makes use of the fact that babies are interested in a moving toy, such as a monkey that claps cymbals together. Using the presentation of the moving toy as a reward, babies can be trained to turn their heads when they hear a change in a sound being presented. First, a sound is played over and over and then the sound is changed, followed by activation of the toy monkey that is otherwise concealed behind dark Plexiglas. The babies turn to look at the monkey when it is activated. After several trials, when the sound being presented changes, the babies turn their heads toward the place where the monkey will appear even before it's activated.

Babies are trained using sound pairs that we know they can discriminate, and then they are presented new sound pairs to see whether they can discriminate the new contrast. Babies sit on their mothers' laps for this procedure, but the mothers wear headsets to prevent them from hearing the sounds and inadvertently providing cues to the babies. A researcher is also in the testing room to get the baby's attention between trials so that the baby isn't already looking toward where the toy will appear before the stimuli are presented. Using primarily the high-amplitude sucking and head-turn procedures,

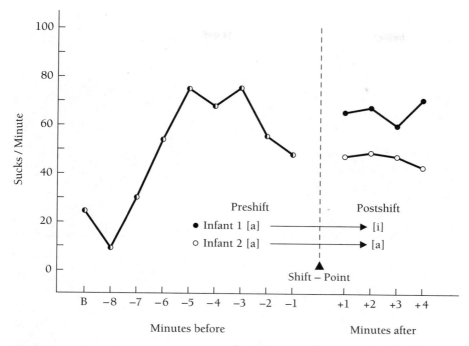

**Figure 3.2** Example of data from the high-amplitude sucking procedure. The left side of the figure shows the average number of sucking responses for two infants presented with the sound [a]. The right side of the figure shows separately the sucking responses for the experimental infant who was presented with [i] and the control infant who continued to be presented with [a].

Source: From "Speech Perception in Early Infancy," by P. K. Kuhl. In S. K. Hirsh et al. (eds.). *Hearing and Davis: Essays Honoring Hallowell Davis*, pp. 265–280. Copyright © 1976 Central Institute for the Deaf. Reprinted by permission.

child language researchers have learned a great deal about what discriminations babies can make among the speech sounds they hear.

## Infants' discrimination of speech sounds

Infants can discriminate essentially all the sound contrasts languages use. For example, infants as young as 4 weeks old can discriminate vowel contrasts such as /u/ versus /ɪ/ and /ɪ/ versus /a/ (Trehub, 1973) and consonant contrasts such as /p/ versus /b/ and /d/ versus /g/ (for a summary, see Aslin, Jusczyk, & Pisoni, 1998). Furthermore, infants' discrimination abilities are language-general; they include the ability to discriminate contrasts not used in the am-

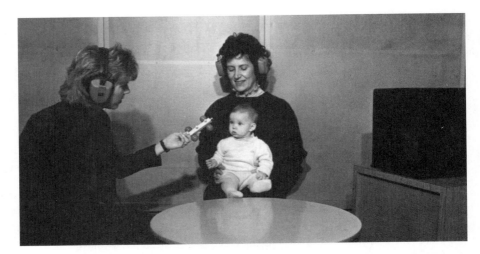

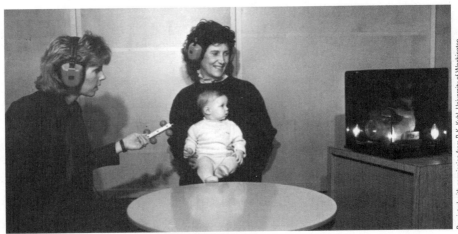

**Figure 3.3**   The head-turn procedure is used to test perception of speech sounds in infants older than 5½ months. Using easily discriminable sounds, researchers train the infant to turn her head when the sound being broadcast in the testing room changes. Once the infant is so trained, the infant's producing a head turn when the sound is changed is taken as evidence that the infant perceived the new sound as different from the old.

bient language. For example, English-learning babies can discriminate vowel contrasts that are present in French but not in English (Trehub, 1976), and they can discriminate consonant contrasts that Hindi uses but English does not (Werker, Gilbert, Humphrey, & Tees, 1981). Many studies have established the range of infant perceptual abilities using contrasts from many different languages (for summaries, see Goodman & Nusbaum, 1994; Kuhl & Meltzoff, 1997; Werker & Polka, 1993).

## Categorical perception

One feature of infants' speech perception—infants' tendency to perceive some consonants categorically—was the focus of intensive research during the 1960s and 1970s. For example, listeners hear one range of acoustic signals all as /p/ and a different range of acoustic signals all as /b/, but no acoustic signal is perceived as something in between a /p/ and a /b/. This phenomenon of **categorical perception,** more properly termed the **phoneme boundary effect,** was first discovered in adult perception and then investigated in infants. The next sections will describe the phenomenon, first as it is demonstrated in adults, and then as it has been observed in infants.

***Categorical perception in adults.*** Demonstrating the phenomenon of categorical perception requires two steps. In the first step, stimuli are constructed to vary along an acoustic continuum. One example of an acoustic continuum is the one that differentiates /p/ from /b/. The difference between /p/ and /b/ is in the duration of the time lag between air passing through the lips and the vocal cords vibrating when producing a syllable. This lag is called **voice onset time** (VOT). For /b/ the lag is very short: about 15 milliseconds (msec). For /p/ the lag is longer, closer to 100 msec. By using a computer, it is possible to artificially create sounds that vary along this VOT continuum, producing sounds in which the lag is 0, 20 msec, 40 msec, 60 msec, and so on. When these sounds are played to adults who then report what they hear, everything with a VOT of less than 25 msec is perceived as /b/, and everything with a VOT of more than 40 msec is perceived as /p/. In fact, there is very little variation among listeners; the **phoneme boundary** between /b/ and /p/ is at about 25 msec VOT. This response pattern is depicted in Figure 3.4.

In the second step of the procedure, pairs of these artificially synthesized stimuli are played to adults who judge whether the two sounds in a pair are the same or different. Sometimes the two sounds really are identical; sometimes they differ by 20-msec VOT. The different pairs are taken from throughout the VOT continuum, so the adult judges are required to discriminate the 0-msec from the 20-msec sound, the 20 from the 40, the 40 from the 60, and so on. The results show that adults cannot distinguish between 0 and 20-msec VOT or between 40-msec and 60-msec VOT, but they can distinguish between 20-msec and 40-msec VOT. It seems, then, that not all 20-msec intervals are equal. Adults cannot detect a 20-msec difference within a phonemic category, but they can detect a 20-msec difference across a phoneme boundary. The phenomenon illustrated in the first step is categorical perception, and the phe-

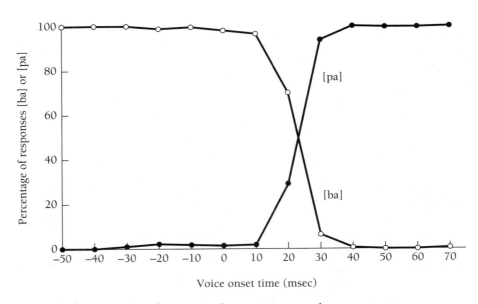

**Figure 3.4** Example of categorical perception results

Source: From "Discriminability, Response Bias, and Phoneme Categories in Discrimination of Voice Onset Time," by C. C. Wood, 1976. *Journal of the Acoustical Society of America*, 1381–1389. Copyright © 1976 American Institute of Physics. Reprinted by permission.

nomenon illustrated in the second step is the phoneme boundary effect, although the term *categorical perception* is frequently used to refer to both.

***Categorical perception in infants.*** The next question asked in the course of research on this phenomenon was whether infants also exhibit categorical perception. In a now classic experiment using the HAS procedure, Eimas, Siqueland, Jusczyk, and Vigorito (1971) demonstrated that infants do show categorical perception. The researchers played artificially synthesized syllables to 1- and 4-month-old babies in three different conditions. In the first condition, babies habituated to a 20-msec VOT sound and then were presented with a 40-msec VOT sound. Babies in this condition increased their sucking when the new sound was presented. (Remember the phoneme boundary between /b/ and /p/ is 25 msec.) In the second condition, babies habituated to either a 20-msec VOT sound or a 60-msec VOT sound and then were presented with a new sound that had a 20-msec longer VOT lag. Babies in this group did not significantly increase their sucking. In a third control condition, babies were presented with the same sound even after they had habituated to it, and no increase in sucking occurred. These findings are depicted in Figure 3.5. They

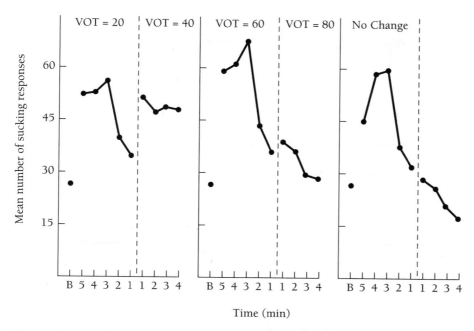

**Figure 3.5** Evidence of categorical perception in infants

Source: Reprinted with permission from "Speech Perception in Infants," by P. D. Eimas et al., 1971. Science, 171, 303–306. Copyright © 1971 American Association for the Advancement of Science.

suggest that babies perceive the VOT continuum the same way that adults do. Everything on one side of the 25-msec boundary is perceived as one sound; everything on the other side is perceived as a different sound. These results suggest that infants sort sounds into phonemic categories, and they do so with little, if any, experience.

***The significance of categorical perception.*** The initial discovery of categorical perception for speech sounds led to the claim that speech perception is special because, for most physical continua, perception does not change abruptly at some point, and the ability to perceive a difference between two stimuli does not change abruptly in the middle of the continuum. For example, categorical perception for the pitch of a sound would be as if the first 44 notes on a piano were perceived as "low" and the second 44 notes perceived as "high," and the only difference you could detect was the difference between notes on the low side and notes on the high side. Categorical perception of the VOT continuum packages sound into the categories relevant for speech.

For a while the finding that even babies perceived VOT categorically was taken as strong evidence that human babies come into the world specially prepared to acquire language. The claim was made that language is unique among human abilities and humans have evolved mechanisms, including perceptual mechanisms, that specifically serve this special ability (for a more detailed history of this argument, see Kuhl, 1987).

Two subsequent discoveries cast doubt on the significance of categorical perception for the argument that language is unique. (There may be other arguments, and we will take that issue up later as well.) One study that burst the uniqueness bubble found that some nonspeech sounds are also perceived categorically (Miller, Wier, Pastore, Kelley, & Dooling, 1976). A second result that cast doubt on the notion that categorical perception is an example of human preparedness for language acquisition was the finding that chinchillas also show the phoneme boundary effect for /b/ and /p/ (Kuhl & Miller, 1975), although chinchillas (small rodents whose main claim to fame is their soft fur) show no other signs of having evolved to acquire language. However, among audiologists, chinchillas are well known as research subjects because the chinchilla ear functions much the way the human ear does, including—it turns out—perceiving the VOT continuum categorically. It seems that the phoneme boundary effect is a property of the mammalian aural system that language uses rather than a specifically linguistic property of auditory perception (Kuhl, 1987; Miller & Eimas, 1994). In fact, language may have evolved to take advantage of this preexisting property of mammalian audition. But whether this property is language-specific or not, it is clear that infants begin life with the ability to discriminate most phonetic contrasts that any target language might require, and their perception of consonant contrasts has a categorical quality (Werker & Polka, 1993).

## Infants' mental representation of speech sounds

Although research on infant speech perception makes it clear that infants have the sensory capacity to discriminate between minimally different phones, that finding does not tell us that infants perceive speech as a series of different phones. In fact, other evidence suggests that the syllable is the effective unit of infant speech perception. On this account, the infant hears /pa/ and /ba/ as different chunks of sound and would similarly hear /pa/ and /bu/ as different chunks of sound. The fine level of analysis that tells us that /pa/ and /bu/ are more different from each other than are /pa/ and /ba/ is not part of how infants mentally represent the sounds they hear.

The proposal that syllables are the units in which infants perceive and mentally represent speech sounds is supported by the following evidence: Using a modified HAS procedure, Jusczyk and Derrah (1987) repeatedly presented a randomly ordered sequence of different syllables (bi, bo, bər, ba) to

2-month-old infants until the infants habituated to the sounds. Then the researchers altered the set of syllables, either by adding /bu/, /du/, or /da/ to the set or by changing all the syllables to begin with /d/. The result was that no matter how much or how little the syllables changed, the infants increased their sucking. Furthermore, the strength of the increased responsiveness was unaffected by the number of phonemes changed. For babies, it seems, a new syllable is a new syllable. A study of 4-day-old infants reached a similar conclusion, finding that the babies could distinguish a sequence of two-syllable sounds (such as *rifo, ublo*) from a sequence of three-syllable sounds (*rekivu, kesopa*); but they could not discriminate a two-syllable sequence with four phonemes (*rifo, ublo*) from a two-syllable sequence with six phonemes (*treklu, suldri*) (Bijeljac-Babic, Bertoncini, & Mehler, 1993). Again, babies seem to process the speech stream in terms of syllables, even though they have the sensory capacity to discriminate among phonemes.

## Infants' recognition of speech sounds

Although the ability to hear the difference between sounds that mark meaning differences in the language is necessary for language acquisition, it alone is not sufficient. The language-learning infant must also be able to ignore differences among acoustic signals that do not mark meaning differences. For example, the language learner must be able to recognize /b/ as /b/ and /p/ as /p/ every time they are produced, even if they aren't acoustically identical. The perceptual mechanisms take care of this distinction for acoustic continua that are perceived categorically. But what about acoustic differences that are not perceived categorically, such as the difference between vowels? And what about the acoustic differences that result from different speakers with different voice qualities? The answer to these questions seems to be that, by age 6 months, infants do treat acoustically different but phonologically equivalent speech sounds as equivalent. Young babies will treat as equivalent acoustically different vowel sounds (Kuhl, 1983), and they will treat as equivalent the same phoneme produced by a male and a female voice (Kuhl, 1980). In the case of vowels, the equivalence classes are organized around prototypes for each vowel (Grieser & Kuhl, 1989).

## Infants' perception of multisyllabic strings

Even these abilities—to hear different speech sounds as different and to recognize the same speech sound as the same across acoustic differences—may be of limited use to the language-learning child if the sounds must occur in isolation. Researchers test babies on contrasts presented in single syllables, such as /pa/ and /ba/, but the language-learning environment presents sounds embedded in a stream of ongoing speech. Discriminating speech sounds embedded in multi-syllabic strings is more difficult for infants than is discriminating isolated contrasts, and the more complex the string, the more difficult it is. This fact was nicely demonstrated in an experiment by Goodsitt, Morse, Ver Hoeve, and Cowan (1984). Using the head-turn procedure, the researchers trained 6-month-old infants to discriminate between /ba/ and /du/, a very easy contrast. Then /ba/ and /du/ were combined with other syllables to see whether the infants were still able to make the discrimination they made between the isolated syllables. The study found that infants could still tell the strings apart, but the discrimination was harder for infants to make when the /ba/ and /du/ were embedded in a complex sequence than when embedded in a redundant sequence. For example, infants correctly discriminated /kokodu/ from /kokoba/ 75 percent of the time, but they were able to discriminate mixed sequences such as /kotiba/ from /kotidu/ only 67 percent of the time. Although this finding suggests that much of the speech babies hear must be a jumble for them, other evidence shows that when the contrasting syllable is stressed, babies can make use of this in distinguishing series of sounds (Karzon, 1985). More generally, there is evidence that babies make use of the prosodic features of input to break the speech stream into meaningful components, which leads us to the next topic of how the particular ways in which adults talk when they are addressing babies may help children crack the language code.

## Infant-directed speech

***The nature of speech addressed to babies.***    In many cultures, adults use a particular way of speaking with babies (Fernald et al., 1989; Grieser & Kuhl, 1988). This style of speech is sufficiently different from the way adults talk to other adults that it has been given its own name—**motherese** (Newport, Gleitman, & Gleitman, 1977)—although the terms **infant-directed speech** or **child-directed speech** are currently more widely used. The prosodic characteristics of infant-directed speech are of particular relevance to prelinguistic babies. When talking to babies, mothers (and fathers and other unrelated adults) use a higher-pitched voice, a wider range of pitches, longer pauses, and shorter phrases (Fernald et al., 1989; Fernald & Simon, 1984, and see summary in Gerken, 1994). In sum, the intonation contour of normal speech is greatly exaggerated in speech addressed to infants and so is likely to highlight some features of speech for language-learning infants. Infant-directed speech is also produced at a slower tempo than adult-directed speech, with the result that vowels are prolonged. It turns out that these vowels are not only longer in duration, but also are more prototypical examples of the particular vowel being produced (Kuhl et al., 1997; Kuhl, 1999). Thus, infant-directed speech might also support language acquisition by providing particularly clean examples of the sounds to be learned.

***Infant-directed speech as a universal signal system.***   It is insufficient for scientific purposes, however, to assume that the existence of a special speech register for talking to infants implies that it serves some useful function. A substantial body of research has investigated how infants respond to infant-directed speech and what infants might learn from it. Several findings make the case that infants prefer to hear infant-directed over adult-directed speech. Anne Fernald (1985) recorded 10 different adult women talking to their 4-month-old infants and to an adult. These tapes were then played to 4-month-olds in an experimental setting in which the infant-directed speech tape was played if the babies turned their head in one direction, and the adult-directed speech tape was played if the babies turned their head in the other direction. The infants chose to hear infant-directed speech more frequently than they chose to hear the adult-directed speech. This preference has also been demonstrated in newborns and 1-month-olds (Cooper & Aslin, 1990), and it holds true across languages— English-learning babies prefer infant-directed Cantonese to adult-directed Cantonese and Cantonese-learning babies prefer infant-directed English to adult-directed English (Werker, Pegg, & MacLeod, 1994).

What is it about infant-directed speech that makes it so interesting to babies? For 4-month-old babies, it seems to be the exaggerated pitch contours. Fernald and Kuhl (1987) found that 4-month-olds preferred to hear infant-directed speech when everything but the melody had been filtered out of the speech signal. However, Cooper and Aslin (1994) found that 1-month-olds demonstrated a preference for infant-directed speech only if the full speech signal was presented: prosody alone was not sufficient. Thus, Cooper and Aslin suggest that infants start out preferring something about the whole speech signal, but they come to prefer even the isolated pitch contours because these are associated with positive interactions with their caretakers.

Whatever the relevant acoustic properties of infant-directed speech are, it seems that mothers naturally produce sounds that interest babies. One possible reason is simply that the exaggerated intonation contours produce a stimulus with high contrast. According to this view, babies like infant-directed speech for the same reason they like bold colors and black on white patterns (Vihman, 1996). Fernald (1992), on the other hand, has suggested that special attention-getting properties of infant-directed speech have a unique basis. She has referred to infant-directed speech as a universal signal system, and she has proposed that it is based in human biology. That is, infant-directed speech is not just talk, it is also a system of calls that have effects on infants entirely separate from the meaning of the words produced. The immediate effects of these calls are to direct the infants' attention and to calm or arouse them, depending on the particular call. In support of this argument, Fernald points out the apparently universal correspondences between intonation and affect (the emotion behind what is said) that hold across languages. When mothers say things like "No!" or "Don't touch that!" the intonation is very different from when they say things like "Good!" or "Clever girl!" These different intonations for both prohibitions and praise tend to be much the same across different languages. Fernald (1989) has demonstrated that on the basis of intonation alone, adults can tell the difference between prohibitions and approval statements addressed to babies.

***The role of infant-directed speech in language acquisition.*** Some researchers have suggested that in addition to regulating attention and arousal, infant-directed speech also provides the gateway to language acquisition. The correlations between intonation and affect may provide infants with their first accessible sound-meaning correspondences. The exaggerated stress patterns may help infants isolate words in the speech stream. One study found that adults learned words in a foreign language better if the words were presented in infant-directed rather than adult-directed speech (Golinkoff & Alioto, 1995). Another hypothesis suggests that the exaggerated prosodic contours of infant-directed speech may give infants the foundation for acquiring their language's grammatical structure.

Support for the notion that the prosodic cues of child-directed speech might assist language learning comes from research that compared infants' processing of child-directed speech and adult-directed speech. In one study, Hirsh-Pasek and associates (1987) presented 7- to 10-month-old infants with tape-recorded samples of child-directed speech into which pauses had been inserted. In some of the samples, the pauses had been inserted at clause boundaries; for other samples, the pauses had been inserted within clauses. The researchers found that the babies preferred to listen to the speech samples that were interrupted at clause boundaries. This finding suggests that clauses are perceptual units for young infants. In a subsequent study, Kemler-Nelson, Hirsh-Pasek, Jusczyk, and Wright Cassidy (1989) repeated the same procedure, this time using samples of child-directed speech with half of the infants tested and samples of adult-directed speech for the other half. Infants preferred only the uninterrupted clauses in the child-directed speech condition. When the speech samples were adult-directed speech, it didn't matter where the pauses were inserted. These results suggest that prelinguistic infants can identify clauses in child-directed speech but not in adult-directed speech. However, see Fernald and McRoberts (1996) for a different interpretation.

The proposal that infants find important clues to language structure in the prosodic characteristics of the speech signal is known as the **prosodic bootstrapping hypothesis.** A more-encompassing proposal, that properties of the sound signal other than prosody contribute to language learning, is known as the **phonological bootstrapping hypothesis** (for a comprehensive treatment, see Morgan & Demuth, 1996). We will consider how the phonological properties of language might be involved in lexical and grammatical development in Chapters 4 and 5. There we will also consider how properties other than the phonological properties of infant-directed speech might be involved in language acquisition.

When we consider the arguments offered regarding the role of infant-directed speech in language development, we also have to consider cultural differences in the speech addressed to children. Although it is often claimed that the special features of infant-directed speech are universal, there are dissenting voices (Ingram, 1995; Ratner & Pye, 1984). Furthermore, in many cultures—including the cultures of Samoans (Ochs, 1982; Schieffelin & Ochs, 1986), Papua New Guineans (Schieffelin, 1979, 1985), aboriginal groups in Australia (Bavin, 1992), Mayans in Mexico (Brown, 2001), and U.S. African Americans in the rural South (Heath, 1983)—adults simply do not address speech to prelinguistic infants. In these cultures, infants are loved, held, and cared for but not talked to, yet they learn to talk. The fact that language acquisition is universal whereas infant-directed speech may not be raises the question of how important the properties of infant-directed speech can be in explaining language acquisition. One possibility is that it is not important for language development. Another possibility is that it is not necessary, just useful. In this latter case, we would expect children who do not hear infant-directed speech to acquire language at a slower pace. There are some suggestions in the literature that this might be the case, but we do not know enough about language development in other cultures to come to any firm conclusion.

## The influence of the target language on infants' speech perception

Up to this point, we have focused our discussion of infants' speech perception on describing the initial state of the language-learning infant. That initial state includes the perceptual abilities language acquisition will require, and it also seems to include a preference to attend to the kind of sound signal likely to be linguistically relevant—that is, infant-directed speech. Before leaving the topic of infant speech perception, we also need to consider the changes that occur during infancy. As was the case for prelinguistic sound production, we can see in prelinguistic speech perception that well before babies talk, they have learned something about the particular language to which they have been exposed.

***The tuning of phonemic perception.*** Although infants start out able to make essentially all the discriminations language acquisition will require, they do not remain in that initial state. The infants soon become, like adults, less able to discriminate some contrasts that are not used in their ambient language. An experiment by Werker and Tees (1984) demonstrated the influence of the linguistic environment on infants' speech perception. Werker and Tees took advantage of the fact that Hindi and Inslekepmx (the language spoken by the native Salish of British Columbia) have consonant contrasts that English does not. Using the head-turn procedure, the researchers found that 6- to 8-month-old English-learning infants could make these Hindi and Inslekepmx discriminations, but very few could do so at 10 to 12 months old. In contrast, 11- and 12-month-old Hindi-learning and Inslekepmx-learning infants were still able to make phonemic distinctions in the language they were acquiring. Effects of the target language on vowel discrimination have been found in infants as young as 6 months old (Kuhl, Williams, Lacerda, Stevens, & Lindblom, 1992). Vowel perception may be affected before consonant perception because there are fewer different vowels than consonants; thus infants hear each vowel more frequently than they hear each consonant (Gerken, 2002).

It appears that even before babies know anything about the meaning of the sounds they hear, they are paying attention to the acoustic properties of those sounds. A baby hearing a language in which /d/ and /t/ are different phonemes, for example, will hear many clear examples of /d/ and /t/ and not much that is in between. If there were a language in which the contrast between /d/ and /t/ were not phonemic (for example, /b/ and /v/ are not different phonemes in Spanish), then babies would be likely to hear adult speakers producing sounds that cover the whole acoustic continuum from /d/ to /t/. If babies are paying attention to acoustic properties and the frequencies with which they occur, babies in the first case should learn that there are two distinct sounds on the /d/–/t/ continuum; babies in the latter case would not. Maye, Werker, and Gerken (2002) tested the hypothesis that this sort of learning could account for ambient language effects on infant speech perception. They gave 6- and 8-month-old infants two different types of experience hearing sounds along the /d/–/t/ continuum. Some infants heard sounds near the endpoints more frequently than they heard sounds in the middle of the range (a bimodal distribution of experience); other infants heard sounds in the middle more frequently than sounds at either end (a unimodal distribution of experience). Next, the infants' abilities to make the /d/–/t/ discrimination was tested. The infants who heard the bimodal distribution were able to distinguish between /d/ and /t/; the babies who heard the unimodal distribution could not. A similar process by which experience creates categories of sounds based solely on acoustic properties has been proposed to account for ambient language effects on vowel perception (Kuhl, 1999; Kuhl & Meltzoff, 1997).

It is important to note, however, that the effect of early experience is not absolute. Although experience with the target language results in a decline in the ability to perceive unused contrasts, the loss of the ability to make nonnative discriminations is neither total nor across the board. Some contrasts remain easy even for nonnatives, and the perception of the difficult contrasts can be improved with training (Best, 1994). Also, regarding vowels, the effect of language experience on perception seems to be stronger in infancy than in adulthood (Werker & Polka, 1993). Thus, the nature of the effect of experience seems to be an adjustment of attention rather than a change in basic sensory capacities (Best, 1994).

***Learning the sound patterns of one's language.***   Newborns can distinguish utterances in their native language from utterances in another language (Mehler et al., 1988). In a study by Mehler and colleagues, babies born to French-speaking mothers heard tapes of French and Russian speech, and the babies' sucking rate—as an indicator of their levels of arousal—was measured as they listened to the tapes. The babies showed more arousal when they heard French than when they heard Russian. When babies of mothers who spoke a language other than French or Russian were played the French and Russian tapes, these babies showed no difference in arousal to the two tapes. The results of this study suggest that French and Russian are not intrinsically different in how interesting they are to babies. However, if one language is familiar, it is more interesting, and newborns show evidence of familiarity with the particular language their mothers spoke.

This finding raises the question of what the babies remember. The uterus is a noisy environment, and the fetus is surrounded by fluid—not exactly ideal listening conditions. Part of the answer seems to be that babies hear and remember the prosodic contour of the speech their mothers produced while the babies were in utero. As evidence that prosodic cues are what distinguished French from Russian for the infants in the preceding study, when the French and Russian speech samples were filtered so that only the prosodic cues remained, the main findings of the study were replicated (Mehler et al., 1988). French and Russian have very different prosodic characteristics. If babies represent the sound of a language in terms of its prosodic features, they should have a hard time distinguishing between prosodically similar languages. This is exactly what Nazzi, Bertoncini, and Mehler (1998) found. Using all low-pass filtered stimuli, in which the particular sounds are lost and only the prosody remains, they found that newborns were able to discriminate between English and Japanese and between English and Spanish or Italian, but not between English and the prosodically similar Dutch and not between Spanish and the prosodically similar Italian.

By the age of 9 months, infants are able to tell their language from another on the basis of sound patterns without relying on prosody. Just as English-speaking adults can recognize *geslacht* and *woestign* as foreign words based on their sounds, so too can 9-month-olds. Jusczyk, Friederici, Wessels, Svenkerud, and Jusczyk (1993) presented American and Dutch 6- and 9-month-old babies with American and Dutch words. At 9 months, but not at 6 months, the American infants listened longer to the American words, and the Dutch infants listened longer to the Dutch words. When only the prosodic contours of the words were presented, there were no preferences. (English and Dutch have very similar prosodic characteristics.) This result suggests that by 9 months, infants have learned something about the kind of sound patterns that characterize their language.

## PHONOLOGICAL DEVELOPMENT ONCE SPEECH BEGINS

We have thus far described the prelinguistic period in children's development of the production and perception of speech sounds. We turn now to phonological development once speech begins. The fundamental question about phonological development during this period concerns how children mentally represent the acoustic properties of words and, even more basically, how children represent the phonological system of their language. These questions are puzzles because prelinguistic infants seem to know much more about the sound structure of their language than children use when they begin to understand and produce words. We present first the data on word recognition and production, followed by a discussion of current models of phonological representation. Last, we briefly review the topics of cross-linguistic and individual differences in phonological development, and we introduce the topic of the development of phonological awareness.

### Word perception

***Word learning.***    It would seem that infants' abilities to discriminate phonemic contrasts should put them in an excellent position to begin learning words. That is, 1-month-olds can tell that /p/ and /b/ are different sounds, so 1-year-olds should have no trouble learning that *pat* and *bat* are different words. In fact, however, young 1-year-olds do have trouble with this sort of task. Werker and her colleagues (Werker, Fennell, Corcoran, & Stager, 2002) presented 14-month-olds and 18- to 24-month-olds with two different object–sound pairs. For example, the infants saw a plastic model of a molecule and heard *dih* over and over until they habituated, and they saw a toy crown while hearing *bih* over and over until they habituated. Then the object–sound pairings were switched. The question is, did the infants show they noticed that what used to be called *dih* was now *pih* by resuming interest in what was presented? The answer is that 14-month-old infants did not, but 18-month-old infants did. We know it is the similarity in sound that caused the difficulty for the 14-month-olds, because 14-month-olds were successful at this task when the pairs of sounds were phonetically very different (Werker, Cohen, Lloyd, Casasola, & Stager, 1998).

Other researchers have also found that very young children fail to distinguish newly taught words if the words differ by only one segment (Shvachin, 1948/1973; Garnica, 1973). According to Werker et al. (2002), the reason is that the multiple demands of the word-learning task do not leave the child with sufficient resources to register all the phonetic details of newly encountered words. When they are busy paying attention to a new object and a new sound sequence, children create only a rough representation of what the new sound sequence is like. That rough representation is not sufficient to distinguish *dih* from *bih*.

***Word recognition.*** According to a widely held view, children have only rough or holistic representations even of words that they know. The evidence that led to this view consists of many findings that in word-recognition tasks children perform differently than adults. In general, they are less sensitive to differences between words at the level of individual phonetic segments and base their judgments on syllables or whole words (Walley, 1993).

More recent evidence, however, suggests children do represent words they know in some phonetic detail. Swingley and Aslin (2000) presented 18- to 23-month-olds with familiar words that were either pronounced correctly or incorrectly. The incorrect pronunciations changed only a single segment (e.g., *baby* was pronounced *vaby*). The infants' task was to look at the matching picture out of two presented on a screen in front of the baby (e.g., a picture of a baby versus a picture of a dog). In this study, the babies looked more to the matching picture than the nonmatch even when the word was pronounced incorrectly, but they were faster at looking to the matching picture when the word was pronounced correctly. In this case, the babies' overall looking indicates that *vaby* works as well as *baby*, suggesting that infants' lexical representations may lack phonetic detail. The speed of response data, however, show that infants are sensitive to even a single segment difference. Measuring the speed with which children looked to the matching picture was made possible by a new technique for monitoring infants' eye movements. Eye movements reveal what children are gleaning from the speech they hear—as they hear it. Other work using eye tracking has also shown that very young children process words in a segment-by-segment manner. For example, it takes 2-year-olds longer to differentiate *dog* and *doll* than to differentiate *tree* and *truck* because the parts of *dog* and *doll* that are the same have a longer duration than the parts of *tree* and *truck* that are the same (Swingley, Pinto, & Fernald, 1999). If children do mentally represent words in their lexicons as sequences of phonetic segments—just as adults do—then we are left without an explanation for why children perceive and produce words with less accuracy than adults. We turn now to the data on early word production— which has also motivated the view that children represent the sounds of words in a holistic fashion.

## Word production

***First words.*** Children's first words have a simple syllable structure: They are either single syllables or reduplicated syllables, such as *baba* and *dada*. First words also use a small inventory of vowels and consonants (Ingram,

1999); the particular sounds that appear in first words are the same sounds that were evidenced in children's late babbling and transitional forms. Leonard, Newhoff, and Meselam (1980) studied the initial consonant sounds in the first 50 words spoken by children acquiring English. They found that the sounds most common in children's babble were also most common in early vocabularies and that some sounds in the adult language were conspicuously absent in children's productions. For example, /m/, /b/, and /d/ were consistently present, and /θ/, /ð/, /l/, and /r/ were consistently absent. This general description not withstanding, the researchers also found considerable variety across children in the phonemes in their first 50 words.

Although researchers can describe the sounds in children's first words in terms of the presence and absence of particular phonemes, this does not mean that words are a sequence of phonemes in the minds of children at this point. In fact, it has been proposed on the basis of production data that early word representations are of the whole word—not analyzed into separate phonemic segments. One sort of evidence for this view is the lack of consistency in the ways children produce sounds during this stage. The same sound may be produced different ways in different words in the target language. So, for example, the initial sounds in the words *purse* and *pretty,* which are the same in adults' productions, may be different in the child's productions (Ferguson & Farwell, 1975; Walley, 1993).

The production of **phonological idioms** is a particularly striking inconsistency that suggests some whole-word representations. This term refers to words the child produces in a very adultlike way, while still incorrectly producing other words that use the very same sounds. Some frequently used phonological idioms persist into later stages of development, whereas less frequently produced words get assimilated into children's developing general patterns for producing speech sounds (Menn & Stoel-Gammon, 1995). Children's pronunciation of these assimilated idioms may actually become less adultlike for a while (Stemberger & Bernhardt, 1998).

**The development of phonological processes.**    Around 18 months of age children's productions become more consistent, although not adultlike. They appear to have developed systematic ways in which to alter the sounds of the target language so that they fit within the repertoire of sounds they can produce. These systematic transformations are called **phonological processes** (Menyuk, Menn, & Silber, 1986). Many phonological processes are common to all children acquiring the same language, and they give young children's speech certain characteristic features. For example, pronouncing *bottle* as /baba/ or *Mommy* as /mama/ results from the process known as reduplication, in which one syllable, usually the first, is duplicated. Another common process is the substitution of stops for fricatives, so that *church* becomes /tʌrč/. This particular example illustrates that a process can be applied to a sound in

---

**Box 3.2   Common phonological processes in children's speech**

*Whole word processes*

*Weak syllable deletion: omission of an unstressed syllable in the target word*

    banana [nænæ]
    butterfly [bʌfaɪ]

*Final consonant deletion: omission of the final consonant in the target word*

    because [pikʌ]
    thought [fɔ]

*Reduplication: production of two identical syllables based on one of the syllables in the target word*

    Sesame Street [si:si]
    hello [jojo]
    bottle [baba]

*Consonant harmony: one of two different consonants in the target word takes on features of another consonant in the same word*

    duck [gʌk]
    tub [bʌb]

*(continued)*

---

one position in a word but not to the same sound in a different position. Consonant clusters tend to be reduced, so *school* becomes /kul/, and glides are often substituted for liquids, so that rabbit is pronounced /wæbɪt/. Deletion, particularly of word-final consonants, is very common in children's early speech. Common phonological processes and some examples are listed in Box 3.2.

Often more than one process is applied to a word, making the relation of the child's attempt to the target language less than obvious. For example, one early "word" observed in the speech of a 2-year-old boy was /bu/. This child consistently used his word /bu/ to refer to his urine and feces as he proudly flushed them down the toilet. The fact that /bu/ doesn't sound like any related word in English suggests that maybe this was an invented, idiosyncratic form.

---

**Box 3.2**   *(continued)*

*Consonant cluster reduction: omission of one of the consonants of a cluster in the target word*

    cracker [kæk]

*Segment substitution processes*

*Velar fronting: a velar is replaced by an alveolar or dental*

    key [ti]

*Stopping: a fricative is replaced by a stop*

    sea [ti]

*Gliding: a liquid is replaced by a glide*

    rabbit [wæbɪt]
    Lissa [jɪ sə]

Whole-word processes, which alter the adult word most drastically, are especially typical of younger children (up to age 3 or 4), whereas in some normally developing children, some of the segment substitution processes persist into the early school years (Vihman, 1988).

---

However, it is possible to explain the derivation of /bu/ from the target language word *poop* in the following way: First, apply the common process of deletion of the final consonant. That changes *poop* to /pu/. Then apply the less common, but certainly not bizarre, process of voicing initial voiceless consonants. That changes /p/ to /b/ and yields /bu/. Some children may have a great many idiosyncratic processes, making their speech difficult for unfamiliar people to understand, though quite comprehensible to their parents and quite lawful to the linguist.

    In addition to these processes for transforming words in the target language to sound sequences within the child's articulatory abilities, children may adopt other strategies when confronted with a new word. One strategy is simply to avoid acquiring new words that use sounds that are not in their repertoires (Schwartz & Leonard, 1982). Alternatively, children may assimilate a new word either to another similar-sounding word in their lexicons or to a preexisting whole-word sound pattern (termed a **canonical form**). For example, a child might modify all words to fit the pattern *consonant + vowel + /j/ + vowel +consonant*. One child pronounced the word *panda* as /**pajan**/, the word *berries* as /**bjas**/, and the word *tiger* as /**tajak**/ (Priestly, 1977, in Vihman, 1988a). Some children seem to modify all new words to fit a small set of canonical forms; other children use a few canonical forms along with a more elaborate system of phonological patterns. The need for these processes gradually declines as children become able to produce more and more of the sounds in their target language. The whole-word processes, which alter the adult word most drastically, are especially typical of younger children (up to age 3 or 4); some of the segment substitution processes, in contrast, persist into the early school years (Vihman, 1988).

***General patterns of phonological development.*** Some speech sounds seem to be harder for children to produce than others, and therefore some general patterns exist in the order in which different speech sounds appear in children's productions. We have already seen that some sounds are common in children's babble and first words. Other sounds still cause difficulty to many children at the age of 5 or 6 years. Normally, children sound adultlike in their phonology by the time they are about 7 years old. Sander (1972) summarized the data on the age at which different speech sounds appear in the speech of children learning English. His age estimates, shown in Figure 3.6, relate to what he terms the "customary" production of a sound, which he defines as the age at which a majority of children can clearly articulate that sound in two out of three word positions. However, several factors limit the usefulness of such norms as descriptions of phonological development (Menyuk & Menn, 1979). First, the likelihood that a sound will be articulated depends both on the sound's position in the word and on the neighboring sounds in the word. Furthermore, the factors of word position and neighboring sounds affect different sounds differently. For example, fricatives, such as /f/ and /s/, tend to be produced first in word-final position and to appear only later as the initial sound in a word. In contrast, stops, such as /p/ and /g/, tend to be produced first in word-initial position.

***The relation between perception and production.*** The fact that a child pronounces something in an immature way does not mean that the child is unaware of the difference between that pronunciation and adult pronunciation. For example, a child named Alissa pronounced her name as though it were "yitya" for a long time. However, if someone else teasingly called her "yitya," she became quite incensed. This phenomenon is sometimes referred to as the "fis" phenomenon, following an oft-cited example of one child's refusal to accept "fis" as the label for his toy fish, even though "fis" was how

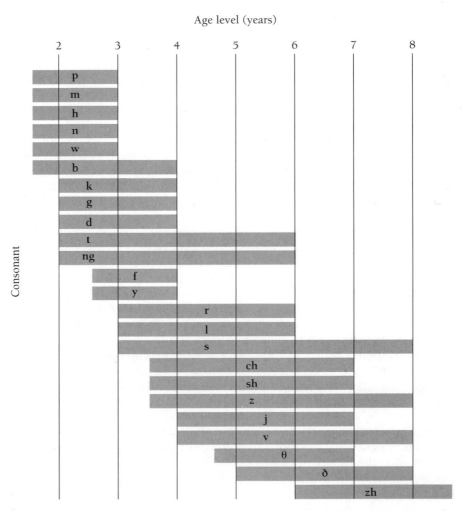

**Figure 3.6**  Average age estimates and upper age limits of customary consonant production in the speech of children acquiring English

Source: From "When Are Speech Sounds Learned?" by E. K. Sander, 1972. *Journal of Speech and Hearing Disorders*. 37, 55–63. Copyright © 1972 American Speech-Language-Hearing Association. Reprinted by permission.

the child produced the word (Berko & Brown, 1960). Such anecdotes are common (see, for example, Butler, 1920), and they tell us that children's mispronunciations do not necessarily imply that children have incomplete mental representations of how the word is supposed to sound. The results of systematic research on the relation of production and perception suggest that this is true only some of the time (Eilers & Oller, 1976). Some contrasts are difficult to discriminate—for example /θ/ from /f/, and /r/ from /w/—and production errors involving these consonants may have a basis in perception (Vihman, 1996).

## The mental representation of words and speech sounds

Do children have adultlike representations of words from the beginning, or do they move from holistic to segmentally based representations? A related question is whether children have representations of all the phonemic contrasts in their language from an early age or whether they only gradually achieve a system in which contrasting phonemes have distinct mental representations. These are the phonological versions of a larger question that often arises in discussions of development: the question of the continuity of development. In discussing the evolution of language in Chapter 2, the issue was continuity in phylogenetic development (i.e., development across species); here the issue is continuity in ontogenetic development (i.e., development within an individual). In both cases, the question is whether there is a qualitative change from one kind of thing to another in the course of development or whether, instead, the same sort of thing exists at all points in development. In the case of discontinuity, the problem is explaining the shift in the underlying system. In the case of continuity of the underlying system, the problem is explaining the development changes in behavior.

The dominant view for some time has been discontinuity. The argument has been that children initially have holistic representations of how words sound and that their phonological systems do not capture every contrast in sound that is used by the adult language. (That is, for example, that there is a point at which /r/ and /w/ not only are confused in perception, and sound alike in production, but actually are not distinct entities in the child's mental representation of the sounds of his language.) Children are motivated to move from holistic to segmental representations, and thus, a system for segmental representations, by vocabulary growth.

The argument is as follows: When children have a small vocabulary, both receptively and productively, global representations of word sounds may be sufficient to distinguish one word from another. As vocabulary grows, however, words start to overlap in their acoustic properties and more detailed representations are necessary in order to keep different words apart. According to this argument, vocabulary growth is a major cause of the move from holistic to phonetically-detailed word representation. In order to support the more detailed representations of the sounds of words, children need a mental system of the sounds that words are composed of. This system is the phonological system of the language, and the argument often made is that lexical development is the factor that pushes the child to a phonological analysis of his language and to the representation of a phonological system (see Beckman & Edwards, 2000; Gerken, 1994; Walley, 1993).

This argument is consistent with evidence that phonemic representation of words begins at around the time that vocabulary size increases dramatically—the word spurt at 18 months. It is also consistent with the finding that the ability to learn new words with minimal phonetic differences in the Werker et al. experiment was not related to age, but actually was more a function of children's vocabulary size than it was a function of their age. Another source of data that has been marshaled in support of this argument has to do with what are called similarity neighborhoods in children's lexicons. The neighborhood of a word is all the other words in the vocabulary that differ by only one phoneme. At one point in the history of this debate, the argument was made that neighborhood density increases as vocabulary grows—that is, in a bigger vocabulary each word resides in a denser neighborhood (Charles-Luce & Luce, 1990). On the other hand, more recent analyses show that the proportion of words in a child's vocabulary that are "neighbors" declines with increasing vocabulary size (Coady & Aslin, 2003). At present, both the continuity of early lexical representations with adult lexical representations and the nature of early representation of phonological systems are very much open questions.

## Cross-linguistic differences in phonological development

The order in which sounds appear in children's speech is influenced by properties of the target language. For example, for children acquiring English, /v/ is a relatively late-appearing sound. However, among children acquiring Swedish, Bulgarian, and Estonian, /v/ is a much earlier acquisition (Ingram, 1988). Such cross-linguistic differences indicate that the difficulty of producing different speech sounds cannot entirely explain why some sounds are acquired earlier than others. Ingram (1988, 1999) suggests that the function different speech sounds serve in the language is another important factor. In English, /v/ is relatively infrequent, and children can get fairly far making different words sound different without mastering /v/. In contrast, in Swedish, Bulgarian, and Estonian, /v/ is more important to marking the difference between different words. The relevant factor according to Ingram's functional hypothesis is not the frequency with which children hear the sound but rather the frequency with which the sound is used in different words. For example, in English, the initial sound in *the* and *this* is very frequently heard because it is used in a few very high-frequency words. However, because that sound is not involved in many different words, its functional significance is low, and it is acquired late in children acquiring English. In sum, sounds that appear early may not always be sounds that are easy to produce. Rather, they may be the sounds that carry information in the phonological system. On the other hand, Ingram (1989) suggests that it would not be surprising to find that languages tend to assign the greatest functional loads to sounds that are easy to produce.

## Individual differences in phonological development

Even children acquiring the same language vary in their phonological development. One difference is the rate of development: Some babies start to babble earlier than others, and some babies acquire the ability to produce adult-sounding words earlier than others. Although severe difficulty in producing speech may be a sign of some underlying language or hearing disorder, normal language development includes a wide range in the rates of development. Figure 3.6 gives a rough indication of the range observed.

There are individual differences in aspects of phonological development other than rate. As mentioned earlier, some children in the babbling stage are "intonation babies," who babble long strings of jargon with the intonation contour of the target language. Other children are "word babies," who tend to produce one short babble sequence at a time (Dore, 1975). Children also differ in the particular sounds they produce. Some children, for example, produce many nasal sounds; others produce few. These differences may be due to differences in articulatory ability, but some children just seem to like certain sounds (Vihman, 1993).

At a later point in development, children differ in the approaches they take to constructing a phonological system. Some children rely heavily on whole-word processes, assimilating adult words to a few patterns and avoiding unassimilable words. Other children have a larger repertoire of segmental phonological processes. Also, children differ in the particular processes they use in transforming target words in their own speech. For example, children who like to use reduplication will be good at maintaining the multisyllabic nature of adult words even if they cannot quite produce all the individual sounds. So, a child who reduplicates might produce *blanket* as /baba/, whereas another child less inclined toward reduplication might say /bat/.

## The development of phonological awareness

Earlier we made the point that all competent speakers and hearers know the phonology of their language, even though they are not aware of that knowledge. So, for example, all speakers pluralize *bug* with /z/ and *bike* with /s/, although most speakers couldn't say why. However, adults do have some conscious awareness of the sounds that make up the speech they hear. Adults can rhyme, and count syllables, and think of five different words that begin with /t/. This is called phonological awareness. Children show some signs of phonological awareness beginning around 2 years; they play with the sounds of words and they appreciate rhymes and alliteration (as in Dr. Seuss books). The development of phonological awareness is of central importance in considering the relation between oral language and literacy, because children's levels of phonological awareness predict their success in learning to read. We will consider the topic further in Chapter 9 when we discuss children's acquisition of literacy.

## MODELS OF PHONOLOGICAL DEVELOPMENT

Having described the course of phonological development, it is now time to consider explanations of phonological development. We can organize the proposed explanations under four headings: (1) behaviorist models, (2) biologically based models, (3) cognitive problem-solving models, and (4) connectionist models. Each model is a proposed answer to the question, How do children learn to distinguish and produce the sound patterns of the adult language? The models focus on early phonological development, which is where the most dramatic changes occur.

### Behaviorist models

In the heyday of behaviorism in the 1950s, researchers attempted to account for children's phonological development using the behaviorist mechanisms of imitation and reinforcement (for example, see Mowrer, 1960; Skinner, 1957). According to these accounts, babies produce the sounds they do because they imitate the sounds they hear and because they receive positive reinforcement for doing so. Over time, the sounds babies produce come to match the sounds of the target language because these are the sounds that babies have imitated and that have been reinforced.

This explanation has a few problems. First, it ignores the role of maturational processes in accounting for infants' changing sound repertoires. Some sounds seem to be late appearances in children's babbling because they are difficult to produce, not because children are not reinforced for producing them. This leads us to the second problem with the behaviorist account: that parents do not selectively reinforce speech sounds. Many parents express delight at every burp and raspberry their babies produce, and those children acquire the phonology of the target language nonetheless. Although these babies may also burp and make raspberries with high frequency, that does not seem to interfere with their phonological development.

The most serious problem for a behaviorist account, however, is the fact that the development of phonology is more than just the development of a repertoire of sounds. It is the development of a system of regularities (such as the voicing assimilation rule), and it is coming to know the relation between sounds (such as knowing that the voiceless equivalent of /d/ is /t/). This knowledge is not conscious knowledge, and it is not available to be rein-forced. Because behaviorist accounts of phonological development, and of language development more generally, operated with fundamentally mistaken notions of what language knowledge and language development are, behav-iorist accounts were not taken very seriously for long. Although many unre-solved issues remain regarding how children acquire the phonology of their language, virtually everyone agrees that 1950s-style behaviorism is not a seri-ous candidate for an explanation.

This somewhat harsh dismissal of behaviorism should not be taken to mean that responding to babies' vocalizations has no effect; it does. Bornstein and Tamis-LeMonda (1989) found that babies vocalize more if they have mothers who are very responsive to the babies' vocalizations. Oller, Eilers, Basinger, Steffens, and Urbano (1995) found that babies living in extreme poverty, who tend to get less verbal stimulation than do more advantaged ba-bies (Hart & Risley, 1995), also tend to produce less babbling. Rheingold, Gewirtz, and Ross (1959) demonstrated experimentally that smiling in re-sponse to a baby's vocalization causes the baby to vocalize more. Other findings suggest that mothers may encourage their children's language devel-opment by responding contingently to their infants' prelinguistic vocalizations (Velleman, Mangipudi, & Locke, 1989). Thus, a responsive environment does seem to support vocal development and perhaps also helps language devel-opment proceed. (Other ways in which parents' responses to their children do and do not influence language development will be considered in later chapters.) The problem with behaviorism is not that it is wrong but that it is insufficient. A theory of phonological development needs to explain why de-velopment follows the path it does (as opposed to other paths), and it needs to explain how the ultimate achievement of the phonology of a language is possible.

## Biologically based models

Some researchers argue persuasively that biological factors shape both the course of phonological development and its ultimate result—namely, the phonological properties of the world's languages. According to Locke (Locke, 1983; Locke & Pearson, 1992), infants' first sounds are the sounds the human vocal apparatus is most inclined to produce, given its anatomical and physio-logical characteristics. Sound production is shaped by motor capacity, and the development of sound production is shaped by the development of motor ca-pacity. This biological basis to vocal development is the reason, according to Locke (1983, 1993), for the similar early sound repertoires of children acquir-ing different target languages.

The same biological factors that shape phonological development may shape adult languages as well. The sounds that appear early in infants' vocal productions are also common sounds among the world's languages, and sounds produced late in the course of development tend to be rare in the world's languages. For example, /m/ is among the first sounds babies produce, and 97 percent of the languages studied have /m/ among their phonemes. In contrast, the American /r/ is a sound that causes difficulty for children even into the school years, and this sound is a phoneme in only about 5 percent of the world's languages. A role for biology—or physiology—is also suggested by the fact that the phonological processes young children employ are also seen in processes used in adult languages (Donegan & Stampe, 1979; Stemberger & Bernhardt, 1998). For example, children commonly substitute voiceless for voiced consonants at the ends of words, such as pronouncing bad as /bæt/, and many languages have a rule that voiced consonants are pronounced as their voiceless counterparts in word-final position (e.g., *knives-knife, leaves-leaf*) (Vihman, 1988a).

Although no one would argue that motor capacity and its development are irrelevant to phonology and phonological development, researchers disagree about the importance of biology compared with language experience. The influence of the ambient language on the sounds produced in early babbling is a matter of some controversy (Oller & Eilers, 1998), but it is probably not zero. There is also evidence that how those sounds are used in the target language influences which sounds will be common in young children's early speech (Ingram, 1988; Pye, Ingram, & List, 1987). Finally, there is no doubt that the ambient language influences early speech sound discrimination (Kuhl et al., 1992; Werker & Tees, 1984). Thus, an account of phonological development also has to explain how experience exerts its effects.

## The cognitive problem-solving model

A long-standing view of phonological development is that children figure out the phonology of their language as a solution to the problem of how to sound like adults and to distinguish among the words they know when others talk to them (Ferguson & Farwell, 1975; Macken & Ferguson, 1983). This is the model of phonological development associated with the view that initially, children's word representations are whole-word representations and only later, when a child's capacity for mental representation is sufficient, are words analyzed into their segmental components, with contrasting features.

This cognitive view differs from a strong biologically based account of phonological development in placing a greater explanatory burden on the child's active problem-solving efforts than on the unfolding of a biologically determined course of development. One test of these competing views is the extent of individual differences in phonological development. The problem-solving view predicts substantial individual differences on the logic that different children might, at least initially, solve the problem of figuring out their language's phonology in different ways. Also, the view that vocabulary development provides the impetus for phonemic analysis predicts individual differences arising from differences in the vocabularies children acquire (Walley, 1993). In contrast, the biological view suggests that the course of phonological development should be more similar across children because all children share the same essential biological makeup. The data on individual differences are inconclusive, however, because different procedures for analyzing children's phonetic inventories give different pictures of the degree of variability and because individual differences can also result from individual differences in biological makeup.

The cognitive problem-solving view, because it is associated with the position that children initially represent the sounds of words as unanalyzed wholes, also differs from views that attribute more phonological knowledge to children earlier in development. An alternative view, with roots in a theory proposed by the Russian linguist Roman Jakobson in 1941 (translated into English in 1968), holds that children represent the underlying structure of the sounds of words from the very beginning of language. Children don't sound like adults, of course, but their mental representations of the sounds of words are not different in kind from those of adults (Ingram, 1999). As already discussed, recent work on word recognition suggests that young children have more phonetic detail in their lexical representations than was thought previously (Swingley & Aslin, 2000). The problem remains, however, that there are many differences between children's and adults performance on phonological tasks that need an explanation.

## The connectionist approach

Most recently connectionist models of phonological development have been proposed. As we discussed in Chapter 1, connectionism is a relatively new approach to modeling all human cognitive processes. There are connectionist models of pattern recognition, of learning, and of other aspects of language development. Here we will give an overview of how the phonological processes of young speakers and their eventual decline would be described in connectionist terms, based on an account by Stemberger (1992).

A central tenet of connectionism is a belief that rules are not necessary to describe the regularities of human behavior. One example of unnecessary rules is the phonological processes described in Box 3.2 that have been proposed to account for the systematic differences between the sound of words in the target language and the sound of words as children produce them. Instead of the processes view that children systematically transform the targets and then utter this transformed word, in the connectionist view children try to approximate the target word and make an error, saying /wæbɪt/, for example, instead of /ræbɪt/.

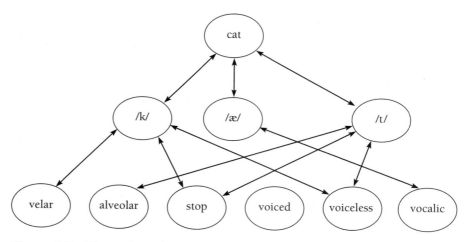

**Figure 3.7**    Illustration of a partial connectionist model of phonology

Source: From "A Connectionist View of Child Phonology," by J. P. Stemberger. In C. A. Ferguson et al. (Eds.). *Phonological Development*, pp. 165–189. Copyright © 1992 York Press. Reprinted with permission.

The test of such a model is whether it can account for the systematic na-ture of children's "errors." According to the connectionist model, in the pro-cess of producing a word like *cat,* a mental unit corresponding to the word is activated (presumably by the intention to say *cat*). That mental unit is con-nected to units that correspond to the phonemes in the word cat—/k/, /æ/, /t/—and those units are connected to the features that make up the sounds: voiced, stop, and so on. The hypothesized units and their interconnections are depicted in Figure 3.7. When the cat unit is activated, that activation spreads downward and eventually reaches the units connected to the actual muscles involved in speech production.

According to this model, children err because their connections are not yet adultlike. For example, cat is pronounced /tæt/ because the connection from the phoneme /k/ to the feature velar is weak. In fact, some features may be weakly connected to everything initially—that is, some features may be inac-cessible. (Inaccessibility could have a motoric basis.) In such a case, velars would be systematically absent from a child's productions, replaced by a sound that shared all the strongly connected features but was missing the weakly con-nected features; so /k/ would be replaced by /t/, and /g/ by /d/. The process of phonological development, according to this account, is the process of setting up the connections. This process begins in the vocal play that precedes babbling and continues until phonological development is complete.

# ● SUMMARY

The acquisition of phonology consists of learning to "distinguish and produce the sound patterns of the adult language" (Vihman, 1988a, p. 61). It also consists of learning and coming to mentally represent the structure underlying those sound patterns. At birth the child has the ability to distinguish virtually all the sounds all languages use, at least when the sounds are presented in isolation. The newborn produces no speech sounds, however. During the first year of life, speech sounds gradually emerge, beginning with vowel-like coos at 6 to 8 weeks of age, followed by some consonant sounds, followed by true babbling. By the end of the first year, children are typically babbling sequences of syllables that have the intonation contour of their target language.

The factors that underlie these developments include physical growth of the vocal apparatus, neurological development, and language experience. Language experience shows its influence on both the perception and the production of speech sounds. Although 4-month-old infants demonstrate that they can hear the difference between virtually all the sounds languages use, 1-year-olds cannot. Like adults, although not necessarily to the same degree, 1-year-olds have lost some of the ability to hear contrasts that are not present in the language they are acquiring. Language experience shows its influence on early sound production as well. The babbling of 10-month-old infants has elements of both the prosodic features and the particular sounds used by the infants' target language.

Children's productions are not adultlike. Initially children appear to tackle the task of articulating words on a word-by-word basis. Around the age of 18 months, children seem to develop systems for mapping the phonemes in the target language to sounds within their own, more limited repertoires. Many of these mapping rules—or phonological processes—are common across children, giving all young children's speech characteristic features, such as pronouncing bottle as /baba/ or rabbit as /wæbɪt/. The use of these processes declines gradually as children's articulatory abilities develop.

Also, which sounds are acquired early and which sounds appear later depends to a degree on how important those sounds are to marking distinctions in the target language. The full repertoire of speech sounds develops only gradually, with children typically sounding adultlike by about 7 years of age.

When and how children achieve a mental representation of the underlying phonological system is a central topic in the study of phonological development. One view holds that phonological development is discontinuous. According to this view, children's early representations are not like the phonological representations of adults. Rather, children initially represent words as unanalyzed wholes and only later come to represent words as sequences of phonemes. The alternative view of phonological development as continuous holds children mentally represent the phonetic features of words, and, in that respect, children's systems are adultlike from the beginning.

One widely held account of phonological development describes it as an active (although not necessarily conscious) problem-solving process for the child. With respect to production, children try to sound like the adults around them and try to figure out a system for doing so. With respect to comprehension, children need a system for representing the sounds of the words they know in sufficient detail to distinguish one word from another. There is also good evidence that biology plays an important role in shaping both the course of language development and its end result. Some sounds are harder to produce than others. These sounds are less frequently used by the languages of the world, and, on average, children acquire them later. However, another factor influencing the order of speech sound development is how important different sounds are to marking distinctions in the language. One new approach to modeling phonological development, the connectionist approach, proposes a very different view of how phonological knowledge is represented and of what causes the transformations of adult sounds in children's productions.

# KEY TERMS

distinctive feature

phone

phoneme

allophone

voicing

articulatory phonetics

phonetic features

place of articulation

manner of articulation

stops

fricatives

vegetative sounds

cooing

vocal play

expansion stage

marginal babbling

canonical or reduplicated babbling

nonreduplicated or variegated babbling

prosody

jargon

babbling drift

protowords

high-amplitude sucking technique (HAS)

habituation/dishabituation

head-turn technique

categorical perception

voice onset time (VOT)

phoneme boundary

phoneme boundary effect

motherese

infant-directed or child-directed speech

prosodic bootstrapping hypothesis

phonological bootstrapping hypothesis

phonological idioms

phonological processes

canonical form

phonological awareness

cognitive model

connectionist models

# REVIEW QUESTIONS

1. How would you convince your friend, who claims to know nothing about phonology, that she knows the difference between voiced and voiceless consonants?
2. What is the difference between a speech sound (or phone) and a phoneme?
3. List and describe the five stages of prespeech vocal development.
4. What have 10-month-old babies learned about the sounds of their language?
5. Why is a normative description of the development of speech sounds (such as Figure 3.6) only a very rough description of phonological development?
6. What are phonological processes? How are they significant?

7. What influence might lexical development have on phonological development?
8. What is phonological awareness?
9. What evidence supports the view that phonological development is the result of biological processes?
10. What evidence supports the view that phonological development is the result of children's active problem solving?
11. What claims and evidence about phonological development are consistent with a continuous view of phonological development, and what claims and evidence suggest children's phonological systems are different in kind from adults'?

# LEXICAL DEVELOPMENT: LEARNING WORDS

## LEXICAL KNOWLEDGE IN ADULTS

As an adult, you know tens of thousands of words. The vocabulary of an average English-speaking college student has been estimated at 150,000 words (Miller, 1977). Perhaps even more impressive is the fact that the average first-grader has a vocabulary of more than 14,000 words (Templin, 1957). In this chapter, we consider what this word knowledge consists of and how children acquire it.

### The mental lexicon

Think about what you know when you have a vocabulary of more than 100,000 words. You have in your head something like a dictionary with 100,000-plus entries. Each entry consists of a word and the things you know about that word. One sort of word knowledge you have is phonological: You know how to pronounce the word. Another sort of knowledge is grammatical: You know how to use the word in combination with other words. And another sort of knowledge—the central information about each word found in a dictionary—is its definition: You know what the word means. This knowledge of words that adults have—this dictionary in the head—is termed the **mental lexicon.** The study of lexical development is the study of the child's acquisition of a mental lexicon.

There are many questions to ask about lexical development: When does lexical development start? What words do children learn first? Are some words easier to learn than others, and why? What do children know about the words they use? How do children learn the words of their language? Before we turn our attention to these questions regarding lexical development, we need to consider a very basic question about lexical knowledge in adults: "What is a word?"

### What is a word?

A **word** is not just any set of sounds (or gestures) that communicates a meaning. If I point to something out of my reach and whine, you can probably figure out that I want what I am pointing to. However, neither my point nor my whine is a word. So what is a word? First of all, a word is a symbol. That is, it stands for something without being part of that something. Furthermore, the relation between words and what they stand for is arbitrary. Pointing and whining fail by this criterion. Many behaviors communicate meaning but are not symbols and therefore are not words. Babies' crying because they are hungry, dogs' barking because they need to go outside, and adults' shivering because they are cold all convey information; but neither the cries, the barks, nor the shivering are words because none is a symbol.

Words are more than arbitrary symbols; they are symbols that can be used to refer to things. The notion of **reference** is difficult to define, but it is crucial to discussions of lexical development. For a word to be used consistently in combination with a particular object is not sufficient to qualify that word use as referential. To borrow an example from Golinkoff, Mervis, and Hirsh-Pasek (1994), "one can say 'yikes!' each time one sees a particular cat, but that is not necessarily the same thing as referring to the cat" (p. 130). That is, reference involves words "standing for" their referents, not just "going with" their referents (Golinkoff et al., 1994).

As adults we use words referentially all the time, and nonreferential uses are the exception. (Greetings and social routines might be considered examples of nonreferential language use.) For young children, however, the referential status of the words they use is one issue that comes up in describing children's early lexical development. Describing lexical development involves more than just describing what words children say and when they say them. We are actually concerned with the development of children's mental lexicons: the knowledge inside their heads. Therefore, researchers who study lexical development are interested both in the words children say and in the knowledge underlying the use of those words. With that in mind, we turn now to a description of lexical development.

## THE COURSE OF EARLY LEXICAL DEVELOPMENT

### First words

Children usually produce their first words sometime between 10 and 15 months of age (Benedict, 1979; Fenson et al., 1994; Huttenlocher & Smiley, 1987). These first words may be hard to distinguish from the earlier protowords described in the previous chapter on phonological development. The critical difference is the fact that although protowords are sound sequences that seem to have consistent meaning for the child, the particular sounds of protowords are not derived in any obvious way from the language the child is learning. In contrast, true first words are approximations of words in the target language, even if somewhat rough approximations.

***Many first words are context-bound.***   Like the protowords that preceded them, the first words children use are often tied to particular contexts (Barrett, 1995). One famous example of such **context-bound word use** comes from Allison Bloom as reported by her mother, the well-known child language researcher Lois Bloom. Allison produced the word *car* at the age of 9 months, but she said "car" only when she was looking out her apartment window at cars on the street below (Bloom, 1973). She did not say "car" when she saw a car close up or when she saw a picture of a car in a book. Similarly, at the age of 12 months, Martyn Barrett's son Adam used the word *duck* only when he was hitting one of his toy yellow ducks off the edge of the bathtub (Barrett, 1986). He never said "duck" while playing with these toy ducks in other situations, and he never said "duck" while looking at real ducks. Barrett's interpretation of this behavior was that Adam "had not yet learned that the word duck could be used to refer to either his toy ducks or real ducks. Instead, his behavior suggests that he had simply identified one particular event in the context of which it was appropriate for him to produce the word duck" (Barrett, 1986, p. 40).

Even when word use is not limited to a single context, as in the preceding examples, children's use may be limited in ways that suggest their understanding of the word's meaning still falls short of adultlike representations of word meanings. For example, *more* might be used only as a request and not to comment on recurrence, and *no* might be used only to indicate refusal (Gopnik, 1988). Although these uses are more general than Allison's use of *car* and Adam's use of *duck,* these uses suggest that the child's mental representation of these words is only that words are what you say to accomplish a particular goal. On the basis of data from hundreds of American and Italian children, Caselli and colleagues (1995) concluded that children's first words may always be parts of routines or language games. Such situation-specific or function-specific understandings of word use are crucially different from adults' mental representations of words as symbols that refer.

**Is there a prelexical stage of word use?**    Because the understanding of word meaning that seems to underlie children's early context-bound words is so different from adults' mental representations of word meanings, some have argued that these context-bound words are not really words at all. Behrend (1990) suggested that these words are merely responses elicited by particular environmental conditions, similar to the reaching and pointing gestures of prelinguistic children. Behrend termed these context-bound words prelexical.

But if these first words are not really words, then when do real words appear? This question is important, in part because we want to know if the context-bound nature of early words reflects some internal limitation in the child. Are word meanings tied to particular contexts because there is something about these particular words that children do not know, or is there something about words in general that children don't know? That is, are the words prelexical, or is the child prelexical?

To answer this question, we need to know (1) whether there is a stage during which the child uses words only in these prelexical ways or (2) whether these prelexical words in children's vocabularies coexist with truly **referential words.** Some researchers argue that context-bound words appear first and that truly referential words must await some cognitive development in the child (for very different versions of this hypothesis, see Gopnik & Meltzoff, 1987; Nelson & Lucariello, 1985). Other researchers have found evidence that suggests otherwise.

**First words can also be referential.**    An example of evidence of referential word use among children's first words comes from research by Harris, Barrett, Jones, and Brookes (1988), who analyzed the first 10 words produced by four children using diaries their mothers kept of the children's word use. Harris and

**Table 4.1   Four children's first ten words**

| Word type | CHILD | | | |
| --- | --- | --- | --- | --- |
| | James | Jacqui | Jenny | Madeleine |
| Context-bound | mummy | wee | choo-choo | there |
| | go | hello | bye-bye | hello |
| | quack | mummy | there | here |
| | there | here | | bye-bye |
| | buzz | no | | |
| | moo | down | | |
| | boo | more | | |
| | | go | | |
| Nominal | teddy | Jacqui | teddy | teddy |
| | ball | bee | doggy | shoes |
| | | | moo | brum |
| | | | shoe | woof |
| | | | car | baby |
| Nonnominal | more | | mummy | yes |
| | | | no | |

Source: From "Linguistic Input and Early Word Meaning," by M. Harris et al., 1988, *Journal of Child Language, 15,* p. 83. Copyright © 1988 and reprinted with the permission of Cambridge University Press.

colleagues were able to categorize children's first words into three groups, as shown in Table 4.1. The largest category was context-bound words, containing 22 of these 40 first words. Contextually flexible **nominals,** or names for things, were the next most frequent, accounting for 14 of the 40 words. Last, four words were contextually flexible in their use and were not nominals.

It is interesting to note that the same word that is context-bound for one child may be contextually flexible for another. For example, Jacqui, who participated in the study by Harris and colleagues (1988), said "no" only when refusing something that was offered by her mother, so for Jacqui *no* was a context-bound word. In contrast, Jenny said "no" while pushing a drink away, while crawling to a step she was not allowed to climb, and while refusing a request by her mother. For Jenny, *no* was contextually flexible.

**Why are some words context-bound and others referential?**    If children are capable of acquiring referential words from the start, then why are some words not represented that way? It could be that limited experience produces limited understanding. However, not all of children's limited understandings seem explainable in this way. Children seem to not make use of the full range of their linguistic experience. In their study of children's first 10 words, Harris and associates also looked at how the mothers used these words and found that mothers used their children's first words in contexts other than the ones in which their children used them. The children, it seems, had extracted narrower meanings than their experience would have supported. The reason the children did not use their experience to build contextually flexible representations of word meanings may be that distilling the common meaning from a variety of contexts of use takes time for the beginning language learner. Some words get used before that common meaning has been inferred. The particular narrow meaning the children inferred does make sense given the children's experience hearing the word. Harris and associates found that for 18 of the 22 context-bound words, the child's sole use was the same as his or her mother's most frequent use.

***Context-bound words become decontextualized.*** Words that are at first context-bound gradually become decontextualized (Barrett, 1986; Bates, Benigni, Bretherton, Camioni, & Volterra, 1979; Dore et al., 1976). For example, about 2 weeks after Barrett's son Adam first said "duck" while hitting toy ducks off the edge of the bathtub, he began to say "duck" in other settings as well. The description of the beginning of lexical development that emerges from studies of this early stage is one in which children start out with at least two kinds of lexical entries for the words they use. One kind of lexical entry is situation-specific: This is a word you can say in this particular circumstance. The other kind of lexical entry is more adultlike: This is a word that encodes this meaning, and you can say it whenever you wish to express this meaning. Although some words enter the lexicon as context-bound words and gradually become decontextualized, other words are contextually flexible from the time the child first uses them.

## Vocabulary development from first words to 50 words

For several months after the appearance of their first words, most children plod along, adding words to their vocabulary slowly at first but with increasing speed as they approach the achievement of a 50-word vocabulary. Sometime around 18 months of age, but ranging from 15 to 24 months, children achieve a productive vocabulary of 50 words. The results of Katharine Nelson's (1973) longitudinal study of 18 children can be used to illustrate the course of lexical development from the first word to the 50-word vocabulary. Each mother in Nelson's study kept a diary and recorded each new word her child produced, along with the date and notes about the context in which the word was used. The mothers kept records until their children had acquired 50 words. From these records, Nelson was able to analyze the content of chil-

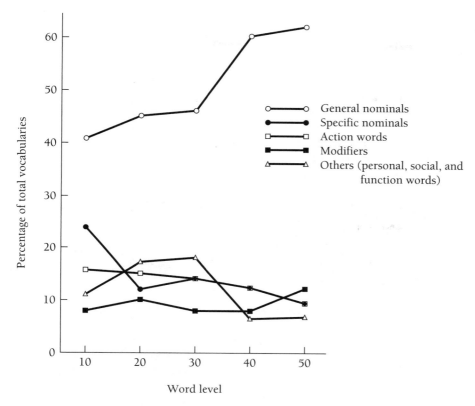

**Figure 4.1**   Lexical growth from 10 to 50 words, by word type

Source: From "Structure and Strategy in Learning to Talk," by K. Nelson, 1973, *Monographs of the Society for Research in Child Development,* 38. Serial No. 149. Copyright © 1973 The Society for Research in Child Development, Inc. Reprinted by permission.

dren's 50-word vocabularies and the course of their lexical development to that point. Nelson classified the children's words into six different categories: (1) Specific nominals, such as *Mommy, Daddy, Rover* (2) General nominals, including common nouns such as *dog, ball, milk* and pronouns such as *he, this* (3) Action words, such as *go, up, look* (4) Modifiers, such as *big, all gone, outside, mine* (5) Personal social words, such as *no, want, please* (6) Grammatical function words, such as *what, is, for.* Nelson found that nominals (general and specific) were the largest single category of children's words, from the first 10 words to the 50-word mark. She also found that the proportion of general nominals in children's vocabularies increased as vocabulary size increased during this period. Her results are illustrated in Figure 4.1.

## Vocabularies at the 50-word mark

***The content of children's 50-word vocabularies.*** The vocabularies of very young children are not just small versions of the vocabularies of older children and adults; they differ in the kinds of words they contain. Not surprisingly, children's first words reflect their experiences. They know names for people, food, body parts, clothing, animals, and household items that are involved in children's daily routines (Clark, 1979). Routines are also the source of early expressions such as *night-night* and *bye-bye*. First verbs include labels for actions that are part of children's routines (e.g., *eat, drink, kiss, sing*) and verbs with more general meanings that are frequent in children's input (*look, go, come, do*) (Naigles & Hoff, in press).

One feature of early vocabularies that has received a great deal of attention is the predominance of nouns (Bates et al., 1994; Benedict, 1979; Dromi, 1987; Goldin-Meadow, Seligman, & Gelman, 1976; Gentner, 1982; Gentner & Boroditsky, 2001). For English-speaking children with vocabularies between 20 and 50 words, fully 45 percent of their vocabulary consists of nouns, compared with 3 percent for verbs (Caselli et al., 1995).

***What determines the content of early vocabularies?*** Gentner (1978, 1982) argued that children acquire nouns before verbs (and hence nouns dominate early vocabularies) because the meanings nouns encode are easier for children to learn than are the meanings verbs encode. Nouns refer to entities or things (like tables, chairs, birds, or dogs), and young children can have an understanding of things based on their perception of the physical world. Verbs, on the other hand, express relationships among things; for example, *give* entails somebody giving something, and *go* entails somebody going somewhere, and these relational meanings are less available to young children through nonlinguistic experience. This is referred to as the **natural partitions hypothesis**—that the physical world makes obvious the things that take nouns as labels whereas the meanings that verbs encode have to be figured out from hearing the verb in use. The reason verb meanings must be figured out from use is that they do not naturally emerge from the structure of the world, leaving open the possibility that verb meanings will vary from language to language. This latter part of the hypothesis is the **relational relativity hypothesis** (Gentner & Boroditsky, 2001). In support of this view, Gentner (Gentner, 1982; Gentner & Boroditsky, 2001) refers to linguistic work showing that noun meanings are more common across languages than verb meanings. For example, if you were to learn Spanish, you would find direct equivalents for the English words *dog, cat, table,* and *chair.* Verbs of motion would be another matter. The most frequently used English motion verbs tend to include the manner of motion in their meaning (e.g., *walk, run, drive*). Spanish, in contrast, tends to include the direction of motion in the verb (*salir* [to exit], *escalar* [to go up], *entrar* [to enter]). Such verbs exist in English, *en-*

*ter* and *exit*, for example, but they are less frequently used. The point is, according to the natural partitions and relational relativity hypothesis, in learning nouns children need only learn the labels for meanings they already have, whereas in learning verbs children have to figure out how meaning is packaged by their language.

A different hypothesis attributes the source of the noun bias in children's early vocabularies to the nature of children's early understanding of how types of words and types of meanings are linked. According to Waxman (1994), children understand that certain kinds of nouns (i.e., count nouns) label objects at the very beginning of language acquisition. Understanding that other kinds of words are linked with other kinds of meanings (e.g., adjectives label properties) comes later. Children's first words, then, are the words they first know how to link to meaning.

Alternatively, it has been argued that the child's cognitive or linguistic understandings have nothing to do with why some words are acquired earlier than others. Rather, it is a language-learning problem. Early vocabularies will, of necessity, be dominated by the kinds of words children can learn by mapping the sounds they hear onto the nonlinguistic context (Snedeker & Gleitman, 2004). Only later when children know some language can they use the linguistic context as a source of information. The easiest words to learn through observation are concrete nouns. Evidence that the meanings of nouns are clearer from context than the meanings of verbs comes from a study in which silent videotapes of mother–child interaction were played for adults whose job it was to guess the word that was uttered at the moment a beep was inserted into the tape. Adults were able to identify 45 percent of the nouns they had to guess, but only 15 percent of the verbs (Gillette, Gleitman, Gleitman, and Lederer, 1999).

Another relevant factor has to do with how the particular language being acquired illustrates nouns and verbs. Children acquiring Korean, Japanese, and Mandarin (Chinese) show less of a noun bias than children acquiring English (Fernald & Morikawa, 1993; Gopnik & Choi, 1995; Tardif, Gelman, & Xu, 1999). In these languages, a verb is often the final word in a sentence, and this position may be particularly salient (that is, noticeable) to children. Also, the grammars of these languages allow noun dropping, thus making verbs relatively more frequent in the input. The culture in which a language is used also shapes input and affects children's vocabulary development. American mothers—at least the middle-class mothers most frequently studied—spend a great deal of time labeling objects for their babies. Fernald and Morikawa (1993) found that Japanese mothers do so much less frequently.

## Overextensions and underextensions of first words

Even after words no longer have the context-bound meanings of some very first words, children do not always use the words they produce in adultlike ways. Sometimes children may use words in a more restricted fashion, such

### Table 4.2   Examples of children's overextended word uses

| Word | Referents |
|---|---|
| ball | ball, balloon, marble, apple, egg, wool pom-pom, spherical water tank (Rescorla, 1980) |
| cat | cat, cat's usual location on top of TV when absent (Rescorla, 1980) |
| moon | moon, half-moon shaped lemon slice, circular chrome dial on dishwasher, ball of spinach, wall-hanging with pink and purple circles, half a Cheerio, hangnail (Bowerman, 1978) |
| snow | snow, white tail of a spring horse, white flannel bed pad, white puddle of milk on floor (Bowerman, 1978) |
| baby | own reflection in mirror, framed photograph of self, framed photographs of others (personal data) |
| shoe | shoe, sock (personal data) |

as using *dog* to refer to collies and spaniels but not to chihuahuas. Such narrower uses are called **underextensions.** More noticeably, children sometimes use their words more broadly than the meaning truly allows, calling all four-legged animals *doggie* or, more embarrassingly, calling all adult males *Daddy.* These overly broad uses are called **overextensions,** and at one time these uses were thought to reveal the meanings that children had assigned to these words in their mental lexicons. Overextensions were taken as evidence of incomplete meanings (e.g., Clark, 1973). For example, the child who calls all four-legged animals *doggie* knows something about the meaning of *doggie,* but doesn't know all the features unique to dogs that are not present in horses, cows, and bears. Ultimately, however, a large body of research on early word meanings in general and on overextensions in particular suggested that this account was incorrect.

Children's overextensions can be highly variable and difficult to capture with the notion that one or two features of a word's meaning are missing. For example, Bowerman (1978) reported that her daughter used the word *moon* to refer to the moon, to a ball of spinach, to hangnails she was pulling off, to half a Cheerio, to curved steer horns mounted on a wall, and to the magnetic capital letter *D* she was about to put on the refrigerator, to list a few. Another child used the word *baby* first to refer to a framed picture of himself that his mother had just labeled *baby.* Then he used *baby* in reference to his own reflection in a mirror, and then he used *baby* to refer to any framed photograph (personal data). In all cases, the overextended uses have some component of meaning in common with the original referent of the word, but they don't seem consistent with a single, incomplete meaning like the earlier *doggie* example. These and other examples of overextensions are presented in Table 4.2.

The idea that overextensions provide a window onto the nature of the early lexicon was also quashed by careful research, which pointed out that although overextensions are very noticeable when they occur, they are actually not very common. Rescorla (1980) followed six children from age 12 months to 18 months and reported that 33 percent of the children's word uses were overextended, but only a few different words accounted for a disproportionate share of those overextensions. Furthermore, there is good evidence that overextensions occur for reasons other than incomplete word meanings (Hoek, Ingram, & Gibson, 1986; Hudson & Nelson, 1984; Huttenlocher & Smiley, 1987). That is, it is not that the child really thinks that the word for horse is *dog;* the child just doesn't know or can't remember what the horse is called and wants to make some comment on it, and *dog* is the closest word the child can find in his or her vocabulary. Rescorla (1980) found that the incidence of overextensions declined as children acquired more differentiated vocabularies (for example, learning words for animals other than *dog).* Other findings indicate that overextensions in comprehension are rare and are not predictable from overextensions in production, which further contests the idea that overextensions reflect underlying semantic representation (Chapman & Thompson, 1980; Fregmen & Fay, 1980; Huttenlocher, 1974; Kay & Anglin, 1982; Naigles & Gelman, 1995).

## The word spurt

As previously mentioned, lexical development starts slowly for most children. During the first months after speaking their first words, children add an average of 8 to 11 words to their vocabularies each month (Benedict, 1979). During these months of slow lexical growth, exposure to a new word does not necessarily result in word learning. Another characteristic of this period is that words that were apparently learned at one point do not necessarily become permanent additions to children's productive vocabularies.

For many children, lexical development seems to shift into a different gear at about the 50-word milestone. In this new gear, the rate at which new words appear in the children's vocabularies increases from 8 to 11 words per month to an average rate of 22 to 37 words per month (Benedict, 1979; Goldfield & Reznick, 1990). In fact, Nelson's study of lexical development ended at 50 words partly because word learning was too rapid for most mothers to keep up with after that. In this later period of rapid lexical growth, children often learn a new word after only a single exposure.

A great deal of attention has been given to this increase in the word learning rate, which has been called the *word spurt,* the *word explosion,* and the *naming explosion*. This spurt occurs for most children sometime around the

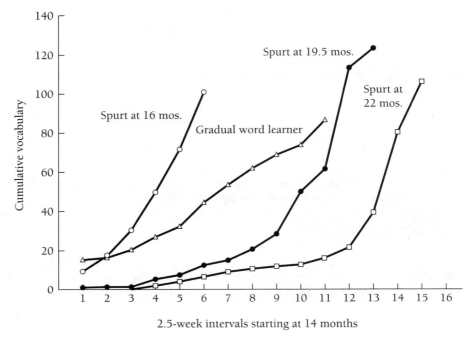

**Figure 4.2** Patters of lexical growth shown by four different children

Source: From "Early Lexical Acquisition: Rate, Content, and the Vocabulary Spurt," by B. A. Goldfield and J. S. Reznick, 1990, *Journal of Child Language 17,* Cambridge University Press.

achievement of a 50-word productive vocabulary or around the age of 18 months (Benedict, 1979; Bloom, 1973; Nelson, 1973). We will first consider the evidence that some "shifting of gears" occurs and then consider proposals for what causes that shift.

**What is the word spurt?** Although many observers have reported a marked increase in the vocabulary growth rate during the second year of life (Benedict, 1979; Bloom, 1973, 1994; McShane, 1980; Nelson, 1973), there is disagreement as to whether all children show this pattern or whether such a thing as a spurt exists at all. Goldfield and Reznick (1990) have claimed that only some children show a spurt and that other children show more even rates of vocabulary development. These researchers carefully documented the rate of vocabulary development in 18 children whom they studied from the age of 14 months until each child achieved a 75-word vocabulary. Examples of four different growth curves shown by children in Goldfield and Reznick's study are illustrated in Figure 4.2. Thirteen of the eighteen children showed a word spurt, or surge, in the rate of vocabulary growth, which occurred at ages as early as 14 months and as late as 21 months. However, 5 of the 18 children achieved vocabularies of 75 words or more without any spurt at all. Instead, these five children showed a linear pattern of vocabulary growth in which their vocabularies increased at a constant rate. Another finding from this study was that the children who showed a vocabulary spurt showed a large, concurrent increase in the proportion of object labels in their vocabularies, whereas the "nonspurters" did not. It is possible, however, that Goldfield and Reznick stopped their study too soon and that they would have seen spurts in all the children if they had followed them long enough. Mervis and Bertrand (1995) followed some apparent nonspurters past the 75-word point and found that these children eventually did show a vocabulary spurt. (But see Goldfield & Reznick, 1996, for an alternative view.)

On the other hand, P. Bloom (2000) has claimed that the word spurt is a myth. Children do increase the rate at which they acquire new words, but, Bloom argues, the change for most children is a gradual increase rather than an abrupt change in rate. Of course, abrupt changes may occur in individual cases. A child may briefly plateau, in which case a return to lexical growth might look like a spurt. Also, a child's circumstances might change. The child who goes on vacation and is exposed to many new things will increase his rate of vocabulary learning. Many such stories are possible. Bloom's point is that there is no general developmental phenomenon that needs an explanation.

***What causes changes in word learning efficiency?***    The dominant view for a long time, however, has been that there is a spurt in vocabulary growth, and a great deal of research has been aimed at explaining what might change in the child to account for this spurt. In support of the view that word learning ability does change, there is evidence that children younger than 18 months or with vocabularies of fewer than 50 words are not as good at learning new words in an experimental situation as are older children or those with larger vocabularies (Lucariello, 1987; Oviatt, 1982). Of course, these two groups of children could be at different points in a continuous curve, rather than on different sides of a qualitative shift.

Various proposals address the question of what internal changes might underlie this change in the ability to learn new words. According to some accounts, the onset or maturation of internal word-learning constraints occurs at this point (e.g., Behrend, 1990; Mervis & Bertrand, 1994). According to other accounts, reaching the threshold of a 50-word vocabulary gives children a basis for figuring out principles of how the lexicon works (e.g., Smith, 1995, 2001). McShane (1980) suggested children achieve a "naming insight" at which point they realize that everything has a name. It has also been pointed out that children's phonological abilities influence their very early vocabularies (Vihman, 1996), raising the possibility that changes in the nature of children's phonological systems contribute to the word spurt. Finally, it has been proposed that the critical underlying change comes from ongoing cognitive development. Gopnik and Meltzoff (1986) found that children begin to show a cognitive understanding that objects can be grouped into categories about the same time that they become very good at learning object labels—which, after all, label object categories, not individual objects. However, attempts to replicate that finding have failed, suggesting that if such cognitive changes do contribute to the word spurt, they are only part of the story (Gershkoff-Stowe, Thal, Smith, & Namy, 1997). More generally, it is possible that many changes in children's word-learning abilities occur after word learning begins with the result that word learning becomes increasingly efficient. When critical points in these developments coincide, the rate of word learning might change abruptly—and could be called a spurt.

## Early word comprehension

At this point, we have described lexical development only in terms of the words children say. The course of word comprehension is another source of evidence of the internal changes that occur as children's mental lexicons develop. Clearly, word learning begins months before children speak their first words. Both anecdotal reports (Vihman, 1988a) and experimental demonstrations show that children as young as 5 months selectively respond to certain words (Mandel, Jusczyk, & Pisoni, 1995). The first word children seem to respond to is their own name. Anecdotal evidence that infants recognize their own names is common; for example, a baby sitting in an infant swing is apparently ignoring the conversation going on behind her but turns around to look when someone mentions her name (personal data). Experimental evidence is also available. Mandel and associates (1995) demonstrated, using the head-turn procedure described in Chapter 3, that 5-month-old babies preferred their own name to prosodically similar foils.

At around the age of 8 months, children begin to understand a few phrases, such as "Give me a hug," "Stop it," and "Come here" (Fenson et al., 1994). Shortly after that—between the ages of 8 and 10 months—children start to understand the meanings of individual words. Fenson and colleagues studied more than 1000 children in the United States using the MacArthur Communicative Development Inventory, which assesses children's comprehension and production vocabularies from mothers' reports, and found that 10-month-old children's comprehension vocabularies ranged from an average of 11 words (for the bottom 10 percent of children tested) to an average of 154 words (for the top 10 percent). At 16 months of age, children have comprehension vocabularies between 92 and 321 words. Compare this with production vocabularies that are typically zero at 10 months and under 50 words at 16 months, and it becomes clear that comprehension vocabularies are acquired earlier and grow faster than production vocabularies. Other, smaller-scale studies have also found that early comprehension vocabularies are larger than production vocabularies (Benedict, 1979; Goldin-Meadow, Seligman, & Gelman, 1976).

Comprehension and production vocabularies differ not only in size but also in content. Both Benedict (1979) and Goldin-Meadow and associates found proportionately more verbs in children's comprehension vocabularies than in their production vocabularies. Gentner (1978) suggests that this imbalance may occur because communication works adequately with a minimal verb vocabulary. For example, the single verb *go* can be combined with *night-night, car,* and *park* to convey the meanings of three verbs: *sleep, drive,* and *play.*

Although comprehension generally precedes production and comprehension vocabularies are larger than production vocabularies, some words may appear in production first. When children have context-bound word meanings or word meanings that are narrower than the adult meanings, they tend to use those words correctly, even though they don't fully know what the words mean. Isolated words with context-bound meanings can coexist with a large and fairly adultlike vocabulary. For example, the preschool child who said he was "late" to school that morning defined late for the inquiring researcher as "when I get to school and everyone else already has their boots off" (Keller-Cohen, personal communication, 1978). Thus, if not pressed for definitions, children can sometimes appear more competent verbally than they really are.

## INDIVIDUAL DIFFERENCES IN LEXICAL DEVELOPMENT

Thus far in this chapter, we have been trying to construct an account of the normative course of lexical development. That is, we have been trying to describe how lexical development generally proceeds. In describing this normative course, we always gave age ranges for the achievement of various landmarks because children vary in the rate at which they develop. But our focus has been on abstracting that which was common among all children. Now we will focus on the ways in which children differ in the courses of lexical development they follow and the rates at which they proceed.

### Individual differences in language style

***First words.*** Characterizing first words as context-bound seems to be more true for some children than for others. Some children's vocabularies consist almost entirely of referentially used words from the start. Other children acquire many context-bound words even as their acquisition of referential words proceeds. What underlies these differences? One factor, already discussed, may be the contexts in which children hear the words. Words taught as labels and given explicit definitions may be more likely to be used referentially from the beginning than words the child picks up from context. Particularly if a word is used almost exclusively in a single context, the child would have no basis for figuring out its more generalizable meaning. For example, Ferrier (1978) reported that her daughter thought *phew* was a form of greeting because that's what her mother said to her when she entered her room each morning. Her mother was responding to the smell of the diaper the baby had worn for the past 12 hours, but the baby didn't know that.

Another factor that may influence the number of context-bound first words is the child's approach to the language acquisition task. Some children seem to be more analytic about language learning than others. The most analytic children divide the speech stream into small bits (words or even parts of words), whereas other children proceed in a more holistic manner, acquiring big chunks (Peters, 1983). For example, *Don'tdothat* appeared as a single big chunk in the early vocabulary of one little boy (personal data). Such big chunks are more likely to be associated with certain interactive functions or with whole events than with particular referents. As we saw in the studies by Barrett (1986) and Harris and associates (1988), however, single words can have contextually bound meanings. So the distinction between analytic and holistic approaches does not seem adequate to fully explain individual differences in the use of context-bound words.

Another way in which children differ, which may have something to do with this difference in lexical development, is the extent to which children are risk takers (Peters, 1983; Richards, 1990). Some children may jump into talking with a minimal understanding of what they are saying, whereas other children may be more cautious, not using words until they are sure of what they mean. The more cautious children would be expected to produce fewer context-bound words if children at this point in development know that their understanding of context-bound words is incomplete.

How social they are is one last sort of difference among children that might have something to do with who uses many context-bound words and who uses primarily referential words. A child who is very interested in social interaction would want a vocabulary of words to use in particular situations. Also, such a child might be more driven to use whatever means is available for interaction and thus be more likely to talk when his or her understanding of word meaning was still incomplete and tied to particular settings. A child who is less social, or who is good at maintaining interaction nonverbally, may have little use for words that serve only a social function and so may wait longer to talk, at which point the child's understanding of word meaning is more likely to allow contextually flexible usage.

***Referential and expressive language users.*** Most of the work on individual differences in children's styles of lexical development focuses on vocabularies at the 50-word mark. In Nelson's (1973) study of the lexical development of 18 children, she found that some children's vocabularies had much larger percentages of nominals than others' did. For example, one child had 38 nominals among her first 50 words, whereas another child had only

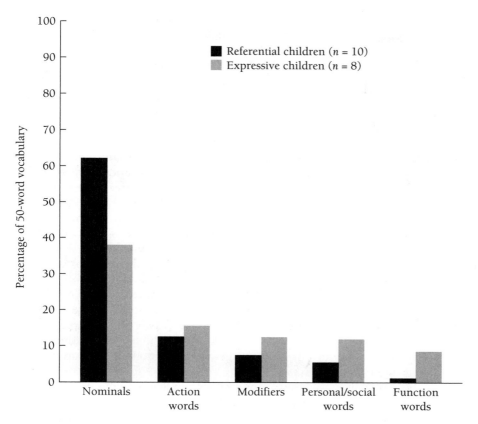

**Figure 4.3**   The composition of 50-word vocabularies for referential and expressive children

Source: Based on data in Nelson, 1973.

17. Nelson also argued that the children who used fewer nominals did not make up the difference evenly with words from other categories. Rather, children with fewer nominals tended to have more personal/social words. Nelson concluded that these two kinds of early vocabularies—one dominated by object labels and the other including many more personal/social words—represent two different styles of language use. Nelson labeled the children with more object labels in their vocabularies referential, and she called the children with relatively fewer object labels and more personal/social words expressive. The composition of the vocabularies of the referential and expressive children in Nelson's study is depicted in Figure 4.3. Two things about the difference between referential and expressive children should be noted. First, these two types of language

learners represent two ends of a continuum, and most children fall somewhere in between. Second, even when comparing the extremes, the difference is one of degree; all children have some object labels and some personal/social words in their early vocabularies. Nonetheless, the difference between a referential style and an expressive style inspired a great deal of subsequent research on (1) what these differences actually reflect about the language learner, (2) where these differences might come from, and (3) what other sorts of differences in language acquisition these styles might be related to.

***Sources of the referential/expressive difference in lexical development.*** Some children may have more referential vocabularies than others because of differences in their language-learning experiences. Some mothers spend a great deal of time teaching their children labels, and these children accordingly acquire large numbers of object labels. Support for this view includes the finding that the proportion of nouns in children's early vocabularies is related to the frequency with which their mothers produce descriptive utterances containing nouns (Pine, 1994). Also, referential children are more likely than average to be the firstborn of college-educated parents (Goldfield & Reznick, 1990; Nelson, 1973). Later-born children have a higher number of unanalyzed chunks in their vocabularies (Pine, 1995). More-educated mothers may be more likely to engage in explicit labeling (Lawrence & Shipley, 1996) and are more likely to have the time to do so with their first children. Children who are not the firstborns of college-educated mothers pick up more of their language from context.

Some researchers have also proposed that individual differences in early vocabularies reflect differences in the children, not just in their input. Nelson postulates that the referential/expressive difference in the content of early vocabularies reflects differences in the views children hold about the use of language. Some children seem to regard language as a vehicle for referring to objects. Perhaps these children are inherently more interested in the world of objects than other children are, or maybe their mothers play word games with them and thus teach them that reference is the point of language. In either case, a vocabulary dominated by object labels suits the function to which these children put their emerging linguistic abilities. Other children seem to regard language as a vehicle for social interaction, either because they are inherently more social or because of the situation in which they are placed. Accordingly, a vocabulary of personal/social words best suits the function of language for them.

Others have suggested that the referential/expressive difference is related to the analytic/holistic dimension of difference referred to earlier regarding individual differences in first words (Peters, 1983). According to Bates, Bretherton, and Snyder (1988), children who approach language analytically are more likely to be referential, and children who approach language holistically are more likely to be expressive. Bates and associates also hypothesized that the analytic/

holistic difference in approach may reflect differences among children in the parts of the brain doing the work of language acquisition.

***The significance of the referential/expressive distinction.***    For whatever reason, referential and expressive children seem to follow different routes in their early lexical development. It is not clear, at this point, whether these are two routes to the same place or whether referential and expressive children will continue to differ in the course of their later language development.

One proposal that was made and rejected hypothesized that the referential style is superior to the expressive style and is associated with more rapid language development. The referential style initially may have seemed to be associated with more rapid learning for two reasons. First, Nelson (1973) found that the referential children in her study took less time between acquiring their first word and achieving a 50-word vocabulary. Second, Bates and associates (1988) found that among a group of 13-month-olds with vocabularies ranging from 2 to 32 words, the children with proportionately more object labels had the larger vocabularies. However, neither finding implies that the referential children should be more precocious language learners. In Nelson's study, both referential and expressive children reached a 50-word vocabulary at the same age. The referential children produced their first word later than the expressive children, so the time they took to go from 1 to 50 words was less. In Bates, Bretherton, and Snyder's study, the children's vocabularies were different sizes at the point when referential style was assessed. The graph in Figure 4.1 clearly shows that, up to a 50-word vocabulary, children with larger vocabularies would have proportionately more object labels. In sum, variation in style and rate of vocabulary development are separate phenomena, and the referential/expressive distinction properly applies only when the size of vocabulary is held constant (Bates et al., 1994; Pine & Lieven, 1990). But if differences in style are not the source of differences in the rate of vocabulary development, then what is?

## Individual differences in the rate of lexical development

Some children reach the 50- and 100-word milestones at younger ages than others. To put the same phenomenon another way, the vocabularies of children of the same age vary enormously in size. The MacArthur Inventory data referred to earlier (Fenson et al., 1994), for example, show that even excluding the top and bottom 15 percent of children, the range in productive vocabulary size among 16-month-olds is between 0 and 160 words, and the range for 24-month-olds is between 50 and 550 words. These data, and data for the ages 16 to 30 months, are presented in Figures 4.4 and 4.5. For a discussion of the individual differences in these data, see Bates, Dale, and Thal (1995).

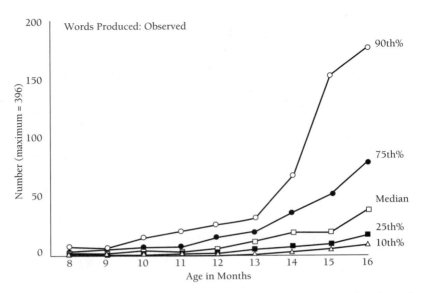

**Figure 4.4**   The range of individual differences in vocabulary size from 8 to 16 months

Source: From L. Fenson, P. S. Dale, J. S. Reznick, E. Bates, D. Thal, S. J. Pethick (1994), Variability in early communicative development. *Monographs of the Society for Research in Child Development*, No. 242, V. 59, no. 5. Copyright © 1994 Blackwell Publishing. Reprinted with permission.

Understanding why children differ in their rates of vocabulary development is potentially of both practical and scientific significance. With respect to practical concerns, a child with a small vocabulary compared to his age-mates will have difficulty understanding in school and difficulty with the materials designed for reading instruction. With respect to scientific concerns, an understanding of the sources of individual differences in vocabulary development should contribute to understanding of the basic process that underlie vocabulary development in all children. The factors identified by research thus far as relevant to individual differences in vocabulary development can be organized under two headings: environmental factors and child factors.

***Environmental factors that influence the rate of lexical development.*** Children's language experience clearly affects their vocabulary development. One relevant aspect of experience is the sheer amount of talk that children hear. Studies that have measured the amount of speech mothers address to their young children and the children's vocabulary growth have found that children who hear more speech add words to their vocabularies at a faster rate (Hoff & Naigles, 2002; Huttenlocher, Haight, Bryk, Seltzer, & Lyons, 1991). Dif-

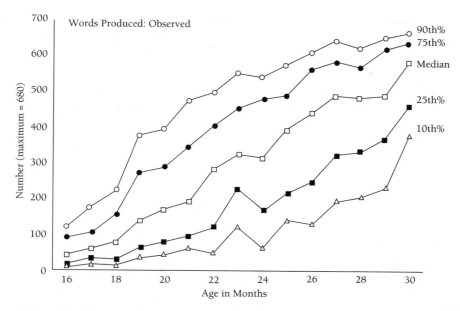

**Figure 4.5** The range of individual differences in vocabulary size from 16 to 30 months

Source: From L. Fenson et al. (1994), Variability in early communicative development. *Monographs of the Society for Research in Child Development,* No. 242, V. 59, no. 5. Copyright © 1994 Blackwell Publishing. Reprinted with permission.

ferences in the amount of speech children hear may contribute to explaining some of the differences in vocabulary development that are associated with birth order and socioeconomic status. The effects of birth order are small and not always found, but when they are found, they consistently show that first-born children have a slight advantage in vocabulary development over later-born children (Fenson et al., 1994; Hoff-Ginsberg, 1998a; Pine, 1995). A likely cause of this difference between firstborn and later-born children may be the different amount of one-to-one interaction they experience with an adult. The effects of socioeconomic status (SES) on vocabulary development are also small at the beginning of language development, but these effects grow larger over time and always show that children of more-educated parents have larger vocabularies than children of less-educated parents (Fenson et al., 1994; Hart & Risley, 1995; Hoff-Ginsberg, 1998a). A role for the environment is implicated by the many findings that more-educated mothers talk to their children more than less-educated mothers do (Hart & Risley, 1995; Hoff-Ginsberg, 1994; Hoff, Laursen, & Tardif, 2002).

The amount of speech children hear is not the only property of language experience that affects vocabulary development. The nature of the speech children hear matters as well. Hearing a rich vocabulary that includes many different words and rare or sophisticated words is associated with more rapid vocabulary development than hearing a more restricted and simpler vocabulary (Hoff & Naigles, 2002; Weizman & Snow, 2001). This is another property of child-directed speech that varies as a function of maternal education and contributes to the SES-related differences in children's vocabularies (Hoff, 2003).

Beyond hearing lots of speech that uses a rich vocabulary, other properties of the speech that children hear affect their vocabulary development. It helps, particularly for children under 18 months, if the timing of speech is responsive to child verbalizations and if the content of the speech is related to the child's focus of attention. Several studies have found correlations between measures of maternal verbal responsiveness or mother–child mutual engagement and children's subsequent vocabulary development (Tamis-LeMonda, Bornstein, Kahana-Kalman, Baumwell, & Cyphers, 1998; Tomasello & Todd, 1983). It has also been demonstrated experimentally that 17-month-olds are more likely to learn words that label their current focus of attention than words that label something they are not attending to (Tomasello & Farrar, 1986). In older children, vocabulary growth is predicted by the informativeness of the context in which mothers present new words (Weizman & Snow, 2001). Mothers who not only use words that are new to their children but who also say something about what the word means have children who build their vocabularies at faster rates. The value of information about word meaning may explain why children's vocabulary development benefits from mothers using longer, as opposed to simpler and shorter, sentences (Bornstein, Haynes, & Painter, 1998; Hoff & Naigles, 2002; Hoff-Ginsberg, 1998b). Longer sentences are more likely to contain explicit information about word meaning (e.g., *That's a bat.* versus *That's a bat hanging upside down in his cave.*), and longer sentences are more likely to contain other, syntactic clues to word meaning. (We will explain this argument regarding syntactic sources of information in the next section.)

***Child factors that influence the rate of lexical development.***    Although differences in language-learning opportunities account for a great deal of the individual differences in vocabulary size, children are not completely passive in the process. It takes two to achieve the mutual engagement that benefits language-advancing interaction. Some children develop the joint attention skills that mutual engagement requires at a younger age than others, and this aspect of development predicts later language development (Carpenter, Nagell, & Tomasello, 1998). Personality may also play a role. Children who are very outgoing may elicit more input, which in turn may support more rapid language development (Slomkowski, Nelson, Dunn, & Plomin, 1992). More generally, a temperament that results in the child being attentive to his environment and easy for others to interact with may promote language development (Bloom & Capatides, 1987; Dixon & Smith, 2000).

There may also be individual differences in specific language-learning skills that children bring to bear on the task of lexicon building. One skill that contributes to word learning is **phonological memory**—the ability to remember a sequence of unfamiliar sounds. Gathercole and Baddeley (1989) tested the phonological memory skills and vocabulary size of 100 children, first at the age of 4, and then a year later at age 5. They found that children with better phonological memory skills had more advanced vocabularies at both ages. Even more important, phonological memory tested at age 4 predicted vocabulary one year later, even when earlier vocabulary and nonverbal intelligence were factored out statistically (Gathercole, Willis, Emslie, & Baddeley, 1992). It makes sense that remembering how newly encountered words sound is a prerequisite to learning what those words mean. In Chapter 7, we will see that phonological memory is also implicated in cases of impaired language-learning ability.

Another finding that suggests there are differences among children in word-learning ability—without suggesting exactly what that ability consists of— is the frequent finding of sex differences in vocabulary size or word-learning ability. The sex difference is small and not always present, but several studies have shown girls to be more advanced in vocabulary development than boys (Bauer, Goldfield, & Resnick, 2002; Fenson et al., 1994; and for a review, see Klann-Delius, 1981). Some studies have found that mothers talk more to girl babies than to boy babies (Cherry & Lewis, 1978; Halvorsen & Waldrop, 1970), suggesting a possible experiential basis to the observed sex differences. However, girls sometimes demonstrate word-learning skills that boys of the same age do not (Katz, Baker, & Macnamara, 1974; Naigles, 1995). Huttenlocher and colleagues (1991) found a sex difference in the rate of vocabulary growth that could not be accounted for by different amounts of input. An early sex difference in word-learning ability could reflect the differing maturation levels of girls and boys; as infants, girls are physically more mature than boys.

Thus far we have described the normative course of lexical development and the individual differences that have been observed. These are the outward manifestation of the internal process of word learning. We turn now to a consideration of what that internal process entails.

## THE PROCESS OF WORD LEARNING

At first glance, word learning may seem fairly straightforward. Someone holds up a cup and says, "This is a cup," and then the child knows the word *cup*. Similarly, the word *ball* is uttered in the presence of a ball, and so on. The child takes the word uttered to be the label for the thing that is there, and that's all there is to it. But let's examine this scenario a little more closely. In order for the experience of hearing a sound sequence, say /kʌp/, to result in the child adding a new word, *cup*, to her mental dictionary, the child must identify that sound sequence as a separate word, the child must figure out what the newly encountered word refers to, the child must know what else the word can be used to refer to besides the particular item that is the first referent, and last, in order to use or understand the word later, the child must be able to remember what the new word sounded like. We consider each of these problems in turn.

## Word segmentation

The first problem for the child is how to find the word within the stream of speech. Someone says, "Thisisacup." To learn what *cup* means, the child must identify *cup* as a word. In writing we put spaces between words to separate them, but speakers do not reliably pause between words. The child must find the word boundaries some other way; this is called the **speech segmentation** problem. Of course, sometimes children make mistakes, such as thinking that "elemeno" is one letter in the alphabet (see others in Box 4.1); but children must get it right most of the time or they couldn't acquire language. How do they distinguish word boundaries?

One fact about words is that they occur over and over. The evidence discussed in Chapter 1, that 7-month-old babies can learn distributional regularities in the sounds they hear (Saffran et al., 1996), suggests that babies identify words in the speech stream in part by recognizing recurring sound sequences. Babies may first use statistical learning to isolate words in the speech stream and then use that knowledge to learn other cues to word boundaries in their language. Stress, or rhythm, is one other cue. In English, for example, a stressed syllable is likely to signal the beginning of a new word, and by 9 months, babies acquiring English use stress patterns as a clue to word boundaries (Thiessen & Saffran, 2003). Evidence from infants acquiring other languages suggests, more generally, that infants attend to the rhythmic properties of speech, learn the rhythm of their particular language, and use that rhythm to segment the speech stream (Cutler, 1994, 1996; Mehler, Dupoux, Nazzi, & Dehaene-Lambertz, 1996; Thiessen & Saffran, 2003). Phonotactic cues also provide word boundary markers. For example, in English the sound sequence "topdog" is not likely to be a single word because two stop consonants are not usually adjacent within a word. Babies seem sensitive to this, and by 9 months they prefer to hear sound sequences consistent with the phonotactics of their language rather than foreign words (Jusczyk, Friederici, Wessels, & Svenkerud, 1993).

Some of the special characteristics of child-directed speech might also help children with speech segmentation (Ratner, 1996). Utterances directed to children are short, with few word boundaries to find. Also, child-directed

---

### Box 4.1 Examples of children's speech segmentation errors

*Family interaction:*

Father: Who wants some mango for dessert?
Child: What's a semmango? (Ratner, 1996)

*Children's attempts to say the "Pledge of Allegiance":*

" . . . and to the flag of the nine of states . . . "
" . . . and to the republic for witches stands . . . "
(Chaney, 1989)

*Child''s version of a line from the Bob Dylan song:*

"The ants are my friends, they're blowin' in the wind."
(Pinker, 1994)

*Mother and child reading a book:*

Child: I know why he's called Don Quixote. It's because he's riding a donkey. (personal data)

---

speech involves a small vocabulary, so the same word is presented in many different utterances. And, when adults are trying to teach children a new word, they tend to stress that word and to put it in sentence final position (Ratner, 1996). Both stress and final position seem to make a sound salient to young children (Echols & Newport, 1992). There is evidence that new words presented in sentences produced with infant-directed intonation are easier to learn than are words presented in adult-directed speech (Golinkoff & Alioto, 1995). Part of this advantage may be the exaggerated intonation of infant-directed speech, which helps the listener extract the word to be learned.

## Word-referent mapping

Once a child has successfully identified a word in the speech stream, he or she must tackle the next problem: to what does this new word refer? How does the child know that it is the cup that is being labeled rather than the cup's handle, the cup's color, the material the cup is made of, or the contents of the cup? Or maybe the word being uttered in the presence of a cup is not a label at all but a command to do something, like drink. The possibilities are limitless. This problem is known as the **mapping problem.** The philosopher Quine (1960) described the child's problem as follows: An infinite number of hypotheses about word meaning are logically possible given the data the child has. Yet children tend to figure out the meaning of the words that they hear. In fact, children are remarkably able word learners. From about 18 months, when word learning takes off, until 6 years, children must learn an average of nine new words a day (Carey, 1978). How do they do it?

It appears that children begin by making an initial **"fast mapping"** between a new word they hear and a likely candidate meaning. Carey (1978) demonstrated that children who have heard a new word only once have already developed hypotheses about what that word means. Several different researchers have demonstrated this fast-mapping process experimentally in a procedure such as the following (e.g., Dollaghan, 1985; Mervis & Bertrand, 1994): A child is presented with an array of four objects that includes three familiar objects for which the child has a word (e.g., a bottle, a cup, and a ball) and one unfamiliar object the child would not have a word for (e.g., an egg piercer). Then the experimenter asks the child, "Can I have the ball?" After the child indicates the ball, the experimenter asks "Can the I have the zib?" By the age of 20 months, using this procedure, many children can conclude, on the basis of only this experience, that *zib* must be the name of the egg piercer. With fewer items to choose from, children as young as 15 months can successfully map a new word onto a new object (Markman, Wasow, & Hansen, 2003), and children as young as 13 months are capable of learning new words on the basis of only a few exposures (Woodward, Markman, & Fitzsimmons, 1994). The question is, how? Several explanations have been proposed, each relying on a different source of potential help to the child.

***Lexical principles as guides to word learning.***   Word learning would certainly be facilitated if children did not have to consider all of the many possible meanings each time they heard a new word. Some contend that children do not, in fact, consider all possible meanings but instead enter word-learning situations with several assumptions or principles about how the lexicon works. These **lexical principles** guide the child by constraining the possible interpretations of new words that children must consider (Behrend, 1990). Two proposed **word-learning constraints** are the whole-object assumption and the assumption of mutual exclusivity (Markman, 1991, 1994).

The **whole-object assumption** is the child's assumption that words refer to whole objects. According to this proposal, children assume that every new word they hear refers to some whole object rather than to part of an object or to a property of the object. This eliminates "white," "handle," "being held in a hand," and the like as possible meanings of *cup*. The existence of such an assumption is supported both by evidence from word-learning experiments (Markman & Wachtel, 1988; Mervis & Long, 1987; Taylor & Gelman, 1988; Waxman & Markow, 1995) and by errors young children make. For example, it is not uncommon for very young children to think that *hot* is the label for the stove, given the common experience of hearing "Don't touch it; it's hot," in reference to the stove.

The **mutual exclusivity assumption** is the assumption that different words refer to different kinds of things. So, for example, members of the category labeled *dog* do not overlap with members of the category labeled *cow*. Evidence that suggests children actually operate according to such an assumption consists of experimental studies in which children are given an array of familiar objects for which the children have a label and one object that is novel and nameless. Given the instruction "Show me the *x*," where *x* is some nonsense syllable chosen to function as a new word, children pick the object for which they do not yet have a word, seemingly indicating that they assume the new word cannot be a synonym for any of the words they already know (Markman & Wachtel, 1988). In fact, by 18 months, children hearing a novel word will look around for a novel object rather than take the novel word as a label for something familiar that is in view (Markman et al., 2003). The mutual exclusivity assumption also provides a basis for overriding the whole-object assumption, which children must do in order to learn terms for parts and properties of objects. So, if a child knows the word *cup* and her mother says, "This is a handle," the child won't take *handle* to be a synonym for *cup* but will look for something else to be the referent of the new term.

***Pragmatic principles as guides to word learning.*** A somewhat different view of what children know comes from Clark (1993, 1995) who has proposed that word learning is supported by children's understanding of **pragmatic principles** (principles about how language is used). According to the **principle of conventionality,** the meaning of a word is determined by convention; it has to be agreed upon and observed by all members of a language community. Language wouldn't work if people just made up their own words for things, and children seem to know that; they try to learn the meanings of the words they hear. According to the **principle of contrast,** different words have different meanings. This principle is a close variant of the mutual exclusivity assumption but differs in that it allows for multiple labels with different meanings, such as *dog* and *animal,* whereas mutual exclusivity does not. As a practical matter, the two principles would have the same effect in many situations. When a child hears the word *cup* in the presence of a cup, the child would exclude possible meanings such as "container for liquid" and "juice" if the child already knows the words *bowl, glass,* and *juice*.

***Social-pragmatic understandings as word-learning guides.*** Children may also find support for solving the mapping problem in their understandings of the conversational process and the intentions of their conversational partners. Gathercole (1989) proposed that children expect a novel word to have a new meaning, not because they know a linguistic principle, but because they assume the speaker is trying to communicate and thus would not have used an unfamiliar term if a familiar one would have sufficed. More generally, it has been argued that children figure out the meaning of the new words they hear by figuring out the communicative intentions of the other speaker (P. Bloom, 2000; Diesendruck & Markson, 2001; Tomasello, 2001). Cast in this form, the mapping problem is not the logical problem posed by Quine but the social problem of figuring out the meanings that others are trying to convey.

Many experimental findings document children's abilities to read a variety of social clues to speakers' intentions and to use these inferred intentions as a basis for word learning. For example, Baldwin (1993) found that by 18 months of age (but probably not before), children can follow a speaker's gaze and use it as a clue to word meaning. That is, children will take a novel word as the label for what the speaker is looking at, not what they themselves are looking at. As another example, Akhtar, Carpenter, and Tomasello (1996) found that 2-year-olds will infer that a novel label produced with an expression of surprise refers to an object that is also novel to the speaker. And Tomasello and Barton (1994) found that 24-month-olds could distinguish accidental from intentional actions. If an experimenter said, "Let's go *twang* it" and then did something accidentally (that is, clumsily) followed by doing something intentionally, children took *twang* to refer only to the intentional action.

***General learning processes as the basis of word learning.***    There is an alternative to both the view that mapping depends on internal constraints and the view that successful mapping depends on children's abilities to know the communicative intentions of their conversational partners. Linda Smith and her colleagues have proposed that general processes of attention and learning can, in fact, explain the sorts of phenomena that lexical principles and sociopragmatic skills have been invoked to explain (Smith, 2001). For example, Samuelson and Smith (1998) argue that children do not need to understand that a new item is novel to the speaker in order to infer that the speaker is labeling that item. Rather, the item's newness in the physical context makes it salient to the child, who then attaches the new word to the physically most salient item.

***Input as a source of support.***    The way in which people talk to children makes word meaning in context much less ambiguous than it seemed to Quine. Compared with speech among adults, speech directed to children is overwhelmingly about the here-and-now. We tend to talk to young children about what is currently going on rather than about past or future events. This feature of child-directed speech makes the child's task of mapping words to their referents easier than if the child were watching speeches on the senate floor, for example. Furthermore, in talking to children, adults also provide explicit instruction about word meanings. Adults offer new labels (e.g., That's a chair) and corrections of children's imprecise lexical choices (e.g., Ch: Mommy, where my plate? M: You mean your saucer? Ch: Yeah.) Adults also provide information about word meanings (e.g., It's called an eel. It's like a snake only it lives in the water.) (Clark, 2002; Gelman, Coley, Rosengren, Hartman, & Pappas, 1988). The evidence that variation in mothers' child-directed speech predicts their children's vocabulary development suggests that the environment can meaningfully support the word-learning process.

Despite this evidence of environmental support, it is nevertheless unclear that environmental supports are sufficient to explain how children succeed. Sometimes speech doesn't refer to the nonlinguistic context as the child perceives it, and social cues may not always be provided. For example, a child's mother may open the door and say, "Whatcha doing?" not "This is a door"; or the mother may say, "Eat your peas," when the child's thoughts are entirely elsewhere (for a more developed argument in this regard, see Gleitman, 1990).

***Syntax as a clue to word meaning.***    Another potential source of information about word meaning is the structure of the language itself. A poem in Lewis Carroll's *Through the Looking Glass* begins, "Twas brillig, and the slithy toves did gyre and gimble in the wabe." Although you certainly have never seen a slithy tove, you can probably figure out that *toves* are things of some sort and that *slithy* is some property of those toves. Similarly, you can figure out that *gyre* and *gimble* are actions, although of what sort of actions you cannot be sure.

It is a fact about language that different grammatical classes tend to have different sorts of meanings. Nouns tend to refer to things, verbs to actions, and adjectives to properties of things. Once children have acquired enough grammar to identify nouns, verbs, and adjectives (using the same cues you did to interpret Lewis Carroll's poem), children can use the grammar as a clue to meaning. Roger Brown (1957) demonstrated that children use grammar as a clue to meaning by showing preschool children a picture of a pair of hands kneading a mass of material in a container. He described the picture as *sibbing* to some of the children, as *a sib* to some of the children, and as *some sib* to others. Children interpreted *sib* as describing the action, the container, or the material, respectively, depending on which form they heard.

Other studies also have found that preschool children use grammar to infer the meaning distinction between proper nouns like *Lassie* and common nouns like *dog* (Gelman & Taylor, 1984) as well as between nouns and adjectives (Gelman & Markman, 1985; Hall, Waxman, & Hurwitz, 1993). Gelman and Markman's study is illustrated in Figure 4.6. Syntax provides clues not only to whether a word refers to an object or to an action, but also to what kind of action is being referenced. Verbs with different meanings can appear in different kinds of sentences. For example, a verb like *hit* means to do something to someone else. It usually appears in a sentence like *Tom hit Jerry,* in

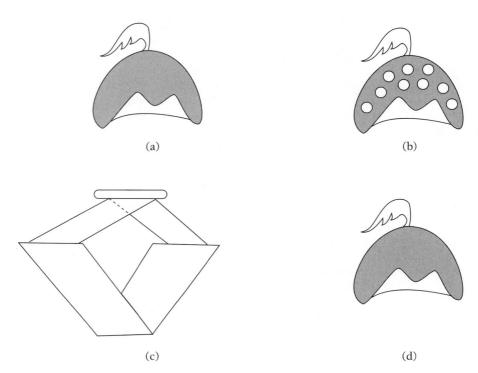

**Figure 4.6** Syntax as a clue to word meaning. Four-year-olds pick (b) when told, "Find the fep one," and they pick (c) when told, "Now find the fep." These responses suggest that 4-year-olds can use the syntax of a sentence to distinguish between words that imply a contrast between members of the same category (adjectives) and words that do not imply such a contrast (common nouns).

Source: From "Adjectives vs. Nouns," by S. A. Gelman and E. M. Markman, 1985, *Journal of Child Language,* 12, p. 135. Copyright © 1988 and reprinted with the permission of Cambridge University Press.

which the verb is preceded by one noun, the doer, and followed by another noun, the recipient of the deed. In contrast, verbs like *laugh* that refer to an action with no recipient appear in sentences like *Tom laughed,* in which there is just one noun, the doer.

Letitia Naigles (1990) found that 2-year-olds used the correspondence between sentence structure and verb meaning to learn the meaning of new verbs. Naigles showed children a videotape depicting a novel action that could be interpreted as either something one person did to another or something two people did together. Different children heard different sentences with a novel verb accompanying the action, and then all were tested to see how they interpreted the new verb. It is no small feat to figure out how 2-year-olds are interpreting anything, so the experimental method had to be ingenious. First, the children watched the action, which consisted of a rabbit repeatedly pushing a duck down into a squatting position with its left hand while at the same time both the rabbit and duck were making circles in the air with their right hands. (The rabbit and duck were actually people—probably graduate students—dressed in costumes.) Some children heard the sentence *The rabbit is gorping the duck,* and other children heard the sentence *The rabbit and the duck are gorping.* If these children used the sentence structure as a clue to verb meaning, the children who heard the first sentence should infer that *gorping* refers to what the rabbit did to the duck, whereas children who heard the second sentence should infer that *gorping* refers to what both the rabbit and duck did (arm circling). As expected, when the two different actions were presented separately, the children picked the meaning consistent with the sentence structure they had heard. Naigles's method for eliciting the children's responses was to show two actions simultaneously on two TV screens. One screen showed the rabbit pushing the duck down and doing nothing else; the other screen showed the rabbit and the duck making hand circles. The children were asked, *"Where's gorping now? Find gorping!"* The children who had heard the initial sentence *The rabbit is gorping the duck* looked longer at the screen on which the rabbit was pushing the duck down. The children who had heard the initial sentence *The rabbit and duck are gorping* looked longer at the screen on which the rabbit and duck were making hand circles. The proposal that knowledge of language structure is generally useful for learning new verbs is termed the **syntactic bootstrapping hypothesis,** and it is supported by a variety of experimental and naturalistic evidence (see Fisher, Hall, Rakowitz, & Gleitman, 1994; Gleitman, 1990; Naigles, 1995; Naigles & Hoff-Ginsberg, 1995; 1998).

The foregoing proposals for how children solve the mapping problem invoke very different notions of the nature of the word-learning process. If word learning is guided by lexical principles that are specific to language and not learned from experience, then word learning depends on language-specific innate knowledge. If word learning depends on children's ability to read their conversational partners' communicative intentions, then word learning is a social process that depends on sophisticated social cognitive skills. If word learning can be explained in terms of the operation of general attention and learning processes, then word learning is one more result of general cognitive processes applied to experience. This is currently a much debated issue (see, for example P. Bloom, 2000; Markson & Bloom, 1997).

Despite the very different notions of the word-learning process that these proposals entail, they are not mutually exclusive. It is quite likely that many, if not all, of these processes play a role (Woodward & Markman, 1998). To further complicate matters, the role these processes play may well change with development. For example, younger children seem more dependent on their caregiver's responsiveness than older children; older children (i.e., older than 18 months) are better at following their caregiver's lead (Hoff & Naigles, 2002). Older children have the benefit of the vocabulary and syntax they already know; children at the beginning of lexical development do not and are dependent on correspondences between the speech they hear and the accompanying nonlinguistic context (Snedeker & Gleitman, 2004). Any account of word learning, whether in terms of constraints, **sociopragmatic cues,** or syntactic cues (or some combination of those), will also have to account for developmental changes in word learning. (For proposals in this regard, see Golinkoff et al., 1994; Waxman, 1994.)

## Word extension

When children fast map a new word onto a referent, the process of creating a lexical entry is not complete. The child who correctly infers the referent of "cup" when he first hears it, still has to figure out what else "cup" might refer to. Is "cup" a proper name, like *Lassie* or *Versailles*, referring only to a particular individual (dog or palace), or does it refer to other things as well. If the latter, what other things? This is the problem of word **extension.** We saw earlier in this chapter that children may overextend or underextend some early-acquired words. Most of the time, however, children get it right. The question again is how, and the proposed answers again include reference to language-specific principles, to clues from input, and to understandings based on the application of domain-general learning procedures to language and language experience.

One language-specific principle that would help accurate word extension is the taxonomic assumption, which holds that words refer to things that are of the same kind. A taxonomy is a system of classifying things into categories. So when the child hears the word *dog* in the presence of a dog (and assumes that it is the whole dog that's being referred to, thanks to the whole-object assumption), then the taxonomic assumption leads the child to think that dog will also refer to other dogs but not to things that are thematically related to dogs, such as collars, leashes, or bones.

This assumption about word meanings may be crucial for word learning, because preschool children show a preference for making thematic groups on many nonlinguistic tasks. For example, if you give children a jumble of toys—including toy people, animals, and vehicles—and ask the children to "put together the things that go together," children who are age 7 or older will sort the collection into a group of animals, a group of people, a group of vehicles, and so on. However, given the same toys and same instructions, preschoolers will put a person with a car because the person drives the car (Markman, 1989). But if preschoolers have this inclination to form thematically related groupings, why don't preschoolers hypothesize that words refer to thematically related sets of things? The taxonomic assumption asserts that children know that words don't work that way.

Evidence that children actually operate according to the taxonomic assumption in word learning comes from Markman and Hutchinson (1984), who found that preschool children override their inclination to group thematically related things when presented with a new word. Markman and Hutchinson used a puppet to present a picture (say, of a dog) to 2- to 3-year-old children, and then presented a choice between a thematically related item (dog food) and a taxonomically related item (a dog of a different breed). In the "no word" condition, the puppet pointed to the first picture (of a dog) and said, "Look carefully now. See this?" When the next two choices were presented (the other dog and the dog food), the puppet said, "Find another one that is the same as this." In the "word" condition the puppet introduced the first picture by saying, "See this? It is a sud." And when presenting the other choices, the puppet said, "Find another sud that is the same as this sud." Children in the "no word" condition chose the taxonomically related choice 59 percent of the time. In contrast, children in the "word" condition made the taxonomic choice 83 percent of the time. That is, even though these children think that thematically related things such as dogs and dog food "go together" (41 percent of the time), they don't think that words label things that "go together." Children assume that words label things that are of the same kind.

The question then becomes, how do children decide what things are of the same kind? Evidence suggests that children have a few ideas about the kinds of things there are in the world before they begin the word-learning task. For example, children seem to make, on a nonlinguistic basis, a conceptual distinction between objects (like cups and sticks) and substances (like sand and clay). Soja, Carey, and Spelke (1991) presented children with a new word by saying, "This is my blicket" as she showed them either an object or a substance. (The objects were things like apple corers and honey dippers and the substances things like face cream and hair gel, all of which 2-year-olds are unlikely to have words for.) After the initial word-learning trials, the child was then given two things to choose from and was told, "Point to the blicket." The choices were constructed to make the children reveal the meaning they had construed for the new term, blicket. So, if the child first saw a plastic honey dipper, the child would then have to choose between a wooden honey dipper and pieces of plastic. If the child first saw a glob of face cream, the child would then have to choose between a similar-shaped glob of hair gel and an arrangement of lots of little dots of face cream. Two-year-old children who first saw the plastic honey dipper chose the wooden honey dipper; they thought blicket referred to the form, not the substance. Two-year-olds who first saw the glob of face cream chose the arrangement of little dots of face cream; they thought blicket referred to the substance, not the form.

Thus, Soja and colleagues concluded that 2-year-olds have separate mental categories of objects and substances. They see a plastic honey dipper as one example of honey dippers (the object), not one example of plastic; and they see a glob of face cream as one example of face cream (the substance), not one example of globs. Children then use this way of organizing the world (known as their ontological categories) to guide their inductions of word meaning. The researchers concluded, consistent with the taxonomic constraints position, that children take words as referring both to the whole thing present in the nonlinguistic context and to other things of that kind. The child's ontological categories are the kinds of things the child thinks there are.

The object–substance distinction isn't sufficient as a basis for lexical extension. For example, the child needs to decide when objects are of the same or different kinds. One basis for extension might be function—if it works like a honey dipper, then it is a honey dipper. Another basis might be appearance—if it looks like a honey dipper, then it is a honey dipper. Evidence for both a functional and appearance basis to word extensions has been found. Furthermore, among aspects of appearance, shape, rather than color or texture, seems to guide extension (Smith, Jones, & Landau, 1992). Attention to shape appears to increase with development. Smith (1995, 2001) argues that the bias to use shape as a basis for word extension emerges after the child has a vocabulary of 50 words or so, because many early-acquired common nouns do, in fact, refer to categories of similarly-shaped things.

The issues regarding the roles of function and appearance and, within appearance, of shape as a basis for extension may miss the real point about how children decide when something new is another example of a particular category. For objects that are human-made (i.e., artifacts such as honey dippers as opposed to natural kinds such as plants and animals), evidence suggests that children and adults make decisions about categorization based on what they think the intention of the maker was. Function and appearance matter only because they serve as clues to the creator's intention (Gelman & P. Bloom, 2000). That is, if it was made to be a honey dipper, then it is a honey dipper—even if it is an odd-looking, not particularly effective honey dipper. Experimental findings show that young children do consider the intention of the creator in categorizing and labeling things (Bloom & Markson, 1998; Gelman & Bloom, 2000). For example, Gelman and Ebeling (1998) asked 2-year-olds to name the thing portrayed in a picture. Some of the pictures were described as purposefully created, others as created by accident. The children were more likely to call a bear-shaped blob a bear if they thought it was made on purpose than if they thought it was the result of an accident.

## Lexical entry storage

Let's return to our imaginary child who has now isolated the sound sequence /kʌp/, accurately mapped it onto its immediate referent, and correctly inferred that it also can be used to refer to other "small open containers, usually with a flat bottom and handle, used for drinking" (*American Heritage Dictionary*, 1985).

All this does the child no good if the next time he wants to make such reference, he cannot remember the sound sequence. (If this seems a trivial problem, think of trying to learn six new words in a foreign language every day. You have to remember the word meanings, but you also have to remember the words.)

As we saw in the discussion of individual differences in vocabulary development, phonological memory appears to be a significant component of word-learning skill. In order to create a new lexical entry, the child must also have a phonological system that distinguishes /kʌp/ from /pʌp/ and /kʌb/ and so on. We know from the studies of infant perception reviewed in Chapter 3 that children can hear these differences, but having a way of mentally representing these differences may be another matter. According to some, it is the need to make distinctions in a growing mental lexicon that pushes the child to develop a system of phonological representation (see Walley, 1993). The particulars of just how lexical development and phonological development are related remains an open question at this point, but entries in the mental lexicon are, at some point in development, sequences of phonemes, and thus creating lexical entries must depend on phonological knowledge.

## THE RELATION OF WORDS TO CONCEPTS

Up to this point, we have been discussing the acquisition of word meaning assuming that the child's problem is to decipher what ideas or **concepts** words encode, but we haven't considered how the concepts themselves might develop. In a sense this is proper, because this is a book about language development, not cognitive development. However, the relation between words and concepts is too intimate to do a good job of talking about one without talking about the other.

The meanings of words are functions of the concepts the words encode. Words with different meanings encode different concepts. To illustrate with our *gorping* example from the previous section, the meaning of *gorp* as "pushing into a squatting position" encodes the concepts of motion and causality (among others), whereas the meaning of *gorp* as "making circles with the arms" encodes motion but not causality. The task of determining what concepts words encode is simpler for common nouns. Concepts encoded by words like *juice* and *dog* are mental categories that include everything that is juice or dogs, respectively, and exclude everything else.

### Words map onto preexisting concepts

To learn the meaning of the words *juice, dog,* or *gorp,* the child must have the concepts of juice, dog, or motion and causality. Usually the relationship between concepts and words is described as one in which the concepts develop first, independent of language. Some concepts may well be innate in the child. For example, motion is a good candidate for an innate concept because the infant's perceptual apparatus detects motion from birth. Other concepts develop as a result of the child's nonlinguistic experience in the world. The kinds of word meanings children consider, according to such an account, are a function of the kinds of mental categories children have. However, learning words cannot be solely a matter of learning labels for preexisting concepts.

***Lexical organization differs from conceptual organization.*** Words do not always map onto concepts one-to-one. Sometimes children have concepts for which there is no word in their language, and so they may invent words to fill these lexical gaps. For example, one child invented the words *couch hole* and *pee mat* (personal data). Couch holes are the cracks between cushions that a 2-year-old has to be careful to avoid when walking across a couch. A pee mat is the bathmat in front of the toilet the same 2-year-old stood on when urinating. Lexical gaps, however, are not the biggest problem in learning how words map onto concepts. A far more pervasive problem is that words mark some, but not all, conceptually available distinctions, leaving children to figure out how their language divides the world into word-sized packages (Bowerman, 1978).

The fact that there are many different ways a language could potentially map words onto concepts is best illustrated by comparing languages that do this differently. In Spanish, one word means both "fingers" and "toes." (In English, there is a single word for these things—digits—but it is not used very frequently.) In Navaho, there is one word for both "head" and "human hair" and a separate word for "animal hair" (Miller, 1981). English has a huge vocabulary of color terms (including terms like *puce, magenta,* and *turquoise* in addition to the basics), whereas some languages have fewer than half a dozen color terms. What verbs encode also differs across languages (Talmy, 1985). In English, verbs tend to encode both motion and the manner of the motion, so we have many different verbs for different manners of motion, like *run, skip,* and *slide.* In Spanish, verbs tend to encode direction rather than manner. (Again, English has such verbs, such as *exit* and *enter,* but they are less commonly used.) This difference is illustrated in the Spanish and English descriptions of the scene in Figure 4.7.

***Learning lexical organization.*** In learning the lexicons of their languages, children must determine which cognitive distinctions are marked in their language and which are not. This level of organizing the world that mediates between cognitive organization and language is called **semantic organization.** Acquiring a language includes learning its semantics—that is, learning how meanings are linguistically realized. In this chapter, we discuss how children learn the semantics of their language with respect to the lexicon—that is, **lexical organization.** We will discuss semantics again in the next chapter with respect to the grammar.

The process children go through in figuring out the semantic level of organization is interestingly revealed in Carey's (1978) study of word learning. Three-year-old children were exposed to a novel word in a naturalistic con-

**Figure 4.7**    To describe this scene, an English speaker would say, "The girl is running out of the house," encoding the manner of the motion in the verb. A Spanish speaker would say,"La niña está saliendo de la casa" (the girl is leaving the house), encoding the direction of the motion in the verb (Naigles, Eisenberg, & Kako, 1992). Thus, learning a lexicon includes learning how your language packages meaning into words—that is, learning lexical organization.
Source: From Acquiring a Language-Specific Lexicon: Motion Verbs in English and Spanish, by L. Naigles, A. R. Eisenberg, E. T. Kako. Paper presented at the International Pragmatics Association conference, Belgium, November 1992. Reprinted with permission. Drawing courtesy of Qi Wang.

text. The word was *chromium,* and it was used to refer to the color olive. (Carey made sure that none of the children had a word for olive or knew the word *chromium* before the study started by giving them a pretest with color chips.) The children's preschool was equipped with two identical trays, one blue and one chromium. In the course of setting up for a snack, the preschool teacher asked each child to "Bring me the chromium tray; not the blue one, the chromium one." The children also had a second exposure to the word chromium a week later using the color chips.

The interesting finding of the study came 5 weeks later, when the children were tested by being presented with several color chips, including familiar colors and olive. The children were asked what color each chip was. None of the 14 children in the study had learned to call olive "chromium." But they had learned something because they changed what they called "olive." Two children who had called olive "green" on the pretest said that they did not know what to call it. Six children called olive a color term—gray, blue, or brown—they had not applied to olive before and did not yet use appropriately. What this shows is that although the children had not learned the word chromium, they had learned that olive was a color that had its own name. As mentioned in a previous section, Carey dubbed this process fast mapping, emphasizing that this initial fast mapping was only a partial mapping of the new word onto the conceptual domain of color, because none of the children had fully figured out that chromium meant olive.

Although after one exposure children had only begun the process, Carey's study shows that children use input to figure out that a particular concept (in this case, the color olive) is lexicalized (has a name) in the language, even if they don't know what the name is. There is also evidence that lexical development may include learning broader principles about what gets lexicalized in one's language. As discussed earlier and illustrated in Figure 4.7, languages differ in how they package meaning in verbs. For example, in Spanish, motion verbs generally encode the path of a motion (in English, these would be verbs like *exit* and *enter*), whereas in English, verbs generally encode manner (e.g, *run, walk*). Adult Spanish and English speakers appear to have learned this, because if they are given a novel verb presented with a videotaped motion (e.g., "She's kradding toward the tree" or "She's kradding the tree"), adult Spanish speakers tend to favor a path interpretation and adult English speakers favor a manner interpretation. Consistent with the theory of syntactic bootstrapping, the sentence frame in which the verb appears has an influence as well (Naigles & Terrazas, 1998).

Additional evidence that children do learn language-specific lexicalization patterns comes from a comparison of the early description of motion by children acquiring Korean and English (Choi & Bowerman, 1991). In English, the same words are used to describe the path of motion (such as *up* or *down*) regardless of whether the motion is caused ("He pushed me down") or spontaneous ("I fell down"). In Korean, however, the direction of motion is part of the meaning of the verb (like *ascend* and *descend*), and different verbs are used for caused and for spontaneous motion. This means that in Korean, path is lexicalized along with cause, and in English, path is lexicalized independent of cause.

Very young English and Korean speakers seem to know this. One-year-old English-speaking children commonly use the words *down* and *up* for both spontaneous and caused motion to mean "put me down" or "I fell down." However, Korean children do not extend verb meanings in this way. Even children under the age of 2 respect the caused/spontaneous distinction in their use of motion verbs. That is, from the very beginning, Korean children seem not only to be learning Korean words but also to be figuring out how Korean words divide meaning into lexicalized components.

## Words influence conceptual development

Thus far, we have been taking the commonly held view that cognitive organization comes first and that children learn semantic organization as they map words onto concepts. Other relationships between cognition and language are possible. For example, language might influence cognition. Spanish speakers might really think of fingers and toes as being more similar to each other than English speakers do. English speakers might consider manner of motion to be more central to action than Spanish speakers do. This hypothesis, that language influences thought, was first developed by linguist Edward Sapir and his student Benjamin Lee Whorf. Known as the **Whorfian hypothesis,** or the **linguistic relativity hypothesis,** this position states that the way our language "carves up" the world influences how we think about the world. This hypothesis has inspired a large body of research on the thought processes of adults who speak different languages. Fewer empirical studies have been done with children, but some researchers suggest that characteristics of the language children are acquiring exert an influence on their cognitive development.

As we discussed earlier in this chapter, some languages seem to make it easier to learn verbs than others. In Japanese and Korean, verbs are more frequent and more salient in input than they are in English, and children acquiring Japanese and Korean seem to acquire verbs relatively earlier in the course of lexical development than children acquiring English do. The Whorfian hypothesis would predict that children acquiring Japanese and Korean should acquire the concepts encoded by verbs at a younger age than would children acquiring English (Gopnik & Choi, 1990). Some evidence supports this Whorfian prediction. Gopnik and Choi studied both early lexical development and early cognitive development in children acquiring Korean and in children acquiring English (Gopnik & Choi, 1995; Gopnik, Choi, & Baumberger, 1996). They found that Korean-speaking children used verbs earlier and acquired concepts of means/end relations (the kind of things that verbs encode) earlier than English-speaking children did. In contrast, English-speaking children had larger naming vocabularies and also showed a more advanced understanding of object categorization. In a similar vein, there is evidence that 3- to 5-year-old children acquiring Spanish sometimes use grammatical gender as a basis for categorizing when asked to sort familiar objects (Martinez & Shatz, 1996) and that children acquiring languages that explicitly mark beliefs that are false (i.e., a different word refers to thinking things that are true and thinking things that are false) acquire an understanding that beliefs can be false just a little earlier than children acquiring languages (for example, English) that do not mark that distinction (Shatz, Diesendruck, Martinez-Beck, & Akar, 2003).

Although this idea that characteristics of the input language make some concepts more salient and easier to learn than others goes somewhat against the more mainstream view of the primacy of cognition, such a notion has been proposed before. In a classic article on children's word learning, Roger Brown (1958b) suggested that the particular words adults use when they talk to children can influence children's cognitive organization. For example, when a child points to a tree and says, "What's that?" it's up to the adult whether to say "maple" or "tree." The child whose parents say "oak," "maple," and "dogwood" will develop more differentiated mental categories of trees than will the child whose parents say "tree." The word the adult provides serves as "an invitation to form the concept." In actuality, the effects of parental naming practices on cognition may be hard to untangle from the effects of other information. It would be odd for an adult to label oaks, maples, and dogwoods individually without also pointing out some of their distinctive characteristics. Mervis and Mervis (1988) have argued that such demonstrations of important attributes play the greatest role in children's category evolution.

Other evidence suggests that words may prompt even very young children to form categories. That is, hearing different items referred to by the same word leads children to notice how they are similar and to form a category that includes them all. For example, Waxman and Markow (1995) presented 12- and 13-month-old infants with four different toy animals and then measured the children's interest in a fifth animal. Some children heard all the animals receive the same label (i.e., "Do you like that *X*?"), whereas other children were introduced to the animals without any label presented (i.e., "Do you like that?") The children who heard the label showed less interest in the fifth animal than the children who heard no label. It is as though for the children who heard all the animals given the same label, the fifth animal was one more boring example of the same kind of thing. For the children who heard no label, and thus formed no category that included all these items, the fifth item was novel and interesting. A similar effect of labels as invitations to form categories has been demonstrated in children as young as 9 months old (Balaban & Waxman, 1997).

## Words and concepts develop together

Another proposed relationship between cognitive development and lexical development also has empirical support: the relationship of simultaneous development. Concepts don't develop first and wait for the words, nor do the words prompt the development of the concepts. Rather, words and concepts develop together. Gopnik and Meltzoff (1984, 1986) followed children longitudinally, measuring their understanding of particular concepts and also tracking their vocabulary. They found a close correspondence between the appearance of words that encode disappearance, like *gone,* and the age at which children were successful on a nonlinguistic task that measures understanding that objects are permanent. (Young babies seem not to fully understand that objects continue to exist when they are out of view.) Gopnik and Meltzoff also found a close correspondence between children's development of the understanding of means/ends relationships and the children's first use of words that encode success or failure, such as *there* or *uh-oh.* Gopnik and Meltzoff proposed that "children acquire words that encode concepts they have just developed or are in the process of developing" (Gopnik & Meltzoff, 1984, p. 495).

In fact, it has been suggested that the beginning of word learning itself may coincide with infants' mental individuation of the different sorts of objects they encounter (Carey, 1994; Xu & Carey, 1995, 1996). Xu and Carey found evidence that before about the age of 11 months, infants' understanding of the world may be very different from ours. Imagine you saw a book emerge from behind an opaque screen and then return; then you saw a cup emerge from behind the screen and then return. What would you think was behind the screen? A book and a cup, most likely. If the screen were removed and only a cup was there, you would be surprised. However, you would not be surprised if the screen were removed and both objects were there; that would be just what you expected. When Xu and Carey performed this demonstration with babies, they found a difference between the responses of 10-month-olds and 12-month-olds. The 12-month-olds looked longer at the cup than at both objects, and looking longer is what babies do when they are surprised. Thus, the 12-month-olds responded the way adults would. In contrast, 10-month-olds, as a group, showed no surprise at seeing only a single object and thus no evidence that they expected two objects to be behind the screen (Xu & Carey, 1995, 1996). (There were actually several trials with different sets of objects.) It is as if 10-month-olds perceive things as "objects" but not as separate, different objects. Twelve-month-olds, on the other hand, share the adult view that a cup and book are two different things, not one thing that takes on different forms as it moves through space.

Xu and Carey's findings suggest a striking coincidence between the nonlinguistic development of concepts of books, cups, and other things as individual, countable things and the comprehension of words that label these categories of individual things ("count nouns"). A corollary of the claim that concepts of individual objects develop with comprehension of words for those objects is the claim that even the youngest word learners share the adult understanding of what count nouns mean: They refer to instances of countable things. This position contradicts some earlier proposals about the nature of children's first semantic representations offered to explain children's overextended word uses.

## ● SUMMARY

Words are symbols that can be used to refer to things, actions, properties of things, and more. Adults' knowledge about words is stored in the mental lexicon. The process of children's lexical development is the process of learning the words in the target language and organizing them in the mental lexicon.

Children may begin to recognize some words as early as 5 months of age and to truly understand word meanings around 10 months of age.

Children typically produce their first word around their first birthday. The course of vocabulary development is slow at first. On average, children take approximately 6 months to acquire a productive vocabulary of 50 words. At the point of achieving a 50-word vocabulary, typically around age 18 months, many children show a word spurt, in which the rate of vocabulary development increases dramatically. Cognitive changes in the child probably contribute to this word spurt.

From the beginning of lexical development, children vary in both the size and content of their lexicons. A great deal of research suggests that early vocabularies of English-speaking children tend to be dominated by general nominals, or object labels. However, individuals differ in the extent to which this is true. Some children have proportionately fewer object labels than others and proportionately more words or expressions that serve social-interactive functions. Also, cross-linguistic and cross-cultural differences in the relative dominance of object labels in early vocabularies suggest that both the nature of the language and the sociocultural uses to which it is put influence the content of early vocabularies. Two factors that affect the size of children's vocabularies are their phonological memory skills and the amount of speech addressed to them.

The words children utter when they first begin to talk may not have the same sort of representation in the children's mental lexicons as adults' words have in adults' mental lexicons. The meanings of some of children's first words seem tied to particular events or contexts, and, even later, children may not fully understand the meanings of all the words they use. Such immature word knowledge seems to be the exception, however. For the most part, children do a remarkable job of correctly figuring out the meanings of the words they hear. This accomplishment is notable because most situations in which a new word is heard leave room for many possible interpretations of that new word.

Accounting for how children manage to learn words as quickly and accurately as they do is the main arena in the study of lexical development where different theoretical orientations clash. Proposals consonant with a nativist view of language development suggest that children know something about how words work before they learn any words. This prior knowledge constrains the universe of possible solutions to the word-learning problem and makes it solvable. One sort of counterproposal claims that children can find all the information they need for word learning in the social context in which words are encountered; another argues that ordinary processes of attention and memory explain word learning.

Words are not the only elements in the mind that represent things in the world. Children and adults also have nonlinguistic concepts. Conceptual development influences lexical development, as children acquire words for newly developed concepts. Lexical development may also influence conceptual development, as new words stimulate the development of new concepts. Because not every concept has a word, part of the process of lexical development is learning lexical organization, or how the words in the target language map onto nonlinguistic concepts.

## ● Key Terms

mental lexicon

words

reference

context-bound word use

referential words

nominals

natural partitions hypothesis

relational relativity hypothesis

underextensions

overextensions

word spurt

referential and expressive language styles

phonological memory

speech segmentation problem

mapping problem

fast mapping

lexical principles

word-learning constraints

whole-object assumption

mutual exclusivity assumption

pragmatic principles

principle of conventionality

principle of contrast

syntactic bootstrapping hypothesis

sociopragmatic cues

word extension

taxonomic assumption

concepts

semantic organization

lexical organization

Whorfian hypothesis, or linguistic relativity hypothesis

## ● REVIEW QUESTIONS

1. Give examples of the kinds of questions we ask when we study lexical development.
2. What is a word? Explain the difference between a baby's reaching gesture and true words.
3. What is the difference between context-bound word use and referential word use? Why is this an important distinction?
4. What kinds of words make up children's early vocabularies? Why do children learn these words as opposed to other kinds of words?
5. What is the word spurt? Discuss the proposed explanations for the word spurt.
6. What is the relation between word production and word comprehension in early lexical development?
7. Describe the kinds of individual differences in lexical development style that have been observed. What might account for these differences?
8. What factors appear to play a role in accounting for differences in the rate of lexical development?
9. What's the mapping problem, as the philosopher Quine described it?
10. What are constraints on word learning? Define and illustrate with an example.
11. What claims are made by the sociopragmatic view of word learning?

12. Give an example of how syntax provides clues to word meaning and an example of evidence that children use those clues in figuring out the meaning of newly encountered words.
13. Define and explain the difference between conceptual organization and lexical organization.
14. Outline three proposed relations between the development of concepts and the acquisition of words that encode those concepts. What kind of evidence would support each view?
15. Which proposed solutions to the mapping problem entail the most nativist views of lexical development? What are the most experientially based proposals?
16. Find examples of evidence in this chapter that support the views that (a) children's lexical development is guided by properties of the speech they hear and (b) children's lexical development is guided by internal properties of children's minds.
17. To what extent are the several proposed solutions to the mapping problem incompatible, and to what extent could they all be true to some degree?

# THE DEVELOPMENT OF SYNTAX AND MORPHOLOGY: LEARNING THE STRUCTURE OF LANGUAGE

Thus far we have described children learning the sounds and the words of their language. Sometime, typically between 18 months and 2 years, children start to put words together. The development of this ability to combine elements of the language is the next facet of language development we will consider. Because elements are not combined haphazardly but only in certain structures, we refer to this aspect of language development as the development of language structure. As we did regarding phonological and lexical development, we will begin our discussion of children's development of language structure with a description of the endpoint of that developmental process. We will not attempt a comprehensive description of adults' knowledge of linguistic structure but rather will focus on the basic aspects of grammar we need to understand the discussion of development that follows.

## SOME FEATURES OF ADULTS' KNOWLEDGE OF LANGUAGE STRUCTURE

### The productivity of language

When mature speakers talk, most of the sentences they produce are sentences they have never produced or heard before. When mature speakers understand the sentences others produce, it's almost always a matter of understanding sentences they have never heard before. This characteristic of language and of language knowledge—that speakers and hearers have the capacity to produce and understand an infinite number of novel sentences—is referred to as the **productivity or generativity of language.** The productive nature of language has a very important implication both for linguistic theories that try to describe adults' linguistic knowledge and for psychological theories that try to explain how children achieve that knowledge. Knowledge of language is not knowledge of a list of sentences from which to select as the occasion demands; rather, it is knowledge of a system that allows speakers to produce an infinite number of different sentences from a finite inventory of words. The two components of that productive system are syntax and morphology.

### Syntax

Let's say that you want to communicate that John kissed Mary. If you know the words that refer to "John," "Mary," and "kissed," you also need to know the order in which these words must be combined to produce the sentence "John kissed Mary." If you said instead "Mary kissed John," that would mean something different, and if you said *"kissed Mary John," that would be ungrammatical. (It is a convention in linguistics to put an asterisk in front of ungrammatical constructions.) So when you know a language, you know a system for putting words together. **Syntax** is the component of grammar that governs the ordering of words in sentences.

*"I understood each and every word you said but not the order in which they appeared."*

**Figure 5.1**  Source: Copyright © The New Yorker Collection 1999 William Haefeli from cartoonbank.com. All rights reserved.

How best to characterize speakers' and hearers' syntactic knowledge is currently a topic of hot debate. We will begin by presenting the arguments for the position that syntactic (and morphological) knowledge consists of a system of rules that operate over abstract or symbolic representations. This is probably the most widely held view in the field, and it certainly is the view that has provided the framework for most of the research on syntactic development. We will consider the alternative, connectionist view in later sections of this chapter.

In the standard, rule-based approach, we would account for your ability to produce and understand "John kissed Mary," by positing that you know a rule. The simplest rule would be something like the following:

Sentence → John + kissed + Mary

The problem with this rule is its limitation: It generates only one sentence. If each rule generates only one sentence, then to produce an infinite number of sentences you would need a grammar system with an infinite number of rules. Such a system is not productive, and because we know that the system adults have is productive, the grammar must be of a different sort. The solution to the problem of accounting for the productivity of syntactic rules is to posit rules that operate over linguistic entities bigger than individual words. For example, we could posit the following rule:

Sentence → agent of action + action + recipient of action

This would account for "John kissed Mary," "Mary kissed John," "John Wilkes Booth shot Abraham Lincoln," and many more sentences as well. Although categories such as agent and action allow a productive system, such categories cannot handle all the kinds of sentences speakers produce and listeners understand. For example, we would run into problems if we tried to use the preceding rule to account for "John resembles Mary" because *John* is not an agent of any action, *resembles* is not an action, and nothing is being done to Mary at all.

To solve this problem, we could try to figure out a new set of categories that would handle this kind of sentence and add those categories to the grammar. A better way, however, would be to posit even more abstract categories—categories that would include *kiss* and *resemble* as instances of the same kind of thing and that would include John both when he was kissing and when he was resembling. These categories are the familiar categories of Verb and Noun. By writing rules that operate over categories such as Noun and Verb, we can account for all the sentence examples just listed with a rule like this:

Sentence → Noun + Verb + Noun

At this point we have worked our way up to a system in which the rules operate over symbols, because *Nouns* and *Verbs,* as such, never appear in sentences. Rather, Nouns and Verbs are symbols, or variables, that stand for a variety of different possible instances in the definition of a sentence. The instances appear in the sentence, but not in the rule. Even this treatment is overly simple. As you are very aware, more kinds of words than just nouns and verbs get combined in sentences, and more kinds of sentence structures than the simple examples just listed get produced. Although we won't attempt anything like a full treatment of syntax in this book, we need to establish two more pieces of information about adults' syntactic knowledge before we can talk about children's syntactic development. One piece is a further elaboration of the kinds of categories rules operate over; the other concerns the kinds of structures the rules build.

The categories that linguistic rules operate over seem to divide fairly neatly into two types. One type, termed **open-class words,** content words, or **lexical categories,** consists of the categories noun, verb, and adjective. (The different terms come from different linguistic theories. Here we introduce the terminology so that you will be able to recognize the terms in other sources, but we will not attempt a treatment of the linguistic theories themselves.) The words in these categories do most of the work of carrying the meaning of a sentence. They are called "open" classes because you can always invent a new noun, verb, or adjective and use it in a perfectly grammatical (if not particularly meaningful) sentence (for example, "the blick gorped the fepish woog.") The other type of word category is the **closed-class words,** also called function words or **functional categories.** These are auxiliaries like *can* and *will,* prepositions like *in* and *of,* complementers like *that* and *who,* and determiners like *the* and *a.* They are called closed-class words because you can't really invent new ones, and they are called function words or functional categories because their main role in the sentence is to serve grammatical functions rather than to carry content.

The last crucial feature about grammatical knowledge concerns the nature of sentence structure. Sentences are not merely linear arrangements of content and function words: They have hierarchical structure. Consider the following sentences:

John Wilkes Booth shot Abraham Lincoln.

A Confederate sympathizer shot the 16th president.

The clever runner stole second base.

The catcher swore.

Although each sentence would have a different description in terms of the sequence of nouns, verbs, adjectives, and so on, all these sentences are similar at another level of structure. They are all accounted for by one set of rules:

Sentence → Noun Phrase + Verb Phrase

Verb Phrase → Verb + (Noun Phrase)

Noun Phrase → (Determiner) + (Adjective) + Noun

These rules say that a sentence is made up of a Noun Phrase plus a Verb Phrase; that a Verb Phrase comprises a Verb plus an Optional Noun Phrase; and that a Noun Phrase comprises a Noun optionally preceded by a Determiner, an Adjective, or both. These three rules generate a large number of sentences (limited only by the number of different nouns, verbs, and so on in your vocabulary), and they also describe the hierarchical structure of sentences.

Words are combined to form phrases, and phrases are combined to form simple sentences.

Complex sentences are formed by combining simple sentences, and this is how the system acquires the capacity to generate an infinite number of sentences with a finite vocabulary. You can endlessly conjoin sentences ("The runner stole second base, and the crowd roared"), and you can embed sentences in larger sentences. For example:

The catcher swore.

The umpire noticed that the catcher swore.

The crowd saw that the umpire noticed that the catcher swore.

In sum, then, the standard linguistic account of speakers' ability to produce combinations of words that they have never heard before but that form grammatical sentences in the language is to posit that speakers know a system of rules that specifies how words belonging to different linguistic categories can be combined into structured sentences. The rules we have discussed are far from constituting the entire system for English, but they illustrate some basic features of syntactic knowledge we want to account for in discussing language development. That is, we need to explain the origin of rules and of the linguistic categories over which the rules operate.

## Morphology

It is easy for English speakers to think of sentences as combinations of words. However, the units that are combined in language include something smaller than words. To illustrate what is referred to as the **morphology** of language, consider the following:

One book

Two books

In English, a plural noun is usually indicated by adding an *s* to the end of the singular form. This *s* means something; it indicates the plurality of the noun. Even though the *s* conveys meaning, it does not stand by itself as a word. In linguistics, this kind of language unit is called a **bound morpheme— morphemes** being the smallest units of meaning. Most units of meaning in English are words that stand alone, and these are **free morphemes.** However, bound morphemes, such as the plural marker, must be attached to a word. (We are talking in this chapter about grammatical morphology, also known as inflectional morphology. Inflectional morphemes add grammatical information to words, but they do not change the meaning or the grammatical category of the word. That is, *cats* is just more of the same thing that *cat* is, and they are both nouns. This is in contrast to derivational morphemes (e.g., the *er* in *dancer* and *runner,* the *ish* in *pinkish* and *smallish*), which actually form new words, potentially of a different grammatical category. That is, *run* refers to a manner of locomotion and is a verb; *runner* refers to a person who locomotes in that manner and is a noun. (The acquisition of the word formation processes that involve derivational morphemes will be discussed in Chapter 9.)

The English language does not have a very rich morphological system, and the bound morphemes in English are few. Other examples include the *s* that goes on the end of a verb to indicate a third person singular subject ("He talks"), the *ed* that goes on the end of a verb to indicate past tense ("He talked"), and the *ing* that goes on the end of a verb to indicate progressive action ("He is talking").

Other languages have very rich morphological systems. In such languages, the form of a noun is different depending not only on whether the noun is singular or plural but also on whether the noun is the subject of the sentence, the direct object, or the indirect object—and that would be just part of the morphological system. For example, compare the following English and Hungarian sentences:

The boy gave a book to the girl.

A fiú egy könyvet adott a lánynak. (The boy a book gave the girl.)

In Hungarian the morphemes at the end of the nouns indicate the noun's role in the sentence. The *et* at the end of *könyvet* indicates the role that in English is the direct object, and the *nak* at the end of *lánynak* indicates the role that in English is the indirect object. (For readers who know other languages that have a similar system, these are the accusative and dative markers, respectively.) English has remnants of such a system in the pronoun system, where *he* or *she* indicates the subject of a verb and *him* or *her* indicates the object. However, English speakers primarily rely on the order of words in the sentence to indicate the words' roles.

For children acquiring languages with rich morphological systems, morphological development is a larger component of language acquisition than it is for children acquiring English. Although in this chapter we will focus on the acquisition of English, child language researchers also study children acquiring languages that are unlike English. This research is important because one of the goals of studying language development is to understand the mental processes that make language development possible. If we looked only at children learning English, we would risk creating a description of mental processes that would be adequate only for acquiring English. Such mental processes are obviously not true of children, because children can learn whatever language is spoken around them.

To summarize, syntax and morphology are the systems for combining units of meaning. Syntax refers to combining words into sentences, and morphology refers to building words. All speakers of a language know the rules of both syntax and morphology as well as the categories and structures these rules operate over. But before we begin describing children's acquisition of the rules of language, it is important to understand just what sort of rules we are talking about.

## Descriptive versus prescriptive rules

The knowledge of the rules of language that speakers or hearers possess is not explicit. Unless you have taken a course in linguistics, you wouldn't be able to explain these rules. Rather, you would simply follow these rules. We illustrated this kind of rule knowledge with respect to phonological rules in Chapter 3, and the same thing applies here to the rules of syntax and morphology.

The implicit rules we address in this chapter are not like the **prescriptive rules** of grammar taught in an English class. An English class teaches the current standard of language use for educated speakers and writers. Linguists, in contrast, take whatever people do as "correct" and try to describe the patterns in it. One way of seeing the difference between the **descriptive rules** that linguists write and the prescriptive rules taught in English class is to compare the outcome of breaking those rules. What would happen if you turned in a paper to English class with the following sentence?

Me and Tiffany went to the mall.

You will be corrected, because that form is unacceptable in formal writing, even though it is a form that people say all the time. On the other hand, if you just string words together in violation of word order rules, you might get something like this:

*mall the to went me Tiffany and

This is something that no one would ever say and that everyone would agree is ungrammatical. The study of language acquisition is the study of how children learn the language used by the adults around them. Thus, we are concerned with the acquisition of the descriptive rules that disallow *"mall the to went me Tiffany and," not the prescriptive rules that deem "Me and Tiffany went to the mall" "bad grammar."

Having thus established the purpose of this chapter, we will begin our discussion of children's development of syntax and morphology with a brief overview of the ground to be covered.

## AN OVERVIEW OF GRAMMATICAL DEVELOPMENT

After several months of talking in single-word utterances, children begin to put two words together in sentences like "Daddy shirt," "Off TV," and "Pretty tower." These first word combinations tend to be missing function words and the bound morphemes that mark plural, possessive, or tense. Next, children start to produce longer utterances, combining three and more words. As children start to put words together in longer sequences, they also start to add the function words and bound morphemes that were missing in their first word combinations. Children's first sentences are usually simple active declarative sentences; negative sentences and questions, for example, appear later. The last major syntactic development is the production of multiclause sentences. This course of development usually begins some time before the child's second birthday and is largely complete by the age of 4 years.

The foregoing outline, while true, ignores completely the individual differences that exist. It also ignores the development of grammar as it is evidenced in comprehension. Our next task is to fill in and supplement this sketchy outline. We will begin with what has historically been the primary database for describing grammatical development: the utterances children produce. We will describe the transition from single-word speech to the production of word combinations, and we will follow the course of development in production through to the production of complex sentences. We will then turn to the topics of individual differences in the course of development and the measurement of grammatical development. Following that, we will review studies of comprehension for further evidence of what children know about the grammar of their language at different developmental points. Having thus described the course of development, we will then look at the theoretical issues in the field regarding how to describe children's linguistic knowledge at different points in development and how to account for the changes that occur.

## EARLY MULTIWORD UTTERANCES

The first evidence of grammatical knowledge in production comes when children combine units of the language in a single utterance. For children acquiring English, the units are typically words, and, thus, the beginning of structured speech is marked by the appearance of multiword utterances. However, many children produce **transitional forms** that can blur the distinction between the one-word and two-word stages of language production.

### The transition from one-word speech

***Vertical constructions.***   Before they produce two-word utterances, some children utter successive single-word utterances that seem to be related to each other in meaning in the same way that the words in a two-word utterance are. For example, one little girl who woke up with an eye infection pointed to her eye and said, "Ow. Eye" (personal data). In this case, each word had the same intonation contour as if it had been said by itself, and the two words were separated by a pause. However, the expressed meaning clearly involved a relation between the two words. At this stage, children also sometimes produce a single-word utterance that builds on someone else's previous utterance. Scollon (1979) called these sequences "vertical constructions," because when researchers transcribe what children say, they write each utterance on a new line. A two-word sentence, in contrast, would be a horizontal construction and would be written on the same line in transcription.

***Unanalyzed word combinations and "word + jargon" combinations.*** There are other transitional forms besides these vertical constructions. Most children have at least some multiword phrases in their repertoires that have been memorized as unanalyzed wholes; these phrases therefore do not reflect the development of the ability to combine words (Peters, 1986). *Iwant* and *Idontknow* are examples of unanalyzed wholes common in children's early language. Some children—typically those who have been producing long strings of jargon since their babbling days—produce utterances longer than one word by inserting one clear word into what is otherwise an incomprehensible babble sequence. The result can sound something like "mumble mumble mumble cookie?" To further complicate matters, all these transitional phenomena may exist simultaneously, so that one child's first multiword utterances may include some rote-learned wholes, some "jargon + word" combinations, and some truly productive word combinations.

## Two-word combinations

***The beginning of a productive system.*** At some point, truly productive word combinations begin. We say that children have a productive system when they use the words in their vocabularies in different combinations. A sample of the two-word utterances produced by one child during a one-month period is presented in Box 5.1 (from Braine, 1976). The variety of utterances in this table suggests that the boy who produced these utterances was able to combine the words in his limited vocabulary productively. For example, he could say that anything is big or little; he could say that Daddy and Andrew walk and sleep. (And you would predict from the appearance of the utterance "Daddy sit" on this list that the child could also produce "Andrew sit.") It's also a good bet—and crucial to the claim that the child has a productive system—that these utterances were not just reduced imitations of sentences he had heard adults produce. The test would be to introduce this little boy to a new person, Emily. If his linguistic knowledge were productive, he should immediately be able to produce "Emily sit," "Emily walk," and so on.

## Box 5.1  Examples of one child's two-word utterances

*Possessives*

| | | | |
|---|---|---|---|
| daddy coffee | Andrew book | daddy book | daddy eat |
| daddy shell | daddy car | mommy book | juice daddy |
| mommy shell | daddy chair | daddy bread | daddy juice |
| Andrew shoe | daddy cookie | Elliot cookie | Mommy butter |
| daddy hat | daddy tea | Elliot diaper | daddy butter |
| Elliot juice | mommy tea | Elliot boat | |
| mommy mouth | daddy door | | this Nina |

*Property-indicating patterns*

| | | | |
|---|---|---|---|
| big balloon | little shell | all wet . . . | red balloon |
| big hot | little ham | mommy . . . | blue stick |
| big shell | little water | all wet | |
| big juice | little light | daddy all wet | hurt Andrew |
| big pants | little wet | daddy all | hurt fly |
| big lion | little step | wet | hurt knee |
| big water | little boy | all wet ball | hurt plane |
| big light | little bird | shirt wet | hurt hand |
| big step | little tobacco | wet nose | |
| big jump | little banana | shoe wet | old cookie |
| big boy | little spilt | wet diaper | old apple |
| big bird | little hurt | | old cup |
| big tobacco | | hot sand | old stick |
| big banana | all wet . . . | hot fire | old egg |
| | water . . . | hot tea | |
| little hat | all wet | hot ball | |
| little duck | all wet pants | blue shirt | |

*Recurrrence, number, disappearance*

| | | | |
|---|---|---|---|
| more glass | two plane | two car | one daddy car |
| more boy | two stick | two diaper | |
| more raisins | two ducks | two tobacco | all gone big |
| more shovel | two spoon | two raisins | stick |
| more "O" | two fly | two daddy | all gone stick |
| | two shoe | door | all gone bee |
| other door | two bird | two daddy | all gone |
| other pin | two pipe | two mommy | stone . . . |
| other ball | two door | two squirrel | all gone |
| other hand | two cup | two bread | |

*(continued)*

**Box 5.1**     *(continued)*

*Locatives*

| | | | |
|---|---|---|---|
| sand ball | "ON" | hand eye | "IN/TO" |
| hand hair | "IN" | stone outside | "TO" |
| ball house | "IN/TO" | key door | "TO" |
| man car | "IN" | raisin cup | "IN/TO" |
| fly light | "ON" | dog house | "ON" |
| sand toe | "ON" | feet light | "TO" |
| sand water | "IN/TO" | | |
| sand eye | "IN" | in there . . . old apple | |
| daddy . . . hot ball | "TO" | | |
| ball daddy | "TO" | milk in there | |
| stick car | "IN" | down there car | |
| rock outside | "TO" | | |

*Actor/action*

| | | | |
|---|---|---|---|
| mommy sit | daddy work | boy walk | Andrew sleep |
| daddy sit | daddy sleep | man walk | daddy work |
| Andrew walk | daddy walk | Elliot sleep | stone daddy |

*Other combinations*

| | | |
|---|---|---|
| have it egg | eat fork | back eat |
| have it milk | bite top | up bed |
| have it fork | bite block | |
| | bounce ball | mommy girl |
| dirty face | broke pipe | daddy boy |
| dirty mouth | ride car | |
| dirty feet | walk car | orange juice |
| clean socks | ride daddy | apple juice |
| spilt bread | walk daddy | grape juice |
| spilt raisin | | drink water |
| | daddy window | butter honey |
| boom-boom tower | window byebye | sock shoe |
| boom-boom car | hat on | sit down |
| boom-boom coffee | socks on | lie down |
| boom-boom plane | out car | |
| boom-boom chair | out chair | |
| | back car | |
| eat dessert | back raisin | |

---

**Box 5.2  Relational meanings expressed in children's two-word utterances**

| Meaning | Example |
|---|---|
| agent + action | Daddy sit |
| action + object | drive car |
| agent + object | Mommy sock |
| agent + location | sit chair |
| entity + location | toy floor |
| possessor + possession | my teddy |
| entity + attribute | crayon big |
| demonstrative + entity | this telephone |

---

Source: Based on Brown, 1973.

***Meanings in two-word utterances.*** Although we say that children's systems are productive when children can put words together in novel combinations, children's first word combinations are limited in the range of relational meanings expressed. (The term **relational meaning** refers to the relation between the referents of the words in a word combination. So, for example, in the utterance "my teddy," the word *my* refers to the speaker and the word *teddy* refers to a stuffed animal. The relational meaning is that of possession.) Roger Brown (1973) proposed a list of eight relational meanings that he claimed accounted for the majority of the meanings children express in their two-word utterances, even children acquiring different languages. These meanings, with examples drawn from many different children, are listed in Box 5.2. According to Brown, the child's grammar at the two-word stage is a vehicle for expressing a small set of semantic relationships. The particular semantic relationships expressed at this stage reflect the level of cognitive development typical of children of this age. The particular words, of course, reflect the language the children have been exposed to. So, according to this view, cognitive development provides the categories of early **combinatorial speech,** and input in the target language provides the lexical items that fill those categories.

## Three-word and more combinations

For some children, the two-word stage lasts for several months. For other children, the two-word stage is brief and barely identifiable as a separate stage before utterances with three and more words are produced. Of course, children continue to produce one- and two-word utterances. What changes with

---

**Box 5.3   Examples of multiword speech**

All the utterances longer than two words produced by one 2-year-old child during breakfast:

I want some eggs.

Where'd it go?

I watch it.

I watching cars.

Here it comes.

Daddy get you.

Put it table.

I see it.

---

Source: From data described in Hoff-Ginsberg, 1991.

development is the upper limit on the length of utterance children can produce. Box 5.3 is a sample of all the three-word utterances produced by one 2-year-old child in the course of having breakfast. This child had just started to put three words together; most utterances were one or two words long and only one was longer than three words. These sentences illustrate several typical characteristics of children's speech at this stage.

When children start to put three words together, many of the meanings expressed are combinations of the relational meanings in two-word combinations, with the redundant terms mentioned only once. For example, the sentence "I watch it" could be described as a combination of "agent + action" (I watch) and "action + object" (watch it). Also, children's utterances at this stage are almost exclusively about the here-and-now. Even 3-year-olds rarely mention absent or imaginary events (Sachs, 1983). However, it is important to point out that these generalizations do not hold perfectly. Not all meanings expressed fit the description of combinations of the two-word relational meanings, and not all utterances refer to the here-and-now. For example, one of the sentences in Box 5.3 refers to an absent person, Daddy. (For a more elaborate description of the meanings in early multiword speech, see Bloom, Lightbown, & Hood, 1975.)

In terms of structure, two characteristics of these early multiword sentences are noteworthy. First, early sentences tend to be affirmative, declarative statements, as opposed to negations, or questions. Second, certain types of words and bound morphemes consistently tend to be missing. Because the omission of certain words and morphemes makes children's utterances sound like the sentences adults used to produce when writing telegrams in which the sender paid by the word, children's speech at this point in development has been termed **telegraphic speech** (Brown & Fraser, 1963). (Telegrams have been replaced by overnight mail and e-mail, but the term has remained.) The telegraphic quality of children's early speech has been the focus of considerable research attention.

## The telegraphic nature of early combinatorial speech

The words included in the early sentences of children acquiring English are primarily words from the major grammatical categories of nouns, verbs, and adjectives. The missing elements are determiners, prepositions, auxiliary verbs, and the bound morphemes that go on the ends of nouns and verbs. These missing forms are called **grammatical morphemes** because the use of these words and word endings is tied to particular grammatical entities. For example, *the* and *a* can appear only at the beginning of a noun phrase; *ing* is typically attached to a verb. Although these grammatical elements do carry some meaning, they seem to carry less meaning than do the nouns and verbs in the utterance (Brown, 1973). Rather, their primary function is structural; they are "the linguistic hooks and eyes that hold sentences together" (Menken, 1935, reprinted 1999, p. 88).

Exactly why these grammatical functors (i.e., function words) and inflections are omitted is a matter of some debate. One possibility is that the omitted words and morphemes are not produced because they are not essential to meaning. Children probably have cognitive limitations on the length of utterance they can produce, independent of their grammatical knowledge. Given such length limitations, they may sensibly leave out the least-important parts. It is also true that the omitted words tend to be words that are not stressed in adults' utterances, and children may be leaving out unstressed elements (Demuth, 1994). Some have also suggested that children's underlying knowledge at this point does not include the grammatical categories that govern the use of the omitted forms (Atkinson, 1992; Radford, 1990, 1995), although other evidence suggests it does (Gerken, Landau, & Remez, 1990). For example, 18-month-olds, but not 15-month-olds, listen longer to passages that use grammatical functors correctly than to passages that are identical except that the grammatical functors are incorrect (Santelmann & Jusczyk, 1998). We will return later in this chapter to the question of what grammatical knowledge underlies children's early sentences.

## AFTER TELEGRAPHIC SPEECH

The typical 2-year-old speaker of English puts words together in short affirmative, declarative sentences that are missing many obligatory morphemes. Between the ages of 2 and 3 years, children fill in the parts that were missing in their early utterances, they expand the range of sentence forms they use, and they begin to use longer and structurally more complex utterances. We will review each of these developments in turn.

## Morphological development in children acquiring English

The missing forms in children's telegraphic speech begin to appear in utterances around the time that the first three-word utterances appear. In his famous longitudinal study of the three children known to child language researchers by their pseudonyms, Adam, Eve, and Sarah, Brown (1973) tracked the appearance of 14 grammatical morphemes of English. Brown's careful study of the emergence of grammatical morphemes allows us to make some generalizations about children's transition from being beginning telegraphic speakers to having full command over the use of these forms. One generalization is that this transition takes quite a long time. Although the first grammatical morphemes typically appear with the first three-word utterances, most grammatical morphemes are not reliably used until more than a year later, when children are speaking in long, complex sentences. A second generalization is that the acquisition of grammatical morphemes is not an all-or-none phenomenon—either for the morphemes as a group or even at the level of individual morphemes. Different morphemes first appear at different times, and a long period of time passes between the first time a morpheme is used and the time it is reliably used in contexts where it is obligatory (Brown, 1973; Wilson, 2003). Figure 5.2 shows the gradual development of the progressive *ing* and the plural *s* in one child's spontaneous speech.

A third generalization that can be made is that the order in which the 14 different morphemes are acquired is very similar across different children. Brown found that Adam, Eve, and Sarah acquired these 14 morphemes in similar orders, although their rates of development were quite different. De Villiers and de Villiers (1973) found that that same general order of development was true in a sample of 21 children at different levels of language development. That is, children who had only a few grammatical morphemes were likely to have only those that first appeared in Adam, Eve, and Sarah's data. Children who had a late-appearing morpheme were likely to have all the earlier-appearing ones as well. The order of appearance found in these studies is presented in Box 5.4.

## Morphological development in children acquiring languages other than English

If one looked only at the acquisition of English, it would appear that ordering content words is easier for children to learn than grammatical morphology. To the English-speaking adult, the task of learning word-order rules seems intu-

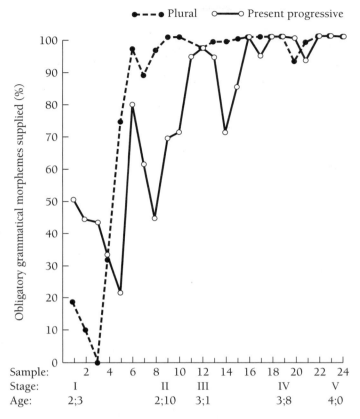

**Figure 5.2**  The development of the progressive and plural inflections in one child's speech

Source: Reprinted by permission of the publishers from *A First Language: The Early Stages,* by Roger Brown. Cambridge, Mass.: Harvard University Press. Copyright © 1973 by the President and Fellows of Harvard College.

itively much easier than the task of learning a morphologically rich language. Where the child learning English needs merely to learn that subjects precede and objects follow the verb, the child learning Hungarian must learn to make 18 different distinctions among roles of nouns and to add a different suffix to the noun depending on the role it serves. For example, where in English one says "John kissed the girl" and "John gave the book to the girl," in Hungarian the form of *girl* would be different in each sentence—and different in potentially 16 more ways depending on just what the girl did or was having done to her. Although this sort of system seems much more complex than the system in English, it is not necessarily more difficult for children to learn. Chil-

---

### Box 5.4 Fourteen grammatical morphemes and their order of acquisition

1. present progressive (+ *ing*)
2.–3. *in, on*
4. plural (+ *s*)
5. past irregular (for example, *came, went*)
6. possessive (+ *'s*)
7. uncontractible copula (*am, is, are, was, were*)
8. articles (*a, the*)
9. past regular (+*d*)
10. third person regular (+*s;* for example, *she talks*)
11. third person irregular (for example, *does, has*)
12. uncontractible auxiliary (*am, is, are, has, have*)
13. contractible copula (*'m, 's, 're*)
14. contractible auxiliary (*'m, 's, 're* when combined with +*ing;*
    *'ve, 's* when combined with a past participle such as *has been*)

Source: Reprinted by permission of the publishers from *A First Language: The Early Stages,* by Roger Brown, Cambridge, Mass.: Harvard University Press. Copyright © 1973 by the President and Fellows of Harvard College.

---

dren learning English may learn morphology relatively late because it is not as salient or important a part of the grammar. Children learning languages that have rich morphology have been reported to learn morphology earlier in the course of language development than do children acquiring morphologically impoverished languages (Berman, 1986; Peters, 1995). In fact, children acquiring Turkish have been reported to produce inflected forms (that is, words with grammatical morphemes) before they combine words (Aksu-Koc & Slobin, 1985). On the other hand, the telegraphic quality of children's early word combinations has been reported in studies of children acquiring morphologically richer languages including Finnish, German, Luo (spoken in parts of Kenya), and Kahluli (spoken in Papua New Guinea) (Brown, 1973; Mills, 1985; Schieffelin, 1985).

Examination of the factors that influence the difficulty of learning grammatical morphology adds an important dimension to the study of grammatical development, as such examination reveals more general principles of what makes aspects of grammar easy or difficult for children to acquire than could the study of English alone. Two factors seem to influence the ease of learning grammatical morphology. One is characteristics of the child. Given a language that uses both word order and morphology, children will differ in whether their early utterances rely more on word order or morphology, depending, it seems, on what aspects of speech they are inclined to attend to (Clancy, 1985; Peters, 1997). The characteristics of the language also seem to matter. A system that is regular or predictable, such as Turkish, results in fewer errors committed by children learning the system than a system with many exceptions such as Russian (Berman, 1986; Maratsos, 1983, 1998). Within a language, some grammatical morphemes seem easier to acquire than others. Morphemes are easy to acquire when they are frequent and have a recognizable form (i.e., a form that stays the same across linguistic environments, unlike the English plural, which takes on three different forms, /s/, /z/, or /əz/, depending on the context). Other factors that make a morpheme easy to acquire are a fixed position relative to the stem they attach to and a clear function. It also seems to help if the morpheme is easy to segment from the stem and if the rhythm of the language makes the morphemes perceptually salient (Peters, 1998). One factor that clearly does not make a difference is complexity as it is perceived by English-speaking adults. Languages with inflectional systems that both seem impossible to learn and really do cause difficulties for second language learners are not necessarily systems that cause difficulty to children, and although children do produce occasional errors, morphological development is, like syntactic development, relatively error free (Maratsos, 1998).

## The development of different sentence forms

To return to our discussion of the acquisition of English, another syntactic development that typically begins around the time the first grammatical morphemes appear is the development of sentence forms other than the basic affirmative, declarative form. In English, forming negative statements, questions, and passives requires auxiliary verbs. Auxiliaries are among the last grammatical functors children acquire, but children do not wait until they have acquired the adult means of expression to make negative statements or to ask questions. Initially they indicate negation or questioning without auxiliaries. (Typically children use *can't* and *don't* long before they use *can* and *do,* and *can't* and *don't* seem to be used as unanalyzed negative markers, much as *not* is used. Therefore, *can't* and *don't* are not counted as auxiliaries.) As children's syntactic abilities develop, the form of their negative statements and questions changes.

***Expressing negation.*** The earliest linguistic means of expressing negation that children acquiring English use is to tack on a negative marker (typically *no* or *not*) to the beginning or end of the sentence. Some children also mark negation nonlinguistically by shaking their heads as they utter an affirmative

---

**Box 5.5   Children's negative sentence forms, in order of development**

1. *Sentences with external negative marker*
   No . . . wipe finger
   No the sun shining
   No mitten
   Wear mitten no

2. *Constructions with internal negative marker but no auxiliaries*
   I can't see you
   I don't like you
   I no want envelope

3. *Constructions with auxiliaries*
   I didn't did it
   Donna won't let go
   No, it isn't

Source: Examples are from Adam, Eve, and Sarah, as reported in Klima & Bellugi, 1967.

statement. Following these sentence-external means of marking negation, children produce utterances in which the negative marker is inside the sentence (such as "I no want go in there"), but the sentences are still not adultlike because they do not use auxiliaries. Finally, as children acquire auxiliaries, their negative expressions take the adult form. Examples of these different types of linguistic expression of negation are provided in Box 5.5.

***Asking questions.***   English-speaking children's first expression of questions is also affected by the late acquisition of auxiliaries. Describing the development of question forms is a little more complicated than describing the development of negation because there are two types of question forms. **Yes/no questions** can be answered with either "yes" or "no." **Wh- questions** begin with *wh-* words, such as "who," "where," "what," "why," or "when," and also include "how." Children's first yes/no questions are typically marked only by intonation. At this stage, wh- questions are typically affirmative statements with a wh- word at the beginning, such as "What that is?" Next, auxiliaries appear in questions. In yes/no questions, auxiliaries are added to the beginning of the utterance, which suffices to construct a grammatical yes/no question

---

**Box 5.6    Children's question forms, in order of development**

|  | **Yes/no questions** | **Wh- questions** |
|---|---|---|
| 1. *Constructions with external question marker* | Mommy eggnog?<br>I ride train?<br>Sit chair? | Who that?<br>What cowboy doing?<br>Where milk go?<br>What a bandaid is? |
| 2. *Constructions with auxiliaries— but no subject auxiliary inversion in wh- questions* | Does the kitty<br>   stand up?<br>Oh, did I caught it?<br>Will you help me? | Where the other<br>   Joe will drive?<br>What you did say?<br>Why kitty can't<br>   stand up? |
| 3. *Subject-auxiliary inversion in wh- questions* |  | What did you doed?<br>What does whiskey<br>   taste like? |

Source: Examples from Klima & Bellugi, 1967, and personal data.

(such as "Will it fit in there?"). At this stage, however, wh- questions are still not adultlike because children do not invert the subject and auxiliary, instead producing utterances like "What a doctor can do?" Once subject-auxiliary inversion has been acquired, wh- questions are adultlike in form. Box 5.6 lists examples of children's question forms in their typical order of appearance.

***Using passive forms.***    Passives are rare even in speech among adults, but they are useful when the speaker wishes to make the object of the verb prominent, as in *My cat got run over by a bus,* or when the speaker does not wish to specify the agent of the action at all, as in *Mistakes were made.* By the age of 3½ years, children produce passive forms in their spontaneous speech, and the frequency of passives in children's speech continues to grow, even after age 5 (Budwig, 1990). Passives that use the verb *to be* (e.g., *It can be putten on your foot*) are more frequent than *get* passives (e.g., *He got punished*), and these two forms of passives tend to be used to express different sorts of meanings—both by adults and by children from the time they first begin to produce passives. *Get* passives tend to be used to describe something negative that happened to an animate entity—a person or animal (e.g., *The boy got punished*), whereas *be* passives tend to be about inanimate things (e.g., *They [the pieces of paper] have just been cutten off* [personal data]).

---

**Box 5.7    Children's complex sentences, in order of development**

1. *Object complementation*
   Watch me draw circles.
   I see you sit down.
2. *Wh- embedded clauses*
   Can I do it when we get home?
   I show you how to do it.
3. *Coordinating conjunctions*
   He was stuck, and I got him out.
   When I was a little girl I could go "geek-geek" like that, but now
   I can go "this is a chair."
4. *Subordinating conjunctions*
   Here's a set. It must be mine if it's a little one.
   I want this doll because she's big.

---

Source: Examples from Limber, 1973.

***Producing complex sentences.***    After the development of grammatical morphemes and different sentence forms is well under way, the next grammatical development is the appearance of sentences that contain more than one clause. There are many different types of **complex sentences,** and some appear in children's spontaneous speech much earlier than others do. Box 5.7 contains examples of the different types in their approximate order of development. The first complex sentences appear after children are regularly producing four-word utterances (Bowerman, 1976), typically around the age of 2 years. From the age of 2 to 3 years, children add to their repertoire of complex constructions and use them with increasing frequency (Bloom, 1991). Children use most of the different complex sentence types by the age of 4 (Bowerman, 1979; Limber, 1973).

## INDIVIDUAL DIFFERENCES IN GRAMMATICAL DEVELOPMENT

Children differ in both the rate and the course of grammatical development. The differences in rate are the most obvious. Some children produce multiword utterances at age 18 months, whereas others do not start combining words until they are 2 years old. Less obvious than differences in when children start to combine words are differences in the kinds of multiword utterances children produce. Some children's early multiword utterances are rote-learned as wholes; other children's are combinations of separate words from the start.

The different kinds of multiword utterances children produce seem to reflect different approaches to the task of syntax acquisition. These differences in syntactic development may originate in differences in what children attend to and therefore how children perceive the speech they hear. Some children pay attention to syllables and phonemes; others pay more attention to the overall prosodic "tune" (Peters, 1997). The tune approach, which has also been termed **holistic,** or top-down, results in many unanalyzed chunks (Bretherton, McNew, Snyder, & Bates, 1983; Peters, 1986). Children who take this approach can sometimes produce impressively long utterances with little combinatorial ability. For example, a 2-year-old who stores chunks in memory might be able to say "I don't wanna go nightnight" by combining just two units—*Idontwanna* and *gonightnight*. The other approach of breaking down speech into smaller units and then combining them has been termed **analytical,** or bottom-up. Although children eventually must figure out the smallest units and how to combine them, the holistic approach to combinatorial speech is not necessarily a dead end. Some children may "break into structure" (Pine & Lieven, 1993, p. 551) by starting with unanalyzed phrases and then identifying slots in these phrases that can be occupied by different lexical items. At this intermediary stage, a child may have a repertoire of rules that allow very limited productivity, like the following:

Sentence → There's the + $x$

Sentence → Me got + $x$

Sentence → Wanna + $x$

A similar account of children's first word combinations was suggested by Braine (1976), who called such rules limited-scope formulas.

Most children use both the top-down and bottom-up strategies, and most children include both unanalyzed chunks and smaller units in their early sentences. However, children vary in how much they rely on one strategy versus the other, and the route to syntax some children take seems to be extremely holistic or extremely analytic.

## MEASURING GRAMMATICAL DEVELOPMENT

As children gradually master the grammar of their language, they become able to produce increasingly long utterances. This is true not only when length is counted in words but even more so when length is counted in morphemes. For example, a telegraphic sentence such as "I watch it" has a length of three words and three morphemes. A nontelegraphic version of that sentence, "I am watching it," has a length of four words and five morphemes; -ing is a separate morpheme although not a separate word. Because length in morphemes is a good index of the grammatical complexity of an utterance, and because children tend to follow similar courses of development in adding complexity to their utterances, the average length of children's utterances (counted in morphemes) has been widely used as a measure of children's syntactic development.

The relation of **mean length of utterance (MLU)** to age for the three children Adam, Eve, and Sarah is depicted in Figure 5.3. Even among these three children, there were large differences in the age at which each began to show evidence of grammatical development. And because the range of individual variation in the rate of syntactic development is so great, age is not a good indicator of a child's level of grammatical development. Thus, knowing that a child is 18 months old doesn't tell you very much about that child's level of productive language. It would be normal for an 18-month-old to be talking in single-word utterances or in three-word sentences. Describing a child in terms of MLU provides a sharper picture of the child's level of productive language—at least up to an MLU of 3.0 (Rondal, Ghiotto, Bredart, & Bachelet, 1987). However, children with similar MLUs can differ in the nature of their utterances; some children lengthen their utterances primarily by adding content words and others do so by adding bound morphemes (Rollins, Snow, & Willet, 1996). In any case, after MLU exceeds 3.0, its usefulness as a predictor of the complexity of children's utterances declines (Klee & Fitzgerald, 1985).

For children acquiring English, MLU has also been used as the basis for somewhat arbitrarily dividing syntactic development into five stages. We can use this stage terminology to summarize the major developments in the course of children's acquisition of the syntax and morphology of English we have just described. In Stage I (MLU + 1.01 to 1.99), children begin to combine words. In Stage II (MLU = 2.00 to 2.49), children begin to add grammatical morphemes to their word combinations. In Stage III (MLU = 2.50 to 2.99), children begin to use different sentence modalities (negative and question). In Stage IV (MLU = 3.00 and up), children begin to use complex sentences. New forms of complex sentences emerge in Stage V. Miller and Chapman (1981) collected data on 123 largely middle-class children to establish norms for the age at which most children reach each stage. The MLU boundaries and the age at which roughly two-thirds of children are at each stage are presented in Table 5.1.

## THE DEVELOPMENT OF COMPREHENSION OF STRUCTURED SPEECH

Having described grammatical development in terms of what children produce, we now turn to studies of what children understand. The picture of grammatical development that can be constructed from studies of compre-

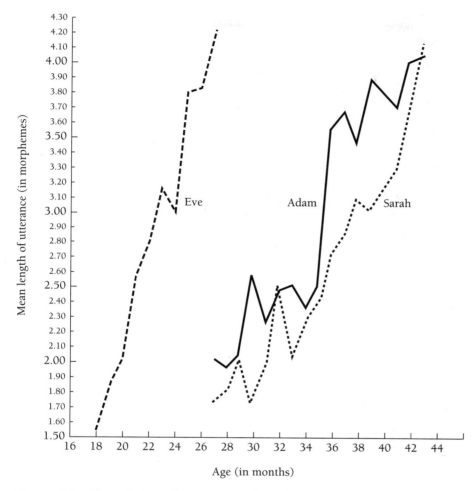

**Figure 5.3**  The relation of MLU to age for Adam, Eve, and Sarah

Source: Reprinted by permission of the publishers from *A First Language: The Early Stages,* by Roger Brown. Cambridge, Mass.: Harvard University Press. Copyright © 1973 by the President and Fellows of Harvard College.

hension is not as continuous as the picture that emerges from studies of production. There is no such thing as a record of spontaneous comprehension that would be the counterpart to the transcripts that are records of children's spontaneous productions. Instead, to find out what aspects of grammatical structure children understand, one must devise a way of testing for comprehension of particular structures. Simply talking to children and seeing whether they respond appropriately is not sufficient because children have a variety of

**Table 5.1   Stages of grammatical development and normative age ranges**

| Stage | MLU | Age range |
|-------|-----|-----------|
| Early I | 1.01–1.49 | 16–26 months |
| Late I | 1.50–1.99 | 18–31 |
| II | 2.00–2.49 | 21–35 |
| III | 2.50–2.99 | 24–41 |
| Early IV | 3.00–3.49 | 28–45 |
| Late IV/Early V | 3.50–3.99 | 31–50 |
| Late V | 4.00–4.49 | 37–52 |
| Post V | 4.5+ | 41— |

Source: From "The Relation between Age and Mean Length of Utterance," by J. F. Miller and R. S. Chapman, 1981, *Journal of Speech and Hearing Research*, 24, 154–161. Copyright © 1981 American Speech-Language-Hearing Association. Reprinted by permission.

ways of responding appropriately, even without truly understanding the structure of what they hear. These strategies for responding are sufficiently successful that if you ask parents of 1-year-olds how much their children understand of the speech that they hear, most parents will answer, "Everything" (Hoff-Ginsberg, 1991). (The next most frequent answer is "too much.") Although it's not the business of child language researchers to delve into the details of what constitutes "too much" language comprehension for some parents, researchers have tackled the question of whether children understand "everything." In the next sections, we will first discuss the strategies children use that sometimes mislead parents and others into thinking children have more competence than they do. Then we will describe the course of grammatical development suggested by controlled studies of comprehension.

## Strategies children use

Children have **response strategies** that enable them to respond to speech they only partially understand. Very young children are particularly likely to respond to speech by doing something (Shatz, 1978a, 1978b). This action strategy allows children to produce appropriate responses to much of what is typically said to them. For example, when a child's mother says, "Why don't you play with your blocks?", the child knows that playing with blocks will probably satisfy her mother; and when her mother asks, "Where are your shoes?", the child knows that getting her shoes is probably what her mother wants her to do. However, the success of this strategy depends on the child's ability to figure out the correct action without fully understanding the sentence.

Occasionally, children's strategies trip them up and reveal their syntactic ignorance, as in the following example provided by Robin Chapman (1978). Chapman's young son was standing in the living room when his father asked, "Do you need a dry diaper?" The little boy felt his diaper, ran to his room, and returned with a clean diaper in hand. At this point, the child appeared to have fully understood his father's question. After the boy was changed, his father said, "There, now you have a dry diaper," and the little boy ran to his room to return with more clean diapers. In doing so, the child revealed that all he really understood of what was spoken to him was the word *diaper* and that he knew just one thing to do with diapers. Chapman (1978) described children at this stage as deriving sentence meaning from knowledge of the world rather than from knowledge of syntactic structure.

To find out what children know about syntactic structure, it is necessary to set up a situation in which knowledge of the world is insufficient to yield a correct response. Even then, children have strategies that they use before they have achieved full understanding. In this case, the strategies are sentence comprehension strategies rather than response strategies. One sentence comprehension strategy is a word-order strategy, which treats whatever is mentioned first in the sentence as the subject and whatever is mentioned second as the object. This strategy allows children to correctly act out "The swing bumps the kitty" and "The kitty bumps the swing." However, this strategy produces incorrect responses to passive sentences, such as "The swing was bumped by the kitty." A similar strategy that children use in interpreting complex sentences with two events is the order-of-mention strategy. This strategy works for interpreting sentences such as "John played before Mary sang," but it yields misinterpretations of sentences such as "John played after Mary sang" or "Before Mary sang, John played." Another strategy children use, even at this later stage, involves recourse to world knowledge. This probable-event strategy allows children to correctly act out sentences like "The mouse was chased by the cat," even though the word order strategy doesn't work here. However, children using this strategy will reverse the sequence of events when presented with nonprobable sentences, such as "I broke my balloon because I cried."

In normal interaction, the strategies children use tend to serve them well, and for that reason children may appear to understand "everything" even when child language researchers can prove that they do not. But if children do not understand everything, they do know more about the grammar of their language than they reveal in their spontaneous productions. We turn now to a description of what children know about the grammar of their language and when they know it, based on studies of children's comprehension.

## Children's comprehension of meaning in sentence structure

***Comprehension of relational meanings in word combinations.*** Children who produce only single-word utterances appear to know something about the meanings that arise from putting words together. Sachs and Truswell (1978) found that children who were all one-word speakers (and between 16 and 24 months old) could correctly respond to unlikely two-word instructions such as "kiss keys" and "tickle book." Hirsh-Pasek and Golinkoff (1991) demonstrated comprehension of the relational meanings in two-word combinations in even younger children. Using the preferential looking paradigm used in the "gorping" experiment described in Chapter 4, Hirsh-Pasek and Golinkoff presented 13- to 15-month-old children with a sentence like "She's kissing the keys." As the children heard this sentence, two videotaped scenes were presented simultaneously on two different screens. On one screen, a woman was kissing keys and holding up a ball; on the other screen, a woman was kissing a ball and holding up keys. Thus, kissing and keys were depicted in both scenes, but kissing keys was depicted in only one scene. These very young children looked longer at the action that matched the sentence than at the nonmatching action. In doing so, these children demonstrated that they knew that words together carry a meaning beyond the meaning of each word individually. Understanding that meaning is carried not just by words but by word combinations is the kernel of understanding grammar. Next the child must learn that particular sorts of combinations yield particular sorts of meaning.

***Comprehension of meaning in the structure of word combinations.*** In English, the order in which words are combined carries meaning, and children learning English show that they are aware of language-typical word-order patterns and that they are sensitive to the meaning carried by word order before they produce word combinations. Using the sort of procedure described in Chapter 3 (in which an infant's preference between two sets of auditory stimuli is measured by how much time the infant does what is needed to get the experimenter to play that tape), Fernald and McRoberts (1995) found that 12- and 14-month-old infants (but not 10-month-old infants) preferred to listen to sentences presented in normal word order over sentences with scrambled word order—even with all prosodic features held constant. Of course, this doesn't mean that the 12-month-olds knew what the sentences meant, but it does mean they knew something about the word-order pattern in their language. When Fernald and McRoberts presented normal and scrambled Spanish sentences, children learning English showed no preference, but children learning Spanish did. Children do show sensitivity to meaning carried by word order by the age of 16 months. Using the preferential looking paradigm, Hirsh-Pasek and

Golinkoff (1991) found that 16- to 18-month-old children, most of whom were one-word speakers, could distinguish between the meanings of contrasting pairs of sentences such as "Where is Cookie Monster washing Big Bird?" and "Where is Big Bird washing Cookie Monster?"

There's more to syntax than word order. Hirsh-Pasek, Golinkoff, and Naigles (1996) found, again using the preferential looking paradigm, that 28-month-old children are sensitive to the difference in meaning among the sentences "Find Cookie Monster and Big Bird turning" (both creatures are turning), "Look, Cookie Monster is turning Big Bird" (only Big Bird is turning), and "Cookie Monster is turning with Big Bird" (they're both turning). All these sentences had Cookie Monster, Big Bird, and turning in them, but who is turning and whether he is turning independently or as a result of somebody else's action is signaled entirely by sentence structure. By the age of 28 months, when most children are still saying things like "I watching cars," children are sensitive to these structurally carried distinctions in meaning.

Children also seem to know that grammatical morphemes do something in a sentence before they are actually producing grammatical morphemes in their own sentences. Shipley, Smith, and Gleitman (1969) found that children who were telegraphic speakers were more likely to respond to a well-formed command, such as "Throw me the ball," than to a command that matched their own productive speech, such as "Throw ball." Of course, children in this case might know only that the telegraphic utterance isn't quite right, rather than understanding any information carried by the omitted morphemes.

There is also evidence that children actually derive information from the function morphemes that they hear before they have control over the use of these morphemes in production. Gerken and McIntosh (1993) found that children with MLUs greater than 1.5 were better able to find the correct picture when told "Find the dog for me" than when they were given an ungrammatical sentence in which the wrong function morpheme was used, such as "Find was dog for me." Other findings presented in Chapter 4—that children use the presence of a determiner to decide if a new word is a common noun (*the zav*) or a proper noun (*Zav*) (Gelman & Taylor, 1984; Katz et al., 1974)—also indicate sensitivity to the meaning these grammatical forms carry.

Up to this point, we have described a course of grammatical development in which children show that by 12 months of age they have learned what word combinations in their language sound like (we say "learned" because the preference for normal word combinations is language specific and not in evidence at 10 months). By 13 to 15 months they know that words together mean something more than the meaning of both words individually, and by 16 to 18 months they know the meaning carried by the basic word order pattern of the language. By the time they reach an MLU of 1.5, they know something about grammatical morphemes, and by 28 months, they are sensitive to distinctions among more-complicated sentence structures (see Hirsh-Pasek &

Golinkoff, 1996, for a summary of much of this work). Two basic conclusions can be drawn from this account. First, the sequence of grammatical development that occurs in comprehension is like the sequence seen in production, but it occurs earlier. (The duration of the lag between achievement in comprehension and evidence in production is different for different children. Thus, an individual child's comprehension skills are not a very good predictor of that child's level of productive grammar [Bates et al., 1988].) Second, grammatical competence is achieved very early. This latter fact places constraints on the kind of account of grammatical development that is plausible. However grammar is acquired, it is a process that is accomplished quickly and by very young children.

In addition to showing that children have grammatical knowledge earlier than they display it in production, comprehension studies offer the possibility of finding out things that children know about grammar that you would never see in production. At this point in our description of children's grammatical development, we are going to jump ahead to consider older children and more complex structures. Having established that children know the basics of grammar when they are still babies or toddlers, we now turn to evidence that children know a great deal more than the basics while they are still preschoolers.

### Successful comprehension of complex sentences by preschoolers.
Imagine that you were told the following story:

> Once there was a boy who loved climbing trees in the forest. One afternoon he slipped and fell to the ground. He picked himself up and went home. That night when he had a bath, he saw a big bruise on his arm. He said to his Dad, "I must have hurt myself when I fell this afternoon." (de Villiers, 1995a, p. 23)

After hearing this story, suppose you are asked, "When did the boy say he fell?" There are two possible answers to this question—"in the afternoon" or "at night"—because there are two possible interpretations of what *when* is asking about—the "saying" or the "falling." On the other hand, if you are asked, "When did the boy say how he fell?" then the only possible answer is "at night" because the only possible interpretation of what when is asking about is the "saying." When Jill de Villiers and Thomas Roeper (1995) presented 3- to 6-year-old children with stories and sentences like these, they found that even 3-year-olds knew that there were two possible interpretations of the first question and that the word *how* in the second question form made only one interpretation possible. Children's performance in response to questions like these makes it clear that they know subtle aspects of complex syntax at a very young age (de Villiers, 1995a).

***Difficulties understanding co-reference relations in complex sentences in older children.*** The previous section described very sophisticated linguistic competence in fairly young children and is consistent with the frequently expressed view that the acquisition of grammar is essentially complete by age 4. On the other hand, some constructions cause difficulty even for older children. For example, given the sentence "John is easy to see," children have difficulty figuring out who is easy to see and who does the seeing. Given the sentence "John promised Bill to go," children have difficulty figuring out who does the going and what John told Bill he would do. Given the sentence "The zebra touched the deer after jumping the fence," children have difficulty figuring out who did the jumping—the zebra or the deer. All the interpretive difficulties in these sentences concern whom or what is being referred to. In linguistic terminology, the problem is in interpreting the co-reference relations in these sentences.

Carol Chomsky (1969) studied comprehension of these sentence forms in children aged 5 to 10 years, and on the basis of her data she countered the then-prevailing view that language acquisition was complete by the age of 5. She found that most 5-year-old children have difficulty with such sentences and that some children do not fully master them until 9 years of age. She argued that 5-year-old children have not acquired all the structural principles of the grammar and that they rely, as younger children do, on strategies that look to meaning, context, or surface properties of the sentence for clues to sentence interpretation. For example, Chomsky found that children often interpret the noun phrase that is closest to the verb as the subject of that verb. This often works, but not for sentences like "John promised Bill to go," in which it is John, not Bill, who will do the going.

This conclusion is where the matter rested for many years after Carol Chomsky's work. Syntax development after age 5 years received very little research attention until the 1980s, when the theory of Universal Grammar proposed by Noam Chomsky (Carol Chomsky's husband) made the source of difficulty in the preceding sentences central to linguistic theory and to the Universal Grammar (UG) approach to language acquisition. Remember, according to the Universal Grammar approach, UG is innate in all children. Furthermore, according to current UG theory (which is the Government and Binding [GB] theory first proposed by Noam Chomsky, 1981), a component of UG handles co-reference relations. Thus, there is a seeming contradiction: UG is innate and UG handles the interpretation of co-reference relations, yet children (who are held to have UG in their heads) have difficulty interpreting co-reference relations.

Presently two competing sorts of explanations are offered for children's non-adultlike performance with such sentences. One is essentially similar to the account Carol Chomsky proposed in 1969. It holds that children do not have the adult system, and they interpret sentences using strategies that depend on the meaning or pragmatics of surface features of the sentences, rather than on purely linguistic principles (e.g., Goodluck, 1991; Hsu, Cairns, & Fiengo, 1985). The other argues that children have full adult knowledge but cannot display it because of performance limitations (e.g., Grimshaw & Rosen, 1990; Sherman & Lust, 1993). The two positions are importantly different and apply much more broadly than to the interpretation of co-reference relations. The first position asserts that developmental change in children's underlying grammars occurs; children's initial systems are not the same as adults' grammatical systems. The second asserts that the underlying system stays the same, even though performance does change. We will return to this issue later when we consider the continuity or discontinuity of development.

## Sometimes production precedes comprehension

Before we leave the topic of children's comprehension of grammatical structure, we need to point out exceptions to the general pattern in which competence in comprehension precedes competence in production. Sometimes children are unable to show that they understand the grammatical structures they produce in their own spontaneous speech. One reason for this inability may be difficulties in demonstrating comprehension in the way a particular testing situation requires. It is also possible for children to use structures correctly in a limited way without necessarily knowing everything about those structures. For example, young children can correctly use if–then statements describing contingent relations they are familiar with (such as, "If I'm a good girl and eat my beets, then I can have ice cream"), but these children could not understand the logical implications of all if–then statements that might be presented to them (such as, "If Socrates is a man and all men are mortal, then Socrates is mortal"). Also, it has been argued that children can demonstrate competence in the supportive context of describing familiar events that they cannot demonstrate in experimental settings (French, Lucariello, Seidman, & Nelson, 1985) and that sentences presented in isolation may be more difficult to understand than sentences presented in context (de Villiers & Roeper, 1995).

## WHAT IS THE NATURE OF CHILDREN'S GRAMMARS?

So far in this chapter, we have simply described the different kinds of sentences children become able to produce and understand as they acquire the syntax and morphology of their language. We now need to back up and consider what children know about the underlying grammar at different points in the course of development. As we have seen, some of children's first multiword utterances appear to be partially or entirely memorized routines. We would not want to credit children at that early point with any understanding of grammar. However, this rote basis for producing multiword utterances doesn't last very long, and it doesn't account for very much of what young children say. When children can produce a variety of word combinations (such as those in Boxes 5.1 and 5.2), and when they regularly add grammatical morphemes to indicate plurals and past tense, children have some productive system underlying the syntax and morphology of their speech. By most accounts, the form of this underlying knowledge is a system of rules.

## Evidence that children know grammatical rules

Three kinds of evidence support the contention that children know rules: (1) regular patterns found in children's word combinations, (2) errors children make that seem to reflect overapplication of rules, and (3) children's performance in experiments that shows they know how to use words they have never heard before in grammatical constructions. We will review each of these types of evidence in turn.

***Patterns in early word combinations.*** There is order or systematicity in the way children put words together; their word combinations are not "word salad." For example, in the two-word combinations in Box 5.1, possessive relations are consistently expressed in the form of "possessor + possessed object" ("my teddy"), and actor/action combinations are consistently "actor + action" ("Daddy sit"). When psychologists and linguists find order in behavior, they tend to describe that behavior as rule-governed. We account for the consistent word-order patterns across a variety of newly produced utterances in adult speech by attributing a productive rule to adults; similarly, the child's production of many different utterances that all have consistent word order seems to require a rule-based explanation.

***Overregularization errors.*** Another piece of evidence that children know rules is the fact that children make errors in spontaneous speech that seem to be overapplications of rules. For example, one 4-year-old consistently said "amn't I," as in "I'm a good boy, amn't I?" (personal data). This is not something that he heard, but it is a sensible overapplication of the rule that forms a tag question by inverting the subject and the form of the verb *to be*. In American English, we say "You're good, aren't you?" and "He's good, isn't he?" but "I'm good, amn't I?" is an exception to the rule. The 4-year-old who said "amn't I" had learned the rule but not the exception.

In the domain of morphology, applying a rule to a word that is an exception in the language results in the production of plural forms such as *footses* or *toothes* or past-tense forms such as *goed* or *breaked*. These errors are called **overregularizations** because the child has made an irregular part of the language regular. One aspect of these overregularization errors that has received considerable attention is the fact that children will produce them after they have already been heard to say the correct irregular form, such as *went* or *broke*. So, in this case, it can't be that the children do not yet know the exceptions to the rule; they know the exception but apply the rule anyway.

Exactly why children overregularize when they already know the irregular form is a matter of debate. It has been argued that the same analytical tendency and search for patterns that allows children to learn the rule results in the rule's overriding the rote-learned exceptions. Some children overregularize more than others, perhaps because they have a particular affinity for regular systems (Maratsos, 1993). However, overregularizations are always fewer than children's correct uses of the irregular forms, and overregularization errors are infrequent for most children. Analyzing 11,521 irregular past-tense verb forms in the speech of 83 children, Marcus and associates (1992) found a 2.5 percent median rate of overregularization errors. In a similar analysis of plural noun forms, Marcus (1995) found an 8.3 percent median overregularization rate. Marcus and colleagues suggested that in talking, children sometimes fail to retrieve the irregular form from memory. (According to this account, the retrieval failure rates must be 2.5 percent for verbs and 8.3 percent for nouns.) When retrieval of the irregular past-tense form fails, the regular rule for past-tense formation applies as a sort of default. Adults make overregularization errors too, they claim, although less frequently than children because adults have fewer retrieval failures.

***Experimental tests of rule knowledge.***     The final sort of evidence that children have rules is their ability to use novel forms. In the domain of syntax, children who are taught a novel verb in one sentence structure show that they know how to use that verb productively in other sentence structures. For example, 4-year-old children who are told "The pig is pilking the horse" can later say, "The horse is being pilked by the pig" (Pinker, Lebeaux, & Frost, 1987). Similarly, children who hear "I'm mooping a ball to the mouse" can then say, "I'm mooping the mouse a ball" (Gropen, Pinker, Hollander, & Goldberg, 1991). (Just when this productivity develops is a matter of debate. Some findings indicate that 2-year-olds are not willing to use verbs in new sentence structures (Tomasello, 2000); other findings suggest there is some productivity in verb use from the very first instances of verb use (Naigles & Hoff, in press).

In the domain of morphology, the classic demonstration of children's productive knowledge is Berko's "wug test," which was also mentioned in Chapter 3. Berko (1958) tested children's knowledge of inflectional rules by giving children nonsense words and asking them to supply the inflected forms (the forms with the grammatical inflections added). Berko found that children as young as 4 years old knew that the plural of *wug* must be *wugs* and that the past tense of *blick* must be *blicked,* thus demonstrating that "their linguistic knowledge went beyond the individual words in their vocabularies, and that they had rules of extension that enabled them to inflect the nonsense words" (Gleason, 1992, p. 10).

As was mentioned in Chapter 1, some argue for another explanation of the regularities in children's speech, including the foregoing evidence cited in support of the contention that children know rules. According to the connectionist view, the knowledge that underlies the regularities in children's productions—including their novel productions—is not knowledge of rules but is the stored memory of the regularities previously experienced in input. Those who hold the view that language is the outcome of rules fiercely debate those who hold the view that language is the outcome of associative memory. However, that is not the only debate. Those who assume that children know rules disagree on the nature of those rules.

## Questions about the nature of early grammatical rules

***Is early grammar semantically based?*** It has been suggested that 2-year-olds have a **semantically-based grammar,** in contrast to the **syntactically-based grammar** of 4-year-olds and adults. To explain this position, it is necessary to review an important claim about adult grammars that was made in the first section of this chapter. That claim states that the rules adults have are rules for combining grammatical categories like Noun and Verb. Nouns and verbs are defined in terms of how they function in a sentence. A noun is anything that fills the Noun slot in a sentence. A noun can be a person, place, or thing, as you may have learned in elementary school, but it does not have to be. The first nouns in the following sentences include a person, an action, an internal state, and an attribute:

Melissa is the class president.

Swimming is good exercise.

Hunger is a common problem in many parts of the world.

Blue is my favorite color.

What makes *Melissa, swimming, hunger,* and *blue* all nouns is the fact that they fill the same slot.

In children's sentences, however, the variety of meanings in words that fill the first Noun slot is clearly less than the variety of meanings adults express. For this reason, some have proposed that the rules underlying children's early word combinations operate over semantic categories (Bowerman, 1973). This position is essentially what Brown (1973) said about the system underlying children's first word combinations. The categories that are combined are semantic categories such as agent, action, and location, not Noun and Verb. Radford (1990, 1995) has made a similar suggestion, arguing that children's early sentences are purely combinations of lexical categories in thematic (meaning-based) structures.

***Are early rules lexically based?***   Another proposal for how children could combine words without syntactic categories argues that the rules are lexically based, or specific to individual words. Some of the limited-scope formulae (to use Braine's [1976] term) or partially analyzed phrases (to use Pine & Lieven's [1993] term) may be examples of rules that are only partially productive because they are anchored by specific lexical items. Tomasello (1992b) has made an even stronger claim, arguing that all of children's multiword utterances might initially be generated by lexically based rules. Referring to the diary record of one child's first word combinations, he claimed that all the multi-word utterances this child produced (at this early stage) involved words that would be categorized as verbs in the adult system; however, there was little consistency across different verbs in the kinds of structures the verbs appeared in. Rather, each verb appeared in different structures. Tomasello (1992b) argued that at the age of 2 years, children do not have the category Verb at all. Instead, 2-year-olds have a vocabulary of particular verbs, each associated with its own possible structures.

In support of this contention, Theakston, Lieven, Pine and Rowland (2001) found in a sample of nine 2-year-olds that the children tended to use particular verbs in particular frames, not in the full range of allowable frames. Another sort of evidence for this argument is the results of an experiment in which 2-year-olds were exposed to novel (nonsense) verbs (Olguin & Tomasello, 1993). In the course of play, an experimenter would say things to the children, such as "Oh look, gaffing!" and "See that? Ernie's chamming!" Later, the children used these newly learned verbs in their spontaneous speech but not productively with structures or even tense markings that had not been modeled. Bloom (1991) made a similar argument with respect to the knowledge that underlies young children's verb morphology. She argued that when children first begin to add inflectional endings to verbs, children know only that certain words can take different forms (such as *fit/fits, play/playing*), not that inflections apply to all members of a syntactic category.

Recently, Tomasello (2003) has argued that even these limited, lexically based rules may not be the right way to characterize children's linguistic knowledge. He claims that the production of an utterance is not a process of putting together words and morphemes, following the rules of the grammar. Rather, producing utterances is a matter of "cutting and pasting" larger chunks that are heard and remembered from earlier conversations. Adults' linguistic knowledge, Tomasello (2003) argues, also consists of chunks of previously heard patterns of usage, although these chunks (or constructions) may include variables or slots that can be filled by a number of items. For example, *Where's X?* is a construction, and X can be replaced by any noun.

The same researchers who have argued that 2-year-olds do not have an abstract Verb category or rules that operate at that abstract a level have suggested that children at this age do have a Noun category. For example, Bloom, Lightbown, and Hood (1975) argued that the initial nouns in children's utterances do include some variety in expressed meanings. They observed that children produce sentences including the following:

Lois watch Gia

The bag go

Kathryn jump

Bloom and associates argued that, in these sentences, the first Noun slot is assigned the following different semantic roles: noticer (Lois), object (the bag), and actor (Kathryn). Valian (1986), who also used children's spontaneous speech as the database, argued that 2-year-old children show evidence of the major syntactic categories (Valian didn't look at verbs in this study) because children use words from these categories in a range of appropriate syntactic structures. Experimentally, Tomasello and colleagues have found that children use newly learned nonsense nouns in structures and with inflectional morphology that had not been modeled in their learning experiences, but children tend to stick to uses they have heard with respect to new verbs.

In sum, the foregoing data suggest that 2-year-old children have the syntactic category Noun and use it productively, but the data are less clear about the status of the category Verb in children's grammars. It is clear that children initially use verbs in a narrower range of syntactic environments than the language allows, but there are alternative explanations besides the one that children do not have the category Verb. Perhaps children produce less than they know because the demands of formulating complex utterances are too great (Valian, 1991). Or perhaps children don't know the full meaning of the verbs they use. As we discussed in Chapter 4 on lexical development, the meanings of verbs are less accessible than the meanings of nouns. Also, in order to know the full range of possible uses of a verb, it is necessary to fully know what the verb means; this is less true for nouns. For example, if you hear the sentence "He blicked," you cannot know if the sentence "He blicked Sally" is grammatical unless you know whether blicking is the sort of thing one person can do to another. (That's why *"He laughed Sally" is ungrammatical.) The issue of what sort of categories children have underlying their early word combinations is important because it has implications for two major issues in explaining the acquisition of the adult grammar: one is the issue of what is innate, the other is the issue of continuity. We turn to a fuller discussion of these issues in the following section.

## ISSUES IN EXPLAINING THE ACQUISITION OF GRAMMAR

The previous sections described the developmental changes in the structures that children produce and understand and considered proposals for developmental changes in children's underlying grammatical knowledge. We now turn to the question of what kind of process could produce these developmental changes. In addressing this question, we return to some of the major issues in the field that were outlined in Chapter 1.

## Nature or nurture?

It is obvious that children have some quality of mind that explains why they learn to talk but kittens, for example, do not (Pinker, 1984). It is not obvious what that quality is. One possibility is the fact that children are much smarter than kittens. In that case, somehow general cognitive processes must be sufficient to account for language acquisition, and there are several proposals to this effect. An alternative possibility holds that children acquire grammar but kittens do not because the acquisition of grammar is preprogrammed in the human genetic blueprint but not in the cat's. There are proposals that significant aspects of grammatical knowledge are innate, the motivation for which is largely the view that there is no way to explain the acquisition of grammar otherwise. We will not resolve the debate over the innateness of grammar here, but we will review some of the evidence that has been marshaled on both sides of the argument.

***Is innate grammar possible?***    To many people the idea that grammar is innate is preposterous. First, babies don't talk, and second, how can something as specific as a grammatical rule be specified genetically? Also, many people believe that to say some aspect of language is innate is effectively to give up trying to explain it. However, many human characteristics are innate, even extremely specific ones that are not present at birth. Take the example of motor development. At birth, babies cannot do very much physically. However, with maturation, babies go through a sequence of stages from rolling over, to sitting up, to crawling, to standing, and to walking. Furthermore, fairly specific human behaviors, such as smiling when one is happy, appear to have a genetic basis. Although we speak colloquially of babies' "learning" to walk, this development is not learning in the usual sense of the word. Both the development of smiling and the development of walking are the result of maturation.

Some have argued that "learning" to talk has much in common with "learning" to walk. Babies do not talk at birth, but they go through a sequence of stages in the production of prespeech sounds, words, and then word combinations. This reliable sequence of development cannot be attributed to any schedule of instruction the environment provides, and therefore it must reflect some underlying maturational process at work (Gleitman, 1981). No one knows exactly what a biological explanation of grammar would look like, but that shouldn't exclude innateness as a possibility.

***Is innate grammar necessary?***   Most of the arguments for grammar's innate basis are not arguments based on evidence for such a genetic basis. Rather, the argument holds that general learning mechanisms are too weak to accomplish the acquisition of grammar and that regardless of the learning mechanism, the speech that children hear is inadequate to support the acquisition of grammar. Thus, grammar must be innate because there is no way to learn it. The argument that input is inadequate was made first by Noam Chomsky and is known as the poverty of the stimulus argument. The stimulus is the speech that children hear, and its poverty is its inability to support the acquisition of grammar. There are two aspects to the poverty of the stimulus argument. One is the assertion that it is impossible in principle for children to figure out the generative system underlying language just from hearing examples of sentences. The other is Chomsky's claim that the speech children hear is full of errors, false starts, slips of the tongue, and so on, giving children a very bad database from which to work.

These claims that support the contention that grammar must be innate have been countered, although the adequacy of the counterarguments is disputed. The assertion that cognitive mechanisms are inadequate has been countered (1) with proposals of how general cognitive mechanisms could achieve aspects of grammatical knowledge and (2) with evidence that general cognition does contribute to grammatical development. The assertion that the input is inadequate has been countered with evidence that the speech children hear is not so impoverished as Chomsky had supposed and that it does play a significant role in grammatical development.

## Can general cognitive processes account for grammatical development?

***The connectionist approach.***   The **connectionist view** argues that language development is the result of "the interaction between general learning mechanisms and a richly structured environment" (Plunkett & Schafer, 1999, p. 51). In this assertion, connectionism directly counters both the claimed inadequacy of the learning mechanism and the poverty of the stimulus assertion that are the foundations of Chomskyan nativism. Connectionist models also reject the view that morphosyntactic knowledge is knowledge of a system of rules that operate over abstract categories. The primary method of empirical testing for a connectionist model is to implement it as a computer program, feed data to the program, and see whether the program can, after grinding away at the data for a while, produce some language-like function that it could not produce initially. Many such efforts have shown that connectionist models can accomplish many language-learning tasks (Elman, 2001). However, the tasks that these programs accomplish are little pieces of the entire language acquisition task. It is not clear that the gap between what these computational models do and what children do is bridgeable with the same sort of learning mechanism, or whether what children ultimately accomplish can be accounted for with rules and abstract categories.

Other issues that arise in considering the implications of connectionist simulations concern how similar to the data that children actually get are the data fed to the computational model and how much "knowledge" is built into the model at the start. In principle, there could be a connectionist model that is a computer-based program of a learning mechanism that starts out with a great deal of preprogrammed knowledge about language that is represented as rules that operate over variables (linguistic categories such and Noun and Verb are variables, because in actual sentences they can be replaced by many different instances of the category). In such a case, the connectionist model is different only in form, but not in substance, from nativist, domain-specific models of a language acquisition device. For that reason, the implications of particular connectionist simulations depend on how the program actually works. Put another way, there is no such thing as evaluating connectionism against the symbolic, language-specific, and nativist approach it seeks to replace. Rather, individual connectionist implementations must be evaluated one by one. As was also discussed in Chapter 1, the real contest is between the symbolic approach and "eliminativist connectionist" models that operate without any internal devices that function as symbols (see Fodor & Pylyshn, 1988; Marcus, 1998).

***Evidence of children's learning capacities.***        Because one of the foundations of Chomskyan nativism is the assertion that the child's learning mechanisms are inadequate to the task of language acquisition, evidence that children are powerful learners is taken by some as evidence against Chomskyan nativism. Thus, one line of research that suggests that general learning mechanisms make a substantial, if not fully explanatory, contribution to language acquisition is the research on infant learning introduced in Chapter 1. If babies as young as 7 months can learn the distributional regularities in their input (Saffran, Aslin, & Newport, 1996) and even to generalize from those regularities to new instances (Marcus, Vijayan, Bandi Rao, & Vishton, 1999), they might be able to use those mechanisms to acquire the grammar of their language. In fact, 1-year-olds have demonstrated the ability to distinguish sound sequences that differ only in whether they are consistent with the abstract, underlying grammar that generated previously presented sound sequences. In other words, 1-year-olds can learn a miniature grammar (Gomez & Gerken, 1999). In some cases, these learning capacities have been shown also to apply to nonlinguistic stimuli (Aslin, Saffran, & Newport, 1999). In other cases, it is not clear whether these learning abilities are general or domain specific. It is fair to say, however, that the recent evidence of infants' abilities to extract patterns from the sounds they hear has seriously challenged the Chomskyan assertion that language must be innate because it could not be learned.

Another line of work suggests that learning from input—even imperfect input—might help a child achieve grammar. Usually children hear the language they will acquire from native and expert speakers of that language. For some deaf children, however, the circumstance of language exposure is different. Singleton and Newport (1987) studied the sign language acquisition of a child whose only exposure to sign was the signing of his parents. His parents were deaf, but they had both learned sign after the age of 15. Experimental tests of their ASL competence revealed they had a very imperfect mastery of verb morphology, and thus they could provide their child with only an errorful sample of verb morphology. Nonetheless, this child surpassed his parents in terms of his ability to use verb morphology and scored, on experimental tests, on par with children exposed to the signing of native users. Singleton and Newport suggest that the child was able to do this by finding and storing the regularities that did exist in his parents' signing and essentially ignoring the data that didn't fit the pattern. It appears from this result and others (Newport & Aslin, 2000) that children have available to them learning mechanisms that are very good at extracting patterns from input, thus lessening the dependence of the language acquisition process on either data that perfectly reveal the systematicity of language or innate knowledge that obviates the need for finding the systematicity in input.

**The relation between cognitive development and grammatical development.** Another approach to making the case that general cognitive processes contribute to grammatical development is to look for aspects of development outside the domain of grammar that are correlated with grammatical development. If the pace of grammatical development appears to be linked with the pace of other developments, then a common underlying mechanism may exist. Any mechanism common both to grammar and to something else must be somewhat general. A large body of research, much of it produced by Elizabeth Bates and her colleagues, takes this approach and draws the conclusion that general cognitive processes are at work as children learn the grammar of their language.

For example, Bates, Bretherton, and Snyder (1988) followed 27 children from the age of 10 months to 28 months, collecting data on several aspects of the children's language production and comprehension along the way. They then analyzed these data to see which aspects of development were related and which were not. They found that measures of the children's lexical development at ages 13 months and 20 months were strongly related to measures of their grammatical development at 2 years. Bates and colleagues argued on this basis that a common cognitive process underlies both.

Some researchers have also attempted to find relations between grammatical development and completely nonlinguistic aspects of cognitive development. Shore, O'Connell, and Bates (1984) investigated the relationship between children's ability to combine words in sentences and their ability to combine elements in symbolic play. They found that 20-month-olds who produced longer play sequences (such as pretend to pour a drink, then pretend to drink it, then pretend to wipe your mouth as opposed to pretend to pour a drink and then move on to a new activity) also produced longer utterances. This research approach starts with the statistical evidence that some common process or processes exist and then tries to infer what those processes might be. However, although statistical analysis can tell you that things are related, it does not clearly tell you why. (For a discussion of some hypothesized processes see Bates et al., 1988.)

***Models of language induction.*** The case for general cognition as the mechanism of grammatical development has also been explicit in several hypotheses about how particular aspects of language are acquired. For example, Braine (1992) and Maratsos and Chalkley (1980) proposed models to explain how children could learn grammatical categories. According to Braine (1992), children start out with categories, such as actor and action, that have their basis in general cognition. Then, as children hear sentences with other words filling the actor slot, children broaden that category until it includes anything with the same privileges of occurrence as actors. At that point, the category is a formal grammatical category.

In Maratsos and Chalkley's (1980) account, the primary basis on which children construct grammatical categories is not the meanings of words but their distributional properties—that is, where in sentences they appear and with what other elements they combine. For example, children figure out that the words that take *s* in the third person singular also take *ed* to indicate past tense and take *ing* to indicate present progressive. This correlation would be the basis for inferring the category Verb from properties of the speech children hear. More generally, Maratsos (1998) has argued that the acquisition of grammar is a "data sifting-induction process" in which the child stores input heard in many different situations and sifts through that database to find the patterns that hold up over all the data. For example, when a child exposed to English hears a verb with *ed* affixed just once, the verb could signal a number of possibilities. (This is essentially like the mapping problem described in the discussion of lexical acquisition.) Across all the utterances heard, however, the only thing that should reliably occur with *ed* is that the action occurred in the past. Similarly, a child exposed to Turkish and hearing *u* at the end of some nouns would need to sift through a great deal of data in order to discover the only thing that is reliably true when a noun ends in –*u,* that the noun is the recipient of the action of the verb. (English signals this with word order.)

Another, not incompatible, view holds that the correlation between prosody and syntax helps children learn syntax (Morgan, 1986; Morgan & Demuth, 1996). For example, speakers pause at phrase boundaries, thus providing a clue to language structure. Such prosodic bootstrapping might be particularly helped by the exaggerated prosody of child-directed language.

## The role of language experience

***The nature of the speech children hear.***   Long before connectionist proposals gave new theoretical significance to the study of input, child language researchers were studying mothers' speech to their children and challenging the Chomskyan claim that the language children hear is errorful. It turns out that when adults talk to children, their speech has very few grammatical errors (Newport, Gleitman, & Gleitman, 1977). Speech to children has other characteristics that might make it a good database from which to figure out a language's grammar. Conversation with children tends to be about the here-and-now, so it is easier to understand what is being said from the extralinguistic context than it would be in most adult-to-adult conversations. Also, adults talking to children use gestures to secure children's attention, so the speech children hear is likely to be about the things the child is focusing on (Zukow, 1990).

Speech to children also has properties that may be more directly related to children's acquisition of language structure. Speech to children is very repetitious. Caregivers say things like, "Put the doll in her crib. Yes, the doll. That's right, in her crib." They also repeat and expand children's utterances:

Child: Milk.
Adult: You want some milk?

These repetitions and expansions of children's incomplete utterances might serve as little language lessons, revealing the component structures that make up sentences. Also, prosodic features of speech, which tend to be exaggerated in speech to children, may provide cues to syntactic structure. For example, pauses and changes in intonation tend to occur at phrase boundaries ("Little Red Riding Hood *pause* lived with her mother *pause* at the edge of the woods"). Also, open-class words tend to receive stress, and closed-class words tend to be unstressed, providing cues to that grammatical distinction. Additionally, nouns and verbs have phonological differences: Nouns tend to have first syllable stress, and verbs have second syllable stress (for example, compare the noun and verb versions of the word *record*) (Kelly, 1996). The hypothesis that children use these phonological cues to break into grammatical structure is known as the **phonological bootstrapping hypothesis.** Often, because prosodic cues seem particularly important, it is known as the **prosodic bootstrapping hypothesis.** (See Morgan & Demuth, 1996, for a full discussion of this hypothesis.)

The other side of the argument points out that some of these hypothesized cues to language structure are unreliable (Fernald & McRoberts, 1996; Pinker, 1984). For example, when the subject of a sentence is a pronoun, pauses don't separate the subject from the rest of the sentence but occur elsewhere ("She went *pause* to Grandmother's house"). Furthermore, these hypothesized little language lessons do not cover everything children need to know about their language's grammar. Even if children do use the properties of the speech they hear to learn the basic structural components of their language, where do they find the information that tells them that "When did the little boy say he hurt his arm?" has two interpretations but "When did the little boy say how he hurt his arm?" has only one (de Villiers, 1995b)? Last, a frequently made argument against attributing much importance to the role of input in grammatical development is the observation that in many cultures of the world people simply do not talk to prelinguistic children, yet these children acquire language too.

This last objection may not be as damning as it first appears. Lieven (1994) suggested a way to reconcile the fact that some children acquire language without being spoken to by adults with the hypothesis that adults' child-directed speech significantly contributes to grammatical development. One part of the solution is to point out that siblings and older children may talk to young children, although a variety of evidence suggests that the child-directed speech of older children does not have all the potentially supportive properties of adults' child-directed speech (Barton & Tomasello, 1994; Hoff-Ginsberg & Krueger, 1991). Another part of the solution is to suggest that children who learn language from the speech they overhear are more likely to learn grammar through rote-learning large chunks and then later analyzing their internal structure (Lieven, 1994). Finally, Lieven proposes that in cultures where children are not directly talked to, children may learn to talk more slowly as a result. If children who are not directly addressed by adults acquire grammar in a different way or less rapidly than do children who are directly addressed, then the fact that they do acquire language does not mean that input plays no role when it is available. To the contrary, if differences in grammatical development are associated with differences in input, input may be playing a role.

***The relation between the speech children hear and grammatical development.*** Even within cultures where children are talked to, children's language-learning experiences vary. One approach to investigating the role of language experience is to look for relations between variability in experience and variability in grammatical development. Such research has yielded evidence that the input children receive contributes significantly to their acquisition of grammar. Although the effect of the amount of input on grammatical development is less than that on vocabulary development (Hoff-Ginsberg, 1998), there does seem to be some effect. Children who attend day care centers that provide more one-to-one contact with an adult develop language more rapidly than children who attend day care centers with less one-to-one adult contact (McCartney, 1984; NICHD Child Care Network, 2000). Other evidence indicates that firstborn children begin to combine words at a slightly younger age than do later-born children (Hoff-Ginsberg, 1998). In both cases,

**Figure 5.4** Social interaction with others provides the context for language learning, but the types of social interaction that children experience vary from culture to culture. One important question for child language researchers concerns how children make use of their varying experiences in accomplishing the feat of language acquisition.

differences in the amount of adult speech addressed to the children is a likely explanation for the observed differences in language development. Lastly, in an experiment in which children were given extra experience hearing and repeating wh- questions, Valian and Lyman (2003) found that more such experience resulted in better performance in accurately imitating such questions. (Children tend to be very bad at imitating grammatical structures outside their competence.) Valian and Lyman argued that more exposure to a structure provides the child more opportunities to attend to and analyze the structure. Analysis of structure, they argue, is the basis of grammatical development.

Particular properties of the speech children hear also seem to be related to grammatical development (Hoff-Ginsberg, 1999; Hoff-Ginsberg & Shatz, 1982; Richards, 1994). For example, studies of mother–child conversation and its relation to child language development have shown that both the frequency with which mothers produce partially repetitious sequences (like "Put the doll in the crib. That's right, the doll") and the frequency with which mothers expand or slightly change their children's prior utterance are associated with more rapid grammatical development (Hoff-Ginsberg, 1985, 1986; Nelson, Denninger, Bonvillian, Kaplan, & Baker, 1984; Newport et al., 1977). Consistent with Valian and Lyman's (2003) argument, these sorts of utterance pairs may prompt particularly useful structural analysis on the part of the child.

Although there is good evidence that children use the speech that they hear in figuring out the grammar of their language, there are also limits to what can be explained on that basis. The differences in the rate of language acquisition associated with differences in experience are small. Furthermore, the same studies that find that some aspects of grammatical development are related to input also find that many aspects of grammatical development are unrelated to input (Gleitman, Newport, & Gleitman, 1984; Newport et al., 1977). In addition, experience might often mislead children. Language is full of situations in which an active problem solver, trying to figure out the rules of grammar from the patterns in the sentences heard, would come up with overly general rules. For example, imagine you heard the following sentences:

John gave Mary the book.

Nicholas tossed Alex the keys.

Alissa threw Mark the ball.

You might, on the basis of this experience, construct a rule that allowed verbs to be followed by two objects. (The structures in the preceding examples are called double-object constructions.) The rule you constructed could lead you to produce the following ungrammatical utterances:

*John carried Mary the book.

*Nicholas said Alex something.

The verbs *carry* and *say,* however, need a different construction: "John carried the book to Mary" and "Nicholas said something to Alex."

In fact, children do overgeneralize the double-object construction to verbs that do not allow it, such as "I said her no" and "Shall I whisper you something" (Bowerman, 1988). Any theory of language acquisition has to explain how children recover from such **overgeneralizations.** Just hearing examples of grammatical sentences is not sufficient. No matter how many times you hear "John carried the book to Mary," that experience wouldn't tell you that it's not possible to say *"John carried Mary the book." One thing that would solve the problem for the learner is correction, or **negative evidence.** Because the availability of negative evidence has crucial implications for attempts to account for learning language from input, whether or not adults provide and children use this kind of feedback is hotly debated.

***The role of feedback.*** In 1970 Roger Brown and Camille Hanlon studied the mothers' speech in the transcripts of Adam, Eve, and Sarah, and they found that the mothers did not correct their children's ungrammatical utterances. The mothers did correct factual errors, mispronunciations, "naughty" words, and some overregularizations, such as *goed*. However, syntactic errors such as "Why the dog won't eat" passed without comment. On the basis of this finding, the general consensus for a long time was that children do not receive negative feedback.

More recently, others have looked more closely to see whether parents respond differentially to children's grammatical versus ungrammatical utterances in ways that are more subtle than overt correction but are nonetheless potentially useful to the child. Bohannon and Stanowicz (1988) found that adults were more likely to repeat verbatim children's well-formed sentences than their ill-formed sentences, and adults were more likely to repeat with corrections children's sentences that contained errors. Also, adults were more likely to ask for clarification of ill-formed sentences. Chouinard and Clark (2003) also found that adults reformulate their children's errorful utterances more frequently than they repeat or revise their error-free utterances. Other studies have also found differences in the frequencies of different kinds of parental responses, depending on the grammaticality of children's speech (for example, Demetras, Post, & Snow, 1986). It is unclear, however, just how children use such parental behavior as a guide to language acquisition. Children clearly cannot depend on being corrected if they produce an ungrammatical utterance. Although researchers can find a statistical difference between responses to grammatical and ungrammatical utterances by looking at hundreds of children's utterances, it is not clear that children could ever discern a pattern in their parents' behavior. Marcus (1993) has estimated that a child would have to say the same ungrammatical sentence 85 times to have enough data to determine that the sentence was ungrammatical. Chouinard and Clark (2003) argue, in contrast, that children understand when an adult utterance is a correction because they can tell that although the form is different, the intended meaning is the same. They also argue that children frequently directly acknowledge such corrections or use the new forms in their subsequent utterances, thus suggesting that the children recognize the reformulations as corrections and pay attention to them.

In sum, research points to ways in which children's language experience provides a rich database from which they might figure out the structure of language. Furthermore, evidence that aspects of children's language experience influence the rate of their language development suggests that children are actually using that database in acquiring language. On the other hand, research on language experience has not demonstrated how language experience could be sufficient to explain the acquisition of grammar.

## Continuity or discontinuity in grammatical development

Another issue with regard to grammatical development, besides whether nature or nurture provides an explanation, is whether development itself is continuous or discontinuous. We will illustrate the issue with the aspect of grammar that is the focus of much of this debate: the origin of grammatical categories. Remember, categories such as Noun and Verb are, by most accounts, crucial to a productive system. Also remember that it is not at all clear that very young speakers have grammatical categories. Some have suggested that children's first word combinations are based either on structures learned word-by-word or on semantically based categories. If the latter is the case, then children start out with a very different kind of system than adults have, and somewhere in the course of development they undergo a qualitative change. Such a change has been likened to the metamorphosis that tadpoles undergo to become frogs (Gleitman, 1981). Accounting for the change is known as the **tadpole–frog problem,** and how to solve the tadpole–frog problem is a central issue in accounting for grammatical development.

***Arguments for continuity.***     Pinker (1984) has argued that continuity in development should be assumed unless the data prove otherwise. The argument for this **continuity assumption** is that the fewer changes a theory has to account for, the more parsimonious the theory will be. In keeping with the continuity assumption, Pinker proposed that children are innately equipped with grammatical categories, and thus there is no metamorphosis to account for. Such a proposal solves the tadpole–frog problem by saying there are no tadpoles: They're frogs from the very beginning (Levy, 1983).

There is another way to meet the continuity assumption, aside from crediting young children with formal grammatical categories. That way is to describe the endpoint of development differently. If the system the child ultimately achieves does not have rules that operate over arbitrary, formal categories, then there is no tadpole–frog problem because there are no frogs. Some functionalist and cognitive theories of language essentially redefine linguistic competence in a way that takes the problem out of the tadpole–frog problem (for example, Van Valin, 1991; see Tomasello, 1992b, 2003). The connectionist proposals we will review later also fall into this category of avoiding the tadpole–frog problem by getting rid of the frogs.

***Maturation as the mechanism of discontinuous development.***     A solution to the tadpole–frog problem that is equally as innatist as crediting children with inborn syntactic categories is the proposal that syntactic categories appear later as the result of biological maturation. This position accepts the evidence that children's early speech does not require crediting children with a syntactically based grammar and explains the change from a semantic to a syntactic system as a result of maturational processes. According to this view, children begin to combine words with whatever pregrammatical system they can figure out using general cognition and language experience; however, their systems undergo a qualitative change when their innate grammatical knowledge matures, sometime during the third year of life (Atkinson, 1992; Radford, 1990). The analogy to the physical changes that occur at puberty is typically used to argue for the reasonableness of such an assertion. The genetic program for these changes is innate, even though the changes themselves occur well after infancy.

***Learning from input as a mechanism for change.***   Another possibility is that children initially have word-by-word or semantically based systems, but revise their categories on the basis of the speech that they hear. (Proposals to this effect were reviewed in the section on general cognitive mechanisms.) Discontinuity is not a problem if you can explain how the metamorphosis occurs.

## THEORETICAL POSITIONS ON THE ACQUISITION OF GRAMMAR

We have outlined some of the issues any theory must address if it is to account for children's acquisition of language structure. We turn now to a discussion of the major theoretical positions taken in attempting to construct such an account.

### The behaviorist account

If you ask the proverbial man on the street how children learn to talk, you are likely to get the answer that children learn to talk by imitating adults. This "folk psychology" belief somewhat resembles the explanation of language development that behaviorist psychology proffered in the 1960s. According to a behaviorist account of language development, children imitate what they hear, and they are reinforced when they get it right and are corrected—or at least not reinforced—when they get it wrong. Obviously, this account is inadequate because the adult language ability is not confined to repeating sentences that have previously been heard. Somewhat more sophisticated behaviorist accounts tried to handle the productivity of language in terms of "grammatical habits," or word-association chains in which each uttered word serves to elicit the next word in the sentence (Staats, 1971).

Such attempts to account for children's language development and adults' language ability in behaviorist terms were fairly short-lived and unsuccessful. In 1959 Noam Chomsky wrote a scathingly negative review of B. F. Skinner's (1957) attempt to account for language in behaviorist terms, and he was successful in convincing the scientific community that adult language use cannot be adequately described in terms of sequences of behaviors or responses (Chomsky, 1959). Because the behaviorists' notion of the endpoint of development was wrong, the behaviorist theory of achieving that endpoint was inadequate as a theory of language acquisition.

The issues of how to describe the endpoint of development and how to describe the process of development remain inextricably linked. If we assume, as many researchers do, that knowing how to talk consists of knowing a system of rules that operate over grammatical categories, then the question of language development becomes how children learn the rules and the categories. There are essentially two positions in current contention to explain this development: the innate grammar position and the social/cognitive position.

## The innate grammar position

The **innate grammar position** is the view that the acquisition of language is significantly supported by innate syntactic knowledge and language-specific learning procedures. This view of how language is acquired is associated with a particular approach to studying how grammar is acquired—the learnability approach discussed in Chapter 1. It begins with a description of the endpoint, constructs a theory that fits known developmental facts, and fills in what is not known to arrive at a theory sufficient to explain language acquisition. In such an approach, there is no hesitation to attribute innate knowledge to the child if such knowledge seems necessary to account for the acquisition of grammar. We will discuss two different theories that have in common this strong commitment to learnability and the assumption that children start out with substantial innate syntactic knowledge.

***Semantic bootstrapping and linking rules.***   We may be able to overcome the insufficiencies in accounting for how children could learn the syntactic categories of language and the rules for combining those categories if we give the child a head start in the form of innate knowledge. This is essentially what the theory of language acquisition proposed by Steven Pinker (1984, 1989) does. According to this theory, children innately know the categories of Noun and Verb, but they have to figure out the rules for ordering these categories in sentences. But they are helped here, too, because they know innately that agents are likely to be subjects, objects affected by action are likely to be direct objects, and so on. All that children need to figure out in the sentences they hear is which words are nouns and which are verbs, which noun is the agent that performs the action, which noun is the object that is acted upon, and so on. From that information, children can construct the rules for ordering these elements in sentences. Of course, the full theory is far more complicated, because sentences have more parts than just nouns and verbs, and sentence structures can be far more complex than just "subject + verb + object." But this little bit of the theory will serve to illustrate this position.

A crucial component of this theory is the assertion that children can identify the nouns and verbs in the sentences they hear. They can do this, according to Pinker, because they know that nouns tend to refer to persons or objects and that verbs tend to refer to actions. Thus semantics provides the entrée into the system—hence the label **semantic bootstrapping.** However, semantic bootstrapping depends not only on what the child knows but also on what the child hears. If children hear "John throws the ball" in the presence of John throwing the ball, they could—assuming the postulates of this theory—correctly assign words to syntactic categories and even figure out that *John* is the subject of the sentence and *the ball* is the direct object. But if instead children heard "John, you'd better not break another window," under semantic bootstrapping theory they would have trouble assigning words to syntactic categories. It can be argued that children usually can map words in the sentences they hear to their referents and thus to their syntactic category, because there is generally a good match between what adults say to children and the accompanying extralinguistic context. However, it is still the case that a mother coming home from work at the end of the day is more likely to say, "Hello, Alfred, whatcha been doing all day?" than she is to say, "Hello, Alfred, I'm opening the door" (Gleitman, 1990). The fact that even child-directed speech is not just a running commentary on the nonlinguistic scene is also a problem for many cognitive accounts of how children could figure out language by trying to match sentences to scenes. However, it is a fatal problem only for a theory that claims semantic bootstrapping as a crucial mechanism and that also claims to be sufficient to account for the acquisition of grammar.

Criticism has also been leveled at the proposal that children know innately that agents are likely to be subjects and affected objects are likely to be direct objects (this is one example of a **linking rule**). One sort of evidence against innate rules linking grammatical notions like "subject" to semantic roles like "agent" is that languages differ in the semantic roles that serve the grammatical function of subject. Some languages (called ergative languages) do not have true subjects, yet children acquire these languages without difficulty (Maratsos, 1988; Pye, 1992). Closer to home, children do not seem to produce sentences that conform to the supposedly basic "agent + action + affected object" structure any earlier than they produce sentences in which the subject is not a true agent and the verb is not really an action (such as *Ernie got spoon, Tasha have it*) (Bowerman, 1990).

Pinker's theory is the most complete and precise theory of how children might learn the rules of their language. As we have seen, there is reason to question some of its most important tenets. It is harder to find fatal flaws in the alternative social/cognitive position because that position's claims are less precise. If by now you have concluded that it is impossible to explain how children learn the rules of their language, you are in good company. The next two theories we will discuss eliminate the need for rule learning, albeit in very different ways.

***Principles and parameters theory.***   Children do not need to learn rules if *all* the rules are innate. According to the **principles and parameters theory,** the grammar that defines human language is innate in the child, and that grammar consists of a set of principles true for all languages and a set of parameters that define the range of possible differences among languages. The task of acquiring the grammar of a particular language is merely to set the language-specific parameters. There are no language-specific rules to be learned.

This nativist model of acquisition assumes, and depends on, the correctness of the principles and parameters approach to describing languages, according to which almost everything about grammar is universal and variation can be described in terms of parameters. We can illustrate that argument with respect to phrase structure: All languages have noun phrases and verb phrases, and these phrases contain a head (i.e., the noun or the verb) and other words that modify the head in some way. In English, the head comes before the modifiers. We say "the house that Jack built," in which *house* is the head and *that Jack built* is the modifier. We say "the farmer milked the cow with the crumpled horn," in which *milked* is the head of the verb phrase and *the cow with the crumpled horn* modifies milking—and *with the crumpled horn* also modifies *cow*. In fact, whatever the nature of the head of the phrase and whatever the modifiers might be, the modifiers always follow. This is why English is labeled a right-branching language.

Other languages are different. Although they all have phrases with heads and modifiers, in some languages the modifiers precede the head. Japanese is such a language. In Japanese, to say "the farmer milked the cow," you say the equivalent of "the farmer the cow milked." Japanese prepositions follow rather than precede nouns. In English, one says "to Sally"; in Japanese, it would be "Sally to." Japanese is a left-branching language. The notion that there are phrases with heads and modifiers, then, is a universal principle of language and could, conceivably, be innate. The direction of branching is language specific, but there are only two possibilities: right or left. Thus, the direction of branching is called a parameter. According to the principles and parameters theory, all of linguistic knowledge can be described in terms of a few universal principles and language-specific parameters. The parameters must be set on the basis of hearing input, but because the options are limited, input is necessary only to "trigger" parameter setting. No data-crunching induction process is required. Furthermore, because many properties of a language follow from the setting of one parameter, the number of parameters to set is limited. This view has great theoretical elegance. Unfortunately, other than this illustration of right- and left-branching languages, it is not clear what the parameters are or how all the variation among languages in the world would be captured by a theory that works within the constraints of a principles and parameters framework. There have been many attempts, but they have not held up under empirical test, and the failure of efforts to describe language variation in terms of principles and parameters casts doubt on the feasibility of accounting for language acquisition within that framework (Maratsos, 1998).

## The social/cognitive position

According to the **social/cognitive view** of language acquisition, the starting point of language acquisition is provided by general cognition, as are the mechanisms of language development. The requisite experience for language acquisition is social interaction with other speakers. This position is not one person's theory; rather, it is a school of thought that encompasses a variety of more specific proposals about how children's early language experience, in interaction with children's active efforts at figuring out language, results in the course of language development we observe (Bloom, 1991; Snow, 1989; Snow, Perlmann, & Nathan, 1987; Tomasello, 1992a, 2003). The social/cognitive position is also associated with the developmental approach to investigating language acquisition (see Chapter 1 and Bloom, 1991, 1998). Disagreement exists among theories that would fall under this heading regarding how much of the information necessary for language acquisition depends on the social nature of the interactions in which children hear speech and how much of language acquisition is the result of asocial cognition (Maratsos, 1998; Tomasello, 2003). That disagreement is similar to the dispute regarding how much of the mapping problem in lexical acquisition is solved by sociopragmatic sources of information and how much of the mapping problem is solved by asocial processes of attention and memory.

Much of the work that is relevant to an evaluation of the social/cognitive position has already been discussed in this chapter. There is evidence that children have powerful learning mechanisms available to them and that at least some of these mechanisms are domain general, which supports the notion that general cognition could importantly contribute to language acquisition. There is evidence that the information provided in the speech children hear—that is, the structural properties of input—affects the development of grammatical knowledge, which supports the notion that learning from input does contribute to language acquisition. There is evidence that children's experience in conversation—that is, pragmatic aspects of input—affects their language development, which supports the notion that social interaction contributes in an important way to language development. However, the problem of sufficiency remains. There is at present no explanation of how experience in combination with general cognitive abilities is sufficient to account for children's acquisition of the rules of grammar. This is perhaps to be expected in what is a fairly young field. Some time in the future, when we know more about how children use their experience, there could be such an account.

## Connectionism

Connectionism has already been mentioned several times as one of the major approaches to explaining language acquisition. It is consistent with the claim that general learning mechanisms can account for language acquisition—connectionist mechanisms of learning are domain general. Connectionism is not, however, an alternative to nativism as an explanation of how children learn rules. To recap briefly, connectionism is a theory of cognition according to which seemingly rule-governed behavior—such as speaking a language—

can be explained without recourse to underlying rules. Connectionism, then, solves the problem of accounting for children's rule learning by saying there are no rules for children to learn. Rather, what underlies language is a network of interconnected units. The process of language development is a process of getting right the relative strengths of the connections in the network.

The dispute between this view and the rule-based, symbolic processes view is clearly revealed in their differing accounts of morphological development—specifically the morphology of past-tense formation in English (see, for example, Daugherty & Seidenberg, 1994; Pinker & Prince, 1994; Plunkett, 1995; Plunkett & Marchman, 1991). A connectionist model of past-tense formation starts out with units that correspond to the sounds of verb stems and the sounds of verb endings. The model is fed "experience" in which certain stem sounds appear with certain ending sounds, and the model increases the strength of those particular connections. In its final state, the model can generate the past tense of novel forms based on the similarity of the novel form to stored forms. So, if we gave the model the Berko test and asked it to form the past tense of *blick,* it would produce *blicked* based on the similarity in sound of *blick* to *kick* and *lick* and past exposure to *kicked* and *licked.* Just how successful connectionist models are at mimicking what every 4-year-old can do is a matter of considerable debate (Daugherty & Seidenberg, 1994; Pinker & Prince, 1994; Plunkett, 1995; Plunkett & Marchman, 1991).

According to the symbolic processes view, in contrast, we do not form the past tense of new verbs because of the similarity of their sound to verbs we already know. What we do, as adult speakers, is apply the rule, "add *ed.*" It is easy to demonstrate this fact with what psychologists call an armchair experiment. Sitting in your armchair, you can easily retrieve the irregular past tense form of the verb *to ride;* it is *rode.* What happens if you imagine a new verb that sounds exactly the same as *ride* but isn't *ride?* If you want to say that someone was such an amazing pioneer that she matched and exceeded the accomplishments of the first female astronaut, Sally Ride, you could say that she "out-Sally *Rided* Sally Ride." You would never say that anyone "out-Sally *Rode* Sally Ride." This evidence suggests that we have a rule that applies as the default to new verbs even when they are phonologically similar or identical to old verbs (Marcus et al., 1992).

At this point, connectionism's potential to account for the acquisition of syntax and morphology is an open question. To some people, the connectionist approach is attractive because it holds the promise of accounting for language and language acquisition using the same mechanisms that could also account for other cognitive processes. To others, though, such an approach to language cannot possibly succeed because it assumes a theory that is wrong in its description of the endpoint of development (Marcus et al., 1992).

# • SUMMARY

Around the age of 18 months to 2 years, children begin to combine words. This milestone marks the beginning of structured language. Children's two-word combinations are followed by utterances that are three and more words long, and as children's utterances get longer, they also become increasingly complex. Children's first sentences tend to be simple declarative sentences lacking many of the grammatical morphemes, such as verb endings and auxiliary verbs, present in adults' speech. For this reason, children's early speech is described as telegraphic. Beginning around the time children start to put three words together, they begin to use grammatical morphemes. They start to produce questions and negative statements, whose form changes as children acquire the syntactic means of adult grammatical expression. By the time children are 4 years old, they can produce complex sentences, and it is said that at this point they have essentially mastered the grammar of their language.

There are individual differences in the early stages of the development of multiword speech. Some children rely heavily on rote-memorized phrases, and other children approach language more analytically—producing novel word combinations from the start. However, there is sufficient commonality among children in the course of syntactic development for the mean length of a child's utterances to be a useful measure of that child's level of grammatical development, at least up to an MLU of 3.0. Because the rate of syntactic development is extremely variable across children, age is not a good indicator of a child's level of grammatical development.

Children seem to know more about grammar than they demonstrate in their speech. For example, children who produce only one word at a time understand the relational meanings in two-word utterances. However, children often appear to understand everything that is said to them, and that is not the case. Children have a variety of strategies for interpreting and responding to sentences that they do not fully understand, and these strategies make children seem more grammatically competent than they really are.

Although the facts of the developmental changes that occur in children's speech are relatively clear, the explanation of those facts is not. One source of contention concerns how to describe the system of knowledge that underlies children's structured speech. Children's initial sentences seem to be combinations of semantically defined categories, such as actor and action. Children do not produce the kind of sentences that require knowledge of abstract grammatical categories such as Noun and Verb. However, if children start out with a semantic system and end up with an abstract syntactic system, there needs to be an explanation of how that change occurs. According to one view, the explanation is in the maturation of an innate grammar. According to another view, the explanation is in the learning procedures children apply to the speech they hear. Still other views argue that the adult system is not the abstract, syntactic system that most assume it is, thus redefining the problem. The debate over the innate and experiential contributions to the acquisition of grammar is fierce and unresolved at this point.

Current theories of grammar acquisition cover the spectrum from the most experientially based to the most innatist views. According to the social/cognitive position, the achievement of grammar is the result of children's applying general cognitive procedures for the acquisition of knowledge to the language they hear in social interactions. In contrast, the innate grammar view holds that significant aspects of linguistic knowledge are genetically preprogrammed. The most strongly innatist view is that of the principles and parameters approach, according to which the child has innate knowledge of Universal Grammar and uses language experience only to set parameters that vary across languages. According to the connectionist approach, the process of acquiring a grammar is the process of the patterns in input fixing the relative weights of connections in a network of units.

## ● KEY TERMS

productivity or generativity of language

syntax

open-class words

lexical categories

closed-class words

functional categories

morphology

bound morpheme

morphemes

free morphemes

prescriptive rules

descriptive rules

transitional forms

relational meaning

combinatorial speech

telegraphic speech

grammatical morphemes

yes/no questions

wh- questions

complex sentences

analytical versus holistic approach

mean length of utterance (MLU)

response strategies

overregularizations

semantically based grammar

syntactically based grammar

connectionist view

phonological bootstrapping hypothesis

prosodic bootstrapping hypothesis

overgeneralizations

negative evidence

tadpole–frog problem

continuity assumption

innate grammar position

semantic bootstrapping

linking rule

principles and parameters theory

social/cognitive view

## ● REVIEW QUESTIONS

1. What is meant by the productivity of language, and what is its significance for the task of explaining language acquisition?

2. What aspects of language structure have children acquired, and what have they not acquired, when they produce telegraphic speech?

3. What is the difference between a holistic and an analytical approach to the acquisition of grammatical structure? What would be evidence for each in children's speech?

4. It often seems to parents that young children understand "everything." What is the evidence that this is not true, and why do children often appear to understand more than they do?

5. Based on evidence from comprehension studies, what is the developmental timetable for the acquisition of grammar?

6. What kind of evidence supports the claim that children acquire rules in acquiring the syntax and morphology of their language?

7. What are the differences among a lexically based, a semantically based, and a syntactically based grammar? Give one example of evidence for attributing each to children.

8. What is the tadpole–frog problem? Outline the possible solutions.

9. Outline the arguments for and against innate grammar as an explanation of the acquisition of grammar.

10. What assumption about children's language input is necessarily entailed by any proposal to account for the acquisition of grammar in terms of general cognitive processes?

11. What is negative evidence? Why is the availability of negative evidence to children an important issue?

12. What is semantic bootstrapping? What does semantic bootstrapping propose to explain? What does this hypothesis assume about children? What does it assume about children's language experience?

13. How is the connectionist account unique among theories of the acquisition of grammar?

© Erika Stone/Photo Researchers, Inc.

# COMMUNICATION AND LANGUAGE IN DEVELOPMENT

In the previous chapters, we have described children's development of language; in this chapter, we focus on communication. Although language is used to communicate, language and communication are not the same thing. For instance, a typical 15-month-old has very little language but can be highly communicative, using gesture and vocalization. In this chapter, we consider the child's development as a communicator, including both the development of communication before language emerges and children's development of skill at using language to communicate. Because we will have an eye toward the endpoint of development as we consider both prelinguistic communication and linguistic communicative skill, we begin this chapter, as we have other chapters, with a description of what adults know.

## THE NATURE OF COMMUNICATIVE COMPETENCE

Linguists and language researchers make a distinction between **linguistic competence,** which is the ability to produce and understand well-formed, meaningful sentences, and **communicative competence,** which is the ability to use those sentences appropriately in social interaction (Hymes, 1972). (Sometimes the term communicative competence is used to include linguistic competence [see Foley & Van Valin, 1984]; we will use it in its narrower sense.) The knowledge that constitutes communicative competence consists of several overlapping domains of knowledge. **Pragmatic knowledge** concerns understanding the communicative functions of language and the conventions that govern the use of language in order to communicate. **Discourse knowledge** concerns the use of language in units larger than a sentence; conversations and narratives are two such larger units. **Sociolinguistic knowledge** concerns how language use varies as a function of sociological variables such as status, culture, and gender. We consider the nature of each of these sorts of knowledge in turn.

### Pragmatic competence

Just as we looked to linguists' analyses of language structure as a guide to what we must account for in describing children's development of language structure, we now look to analyses of communication as a guide to what we must account for in describing children's communicative development. Some of the most explicit accounts of what constitutes communication come from the academic discipline of philosophy, specifically the philosophy of language.

***Speech acts.*** The work of the philosophers of language J. L. Austin and John Searle has been particularly influential in the study of children's pragmatic development. According to Austin, speaking is not just uttering sen-

---

**Table 6.1   Speech act components**

| Component | Definition | Examples |
|---|---|---|
| illocutionary force | intended function | request, query, promise |
| locution | form | declarative, imperative |
| perlocution | effect | obtaining requested object, directing other's attention |

---

tences that describe events but "doing things with words" (Austin, 1962). Each sentence a speaker utters is a **speech act.** Austin often illustrated this point with examples such as a judge uttering the sentence "I now declare you husband and wife," which, in the context of a marriage ceremony, has the effect of marrying two people. However, the notion that speaking is performing acts applies to all speaking. The kinds of acts performed are promising, requesting, referring, describing, arguing, demanding, and others (Searle, 1969).

A speech act has three components: (1) its intended function (its **illocutionary force**), (2) its linguistic form (its **locution**), and (3) its effect on the listener (its **perlocution**). Table 6.1 lists these components and some examples. We can illustrate these different components of the speech act using the following example of one child's communicative behavior (Rees, 1978): Dennis the Menace appears at his neighbor's front door and says, "My mother wants to borrow a cup of ice cream." In this example, the intended function, or illocutionary force, of Dennis's speech act is to request ice cream, and the form, or locution, is that of a declarative sentence. The effect, or perlocution, of this particular speech act is unknown. Dividing speech acts into components is useful for the study of communicative development because it makes it possible to ask separate questions about the development of children's communicative intentions, the development of the forms of language, and the development of the ability to achieve desired effects.

***Intentionality.***    Of the three components of speech acts—intentions, forms, and effects—the intentions that underlie communication are the most difficult to specify. In fact, it could be argued that intentionality is irrelevant to the question of whether communication is taking place, and, indeed, intentionality is not central to the concerns of some who study communication. For example, people who study nonverbal communication study messages that are often unintended (for example, Birdwhistell, 1970). However, in studying the development of communicative competence, we are not asking whether communication is taking place but rather whether the child is communicating. This focus on what's inside the mind of the communicator makes **intentionality** a crucial part of the definition of communication. With that definition, then, it is insufficient that a behavior be interpretable for it to be communicative. For example, if someone sneezes, you may be able to infer that she or he has a cold. However, sneezing is a reflex and not necessarily a communicative act. (If one pretended to sneeze in order to signal that one was feeling ill, that would be communicative.)

Beyond asserting that intentionality is necessary for communication, we can also ask what kind of intentions are involved in communication. It seems, for example, that the intention that is really behind communication is not just the intention to accomplish something. In the preceding example, Dennis's communicative intention was not just to get ice cream. Rather, the intention that underlies true communication includes the intention to create a belief in the listener's mind (Grice, 1957; 1969). If Mrs. Wilson had responded to Dennis that she didn't have any ice cream, we would judge the communication to have been successful, even though the goal of getting ice cream was not achieved. Although the effort to obtain ice cream would have failed in that case, it would not have been a failure of communication. This distinction between the intention to achieve a goal and the intention to make contact with another mind will be an important distinction when we talk about the understandings that underlie children's development of communicative behavior.

***Form-function mappings and the role of context.***    The example of Dennis talking to Mrs. Wilson also illustrates another important point about language use that speech act analysis reveals. Although Dennis's sentence was a declarative statement about his mother's need state, his purpose in uttering that sentence was to make a request. The intended function of language may be different from its form and its literal meaning. In fact, speakers use a variety of different forms for the same function. For example, the request that someone open a window can be made with any of the following utterances:

Open the window.

Would you open the window?

I'd love some fresh air.

It sure is stuffy in here.

These different forms of request for a window to be opened would not be equally appropriate in all settings. A parent might say "Open the window" to a child but may be less direct when talking to a peer. Regarding the

---

**Box 6.1   One form, multiple functions: "Good morning" as greeting, declarative, and directive in J. R. R. Tolkien's *The Hobbit***

"Good morning!" said Bilbo, and he meant it. The sun was shining, and the grass was very green. But Gandalf looked at him from under long bushy eyebrows that stuck out further than the brim of his shady hat.

"What do you mean?" he said. "Do you wish me a good morning, or mean that it is a good morning whether I want it or not; or that you feel good this morning; or that it is a morning to be good on?"

"All of them at once," said Bilbo.

*and later, after some conversation between Bilbo and Gandalf*

"Good morning!" he (Bilbo) said at last. . . . By this he meant that the conversation was at an end.

"What a lot of things you do use *Good morning* for!" said Gandalf. "Now you mean that you want to get rid of me, and that it won't be good till I move off."

Source: From *The Hobbit,* by J. R. R. Tolkien, Ballantine Books, p. 18–19. Copyright © 1937, 1938, 1966. Thirty-seventh printing: September 1972.

---

development of communicative competence, we can ask when and how children acquire a repertoire of different forms to express the same function and when and how they learn to use the form that is appropriate for the circumstance.

## Discourse competence

Using language to communicate typically involves stretches of speech that are much longer than a single sentence. These longer stretches can involve two or more people talking, in which case they called **conversations.** Sometimes one speaker talks at length, as in a lecture, a sermon, or a narrative. Of these forms of extended monologue, **narratives,** or stories, are the most extensively studied. Communicative competence includes knowing how to participate in conversations and how to produce monologues such as narratives.

---

### Box 6.2    Grice's conversational maxims

*Quantity:* Make your contribution as informative as is required; provide neither too much nor too little information.

*Quality:* Try to make your contribution one that is true; do not say what you believe to be false or that for which you lack adequate evidence.

*Relation:* Be relevant.

*Manner:* Be perspicuous (that is, be clear—brief, orderly, unambiguous).

---

Source: From Grice, 1957, 1975.

If a man were a guest on a talk show and answered each question with a single-word response, we would judge him to be a poor conversationalist, and he probably would not be invited back. Similarly, someone who never lets anyone else talk or who always talks about his or her latest vacation regardless of what others are talking about is also being a poor conversationalist. What makes someone a good conversationalist? According to Grice (1957; 1975), there are two basic rules of conversation. The first rule is to take turns (see also Sacks, Schegloff, & Jefferson, 1974, for a description of turn taking in adult conversations). The second rule is to be cooperative. This cooperative principle of conversational participation includes four more specific maxims (or rules of conduct) having to do with the quantity, quality, relation, and manner of conversational contributions. These Gricean maxims are listed in Box 6.2. Like the rules of grammar that we discussed in Chapter 5, these rules are descriptive, not prescriptive. They are rules that describe how conversations work; violating these descriptive rules causes a breakdown in the interaction. The poor conversationalists in the preceding examples violated some or all of these rules. In studying children's development as conversationalists, we can ask when their participation in conversation starts to follow these rules—when they learn to take turns and when they become able to provide the right amount of relevant information in a clear manner. (Child language researchers have left the study of learning to be truthful to other disciplines.)

Children must also acquire skills in order to produce text, or stretches of speech, on their own. Sustaining talk without a conversational partner and making that talk coherent place unique demands on a speaker's communicative competence. The beginnings of narrative development can be found in the spontaneous descriptions of past events children produce in conversation, starting before the age of 3 years. The complete course of narrative development can extend into adulthood. In this chapter, we will provide an outline of the developmental changes that are observable during early childhood.

## Sociolinguistic competence

***Registers.*** Language is used differently in different social settings. The way students talk to their friends in the dormitory is different from the way they talk to the same people in a classroom discussion. Language is also used differently in talking to different people. For example, the ways in which you would talk to a child, a friend, a parent, and a professor are different. Styles of language use associated with particular social settings are called **registers** (Chaika, 1989). Learning to use different registers appropriately, depending on the conversational setting, is one of the tasks children must accomplish in acquiring communicative competence.

***Dialects and cultural variation in language use.*** Language is also used differently by different social groups. For example, a typical conversation between New Yorkers might seem extremely rude to a Southerner, and many of the kinds of conversations that occur among men are different from the kinds of conversations that occur among women (Tannen, 1990). The way adults talk to children is different among working-class white or African Americans than among mainstream, middle-class white or African Americans (Heath, 1983). **Dialects** are variations within a language that are a function of who the speaker is. Although some of the most obvious differences among dialects are in pronunciation, dialectical variation appears in the lexical, syntactic, and stylistic aspects of language as well.

The norms for how language is used in interactions vary widely from culture to culture, and these differences are separate from the fact that the cultures speak different languages. For example, conversations between mothers and children are different in Japan than in the United States (Clancy, 1986), and they take a third form in Samoa (Ochs, 1988). One thing children learn as they acquire communicative competence is to use language in the particular way their social group uses language. The process of learning the language style of one's particular group is called **language socialization.** In describing children's language socialization, we can ask when group-specific styles emerge in children, and we can ask how a culture transmits its particular style of language use to its children. Having thus outlined what the child must learn to achieve communicative competence, we return now to the infant to ask when communication begins.

## THE COMMUNICATIVE FOUNDATIONS OF LANGUAGE DEVELOPMENT

### Prelinguistic communicative development

Most adults in Western culture believe that communicative interaction with infants begins well before infants begin to talk. Infants emit behaviors such as crying, fussing, and smiling that caregivers use as clues to infants' internal states. However, the fact that adults can interpret these signals—no doubt accurately—does not mean that the infants intended to send these signals. There is no reason to think that infants' early expressions of their emotional states are anything other than automatic responses to internal states, as in sneezing or coughing. In sum, young infants have effects on their listeners, but there is no evidence that they have intentional control over those effects (Bates, Camaioni, & Volterra, 1975).

If very young infants do not intentionally communicate, when does intentionality first appear? Because we cannot know with certainty what another person's intentional state is, questions about the intentions underlying young children's communicative behavior are very difficult to answer. However, the difficulty of answering the question about infants' intentionality has not stopped researchers from trying.

Bates and colleagues (1975) described the course of the development of intentional communication based on a study of three little girls, starting when the children were 2 months, 6 months, and 12 months old and following each for approximately 6 months until their developmental courses overlapped. The researchers went to the children's homes every 2 weeks with notepads and videotape recorders looking for spontaneous communicative behavior. They described three phases in the development of communication: perlocutionary, illocutionary, and locutionary phases.

***Having effects.***   In the first, or perlocutionary, phase, children have effects on their listeners; but the signals that have effects are not produced with the intention of communicating to a listener. For example, the child who wants an object that is out of reach may try to get it and may make a fuss in the process. The mother may observe the child, infer the child's desires, and get the object for the child. In this case, the child's behavior had the effect of obtaining the object, but there was no effort to communicate with the mother. Bates and associates (1975) described such an example in one of the children studied when the child was 9 months old:

> In an effort to obtain a box that her mother is holding in her arms, Carlotta pulls at the arms, pushes her whole body against the floor, and approaches the box from several angles. *Yet during the entire sequence she never looks up into her mother's face.* (p. 214; italics added)

***Having intentions.*** In the second, or illocutionary, phase, children become aware that their behavior can be used to communicate with others. More specifically, at around age 10 months, children come to understand that other people can be helpful in satisfying one's goals and that it is possible to elicit this help by communicating with them. For example, a child who wants something will not just reach and fuss but will actively try to elicit another's aid in obtaining that object. Bates and colleagues (1975) provided an example by the same child Carlotta, this time at the age of 11 months:

> Carlotta, unable to pull a toy cat out of the adult's hand, sits back up straight, *looks the adult intently in the face,* and then tries once again to pull the cat. The pattern is repeated three times, with the observer refusing to yield the cat, until Carlotta finally manages to pull the object away from the adult. (p. 215; italics added)

Bates and colleagues describe such communicative behaviors as protoimperatives; that is, these behaviors serve the function of imperatives (commands). They have both the illocutionary force and perlocutionary effect of imperatives—all they lack is the locutionary content.

Another kind of communicative behavior that develops during this prelinguistic phase is the protodeclarative. In contrast to protoimperatives, in which adults are used as a means to obtain objects, with protodeclaratives children use objects to obtain adult attention. For example, a child might point to an object while making noise to attract adult attention, being satisfied only when the adult looks where the child is pointing and acknowledges the child's gesture. Again, there is an important distinction between the behavior that counts as a protodeclarative, and therefore a communicative behavior, and earlier noncommunicative behavior. Before using a pointing gesture to direct adults' attention, children point to things when they are unaware of being observed, and they point to things without any effort to obtain adult attention (Bates et al., 1975).

***Using conventional signals.*** The third, or locutionary, phase of speech act development begins when children's communicative behavior includes using language to refer. As we saw in the discussion of context-bound versus referential word use in Chapter 4 on lexical development, sometimes first words are not used referentially. Because first words can be used nonreferentially, the locutionary phase in speech act development does not suddenly begin with the child's first words. Rather, there are degrees within the locutionary stage. Sounds may first be used consistently in certain contexts but in somewhat idiosyncratic ways. For example, Bates and colleagues (1975) described one child using the sound "Mm" with a pointing gesture to indicate a request. Slightly more advanced, but still not referential, is using a word such as *bam* when knocking over constructions made out of blocks. The relevant distinction here is that

---

**Box 6.3   Summary of speech act development**

*Phase 1: Perlocutionary (Birth–10 mos.)*

Behavior has consequences but is not produced with communicative intent.

*Period 2: Illocutionary (10–12 mos.)*

Behavior has communicative goals but does not use the forms of the target language.

*Period 3: Locutionary (12 mos. + )*

Behavior has communicative intentions and adultlike forms.

---

Source: Based on Schwartz, 1983.

"bam" is part of the activity of knocking down blocks, not a symbol that stands for and can be used to refer to the activity of knocking down blocks. Gradually children come to use language referentially, and at that point all three components of speech acts are in place. Box 6.3 summarizes these phases of speech act development.

## The emergence of communicative intent in infancy

A major milestone in speech act development is the change from the perlocutionary to the illocutionary phase. It is important to note that several other researchers have also described a change in infants around the age of 10 months. According to Sugarman (1984), before this milestone is reached, infants are able to relate to an object or to another person but not to both at the same time. An example of relating to an object would be playing with a rattle or looking at a mobile over one's crib. An example of relating to another person would be smiling or cooing. What emerges around age 10 months is the ability to relate to another person about an object. Sugarman-Bell (1978) described this development as the "coordination between actions and vocalizations" (p. 49).

Trevarthen and Hubley (1978) also described what seems to be the same change in infants at around age 10 months. Before this point, infants may share themselves with others; Trevarthen and Hubley call this **primary intersubjectivity.** After this point, infants share their experiences with others; this is **secondary intersubjectivity.** The convergence of the research suggests that a maturational change occurs in infants at around 9 to 10 months of age, and that change permits the emergence of intentionality.

***The development of joint attention skills.*** **Joint attention** is another term that has been used to characterize the state in which the child and an adult together attend to some third entity. Recently, children's development of the capacity for joint attention and the role of joint attention in language acquisition have been the topic of substantial research attention. A key notion in this work is the idea that when infants follow the gaze of another—or, somewhat later in development, when they seek to direct the attention of another—they are demonstrating an understanding that other people are like them. That is, infants understand that other people also can attend to things and can have intentions to communicate. According to this view, infants understand that in episodes of joint attention they are making contact with another mind, and that basic social desire to meet other minds along with the capacity to do so are the developmental precursors and the foundation of communicative and linguistic development.

***The role of joint attention skills in language development.*** One sort of evidence that supports the view that joint attentional states are the foundation of language development are findings that infants who are more precocious at developing joint attention skills are also more advanced in later measures of language development (Camaioni & Perucchini, 2003; Morales, Mundy, & Rojas, 1998; Mundy & Gomes, 1998). The joint attention skills measured in these studies include both pointing (to direct the attention of another) and following another's eye gaze. Another sort of evidence is the co-occurrence of severe impairment in joint attention skills and impairment in language in individuals with autism.

There are dissenters from this view that infants have an understanding of others' minds and that this social/cognitive accomplishment underlies language acquisition. Critics have argued that infants' and very young children's seemingly communicative behaviors do not reflect such sophisticated understandings of other minds (e.g., Moore & Corkum, 1994; Shatz & Watson O'Reilly, 1990), but are learned instrumental behaviors. That is, children produce social and communicative behaviors because they like the outcome, not because they want to meet another mind. Camaioni and Perucchini (2003) provide evidence that both may be true. They distinguished two kinds of pointing behavior in 11-month-olds: pointing for imperative purposes (e.g., the baby points at something he wants) and pointing for declarative purposes (e.g., the baby points at something just to get another person to look at what he is looking at). Camaioni and Perucchini found that children who were high in the use of declarative pointing at 11 months were later more advanced in language than children who were low in the use of declarative pointing. In contrast, children's imperative pointing was unrelated to later language development. They hypothesize that declarative pointing does reveal an understanding of other minds, whereas imperative pointing requires only understanding that others can serve instrumental purposes.

It is also possible that joint attention skill and language development are related for reasons other than joint attention reflecting communicative understandings that are the foundation of language. Early joint attention skills might reflect early brain maturation, which is independently related to language development. Support for this hypothesis comes from findings that brain maturation, measured by EEG coherence, is correlated with joint attention skill in 14-month-olds (Mundy, Fox, & Card, 2003). Also, the child's interest in achieving joint attention might reflect a more basic interest in social interaction, which later expresses itself in language. Support for this hypothesis comes from findings that measures of infants' initiations of joint attention predict expressive language development, whereas measures of infants' responsiveness to others' joint attention bids predicts language comprehension (Mundy & Gomes, 1998). A third possibility is that children with more advanced joint attention skills experience, as a result, more communicative interaction of the sort that supports language development. Support for this hypothesis comes from findings that infants' responsiveness to joint attention bids at 14 months predicted both their language development and the amount of joint attention they experienced in mother–child interaction at 18 months (Markus, Mundy, Morales, Delgado, & Yale, 2000). On this account, it is not the capacity for joint attention per se that leads to language development but rather the interactions that joint attention allows. Several findings in the literature show that the more time infants spend in joint attention with an adult speaker, the more rapid is their development of language (Carpenter, Nagell, & Tomasello, 1998; Tomasello, Mannle, & Krueger, 1986; Tomasello & Todd, 1983).

## The role of prelinguistic interaction in language development

It is not only children's capacities that predict the amount of time they spend in joint attention with caregivers. Caregivers' behavior makes a difference as well. If it is really the experience of joint attention that underlies the relation between infant joint attention skills and language development—rather than some underlying ability that contributes separately to joint attention and language skill—then mutual engagement that is the result of caregivers' behavior ought also to be related to children's language development. To pursue this hypothesis, we turn to descriptions of caregivers' behavior with prelinguistic infants and the relation of that behavior to language development.

In Western cultures, mothers typically treat babies as conversational partners from birth. Young infants do not do much in terms of holding up their end of the conversation, but mothers build conversational sequences around the smiles, burps, and other noises their infants do produce. The following example from Snow (1977) illustrates this kind of interaction.

| | |
|---|---|
| 3-month-old: | (smiles) |
| Mother: | Oh what a nice little smile! |
| | Yes, isn't that nice? |
| | There. |
| | There's a nice little smile. |
| 3-month-old: | (burps) |
| Mother: | What a nice wind as well! |
| | Yes, that's better, isn't it? |
| | Yes. |
| 3-month-old: | (vocalizes) |
| Mother: | Yes. |
| | Yes! |
| | There's a nice noise. |

Researchers have suggested that through such interactions, adults draw infants into communicative exchanges that become the basis for the later emergence of true intentional communication (Camaioni, 1993; Locke, 1993). Snow has described this phenomenon as mothers "pulling intentionality out of the pre-intentional child" ("Baby Talk," 1984).

Other empirical evidence suggests that infants' experiences with responsive partners may help children discover that communication is possible. Bell and Ainsworth (1972) studied the responsiveness of 26 mothers to their infants' crying over the first year of the infants' lives. Observers visited each home at approximately 3-week intervals, recording the frequency of infant crying episodes, the length of time the infant cried without obtaining a maternal response, and the effectiveness of maternal interventions at calming the baby. Bell and Ainsworth found that infants who had the most responsive mothers when they were 6 to 12 months old cried less at the age of 12 months than did the infants with less responsive mothers. Also, the infants who cried less at 12 months were more communicative in terms of both their vocalizations and their nonvocal behavior.

Even for somewhat older children, experiencing a responsive mother (or other caregiver) appears to promote language development. For example, children whose mothers are responsive to their vocalizations at 13 months produce their first word earlier and reach a 50-word vocabulary earlier than children who have less responsive mothers (Tamis-LeMonda, Bornstein, Kahana-Kalman, Baumwell, & Cyphers, 1998). Also, children whose mothers follow the child's focus of attention in their talk when the children are 13 months old have bigger vocabularies at 22 months (Akhtar, Dunham, & Dunham, 1991). The importance of individual differences in joint attention skills and maternal responsivity to language development appears to decline after the age of 18 months (Morales et al., 2000), perhaps because by that age, all normally developing children can follow the speaker's lead (Hoff & Naigles, 2002).

## The role of communication in language development

***Communication as the motivation for acquiring language structure.*** If you ask the proverbial man on the street why children learn to talk, a likely answer is some form of the following: Children learn to talk in order to communicate with others. In fact, it is common to hear grandmothers (particularly the mothers-in-law) blame a child's perceived slow development in language on the mother who "gives him everything he wants so the child has no reason to learn to talk." Within the field of child language, some theories similarly explain language development as motivated by the urge to communicate, although they would not necessarily agree with that grandmother's diagnosis. Bloom (1993) proposed that children acquire language in order to express what they are thinking, and Snow (1999) proposed that the desire to share experience is the foundation for language development. Consistent with this view, others have suggested that a communicative partner is essential for language acquisition. Without a partner, isolated children do not invent language (Shatz, 1994b). Finally, it has been suggested that when children fail to be understood, the failure prompts them to find new and better ways of communicating (Golinkoff, 1983; Mannle & Tomasello, 1987).

There are, of course, counterarguments to these proposals. First, even if communication is the motivation for language acquisition, that alone doesn't explain how children learn the intricacies of grammar. To suggest that somehow social understandings yield noun declensions and auxiliary verb systems has been described as wishful thinking (Maratsos, 1998). Second, recent evidence of infants' abilities to learn patterns in input suggests that the kind of learning that contributes to the acquisition of grammar is neither difficult for young children nor dependent on a communicative motive. A third counterargument holds that this view attributes too much social understanding to the child. If 1-year-olds are really learning to talk in order to communicate, they must be able to think that they know something that their listener does not and that the way to get the listener to know this unshared information is to vocalize in a particular manner. According to some, that's a great deal with which to credit a 1-year-old (Locke, 1999).

***Language function as the basis of language structure.*** There is an argument that the urge to communicate plays more than just a motivational role in language acquisition. According to this sort of account, words are social conventions that children learn by understanding the communicative intentions of the speaker who utters a novel word (Carpenter, Nagell, &

Tomasello, 1998). Grammatical categories, too, may be reduced to communicative functions. For example, grammatical subjects tend to be message topics (Bates & MacWhinney, 1982). One school of functional grammar claims to be able to do the work of a Chomskyan, generative grammar entirely with categories that have a functional basis. Thus, learning grammar is simply the outcome of learning to communicate (see, for example, Foley & Van Valin, 1984; Van Valin, 1991). This theory was one of those described in Chapter 5 on grammatical development as solving the tadpole–frog problem by getting rid of the frogs. Of course, to some, that is exactly the problem with this approach: It denies the complexity of what children acquire (O'Grady, 1999; Shatz, 1992).

***Language function as the gateway to language structure.***   Another possible relation between the communicative function of language and the acquisition of language structure is one in which children start out with a functionally based system and later move to a formal system. This view is consistent with claims that children's first words and even multiword expressions have only functional meanings (Ninio, 1995), not semantic or syntactic structure (Snow, 1999). Language is initially acquired as a system to perform communicative functions that later serve as bootstraps to a formal system. Snow (1999) has termed this **pragmatic bootstrapping.** She argues that children first understand that it is possible to influence another's action by one's own behavior, which leads then to the production of speech acts. As speech acts come to be expressed with increasingly conventional forms borrowed from the adult's system, the child moves toward a language system that is no longer a set of expressions for different pragmatic intents. In support of this position, Snow (1999) cites evidence that the frequency with which 1-year-olds participate in communicative exchanges predicts their later grammatical development.

What is left unaddressed in this account, however, is just how the child makes the transition from the pragmatically based system to the adult's system. Some researchers have argued that children might exploit the correlations between language function and language form to crack the linguistic code (Bates & MacWhinney, 1982; Budwig, 1991). Such a proposal assumes that there are correlations between function and form for children to use and that function is somehow obvious to the child. Some research suggests that children are sensitive to form/function correspondences in language. For example, Choi (1991) found that Korean children under the age of 2 years used different sentence-ending suffixes depending on whether the sentence they were producing was a statement or a request. However, there is nothing remotely like evidence that children's sensitivity to form/function correspondences (or even perfect sensitivity to the form/function correspondences that exist) is sufficient to account for the acquisition of grammar.

***Communicative pressure as the source of communicative development.***
The proposals just described are all versions of the claim that the need to communicate fuels the acquisition of language form. A more limited effect of communicative pressure that has been proposed holds that communicative need does not affect linguistic development per se but does influence communicative development. For example, taking a somewhat different position from Mannle and Tomasello (1987), Barton and Tomasello (1994) proposed that interaction with fathers and siblings promotes skills that are communicative rather than purely linguistic. This proposal is supported by the evidence that younger siblings learn to interject themselves into others' conversations (Dunn & Shatz, 1989) and that later-born children are more skillful than firstborn children at producing contingent replies with minimal linguistic resources (Bernicot & Roux, 1998; Hoff-Ginsberg, 1998).

There is another example of children's learning communicatively relevant but not particularly linguistic skills that their environment demands. Children who live in cultures in which children are not talked to may learn to pay attention to speech among others instead. This must be true to a certain extent, or only Western middle-class children would learn to talk. Ochs (1988) offers anecdotal support for the idea that children who are not actively solicited to engage in conversation become particularly good at paying attention to the conversations that go on around them. Ochs observed that her Samoan research assistants, who grew up in such an environment, were much better at hearing background conversations on audiotape than she was.

***The independence of language function and language structure.*** It has also been proposed that the process of acquiring the structure of language has nothing to do with the fact that language is used to communicate. According to Chomsky, language is a formal, arbitrary system: "language is not intrinsically a system of communication" (1991, p. 51). Others would argue that although language may have been shaped over the course of evolutionary history by its communicative function (Pinker & Bloom, 1990), history has no relevance to the acquisition process (see Hoff-Ginsberg, 1999, for an outline of the theoretical possibilities). We have already reviewed the substantial evidence that being a communicative creature provides a necessary starting point for language acquisition. However, evidence also exists that communicative development and linguistic development are somewhat separable strands of development. For example, firstborn children tend to be more advanced than later-born children in acquiring a lexicon and grammar, whereas later-born children tend to be more advanced than firstborn children in acquiring conversational skill (Bernicot & Roux, 1998; Hoff-Ginsberg, 1998). The fact that the children who are most advanced in communicative skill are not the same children as those who are most advanced in linguistic skill suggests that communicative development and language development are somewhat separate enterprises for the child.

Some individuals with autism provide dramatic evidence of the dissociability of language and communicative skill. Although most individuals with autism have severe language difficulties, there are many cases of high-functioning individuals with autism who have nearly normal lexical and grammatical development but very aberrant pragmatic development. These individuals have acquired language, but they do not use it to communicate. Another illustration of dissociable communicative and linguistic development is provided in a case study entitled "Language without Communication." Blank, Gessner, and Esposito (1979) described a 3-year-old boy whose command of grammar and semantics were appropriate for his age, but whose sociocommunicative skills were severely deficient. For example, in interaction with his parents, this child typically either did not respond at all to his parents' speech or produced a completely unrelated response. When his mother asked, in the context of a pretend game about driving, "Are you going to go in and say hi to daddy?", the child replied, "O.K., here we are in the garage." Further evidence that this child's difficulties were communicative and not linguistic was his inability to understand nonverbal communicative signals, such as a pointing gesture. The cause of this child's communicative inability is unknown, but this case is a striking demonstration of the potential independence of language and communicative development.

## PRAGMATIC DEVELOPMENT

### First communicative intentions expressed in language

Having considered how communication might or might not lead to language per se, we now turn to the question of how children learn to put language to communicative purposes. Research on the development of communicative functions has made it clear (1) that children have a range of communicative intentions before they have the adult linguistic means of expressing those intentions and (2) that not just language but also communicative functions develop in the first few years.

Anne Carter (1978) intensively studied one child during the period just before the child began to use real words. She found that the child systematically used particular sound–gesture combinations to express eight different communicative functions, including requesting help, directing the listener's attention, and expressing pleasure. Table 6.2 lists these communicative schemata (also sometimes termed sensorimotor morphemes). Halliday (1975) described a similar, but not identical, set of functions in the early vocalizations of his subject. Looking at a slightly later point in language development, Dore (1975) identified nine different functions served by the single-word utterances of two children, which he called primitive speech acts (see Table 6.3). Because the children's linguistic means were limited at this one-word stage, they used other, extralinguistic means to indicate illocutionary force. Intonation is one such means. Dore observed one child's use of intonation: *Mama* said with a

**Table 6.2  Eight communicative behaviors produced by one child between the ages of 12 and 16 months**

| BEHAVIOR | | GOAL |
|---|---|---|
| *Gesture* | *Sound* | |
| Reach to object | /m/-initial | getting help in obtaining object |
| Point to or hold out object | /l/ or /d/-initial | drawing attention to object |
| | phonetic variant of *David* or *Mommy* | drawing attention to self |
| Reach to person | /h/-initial | getting or giving object |
| | /n/ or other nasal with prolonged falling intonation | getting help in changing situation |
| Waving hands, slapping | /b/-initial | getting help in removing object |
| Negative headshake | ʔə ʔə | same as above |
| Smile | breathy /h/ sounds | express pleasure |

Source: Adapted from "The Development of Systematic Vocalizations Prior to Words," by A. Carter. In N. Waterson & C. E. Snow (Eds). *The Development of Communication,* p. 130. Copyright © 1978 John Wiley & Sons, Ltd. Adapted by permission.

falling intonation contour was used to label; *mama* said with a rising intonation contour was used to question; and *mama* said with an abrupt rising–falling contour was used to call his mother when she was at a distance (Dore, 1975).

## Expansion of the communicative functions of language

Other studies spanning the age range from 10 to 22 months have documented developmental changes in children's interest in communicating, in the range of communicative intents they express, and in the number of different linguistic forms they use to realize each intention. In a longitudinal study, Snow and colleagues found that the frequency with which children between 14 and 20 months of age produced a behavior with some communicative intent doubled from about 4 per 10-minute period to nearly 8 (Snow,

**Table 6.3   Primitive speech acts at the one-word stage**

| Speech act | Definition | Example |
|---|---|---|
| Labeling | Use word while attending to object or event. Does not address adult or wait for a response. | Child touches doll's eyes and says "eyes." |
| Repeating | Repeats part or all of prior adult utterance. Does not wait for a response. | Child overhears mother's utterance of "doctor" and says "doctor." |
| Answering | Answers adult's question. Addresses adult. | Mother points to a picture of a dog and asks "What's that?" Child answers "bow-wow." |
| Requesting action | Word or vocalization often accompanied by gesture signaling demand. Addresses adult and awaits response. | Child, unable to push a peg through hole, utters "uh uh uh" while looking at mother. |
| Requesting | Asks question with a word, sometimes accompanying gesture. Addresses adult and awaits response. | Child picks up book, looks at mother, and says "book?" with rising intonation. Mother answers "Right, it's a book." |
| Calling | Calls adult's name loudly and awaits response. | Child shouts "mama" to his mother across the room. |
| Greeting | Greets adult or object upon its appearance. | Child says "hi" when teacher enters room. |
| Protesting | Resists adult's action with word or cry. Addresses adult. | Child, when mother attempts to put on his shoe, utters an extended scream while resisting her. |
| Practicing | Use of word or prosodic pattern in absence of any specific object or event. Does not address adult. Does await response. | Child utters "Daddy" when he is not present. |

Source: From "Exploring Children's Communicative Intents," by R. S. Chapman. In J. F. Miller (Ed.), *Assessing Language Production in Children,* pp. 111-136. Copyright © 1981 by Pearson Education. All rights reserved. Adapted by permission of Allyn & Bacon.

**Table 6.4   Examples of communicative intentions expressed by 1½-year-old children**

Calling hearer to attend to speaker.
Greeting on meeting.
Request/propose the initiation of a new activity.
Request/propose the continuation of a new activity.
Request/propose the repetition of an action.
Propose object to act on; action known.
Propose an act on a known object.
Propose a location for a known act on a known object.
Agree to do as requested.
Refuse to do as requested.
Propose the ending of an activity.
Statement discussing a joint focus of attention.
Statement discussing a recent event.
Statement discussing a past or future event.
Agreeing with a proposition.
Disagreeing with a proposition.
Correcting an utterance.
Yes–no question requesting clarification of utterance
Affirmative answer to yes–no questions.
Negative answer to yes–no questions.
Verbal move in telephone game.
Verbal move in peek-a-boo game.
Mark object transfer.
Mark completion of action.
Mark the falling of an object.
Exclaim in disapproval.
Exclaim in distress.
Exclaim in surprise or enthusiasm.

Source: From Ninio (1995).

Pan, Imbens-Bailey, & Herman, 1996). The parents' rate of communication during that time stayed constant (Pan, Imbens-Bailey, Winner, & Snow, 1996). Ninio (1995) studied children from 10 to 22 months old and found that in 30 minutes of interaction, the number of different communicative intents the children expressed increased from an average of 3 to an average of more than 30. Children also started out with just one way of expressing each intent—that is, one way to express distress, one way to propose a new activity, and so on—but at 22 months the children had multiple linguistic ways of performing many communicative functions. To capture the range of communicative intention at this point in development, Ninio used a system with 65 different categories. Examples of those functions are presented in Table 6.4.

Included in this expansion of communication functions between 1 and 2 years is a new kind of communicative behavior that emerges in children sometime around age 16 to 18 months, on average. Examples of this new function include the primitive speech acts of repeating, answering, and requesting. These utterances have functions that need to be defined in terms of the ongoing discourse; they serve either to respond to prior speech or to elicit further speech. These utterances still have communicative functions that can be defined at the utterance level—they request, they protest, and so on. However, unlike children's very first communicative behaviors, these newer types of speech acts need to be defined in terms of larger discourse context as well; the children are starting to be conversationalists. Another development in the meanings children express occurs by age 24 months, when children start to refer to absent objects and events and to use language imaginatively, as in pretend play. These first references to past events are the beginning of narrative development.

## DISCOURSE DEVELOPMENT

### The nature of young children's discourse

If you could be a fly on the wall in a preschool classroom, you would overhear conversations between children such as the following exchange, which occurred between two 4-year-olds (Schoeber-Peterson & Johnson, 1991).

> Child 1: I'm gonna put on my gloves. Are you finished making your
> dog, honey?
> Child 2: Almost.
> Child 1: Good.
> Child 2: I'm gonna get his nose on. Some of the parts are the same.
> This mechanical dog is more than I thought it was gonna be.
> He's taking it back. This will work.
> Child 1: This is nice. Oh, this is nice.

This conversation includes exchanges that seem to be examples of true dialogue, as when Child 1 asks, "Are you finished . . . ?" and Child 2 answers, "Almost." This conversation also includes a sequence of utterances in which Child 2 is talking to herself or himself about the toy dog being put together, and that stretch of speech is followed by Child 1's comments, which are unrelated to Child 2's speech. In discussing children's conversations, we start with the observation that conversations between children seem different and, in many ways, less successful than conversations between adults. We will ask two questions about children's conversations: (1) How are they different from adult-to-adult conversations? and (2) What causes these differences?

***Piaget's description of the egocentric child.***   The earliest answers to these questions come from the Swiss developmentalist Jean Piaget. According to Piaget, preschool children's speech is not really communicative (Kohlberg, Yeager, & Hjertholm, 1968; Piaget, 1926). On the basis of his own observations of the spontaneous conversations of young children, Piaget claimed that although children may take turns talking, each speaker's turn has little to do with the previous speaker's turn. Rather, each child is producing his or her own monologue, albeit with interruptions for the other child's monologue. Accordingly, Piaget termed such interactions **collective monologues.**

The preschool child does not participate in true dialogue because, according to Piaget, the child is "unable to place himself at the point of view of his hearer" and has "no desire to influence his hearer or to tell him anything" (Piaget, 1926, p. 9; Schoeber-Peterson & Johnson, 1991). Thus, Piaget proposed two explanations for why preschool children do not engage in true dialogue; one had to do with "skill," the other with "will" (Kohlberg et al., 1968). The skill-based explanation held that children lack the requisite cognitive ability. In Piaget's terminology, preschool children are egocentric. This **egocentrism** is not limited to language use but is a general characteristic of children's thought at this stage. For example, preschool children have difficulty with tasks that require them to indicate what a visual array would look like from a different vantage point. (For a more complete description of Piaget's theory of childhood egocentrism and of research questioning that theory, see Gelman & Baillargeon, 1983.) The will-based part of the explanation Piaget offered claimed that preschool children are not trying to engage in dialogue. It is possible to pursue both explanations in subsequent work on the functions of young children's speech. One line of research pursues the explanation that children are not trying to engage in dialogue and focuses on the functions of children's self-directed, or private, speech. Another line of research investigates in greater depth children's abilities to participate in true conversation with others.

***Private speech.***   Everyone talks to themselves sometimes, particularly when engaged in a difficult task (John-Steiner, 1992). Young children talk to themselves more, and more obviously, than older children and adults do, but like adults, children are particularly likely to talk to themselves when they are alone and engaged in a task or in play (Winsler, Carlton, & Barry, 2000; Winsler, De Leon, Wallace, Carlton, & Willson-Quayle, 2003). Some children produce soliloquies alone in their beds before they fall asleep. Children also produce monologues in the presence of other people, in what would seem to adults to be a more suitable context for conversation. Research on children's nondialogic speech, or **private speech,** has looked at both solitary monologues and at monologues that occur in conversational contexts.

***Solitary monologues.*** Researchers who have studied children's solitary monologues suggest that children use these monologues for language exploration and practice (Gallagher & Craig, 1978; Nelson, 1989; Weir, 1962). In a famous early study of presleep soliloquies, Weir (1962) recorded the presleep narratives of her 2-year-old son by means of a remote-controlled microphone placed in the child's bedroom. Weir found that the child produced sequences such as the following, which she termed a "substitution exercise" (Weir, 1962, pp. 135–136).

> Mommy's too weak
> Alice strong
> Alice too weak
> Alice too weak
> Daddy's too weak
> Mommy's too weak
> Too weak with Barbara
> Be careful Barbara
> Barbara can broke
> Careful broke the [rami]
> Careful broke Anthony
> Careful broke it
> Careful broke the
> Broke the finger
> Broke the Bobo
> Broke the vacuum clean

According to Weir, this child was practicing language. The notion that children practice language in their presleep soliloquies is also supported by Nelson's (1989) study of the presleep narratives of one 2-year-old girl (recorded by means of a microphone her parents hid in her bedroom). This child produced extended narratives about events in her day, and the narratives she produced when alone were longer and more complex than the narratives she produced in conversation with her parents.

The notion that children are practicing or exploring language doesn't mean that this activity is work for them. To the contrary, it is **language play.** The ability to play with language is itself a skill that is manifest in forms as varied as puns and poetry. The tendency to engage in spontaneous language play may be related to skill at language play. For example, kindergarten children who produce high amounts of language play in their spontaneous speech are also better than average at explaining verbal riddles, such as *Why didn't the skeleton cross the road? He didn't have the guts* (Ely & McCabe, 1994; Fowles & Glanz, 1977).

***Vygotsky's theory of the function of private speech.*** According to the developmental theory of Russian psychologist Lev Vygotsky (Vygotsky, 1962, 1978; Wertsch, 1985), the primary function of private speech is not language exploration but behavioral self-guidance. This account of private speech derives from Vygotsky's theory that an individual's cognitive skills develop first in social interaction and then later are internalized. For example, a young child who is unable to perform a task such as putting a puzzle together alone can do so with the help of an adult who provides direction. At a later point in development, the child can do the task alone because the child has internalized the directions originally provided by the adult.

Private speech, in this view, is an intermediary stage during which the child is overtly producing the self-talk that will eventually be internalized. This explanation of private speech would not apply to presleep soliloquies but to situations in which children produce private speech as they are acting on objects. Other research supports the Vygotskyan view that first another person's speech, and then one's own private speech, guides behavior. Evidence shows that the kind of talk adults provide children does improve the children's task performance (Behrend, Rosengran, & Perlmutter, 1992; Wood, Wood, & Middleton, 1978) and that the private speech children produce during a task predicts their later performance on the same task (Behrend et al., 1992). This developmental sequence of first hearing the speech from another, then producing it oneself, and finally producing it internally has nothing to do with conversation per se. However, if children are engaged in a task while simultaneously engaged in conversation, the private speech they produce for self-guidance will intrude into the conversation.

Piaget and Vygotsky, then, provide two different accounts of why young children produce monologue in what most adults would construe to be a conversational setting. The Piagetian view is that the child lacks the requisite ability and interest to be truly conversational. The Vygotskyan view is that the child is doing something else with his or her speech. These two views are not necessarily incompatible (Warren & Tate, 1992). Monologue may be interspersed with dialogic speech for different reasons at different times.

In the next section, we focus on describing children's development of conversational skills. We will see that although Piagetian theory motivated some of the early research on children's development of communicative competence, a more useful theoretical system for organizing the research on children's conversation comes from the work on the philosophy of language with which we began this chapter. Remember Grice's description of the rules of conversation: Take turns and cooperate by making your turn informative, relevant, sincere, and clear. In this section, we discuss developmental changes that occur as children come to behave in accordance with that description. The topic of this section, then, is children's development of the mechanics of conversation, including the development of turn taking, the ability to initiate conversational topics, and the ability to sustain connected discourse with another speaker. We will start this description with evidence from observations of children interacting with adults—usually their mothers. We will find evidence that children know something about the mechanics of conversation from the age of about 1 year, but we will also see that mothers provide substantial support for their children's conversational role. We will turn then to descriptions of children's conversations with peers.

## The development of conversational skill

Although mothers and babies in Western cultures interact in formats that have the structure of conversations, babies do not do much to hold up their end of a dialogue. Very young babies do look at their mothers when their mothers vocalize; however, the turn-taking structure of early mother–child interaction (in those cultures where it occurs) appears to depend on mothers' building a conversational structure around their children's behavior, and it does not reflect infants' interactive skill (Shatz, 1983a). There is no clear landmark that signifies children's entry into conversational participation. Rather, the relative burdens carried by the adult and the child in sustaining conversation gradually become more equal as children develop an understanding that they have responsibilities as conversational participants, as they learn what is required of them to fulfill these responsibilities in different linguistic contexts, and as they master the linguistic devices for meeting these requirements (Shatz, 1983a).

***Responding to speech.*** Children's first understanding about the rules of conversation is the understanding that they are supposed to respond to another speaker's utterance. An early strategy that children employ to fulfill this conversational obligation is to respond with action. That is, when an adult says something to a young child, the child is quite likely to do something rather than to say something in response. This strategy allows young children to respond appropriately to much of what is typically said to them, such as "Why don't you play in the sandbox?" and "Where are your shoes?" The effectiveness of such a strategy in most everyday situations can mislead observers into thinking that children understand much more of what is said to them than they actually do. (See Chapter 5's discussion of sentence comprehension strategies.) However, clever experimenters can reveal when children are using strategic shortcuts to achieve appropriate responses. When Shatz (1978a) asked 2-year-olds questions for which an action response would not be appropriate, she found that sometimes 2-year-olds responded with action anyway. For example, when asked, "Why don't you wear shoes on your head?" one child promptly removed his shoes from his feet and placed them on his head.

***Differential responding to different utterance types.***    Gradually, children start to respond more frequently to talk with talk and also to respond differently to different kinds of utterances (Shatz & McCloskey, 1984). In general, children are more likely to respond to questions than to nonquestions (Hoff-Ginsberg, 1990; Shatz, 1983a). Children under 2 years of age are more likely to respond verbally to "what" or "where" questions than to other question forms. Allen and Shatz (1983) suggested that the word *what* in particular serves as an early signal to the child that action is not an appropriate response. In contrast, "why" questions—perhaps because of their abstract meaning (Blank & Allen, 1976)—seem particularly difficult for children.

In some cases, children's ability to take turns and respond in conversationally appropriate ways actually outstrips their understanding of what is being said. For example, children who cannot correctly identify any colors but who know several color words will reliably answer the question "What color is this?" with a color term, although the particular color term may have only a chance probability of being correct (Shatz, 1983a). A similar case is the preschool child who knows to answer the question "What time is it?" with a number, but who reveals her ignorance with answers such as "four-eighty" (personal data). In other cases, however, children as young as 2 years old also produce appropriately different messages to different kinds of questions. For example, when adults fail to understand a child's utterances, the adult may indicate that failure with a general query such as "What?" or with a more specific query about just part of what the child has said, such as "You want what?" Anselmi, Tomasello, and Acunzo (1986) found that preschoolers were more likely to repeat their entire utterance in response to a general query and to repeat only the requested utterance part in response to a specific query. It seems, then, that 1- and 2-year-olds' abilities to participate in conversation are based on a mixture of partial understandings and strategies for participating despite only partial understandings. What children do seem to understand by the age of 2 years is that in conversation one takes turns, and what one says in one's turn is constrained by what the previous speaker has said. In some cases, children's understanding of those constraints is based more on the form than on the content of utterances.

***Initiating topics.***    Another conversational skill is the ability to initiate topics. **Topics** are what conversations are about, so the speaker who initiates topics determines what the conversation will be about. Susan Foster studied the development of topic initiation using videotaped conversations between five children and their mothers, covering an age range in the children from 1 month to 2 years (Foster, 1986). Foster observed three developmental changes in children's topic initiations: (1) With increasing age, children successfully initiated more topics, (2) the means of topic initiation changed from nonverbal to verbal, and (3) the type of topic children initiated changed. With respect to type, children's first topic initiations were about themselves. Next, children began initiating topics about things in the environment, and last (around the age of $1^{1}/_{2}$ years), children began initiating topics about absent or intangible things.

Foster found that the acquisition of language proceeded in parallel with changes in the success and the type of topic initiations, and it no doubt contributed to these changes. However, Foster (1986) points out that the development of topic initiation skills is not solely a matter of developing language skill. She cites the example of a late talker who was nonetheless highly communicative at the age of 1 year and 10 months:

> On one occasion, when [the child] and her mother were looking at a book together, they came across a picture of a cat. Kate promptly pointed to the door to the back garden. Her mother responded with "Yes, there's a cat outside isn't there sometimes." Kate then said "gone," to which her mother replied, "It's gone now yes. We saw it yesterday didn't we?" (p. 246)

In this case, the child successfully initiated a conversation about an absent cat using only gesture. This example concerns a question that has and will come up several times in this chapter: How independent are communicative development and language development? Here Foster argues for some independence. This example also illustrates another recurring theme—the important contributions of a motivated conversational partner and of shared knowledge between speaker and listener to the success of conversation with young children.

***Repairing miscommunication.***    Even motivated conversational partners do not always understand what children are trying to communicate, and children's attempts at topic initiation are not always successful. A necessary conversational skill is the ability to respond to communicative failures by repeating or revising the message so that it is understood. Studies of children's responses to adults' comprehension failures describe the development of this skill. Beyond description, studies of how children respond to communicative failures may shed light on the intentions behind children's communicative efforts.

As is true for initiating topics, efforts at repairing misunderstood signals can be seen in preverbal children. When adults fail to understand children's noises and gestures, children often persevere, repeating or modifying their signal until they achieve the desired outcome. Golinkoff (1983) labeled such

---

**Box 6.4    An example of the preverbal child's negotiation of a failed message**

Child: (*vocalizes repeatedly until his mother turns around*)

Mother: (*turns around to look at child*)

Child: (*points to one of the objects on the counter*)

Mother: Do you want this? (*holds up milk container*)

Child: (*shakes head "no"*)

Mother: Do you want this? (*holds up jelly jar*)

Child: (*shakes head "no"*)

    (two more offer rejection pairs follow)

Mother: This? (*picks up sponge*)

Child: (*leans back in highchair and puts arms down: tension leaves body*)

Mother: (*hands child sponge*)

---

Source: From Golinkoff, 1983.

interactions "preverbal negotiations of failed messages." Golinkoff (1986) analyzed the mealtime interactions between three mothers and their children over the age range from approximately 1 to 1½ years. During the period studied, roughly half of the children's efforts at communication were initially unsuccessful; but by repeating, revising, or substituting a new signal, the children were ultimately able to be successful 55 percent of the time at 1 year and 72 percent of the time at age 1½. Box 6.4 illustrates one example of such a negotiation.

As children acquire language, both their messages and their repairs become more frequently verbal. There also may be developmental changes in how children repair their messages. Several, but not all, studies of older children's repairs suggest that young children (between 1 and 3 years old) are more likely to simply repeat a misunderstood message, whereas older children (between 3 and 5 years old) are more likely to revise their message (Anselmi et al., 1986; Brinton, Fujiki, Loab, & Winkler, 1986; Furrow & Lewis, 1987; Gallagher, 1977; Tomasello, Farrar, & Dines, 1984; Wilcox & Webster, 1980).

***Sustaining dialogue and contingent responding.***    For conversation to be sustainable for very long, each party's contribution must be relevant to the previous speaker's turn. A salient change in children's conversational abilities after the age of 2 years is an increase in the length of conversation children are able to sustain. Brown (1980) compared the conversations of 21 children

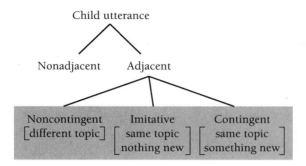

**Figure 6.1**  Categories of child discourse

Source: From "Adult-Child Discourse," by L. Bloom et al., 1976, *Cognitive Psychology,* 8, 521–552. Copyright © 1976. Academic Press, Inc. Reprinted by permission.

who were all 30 months old but who ranged in productive language ability from an MLU of 1.0 to an MLU of 3.0. Brown estimated that the number of topically related utterances children can produce in sequence (related either to their own prior utterance or to intervening utterances by adults) changed from an average of less than 1 utterance at MLU = 1.0 to an average of over 20 related utterances at MLU = 3.0.

Bloom, Rocissano, and Hood (1976) have carefully investigated the development of children's ability to produce related replies. As their database, they used transcripts of adult–child interaction recorded for four children at three different points in the children's development: at Stage 1 (MLU less than 2.0), at Stage 2 (MLU = 2–2.75), and at Stage 5 (MLU = 3.5–4.0). The age range covered approximately 21 months to 36 months. Each utterance by a child was coded in the transcripts as either adjacent (occurring after an adult utterance) or nonadjacent (without a prior adult utterance or with a definite pause). Adjacent utterances were further coded as noncontingent (on a different topic), imitative (on the same topic but with no new information), or contingent (on the same topic and adding new information). The coding scheme is diagrammed in Figure 6.1.

At all stages, most of the children's speech was adjacent, and there was no clear developmental change in the proportion of adjacent speech. Thus, Bloom and associates concluded that from before the age of 2 years, children followed the conversational rule of responding to another speaker. What changed with development was the kind of response children produced. Responses that were noncontingent or only imitative became less frequent as the children got older, and contingent responses became more frequent. The results from this study are graphed in Figure 6.2.

Apparently, initiating a new topic is actually easier for children than producing a response that shares the first speaker's topic and adds new information to it. Bloom and associates explained this finding in terms of the cognitive-processing demands of producing each type of utterance. Producing

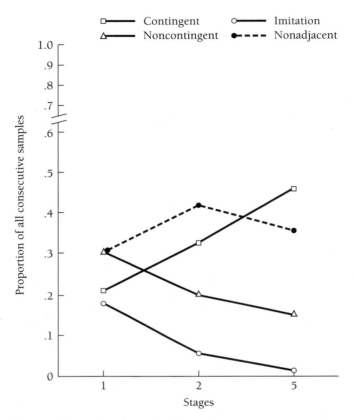

**Figure 6.2**  Developmental changes in the relative frequency of nonadjacent, contingent, noncontingent, and imitative speech

Source: From "Adult-Child Discourse," by L. Bloom et al., 1976, *Cognitive Psychology,* 8, 521–552. Copyright © 1976. Academic Press, Inc. Reprinted by permission.

a spontaneous utterance requires retrieving information from memory to formulate a message and attending to the ongoing interaction. Producing a contingent reply additionally requires attending to the content of the prior speaker's message. Paying attention to three things in formulating a message is more difficult than paying attention to two things.

Bloom, Rocissano, and Hood (1976) also found developmental changes in the kind of contingent responses that children produced. The frequency of contextually contingent responses declined with age, whereas the frequency of linguistically contingent responses increased. Contextually contingent responses refer to the same topic as the prior utterance does but are structurally unrelated to the prior utterance, as in the following example:

Adult: Where's the other sock?
Child: See my sitting on it.

The linguistically contingent form of a reply would be "It is" followed by a prepositional phrase that describes a location. The answer in the preceding example provides the requested information but not in the linguistically contingent form.

In contrast, linguistically contingent responses not only are about the same thing as the prior utterance but also use the sentence structure of the prior utterance, as in the following example:

Adult: Pussycat is calling to wolf. Why?
Child: Because he's up in this building too tall.

Linguistically speaking, "because" is the appropriate form of an answer to a "why" question. This finding of an increase in linguistic contingency suggests that learning to use the structure of language to link utterances in discourse is a later development than simply understanding that conversation requires producing semantically related utterances. However, remember from our discussion of children's turn taking that children seem to know something about the form their reply should take even without fully understanding the meaning of either the question or their answer. As was the case for topic initiating, topic maintenance skills develop along with language skills, but each component of development has some level of independence as well.

***The role of the adult.*** A final point to reiterate about children's conversational competence as evidenced in mother–child interactions is the fact that the mothers helped. In the example of nonverbal topic initiations presented earlier, the success depended as much on the mother as it did on the child. In verbal interactions, mothers also contribute to their children's ability to participate. For example, maternal speech characteristically includes a very high proportion of questions, and children are more likely to respond to questions than to other types of utterances (Hoff-Ginsberg, 1990). Thus, children's responsiveness is due in part to their mothers' efforts at eliciting responses. The children in Bloom and associates' (1976) study were also more likely to produce contingent responses to questions than to nonquestions; the frequency of contingent responding in those data therefore depended in part on the mothers. Finally, in Bloom and associates' data, as the children's linguistically contingent responses to questions increased, the adults increased the frequency with which they asked questions, thus contributing to the observed developmental increase in the frequency of contingent responding.

Other researchers have identified additional means that mothers employ to sustain conversations with young children. For example, Kaye and Charney (1980) described mothers' use of "turnabouts," which both respond to the child's prior utterance and request further response. More generally, mothers' efforts to follow their children's leads in conversation may contribute to sustaining dialogue. Hoff-Ginsberg (1987) found that children were more likely to respond to maternal speech that continued a topic in the child's prior speech than to speech that initiated new topics.

***Young children's peer conversations.*** If mothers help sustain conversation with young children, then a truer, or stricter, test of children's conversational abilities would come from examining children's conversations with one another. In fact, Piaget's description of children as egocentric rather than communicative was based on observations of peer interactions. More recent research on children's peer conversation presents a mixed picture. It is possible to find both examples of egocentric speech such as Piaget described and examples of dialogue that suggest greater communicative competence than Piaget attributed to young children.

Keenan (1974) conducted one of the first studies that challenged the description of preschool children as incapable and uninterested in true dialogue. Keenan recorded the conversations that occurred between her twin 2-year-old sons early in the morning while the twins were alone in their room. (Babies of child language researchers should watch out for hidden microphones.) She found that the children did attend to each other's speech and produced related utterances. However, the children's ability to sustain a topic was limited, and the longest stretches of related exchanges between the children consisted of sound play with no semantic content at all. Box 6.5 presents examples of the Keenan twins' conversations.

Other evidence of conversational competence in 2-year-olds comes from Wellman and Lempers (1977), who studied naturally occurring instances in which 2-year-old children in a preschool setting initiated interaction by pointing out, showing, or displaying something. Wellman and Lempers found that 2-year-olds did initiate such interactions. Eighty percent of these initiations were directed to adults, and only 20 percent to other children. The children's initiations were successful in obtaining a response almost 80 percent of the time, and when they did not receive a response, they tried again with a revised message more than 50 percent of the time. Like Keenan's data, these data suggest that children as young as 2 years old are interested in and capable of engaging others in communicative interaction. Wellman and Lempers' data further suggest that children take into consideration characteristics of their listener, by preferring more competent adult listeners over peers and by adapting their messages to listener feedback. Although such data indicate that preschool children have the will to enter into communicative interactions with others, their skills at doing so are still developing. Garvey and Hogan (1973) observed the free-play interactions of 3- to 5-year-old children and found that children were able to

---

**Box 6.5    Examples of 2½-year-old twins' conversations**

*A topically related sequence:*

Child 1: tree
            see got grass
Child 2: yes I see it
            I see it

*A sound play sequence (nonwords are written
in standard orthography):*

Child 1: wake up
            wake up
Child 2: hake ut *(laughing)*
Child 1: hake ut
Child 2: bake up
Child 1: break ut
            break up
Child 2: wake up
            wake up *(laughing)*

Source: From Keenan, 1974.

sustain sequences of talk that ranged from 4 to 12 or more exchanges in length and that between 21 percent and 77 percent of the children's utterances were contingent on the verbal or nonverbal behavior of others. Schoeber-Peterson and Johnson (1989) studied 4-year-olds' conversations and found that the percent of conversational segments that were dialogue ranged from 23 percent to 70 percent, across 10 different dyads. The length of dialogue that these 4-year-olds sustained for a single topic was shorter than 12 utterances for 75 percent of the conversational topics. On occasion, however, the 4-year-olds sustained topics for much longer stretches of dialogue—even up to 91 consecutive utterances.

One factor that seems to be an important influence on the success of preschool children's conversation is the context in which the conversation occurs. Nelson and Gruendel (1979) suggested that children's ability to sustain dialogue is facilitated when they share knowledge that provides a background for their conversations. In preschool settings, where much of the dialogue occurs in the context of pretend play, the background for interaction is the shared knowledge of routines such as planning a meal or going shopping. In support of this notion, French, Lucariello, Seidman, and Nelson (1985) reviewed evidence from several studies suggesting that when children share contextual knowledge, their conversations are longer and their language use is more advanced than when they do not share background knowledge.

## The development of narrative skill

Speakers can also produce extended discourse without a conversational partner: They can produce monologues. The most studied sort of monologue is the narrative, which is a verbal description of a past event. In ordinary language, narratives are stories. Ultimately, adult speakers are able to tell relatively long, complete stories in an uninterrupted monologue. Children's first narratives, however, occur in the context of conversation.

***The conversational origin of narratives.***     Eisenberg (1985) described three phases in children's development of the ability to talk about past experiences. In the first phase, children's talk about the past is typically elicited and maintained by an adult. The adult provides the **scaffolding** for children's reports of past experience by introducing a past event as a topic ("Did you go to the zoo?") and then eliciting more information on the topic ("What did you see there?"). In these early narratives, most of the content of the narrative is supplied by the adult, and the child supplies single-word responses to the adult's questions.

In the second phase of narrative development, children depend less on the scaffolding of adults' questions, and the children's contributions are longer and introduce new information. However, children's reports of past events during this phase tend to be general descriptions of a kind of familiar event rather than specific descriptions of particular events. For example, a child's recounting of a birthday party might include things that didn't actually occur at that birthday party but that are typical of birthday parties in general. In the third phase, children's narratives depend less on either conversational support or general event knowledge, and they include more information that is unique to the particular event being recounted.

***Adults' scaffolding of children's narratives.***     Some parents provide more useful scaffolding for their children's early narratives than others do. Reese and Fivush (1993) described two different styles in parents' elicitations of past event descriptions from their 3-year-old children. An elaborative style is characterized by questions that help the child say something that moves the narrative forward. In contrast, a repetitive style is characterized by questions that seek the same information over and over again. These two styles are illustrated in Box 6.6.

Box 6.6 **Examples of elaborative and repetitive styles in parents' elicitations of past-event descriptions from 3-year-old children**

*Elaborative style elicitation:*

Parent: Did we see any big fishes? What kind of big fishes?
Child: Big, big, big.
Parent: And what's their names?
Child: I don't know.
Parent: You remember the names of the fishes. What we called them. Michael's favorite kind of fish. Big mean ugly fish.
Child: Yeah.
Parent: What kind is it?
Child: um. ba
Parent: A ssshark?
Child: Yeah.
Parent: Do you? What else did we see in the big tank at the aquarium?
Child: I don't know.
Parent: Remember when we first came in, remember when we first came in the aquarium? And we looked down and there were a whole bunch of birdies in the water? Remember the names of the birdies?
Child: Ducks!
Parent: Nooo! They weren't ducks. They had on little suits. Penguins. Remember, what did the penguins do?
Child: I don't know.

*Repetitive style elicitation:*

Parent: How did we get to Florida, do you remember?
Child: Yes.
Parent: How did we get there? What did we do? You remember?
Child: Yeah.
Parent: You want to sit up here in my lap?
Child: No.
Parent: Oh, okay. Remember when we went to Florida, how did we get there? We went in the _____?

*(continued)*

> **Box 6.6** *(continued)*
>
> Child: The ocean.
> Parent: Well, be—, when we got to Florida we went to the ocean, that's right, but how did we get down to Florida? Did we drive our car?
> Child: Yes.
> Parent: No, think again. I don't think we drove to Florida, How did we get down there, remember, we took a great big _____? Do you remember?

Source: From Reese & Fivush, 1993.

An elaborative style not only helps in the immediate production of a narrative, but also appears to influence the later development of children's ability to produce narratives alone. McCabe and Peterson (1991) found that children whose parents asked useful, elaborative questions when the children were 2 years old produced better narratives when they were 3, and Fivush (1991) found that the complexity and structure of the narratives mothers produced in conversation with their 2-year-olds were related to the complexity and structure of those children's narratives a year later. Similarly, Haden, Haine, & Fivush (1997) found that parents' use of certain narrative devices in joint reminiscing with their children at 3½ years predicted the children's use of those devices in their own narratives at 5½ years. These findings have been interpreted as reflecting the developmental process described by Vygotsky (1962). That is, what children first do in collaboration with an adult, they internalize and later do on their own.

***Developmental changes in children's narratives.*** In addition to the growing independence from adult support, other developmental trends in children's early narrative production include increases in the frequency of spontaneous mention of past events, increases in the length of the narratives produced, increases in the remoteness of the past event, increases in the structural complexity of the stories told, and increases in the use of narrative devices such as orienting to time and place and evaluating the events in the narrative (Haden et al., 1997; Miller & Sperry, 1988; Umiker-Sebeok, 1979). For example, Umiker-Sebeok recorded the peer interactions of 3-, 4-, and 5-year-old children in preschool settings and found that the proportion of conversations that included narratives increased from 23 percent in the 3-year-olds to 35 percent in the 5-year-olds. The average length of the 3-year-olds' narratives was 1.7 clauses, compared with 2.8

---

**Box 6.7   Examples of 3-year-olds' and 4-year-olds' intraconversational narratives**

*3-year-olds*

Child: You know what I was doing?
Adult: What?
Child: I was doing my work.
Adult: Your work?
Child: Like I do at home.

*4-year-olds*

Child: . . . I have two sisters, one with blond hair like me'n the other with long black hair. 'N the one with black hair, when she was four like me, she cut her hair with scissors that aren't for cutting hair. 'N now she has short hair.

---

Source: From Umiker-Sebeok, 1979.

for the 5-year-olds. With respect to complexity, the 3-year-olds' narratives tended to be simply a mention of a past activity. In contrast, the longer narratives of the 4- and 5-year-olds were more likely to have the plot elements of a story. These developmental changes are illustrated in the examples in Box 6.7.

The example of a 4-year-old's narrative in Box 6.7 is an unusually good narrative for a child of that age. Although children's narrative skills increase notably from their first descriptions of past events around the age of 2 years to their more structured stories at 4 years, much is still lacking in 5-year-olds' narratives. Often the narratives 5-year-olds produce are difficult to fully understand unless the listener is already familiar with the event being described, because young narrators fail to provide enough information. At the age of 5 years, children have not fully mastered the tense system, and thus it is sometimes hard to know exactly when events in their stories occurred relative to each other. Often the referents of pronouns are unclear.

Children's narratives improve during the school years. One source of improvement is children's increasing mastery of the linguistic devices necessary to make temporal order and pronoun reference clear and to link clauses together in a single cohesive piece (see, for example, Bamberg, 1987; Berman & Slobin, 1994; Karmiloff-Smith, 1986; Peterson & McCabe, 1988). Another source of improvement in children's narratives is their increasing understanding of the structure of a story. We will describe these developments in more detail in Chapter 9.

## SOCIOLINGUISTIC DEVELOPMENT

### Learning to produce situationally appropriate language

Communicative competence includes the ability to use speech that is appropriate to the circumstance. For example, it would be inappropriate for a child to say to a parent, "Gimme five bucks"; and it would be absurd for an 8-year-old to say to an infant, "It would be awfully nice of you to get out of my way, my dear Mr. Jones" (Becker, 1982). In this case, the social status of the listener determines the appropriate use of language.

Social status of the listener is not the only factor relevant to language use. It would not be particularly communicative to answer a 2-year-old's question about how a car works the same way that you would answer a 10-year-old's question. In this case, the cognitive capacity of the listener is the relevant variable. Sometimes the choice of register depends on multiple factors. In Samoan, there are two speech registers (referred to as "good" speech and "bad" speech), which differ in phonological, lexical, and grammatical features. Which register is appropriate depends on the setting (such as church versus home), the addressee (family member versus Westerner), and the topic of conversation (food preparation versus the Bible). "Good" speech is used in church, in talking to Westerners, and in talking about things like the Bible; "bad" speech is used at home, in talking to family members, and in talking about informal, everyday topics (Ochs, 1988). Using language appropriately requires control over the different styles that different situations require, and it requires knowing when to use what register. Appropriate language use also requires attention to the relevant features of the situation.

***The egocentric child.***    Until at least the 1970s, the Piagetian position that preschoolers are egocentric led most people to assume that children had quite limited abilities to attend to the relevant features of the social setting and to modify their speech accordingly. Support for this pessimistic view of children's communicative competence also came from experimental work on children's **referential communication** skills. In the task used in much of the referential communication research, children are asked to describe one item in an array of objects so that a visually separated listener with the same array can identify the item. Four- and 5-year-old children (who are typically the youngest children tested with this procedure) are not very successful at this task. They provide clues like "Daddy's shirt" as a description of a geometric form and then describe another form as "another Daddy's shirt" (Glucksberg, Krauss, & Higgins, 1975). Such inadequate descriptions have been attributed to children's inability to take into account the needs of their listener. However, examination of children's language use in naturalistic settings often shows more competence than the Piagetian view would predict.

***Children's use of request forms.***   One way to examine children's ability to modify their speech to fit the social situation is to focus on one speech function and look at the different ways in which children express that function in different situations. Children's use of requests has been sufficiently studied to provide useful data in this regard (Becker, 1982). The first step in describing children's use of different forms as requests is to identify the different forms children have available to them. Ervin-Tripp (1976) proposed a system for categorizing request forms based on how direct the form is. For example, imperatives (such as "Give me a fork") are the most direct, need statements ("I need a fork") are somewhat less direct, question-form directives ("Can I have a fork?") even less direct, and hints ("Someone forgot to set a fork at this place") are the most indirect. With a system for categorizing request forms, it is then possible to ask which kinds of forms children know how to produce.

Researchers have found that even telegraphic speakers know more than one way to form a request. For example, they can state their goal ("More juice"), they can issue direct imperatives ("Book read"), or they can state the problem that needs solution ("Carol hungry") (Ervin-Tripp, 1977). Two- and 3-year-olds who have mastered the syntactic form of questions also use question-form requests (such as "Would you push this?" and "Can you give me one car, please?"), and 3-year-olds use hints ("You could give one to me," "You can make a crown") (Ervin-Tripp, 1977). Other researchers have also supported the conclusion that preschool children (between 3 and 5 years old) have more than one form for expressing requests at their disposal (Dore, 1977; Garvey, 1975). If even very young speakers have multiple ways of requesting available to them, then it is possible to ask whether children select different forms from their repertoires depending on the circumstance. The literature clearly suggests that they do. The earliest differential use of request forms has been observed in the study of one 2-year-old girl (Lawson, 1967, cited by Ervin-Tripp, 1976; 1977). This child used simple imperatives in talking to other 2-year-olds at preschool, she usually modified her imperatives by adding *Please* in talking to 3-year-olds, and she used questions when making requests of 4-year-olds. In talking to adults, she used primarily desire statements or questions. At home she also differentiated between her mother and father, being much more direct with her mother. (In this case, it's not clear that perceived status was the relevant factor; her mother may have been more familiar to her [Becker, 1982].)

***Politeness.***   Perceived politeness is at least one of the differences between more- and less-direct forms of request that explains why both children and adults are less direct with higher-status addressees. There seems to be a conversational rule to be more polite with higher-status listeners, and indirect forms are more polite than direct forms. (For a discussion of other understandings implicated by children's use of request forms, see Becker, 1982.)

Children not only use less direct forms with higher-status listeners, but also switch to less direct forms when they are asked to be "nicer." Bates (1976) investigated children's productive control over degrees of politeness by eliciting requests from them. Bates introduced Italian children to a hand puppet representing an elderly gray-haired woman named Signora Rossi (Mrs. Rossi), who had lots of candy. The children were told that Mrs. Rossi would give them a piece of candy if they asked for one. After the children made their request, the experimenter pretended to confer with the puppet and then told the children: "Mrs. Rossi said that she will surely give you a candy. But, you know, she's a bit old, and she likes it when children are VERY, very nice. Ask her again EVEN MORE NICELY for the candy." Regardless of how they formed their second request, the children were given candy. Two main findings emerged from this task: (1) Older children—3 years 5 months to 4 years—used more-varied forms to express requests and were, in general, more indirect than younger children aged 2 years 10 months to 3 years 5 months; (2) Both older and younger children were able to use a different and less direct form the second time they asked.

Thus, evidence suggests that children as young as 3 years of age know to use a less direct form when they are asked to be more polite. Between the ages of 3 and 6, children acquire a variety of different ways of being less direct. Bates also asked the children in her study to judge the politeness of different forms of request and found developmental increases in children's ability to discriminate different forms as being different in politeness. For the most part, the forms produced at a younger age in response to the request to ask "even more nicely" were also the forms that were recognized as polite at a younger age.

***Children's child-directed speech.*** Another aspect of children's sociolinguistic skill that has been studied in some detail is the modifications children make when talking to listeners who are even younger than themselves. Again, a review of the evidence begins with Piaget's (1926) description of children as relatively incompetent. One example of Piaget's research is a study in which 6-year-old children were shown a diagram of a water tap (illustrated in Figure 6.3) and given an explanation of how the tap worked. The children were then required to explain how the tap worked to a peer. Piaget found children's explanations of the water tap to be inadequate in several ways. The children did not order their explanations properly or explain causal connections between elements in the explanation in a way that would ensure listener comprehension (Shatz & Gelman, 1973). (Compare the adult's and child's explanations presented in Box 6.8.) Piaget attributed the poor quality of children's explanations to their egocentrism. Because children cannot consider the perspective of others, they cannot make their messages fit their listeners' needs.

Although the inadequacy of even 6-year-olds' mechanical explanations is not in doubt, the explanation in terms of egocentrism now seems wrong.

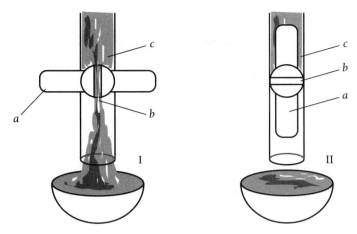

**Figure 6.3**   Diagram of water tap used in Piaget's study of children's communication skill

Source: From Piaget, 1926.

Children may not be able to put together a clear explanation, but it is not because they don't know that different listeners need different messages. When children's speech to other children is examined in the contexts of less difficult tasks or more naturalistic settings, evidence demonstrates that children do adjust their speech depending on their listener's ability. They talk differently to peers than to adults, and they talk differently to younger children than to peers. Shatz and Gelman (1973) asked 4-year-olds to explain to their mothers and to 2-year-olds how a toy dumping station worked. They found that the 4-year-olds' speech to the adult and to the 2-year-old differed on a number of levels. Speech to adults had a longer MLU and more frequently included complex constructions. Speech to 2-year-olds more frequently included devices to secure and direct the listener's attention such as the words *Hey, Look,* and *Watch*. Sachs and Devin (1976) recorded 4-year-olds in free play with their mother, a peer, a baby (between 1 and 2 years old), and a doll. They also found modifications in the 4-year-olds' speech to the baby and to the baby doll. The fact that the children made similar speech adjustments in talking to the doll and to a real baby suggests that the adjustments in speech to the baby are the result of children's knowledge of how to talk to babies, not feedback from the babies themselves.

Children speak differently to 2-year-olds than either to peers or to adults, but children do not speak to 2-year-olds in the same way that adults do. Several studies compared the infant-directed speech of children between 2 and 5

---

**Box 6.8    Adult's and child's explanation of the water tap in Figure 6.3**

*Adult's*

1. Look, these two pictures (I and II) are drawings of a tap.
2. This here (*a*) is the handle of the tap.
3. To turn it off, look, you have to do this with your fingers (move the finger on diagram I and show the result on diagram II). Then it is like this (diagram II).
4. You see (diagram I), when the handle is turned on like this (point to *a* and make horizontal movement), then the canal (point to *b*, call it also the little hole, door, or passage) is open.
5. Then the water runs out (point to *b* in diagram I).
6. It runs out because the canal is open.
7. Look, here (diagram II), when the handle is turned off (point to *a* and make a vertical movement), then the canal (point to *b:* can also be called the hole or door or passage) is also shut.
8. The water can't get through, you see? (point to *c*). It is stopped.
9. It can't run out, because the can (point to *b*) is closed.

*Child's:*

You see, this way (diagram I) it is open. The little pipe (*c*) finds the little pipe (*b*) and then the water runs out. There (diagram II) it is shut and it can't find the little pipe that runs through. The water comes this way (diagram I, *c*) it comes in the little pipe. It is open and there (II) it is shut. Look, you can't see the little pipe any more (II) it is lying down, then the water comes this way (*c*) and wouldn't find the little pipe any more.

Source: From Piaget, 1926.

years to mothers' infant-directed speech and found that when children talk to younger children, there is less talk overall. The speech that children address to a younger child is more directive, has a higher frequency of attention-getting devices and repetitions, has a lower frequency of questions, and is, in general, less attuned to the young child (Dunn & Kendrick, 1982; Mannle & Tomasello, 1987; Tomasello & Mannle, 1985; Vandell & Wilson, 1987).

**Figure 6.4** The ability to modify one's speech when talking to even younger children is part of a 4-year-old's communicative competence.

Tomasello and Mannle (1985) also found that when older siblings interacted with younger siblings, they spent less time than mothers did sharing the attentional focus of the young child. The suggested sources of these differences between the child-directed speech of older children and mothers include differences in the affection felt toward the young child, differences in the motivation or interest in interacting with the younger child, and differences in the competence to engage the younger child (Dunn & Kendrick, 1982; Tomasello & Mannle, 1985). Other evidence indicates that as children get older, their child-directed speech becomes more like mothers' child-directed speech (Gleason, 1973; Hoff-Ginsberg & Krueger, 1991).

In sum, children as young as 4 years demonstrate that they know that one speaks differently to a younger child than to a peer or to an adult. This evidence suggests that 4-year-olds are not as incapacitated with respect to sociolinguistic skill as Piaget's work would lead us to believe. In addition to revising the Piagetian account of the egocentric preschooler, evidence that children modify their speech directed to younger children has also been taken as evidence that children speak "motherese." Although young speakers do respond to their listeners' needs, they do not necessarily do so in the same way that adults do (Ninio & Snow, 1999). Differences in the modifications that 4-year-olds and 8-year-olds and adults make suggest that motherese is not an all-or-none phenomenon and that young children are not as supportive conversational partners as mothers typically are (Hoff-Ginsberg & Krueger, 1991). This may, in fact, be one reason that firstborn children develop some aspects of language slightly more rapidly than later-born children do (Bates, 1975; Hoff-Ginsberg, 1998). (For further discussion of the role of older siblings in children's language development, see also Barton & Tomasello, 1994.)

## Learning culture-specific or group-specific language styles

Registers are varieties of language that depend on characteristics of the setting or the listener. Dialects are varieties of language that depend on characteristics of the speaker, such as region, race, socioeconomic status, or gender. Although differences in accent may be the most obvious differences, dialects vary in stylistic aspects as well. In this section, we ask when and how children come to use language in the style that is typical of their group by focusing on two aspects of group-specific style. First, we will look at the narratives produced by Japanese children and by African American children, comparing those narratives to our earlier description of narrative development that was based primarily on white North American children. Second, we will look at early gender differences in language use.

***Cultural differences in narrative style and development.***    In our earlier account of narrative development, we presented evidence that children's narratives increase in length and structure as children acquire narrative skill. That account needs to be modified, however, because not all cultures value long narratives or narratives with the sort of structure North American children learn to produce.

In Japan, for instance, talking a great deal is viewed negatively. Japanese proverbs such as "The mouth is the source of misfortune" and "Talkative males are embarrassing" illustrate this point of view (Minami & McCabe, 1995). Not surprisingly, then, the personal narratives Japanese children tell tend to be very brief, unembellished accounts of past events. And just as North American mothers with an elaborative style help their children develop the ability to produce long, elaborate narratives, Japanese mothers' interaction with their children fosters the development of a Japanese narrative style (Minami & McCabe, 1995). Compared with North American mothers, Japanese mothers request less description from their children, and they more frequently utter brief acknowledgments of their children's talk. Minami and McCabe suggest that these acknowledgments, which actually interrupt the children's speech, have the effect of stopping the children from talking on at length; and of course fewer requests for description would similarly work to elicit shorter narratives.

Among many African American groups, adults' narratives have a structure different from the structure typical of white middle-class narratives. Not surprisingly, the narrative development of children in these communities follows a different path. On the basis of her research with school-aged African American children and white children in northern California and in Boston, Michaels (1983) described the differences in the following way. The narratives told among white middle-class groups tend to be tightly organized around a single topic. This type of narrative structure has been referred to as **topic centered.** In contrast, the narratives told among African Americans are more likely to consist of a loosely related set of personal anecdotes. This type of narrative structure has been referred to as **topic associating.**

Heath's (1983) description of the narratives told by African Americans in the rural southeastern United States also fits the topic-associating label. In addition, Heath describes narratives as "performances." Good verbal performers within this speech community are skilled at telling narratives in a way that secures and sustains an audience's attention. Stories are often told in a poetic structure, and the nonverbal embellishments that accompany the story are an important part of the performance. Exaggerating the facts to make the story more interesting is also part of good verbal performance. By the standards of this speech community, the narrative about hair cutting in Box 6.7 would not be judged as very good. A good story performance by a 5-year-old in this community is illustrated in Box 6.9. In this example, a 5-year-old boy named Teegie is describing and demonstrating riding his new tricycle.

The child who told the story in Box 6.9 is skilled in the narrative style of his sociocultural group. He has learned a very different style of storytelling than did the little girl who told the story about her sister cutting her own hair. The contrast between these children illustrates two points: (1) Children acquire the stylistic aspects of language use of their own speech community, in addition to acquiring the grammar and vocabulary of the language they hear, and (2) by the age of 5 years, children from different speech communities use language very differently.

What we are discussing here is children's successful achievement of the communicative competencies that are valued in their environment. As long as we are talking about Samoan children learning register variation or Japanese children learning a specifically Japanese style of narrative production, the achievement of these competencies at 5 years is the successful conclusion of the developmental story (although, of course, development may continue after the age of 5 years). However, when we are talking about North American white and African American children acquiring group-specific

---

**Box 6.9   Example of African American narrative style from a 5-year-old**

Zoom. *(racing part-way down the hill, and then falling down)*

Zoom, zoom, zoom, zoom, zoom, zoom, zoom, zoom, zoom, zoom.

Hi ay. *(walking back up the hill, as though he were on a tottering bicycle)*

Hi ay, ay, ay, ay, ay, ay, ay.

Teegie got *(continuing to trudge up the hill with exaggerated motions of a tired old man)*

A bike

A new bike

A bike to ride

See Teegie bike?

Source: From Heath, 1983, pp. 173–174.

styles of language use, the achievement of these competencies at the age of 5 years is not an unmitigated success. And although it may be the end of one story, it is also the beginning of a different story. At the age of approximately 5 years, both white children and African American children begin formal schooling, and the children need to use the oral language skills they have acquired at home in a new setting. A substantial body of research has documented that the way language is used in U.S. classrooms is more similar to the way it is used in white middle-class homes than it is to the way language is used by other groups. Thus, the successful achievement of a minority style of language use places minority children at a disadvantage in school.

***Gender differences in language use.***   The observation that men and women use language in different ways is of interest to more people than just language researchers; it was even the subject of a best-selling book (Tannen, 1990). Gender differences include some domains of vocabulary knowledge (how many male readers of this book know the meanings of the words *mauve, puce,* and *ecru?*), articulation (men tend to say "somethin'" and "workin'"; women more frequently pronounce the final *ing*), and grammar (women's speech is more grammatically correct than men's) (Lakoff, 1975). However, the area of greatest gender difference is in language use.

Several studies identify gender differences in language use in children as young as 3 years old. Preschool girls are more likely to ask an adult for help than preschool boys, even when their need for help (putting a puzzle together) is not greater (Thompson, 1999). Preschool boys tend to be more assertive and demanding in their conversational style, whereas preschool girls tend to be more polite and cooperative. For example, Esposito (1979) found that boys interrupted girls twice as frequently as girls interrupted boys. Sachs (1987) found that boys tended to use simple imperatives in talking to their partner in pretend play (such as "Lie down," "Get the heart thing," "Gimme your arm"). Girls in the same situation used fewer simple imperatives and instead used language that included the other child in planning (such as "Let's sit down and use it," "OK," and "I'll be the doctor for my baby and you be the doctor for your baby").

Given these gender differences in preschoolers' conversational style, perhaps it is not surprising that there are more disputes when preschool boys interact than when preschool girls interact. And, when conflict arises, boys handle it differently than girls do. Amy Sheldon (1990) videotaped same-sex triads of preschool girls and boys at a day care center. She observed that when the boys had conflicts, they frequently issued directives and made threats. The girls, in contrast, tended more to try to negotiate a settlement. Looking at interaction in single-gender and gender-mixed triads, Killen and Naigles (1995) also found that girls used more talk oriented toward conflict resolution than boys did. In addition, Killen and Naigles found that children's discourse style differed depending on the group's gender composition. Children's discourse was less gender-stereotyped in mixed-sex groups than in same-sex groups. Together these descriptions of gender-differentiated language use suggest that the early development of communicative competence includes both the development of gender-specific style and, as we saw earlier with the study of children's child-directed speech, the development of the ability to modify language use based on properties (in this case the gender) of one's conversational partners.

## EXPLAINING THE DEVELOPMENT OF COMMUNICATIVE COMPETENCE

Having described the "what" and "when" of children's pragmatic, discourse, and sociolinguistic development, we now turn to the questions of how and why these developments occur.

## Influences on pragmatic development

We can unpack the question of what explains pragmatic development into the more specific questions of (1) what explains the initial development of communicative intent, and (2) what explains the subsequent growth in children's interest in communicating and in the increasing variety of communicative functions they express. With respect to the emergence of intentionality, evidence suggests that an interest in social interaction with others is a biologically based, universal characteristic of the human species. Furthermore, it appears that some internal prerequisite to the display of this interest matures during the period between 6 months and 15 months, with the result that infants show an increasing interest in and ability to engage with others. There is disagreement about just what infants and children under 3 years understand about communication, but it is clear that they seek communicative interaction. In addition to this internal contribution, it appears that children's interest in communication can be encouraged by maternal responsiveness. Thus, biology provides a core interest and ability, and experience influences the rate at which this interest and ability will be displayed in behavior. It is important to point out, however, that it is difficult to untangle the effects of a responsive environment on the development of communicative intentions, per se, from the effects of a linguistically rich environment on the development of the means to express communicative intentions. That is, mothers' (typically verbal) responsiveness might directly affect communicative development, or it might affect language development, which in turn enables a greater expression of communicative intent.

The next question is what explains the particular communicative functions to which children put their language skills. Very little attention has been paid to explaining the normative course of pragmatic development, in part, perhaps, because there is currently no common description of pragmatic development. There has been some discussion of why children differ in the uses to which they put their language skills. Nelson (1973) addressed this question in her discussion of referential and expressive styles and proposed that children have their own intrinsic cognitive tendencies—to be interested in objects or to be interested in the social world. In addition, children derive notions of the purpose of language from the function to which their mothers put language. Nelson, then, proposed both an internally based cognitive influence and an externally based influence in the form of the model adults provide.

The influence of adult models on children's acquisition of language function is also part of controversial proposals regarding differences in language function associated with socioeconomic status. It has been suggested that adults in different socioeconomic strata use language for different purposes;

therefore, children's development of language function also differs by socio-economic stratum (Bernstein, 1970, 1981; Hymes, 1961; Tough, 1982). For example, Tough (1982) found that mothers with higher education used language to analyze and reflect on experience more than did mothers with minimal levels of education, and this same difference in the use to which language is put was observed in their children between the ages of 3 and 7 years.

In sum, we can conclude, not surprisingly, that both innate characteristics of children and their experiences with other communicative partners influence the emergence and increasing expression of communicative intent. Having specified the two ingredients of pragmatic development, we have to also conclude that at present we do not really know how the two ingredients operate together to produce the developmental result we can observe.

## Influences on the development of discourse skill

In trying to explain the development of discourse skill, we can similarly talk about internal and environmental influences. The internal contribution that has been discussed in the literature consists of general cognitive development, which has been proposed to influence children's conversational skills both because children at different stages of cognitive development have different understandings of how to communicate and because children at different points in cognitive development differ in their processing limitations (Shatz, 1983). The first sort of influence is most clearly illustrated in Piaget's description of the preschool child as egocentric and thus limited in conversational skill. Although more recent research suggests that Piaget's view underestimates both children's conversational abilities and their cognitive abilities, it is nonetheless true that children's conversational skill is limited by their level of cognitive development. For example, the difficulties young children have in producing adequate messages are not primarily linguistic difficulties.

With age and practice, children's processing capacity increases, and this too affects conversation because older children don't have to make the same trade-offs that younger children, with more severe limitations, must make. This argument is predicated on a view of conversation as a cognitive task that places multiple demands on children's cognitive capacity. Children's ability to participate in conversation depends on how many demands are simultaneously being made, on their current processing capacity, and on the efficiency with which they use that processing capacity. This way of thinking about the cognitive requirements of conversation can account for evidence that children's conversational skill is not consistent at any point in development but instead fluctuates, depending on task demands. For example, Bloom, Rocissano, and Hood (1976) found children's utterances were syntactically more advanced when children initiated conversations than when they responded to another's prior speech. According to the researchers, the work of holding in mind what the previous speaker said in order to make one's utterance relevant takes up processing capacity that could otherwise be used to produce a grammatically more complex utterance. There are other examples of children's variable communicative performance depending on the demands of the task (Shatz, 1983a).

The contribution of experience to the development of discourse skill seems to be of two sorts. First, children clearly learn what they hear. For example, children learn to respond to the question "What time is it?" with a number, they learn the narrative style of their culture, and if their parents tell elaborated narratives, so do their children. In addition, children appear to learn what their circumstances require of them. Recall Dunn and Shatz's (1989) finding that children with older siblings develop the ability to intrude into the conversation between the older sibling and the mothers. Between 2 and 3 years of age, the younger children's intrusions become more frequently relevant to the ongoing conversation and more frequently successful at gaining the child entry into the conversation. Additional evidence that children learn the communicative competencies the situation requires may be the finding that later-born children produce more contingent responses in conversation than same-aged firstborn children do, even though their linguistic skills are not more advanced (Hoff-Ginsberg, 1998). The argument is that firstborn children have attentive mothers who will converse with them regardless of what they do, but second-born children need to learn conversational skills if they want to be included.

## Influences on sociolinguistic development

As with the other components of communicative competence, sociolinguistic development depends on a model to learn from and on the development of prerequisite cognitive abilities. In this case the cognitive prerequisites are the abilities to pay attention to the relevant social variables and to take those variables into account in drafting messages. Unlike other areas of language and communicative development, sociolinguistic development is influenced by caregivers' active instruction of their children in particular forms of language use. For example, parents (and others) teach children what to say ("Say *Please* "), prompt children ("What's the magic word?"), and directly praise children for appropriate speech and reprimand them for socially inappropriate speech (Becker, 1990; Ely & Gleason, 1995).

A clear and frequently cited illustration of direct instruction in language use comes from Gleason and Weintraub (1976), who observed mothers and older siblings explicitly coaching young children in the routine of saying "trick-or-treat" as they made their rounds on Halloween. A less explicit means of language socialization is for adults to engage children in the kind of verbal inter-action that demands particular competencies. For example, Eisenberg (1986) and Miller (1986) described adults' teasing of young children in Mexican fami-lies and in white working-class families. One of the mothers in Miller's study ex-plained that the purpose of the teasing was to prepare the children to stand up for themselves in real-life disputes. Perhaps the most subtle form of language socialization is the sort suggested by Reese and Fivush (1993) in their study of parents' elicitations of children's narratives. According to Reese and Fivush, mothers' efforts at eliciting past-event descriptions from their children not only help their children acquire the skill of producing narratives but also communi-cate to the children that narratives are valued in the culture. In like manner, but with different outcomes, the interrupting that Japanese mothers do and the at-tention that African American audiences pay to children like Teegie (Box 6.11) let children in these cultures know what kind of verbal performance is valued.

In summary, it appears that the development of communicative compe-tence has multiple sources of influence. Biologically based social and cognitive capacities mature, making communication interesting and possible. Responsive communicative partners support the development of an interest in communication and the growth of some communicative skills. The need to communicate in less supportive environments may foster the development of other skills. Children observe the communicative behaviors of those around them and reproduce them, and sometimes communicative skills are explicitly taught. Each of the foregoing statements, although probably true, is also very vague. In the previous chapter on syntax, we didn't pretend that a statement to the effect that some things mature and other things are learned from ex-perience constitutes an adequate theory of the development of syntax. And we shouldn't pretend that this summary is adequate as an account of the de-velopment of communicative competence.

## ● SUMMARY

People use language to communicate. The suc-cessful use of language for communicating re-quires knowing more than the phonology, the lexicon, and the morphosyntactic rules of one's language. Other competencies involved in com-munication include understanding the functions of language (pragmatics), knowing how to par-ticipate in conversation and relate a past event (discourse knowledge), and knowing how to use language in a manner that is appropriate to the social situation and valued by your social group (sociolinguistic knowledge). In the first 5 years of life, as children are acquiring language, they are also developing communication skills. At birth, infants are not communicative. Although adults may be able to interpret babies' cries and smiles, babies do not produce these cries and smiles with communicative intent. The first evi-dence of intentional communication appears around the age of 10 months when, for example, babies start to request help from others in ob-taining objects. By the time children are 1 year old, they can be quite communicative, using the few words in their vocabularies along with intonation and gesture to perform such communicative functions as referring to objects, requesting objects, refusing something that is offered to them, and so on.

As children's language abilities progress, language becomes the primary vehicle of communicative acts. Conversational skill also begins to develop during the second year of life as children learn such mechanics of verbal interaction as taking turns, initiating topics, repairing miscommunication, and responding contingently. Initially, children's conversations with adults are very asymmetrical, with adults doing the work of building conversations around children's contributions. As children's conversational skills develop, the relative burdens carried by the adult and child in sustaining conversation become more equal. As children start to produce descriptions of past events in conversation, often in response to adults' questions and with adults' help, a new type of discourse—the narrative—begins to develop. Preschool children also talk to one another, although their lack of conversational skill sometimes limits the success of peer conversations. Children seem interested in conversations with one another from the age of 2 years, and they show some ability to adapt their speech to their listeners' needs from at least the age of 4 years. However, children's conversations tend to be disjointed compared with adult conversations, and children's dialogue is often intermixed with each participant's private speech.

The development of sociolinguistic skill also begins early in the course of language development. Two-year-old children use language differently depending on the social situation. For example, in Samoa, where different speech registers are appropriate in different social situations, 2-year-olds use some aspects of the appropriate register, depending on the setting. In role play, 5-year-olds also demonstrate an awareness that people in different roles—for example, mothers and fathers—use language differently. Another aspect of sociolinguistic development that is well under way by the age of 5 years is the development of the style of language use of one's social group. For example, white middle-class North American children, Japanese children, and some African American children learn to produce very different sorts of narratives, in accordance with the kind of narrative that is valued in their social group. As a second example, preschool boys and girls already differ in the ways they use language in conversation. Normally, the development of communicative competence and the development of language proceed together. However, the correlation between the development of communicative skills and language skills is not perfect. For example, a late talker may be a very skillful communicator using nonverbal means. Cases of atypical development sometimes reveal even more clearly the potential dissociation of communicative and linguistic development.

## ● KEY TERMS

| | |
|---|---|
| linguistic competence | illocutionary force |
| communicative competence | locution |
| pragmatic knowledge | perlocution |
| discourse knowledge | intentionality |
| sociolinguistic knowledge | conversations |
| speech act | narratives |

registers                                  egocentrism

dialects                                   private speech

language socialization                     language play

primary intersubjectivity                  topics

secondary intersubjectivity                scaffolding

joint attention                            referential communication

pragmatic bootstrapping                    topic centered

collective monologues                      topic associating

## ● REVIEW QUESTIONS

1. Define the distinction between linguistic competence and communicative competence.
2. List and define the kinds of knowledge that constitute communicative competence.
3. Describe the course of speech act development.
4. Why is the period around age 10 months considered a major milestone in communicative development? What changes occur in the child?
5. What role does prelinguistic interaction play in the development of communicative competence and in the development of linguistic competence? What claims have been made, and what is the evidence?
6. What are the possible relations between the development of the communicative functions of language and the development of language structure? What sort of evidence would you need to test these proposals?
7. Explain the difference between the instrumental and expressive functions of language. How does this distinction figure in discussions of early language development?

8. What does the Piagetian view of preschool children as egocentric imply about their conversational and sociolinguistic skills?
9. What are the kinds and functions of private speech?
10. Describe the conversational skills of the 2- to 3-year-old. What can children do at this age, and in what ways do they still fall short of adult competence?
11. Describe the narrative skills of the 2- to 3-year-old.
12. Describe the sociolinguistic skills of the 2- to 3-year-old.
13. What is the difference between the narrative style that is typical of mainstream middle-class 5-year-olds and the narrative style that is characteristic of non-mainstream African American children of that age? What is the significance of this difference?
14. How does the language use of preschool boys and girls differ?
15. What are the sources of influence on the development of communicative competence? Illustrate each with an example.

# LANGUAGE DEVELOPMENT IN SPECIAL POPULATIONS

The focus of this book thus far has been on describing and explaining the typical course of language development in children. In this chapter, we turn to a consideration of language development in populations of children who are atypical in language development. Included are children who have conditions such as deafness, blindness, mental retardation, or autism that affect their ability to acquire language. In addition, some children have difficulty acquiring language but appear to be normal in all other aspects of their development. These children are referred to as having specific language impairment.

## WHY STUDY SPECIAL POPULATIONS?

There are two reasons for studying language development in populations other than typically developing children. One is the applied research motive discussed in Chapter 1: Understanding how language development may be affected by other conditions should provide a basis for designing programs to help such children optimize their language development. There is also a basic research motivation for studying language development in different populations: It allows us to ask how different human abilities contribute to the language acquisition process. For example, studying language development in deaf children can help us discover whether language depends on the auditory–vocal channel or whether language is a function of the human brain that can make use of other channels if the typical channel is unavailable. Studying language development in blind children can address questions about the role of the extralinguistic context in language development.

Children who are deaf or blind have normal mental abilities, although their access to information is impaired. What about children who have different mental endowments? Remember, one of the major issues in the field of language development concerns the extent to which language is separate from other cognitive abilities. Looking at language development in children who are mentally retarded provides insights into how language development is affected by other cognitive limitations. Looking at language development in children with autism, who have their own distinctive constellation of mental abilities and limitations, also sheds light on the extent to which the ability to acquire language depends on other human abilities.

Last, children who seem to develop typically in every respect except in language challenge us to identify what aspect of human ability is necessary for language development but not for anything else.

## LANGUAGE DEVELOPMENT AND DEAFNESS

Approximately 1 in 1000 children is born with a severe hearing loss (Carrel, 1977), and some children who are able to hear at birth lose their hearing in infancy, before they have acquired language. In this section, we consider what language development is like for these **prelingually deaf** children, and we consider what the course of their language development can tell us about the process of language acquisition more generally. By limiting our discussion of language development in deaf children in this way, we are excluding cases in which hearing loss occurs after language has been acquired. In such cases, linguistic competence remains, although communication is impaired (Mogford-Bevan, 1993). We also are excluding children with mild-to-moderate hearing loss, who can hear spoken language with the use of hearing aids and whose success at language development is predicted to a large degree by how much hearing ability remains (Meadow, 1980).

A related topic that deserves at least brief mention is the effect of intermittent hearing loss on language development. Many young children have repeated middle ear infections or periodic fluid buildup in the middle ear that causes temporary hearing impairment. Research on the consequences of this condition, known as **otitis media,** for language development has produced inconsistent results. Infants who experienced otitis media before the age of 6 months have been found to be delayed in the onset of canonical babbling and different from infants without such a medical history in the quality of the vowels they produced in their babbling (Rvachew, Slawinski, Williams, & Green, 1996; Rvachew, Slawinski, William, & Green, 1999). The findings of several studies suggest that when children experience hearing loss before 18 months of age, they are at substantially higher risk than other children for language delay during their first 3 years (Friel-Patti & Finitzo, 1990; Shriberg, Friel-Patti, Flipsen, & Brown, 2000; Teele, Klen, Rosner, & The Greater Boston Otitis Media Study Group, 1984; Wallace, Grael, McCaron, & Ruben, 1988). Other studies report small or nonsignificant effects of an early history of otitis media in language skills at 3 years (Campbell et al., 2003; Paradise et al., 2000). Still other studies find that children who have no problems other than early intermittent hearing loss appear to catch up in language development by age 5 (Lonigan, Fischel, Whitehurst, Arnold, & Valdez-Menchaca, 1992; Roberts et al., 2000). Overall, there appear to be real effects on speech and language development of the intermittent hearing loss that accompanies early otitis media, but the long-term impact of otitis media on language outcomes appears to be small (Casby, 2001).

The focus of this section is the population of children who cannot hear—even with hearing aids—the spoken language around them. The primary determinant of the course of language development for these prelingually deaf children is the language environment to which they are exposed. One possible environment is exposure to **sign language,** the manual language used in the deaf community. This is the situation for the approximately 10 percent of deaf children who have a deaf parent. These "deaf of deaf" children are exposed to sign language from infancy, and for these children, the story of their language development is the story of the acquisition of sign language as a first language.

For the 90 percent of deaf children who do not have a deaf parent, the language environment typically depends on the advice given to parents by those who specialize in the education of deaf children. For most of this century, the advice that has been given is to use the **oralist method,** in which deaf children are intensively coached in producing speech and trained in reading lips. Parents traditionally were discouraged from using any gestural communication system with their deaf children in the belief (which now appears to be mistaken) that using gestures or acquiring sign language would interfere with the children's acquiring a spoken language.

More recently, the purely oralist approach has been supplanted by the **total communication** approach to deaf education. The goal of total communication approaches is the same as that of oralist approaches—mastery of spoken English. In total communication approaches (and there are several different ones), oral language is combined with some signing or gestural system. For deaf children who are not exposed to sign and who are trained in one of these methods, language development is the story of **oral language development** in the deaf. The "deaf of hearing" children who are orally educated provide two other topics of interest. One is the "home sign" gestural system that such children invent to communicate with those around them; the other is the outcome when they learn sign language after infancy. The research on late learners of American Sign Language was presented in Chapter 2 because it addressed the hypothesis that there is a critical period for language acquisition.

In this chapter, we begin our description of language development in deaf children with the topic of sign language development in children who are exposed to sign from infancy. We then move to a discussion of oral language development and the home sign systems invented by deaf children who are not exposed to a sign language.

## The acquisition of sign language

***Sign languages are real languages.***    Before discussing the acquisition of sign language, it is important to dispel the common myth that sign language is simply pantomime and not a language at all. Several decades of linguistic analyses of sign languages have clearly established that sign languages are languages. (There are several different sign languages in the world, just as there are many different spoken languages.) The majority of the linguistic work has analyzed **American Sign Language (ASL),** which is used in the United States and the English-speaking provinces of Canada (Klima & Bellugi, 1979; Stokoe, Casterline, & Croneberg, 1965). This work has revealed (1) that ASL has a lexicon, (2) that lexical items in ASL are made up of a finite and discrete number of sublexical components (such as handshape and place of articulation) that are equivalent to phonemes in spoken language, and (3) that ASL has a grammar.

Girl

Tree

**Figure 7.1**  Examples of signs in American Sign Language

One way in which ASL differs slightly from spoken languages is the use of some iconic signs—that is, signs that physically resemble their referents. For example, the sign *TREE* looks something like a tree waving in the wind. Also, ASL uses pointing. For example, pointing to the addressee means YOU and pointing to one's self means ME or I. However, many signs are completely arbitrary or have their iconic source so far back in history that it is of little present use. For example, the sign for girl in ASL may have originated as an imitation of tying a bonnet (Litowitz, 1987). Also, even the iconic signs are conventionalized and therefore must be learned. That is, not any gesture that resembles a tree can serve as the sign for tree. Some examples of signs are illustrated in Figure 7.1. Acquiring a vocabulary in a sign language is thus essentially the same task of learning arbitrary symbol–meaning connections that it is for spoken language. And learning the grammar of ASL is the same task of learning a productive system for expressing meanings with combinations of words and grammatical morphemes that it is for spoken language.

***The course of sign language development.***  For deaf children who have a deaf parent and who are exposed to sign language from birth, the course of sign language development is essentially like the course of the development of spoken language. Children pass through the same stages in the same order. Infants exposed to ASL produce manual babbling, followed by single-sign productions, followed by multisign combinations, followed by morphological development and more complex syntax (Bellugi, van Hoek, Lillo-Martin, & O'Grady, 1993; Newport & Meier, 1985; Petitto, 2000).

Evidence also shows that similar processes underlie the acquisition of both sign and spoken languages. Children acquiring ASL make overregularization errors in their use of morphological markers, producing forms analogous to *goed* or *holded*. Like children acquiring spoken languages, children acquiring ASL persist in their errors and ignore parental corrections, even though parental corrections sometimes involve the parent's actually molding the child's handshape (Bellugi, Van Hoek, Lillo-Martin, & O'Grady, 1993). What is perhaps most striking is that children acquiring ASL make pronoun reversal errors at the same age that children acquiring spoken language do. This error is striking because the signs for pronouns are points, and both deaf and hearing children use pointing gestures to communicate before they have acquired language. Yet the fact that ASL is physically similar in this aspect to prelinguistic communication seems to give it no advantage in acquisition. It seems as if acquiring a linguistic system is a separate enterprise from using prelinguistic communicative gestures, even when the modality is the same (Petitto, 1987; 2000).

Some deaf children learn sign from parents who are not themselves native signers. As mentioned in Chapter 5, this sort of case provides an interesting test of children's ability to learn from imperfect input. It turns out that although the parents make errors typical of late learners of a language, their children do not. Children seem to have the ability to extract the regularities even from errorful data (Newport & Aslin, 2000; Singleton & Newport, 1987).

***The timing of sign language development.*** Deaf infants produce manual babbling, followed by the production of single signs and then sign combinations, so the course of productive sign language development is just like the course of spoken language development. The timing may be a little different, however. The major milestones of producing the first word, achieving a 10-word vocabulary, and producing word combinations appear to be reached earlier by children acquiring sign (Bonvillian, 1999; Bonvillian, Orlansky, & Novack, 1983; Folven & Bonvillian, 1991; Prinz & Prinz, 1979; Schlesinger & Meadow, 1972). (Because signs have the same lexical status as spoken words, ASL researchers use the term *word*.) Although these findings have been criticized as merely overinterpretations of manual gestures—gestures of the sort that young hearing children also produce (Petitto, 1988; 2000)—the claim of early sign production is widely accepted (Newport & Meier, 1985). Hearing infants also seem able to learn to use gestures to communicate slightly earlier than they can use words (Goodwyn & Acredolo, 1993), and this advantage of the manual modality is the basis of programs that teach manual gestures to prelinguistic babies, thus enabling communication in children who would otherwise not be able to communicate (e.g., Acredolo & Goodwyn, 1998).

Such enthusiasm for gesturing notwithstanding, the significance of the earlier timing of gestures compared with spoken words may be limited. The first ASL signs acquired by deaf children tend to be highly context bound—appearing in social routines or produced in imitation of an adult's sign. When only truly referential uses of signs are counted (i.e., extensions of signs to new items), the timing difference disappears. First referential signs in ASL learners and first referential spoken words in children learning an oral language appear around 13 months, on average. Bonvillian (1999) suggests that the early appearance of signs reflects the earlier development of the motor abilities necessary to produce gestures. However, the cognitive requirements for referential use of signs and words develop at the same time in deaf and hearing children. Goodwyn and Acredolo (1993) similarly point out that the slight advantage of the manual modality does not allow symbol use before the prerequisite cognitive developments have occurred.

## Oral language development in deaf children

Deafness is a severe obstacle to acquiring a spoken language, and the story of oral language development in prelingually deaf children is typically not a success story. Although some deaf individuals do learn to lip-read and to speak, most achieve only limited success. Producing speech is also difficult for prelingually deaf children. One report estimates that 15 percent to 55 percent of orally educated deaf people achieve intelligible speech (Jensema, Karchmer, & Trybus, 1978). More important than the difficulty deaf people have in reading lips and talking is the difficulty that prelingually deaf children have in acquiring language through oral means. Many researchers have argued that oralism fails to provide most deaf children with any effective native language. Although there has been less time to evaluate the success of total communication programs, the evidence to date suggests that total communication also has its limitations. Some argue that total communication is more effective than purely oral programs, but the conclusions are mixed (for example, see Moores, 1978; Wood & Wood, 1992). According to Johnson, Liddell, and Erting (1992), both oral and total communication programs deprive deaf children of the opportunity to fully acquire any language. The specifics of what deaf children do and do not acquire in oral language development is best described separately for phonological, semantic, and syntactic development.

***Phonological development.***    Deaf infants sound very much like hearing infants in the first months of life. Deaf infants cry and coo and even begin to babble. (This is true for deaf infants exposed to sign as well.) However, by the babbling stage, deaf infants differ from hearing infants in both the quantity and quality of sound production (Stoel-Gammon & Otomo, 1986), and deaf infants do not produce the canonical clear syllabic babbling typical of hearing 9- and 10-month-olds (Oller, Eilers, Bull, & Carney, 1985; Oller & Eilers, 1988). Some orally trained deaf children do seem to develop a phonological system. For example, these children do things like reduce consonant clusters when they produce words (such as pronouncing *school* as /kul/), showing evidence of phonological processes similar to those seen in the early productions of hearing children. Orally trained deaf children may also show some phonological awareness. For example, they can use lip-read information to identify rhymes (Dodd, 1987). As we discussed in Chapter 3, phonological awareness is related to reading skill, and thus the phonological awareness that orally trained deaf children achieve may help them learn to read, although that is not clear (Mayberry & Wodlinger-Cohen, 1987). In general, the level of literacy achieved by deaf children who have hearing parents is low. The average reading level of deaf high school graduates is roughly the third- or fourth-grade (Johnson, Liddell, & Erting, 1989).

***Semantic development.***    There is not a great deal of research on the topic of semantics in the oral language of deaf children, perhaps because semantic development tends to be the focus of studies of early language development, and there is not a great deal of oral language development occurring in young deaf children. For example, Gregory and Mogford (1981) set out to describe vocabulary development in the oral language of deaf children under the age of 4 years, and they had to exclude the most profoundly deaf children in their sample because there was so little vocabulary to describe.

Two studies suggest that semantic development is similar in deaf and hearing children, although both studies are of the expression and representation of meaning, not of language per se. Skarakis and Prutting (1977) found that 2- to 4-year-old deaf toddlers used their speech and gestures to express the same communicative intents (such as to greet, to request) present in the early speech of hearing children (see Chapter 6 for a discussion of the communicative functions of early language). Also, Tweney, Hoeman, and Andrews (1975) found, using a card-sorting task, that 16- to 18-year-old deaf adolescents categorized words into hierarchical structures similar to those of hearing subjects.

***Syntactic development.***    In prelingually deaf children who are orally educated, syntactic development is delayed, and the endpoint of syntactic development typically falls far short of normal language competence (Mogford, 1993). Various syntactic errors are characteristic of the language produced by orally educated deaf children, even after the age of 10 years (Quigley & King, 1980). The syntactic abilities of hearing-impaired 18-year-olds fall below those of hearing 10-year-olds (Quigley, Power, & Steinkamp, 1977). Box 7.1 illustrates the kind of construction orally educated deaf adolescents produce. The particular type of syntactic errors made by deaf adolescents (educated with either oral or total communication methods) suggests that most deaf children do not fully acquire the grammar of the spoken language (de Villiers, de Villiers, & Hoban, 1994).

---

**Box 7.1    Examples of sentences produced by orally educated deaf students between the ages of 10 and 18 years**

The cat under the table.
John sick.
The girl a ball.
Tom has pushing the wagon.
Beth made candy no.
Beth threw the ball and Jean catch it.
John goes to fishing.
Bill liked to played baseball.
Him wanted go.
Who a boy gave you a ball?
Who TV watched?
The dog chased the girl had on a red dress.

---

Source: From Quigley and King, 1980.

## The creation of home sign systems by deaf children

Children born deaf to parents who cannot sign and who have been discouraged from learning sign language to communicate with their child are in the same situation as the two children whom King Psammetichus sent off to be raised by a shepherd who was not to talk to them. The "deaf of hearing" children are linguistic isolates. Although they typically live in families that love and care for them, their caregivers cannot communicate with them in a language they can perceive. Deaf children in such situations spontaneously use gestures to communicate (Lane, 1984; Lenneberg, 1964). Their gestures are known as **home sign.** Susan Goldin-Meadow and her colleagues (Feldman, Goldin-Meadow, & Gleitman, 1978; Goldin-Meadow, 2003; Goldin-Meadow & Mylander, 1984) studied the home sign systems created by several deaf children to ask the same question that King Psammetichus did: What sort of language does the brain create if it is not given an existing language to learn?

The answer that Goldin-Meadow (1997) suggests based on her study of the home sign systems of several children is that "there is a form that human language naturally assumes" (p. 306), even when it is invented from scratch. The deaf children she studied invented words—that is, gestures that were consistently associated with particular meanings. They combined these words in structured sentences with consistent word order. They had grammatical categories: words that functioned as nouns had a consistently different form than words that functioned as verbs. However, the deaf children Goldin-Meadow studied did not invent a full language, complete with morphology and complex syntax. That seems to require a community of speakers, as in the case of Nicaraguan sign language, which was discussed in Chapter 2.

## Implications of research on language development in deaf children

The literature on language development in the deaf has implications both for deaf education and for our understanding of the process of normal language development. With respect to the applied question of deaf education, the literature makes it clear that deaf children are not handicapped in their ability to acquire language if the language is presented in the visual mode. Thus, the optimal situation for language development is to be born to deaf parents who are themselves native or at least fluent users of sign. However, the issue of deaf education is complicated by two other facts. First, 90 percent of deaf children are born to hearing parents; therefore, they do not have the option of learning sign from native users. Second, language development is not the only goal that parents and educators have for deaf children; usually, the ability to participate in the hearing world and the acquisition of literacy are also goals, and these goals are not automatically achieved when a sign language is acquired.

The problem is somewhat simplified by two other conclusions that emerge from the literature. One is the conclusion that purely oral methods, and even total communication approaches, result in limited success at oral language acquisition. Thus, choosing these routes to the exclusion of sign language for the prelingually deaf child means limiting the level of language competence the child can achieve. To put it plainly, successful oral language acquisition is not really an option for prelingually deaf children. Another conclusion that emerges from the literature is the finding that sign language acquisition does not interfere with what the child can accomplish via oral means (Wilbur, 1979). Therefore, even if the goal is for the child to become as orally competent as possible, there is no reason to deprive the deaf child of access to sign language.

A new and developing technology may change the conclusion that successful oral language development is not an option for the deaf. A device called a **cochlear implant** can bypass the damaged cells in the ear and directly stimulate the auditory nerve. This device must be surgically implanted inside the cochlea—the part of the inner ear where sound is converted to neural signals. This implanted device receives signals that are picked up by a microphone worn behind the ear and that are processed for transmission by a small externally worn device. Cochlear implants have proven to be helpful to postlingually deafened adults (Owens, 1989), but how well they can work for the prelingually deaf is an open question at this point (see Owens & Kessler, 1989; Svirsky, Robbins, Kirk, Pisoni, & Miyamoto, 2000; Tyler & Summerfield, 1996).

The potential of cochlear implants to "cure" deafness raises a political issue for many people. Some members of the Deaf* community argue that deafness is not a disability in need of a cure. Rather, deaf people constitute a culture that is defined, in large measure, by their shared language. Proponents of the "deafness as culture" view agree that there are hardships associated with being Deaf, but they see these hardships as a result of being in a linguistic minority that is discriminated against, not as an intrinsic feature of deafness (Dolnick, 1993; Lane, 1984; and see also Padden & Humphries, 1988, for a discussion of Deaf culture). Proponents of this view object to both oralist (or total communication) methods of education and to cochlear implants because the goal of these approaches is to make the deaf like the hearing rather than to promote Deaf culture. The controversy that surrounded the 1994 Miss America—who was deaf but who communicated orally rather than in sign language—is an illustration of the tensions this issue generates.

In addition to providing the foregoing implications for deaf education, studies of deaf individuals have also yielded information that advances our understanding of language acquisition in general. The similarities between the course of sign language development in deaf children exposed to sign from birth and spoken language development in hearing children suggest that the human capacity for language is not tied to the aural–oral channel (Petitto, 2000). Language is a property of the human brain, not of the mouth and ears. Two things suggest that language development is not the next step after gestures in some continuous course of communicative development: (1) The specific similarities in the acquisition of personal pronouns in sign and spoken language, and (2) the evidence that the similarity of the signs to prelinguistic pointing gestures doesn't help their acquisition as signs. This evidence suggests, in contrast, discontinuity between prelinguistic and linguistic communication (Petitto, 1987). Acquiring a formal grammatical system is a separate cognitive enterprise from figuring out how to communicate, even though, once acquired, that formal system is very useful for communication (see the discussion in Chapter 6 on the relation between communication and language).

## LANGUAGE DEVELOPMENT AND BLINDNESS

Perhaps the first question to consider in discussing language development in blind children is why it should be any different from language development in sighted children. After all, blind children can hear and talk. However, blind children's access to nonverbal communication and to the nonverbal context of communication is limited to what can be perceived through senses other than vision. Many arguments assert that language development builds on nonverbal communication (for example, Bates, Camaioni, & Volterra, 1975;

---

'It is a convention to use the lowercase *deaf* to refer to the audiological condition and the uppercase *Deaf* to refer to a group of people who share a culture.

Bruner, 1977; see also Chapter 6 on the role of prelinguistic interaction in the development of communication) and that language development depends on accessing the meaning of sentences from the observable nonlinguistic context. Therefore, the language development of blind children provides an interesting test of these arguments.

Clearly, blindness does affect communicative interaction and some aspects of language development. Remember from earlier chapters that joint attention between speaker and listener is important for both effective communication in the short run and successful language development in the long run. With blind children, achieving joint attention is more difficult because the usual routes of eye gaze and pointing are blocked (Fraiberg, 1977; Urwin, 1978). Phonological development is also affected by blindness. Blind children make more errors than sighted children in producing speech sounds that have highly visible articulatory movements (such as /b/, /m/, /f/), but they are not different from sighted children in their production of speech sounds produced by nonvisible articulatory movements (such as /t/, /k/, /h/). This suggests that visual information, such as lip configuration, contributes to phonological development in sighted children (Mills, 1987). (This finding is also consistent with the evidence that deaf children can acquire some aspects of phonology on the basis of lip-reading; see Dodd, 1987.)

With respect to vocabulary, blind children have been reported to have fewer words for objects that can be seen but not touched, such as *moon* or *flag,* and more words for things associated with auditory change, such as *piano, drum,* and *bird* (Bigelow, 1987). Also, several studies have indicated that blind children are less likely than sighted children to overgeneralize their words (such as calling a horse *doggie*) (Mills, 1993). In fact, blind children often fail to appropriately generalize words, using new words as names for specific referents rather than as names for categories (Dunlea, 1989), which suggests that visually accessible information plays a role in learning the extensions of categories.

The only reported difference between blind and sighted children in the rate of grammatical development is a delay in blind children's acquisition of verbal auxiliaries—the "helping verbs" such as *can, will, do* (Landau & Gleitman, 1985). Landau and Gleitman observed this delay in a study of three blind children and suggested that the cause for the delay was in the nature of the mothers' speech. Landau and Gleitman found that the mothers of the blind children used more direct imperatives (such as "Take the doll") and fewer yes/no questions (such as "Can you take the doll?") than did mothers talking to sighted children. Other studies of sighted children's language development have found that high rates of imperatives and low rates of yes/no questions in mothers' speech are associated with children's slower acquisition of auxiliaries (Newport, Gleitman, & Gleitman, 1977; see also Chapter 5).

With respect to style of language use, several studies have reported that blind children show a greater use of social routines and unanalyzed, formulaic speech than sighted children do (Dunlea, 1984; Kekelis & Andersen, 1984; Mills, 1993; Perez-Pereira & Castro, 1992; Peters, 1994). For example, Peters (1995) described a blind child who, at 2 years, used the form *Didja* (from "Did you") to introduce sentences about something that just happened. Examples of such sentences and their meanings include the following:

Didja find it. (I found it.)

Didja dump it out. (I dumped it out.)

Didja burp. (I burped.)

Peters (1994) suggests that because blind children are more dependent than sighted children are on speech as a means of social interaction, they are motivated to adopt a "pick it up and use it before you have time to analyze it" (Peters, 1994, p. 200) approach to language.

Blindness also affects conversational interaction. Adults talking to blind children tend to initiate topics more than adults talking to sighted children do; and when blind children introduce topics, they tend to be self-oriented topics (Kekelis & Andersen, 1984). Also, young blind children have difficulty understanding the conversations that go on around them, leading to frustration and sometimes to behavioral problems (Gleitman & Gleitman, 1991).

These differences notwithstanding, the course of language development is remarkably unimpeded by blindness. Blind children who have no other handicapping condition babble, produce first words, produce word combinations, and acquire syntax and morphology on essentially the same timetable as do sighted children. The difficulty that blind children experience in generalizing both word meaning and language use suggests that visual information plays a role in language development. However, the essential success of blind children's language acquisition reveals that language acquisition cannot be simply a process of mapping sounds onto the things and actions to which they refer. Otherwise, the unavailability of referents would pose greater problems for blind children than it does. In fact, it was the successful language acquisition of one blind child studied by Landau and Gleitman (1985) that led to the proposal that children use information in the syntactic structure of sentences as a significant source of information about what verbs mean (see discussion of the syntactic bootstrapping hypothesis in Chapter 4).

## LANGUAGE DEVELOPMENT AND MENTAL RETARDATION

A variety of different conditions result in mental retardation, which is defined by the American Psychiatric Association as "significantly subaverage general intellectual functioning . . . that is accompanied by significant limitations in adaptive functioning" (American Psychiatric Association, 1994, p. 39). Persons with mental retardation form a very heterogeneous group, and different forms of mental retardation have different consequences for language development. The question of how language development is affected by mental retardation is of interest for obvious applied reasons and because it allows researchers to ask how general intellectual functioning is related to language development. If acquiring language is just one more thing humans do with their general intellectual capacity, then impairment in general intellectual capacity should impair language development, and it should do so to the same degree that general capacities are impaired. On the other hand, if language is a separate capacity (the term *autonomy* is often used to refer to this idea of separateness), then there should be some independence, or dissociation, of general intelligence and language ability.

In this section, we will cover the topic of language development and mental retardation selectively, focusing first on persons with Down syndrome, second on the condition known as Williams syndrome, and last on a few individual case studies that have particular relevance for this theoretical issue.

## Language development in children with Down syndrome

Down syndrome is a chromosomal abnormality, present in approximately 1 in 800 newborns, that accounts for roughly one-third of the moderately to severely mentally retarded population (Rondal, 1993). Both the severity of mental retardation and the language development of persons with Down syndrome vary considerably, and some individuals with Down syndrome achieve typical adult-level linguistic competence. However, most do not (Fowler, Gelman, & Gleitman, 1994), and despite the individual differences that exist, it is possible to describe some general characteristics of language development in individuals with Down syndrome.

In general, for children with Down syndrome, language is more impaired than other cognitive functions, grammar is particularly affected among components of language, and production deficits exceed comprehension deficits (Abbeduto et al., 2003; Beehgly & Chicchetti, 1987; Singer Harris, Bellugi, Bates, Jones, & Rossen, 1997; Miller 1992). Looking separately at the components of language development in children with Down syndrome, we find the following developmental courses: The onset of canonical babbling appears to be delayed by about 2 months, and phonological development after infancy is substantially delayed. Phonological processes that are typical of normally developing toddlers (such as final consonant deletion and cluster reduction) continue into adolescence and adulthood (Chapman, 1995). Most adults with Down syndrome have some difficulty producing intelligible speech, although the source of the problems is not clear (Miller, 1992).

**Figure 7.2** Down syndrome is a form of mental retardation that typically results in delayed language development. Individuals with Down syndrome become quite competent communicators, but their vocabulary and the grammatical complexity of their speech are usually below typical adult levels.

Lexical development starts late and proceeds slowly in children with Down syndrome. They typically produce their first word around 24 months—approximately 1 year later than typically developing children but on schedule, so to speak, with respect to mental age. By the time children with Down syndrome are 6 years old, they are more than 3 years behind typically developing children in mental age, and their productive language lags even behind their mental age. That is, a child with Down syndrome who is 6 years old and has a mental age of 3 years is likely to have a smaller productive vocabulary than an average 3-year-old child. Comprehension vocabulary is more on a par with mental age. Perhaps to compensate for their limited vocabulary, children with Down syndrome produce communicative gestures more frequently than typically developing children (Singer Harris et al., 1997).

Grammatical development is the area of language most affected by Down syndrome. Both production and comprehension are delayed relative to mental age, and grammatical development shows an extremely protracted course of growth. Children with Down syndrome cover the same course of grammatical development as typically developing children do, but the children with Down syndrome may take 12 years to do what most children accomplish in 30 months (Fowler et al., 1994). For many individuals with Down syndrome, language development comes to a halt at the age of 12: Stage III, or an MLU of about 3.0, is as far as they get. Fowler (1988) suggests that an IQ greater than 50 may be necessary for progress beyond that point. Most individuals with Down syndrome do not have IQs above 50, and they fail to fully master the grammatical morphology or complex syntax of English (Fowler et al., 1994). This degree of grammatical impairment means that the average 12-year-old with Down syndrome, who has a mental age of no more than 6 years (which would be an IQ of exactly 50), produces speech with the grammatical complexity of the speech of a typically developing child who is 2 to 3 years old (Fowler et al., 1994).

In contrast, communicative and pragmatic development appear to be particular strengths of children with Down syndrome. Beginning at about 6 months, children with Down syndrome vocalize and engage in mutual eye contact (i.e., primary intersubjectivity) more than do typically developing infants. However, children with Down syndrome have trouble achieving secondary intersubjectivity, which requires engagement with another person about some third entity. As a practical matter, very young children with Down syndrome are not good at interacting with a person and playing with toys at the same time (Tager-Flusberg, 1999).

Into the preschool years, children with Down syndrome seem particularly interested in social interaction and less interested in objects, compared with typically developing children. Also, the communicative intentions expressed in their early language productions involve engaging other people more and commenting on the environment less than is typical for children at that language level. Perhaps related to this orientation toward people more than things, children with Down syndrome are particularly competent conversational partners. Compared with typically developing children of the same language level, they are better at maintaining a conversational topic over several turns and are better at repairing or revising their utterances when conversation breaks down (Tager-Flusberg & Anderson, 1991; Tager-Flusberg, 1999). However, in more demanding communicative tasks, adolescents and adults with Down syndrome do not do as well. They perform poorly in referential communication tasks, have difficulty with the kinds of form-function mappings that need to be controlled in order to mark politeness appropriately, and have difficulty controlling reference in narrative production (Rosenberg & Abbeduto, 1993).

What does the language development of individuals with Down syndrome suggest for the role of general cognition in language? On the one hand, the fact that language development is delayed is consistent with the idea that general cognitive factors are involved. On the other hand, many aspects of the language development of persons with Down syndrome are even more delayed than is cognitive development, suggesting that general cognitive development cannot be the only relevant factor. Furthermore, the evidence that different components of language are affected differently suggests there is not one ability that underlies all of language. Whatever the cognitive deficits of children with Down syndrome are, they seem to particularly affect grammatical development.

Part of the problem in using the evidence from children with Down syndrome to explain how general cognitive functioning and language development may be related is the fact that the typically available measure of cognitive development is mental age as assessed by an IQ test. IQ tests provide a useful overall measure of mental functioning, but they may not be sufficiently fine-grained to identify the components of mental functioning that would be interestingly related to language acquisition. This is a problem that is true for the study of other special populations as well.

A recent and potentially fruitful approach to the study of language development in special populations is to establish a cognitive profile of the abilities and inabilities associated with particular syndromes. This description of cognitive functioning can then be linked to descriptions of brain function and structure. This approach promises to be more revealing of the particular cognitive functions that contribute to children's language development (e.g., Bellugi, Mills, Jernigan, Hickok, & Galaburda, 1999; Singer Harris et al., 1997). A particularly interesting and potentially revealing cognitive profile is associated with another form of mental retardation: Williams syndrome.

## Language development in children with Williams syndrome

Individuals with **Williams syndrome** are—by general IQ measures—as mentally retarded as individuals with Down syndrome (Bellugi, Wang, & Jernigan, 1994). Unlike individuals with Down syndrome, however, persons with Williams syndrome speak in long, grammatically complex sentences, use a rich vocabulary, and can tell coherent and complex stories. Williams syndrome is a rare disorder, but the striking contrast between the severe cognitive deficits and the unusual language abilities that characterize individuals with Williams syndrome makes the study of Williams syndrome central to issues regarding the **dissociability of language and cognition.**

The psycholinguistic study of Williams syndrome came about in a rather unusual way. The impetus came from the mother of a child with Williams syndrome. The mother had read a magazine article about Noam Chomsky and Chomsky's theory that there is a "language organ" separate from the rest of human mental abilities. Believing that Dr. Chomsky would be interested in her daughter's unusual language abilities, the mother called him at his office at the Massachusetts Institute of Technology. Chomsky is a theoretical linguist who studies sentences, not children, and he resides in Massachusetts, whereas the mother and daughter lived in San Diego. So Chomsky referred the mother to Ursula Bellugi, who was one of Roger Brown's first students in developmental psycholinguistics and who is the director of the Laboratory for Cognitive Neuroscience at the Salk Institute for Biological Studies in California.

And so it came to pass that late one evening, when Dr. Bellugi was alone in her office and answering her own phone—which laboratory directors at that institute do not usually do—the phone rang and the caller announced to Dr. Bellugi that "Noam Chomsky told me to call you" (Bellugi, personal communication, February 1995). The mother, and subsequently the child herself, convinced Bellugi that Williams syndrome was of interest, and now not only this child but many other children with Williams syndrome have been studied intensively.

The first individuals with Williams syndrome to be studied ranged in age from 11 years to young adulthood. They all displayed a striking discrepancy between their language skills and their level of general cognitive functioning. Although the IQs of individuals with Williams syndrome range from 40 to 70—roughly the same range as individuals with Down syndrome—these individuals give the impression of being even more verbal and more conversational than typically developing children (Singer Harris et al., 1997). Adolescents with Williams syndrome tell coherent and complex stories with great emotional expression (Reilly, Klima, & Bellugi, 1990). They use advanced and unusual vocabulary in their spontaneous speech—words like *surrender, nontoxic, commentator,* and *brochure*—and, when asked, are capable of providing appropriate definitions of these terms. Their spontaneous language is grammatically complex in terms of both grammatical morphology and sentence structure (Bellugi, Wang, & Jernigan, 1993). The contrast between the language and nonlinguistic skills of individuals with Williams syndrome is illustrated in Figure 7.3, which presents a drawing and a verbal description produced by an 18-year-old with Williams syndrome who was asked to draw an elephant.

For a time it appeared that Williams syndrome was evidence that the mental capacity underlying language was separate from general mental capacity, because these individuals were mentally retarded, yet their language appeared to be intact (e.g., Pinker, 1994). However, subsequent research has called those claims into question. Although the language skills of individuals with Williams syndrome are more advanced than their visual-spatial skills, they are not at the level of typically developing children of the same chronological age (Karmiloff-Smith, Brown, Grice, & Paterson, 2003; Mervis, 2003; Singer Harris et al., 1997; Thal, Bates, & Bellugi, 1989). Moreover, both the course of development and the ultimate language competence achieved seem very different from those of typically developing children. In children with Williams syndrome, lexical development precedes the cognitive developments that it usually accompanies. In particular, children with Williams syndrome learn words before they use pointing gestures to refer, and they experience a word spurt before they categorize objects (Mervis, Morris, Bertrand, & Robinson, 1999). Children and adults with Williams syndrome score in the normal range on standardized vocabulary tests, despite scoring in the mentally retarded range on IQ tests. Perhaps it is not surprising, given the discrepancy between their language performance and general cognitive performance, that children

(a)
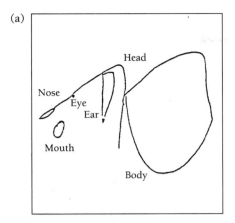

(b) And what an elephant is, it is one of the animals. And what the elephant does, it lives in the jungle. It can also live in the zoo. And what it has, it has long gray ears, fan ears, ears that can blow in the wind. It has a long trunk that can pick up grass, or pick up hay . . . If they're in a bad mood it can be terrible . . . If the elephant gets mad it could stomp; it could charge, like a bull can charge. They have long big tusks. They can damage a car . . . it could be dangerous. When they're in a pinch, when they're in a bad mood it can be terrible. You don't want an elephant as a pet. You want a cat or a dog or a bird . . .

**Figure 7.3** Response of an adolescent with Williams syndrome who was asked to draw and then describe an elephant

Source: From "Williams Syndrome: An Unusual Neuropsychological Profile," by U. Bellugi et al. In S. H. Froman and J. Grafman (Eds.), *Atypical Cognitive Deficits in Developmental Disorders*, pp. 25–26. Copyright © 1994 Dr. Ursula Bellugi, The Salk Institute for Biological Studies, La Jolla, CA. Used by permission.

with Williams syndrome seem to say more than they actually comprehend (Singer Harris et al., 1997).

With respect to grammar, Williams syndrome individuals show clear deficits on standardized tests of morphosyntactic knowledge (Bellugi et al., 1994; Karmiloff-Smith, 1998; Karmiloff-Smith et al., 2003; Singer Harris et al., 1997). In an experimental task designed to assess French-speaking children's ability to infer gender from morphological and phonological cues, French children with Williams syndrome performed less well than typically developing children who were younger than the mental age of the children with Williams syndrome (Karmiloff-Smith et al., 1997).

In terms of pragmatic skills, children with Williams syndrome present a mixed picture. They seem relatively competent as conversational partners (Tager-Flusberg, 1999), although there is something a little odd about the exaggerated way in which they engage their listeners. In fact, from infancy, children with Williams syndrome demonstrate an extreme sociability. In general, they spend more time than typically developing children looking at peoples' faces (Mervis, 2003), and in conversation as well, they spend an unusual amount of time focused on their listener's face. They have high levels of emotion in the stories they tell, but although their narratives are initially impressive, they seem wanting on further examination. An individual with Williams syndrome often cannot answer questions about the stories they tell, and they tell stories with the same high level of dramatic expression no matter how many times they've told the same story and no matter who the audience is (Reilly, Klima, & Bellugi, 1990). Another deficit appears in the comprehension of nonliteral language. Even in adolescence, individuals with Williams syndrome have trouble telling the difference between a joke and a lie. They tend to interpret all language literally, and they treat jokes as lies (Mervis, 2003).

The evidence of excellent lexical development, combined with poor performance on grammar in general and on gender assignment in particular, suggests that children with Williams syndrome have a unique set of abilities that lead them to acquire language in a different manner and with a different outcome than typically developing children (Stromswold, 2000). Children with Williams syndrome appear to be very social and to have unusually good phonological memory skills. Their social inclinations cause them to be communicative, and their memories allow them to acquire those aspects of language that can be acquired by rote. Aspects of linguistic competence that require extracting the regularities underlying grammar are more difficult for them. It seems that they achieve their high levels of verbal performance more by dint of rote memory than by learning the rules of language. Support for this argument comes from evidence that in children with Williams syndrome performance on grammatical tests and performance on memory tests are more strongly related than they are in typically developing children (Robinson, Mervis, & Robinson, 2003). The argument that children with Williams syndrome acquire the language they do in a different way than typically developing children is also supported by findings that the pattern of electrical activity in the brain associated with language performance is different in speakers with Williams syndrome than in the normal population. Furthermore, normal speakers show differences in brain activity depending on whether the task is semantic or syntactic that speakers with Williams syndrome do not show (Bellugi et al., 1999).

What is it about individuals with Williams syndrome that leads them to proceed so differently, and what does that tell us about the process of language acquisition more generally? Karmiloff-Smith and colleagues (1997) have proposed an answer to these questions. The argument starts from the clear evidence that as infants, individuals with Williams syndrome pay an unusual amount of attention to people's faces and voices. (One neurological characteristic of Williams syndrome is hyperexcitability within the cortical areas used for processing acoustic information [Bellugi et al., 1999].) Because the infant brain is plastic and shaped by the kind of processing it does (see Chapter 2), and because infants with Williams syndrome do more processing of faces and voices than most infants do, individuals with Williams syndrome end up with more of their brain devoted to learning what faces and voices do—namely, language. It may seem odd that more space devoted to a task would impede learning, but computer simulations have shown, according to Karmiloff-Smith et al. (1997), that a learning device is driven to extracting rules only when the space is inadequate to memorize everything. Because children with Williams

---

**Box 7.2  Speech sample from D. H., a woman with chatterbox syndrome and a measured IQ of 44**

Researcher: So how long have you been here then?

D. H.: Two and a half years.

Researcher: Uh-huh.

D. H.: And Dad's getting fed up with moving around. He thinks it's time that I settle down—to school, which is fair enough. To him, it . . . he feels it's going to ruin my whole life if I don't settle down sometime.

Researcher: Uh-huh.

D. H.: So I'm gonna have to, at some point settle down, somewhere.

Researcher: Uh-huh.

D. H.: Somehow, Mum didn't mind me moving about, but Dad objected to it because he knew it was bothering me and it was bothering my school work.

---

Source: From Cromer, 1994.

syndrome devote more resources to language learning in infancy, they can memorize more, but as a result when it comes time to extract the system of rules, they do not have a learning device adequate to the task. This argument is somewhat speculative at this point, but it is nicely consistent with Pinker's (1999) argument that learning language requires both an associative memory and a rule-learning system, and it shows how without introducing any new ingredients to explain language acquisition, different kinds of outcomes can be explained in terms of differing relative contributions of two kinds of learning mechanisms.

## Case studies of individuals with mental retardation who have high-level language skills

There have been some other widely discussed cases of persons who are severely mentally retarded but have remarkable linguistic abilities. The woman known in the literature as "D. H." has cognitive deficits so severe that she is unable to put three pictures in correct order to tell a story, she has difficulty naming the seasons of the year, and her IQ has been measured at 44. Yet D. H. can talk up a storm. She not only talks a great deal, but her speech is fluent and grammatically correct (Cromer, 1994). Box 7.2 shows an example of her speech in conversation with the psycholinguist who studied her, Richard Cromer.

D. H. demonstrates what is known as **chatterbox syndrome.** This syndrome has been described in other subjects as well, but D. H. is the individual who has been most carefully studied. Another mentally retarded individual with remarkable language abilities is the woman known in the scientific literature as "Laura" (Yamada, 1990). At the age of 16, Laura performed at the level of a 3- to 4-year-old child on most cognitive tests, but she was able to produce sentences such as these:

> She does paintings, this really good friend of the kids who I went to school with last year and really loved.

> He was saying that I lost my battery powered watch that I loved.

On the basis of cases such as D. H. and Laura, some have argued that the ability to acquire grammar is separate from other nonlinguistic cognitive functions and in fact is separate from the mental ability that underlies the acquisition of semantics and pragmatics; this is the argument for the modularity of syntax (Cromer, 1994; Curtiss, 1988; Yamada, 1990). However, others have argued for a less sweeping conclusion (Shatz, 1994a). Cases in which severe mental retardation is combined with good grammatical abilities make it clear that language need not be as affected as other mental faculties. On the other hand, neither D. H. nor Laura performed at normal levels on a battery of standardized language tests. Therefore, it is not quite accurate to describe the syntactic ability of these individuals as completely spared. And, as suggested earlier in the description of individuals with Down syndrome, we do not have a complete understanding of these individuals' cognitive abilities. It's not that these individuals haven't been fully tested; rather, the current state of the science in cognitive assessment limits what we know about these individuals' cognitive functioning. The content of what Laura and D. H. say suggests that they must have some cognitive abilities that are not typical of individuals with such low IQs. On the other hand, studies of the narratives produced by individuals with Williams syndrome suggest that it is possible to put on a very good linguistic performance with limited knowledge of the grammar and limited understanding of the content of what one is saying.

In sum, mental retardation affects language development. However, the degree of mental retardation present does not straightforwardly predict how language development will be affected. In Down syndrome, language development is more affected than other cognitive skills, as evidenced by the fact that children with Down syndrome show lower-level language skills than typically developing children of the same mental age do. There are also syndromes and individuals in which impressive spontaneous speech is present despite severe mental retardation. These findings serve as a caution that the current state of the science with respect to both cognition and language does not provide a clear picture of the components of either cognitive skill or language skill, nor a clear picture of the relations between skills in the two domains.

## LANGUAGE DEVELOPMENT AND AUTISM

Autism is a severe disorder that always involves impaired language and communication. The characteristic features of autism are impaired social development, delayed and deviant language, insistence on sameness, and onset before age 30 months (Bauman, 1999; Rutter, 1978). That definition includes a wide range of levels of functioning, and for a discussion of language development, it is necessary to distinguish between lower- and higher-functioning persons with autism.

### Language in lower-functioning persons with autism

Approximately 80 percent of autistic individuals score in the mentally retarded range on nonverbal tests of intelligence (Konstantareas, 1993). Those with the more severe cognitive impairments (the lower-functioning persons with autism who compose about 50 percent of the autistic population) either do not speak at all or have **echolalic speech.** Echolalic speech is the meaningless repetition of a word or word group previously produced by another speaker (Fay, 1993). In immediate echolalia, a child might respond to a question by repeating the question or the last word of the question. In delayed echolalia, chunks of previously heard utterances are produced much later. Although these echolalic chunks do not seem to have literal meaning for the autistic individual, they may serve communicative functions, such as maintaining social interaction (Prizant, 1983).

Although efforts have been made to teach language skills to such lower-functioning persons with autism, there have been no clear successes. Practitioners of an intensive behavioral approach, in which children are rewarded for appropriate communicative behavior and occasionally punished for inappropriate behavior, have had mixed results (Lovaas, 1987; Lovaas & Smith, 1988), and even their claims of success have been questioned (Schopler, Short, & Mesibov, 1989). However, some success has been reported for simultaneous communication programs that combine speech with manual signs (Konstantareas, 1993).

For a few years, it appeared that the technique of facilitated communication would enable otherwise low-functioning persons with autism to communicate. In facilitated communication, an individual with autism spells out messages on a keyboard while a facilitator steadies the person's arm. Great successes were initially reported, with formerly mute individuals seeming to write poetry and heart-wrenching accounts of life with their handicap (Biklen,

1990). However, facilitated communication turned out to be a modern-day version of the classic Clever Hans story. Clever Hans was a horse who appeared to be able to solve simple arithmetic problems and who communicated his answers by stomping his hoof the appropriate number of times. However, researchers finally detected that Clever Hans was completely unable to do arithmetic, but he was very good at reading the subtle nonverbal cues in facial expression and body posture his audience inadvertently provided when he reached the correct answer. When the audience didn't know the answer, neither did Clever Hans. Similarly, when subjected to close scientific scrutiny, facilitated communication turned out to be bogus; individuals with autism could answer questions only when the facilitators knew the answers. Thus, the messages that appeared to come from the individuals with autism were actually coming from the facilitators, although the facilitators were unaware that they were subtly directing the arm movements of the autistic individuals whose communication they thought they were only facilitating (Burgess et al., 1998; Regal, Rooney, & Wandas, 1994; Shane, 1993; Smith, Haas, & Belcher, 1994).

## Language in higher-functioning persons with autism

Higher-functioning individuals with autism, who have less-severe general intellectual impairment, do acquire language. However, even in these individuals, language development is both delayed and deviant. The prosodic features of the speech produced by persons with autism are almost always odd, often sounding mechanical (Fay, 1993). Sometimes the speech produced by individuals with autism is also different in terms of pitch, volume, and voice quality (Lord & Paul, 1997; Tager-Flusberg, 1999). Reasons for this may include problems with expressing affect—which would result in monotone speech—and a lack of attention to how others sound and/or a lack of interest in sounding like others (Tager-Flusberg, 1999).

The semantic properties of the language of individuals with autism seems less impaired. Compared with mental-age matched children without autism, children with autism show both similar vocabulary growth (Tager-Flusberg et al., 1990) and similar understandings of word meanings (Tager-Flusberg, 1985). One semantic difference is the fact that children with autism do not use words that refer to mental states, such as *believe, figure, idea,* and *guess* (Tager-Flusberg, 1993). Another difference is in the cues to word meaning that children with autism tend to use. Recall from Chapter 4 that normally developing children use the speaker's eye gaze as a clue to what the speaker is talking about (Baldwin, 1993). Children with autism do this much less and instead are more at the mercy of the coincidence of timing. They take the sound they hear to be the label for what they happen to be looking at, with the result, for example, that one child with autism called a toy truck a sausage because his mother had once said "Tommy, come and eat your sausage" as the boy was looking at his truck (Baron-Cohen, Baldwin, & Crowson, 1997). It has been argued that the underlying deficit in autism is the lack of a theory of mind (Baron-Cohen, Tager-Flusberg, & Cohen, 1993), and the evidence that children with autism often fail to consider speaker intentionality in mapping words to referents is consistent with that argument. Syntactic development in children with autism is slower than in normal children but follows a similar course (Tager-Flusberg, 1981; 1989). However, individuals with autism make use of a narrower range of construction types than do other children, and they particularly tend not to produce questions. Thus, by some measures the grammatical complexity of their speech is lower (Tager-Flusberg, 2001).

It is in the area of communicative competence, rather than linguistic competence, that individuals with autism show the most clear and significant impairment. Even infants with autism differ from normal infants in their nonverbal communicative behaviors. Unlike typically developing infants, they show little interest in people and no preference for their mother's speech (Tager-Flusberg, 1999). They rarely produce the pointing gestures that typically developing children start to use to achieve joint attention around the age of 9 months; and even at age 4 years, their joint attention skills are markedly deficient (Loveland & Landry, 1986; Sigman, Mundy, Sherman, & Ungerer, 1986). Children with autism have difficulty with speaker roles in discourse, and they make pronoun reversal errors. They also have difficulty responding appropriately to indirect requests, which they tend to interpret literally (Paul & Cohen, 1985). Children with autism also differ from typically developing children in the types of speech acts they produce. They produce more identifications (e.g., *That's a car*) and fewer explanations (e.g., *He got a new one because it was broken*). They produce fewer descriptions of ongoing events (e.g., *That's going down now*) and internal state reports (e.g., *I know how to do this*) (Ziatas, Durkin, & Pratt, 2003).

It is difficult to have a successful conversation with an individual with autism. Conversations tend to be limited to a small number of topics—those that are of special interest to the individual with autism (Tager-Flusberg, 1993)—and the nonautistic listener has a hard time learning much from such conversation (Paul, 1987). As stated in Chapter 6, as children's linguistic skills develop, their conversational skills normally develop as well. So, as children acquire language, they become more responsive conversational partners. This responsiveness is shown in an increase in the frequency of contingent responses (responses related to the topic of the other speaker's prior utterance) and an increase in the proportion of contingent responses that add new information (Bloom, Rocissano, & Hood, 1976). That developmental pattern does not hold for children with autism. Their linguistic skills improve with age, but their conversational skills do not. Therefore, even when high-functioning persons with autism have mastered the grammar of their language, they do not use those linguistic skills to contribute new relevant information to the ongoing discourse. They also do not ask questions that would elicit new information (Tager-Flusberg, 1993).

In some ways, the language profile presented by individuals with autism seems to illustrate the dissociability of language and communication and the separate contributions to language acquisition of (1) a computational mechanism for acquiring the grammar and (2) the social/cognitive underpinnings of communicative development (Tager-Flusberg, 1999). High-functioning persons with autism acquire language, but they seem never to be fully communicative. It has been argued that the underlying deficit in autism is the lack of a theory of mind (Baron-Cohen, Tager-Flusberg, & Cohen, 1993). And, recall from Chapter 6, some researchers have argued that understanding other people's minds is prerequisite to true communicative behavior. If both arguments are correct, they converge on an explanation of the communicative deficits observed in individuals with autism. That is, individuals with autism who are not mentally retarded can and do acquire the phonology, the lexicon, and the grammar of language because their computational systems are not impaired. However, they never use that language normally because they lack the social understanding of other minds that underlies human communication.

Like many neat and tidy explanations of psychological phenomena, that story ignores some of the messy facts. The language problems of most individuals with autism are not confined to the pragmatic component of language. Many show linguistic problems much like the problems demonstrated by children with specific language impairment. Also, the underlying deficit in autism is probably not so isolable as a deficit in just theory of mind understandings. Autism has also been described as a disorder of complex information processing systems (Minshew, Johnson, & Luna, 2000), and it has been suggested that a subgroup of children with autism suffer from a linguistic impairment in addition to the impairment that defines autism (Tager-Flusberg, 2003). Thus, the language difficulties experienced by children with autism may reflect impairments in both the computational mechanisms and the social/cognitive skills that underlie normal language development.

## SPECIFIC LANGUAGE IMPAIRMENT

### Who is "specifically language impaired"?

For some children, language development is difficult, even in the absence of any clear sensory or cognitive disorder. Such children begin to talk and to understand spoken language later than other children. They have smaller vocabularies than other children of the same age, and they have difficulty acquiring grammar. The *Diagnostic and Statistical Manual of Mental Disorders* (DSM-IV) (American Psychiatric Association, 1994) uses the term *developmental language disorder* to label this condition, but among speech/language clinicians and researchers, the most frequently used term is **specific language impairment.** Another term for this condition, which is used more by Europeans, is **developmental dysphasia.** Estimates of the incidence of developmental dysphasia or specific language impairment (SLI) range from 5 percent (Leonard, 1998) to 10 to 20 percent (Tallal, 2003).

Children who are diagnosed as having specific language impairment are a heterogeneous group. They all have delayed language in common, but the specifics of the language difficulties may vary from child to child. Identifying subcategories of language impairment is one topic of current research (Levy & Schaeffer, 2003; Miller & Klee, 1995; Tager-Flusberg & Cooper, 1999). Because SLI is diagnosed by exclusion (that is, no hearing impairment, no mental retardation, and so on), children labeled SLI may differ in the causes of their impairment. Nonetheless, it is an interesting fact that some general characterizations of language impairment are possible, and it is to those general characteristics that we now turn.

## Characteristics of language development in children with specific language impairment

***Developmental delay.***    The most obvious feature of the language development of children with specific language impairment is a language delay, which is often greater for production than comprehension. Specific language impairment is typically defined in terms of children's performance on several language tests (Tomblin, Records, & Zhang, 1996). A rough idea of how delayed children with SLI are comes from Stark and Tallal (1981), who stated that children have specific language impairment if their productive language is 1 year behind normal development and their comprehension is 6 months behind (Stark & Tallal, 1981). Many children with SLI are more delayed than that. It is not difficult to find 5-year-old children with SLI whose productive language is like that of typically developing 3-year-olds. The delayed development that characterizes SLI shows up in every area of language: phonology, semantics, syntax, and pragmatics (Leonard, 1979; Menyuk, 1993; Watkins, 1997), although subgroups of children with SLI may not show delay in every area. In particular, it has been suggested that there is a group of children with grammatical SLI whose difficulties are confined to the grammar component of language (van der Lely, 2003).

***Delay or deviance?***    One question that arises in characterizing the language of children with SLI is whether their language is only delayed or whether it is also deviant. The argument for pure delay is that children with SLI produce the same kinds of grammatical structures, use the same kinds of phonological processes, use the same kinds of vocabulary, and so on as typically developing children do—they just do so later in the course of development. It is clear that this characterization of SLI as delayed language development accounts for a great deal of the difference between the language of children with SLI and that of typically developing children.

However, it has also been suggested that the language of (at least some) children with SLI is deviant in addition to being delayed. One argument for deviance refers to examples of errors made by children with SLI that are different in kind from errors that typically developing children make. For example, Grimm & Weinert (1990) describe German dysphasic children as producing utterances with word-order errors both at a higher rate than do typically developing younger children and also with other structural features that are extremely unusual in German. Another argument for deviance proposes that children with SLI (again, at least some) acquire language in fundamentally different ways than typically developing children, do and acquire a different underlying grammar (for example, Gopnik, 1990; 1994; van der Lely, 1994).

The question of whether to characterize the language development of children with SLI as delayed or deviant has theoretical implications. The underlying cause one can posit is different depending on whether the children are thought of as slowly following the same progression as typically developing children do or whether they are thought of as acquiring language in a different way. If their language is simply delayed, then explanations of SLI in terms of impairments in the ability to process input or other general cognitive processes are possible. On the other hand, proposals that children with SLI have deviant grammars are more compatible with the view that there is a selective deficit within a separate language faculty (Clahsen, 1999). We will explore these explanations of SLI in more detail in the next section. Before turning to proposed causes of SLI, however, we need to consider one more view on the delay or deviance issue.

***Asynchrony.*** A potential resolution to the delay versus deviance conflict comes from the recognition that language development consists of development in many subsystems of language: syntax, morphology, semantics, and so on. Within each subsystem, children with SLI may follow the typical developmental course, although with delay. However, various subsystems may be delayed to differing degrees, thus disrupting the usual synchrony of the various components of language development and producing a pattern of language competencies not seen in typically developing children.

For example, many children with SLI seem to be delayed in their acquisition of morphology relative to their acquisition of syntax. Typically developing children begin to add grammatical morphemes to their utterances at the

---

**Box 7.3   A story told by a 4½-year-old child with SLI**

The man got on the boat. He jump out the boat. He rocking the boat. He drop his thing. He drop his other thing. He tipping over. He fell off the boat.

---

Source: From Lindner and Johnston, 1992.

---

**Box 7.4   Examples of sentences produced by a 16-year-old with specific language impairment**

Then he went home and tell mother—his mother—tell what he doing that day.
Then about noontime those guy went in and eat and warm up.
That boy climbing a rope to get to the top the rope.
He want play that violin.
Those men sleeping.
That man in a dark room.
Can I play with violin?

---

Source: From Weiner, 1974.

2- and 3-word utterance stage, so that by the time they produce sentences 6 and 7 words long, they are no longer telegraphic speakers. In contrast, children with SLI may produce 6- and 7-word utterances that are still missing some grammatical morphemes. This type of language use is illustrated in the speech samples presented in Boxes 7.3 and 7.4. Several studies have found that when children with SLI are compared with typically developing children with the same MLU, the children with SLI have deficiencies in morphology (Johnston & Schery, 1976; Leonard, Bortollini, Caselli, McGregor, & Sabbadini, 1992; Steckol & Leonard, 1979).

It is not clear yet whether the notion of asynchrony will solve the delay versus deviance issue. However, competing accounts of the cause of SLI pay close attention to the fact that children with SLI are not equally impaired in all aspects of language. Furthermore, the acquisition of **grammatical morphology**—particularly the tense and agreement markers on verbs, at least for children with SLI acquiring English—seems to be particularly difficult (see Watkins, 1997, and references therein). One account of at least some forms of SLI is that it represents an extended stage in which these verb inflections are optional (Rice, Wexler, & Cleave, 1995). That is, typically developing children go through a stage (the telegraphic speech stage) in which they treat verb inflections as optional, rather than required, and they thus produce sentences like *Daddy wash car* and *Mommy go bye-bye*. Children with SLI, it is argued, stay in this stage a very long time. This view is known as the **Extended Optional Infinitive Hypothesis** (Rice et al., 1995; Rice, 2003; Wexler, 2003). According to the proponents of this view, the decline of this stage in typically developing children is under the control of a maturational timetable, and for children with SLI that maturational timetable is different (Wexler, 2003).

## What causes specific language impairment?

***The language environment of children with SLI.*** Because children with specific language impairment seem to be unimpaired in every other regard, it was thought at one time that the cause of SLI might reside in the environment rather than in the child. To test this hypothesis, numerous studies have investigated the nature of the speech that parents (usually mothers) address to children with SLI. These studies have found some differences between the speech that mothers address to children with SLI and the speech that mothers address to typically developing children. The most consistent findings are that mothers of children with SLI are more directive of their children and do proportionately more of the work of initiating and maintaining dialogue (Grimm, 1993). However, these characteristics of mothers' speech seem to be reactions to the conversational passivity of the children with SLI, rather than independent traits in the mothers (Grimm, 1993).

Two major reviews of the literature on the linguistic environment of children with SLI have concluded that the environment is not the explanation for the children's language difficulty (Lederberg, 1980; Leonard, 1987). These reviews argue that mothers of children with SLI modify their speech to suit their children's abilities in the same way that mothers of typically developing children do. On the other hand, other evidence suggests that in modifying their speech to suit their children's diminished language abilities, mothers of children with SLI may be presenting less useful language input to their children than mothers of typically developing children do (Grimm, 1993; Nelson, Welsh, Camarata, Butkovsky, & Camarata, 1995). For example, Nelson and associates (1995) found that mothers of children with SLI provided fewer responses that were expansions of the child's previous utterance. However, such data suggest merely that the communicative environment of children with SLI may exacerbate their language difficulties. There is no evidence that the input to children with SLI explains their initial problems. Thus, whatever the cause of SLI turns out to be, it seems to

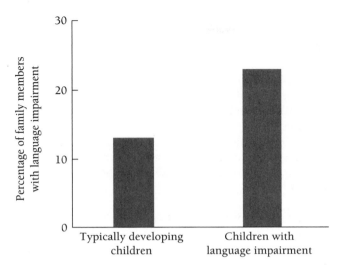

**Figure 7.4**  Familial concentration of specific language impairment
Source: Based on data in Tomblin, 1989.

be a property of the children who have language impairment, not a property of their environments.

***Genetic factors in specific language impairment.***    Whatever that internal cause of specific language impairment turns out to be, it is likely to be something that has a genetic basis. Problems with language acquisition run in families. Neils and Aram (1986) compared the incidence of language disorders in the immediate families of children with and without language impairment. They found that, on average, 20 percent of the family members of children with language impairment also had some language impairment, compared with a 3 percent incidence of language impairment among the family members of unimpaired children. Other studies have also found what is referred to as a **familial concentration** of specific language impairment (Ludlow & Dooman, 1992; Tallal, Ross, & Curtiss, 1989; Tomblin, 1989). Tomblin's data, graphed in Figure 7.4, show that children with language impairment have more family members who also show language impairment than do typically developing children. The most dramatic evidence of genetically transmitted language impairment is the case of one family in which language impairment has been observed over three generations in 16 out of 30 family members (Gopnik & Crago, 1991; Vargha-Khadem, Watkins, Alcock, Fletcher, & Passingham, 1995). In this family, the inheritance pattern suggests that a single dominant gene is at work (Gopnik & Crago, 1991).

However, a single gene or even some other genetic basis cannot be identified for all cases of specific language impairment. Not all persons who are specifically language impaired show exactly the same deficits as the members of the family studied by Gopnik and Crago (1991) in which the genetic basis is clear. In addition, although children with SLI are more likely than typically developing children to come from families in which other members have language impairment, not all children with SLI come from families with such a history. One study of 89 children with SLI found that 70 percent had a family history of language disorder; 30 percent did not (Tallal, Townsend, Curtiss, & Wulfeck, 1991). Furthermore, the children with SLI who did have a family history of language impairment were no different from the other children with SLI in their language skills or IQ.

***Phonological memory and SLI.***    In 1998 the National Institutes of Health held a workshop to define specific language impairment. One goal was to identify markers that could provide a basis for diagnosing children as specifically language impaired based on properties they do show, rather then merely by excluding other causes for their language delay. One property suggested in the report of this workshop was impaired phonological memory, because a deficit in phonological memory is one of the most reliably appearing features of children with SLI (Tager-Flusberg & Cooper, 1999). The standard measure of **phonological memory** is the ability to repeat a meaningless sequence of sounds, known as the nonword repetition task (Gathercole, 1999). As we discussed in Chapter 4, 4- and 5-year-old children who are good at this sort of task tend to have bigger vocabularies than do otherwise equivalent children who are not as good at this task, suggesting that phonological memory is involved in the normal process of language acquisition (Gathercole & Baddeley, 1989). Children with specific language impairment are worse at this task than typically developing children (Bishop, 1995; Conti-Ramsden, 2003; Gathercole & Baddeley, 1990). Furthermore, Bishop (1995) found that this deficit was heritable (has a genetic basis) and can be found even in children whose language impairments were resolved through speech–language therapy. Together these findings suggest that language acquisition depends on phonological memory and that language impairment results when phonological memory is deficient. However, it is also true that some children who are clearly deficient in language, the grammatical SLI subgroup, appear not to be deficient in phonological memory (van der Lely & Howard, 1993; van der Lely, 2003).

***Nonlinguistic cognition in children with SLI.***    One recurring explanation of specific language impairment is that SLI results from deficits in nonlinguistic cognition. On this account, specific language impairment is not so specific after all. Several studies have tested this hypothesis by comparing children with SLI to typically developing children on nonlinguistic cognitive measures. The criteria for diagnosing SLI produce a bias against finding differences between children with SLI and typically developing children on cognitive measures, because any child who scored below age level on an IQ test would not be diagnosed as specifically language impaired. Despite this bias, some differences have been found in research that has looked outside IQ test–type measures of cognitive functioning.

Children diagnosed as having specific language impairment have shown deficits in a variety of cognitive areas, including symbolic functioning, mental imagery, hierarchical planning, hypothesis testing, and reasoning (for summaries, see Johnston, 1988, 1992, 1997; Kamhi, 1993). Weismer (1985) found evidence that children with language impairment have difficulty drawing inferences from stories, even when the stories are presented in a sequence of pictures with no words. Marton and Schwartz (2003) found that the working memory demands of language tasks had greater effects on the performance of children with SLI than on the performance of control subjects, suggesting that children with SLI have greater processing capacity limitations. Some of these cognitive differences may be revealing the cognitive deficits that are the cause of the language impairment. It is also possible that children with SLI perform less well on high-level conceptual tasks than typically developing children of the same age because language plays a role in thought, and thus their language impairment causes some cognitive impairment.

There is one general cognitive difference between children with SLI and typically developing children that is more likely to be a cause than a consequence of the children's language difficulties. At least some children with SLI are more limited in their general processing capacity and therefore process information more slowly than their typically developing peers do (Weismer, Evens, & Hesketh, 1999; Windsor & Hwang, 1999a and 1999b; and see discussion in Leonard, 1998). Of course, if general processing limitations underlie the language problems of children with SLI, we still need an explanation of *how* these general limits result in the particular language profile that is observed. Leonard (2003) has suggested that processing limitations, combined with a poorer phonological memory, make it difficult for children with SLI to represent and hold in their heads enough language data to extract the regularities that lead to linguistic advances.

***Language faculty accounts of specific language impairment.***    Another sort of proposal holds that the difficulties children with SLI experience result from an impairment in some aspect of the grammar acquisition mechanism asserted to be innate in all of us. This language acquisition device (LAD) deficit type of proposal tends to come from those who take the learnability approach to the study of normal language development and who hold the view that a language-specific mental faculty underlies normal language development. With those assumptions, it makes sense to look for what might be wrong with that language acquisition device when language acquisition does not proceed normally, and several such hypotheses have been proposed (see Clahsen, 1999, for a review). To illustrate, Gopnik (1990) proposed the missing features hypothesis to account for the errors produced by the 16 family members with language impairment she studied. According to this hypothesis, the innate grammar of these individuals was missing a piece—the notion that certain features, such as number (for nouns) and tense (for verbs), must be marked. More recently, Gopnik endorsed a different view, termed the *missing rule hypothesis* (Crago & Allen, 1994; Gopnik, 1994; Ullman & Gopnik, 1999). This view postulates that affected members of this family have difficulty learning the implicit linguistic rules that govern the use of grammatical morphology (such as marking number and tense). So, for example, where unimpaired children hear *walk* and *walked* and *jump* and *jumped* and then build a rule for forming the past tense, children with language impairment never use those regularities to form a rule. They manage what they do through rote memorization, and because rote memorization for most is inadequate to the tasks, they often omit these obligatory markers in their speech. (Note that this is similar to the account by Karmiloff-Smith et al. [1997] of language acquisition by individuals with Williams syndrome; the difference is the fact that children with Williams syndrome have better associative memories for acoustic stimuli.)

Gopnik and colleagues have begun research exploring the extent to which the kinds of language problems seen in these family members are characteristic of other people with specific language impairment. However, huge disagreement remains in the field over exactly how to characterize what is wrong with the affected members of this family. In contrast to Gopnik's claim of a language-specific impairment, another research group that has also studied this family found evidence of language disability beyond the inability to form rules. The other team also found general cognitive deficits (as indicated by IQ tests) in the family members with language impairment (Vargha-Khadem et al., 1995). Another example of a specifically linguistic account of the deficit that underlies specific language impairment is the Extended Optional Infinitive Hypothesis (Rice et al., 1995; Rice, 2003; Wexler, 2003). According to this view, an optional infinite stage is part of the normal, genetically controlled and language-specific part of development. In children with SLI, the genetic blueprint is different in this regard, with the consequence that this stage lasts longer, perhaps indefinitely.

***The phonological salience hypothesis.*** Although children with specific language impairment have particular difficulty with grammatical morphology, not all grammatical morphemes are equally difficult for children with SLI. Leonard (Leonard, Sabbadini, Volterra, & Leonard, 1988; Leonard, 1989) suggested that the explanation of why some morphemes are more difficult than others lies in the phonological salience of these morphemes in the speech stream. The morphemes that cause difficulty for children with SLI tend to be unstressed syllables of short duration relative to adjacent syllables (such as *is* in "He is going") or tend not to be whole syllables at all (such as the third person *s* on verbs). Leonard describes such morphemes as having low phonetic substance. If this account is true, then children with SLI acquiring different languages should show different areas of difficulty depending on what morphemes have low phonetic substance in the target language. Cross-linguistic evidence suggests that this hypothesis is consistent with some, but not all, of the data (Crago & Allen, 1994; Leonard, McGregor, & Allen, 1992).

***Specific language impairment as a temporal processing disorder.***
Imagine you were given the following task to perform: You are sitting in front of a metal box with two panels mounted on it—sort of like a typewriter with two giant keys. Now you hear two tones, first a low-frequency tone and then a higher-frequency tone, and you are instructed that the left panel goes with the low tone and the right panel goes with the higher tone. Now you hear a pair of tones in sequence: low-low, low-high, high-low, or high-high. The task is to repeat the sequence you hear in panel pressings: left-left, left-right, right-left, or right-right. This repetition task doesn't appear to be very difficult, and it also doesn't appear on the face of it that being able to do it should be very important. However, this task is quite difficult for some children, and children who find this task difficult are quite likely to have difficulty acquiring language. In a series of studies spanning 20 years, Paula Tallal and her colleagues established that children with specific language impairment have difficulty with this task when the interval between tones is very short. When the tones are separated by more than 400 milliseconds (0.4 second), children with SLI and typically developing children perform similarly on this task. However, when the sequences are presented rapidly, children with language impairment cannot do it. In fact, children with language impairment appear to have a hard time even telling if two tones presented in rapid sequence are two different tones or two presentations of the same tone (Tallal, 1978), and the ability to distinguish rapid auditory cues in infancy predicts later language impairment (Benasich & Tallal, 2002). On the basis of such findings, Tallal has proposed that the deficit underlying SLI is a deficit in processing rapidly presented stimuli. Tallal, Stark, and Mellits (1985) found the same sort of deficit with visually presented stimuli, suggesting that the deficit is not modality specific. The idea suggested by this proposal is that processing speech depends on processing rapidly sequenced acoustic stimuli. Children with impairment in that sort of processing will have difficulty conducting the analysis of speech that language acquisition requires. Evidence from Leonard and associates (1992) suggests that this kind of processing deficit could account for the particular problems with grammatical morphology that characterize SLI. The low phonetic substance positions in the speech stream that make grammatical morphemes difficult to acquire also make sounds difficult to iden-

tify for children with SLI, but not for typically developing children. Using a discrimination procedure developed by Stark and Tallal, Leonard and associates found that children with SLI could discriminate one vowel from another (such as [i] versus [u]). However, the children with SLI could not discriminate between two sequences of sounds that differed only in an unstressed syllable ([dab i ba] versus [dab u ba]) or in a final consonant ([das] versus [da]). Typically developing children could make all three discriminations.

## What is specific language impairment?

The search for the underlying cause of specific language impairment has certainly increased our knowledge of the disorder. As a result of this research, we can describe with some precision which aspects of language are likely to be affected and to what degree. We know that as a group, children with SLI are likely to differ from children who are acquiring language typically in a number of other ways as well. For example, children with SLI show nonlinguistic cognitive deficits, deficits of phonological memory, and difficulty in discriminating and sequencing rapidly presented stimuli. However, the investigation of SLI has not resulted in identifying a single cause of the disorder.

It may be that language development depends on many underlying abilities, and therefore language impairment can have many underlying causes—this view is certainly consistent with the evidence that children with SLI actually represent several different subgroups with different disorders. A more radical proposal has come from Leonard (1987; 1991), who suggested that there is no cause of specific language impairment because there is no such thing as specific language impairment. Instead, he argues, children labeled as SLI simply represent the low end of the distribution of language acquisition ability (whatever that consists of). Language ability varies in the population, as does every other ability. The child with limited musical ability is not called music impaired, nor is the uncoordinated child called sports impaired. Neither should the child with limited language acquisition ability be termed language impaired. This proposal concerns more than just labeling. It claims that there may not be an underlying pathology that causes language impairment. According to Leonard,

> Many children given the label of SLI are not impaired in the sense of being damaged but rather are much less skilled than their peers in such acts as extracting regularities in the speech they hear, registering the conversational contexts in which these regularities occur, examining these regularities for word-referent associations and evidence of phonological and grammatical rules, and using these associations and rules to formulate utterances of their own. (1987, p. 33)

This is not to say that such children should not be treated. Whatever the explanation of the difficulty some children have in acquiring language, those children need help in overcoming their problems with language because of the importance of language skills to academic, social, and occupational success.

# ● SUMMARY

For a variety of reasons, language development in some children does not proceed in its typical fashion. Deafness makes the acquisition of spoken language difficult, if not impossible. However, deaf children who are exposed to sign language in infancy acquire that language according to the same developmental course as hearing children acquire spoken language. Blindness has far less severe consequences for language acquisition. Blind children sometimes fail to appropriately generalize the meanings of words—for example, they may use object labels as if they were names for particular referents rather than names for categories. Blind children also frequently rely on rote-memorized formulaic speech to participate in conversation. However, grammatical development is relatively unaffected by blindness.

Mental retardation has different consequences for language development, depending on the type and severity of the mental retardation. Individuals with Down syndrome typically show language development that is delayed not only in relation to chronological age but also relative to mental age. Although individuals with Down syndrome are conversationally competent, most do not achieve normal adult-level linguistic competence. Some individuals with other forms of mental retardation, including Williams syndrome, display language skills that far exceed their nonlinguistic mental abilities, but even in these cases, language acquisition is delayed and follows a different course than in typically developing children.

Autism is always associated with some degree of both language delay and language deviance. Approximately 50 percent of autistic individuals either do not speak or produce only echolalic speech, in which they "parrot" previously heard utterances with seemingly little comprehension. Higher-functioning autistic individuals do acquire language, but their eventual competence is almost never normal. The most significant language impairment in autistic individuals is in communicative competence. Although high-functioning autistic individuals may acquire normal vocabulary and grammar, they usually fail to use their language for normal communicative interaction.

Some children who seem typical in all other respects nonetheless have difficulty acquiring language. A great deal of research has been directed toward describing the nature of such specific language impairment (SLI) and finding its underlying cause. Children with SLI differ in the nature of their difficulties and, quite likely, in the cause of their difficulties. Nonetheless, some generalizations are possible. As a group, children with SLI have more trouble acquiring grammatical morphology than acquiring syntax or vocabulary, although those functions may be delayed as well. It seems clear that the cause of SLI lies not in the children's environment but in some characteristic of the children themselves. Furthermore, at least for some children with SLI, that characteristic is likely to have a genetic basis, because SLI runs in families. Several hypotheses about the nature of the underlying deficit have been proposed, including deficits in nonlinguistic cognition, deficits in innate grammar, and deficits in the ability to perceive, store, or process language input.

Each of the hypotheses concerning the underlying cause of SLI has some empirical support, but so far no single hypothesis has been able to account for the full range of phenomena that characterize SLI. It has also been proposed that the search for an underlying deficit is misguided. That is, children who are labeled SLI may not have anything wrong with them per se; they simply represent the lower end of the range of human ability to acquire language in the same way that other children represent the low end of the range in musical or athletic ability. Even if this proposal is true, the central importance of language skills to academic and occupational success (unlike musical or athletic ability) makes efforts at remediation crucial.

The study of language development in atypical populations provides information about those populations. It also provides information that could explain typical language development. For example, the fact that the course of sign language development in deaf children is the same as the course of spoken language development in hearing children tells us that the human capacity for language is not specific to one modality. The fact that blind children have difficulty generalizing the meanings of object labels but are unimpeded in their acquisition of grammar tells us that visual information is more important for forming conceptual categories than for forming grammatical categories and learning the rules that operate over those grammatical categories. The course and eventual outcomes of language development in people with different forms of mental retardation tell us that language development does not proceed in lockstep with the development of other mental abilities. Language development may lag behind nonlinguistic cognition, as it does in persons with Down syndrome, or it may exceed nonlinguistic cognitive abilities, as it does in persons with Williams syndrome. Similarly, the relatively spared linguistic competence in individuals with autism, combined with severe social and communicative deficits, tells us that different human abilities are dissociable to some extent. In particular, the language of individuals with autism tells us that acquiring the vocabulary and grammar of language neither depends on nor results in normal communicative interaction. Finally, children with specific language impairment challenge the field to identify just what are the abilities that underlie the human capacity to acquire language.

## ● KEY TERMS

prelingually deaf

otitis media

sign language

oralist method

total communication

oral language development

American Sign Language (ASL)

home sign

cochlear implant

dissociability (of language and cognition)

Down syndrome

Williams syndrome

chatterbox syndrome

autism

echolalic speech

specific language impairment

developmental dysphasia

grammatical morphology

Extended Optional Infinitive Hypothesis

familial concentration

phonological memory

# ● REVIEW QUESTIONS

1. What do researchers hope to learn from studying language development in atypical populations?
2. What is the typical outcome of oral language development in the profoundly deaf?
3. What are "home sign" systems, and what does their form and existence imply about the human capacity for language?
4. Describe and contrast the language skills that are typical of individuals with Down syndrome and Williams syndrome.
5. What sort of relation between language development and cognitive skill is consistent with the evidence from both the Down syndrome and Williams syndrome populations?
6. Describe the language skills of high-functioning individuals with autism. What might explain this pattern of strengths and weaknesses?
7. What are some characteristic features of language development in children with specific language impairment?
8. There are many proposals concerning the nature of the disorder that underlies the symptoms seen in SLI. List and briefly explain each.
9. List one thing that has been learned about normal language development from the study of each of the atypical populations described in this chapter.
10. What does the study of language development in these special populations suggest with regard to the three big issues in the field: (1) the innateness of language, (2) the relation between language and general cognition, and (3) the relation between language development and the development of communication?

# CHAPTER 8

# CHILDHOOD BILINGUALISM

Up to this point, we have considered the process of language development as though children were always exposed to, and therefore acquired, one language. In fact, exposure to more than one language and bilingualism in childhood may be more prevalent than monolingualism. This chapter begins by describing the varied circumstances that result in childhood bilingualism and by providing an overview of the relatively new and growing field of research on bilingualism. Next we turn to the findings of this research to describe the course of bilingual development and to consider the psychological processes underlying bilingual development. We will do so separately for two very different circumstances in which bilingualism develops: one in which children are exposed to two languages from birth, and the second in which children begin life as monolingual speakers but then later acquire a second language while still in childhood. We will then consider whether being bilingual affects cognitive development and the way two languages are represented and processed in the brain. Last, we will turn our attention to an applied and highly politicized issue of concern to bilingual children and their families: bilingual education.

## THE SOCIAL CIRCUMSTANCES OF CHILDHOOD BILINGUALISM

All bilingual children have in common that they have been exposed to two languages. Beyond that, the ways in which children's environments provide exposure to two (or more) languages vary enormously. In some circumstances, children hear two languages from birth and acquire two languages at the same time. This is referred to as **simultaneous bilingualism.** In other cases, children hear only one language for their first few years and later are exposed to another language, which they also acquire. This is referred to as **sequential bilingualism.** Within these categories, there is also variability.

Simultaneous bilingualism requires that the infant be addressed in two languages, but within that constraint there are still various possible environments. One parent or caregiver may be a speaker of a language that is not spoken by any other family members or in the community, but the parent may choose to use that language with the child. For example, an Italian-English bilingual mother married to a monolingual speaker of English, living in a monolingual English-speaking community might choose to speak Italian to her infant, and she would be the infant's only source of exposure to Italian. In contrast, bilingualism in children's immediate environments may reflect bilingualism in the community. For example, French/English bilingual parents in the French/English bilingual community of Quebec might speak French and English to their infant, who would also hear both languages from other sources. When the community is bilingual, a description of the sources of children's experience with each language may be enormously complex. Consider the case described by de Houwer (1995) of a child who lives in the Flemish region of Belgium, where Dutch is the official language but French—the official language of the other half of Belgium—is spoken in many places:

> [The child] goes to a French-medium music school on Wednesday afternoons and a Dutch-speaking preschool on weekday mornings. . . . The paternal grandparents address the child in Dutch, while the maternal grandparents use French. However, the child sees the maternal grandparents every weekday afternoon, and the paternal grandparents only on Sundays. The child's babysitters, who spend approximately three waking hours a week with the child, use exclusively French, and the children that the child regularly plays with also only speak French. . . . (p. 224)

A different sort of example is provided by Nair (1984, cited in Bhatia & Ritchie, 1999), who described the situation of a bilingual child in New Delhi, India. This child lived in a house with grandparents, an uncle, an aunt, and household employees. His father's language and the language of the paternal grandmother who did much of the caregiving was Bengali; his mother's was Malayalam. The parents used their native languages and English to communicate with the child. They used Hindi and English to speak with each other. Through household help the child also heard other Indian languages and dialects. India is the source of many accounts of complicated multilingual situations. It is common there for adults to be at least conversant in four languages: the language of their state, Hindi, the language of a neighboring state, and another tribal language of the region (Khubchandani, 1997). Another fact about multilingual environments is that a great deal of code switching occurs. That is, even within the same conversation with the same participants, multiple languages may be used.

Sequential bilingualism in childhood occurs when a second language is introduced after the acquisition of a first language is well under way, and the circumstances that produce this sort of experience also vary. When a family immigrates to a new language community, the children are exposed to a new language—at least outside the home. Children of immigrants may also hear only their parents' native language for their first several years. Sequential bilingualism also occurs routinely in the many places where children first learn an indigenous or tribal language at home and then the national language at school. This is true for the Inuit of Canada, the Maori of New Zealand, the Saami of Norway, and many other groups (Cummins & Corson, 1997). In all of these circumstances, there are likely to be differences between the home language and the national language in prestige, which complicates the bilingual developmental story. That is, one cannot study bilingual development as a pure test of what happens when the human brain is exposed to two languages. Many social variables are intertwined with the language variables in such children's experience. A further source of complication in children's bilingual language-learning environments is the fact that they change. As household composition changes, as caregiving arrangements change, and as school becomes part of the picture, the amount and kind of exposure to both languages fluctuates (for example, see Pearson, Fernandez, Lewedeg, & Oller, 1997). Because the circumstances that produce bilinguals are so varied, the nature of children's bilingual competence is highly varied. Put another way, bilinguals are a heterogeneous group (Manuel-Dupont, Ardila, Rosselli, & Puente, 1992).

## BILINGUAL DEVELOPMENT AS A TOPIC OF STUDY

The study of childhood bilingualism is rapidly growing—as is the study of bilingualism in general. Two journals devoted to research on bilingualism, the *International Journal of Bilingualism* and *Bilingualism: Language and Cognition,* have appeared in recent years. There is also a journal devoted to the study of trilingualism and more, the *International Journal of Multilingualism.* Knowing three or more languages is less rare than many would imagine, but it is even less researched than bilingualism; in this chapter, we will confine ourselves to the consideration of bilingualism.

This newly increased interest not withstanding, the literature on bilingual development lags behind the literature on monolingual language acquisition in both the number of studies reported and the number of subjects studied. Many studies are based on the diary record of a single child, often the child of a linguist. The best known of these diary studies is still Werner Leopold's four-volume study (1939–1949) of his daughter's bilingual development of English and German. Another strand of research in the history of the study of bilingualism is composed of larger-scale studies of children in immigrant families. The focus of such studies was typically on documenting the children's skill in the majority language, not on the children's development of both languages (for more discussion of the history of the field, see Bialystok, 1991; Hakuta, 1986; Hakuta & McLaughlin, 1996).

Bilingualism is the subject of both basic and applied research. The basic research questions concern (1) how language develops when two languages are acquired during childhood and (2) what the course of bilingual development can tell us about the nature of the language acquisition process. Some of the applied questions are motivated by the social and political circumstances of bilingualism. Immigrant parents want their children to be successful in the new culture but often do not want their children to lose their heritage language and culture. Parents who are monolingual themselves may want to provide their children the opportunity to become bilingual. Parents in both these circumstances may have questions about how best to achieve bilingualism in their children and may have concerns about whether the demands of learning two languages will have negative consequences. Not just parents, but also educators, policy makers, and speech-language clinicians are interested in bilingualism. Educators and policy makers in countries with substantial immigrant populations are understandably concerned about how best to ensure children's acquisition of the majority language. Sometimes this concern appears to clash with the wish of immigrant groups to maintain their language heritage, with the result that bilingual education becomes a political issue. When children in bilingual environments have difficulty with language, speech-language clinicians may confront difficult diagnostic issues. In this chapter, we focus on the psycholinguistic questions that have been raised by the study of bilingual development and touch on the social and political issues that surround bilingualism in the United States. Childrearing, teaching, and clinical concerns are directly addressed in Arnberg, 1987; Genessee, Paradis, and Crago, 2004; Harding and Reilly, 1987; Saunders, 1988; and Tabors, 1997.

## BILINGUAL FIRST LANGUAGE ACQUISITION

*Early bilingualism, bilingual first language acquisition,* and *simultaneous bilingualism* are all terms used to refer to the situation in which a child is exposed to, and thus acquires, two languages from the very beginning of language development. Two major issues are addressed by research on simultaneous bilingual development. The first issue is **language differentiation:** How and when does the child know that he or she is being exposed to two different languages, and does the child build two separate language systems in his or her head or do children build one undifferentiated system using their experience in both languages? The second issue is whether and how bilingual development affects the course and rate of the development of each language: Do bilingual children learn their two languages in the same manner and at the same rate as monolingual children learn one? We will consider the research that addresses each of these questions in turn.

### Language differentiation in bilingual development

Three hypotheses have been offered regarding language differentiation in bilingual development: (1) The fusion hypothesis: children initially create one system that combines the two languages they hear, (2) The differentiation with autonomous development hypotheses: children differentiate the two languages they hear and acquire each uninfluenced by the other, and (3) The differentiation with interdependent development hypothesis: Children differentiate the two languages they hear but the course of the development of each is influenced by the other. (These hypotheses were articulated by Meisel [2001] with regard to morphosyntactic development, but they can be used as a more encompassing framework.)

An early and influential paper argued for initial fusion. Volterra and Taeschner (1978) proposed that bilingual children start by constructing a single system in which one lexicon contains the words in both languages and one system of rules applies. Later, according to this view, bilingual children distinguish two lexicons but apply the same syntactic rules to both languages; and only in a third stage, which is achieved around the age of 3 years, do the children have two fully differentiated systems. This proposal generated a great deal of controversy, with many opponents arguing that in bilingual development children have two distinct and autonomously developing systems from the beginning. The most recent evidence supports the early differentiation position but suggests there are influences of one language on another in the course of bilingual development. This evidence is summarized in the following sections.

***Phonological differentiation.***   The evidence reviewed in Chapter 3 on phonological development makes it clear that children begin to process speech in a language-specific manner from as early as 6 months of age and suggests that their prespeech productions also show some influence of the target language. The question for bilingual development then is whether children exposed to two languages develop two language-specific systems for processing and producing speech in infancy.

We do not, as yet, have an answer to that question. Studies of infants in monolingual environments show that infants as young as 4 days can tell two different languages apart (Mehler, DuPous, Nazzi, & Dehaene-Lambertz, 1996). By 2 months, however, they can only distinguish the language they have been hearing from other languages; they cannot distinguish two unfamiliar languages from each other (Mehler et al., 1996). If they have been exposed to two languages, however, infants at 4½ months can distinguish those two languages (Bosch & Sebastian-Galles, 2001a, 2001b). Together these findings suggest that bilingual experience is shaping speech processing at a very early age, but they tell us only that babies exposed to two languages retain the ability to hear the difference between those languages when without such exposure they might not. The available data do not tell us if the babies listen to each of their languages in a language-specific way or whether they process all speech through a common system. This question is motivated by findings that adult monolinguals do process speech in language-specific ways (Mehler et al., 1996). For example, English words tend to begin with a stressed syllable and adult speakers of English tend to use stress as a clue to word segmentation. Speakers of other languages use other language-specific rhythmic cues, and even highly proficient bilingual adults have been found to use just one set of clues for both their languages (Cutler, Mehler, Norris, & Segui, 1992). The as yet unanswered question is what the development of these language-specific processing procedures would look like in children exposed to two languages from infancy.

The evidence with regard to phonological differentiation in production is slim, and, at this point, also inconclusive. One study of 13 babies between 10 and 14 months old who were exposed to French and English in Montreal found that they did not babble differently in French- and English-speaking contexts. Rather, across contexts, the consonantal features of these babies' babbling resembled those of babies in monolingual French environments (Poulin-Dubois & Goodz, 2001). On the other hand, Maneva and Genesee (2002) report a case study of a French- and English-learning baby, also in Montreal, who did babble differently depending on whether he was interacting with his French-speaking parent or his English-speaking parent.

Case studies of older bilingual children report the children had distinctly different phonological features in their productions depending on which of their languages they were using (Ingram, 1981; Deuchar, 1989). Similarly, Hoffman (1991) describes reports of bilingual development without apparent confusion between the phonologies of the two languages. However, the children whose productions were being described in these studies were at least $1\frac{1}{2}$ years old and 2 years old, respectively, so they could have started with an undifferentiated system that later became differentiated. Other case studies of children at age 3 years report that words in one language are produced with phonological features that belong only to the other language the child is acquiring (Burling, 1959, and Fantini, 1985, cited in Bhatia & Ritchie, 1999). Similarly, a study of 2-year-old Spanish/English bilingual children in south Florida (Navarro, Pearson, Cobo-Lewis, & Oller, 1998) found evidence that, for some children at least, two lexicons and grammatical systems are processed through a single phonological system—that of the dominant language. The evidence comes from the following procedure: words produced by these bilingual children were excerpted from tape recordings and played for judges who were asked to identify the word, and then, if they couldn't identify the word, to identify the target language. The crucial question is whether the target language is clear from the phonological properties of the word, even when the particular word is not clear. The judges could tell at better than chance levels what the target language was, but they were not much better than chance. Over one-third of the children's words were unassignable to a target language on the basis of their phonological properties.

The answer to the question of whether and when phonological differentiation occurs may be different for different bilinguals—large individual differences are a hallmark of such research (Poulin-Dubois & Goodz, 2001), reducing the generalizability of case study findings. In addition, differentiation may depend on factors such as the degree of phonological similarity between the two languages and the bilingual's relative proficiency in the two languages. Even when the evidence comes from the babbling of infants, it is possible that the features of babbling are influenced by how much input the baby receives in each language.

***Lexical differentiation.***    The lexical evidence that is generally considered relevant to the issue of language differentiation in bilingual children is the degree of overlap between the vocabularies of the child's two languages. The argument is made that if children exposed to two languages have words in each language for the same things, then the children have two systems.

Part of the underlying logic for attributing such importance to lexical overlap as evidence of two systems is the view that children acquiring one language operate on the principle of mutual exclusivity. Thus, they would reject a new word that is synonymous with a word they already know if they thought both words came from the same language—they should have only one word per concept. Conversely, then, accepting a new word as having the same meaning as an old word indicates understanding that the two words come from different languages. Consistent with this logic, experimental evidence shows that 4-year-olds do override the mutual exclusivity principle and accept two names for the same object if they perceive the two names as coming from different languages (Au & Glusman, 1990). The question is whether very young children reveal they are also accepting two names for the same thing in the content of their vocabularies. The method is to inventory children's vocabularies in both languages they are acquiring and count the number of translation equivalents (e.g., the word for *dog* in both English and Spanish). What makes the application of this criterion difficult, unfortunately, is that it is not clear how much overlap in vocabularies is necessary to conclude the children have two systems. Clearly, one would not expect complete redundancy because usually children who are exposed to two languages hear them from different people in different contexts and would thus learn different words (Pearson & Fernandez, 1994; Pye, 1986).

The early data on this topic were case studies and were sometimes interpreted as reflecting a single system. The findings and their conflicting interpretations have been summarized by de Houwer (1995). More recently, larger-scale studies have been interpreted as reflecting separation. A study of the Spanish/English bilingual population in south Florida found that for children between 8 and 30 months of age, an average of 30 percent of their vocabularies were translation equivalents. The authors argued that this is a sufficient degree of overlap to suggest that the children are building two separate linguistic systems (Pearson, Fernandez, & Oller, 1995). Similar findings and arguments come also from the study of babies simultaneously acquiring French and English or French and the sign language used in French-speaking Quebec, Langue de Signes Quebecoise (LSQ) (Petitto et al., 2001). Estimates of the degree of overlap in these children's vocabularies range from 36 percent to 50 percent.

***Morphosyntactic differentiation.***   The issue of morphosyntactic differentiation is to many the heart of the issue of whether bilingual children are building one language system or two. The relevant data concern language mixing. If children acquiring two languages have two truly separate systems, then they should not build sentences—a process that depends on grammatical rules—using elements from both languages. They also should not use the rules of one of their languages when producing sentences in the other. If language mixing never occurred, it would be clear that bilingual children have separated the two systems. If, on the other hand, children freely mixed words and rules of their two languages, it would be clear that there is some intrusion. The data fall somewhere in between.

De Houwer (1995), reviewing the diary studies that have addressed this issue, concluded that there was no evidence of a single, fused system. Although language mixing occurs, children mix lexical items but keep the rules of grammar separate (Meisel, 1989). For example, children learning French and German simultaneously do not incorrectly combine French words in German word order or vice versa. Furthermore, Meisel (1989) argued that using words from two languages in a single utterance does not necessarily mean the child fails to differentiate between the two languages. Language mixing could be the result of the child's reaching into one language for a word that he or she doesn't know in the other language (Genesee, 1989). If the person the child is speaking with knows both languages, this is an appropriate communicative strategy.

Another argument against interpreting language mixing as evidence of language confusion is the fact that adults who know two languages often mix them in speaking. Clearly the cause in those cases is not failure to differentiate the two languages. As further evidence of differentiation, children's language mixing generally, although not perfectly, conforms to the same syntactic constraints as adults' language mixing (Paradis, Nicoladis, & Genesee, 2000). That is, neither bilingual adults nor bilingual children jumble words and morphemes from their two languages in any old manner; they follow "rules." Currently, the consensus in the field is that bilingual children do differentiate the morphosyntactic systems of the two languages they are acquiring.

Another source of evidence in support of at least global differentiation is the evidence that bilingual children show awareness of which people in their environment understand which language. A French/English bilingual child, for example, uses French more frequently with those she knows speak only French and English more frequently with those she knows speak only English. Young children don't get this perfectly correct, but they do not randomly select a language regardless of their listener (Deuchar & Quay, 1999; Lanza, 2001; Nicoladis & Genesee, 1996; Petitto et al., 2001).

That is not to say, however, that the two systems develop autonomously. We will consider the evidence for the influence of bilingualism on the development of each language subsequently. First, we tackle a question raised by the current consensus that bilingual children differentiate the lexicons and grammars of their two languages from the very beginning of development—How do they do it?

***How do children differentiate?***   Imagine you are an infant trying (albeit unconsciously) to figure out the system that underlies the speech addressed to you. How could you tell whether you were hearing one language or two (or more)? If you ask the proverbial man on the street this question, the likely answer is that children hearing two languages are in great danger of becoming confused and the remedy for this is to have one parent consistently speak in one language and the other parent consistently speak in the other. This is known as the "one-parent, one-language" principle.

This advice is widely circulated, but it does not have a body of research behind it. It seems to have come from a linguist colleague of Louis Ronjat, whose daughter was the subject of the first diary study of bilingual development (see Reich, 1986; Ronjat, 1913), and to have been perpetuated in the absence of clear evidence to the contrary. There is a ceratin logic to the notion that children will have an easier time keeping the two languages they are hearing distinct if they hear them from different speakers, but there is evidence that suggests this is not necessary. Newborns can discriminate between languages if they are prosodically different, and by 4 months babies with exposure to each language can discriminate between two prosodically similar languages such as Spanish and Catalan (Bosch & Sebastian Galles, 2001b). Also, work on infant speech perception shows that very young babies ignore the speaker in categorizing speech sounds. That is, /ba/ spoken by a male and /ba/ spoken by a female are acoustically very different signals, but babies treat them as the same. Babies seem to know at a very young age which acoustic parameters are linguistically relevant and which are not (Kuhl, 1980). Another reason to think that separation by speaker is not necessary is that it is typically not available. Parents of children who are developing two languages do not universally adhere to the one-parent, one-language principle (e.g., Lanza, 2001), and even parents who claim that they do, in fact do not (Goodz, 1989).

## Bilingualism's effects on the development of each language

The conclusion that bilingual children know, in some sense, that they are acquiring two different languages does not necessarily mean that the development of each language proceeds autonomously. It is still possible that the simultaneous acquisition of two systems affects the development of each of those systems. Two sorts of possible effects can be distinguished: effects on the path of development and effects on the rate of development.

Reviews of the literature by Lindholm (1980) and de Houwer (1995) concluded that in both the course and the rate of development, "bilingual and monolingual development are highly similar" (de Houwer, 1995, p. 244). Petitto et al.

(2001) drew a similar conclusion from their study of babies acquiring either French and English or French and LSQ. This conclusion is problematic for two reasons, however. First, the data come from case studies and small samples of children convenient to the researchers, whose development was compared with descriptions of monolingual development taken from other studies. The children in these studies are likely to be, by and large, an advantaged group. Thus, it could be that bilingual development causes some delay in the development of each language but not so much as to cause these particular children to be outside the normal range of variation in rate of language development. Second, and more generally, the normal range of variation in the rate of development is large. Just because some factor, in this case bilingualism, does not push development outside the normal range does not mean that the factor has no effect.

In order to draw conclusions about the effects of bilingualism on language development, it is necessary to directly compare language development in samples of bilingually and monolingually developing children. Some studies meet this criterion. With respect to precursors of language, findings of such a direct comparison show that babies exposed to one and to two languages begin to produce canonical babbling on the same schedule (Oller, Eilers, Urbano, & Cobo-Lewis, 1997). In contrast, studies of vocabulary development that directly compare bilingual and monolingual children have provided some evidence of delay. Bilingual children 5 years old and older have been found to have smaller comprehension vocabularies in each of their languages than do monolingual children of the same age (Ben-Zeev, 1977; Rosenblum & Pinker, 1983; Umbel, Pearson, Fernandez, & Oller, 1992). Looking at younger children, from 8 to 30 months of age, Pearson, Fernandez, and Oller (1993) found that bilingual children had comprehension vocabularies in each language that were comparable to monolinguals' vocabularies, but in spontaneous speech production, these same children used smaller vocabularies in each of their languages than did their monolingual age-mates. However, bilingual children typically know some words in one language that they do not know in the other, and vice versa. Put another way, their total conceptual vocabularies (all the concepts for which they have a word in at least one language) are larger than their vocabularies in either language. The size of their conceptual vocabularies compares favorably to that of monolinguals, and bilingual children's total vocabularies (the number of words they know in both languages combined) may be larger than the total vocabularies of monolingual children (Oller & Pearson, 2002; Pearson et al., 1993).

The data available to address the effects of bilingualism on grammatical development are similar to, and sometimes the same as, the data on other aspects of bilingual development. There are many case studies of bilingual children and few direct comparisons of samples of bilingually and monolingually developing children. De Houwer (1995) reviewed the work available at that time and concluded that the course of grammatical development in bilinguals was essentially the same as that in children with monolingual development and that it proceeded without major delay. More recently, Gathercole (2002a, 2002b, and 2002c) has directly compared Spanish/English bilingual children to monolingual groups on their command of three different morphosyntactic distinctions: the mass/count distinction in English, grammatical gender in Spanish, and the respective treatments of *that*-trace phenomena in each language. These particular grammatical phenomena are of interest because the first two are specific to each language and thus must, to a certain degree, be learned from input. *That*-trace phenomena, in contrast, are something that every language handles one way or another. In some languages, such as English, "Who do you think has green eyes?" is correct and *"Who do you think that has green eyes?" is ungrammatical. In Spanish, the opposite is true. This phenomenon is part of UG, according to the theory of Universal Grammar, and acquisition should be merely a matter of parameter setting. Thus, a theory of language acquisition that makes reference to UG would predict that acquiring *that*-trace phenomena depends very little on input and thus should be unaffected by bilingualism.

Contrary to that prediction and contrary to the view that bilingualism does not affect the rate of development in either language, Gathercole found, for all three phenomena that she investigated, that the bilingual children lagged behind the monolingual children in mastering the grammar. However, the course of development was not different in bilingual children, and the rate differences seemed to disappear by age 10. This same general conclusion is suggested by a study of French/German bilingual children. Analysis of the errors made in French revealed that the children made errors of the same sort as monolingual French children (the French pronoun system causes problems even for the French), but the period of making errors lasted longer in the bilingual children than in monolingual children (Muller & Hulk, 2001). There are, however, reports of bilingual children showing the intrusion of one language into the other. Ardila (2002) reports that Spanish/English bilingual children sometimes use the English adjective-noun word order (e.g., *a big house*) when speaking Spanish, thus producing errors such as *la grande casa* instead of the correct *la casa grande*, which monolingual speakers do not make. These errors in spontaneous speech are ambiguous with respect to source—bilinguals must not only have two language systems but must also be able to retrieve from those systems as they produce speech. Errors of intrusion could reflect grammatical knowledge or more superficial performance factors of the sort that cause speech errors in everyone upon occasion.

We began this section asking a question that is of both basic and applied interest: Does bilingual development affect the development of competence in each language? The boundaries of the possible answers to this question are defined by two extreme and opposite positions. One is that children can learn two languages as easily as one; the other is that learning two languages is so difficult that simultaneous exposure to two languages in infancy should be avoided. The research just reviewed makes it clear that simultaneous acquisition of two languages is possible, but the research also suggests that the often-expressed notion that for children, two languages are as easy to learn as one may be overstated (Pearson et al., 1997). The practical implications of this conclusion are not solely a matter to be settled by science; they depend also on cultural values. The social/political aspects of bilingualism will be considered further in other sections. Suffice it to say here that if bilingualism is valued by the culture, then one implication of this research is that it needs to be recognized that children who are developing bilingually are learning more than children who are acquiring only one language. They require environmental support for that accomplishment, and the norms for the rate of development may be different.

There are also implications of research on bilingual development for our understanding of the process of language acquisition. One point that research on bilingual development makes clear is that input plays a role in language acquisition (de Houwer, 1995). Not only do children learn the particular languages to which they are exposed, but they appear to learn them in some measure to the degree that they are exposed to them (de Houwer, 1995; Gathercole, 2002a, 2002b, 2002c; Pearson et al., 1997). Very few children get exactly equal amounts of input in two languages. Among children exposed to both Spanish and English in the largely Cuban community of southern Florida, Pearson found that children were unlikely to become competent users of Spanish if Spanish constituted less than 25 percent of their input. Gathercole similarly concluded from her studies of the development of morphosyntax in bilingual children that the frequency with which children hear structures in input plays an important role in their acquisition of those structures. The fact that it takes longer to learn two languages than one and the finding that the rate of mastery of each language depends on the amount of exposure to that language suggests that the process of language acquisition depends more on input than the most nativist of theories would allow.

## SECOND LANGUAGE ACQUISITION IN CHILDHOOD

When children move from one language community to another, they typically acquire the language of that new community. If they retain their native language, they become successive bilinguals, distinct from simultaneous bilinguals who acquire two languages essentially from birth. The cutoff between successive and simultaneous bilinguals is entirely arbitrary (Appel & Muysken, 1987), but research on second language acquisition in childhood rarely discusses children under 3 to 4 years. In Chapter 2, we considered whether children are better at second language acquisition than adults. In this section, we consider the process of learning a second language in childhood and the factors that influence the outcome of that process. We will not try to cover the entire field of second language acquisition. Rather, we will focus on those aspects particularly relevant to the process of learning a second language and becoming bilingual in childhood.

## The course of second language acquisition in childhood

If we returned once more to our proverbial man on the street and asked him what happens when children need to learn a new language, he is likely to say that it is no problem. Children, the saying goes, "soak up language like a sponge." Careful inspection of the data suggests, however, that the ease with which children acquire a second language has been greatly exaggerated. There is no doubt that children do better than adults in terms of ultimate attainment, but they do not achieve this mastery as rapidly as the conventional wisdom would suggest.

When children first move to a new language community they appear to go through stages of using different communicative strategies before they are able to communicate in the new language (Tabors, 1997). They first may use their native language, even though it is not understood. Next, they may go through a nonverbal period in which they communicate through gesture. Then they start to use the new language, but often what children can produce at this first stage of new language use consists of memorized phrases that serve social purposes. Only later do children start to use the new language productively.

When children start to use their new language, they typically make errors. Both children and adults acquiring a second language have been described as going through a period of interlanguage use. The interlanguage is a systematic and rule-governed system, but it is not the same systematic and rule-governed system as the target form of the new language. The differences between the interlanguage and the new language are the source of the errors second language learners make. Some of these errors appear to be like the errors monolingual children make in the course of acquisition (they are called developmental errors), and some seem to reflect the influence of the old language on the new one (these are called **language transfer** errors).

This course of development may take years. One study of school-aged children in immigrant families in English-speaking Canada found that after 18 months of exposure to English-speaking children, only half of these children were native-like in their control of grammatical morphology (Genessee et al., 2004). Furthermore, these findings all pertain to oral language skill. Achieving the level of language proficiency necessary for literacy and academic achievement is an even more challenging task. Cummins estimates that getting to this level of second language achievement takes children between 5 and 7 years (Cummins, 2000).

Second language acquisition in childhood also has effects on children's proficiency in their first language. Sometimes the first language is lost altogether (Fillmore, 1991; 1996). Sometimes the first language is not lost, but the second language becomes the dominant language—the language that is more frequently used and in which the child is more proficient. Jia and Aaronson (2003) have documented this process of dominant language switch for Chinese immigrant children in New York City. They found that children who were under the age of 9 years when they immigrated reported preferring to speak in English over Mandarin after 1 year and were more proficient in English, as measured by several tests of grammatical knowledge and translation, by the end of 3 years. Children over 9 years of age maintained their preference for Mandarin and remained more proficient in Mandarin than English over the 3 years of the study. A switch in language dominance has also been documented in Spanish/English bilingual children in southern California who first learn Spanish at home and then begin to learn English at school at age 5 years (Kohnert & Bates, 2002; Kohnert, 2002). Individuals with this history continue to increase their proficiency in Spanish as they learn English, but they make progress faster in English so that by middle childhood they are more proficient in English than Spanish. The measure in these studies was the speed with which the speakers performed a picture-word verification task, thus the measure is fluency or accessibility of each language. Contrary to what one usually assumes about first and second language proficiency, as adults, individuals with this history are more proficient in their second language than in their native language.

No one has argued that these trade-offs between first and second language proficiency reflect limitations of the brain's capacity to handle two languages. Rather, this outcome reflects the sociology and psychology of language use. The influence of peers and the wider culture converge to make English the preferred language in the United States. This is true even in areas with large bilingual populations. Oller and Eilers (2002) observed that Spanish-English bilingual school-aged children in the Miami area, who attended bilingual schools, nonetheless consistently spoke English to each other outside of their classrooms. The language that is used most, in turn, becomes dominant (Jia & Aaronson, 2003; Oller & Eilers, 2002).

## The process of second language acquisition in childhood

There are many reasons that acquiring a second language might be a different process than acquiring a first language—even in childhood. First, the learner already knows one language, and properties of the first language may influence the sort of hypotheses the child entertains in trying to figure out the second language (Bialystok & Hakuta, 1994; Kellerman, 1986). Evidence of such a process is the widely observed fact that the particular language that is a child's native language influences the errors they make as they learn a second language.

Other questions regarding how second language acquisition might differ from first language acquisition are suggested by the Universal Grammar approach to language acquisition. For example, if first language acquisition involves parameter setting, then does second language acquisition involve resetting those parameters, or is the unset template still available (White, 1996)? As another example, if first language acquisition depends on a language-dedicated mental module, which includes UG, is that module still available for second language acquisition, or does second language acquisition—even in childhood—rely on general cognitive processes (Wong Fillmore, 1991)? The observation that prompts this suggestion is the following: Although virtually all children successfully master a first language, there are enormous individual differences in the success of second language acquisition. The view that the human genome guarantees first language acquisition but that we are left to rely on our differing memories and analytic abilities for second language acquisition seems consistent with this view. On the other hand, there is also evidence that some common underlying language acquisition ability is recruited for both first and second language acquisition. Skehan (1991) found that children's rate of first language development from 3 to 5 years was significantly related to their performance on tests of foreign language aptitude at 13 years.

Second language acquisition in childhood might also proceed differently and have a more variable outcome than first language acquisition because the input conditions are different and highly variable. Children typically do not have the one-on-one dyadic interaction with a speaker of the target language that characterizes the circumstances of first language acquisition, at least in Western middle-class homes. Rather, children tend to be thrown into situations in which they must sink or swim and in which many of their language models are peers. It is interesting, in this regard, to note that Wong Fillmore (1991) has described the process of second language acquisition by children as consisting of their memorizing large chunks of speech to use for communicative purposes and then only gradually analyzing these chunks into their component parts. That description is similar to the way that Heath (1983) described first language acquisition by the children of "Trackton," who also experienced little dyadic interaction but were surrounded by a great deal of speech. Similarly, Bates described her daughter, who learned English as her first language, as having a highly referential style. A few years later when the same child was exposed to Italian, in part by participating in the activities of a large Italian family, she learned socially useful expressions in big, unanalyzed chunks (Bates, Bretherton, & Snyder, 1988).

## Influences on second language acquisition in childhood

The degree to which children master a second language in childhood is a function both of characteristics of the children and of the sociocultural environment in which they are exposed to a second language. The relevant characteristics of the children include both cognitive/linguistic characteristics and social/personality characteristics.

***Characteristics of children that influence second language learning.*** Although there has been a fair amount of research on what cognitive characteristics contribute to successful second language learning, no consensus emerges from that research (Bialystok, 1991; Segalowitz, 1997). Skehan (1989; 1991) has argued, in part on the basis of the correlation between first language acquisition and later language aptitude test performance, that there is a specific aptitude for language learning that applies to both first and subsequent languages and that is different from general intelligence. One likely component of this aptitude is phonological memory. At least in the circumstance of exposure in a classroom setting, children who are better at repeating a new sound sequence after a single hearing are also better at learning a new language (Service, 1992; Service & Kohonen, 1995). Because phonological memory has also been found to be related to vocabulary growth in first language acquisition, it seems reasonable to think that it plays a role in second language learning even when that learning occurs in more naturalistic language-learning settings than the classroom setting that Service and colleagues have studied.

When second language acquisition occurs in more natural contexts, the effect of social personality variables is readily observed and may even overwhelm the differences owing to cognitive/linguistic abilities. In settings in which the speakers of the target language outnumber the target language learners, children who are very sociable appear to learn the language faster than shy, withdrawn children (Wong Fillmore, 1991). Other social/personality characteristics such as a willingness to communicate and low anxiety related to language learning also are associated with successful second language acquisition (Segalowitz, 1997). Of course, these correlations could also reflect the influence of knowing the language on sociability and willingness to communicate (Genessee et al., 2004).

Even within childhood, age affects the outcome of exposure to a second language. The nature of the effect depends on the particular outcome studied. Older children initially make more rapid progress in second language learning than younger children (Snow & Hoefnagel-Höhle, 1978). Ultimate mastery of the grammar and the ability to speak without an accent are better achieved by younger learners, and age effects on these two outcomes have been observed within the range from infancy to late adolescence (Flege, 1995; Johnson & Newport, 1989). The data are particularly clear with respect to accent. Second language learners who begin at 2 years have an advantage over those who begin at 6 years, and those beginning at 6 have an advantage over those who begin at 12 (Flege, 1995).

Finally, children's proficiency in their first language appears to predict their success at learning a second language. This is particularly true with respect to the sort of language proficiency required by academic settings: proficiency in decontextualized language use. Studies of many different immigrant groups, including Finnish immigrants in Sweden, Hispanic immigrants in the United States, and Asian immigrants in Canada, have found that children's academic language skills in their native language predicted their academic language skills in their new language.

***The sociocultural environment and second language learning.*** Another perspective on second language acquisition and bilingualism focuses not on characteristics of individual learners as the factors influencing outcome but on social and political characteristics of the environment in which exposure to a second language occurs. The crucial feature of that environment is the attitude toward acceptance of the groups that speak different languages (Glick, 1987). These sociocultural attitudes in turn affect the attitudes of individual learners. In their work on the achievement of French by English-speaking Canadians, Gardner and Lambert (1972) distinguished two motivations for learning a second language: instrumental and integrative. **Instrumental motivation** included reasons such as needing to speak French for employment purposes. **Integrative motivation** included a desire to be part of the French-speaking community. Gardner and Lambert found that an integrative motivation was associated with more successful language learning. Later, Tremblay and Gardner (1995) expanded that motivational construct to accommodate findings that a constellation of motives, attitudes toward the second language, and beliefs about what contributes to successful second language learning (e.g., is it all a matter of ability, or does effort play a role?) all contribute to predicting second language learning.

Although this more recent work suggests that the distinction between integrative and instrumental motives may be a bit simplistic, it does not contradict the widely held view that language learning is more successful to the degree that the learner is willing to become part of the target language community (Appel & Muysken, 1987). In the same vein, work reviewed in Chapter 2 on the role of identification in accounting for age effects argues that children are sometimes more successful second language learners because they are more likely than adults to identify with speakers of the target languages. The evidence suggests that the best learning occurs in children who become so assimilated by the new speech community that the new language becomes their dominant language (Jia & Aaronson, 1999). On the other hand, it has also been argued that successful language learning need not require giving up one's identity or being assimilated—provided supportive sociocultural attitudes prevail. Taylor (1987) argues that second language learners can retain their cultural identity while seeking positive relations with the majority language group. They can do this only in a larger environment that supports this integrationist ideology. He further argues that a truly bilingual community with balanced bilingual speakers will be sustainable only in such an environment. If the ideology is assimilationist—that is, everyone must become a member of the dominant culture—the native language will be lost. If the ideology is separatist—that is, the two language communities exist side by side without integration—individuals will speak only one of the languages well.

## BILINGUAL LANGUAGE USE: CODE SWITCHING

**Code switching** or code mixing are terms used to refer to bilingual speakers' use of two languages in the same conversation. "Switching" implies a deliberate choice to change languages, whereas the term "mixing" has sometimes been used to imply confusion as the cause. Research has investigated the sociolinguistics of code switching (i.e., what social factors cause it), the psycholinguistics of code switching (i.e, how do people do it), and the linguistics of code switching (i.e., the linguistic constraints on what kinds of mixed utterances speakers produce) (Appel & Muysken, 1987). Linguistic analysis has distinguished different types of code switching. Tag switches involve putting a word or phrase in one language at the beginning or end of a sentence that is otherwise entirely in the other language (e.g., "OYE, when . . ."). Intrasentential switches occur within a sentence (e.g., "I started acting real CURIOSA"), and intersentential switches occur between sentences (Appel & Muysken, 1987). Not all potential possible kinds of switching actually appear. Rather, linguistic constraints restrict where the language switch can occur. For example, subject and object pronouns must match the main verb, and articles must match nouns with respect to language. Spanish/English bilingual speakers would not say *"YO went," *"MIRA him," or *"the CASA." It is also important to distinguish between code switching and the mere borrowing of a word from the other language, which is then integrated phonologically and morphologically into the base language of the utterance (Grosjean, 1982). This particularly happens with new terms for technology (e.g., "EL fax").

When speakers switch codes they seem to do so for a variety of social and communicative purposes. Local switches, within a sentence, may specify who is being addressed, add emphasis by repeating part of the message in the other language, or convey an emotion that is better conveyed in one language than the other (Appel & Muyksen, 1987; Grosjean, 1982). More complete switches from use of one language to the other can set the tone for the conversation. For example, in the common situation in which one language is the majority language (e.g., English in the United States) and the other language that a group of bilinguals speak is the minority language (e.g., Spanish in the United States), using the majority language defines the situation as more formal and less personal, whereas using the minority language emphasizes personal connection (Gumperz, 1976). (This latter use is often awkwardly employed by politicians in the United States who use their poor Spanish in an effort to emphasize their solidarity with Spanish-speaking voters.) More simply, codes are sometimes switched to exclude others from the conversation. Members of the upper class of imperial Russia spoke French among themselves so that their servants wouldn't understand their personal conversations. Thus, in contrast to the notion of language mixing as evidence of confusion, we have the proposal that language mixing is evidence of sociolinguistic skill, which raises the question of when children demonstrate this skill.

Studies of bilingual children's code switching have found that children as young as age 2 years use their two languages in contextually sensitive ways (Genesee, Nicoladis, & Paradis, 1995; Lanza, 1992). Studies of the interactions of French/English bilingual children with their French- or English-speaking parents find a developmental increase in children's use of the parent's same language, with very few cases of addressing the French-speaking parent in English or vice versa by age 5 years (Comeau & Genesee, 2001; Nicoladis & Genesee, 1996). Just what sort of development underlies the developmental increase in pragmatic differentiation is not clear. The children could have been learning to differentiate their two languages, or they simply could have been learning each language well enough to use it when pragmatically appropriate without dipping into the other language in order to communicate. In French-speaking Canada, it is quite likely that both parents had some competence in the other language, and thus the child's switching languages to communicate was not pragmatically bizarre. Furthermore, when children did use a different language from their parent and communication broke down, children as young as 3 years showed awareness of two languages by repairing their misunderstood utterance by switching to the other language (Comeau & Genesee, 2001).

## COGNITIVE CONSEQUENCES OF CHILDHOOD BILINGUALISM

Acquiring language is just one of many things the developing brain accomplishes. Does the task of acquiring two languages have consequences for how the brain performs its other tasks? This is the question of the effects of bilingualism on cognition outside of language development. During the 1930s and 1940s, several studies compared the intelligence test performance of immigrant bilingual children and nonimmigrant (and usually more economically advantaged) monolingual children and found consistently poorer performance among the immigrant children. There were, at the time, two competing explanations of these findings: (1) that the immigrants were genetically inferior and (2) that their bilingualism was to blame. Within the field of psychology, the environmental argument won the day, leading to conclusions that echoed Yoshioka's (1929) assertion that "Bilingualism in young children is a hardship and devoid of apparent advantage" (quoted in Hakuta, 1986, p. 30). This view was overturned by the findings of a study of French/English bilingual children in Canada (Peal & Lambert, 1962), a study that corrected the major flaws of the previous work. In Peal and Lambert's study, the children were balanced bilinguals (relatively equal in their mastery of both languages), unlike the immigrant children who tended to be more competent in their parents' language. The bilingual children also came from the same social class as the monolinguals with whom they were compared. Peal and Lambert found, for the balanced, middle-class sample they studied, that bilinguals performed better than monolinguals on a range of cognitive tests. They concluded, in stark contrast to earlier conclusions, that the bilingual child is a "youngster whose wider experiences in two cultures have given him advantages that a monolingual does not enjoy. Intellectually his experience with two language systems seems to have left him with a mental flexibility, a superiority in concept formation, and a more diversified set of mental abilities. . . ." (quoted in Palij & Homel, 1987, p. 133).

Subsequent studies have looked at more narrowly defined cognitive skills and have found that bilingualism is associated with certain cognitive advantages. Ben-Zeev (1977) compared middle-class 5-year-old to 8-year-old children who were bilingual in Hebrew and English with same-age middle-class monolingual speakers of Hebrew and same-age middle-class monolingual speakers of English. The children were administered several nonverbal and verbal tests. In one test, the children were presented with a physical array of nine different-size cylinders arranged in a 3-by-3 matrix. The children's task was to explain the pattern in the matrix and then transpose it. In another task, the children were told they were playing a game in which an airplane was called a "turtle," and then the child was asked things like "Can the turtle fly?" and "How does the turtle fly?" Ben-Zeev found that the bilingual children were better than the monolingual children both at explaining the pattern in the matrix and at answering questions in the "turtle" example. She concluded that exposure to two languages causes children to develop a mental facility for "seeking out the rules and for determining which are required by the circumstances" (pp. 1017–1018).

Other research on the abilities of bilingual children suggests that bilingual development fosters the development of **metalinguistic awareness,** or awareness of how language works (see Bialystok, 1991). More interestingly, there is also evidence that bilingualism may affect cognitive processing. In a series of studies, Bialystok has found that bilingual children have an advantage over monolingual children in performing tasks that require them to exercise control over attention (Bialystok, 1999; Bialystok & Majumder, 1998). That is, in tasks where the presence of distracting information is what makes the task difficult, bilingual children do better than their monolingual agemates. They do not do better if what makes the task difficult is in the central part of the task that must be attended to. This bilingual advantage in directing attention is true even for nonverbal tasks, suggesting that bilingualism has a general effect on what cognitive psychologists call executive functioning, which is the ability to direct cognitive resources. One caution, however, must be raised about the interpretation of any findings that show bilingual children have an advantage over monolingual children. Children who succeed at becoming bilingual may be a select group. We simply do not know how many children who are exposed to two languages fail to become bilingual, and thus we don't really know how select such samples may be (Diaz, 1983).

## THE BILINGUAL BRAIN

Everything that a person knows is somehow represented in that person's brain. The topic of this section is how two languages are represented in the bilingual person's brain. The question researchers have asked is whether both languages are represented in the same area of the brain or whether different languages are represented in different areas. One motivation for this question is the clinical observation that brain damage in a bilingual individual sometimes has different effects on functioning in each language. A second motivation is the critical period hypothesis. Because bilinguals have often acquired one of their languages later than the other, studying bilinguals provides an opportunity to ask whether age of acquisition affects the neurological bases of language.

When a bilingual individual suffers brain damage, the two languages are not always affected equally, and they may follow different recovery paths. For example, there is a famous case of a man who was a native speaker of Swiss German who also spoke fluent French and some Italian and standard German. When he had a stroke, all languages suffered initially, but all recovered to some extent except Swiss German. He never again could speak his native language (Minkowski, 1927, cited in Obler & Gjerlow, 1999). Another patient with a brain tumor suffered aphasias of different types in her third- and fourth-learned languages, but experienced little damage to her fluency in her first- and second-learned languages (Albert & Obler, 1978). Such intriguing cases suggest that in multilinguals, different languages may be represented in different areas of the brain. However, there are other possible explanations of these unequal effects of brain damage and these nonparallel courses of language recovery. Albert and Obler (1978) suggest that what matters is how much each language is used and that the language most recently used is the most likely to recover first. It is also the case that the striking and memorable cases in which one language is lost and another spared are actually quite unusual. In most cases of aphasia in bilinguals, similar deficits occur in both languages and both languages do, in fact, show parallel courses of recovery (Obler & Gjerlow, 1999). Overall, the data on aphasia in bilinguals have yielded contradictory and confusing results (for summaries see Paradis, 1977, and Vaid & Hall, 1991). One hypothesis that was considered and rejected held that a second language is represented in the right hemisphere, unlike first languages, which are typically represented in the left hemisphere. The failure to find support for that particular pattern of bilingual representation led some to conclude that bilingualism was no different from monolingualism at the neurological level (Vaid & Hall, 1991).

Another approach to studying the neurological representation of a bilingual's two languages is to give normal bilinguals tasks in both their languages and, using brain imagining techniques, look at whether different areas of the brain are recruited depending on the language. The results of this work are also complicated. One reasonably clear conclusion is that many language tasks use the same area of the brain for both first and second languages (e.g., Klein, Milner, Zatorre, Meyer, & Evans, 1995; Klein, Miler, Zatorre, Zhao, & Nikelski, 1999). There is some evidence, in addition, that different regions of the brain are recruited to perform syntactic tasks in a bilingual's two languages—under certain circumstances. For example, Weber-Fox and Neville (1996) studied Chinese/English bilinguals who were all native speakers of Chinese and who began acquiring English at dif-

ferent ages. They recorded the electrical activity of the brain, using evoked response potentials (ERPs), and found that the age at which English was acquired
affected the brain activity associated with performing tasks in the language. Furthermore, the brain activity associated with syntactic processing was more affected
by age of acquisition than the brain activity associated with semantic processing.
Interestingly, age of acquisition had the same pattern of effects on accuracy of
task performance: syntax was more affected by age of acquisition than semantics.
A similar finding emerged from a study using functional magnetic resonance
imaging to locate the brain areas engaging in linguistic tasks (Kim, Relkin, Lee, &
Hirsch, 1997). Early and late bilinguals were given tasks in both their first and second languages. The study found that the same part of Wernicke's area was recruited for tasks in both languages by both groups of subjects. (Roughly speaking,
Wernicke's area is responsible for meaning.) In contrast, the late bilinguals, but
not the early bilinguals, showed that different parts of Broca's area were recruited
for tasks in the first and second language. (Roughly speaking, Broca's area is responsible for syntax.) These findings suggest that the neurological underpinnings
of syntax are different for languages acquired early versus later, but otherwise a
bilingual's two languages make use of the same neurological substrate.

More recent evidence has suggested that it may not be differences in age
of acquisition, but rather, differences in proficiency that result in two languages using different parts of the brain. Typically, late bilinguals are less proficient in their second language than are early bilinguals, and thus, differences
observed between early and late bilinguals could really be differences between more and less proficient speakers of a second language. Another group
of researchers used PET scans to assess the location of brain activation when
bilingual subjects listened to stories in their first and second languages. They
found different areas were used when there were differences in proficiency,
but not when the subjects were highly proficient in their second language—
despite learning it later (Perani et al., 1998).

## BILINGUAL EDUCATION

### Overview

We switch now from the most physiological of bilingualism topics to the most
social. As we have seen in this chapter, bilingualism itself is a social and political phenomenon that is inextricably tangled with the social and political relations
among the groups that speak the two languages. These issues play themselves
out most clearly in the arena of bilingual education. **Bilingual education** is
education in which the curriculum is provided to children in two languages. This
distinguishes it from foreign language instruction, in which the entire curriculum
is provided in the students' native language and a second language is taught in
a separate class. That definition, however, encompasses many different sorts of
programs with differing goals. It includes programs that exist throughout the

world in private schools to which the educated elite send their children in an effort to provide them the benefit of competence in a second language. Bilingual education also includes public programs designed to teach the majority language of the culture to immigrant and native children who speak only a minority language. One system of classifying types of bilingual education programs is presented in Box 8.1, and examples of the languages and countries involved in bilingual education around the world are presented in Box 8.2.

In order to explore the goals, methods, and outcomes of bilingual education in some depth, we focus in this chapter on two very different North American programs. The first, in Quebec, Canada, was designed to teach French to children from homes in which English is spoken at a time when many children from these Anglophone families spoke no French. The second includes the many programs in the United States designed to teach English to immigrant children who speak a variety of minority languages.

## The French immersion program in Canada

One of the largest experiments in bilingual education was begun in the Canadian province of Quebec in 1965. The goal of this **immersion program** was to teach French to the children of the English-speaking population, and the experimental question was whether immersion in French (i.e., delivering part of the curriculum in French) would accomplish that better than standard foreign language instruction without sacrificing competence in English or other content areas. Although the degree of immersion varied from program to program, in all programs children experienced several hours a day of content area instruction in French, for several years during elementary and middle school. Because the program was planned from the beginning with academic consultation, extensive evaluation was part of the program.

Almost 35 years after its inception, the results of the experiment indicated that children who speak the majority language of a community can be successfully taught a minority language if they are immersed in the language at school (Genesee, 2003). (Although both French and English are official languages in Canada, at the time this program began English clearly had majority status.) Immersion resulted in better French proficiency than standard foreign language instruction. Furthermore, when different forms of immersion were compared, it appeared that more hours spent in immersion worked better than fewer, and most, but not all, of the findings suggest that immersion begun earlier worked better than immersion begun later. With respect to other subjects, the children experienced no long-term decrement in their English language skills, although initially, during the grades when the French immersion students were not being explicitly instructed in English and children in the regular program were, the immersion students lagged behind in English language literacy. Based on province-wide testing of math and science knowledge, the immersion students also appeared to learn as much in their content

---

**Box 8.1    Types of bilingual education programs**

| | |
|---|---|
| Type I | Indigenous or native languages are used as the medium of instruction. Often these programs have as a goal saving and revitalizing endangered indigenous languages. Example: Maori language programs in New Zealand. |
| Type II | A national minority language, which may have some official status in the country, is used as the medium of instruction. Maintenance of languages important to the identity of minority groups is often a goal. Examples: Gaelic language programs in Scotland and Basque language programs in Spain. |
| Type III | An international language that is the language of a minority immigrant group is used as the medium of instruction. Often the goal is to help children make the transition to the majority language. Examples: Spanish language instruction in the United States, Finnish language instruction in Sweden, Turkish language instruction in The Netherlands. |
| Type IV | In programs for deaf and hard-of-hearing individuals, manual sign language is used in the classroom in addition to a spoken language. |
| Type V | A minority language is used as the medium of instruction with speakers of the majority language. Examples: French immersion programs for Anglophone Canadians, Spanish/English two-way programs in the United States. |

---

(From Cummins & Corson, 1997)

area classes as students who received instruction in English. In sum, the findings indicated that immersion is a better way to teach a second language to children than standard foreign language instruction and that it can be accomplished without sacrificing first language or content area proficiency (Genesee, 2003).

To return to a question that we considered earlier, does this finding mean that children really can learn two languages as easily as one? The data reviewed earlier with respect to bilingual first language acquisition suggest that the answer is not quite, which raises the question of how children in bilingual education programs could learn just as much content material as children in monolingual programs and learn another language besides. In this case, an an-

---

### Box 8.2    Examples of languages involved in bilingual education around the world

*North America*
| | |
|---|---|
| Spanish/English | United States |
| French/English | Canada |
| Athapaskan/English | Canada |
| Inuktitut/English | Canada |

*Europe*
| | |
|---|---|
| Basque/Spanish | Spain |
| Hungarian/Slovene | Slovenia |
| Turkish/Dutch | The Netherlands |
| Frisian/Dutch | The Netherlands |
| Gaelic/English | Scotland |
| Welsh/English | Wales |

*Scandinavia*
| | |
|---|---|
| Swedish/Finnish | Finland |
| Finnish/Swedish | Sweden |
| Saami/Norwegian | Norway |

*Asia*
| | |
|---|---|
| Cantonese/English | Hong Kong |
| Malay/English | Maylasia |
| Indonesian/English | Indonesia |
| Santali/Hindi | India |
| Kurukh/Hindi | India |

*Africa*
| | |
|---|---|
| Yoruba/English | Nigeria |
| Masai/English | Kenya |
| Luo/English | Kenya |

---

swer was suggested by the children who participated in the bilingual education program. The students consistently reported that they worked harder than students in the regular school program (Genesee, 1983). It is also possible that there are subtle differences in very advanced language skills or content knowledge that standardized tests and provincial exams do not tap. It is nonetheless clear from the results of the Canadian experiment that in these circumstances—one in which both languages are valued and supported in the community—

students through secondary school can achieve fluency and literacy in two languages while still mastering the content appropriate to their grade level.

## Bilingual education in the United States

In the United States, bilingual education is a very different sort of enterprise. The target population is children who speak languages other than English and whose proficiency in English is limited. This was not always the case. Prior to World War I, immigrant groups in the United States typically established schools that provided instruction in their native language. After World War I, however, using a language other than English was regarded as un-American (Faltis, 1997), and bilingual education essentially stopped. Bilingual education began again in the 1960s when large numbers of affluent and educated Cubans settled in south Florida. The goal of the program that they initiated was full bilingualism for their children in English and Spanish. Shortly thereafter, politicians seized upon the idea of legislating bilingual education as a way to help school districts with large numbers of poor, low-achieving immigrant children, particularly in the southwestern United States. This political interest resulted in the Bilingual Education Act of 1968, which provided federal money for local programs designed to meet the needs of children with limited English proficiency.

Bilingual education became the law with a U.S. Supreme Court decision in 1974. In the case of *Lau v. Nichol,* the court declared that school systems that failed to adequately instruct students with limited English proficiency were violating those students' civil rights. Neither the Bilingual Education Act nor the *Lau v. Nichol* decision specified how the students with limited English proficiency were to be provided an education—only that they must be and that federal monies would be available. Different states and local communities have gone about doing this in different ways. Some bilingual education programs have the twin goals of teaching English and maintaining the children's native language, thus producing true bilinguals. Most frequently, the goal of bilingual education in the United States is merely to teach English to immigrant children. Instruction in the children's native language is provided only during a transition period. Typically that period lasts 3 years, after which time children are expected to learn content material in English-only classrooms.

There have been several broad-scale attempts to evaluate the efficacy of bilingual education in the United States, but they have yielded no consistent conclusion (see Faltis, 1997; Oller & Eilers, 2002). Part of the problem is a lack of agreement on the goal of bilingual education. For some, it is that the children become fluent and literate in two languages. For others, the goal of bilingual education is to help children make the transition from their native language to English. Another part of the evaluation problem is the fact that the nature of the programs varies enormously, depending not only on the state and school district, but also on the particular classroom teacher and the population served (Traub, 1999). Thus any general conclusion to the effect that bilingual education is good or bad is likely to be misleading. Furthermore, the issue of bilingual education is so highly politicized in the United States that the findings of the two major government-sponsored studies appear to have as much to do with whether or not they are sponsored by one of the major political parties as with the outcomes for students (Faltis, 1997).

Some narrower conclusions are suggested by Oller and Eilers's (2001) study of Spanish/English bilingual children in Miami, Florida. Half of the bilingual children attended two-way bilingual schools in which 40 percent of their instruction was in Spanish, and half attended immersion schools in which all content was taught in English and children were also given English-language instruction. In this setting, children who attended English immersion programs were more proficient in English than the children who attended two-way programs, but this effect was greater among the kindergarten children and largely gone among the fifth-graders. Also, the advantage was primarily in oral language skill as opposed to literacy skills. One implication of this finding, which is consistent with a great deal of theory and evidence, is that literacy skills are transferable across languages. Training literacy in one language benefits literacy in the other. Oller and Eilers (2002) also found that the children who attended two-way bilingual programs were more proficient in tests of Spanish oral language skill than the children in English immersion programs. Unlike the English advantage associated with immersion, this advantage in Spanish was sustained across grades. Thus, among the fifth-grade bilingual children, the children who had been in two-way programs were better in Spanish and no worse in English than the children who had been in English immersion programs. It appears that it is possible for an educational system to support the acquisition of children's competence in the language they speak at home without cost to competence in the societal language.

## ● SUMMARY

As many as half the world's children grow up exposed to more than one language. Thus, the study of language development must include the study of development in that circumstance. There is not, however, a single circumstance that results in bilingual development. Rather, there is enormous variability in the contexts in which children are exposed to two languages, in the amount of exposure children have to each, and in the age at which exposure to a second language begins. As a result of this variability in language-learning circumstances, the nature of bilingual development is extremely heterogeneous—as is the adult bilingual population. Children who are exposed to two languages from birth appear to differentiate those two languages very early in the course of development, if not from the very beginning. However, in production at least, some bilingual children may use a single phonological system for speaking both languages. When children are acquiring two languages simultaneously, the development of each appears to be slightly delayed compared with monolingual norms, although in the area of grammatical development, the differences disappear by age 10. The reason for the delay appears to be access to input. The amount of input children receive in a language affects the rate at which they acquire the language, and the child who is exposed to two languages receives less input in each than the child exposed to just a single language. It is worth noting, however, that bilingual children acquire two languages in much less than twice the time it takes monolingual children to acquire just one language.

When children begin life as monolinguals but are exposed to a second language later in childhood, the process and sources of influence on the second language development appear to be different from the processes and influences involved in first language acquisition. Perhaps because of the "sink-or-swim" circumstances typical for children who enter a new language community, they often approach a second language by memorizing big chunks and analyzing those chunks into component parts only later. Also, personality variables have a large effect on the success of second language learning: The outgoing

child who is not afraid to talk and make mistakes will do much better than the shy, cautious child. Even within childhood there are age effects on the success of second language learning such that younger learners achieve more native-like grammatical and phonological systems.

There are consequences of bilingualism other than knowing more than a single language. Children who are bilingual have an advantage over their monolingual peers on tasks that require metalinguistic knowledge and in the performance of tasks that require particular control over attention. Bilingual children seem better able to ignore distracting information. Because bilingualism and multilingualism are worldwide phenomena, bilingual education is a worldwide enterprise. However, the particular form of bilingual education, its goals, and its reason for being vary from locale to locale. Because the language a people speaks is central to their identity and because ethnic identity is a highly politicized topic, bilingual education is highly political.

## ● KEY TERMS

simultaneous bilingualism
sequential bilingualism
language differentiation
language transfer
instrumental motivation

integrative motivation
code switching
metalinguistic awareness
bilingual education
immersion programs

## ● REVIEW QUESTIONS

1. What is the issue of language differentiation, and what sort of evidence is used to address the issue?
2. Can children learn two languages as easily as one?
3. How is second language acquisition in childhood different from first language acquisition, in process and in outcome?

4. What is code switching, and why do bilingual speakers do it?
5. What is the best evidence that in some bilinguals, the two languages are represented differently in the brain?
6. Why is bilingual education a political issue, and how does the politics of bilingualism affect children's language learning?

Fall

Fall is great. I like Fall because it is cool. I love Fall because it is prehy. You can burn the leaves. Leaves change color. Fall is a seasan.

By Kirsten

Although children accomplish the basics of language development by the age of 4 to 5 years, language development does not stop at that point. The way children talk continues to change as children master the last difficult aspects of productive phonology, as children's vocabularies grow, and as children come to use more complex constructions and to use them with greater frequency. The kind of talk children produce also changes as they become better able to sustain discourse—both in conversation and in narrative production—and children's speaking and listening skills develop as they become better able to make themselves understood and to understand the messages produced by others. Also, during the school years children develop the ability to understand nonliteral uses of language such as metaphor, irony, and idioms. These changes all are reviewed in this chapter under the heading of Oral Language Development in the School Years. A related topic concerns the effect of schooling itself on oral language skills. The language skills that school demands and the language experiences that school provides differ from the demands and experiences of the preschool period. These are discussed under Oral Language and Schooling.

The third topic in this chapter is the development of literacy. Acquiring the ability to read and write is a central task for children in societies in which children attend school, and success at this task is crucial to the ability to function in a literate society. We begin the topic of literacy by discussing its foundation in the experiences and skills of the preschool period. We then turn to the process of learning to read per se, including a consideration of the sources of individual differences in reading achievement and the highly contentious and politicized question of how reading should be taught.

## ORAL LANGUAGE DEVELOPMENT IN THE SCHOOL YEARS

### Phonological development

By the age of 5 years, children sound as though they have essentially mastered the phonology of their language. Only a few of the later-acquired sounds still cause articulation problems for some children. Coordination of speech production improves during middle childhood, and children become more fluent in producing complex sequences of sounds and multisyllabic words (Vihman, 1988b). With respect to comprehension, children continue to improve in their ability to understand speech under noisy circumstances up to the age of 15 years. These improvements come from children's increased ability to use knowledge of the phonetic patterns of the language, in addition to semantic and grammatical knowledge, to help identify words in a less-than-clear signal (Vihman, 1988b; see also Grunwell, 1986).

There is also evidence that children are continuing to consolidate their underlying phonological representations after the age of 4 or 5 years. An indication of this is improvement in children's ability to perform tasks that depend on the quality of their phonological representations (Goswami, 2000). These tasks include the ability to repeat novel sound sequences (this is a measure of what is termed phonological memory), the ability to rapidly retrieve and produce known words (rapid naming), and phonological awareness (Gathercole & Adams, 1994; Foy & Mann, 2001; Wagner & Torgeson, 1987; Wagner, Torgesen, Laughon, Simmons, & Rashotte, 1993). All these phonological skills are of interest because they predict reading skill—a topic we will return to later. In addition to these incremental changes in phonological knowledge and skill, two new kinds of changes in children's phonology can occur during the school years: Exposure to peers who speak a dialect different from the dialect spoken at home can alter the sound of children's speech, and learning to read an alphabetic writing system affects phonological awareness.

***Accent and dialect changes.***    In the course of early language acquisition, children acquire the particular accent of their caregivers. Accent is not permanently fixed, however, even once phonological development is complete. This is illustrated by a study of accent change in families who moved to the Philadelphia area from other regions of the country (Payne, 1980). Vowels are pronounced differently in Philadelphia than they are elsewhere; for example, *merry* and *Murray* and *ferry* and *furry* sound the same. Payne studied the acquisition of this Philadelphia dialect in transplanted families, focusing on one family with four children. When this family moved to Philadelphia, the children were 3, 5, 6, and 8 years old. Payne examined the children's speech 5 years later, when they were 8, 10, 11, and 13, respectively, and she found that the 10- and 11-year-olds had the strongest Philadelphia accents. The 8-year-old and the 13-year-old had fewer features of the Philadelphia dialect. The explanation Payne offered for this finding was that accent change is the result of peer influence and the age of maximum sensitivity to peer influence is between 4 and 14 years. The 10-year-old and 11-year-old had spent 5 of those years in Philadelphia and only 1 or 2 of those years elsewhere. In contrast, the 13-year-old had spent 4 of those years in another location, and the 8-year-old had spent some of the Philadelphia years at home, exposed to the mother's dialect.

Sometimes adolescents' phonology changes not as a result of moving to a new area but as a result of moving in new social circles. Eckert (1988) studied the speech of Detroit-area adolescents and found that some vowel sounds differed between adolescents who defined themselves as "jocks" and those who defined themselves as "burnouts." Relatedly, Hewitt (1982) described a phenomenon common among black adolescents of Caribbean descent who were born in and live in London. These native Londoners adopt a Jamaican Creole speech for the first time in their lives when they are teenagers. The use of this dialect expresses their black identity, their affiliation with their peer group, and their cultural difference from the larger society. The Jamaican style of speech persists among these adolescents despite the fact (or because of the fact) that it has less prestige in the wider community and is not preferred by the black parents. The social significance of speech in this particular dialect is such that white adolescents who become friends with blacks also sometimes adopt Jamaican pronunciation (Hewitt, 1982).

According to Labov (1970) the influence of peers on dialect is one stage of sociolinguistic development. Labov proposed that up to the age of 5 years, children acquire the basic grammar and lexicon of their language, normally under the influence of parents. Between the ages of 5 and 12 years, children learn the dialect of their peer group. The peer group dialect may be quite different from, and less prestigious than, the mainstream form of the target language, especially for minority children. By the age of 14 or 15, adolescents start to move away from the peer group dialect and toward the more prestigious form of speech, especially in formal situations. The extent to which minority-dialect speakers master and use the mainstream form of speech as adults depends, in part, on the level of education they achieve (Labov, 1970; Romaine, 1984).

The peer influence on dialect is not the automatic result of exposure to a new style of speech. Other influences include the prestige associated with a particular dialect (within the peer group), social pressure from other sources, and identity. Sometimes these other factors can counteract peer influence. For example, Labov (1972) described cases in which teenagers born in Athens to Turkish immigrant families spoke in the Istanbul dialect of their parents because, according to Labov, "The strength and prestige of Istanbul family ties and the value of Istanbul identification seem to have been great enough to resist (peer) pressures" (p. 307). On the other hand, Labov (1972) also cites the case of Swiss-German women who change their dialect as young adults when they marry and move to another village where they would be ridiculed for their native dialect. The role of identity in the dialect one speaks is also illustrated by Labov's (1972) finding that among lifelong residents of Martha's Vineyard, Massachusetts, the extent to which people had the characteristic accent of the region was related to their sociopolitical views about the encroachment of the tourism industry on the life and economy of the island. Those individuals who were more resistant to change had stronger regional accents.

***The development of phonological awareness.***      Remember from Chapter 3 that children show some awareness of the sounds of their language from the age of 2 years. In wordplay, for example, children will spontaneously rhyme or produce a string of words that begin with the same sound. Phonological awareness becomes important and develops substantially in the school years. If you ask preschool children to tap out the number of syllables in a muti-syllabic word, about 50 percent of 4- and 5-year-olds and 90 percent of 6-year-olds can do so (Liberman, Shankweiler, Fisher, & Carter, 1974). Young children also show awareness that a syllable can be further analyzed in two constituents: the onset, which consists of the initial consonant or consonant cluster, and the rime, which consists of the vowel plus any following consonants (Treiman, 1985). In cat, the /k/ is the onset and /æt/ is the rime. Four-year-old children can correctly identify the nonsense words /fol/ and /fir/ as words that will be liked by a puppet whose favorite sound is /f/ (Treiman, 1985), and MacLean, Bryant, and Bradley (1987) report that a "considerable portion" of 3-year-olds can do the same.

Syllables, onsets, and rimes are the smallest units most preschool children can identify. A 3-year-old can hear that the word *cat* is made up of *c* + *at* but not that *at* is made up of *a* + *t*. Treiman (1985) found that 4-year-old children had a harder time recognizing initial consonants when they were part of clusters. For example, the /f/ in syllables such as /flo/ and /fri/ were less recognizable than the /f/ in syllables such as /fol/. Liberman and associates (1974) found that no 4-year-olds and only 17 percent of 5-year-olds were able to tap out the number of phonemes in words. By age 6 years, 70 percent of children could analyze a word into its constituent phonemes. In sum, some phonological awareness develops early, although awareness of phonemes as units (i.e., **phonemic awareness**) is a later development than awareness of syllables, onset, and rimes.

The sources of phonological awareness probably include both experience and innate characteristics of children. The relevant experiences may be secondary language activities that involve the manipulation of the sounds of language, such as songs, nursery rhymes, and word games (Goswami & Bryant, 1990; Mann, 1991). Three-year-olds who know more nursery rhymes also show higher levels of awareness of onsets and rimes even when effect of IQ and socioeconomic status are removed (MacLean et al., 1987), and children who know more nursery rhymes at age 3 are better readers at age 6 (Bryant, Bradley, MacLean, & Crossland, 1989). It could be, however, that having good phonological skills benefits both remembering nursery rhymes and learning to read, rather than nursery rhymes benefiting phonological skills and reading. Reading itself is a secondary language activity, and it may be the biggest cause of phonological awareness. One source of evidence that phonological awareness—particularly awareness of phonemes—depends on learning to read comes from studies that find very low levels of phonemic awareness in adult illiterates (Morais, Cary, Alegria, & Bertelson, 1979) and in Chinese adults (Read, Zhang, Nie, & Ding, 1986). The illiterates, of course, read no writing system, and the Chinese adults read a logographic system in which characters stand for meanings, and only secondarily for syllables, not an alphabetic system in which characters stand for phonemes.

On the other hand, learning to read is not necessary for children to show some awareness of phonemes. Very young children engage in sound play (not all of which involves the phonemic level, of course) and children all over the world (many without benefit of literacy) invent secret languages like pig latin, which depend on the manipulation of phonemes. The evidence of children's spontaneous abilities, combined with the lack of phonological awareness in alphabet-illiterate adults, suggests that phonemic awareness can develop without reading instruction but that in the absence of reading an alphabetic system, this capacity for phonological analysis is lost in adulthood (Mann, 1986, 1991). Whatever the inherent capacity for phonological awareness is, it appears to vary among children and to be heritable. Some children acquire phonological awareness more readily than others (Wimmer, Landerl, Linortner, & Hummer, 1991), and in pairs of identical twins, if one twin has particular difficulty with phonological awareness tasks, the other twin is also likely to have difficulty (Goswami & Bryant, 1990).

## Lexical development

The transition young children make from knowing no words to knowing words is dramatic and has captured a substantial amount of research attention. The lexical accomplishments of older children seem, in contrast, to be less interesting. Vocabulary growth does continue after early childhood, however, and it proceeds at an even more rapid pace than during the preschool years (Anglin, 1993). Three phenomena characterize lexical development after early childhood: (1) growth in vocabulary size, (2) growth in knowledge of word formation processes, and (3) the increasing ability and importance of being able to learn new words from context.

***Growth in vocabulary size.***    Once a child's vocabulary outstrips a caregiver's ability to report on it, it is impossible to compile a list of all the words a child knows. The technique used to estimate children's vocabularies in the school-age years is to take a sample of entries from a dictionary, ask the children to define those words, calculate the percentage of words in the sample that the child knows, and then use that percentage to estimate how many of the dictionary entries the child would know if you had the time and wherewithal to conduct such a test.

Anglin (1993) used this technique to estimate vocabulary size in school-age children. He sampled 1/595th (that is, 434) of the estimated 258,601 entries in an unabridged dictionary and, in an orally administered multiple-choice test, he asked first-, third-, and fifth-graders to choose the best definition for each word. (Actually, he tested them on only 196 of the 434 words that fifth-graders had at least a remote chance of knowing.) The average numbers of test words the children knew at each grade level were 17, 32, and 67, respectively. Multiplying these raw scores by 595 yields the estimates of vocabulary size shown in Figure 9.1. According to these estimates, children's vocabularies increased by 9000 words from first to third grade and by 20,000 words from third to fifth grade.

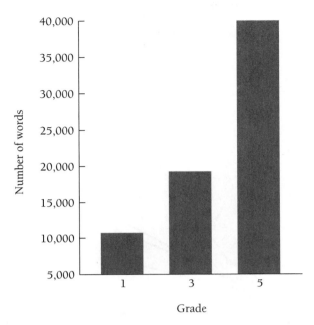

**Figure 9.1**   Estimated vocabulary size at grades 1, 3, and 5

Source: From "Vocabulary Development: A Morphological Analysis," by J. M. Anglin, Society for Research in Child Development, 58, Serial No. 238. Copyright © 1993 The Society for Research in Child Development, Inc. Reprinted by permission.

What accounts for the increase in rate of vocabulary growth during the school years? Anglin suggested that the answer lies in the analysis of the children's vocabularies by type of word. Anglin's test had five types of words: (1) root words (like *closet* and *flop*), (2) inflected words, which are roots plus a grammatical inflection (*boys, soaking,*) (3) derived words, which are roots plus an affix (*sadness:* sad + ness; *preacher:* preach + er), (4) compounds (*payday, milk cow*), and (5) idioms (*lady's slipper:* a kind of orchid; *carrying on:* misbehavior). As Figure 9.2 illustrates, the category of derived words shows a bigger increase between third and fifth grades than between first and third grades. Remember, the test that produced these results was a multiple-choice recognition test. Anglin suggested that the dramatic growth between third- and fifth-grade children's ability to recognize derived words did not reflect an increase in the number of words known but rather an increase in the children's ability to figure out words they had never heard before, using their knowledge of root and affix meanings. An important part of lexical development in the school years, then, is the development of the morphological knowledge that allows children to decipher what new words mean.

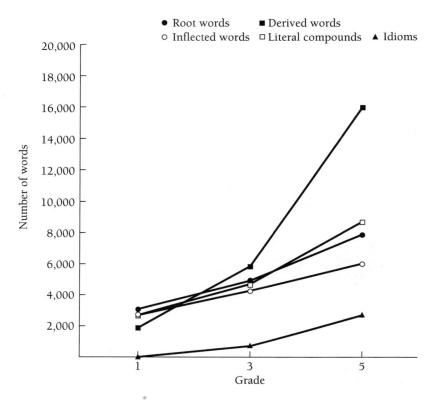

**Figure 9.2**   Vocabulary growth by word type from grade 1 to grade 5

Source: From "Vocabulary Development: A Morphological Analysis," by J. M. Anglin, Society for Research in Child Development, 58, Serial No. 238. Copyright © 1993 The Society for Research in Child Development, Inc. Reprinted by permission.

***Learning word formation processes.***   Imagine I showed you a picture of a birdlike creature and said, "This is a *wug*. What would you call a very tiny *wug*?" (A *wuggie, wuglet,* or *wugling*?) "What would you call a house that a *wug* lives in?" (A *wughouse, wuggery,* or *wughut*?) Or what would you say if asked, "What would you call a man whose job is to *zib*?" (A *zibber*?) These questions may sound familiar to you because they are like other questions Berko (1958) asked of 4- to 7-year old children, who knew that the plural of *wug* is **wug/z/** and that the past tense of *rik* is **rik/t/**.

The children in Berko's study had a harder time with these new questions than they did with providing plural and past-tense forms. (Adults provided the foregoing answers in parentheses.) These questions tap knowledge about **derivational morphology.** In contrast, the tasks of forming plurals and past-tense forms require knowledge of **inflectional morphology.** The difference between the two kinds of morphology is the fact that inflectional morphemes add to a word, but they don't make it into a different word. However, when a derivational morpheme is added to a word, a new word is formed. There is an easy test for determining whether a morphological ending is inflectional or derivational: Most of the time in English you can add inflectional endings after derivational ones, but not vice versa (Aitchison, 1987). So, two people who *zib* for a living are *zibbers*, not *zibser*. Knowing derivational morphology is knowing how to build (derive) new words by adding morphemes to other words, or knowing how to interpret newly encountered words by recognizing their component parts. Creating *wughouse* by combining two existing words is an example of another word formation process, called **compounding.**

Preschool children have been known to coin novel words, as in "Is Anna going to babysitter me?" and "Try to be more rememberful, Mom" (Clark, 1995; see also Becker, 1994; Bowerman, 1985). These lexical innovations show that preschoolers have figured out something about the processes of word formation. However, other data reveal that full control over compounding and derivational morphology is acquired only gradually during later childhood and shows variability even among adults. Compounding appears to be the earliest acquired word formation process. Forty-seven percent of Berko's subjects showed some productive control of word compounding. Very few of the 4- to 7-year-olds in Berko's (1958) study could produce derived words. Similarly, Clark and Hecht (1982) found that when asked questions such as, "What could we call someone who gives things?" 3-year-olds were likely to produce compounds like *giveman,* whereas 5-year-olds consistently used the *-er* suffix to derive forms like *giver.*

Although the first signs of the ability to form compounds may appear early, even adults do not always have full control over the compounding process. In his developmental study, Derwing (1976) found that only 70 percent of adult subjects showed full control of compounding when asked to generate compounds with nonsense words. In another study of adults, Gleitman and Gleitman (1979) revealed that some adults will abandon their knowledge of how compounds are formed under some circumstances. The researchers asked adults to paraphrase straightforward word combinations that included a compound (such as a *black bird-house* or a *black-bird house*) and to paraphrase odd combinations such as *bird house-black* and *house-bird glass.* Although all adults consistently interpreted the straightforward combinations in accordance with the structural principle that makes a bird-house a kind of house and a black-bird a kind of bird, there were individual differences in the interpretation of the odd combinations. Adult subjects who were doctoral candidates tended to interpret the compounds according to the structural principle, even if the resultant interpretation was somewhat far-fetched. For example, if a *house-black* must be a kind of black, then a *bird house-black*

**Table 9.1    Percentage of children and adults able to correctly use word formation processes with nonsense stems**

| Process | Preschool years | Early school years | Middle school years | Junior high/ high school | Adult |
|---|---|---|---|---|---|
| Agentive + er | 7 | 63 | 80 | 86 | 96 |
| Compounding | 47 | 50 | 65 | 79 | 70 |
| Adjective + y | 0 | 30 | 55 | 86 | 100 |
| Instrumental + er | 7 | 35 | 45 | 64 | 59 |
| Adverb + ly | 0 | 13 | 20 | 79 | 81 |
| Diminutive + ie | 7 | 5 | 10 | 14 | 33 |

Source: From "Research on the Acquisition of English Morphology," by B. L. Derwing and W. J. Baker. In P. Fletcher & M. Garman (Eds.), *Language Acquisition,* pp. 209–223. Copyright © 1979 and reprinted with the permission of Cambridge University Press.

might be a "blackener of houses who is a bird." Similarly, if a *house-bird* must be a kind of bird, then a *house-bird glass* could be "a very small drinking cup used by a canary." In contrast, adult subjects who were clerical workers tended to ignore the structural rule and to come up with more plausible interpretations, so that a *bird house-black* was "a black bird who lives in the house" and a *house-bird glass* was "a bird that is made of glass." (Quotations are from participants in Gleitman and Gleitman's 1979 study.)

Knowledge of derivational morphology appears later than knowledge of word compounding. In the same study that tested the ability to produce compounds with nonsense words, Derwing (1976) also tested the productive use of derivational morphology in preschool-age through adult speakers. He found that derivational morphology shows a protracted course of development, with even 17-year-olds not showing full productive control over all morphemes when asked to inflect nonsense stems (Derwing & Baker, 1986). His results are presented in Table 9.1. Tyler and Nagy (1989) similarly found increases in knowledge of derivational morphology up through eighth-graders (who were the oldest children they studied).

The learning process that underlies this protracted development is, according to Derwing and Baker, one of inducing generalizations from input. In their words, "The learning of a morphological rule, surely, depends critically on the discovery of at least a small set of words that succumb to a common morphological analysis" (Derwing & Baker, 1986, p. 327). On the other hand, there is something about morphological processes that children seem to know at a fairly young age, and that evidence is used to argue that some constraints on morphology are innate. Children know that inflectional morphemes (e.g., the plural *s*) are added to words after derivational morphemes, not the other way around. Peter Gordon (1985) discovered that if you ask 3- to 5-year-old children, "What do you call someone who eats rats?" the children will come up with *rat-eater* and not *ratseater,* because you can't have a plural inside a compound. By the same token, children will say that someone who eats mice is a *mice-eater* (not *mouse-eater*) because, although mice is a plural, it is not formed by an inflectional process. Gordon argues that this evidence supports a highly nativist view of the development of morphology because it shows that children obey a distinction—between inflections and derivations—that is not provided in input.

***Word-learning processes.*** When we discussed lexical development in 1- to 4-year-olds, we spent a great deal of time discussing how it is possible for young children to figure out the meaning of newly encountered words. In this chapter, we discuss evidence that with increasing age, children seem to get better at this.

Mabel Rice and her colleagues presented children with new words embedded in an ongoing narration of a cartoon (such as "An *artisan* comes down the road"). They found that 5-year-olds were capable of picking up new words from this incidental exposure, but that 3-year-olds learned almost nothing (Rice, 1990; Rice, Buhr, & Nemeth, 1990; Rice & Woodsmall, 1988). Rice coined the acronym QUIL (for Quick Incidental Learning) for this ability, which seems to emerge only after children have been in the business of learning words for a couple of years. We know from other research that 3-year-olds are capable of fast mapping if they hear a word and see a referent. Thus, this finding of the later emergence of QUIL suggests that, to notice words and identify referents, children aged 3 years and under may be more dependent than older children on certain features of mother–child interaction—such as mothers following their children's attention focus and explicitly labeling objects (see Chapter 4).

Although we do not have developmental data that tell us how the ability to pick up words from context increases after the age of 5 years, clearly the process is complex, and children (and probably also adults) differ in how able they are to learn words. According to Sternberg (1987), the process of learning words from context involves identifying all the relevant information in the context, combining the relevant cues to converge on a definition of an unknown word, and drawing on background knowledge. Consider, for example, the following passage from Sternberg (1987):

> Although for the others the party was a splendid success, the couple there on the blind date was not enjoying the festivities in the least. An acapnotic, he disliked her smoking; and when he removed his hat, she, who preferred "ageless" men, eyed his increasing phalacrosis and grimaced. (p. 91)

To determine from context what the words *acapnotic* and *phalacrosis* mean, you need first to figure out that disliking smoking is a clue to the meaning of *acapnotic*. Next you need to figure out that her preference for ageless men and the fact that his *phalacrosis* showed when he removed his hat are clues to the meaning of *phalacrosis*. If you know that baldness is a condition of aging, that helps too. On the other hand, research has shown that explicit teaching of vocabulary is an effective means of building a stock of known words (Pressley, Levin, & McDaniel, 1987). The fact that vocabulary can be explicitly taught, combined with the fact that most new words are encountered in context, is the source of some disagreement over how to help school-age children increase their vocabularies (see, for example, Nagy & Scott, 2000). Sternberg (1987) has argued that the focus should be on helping children get better at making use of context. Others have argued that, although contextual approaches are useful for inferring what a newly encountered word means, explicit instruction is the best way for building a vocabulary of remembered words (Pressley et al., 1987). In fact, explicit vocabulary instruction is part of many classrooms (McKeown & Curtis, 1987).

## Morphosyntactic development

***Sentence-level developments.***   It is said that by the age of 4 or 5 years, morphosyntactic development is essentially complete. This statement is based on the fact that by this age children's sentences are no longer missing the elements that were missing from their earlier word combinations (i.e., the grammatical morphemes) and children's sentences include all the elements (e.g., adverbial phrases, subordinate clauses) that adults use in their complex sentences. The difficulty children show in understanding the co-reference relations in some constructions (see Chapter 5) is an exception to the general picture of 5-year-olds' mastery of grammar. The grammatical complexity of children's speech does, however, continue to increase after the age of 5, because children use the complex structures at their command more frequently. They more often produce expanded noun phrases, adverbial clauses, subordinate clauses, and so on. (See Scott, 1984, for a more detailed description of these changes.)

***Discourse-level developments.*** Another change in children's grammatical competence after age 5 is that they become able to use syntactic devices to link successive utterances together into longer stretches of discourse. This change can be illustrated with two stories collected by Karmiloff-Smith (1986). Children between 4 and 9 years old were asked to tell a story from a picture book with no text. The story involved a balloon vendor and a boy. A 4-year-old produced the following narrative:

> There's a little boy in red. He's walking along and he sees a balloon man and he gives him a green one and he walks off home and it flies away into the sky so he cries. (Karmiloff-Smith, 1986, p. 471)

The problem here is in the use of pronouns. Without the book, a listener can't tell to whom the different *he*s refer. Each clause by itself—*he sees a balloon man* and *he gives him a green one*—is grammatical, and the pronouns refer appropriately to referents in the picture that is being described. However, the listener can't tell whether the person referred to by *he* is the same from one sentence to the next. The heavy use of *and* to link clauses together is also typical of the narratives produced by children this age (Peterson & McCabe, 1988).

In contrast, a 9-year-old produced the following story:

> A little boy is walking home. He sees a balloon man. The balloon man gives him a green balloon so he happily goes off home with it, but the balloon suddenly flies out of his hand and so he starts to cry. (Karmiloff-Smith, 1986, p. 472)

In this story, the listener can tell to whom the *he*s refer, and the use of pronouns makes the story flow by linking one utterance to the next. Both the 4-year-old and the 9-year-old use the linguistic device of pronominalization (that is, using pronouns to refer to things). The difference between them is that the 4-year-old uses pronouns only to refer to things in the world, whereas the 9-year-old uses pronouns to refer to things in other sentences, thereby creating a cohesive narrative. In sum, according to Karmiloff-Smith, the 4- and 5-year-olds' grammar is a grammar for producing sentences. After the age of 8, children use their grammars for producing text. We consider other aspects of text production in the later section on narrative development.

## Developing conversational skill

Most studies of conversation among children past the age of 5 years examine conversation as a social phenomenon (as in the study of friendship) or as a sociolinguistic phenomenon (as in the study of styles of speech par-

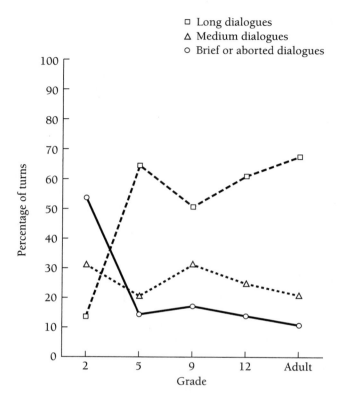

**Figure 9.3** Developmental changes in the percentage of speaker turns occurring in brief, medium, and long dialogues. Dialogues were defined as a sequence of turns on the same topic and were categorized as brief or aborted (between 1 and 10 turns), and long (31+ turns).
Source: Based on data in Dorval and Eckerman, 1984.

ticular to certain social groups). Here we will examine developmental trends in conversational skill during the school-age years. Bruce Dorval and Carol Eckerman (1984) recorded the conversations of acquainted peers using students from second, fifth, ninth, and twelfth grades, and young adults. They found developmental changes that continue trends seen in younger children's conversations. That is, with increasing age, children's contributions to conversation are more frequently relevant to the current topic, and, no doubt as a result, the length of continuous dialogue that the groups can maintain increases. Figures 9.3 and 9.4 illustrate some of Dorval and Eckerman's results.

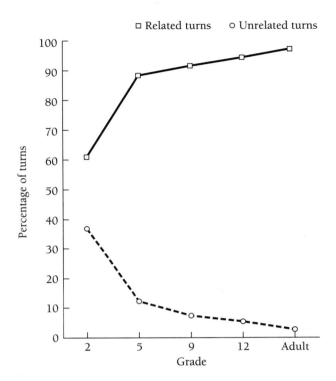

□ Related turns      ○ Unrelated turns

**Figure 9.4** Developmental changes in the percentage of turns in group conversation that are related and unrelated to the conversational topic
Source: Based on data in Dorval and Eckerman, 1984.

The biggest developmental changes in children's ability to sustain conversation come between second and fifth grade. There are, however, other later changes in the quality of conversation that are not revealed in these figures. For example, although the frequency of related turns increased only slightly from fifth to twelfth grade, the kind of related turn changed significantly. Fifth-graders' related turns were more likely to be factually related to the prior turn, whereas twelfth-graders and adults more frequently responded to the feelings or attitudes expressed by the previous speaker (Dorval & Eckerman, 1984). Although there are the developmental changes in conversation that we just described, there is no single kind of adult-level conversation that is the endpoint of development. The kinds of conversations that adults have differ depending on who is talking, what they are talking about, and a host of other variables.

WHY KIDS DON'T HOST TALK SHOWS

*"Don't you hate Eric?"*

**Figure 9.5**    Source: © The New Yorker Collection, 2004 Michael Crawford from cartoonbank.com. All rights reserved.

## Developing a conversational style

Although we saw evidence in Chapter 6 that children develop a style of language use from the time they begin to acquire language, language style is a particularly salient topic in the school years as peer influences grow in importance. Language style, like style of dress, marks one's identity and group affiliation, and these are particularly important to school-age children and adolescents. Some of the work on this topic was reviewed earlier in this chapter under the heading of accent and dialect change. Here we consider the socialization of gender-typed language that occurs during the school years.

Popular books have made it well known that adult men and women have different conversational styles and have argued that much miscommunication occurs as a result (e.g., Tannen, 1990). When adult men and women converse, women are more likely than men to ask questions, to make utterances that encourage responses, and to make use of positive minimal responses such as *mm-hmm* (Fishman, 1978). In contrast, men are more likely than women to interrupt, to ignore the comments of the other speaker, to control the topic of conversation, and to make direct declarations of fact or opinion (Fishman, 1978). One explanation of these differences is that they simply reflect the difference in social power held by men and women (West & Zimmerman, 1977). Another is that the unassertive style of women's speech reflects the personalities women are socialized to have (see Maltz & Borker, 1982, for further elaboration).

According to Maltz and Borker (1982), it is in middle childhood that the mismatch between adult men's and women's conversational styles begins. They argue that men and women participate in conversation in different ways because they learned to converse in different cultures. For boys, the culture was that of the preadolescent and adolescent male peer group; for girls, it was that of the preadolescent and adolescent female peer group. Studies of boys' peer groups find that boys tend to play in large groups that include boys of different social status and even different ages, and that within the group a hierarchical structure places some boys on top and others on the bottom. Nondominant boys are not excluded, although they may be treated badly. The status hierarchy is in constant flux. As Maltz and Borker describe it, "The social world of boys is one of posturing and counterposturing. In this world speech is used in three major ways: (1) to assert one's position of dominance, (2) to attract and maintain an audience, and (3) to assert oneself when other speakers have the floor" (p. 207).

The social world of girls is different. Girls play in small groups or pairs, and the groups tend to be homogeneous in terms of the social status and age of the group members. Nondominant girls have to find other nondominant girls to play with. Within the group, however, play is cooperative and activities are generally noncompetitive. Instead of jockeying for position within a group, as boys must, girls compete for membership in exclusive friendships (Brooks-Gunn & Matthews, 1979; Eder & Hallinan, 1978; Lever, 1976, cited in Maltz & Borker, 1982). According to Maltz and Borker (1982), the social world of girls is one of "shifting alliances and indirect expressions of conflict" (p. 207). Friendships are made and broken with language (Lever, 1976). Sharing secrets cements a relationship; telling secrets breaks off a relationship. While a pair or small group lasts, the function of language is to create and maintain a relationship among equals. This includes criticizing and arguing in ways that don't threaten, not acting "bossy," and accurately interpreting others' indirect signals so that you don't mistakenly think that you are accepted by the group only to have your secrets revealed.

Maltz and Borker (1982) argue that as a result of experiencing these different socializing pressures in childhood, men and women have different cultural rules for how to carry on a conversation. When speakers from different cultures meet and interact, miscommunication can occur. For example, women use language in conversation simply to keep the conversation going. Women's conversation maintenance devices include minimal responses such as "mm-hmm," which indicate that they are listening, and questions, which simply request that the other speaker keep talking. Men, in contrast, don't use language for conversational maintenance. When men say "mm-hmm," it means that they agree, and when they ask a question, it is a request for information. Women (incorrectly) take men's lack of minimal responses as a sign that the men are not listening and are irritated that their questions elicit advice when what they wanted was supportive talk. Men (incorrectly) take women's "mm-hmms" to mean agreement and find it irritating that women don't answer their questions.

## Developing narrative skill

Children begin to recount past events in the context of conversation with others. As we saw in Chapter 6, adults elicit narratives from young children, asking them to describe their day or trip to the zoo or some other event to someone who was not there. Even at the age of 5 years, however, most children's narratives are fairly short and often not particularly coherent. The ability to produce long, coherent, cohesive narratives without external conversational support is really a development that occurs during the school years.

***What makes a good story?***    Mature stories have the properties of coherence and cohesion. **Coherence** refers to the structure of a story; the sequence of events must be related to each other in a meaningful way (Shapiro & Hudson, 1991). **Cohesion** refers to the use of linguistic devices to link sentences together. Thus, the developments that underlie narrative development are the learning of story structure and the mastery of the linguistic devices that produce cohesion. The developments that enable linguistic cohesion were reviewed in this chapter in the section on morphosyntactic development. Here we focus on story structure.

***Story structure.***    The term **story grammar** has been used to refer to the structure all stories follow. (This work focuses on mainstream, Western stories. As is the case for other forms of narrative, what makes a well-structured story may vary from culture to culture.) Even within work on mainstream, Western stories, different researchers have proposed somewhat different grammars. Most, however, agree on the following: (1) A story consists of a setting and one or more episodes (Johnston, 1982, based on Stein & Glenn, 1979); (2) the setting includes both the place ("once upon a time in a far-away kingdom") and the characters ("there lived a girl named Cinderella, with her stepmother and three ugly stepsisters"); and (3) each episode includes an initiating event (an announcement of a ball to which all the eligible young maidens of the land are invited), a problem or an obstacle (nothing to wear and no means of transportation), and a resolution of the problem (action by the Fairy Godmother). Actually, the full story of Cinderella has several episodes. Accounts of past events that do not have this structure are judged by adults to be either poor stories (McCabe & Peterson, 1984) or not stories at all (Stein, 1988).

Various methods have been employed to elicit stories from children in order to examine the development of story structure. Perhaps the most straightforward is simply to ask children to make up a story. Studies employing this method have found a clear developmental progression in the structure of the stories children tell. Often, young children's stories are descriptions of past events that are more like fragments of a story than a united whole. For example, although 5-year-olds' stories are likely to have setting information and some initiating event, they often leave episodes unresolved (Nelson & Gruendel, 1981). By the age of 6 years, children are usually able to produce a single-episode story that includes all the major story components (Kemper, 1984). From age 6 to 10 years, children develop the ability to produce stories with multiple coordinated events and embedded events. Another developmental change is the inclusion of reference to the internal motivations or mental states of the actors in a story. Two-year-olds' stories tend to contain actions alone, with no account of why those actions were produced. Mention of internal motive does not begin until around age 8 and is not consistently present until later (for example, Hudson & Shapiro, 1991; Kemper, 1984). Botvin and Sutton-Smith (1977) elicited fantasy narratives from 220 children between 3 and 12 years old and scored the narratives in terms of structural complexity. They found that with increasing age, children's stories in-

---

**Box 9.1   Developmental changes in the structural complexity of children's fantasy narratives**

*Level 1 stories (typical of 3-year-olds):*

Consists of a series of associated events without the structure of a story.

> A little duck went swimming. Then the crab came. A lobster came. And a popsicle was playing by itself.

*Level 3 stories (typical of 6-year-olds):*

Contains major plot elements but reference to internal states and motivations tend to be absent. Stories tend to contain only a single episode.

> Once there was a little girl. She went walking in the woods and soon it was dark. It was so dark that she couldn't find her way back home. She cried and cried. An owl heard her and asked if

*(continued)*

**Box 9.1**   *(continued)*

she was lost. She said yes. The owl said he would help her find her way home. He flew up in the air and looked around. After finding out which way to go he said, "Okay, follow me." Then he led the girl out of the woods and showed her the way home. When she got back home she was so happy. She gave the friendly owl a kiss and thanked him and told her parents she would never go walking in the woods again by herself. The end.

*Level 5 stories (typical of 9-year-olds):*

Episodes are well developed and a story often consists of multiple episodes. Internal motivations are included.

Once Batman and Robin were in a haunted house. Robin fell through a trap door in the floor and landed in an underground river. Robin pressed his magic watch to signal Batman for help. Batman heard the signal and looked all over the house for Robin. Then he saw the trap door. He lowered a rope from his Bat belt and pulled Robin out of the water. Then they heard a scream. They thought it was a girl, but it was Spiderman. They looked around and the screams seemed to come from the attic.

Batman and Robin ran up to the attic to save the girl but Spiderman was hiding behind the door waiting for them. When they came in Spiderman threw an extra strong Spider net over them. They tried to get out but they couldn't. "I've got you now," he said. "I'm going to kill you, and Wonderwoman and I are going to take your Batmobile and live in your Bat Cave." But Batman told him that he had a special key for the Batmobile and Bat Cave. And when Spiderman came over to get the key Batman hit him right in the face and knocked him down. Then Batman and Robin got out of the net and beat up Spiderman and put him in jail so he wouldn't bother them anymore. The end.

Source: From "The Development of Structural Complexity in Children's Fantasy Narratives," by G. J. Botvin and B. Sutton-Smith, 1977, *Developmental Psychology*, 13, 377–388. Copyright © 1977 American Psychological Association. Reprinted with permission.

cluded an increasing number of story-grammar components. The types of stories typical for 3-year-olds, 6-year-olds, and 9-year-olds are described in Box 9.1.

Another technique for eliciting stories from children is to provide children with a sequence of pictures and ask them to tell the story that is happening in the pictures. One sequence of pictures that has been used in several studies of children's narrative development is a wordless book by Mercer Mayer, *Frog, Where Are You?* (Mayer, 1969). The story in this book begins with a pet frog escaping, after which a sequence of misadventures befall a boy and his dog as they search for and eventually find the missing frog. This book has been used by at least 150 different researchers studying children acquiring 50 different languages (Berman & Slobin, 1994). Although you might think that providing children with the story in pictures would eliminate developmental differences in plot structure, that doesn't happen. The 3- and 4-year-olds tend to describe each picture individually rather than tell a connected story. From school-age up, children do organize the events into longer stretches and make reference to the goal of finding the frog. However, only adults consistently organize the entire sequence of events into a single whole (Berman, 1988). Examples of narratives elicited with one picture contained in the Mayer book are listed in Box 9.2.

***The course of narrative development.*** Narrative development continues into late childhood and even into adulthood, not only because the separate types of knowledge on which narrative production depends take a long time to acquire, but also because the task of coordinating these various knowledge structures, linguistic devices, and communicative considerations is substantial. There is evidence that the cognitive demands of the storytelling task interfere with children's ability to tell a story, even when the children have the component competencies. For example, Shapiro and Hudson (1991) used a picture-eliciting task with 4- and 6-year-olds and found that the children used more sophisticated linguistic devices to achieve cohesion when the pictures provided the goal, the obstacle, and the solution than when the pictures provided only a sequence of events and the children had to invent these story components. The task of producing a narrative, like the task of participating in conversation, makes both content and processing demands of the speaker. When the processing demands exceed their capacity, children make trade-offs (although not necessarily consciously), so that the use of linguistic devices to achieve cohesion is more sophisticated when less effort is required to achieve coherence (see also Shatz, 1985).

As was the case for conversation, there are developmental changes in narrative production, but there is not a single endpoint that all speakers achieve. In this chapter, we have considered only the development of the minimal adult-level ability to produce a narrative. We haven't considered how great authors develop their skills or even what distinguishes great stories from

---

> ### Box 9.2   Developmental changes in picture-elicited narratives
>
> The narrators are describing an episode in which a boy climbs a tree, the boy causes an owl to emerge from a hole in the tree, and the owl causes the boy to fall (Berman & Slobin, 1994, pp. 13–14).
>
> *5-year-old:*
>
> > And then he goes up there. And then an owl comes out and he falls.
>
> *5-year-old (more advanced):*
>
> > And the boy was looking through the tree when a owl came out and bammed him on the ground.
>
> *9-year-old:*
>
> > The owl came out of its tree, and scared the little boy. The little boy fell.
>
> > (Note reference to internal state, *scared.*)
>
> *Adult (translated from German):*
>
> > Poor Tom has also not found the frog in the tree, but has scared an owl to death, who now comes flying out of the tree and scared Tom so much that he loses his grip on the tree and falls splat on his back, falls down on the ground.

ordinary ones. That topic is more central to the discipline of literary theory but has also been considered by psychologists who study language (see Bruner, 1986; Winner, Gardner, Silberstein, & Meyer, 1988).

## Developing speaking and listening skills

Despite their impressive linguistic accomplishments, most 5-year-olds have a way to go in using the knowledge they have acquired to effectively produce and understand messages. As we saw in Chapter 6, it is not that children are completely incapacitated by egocentrism; even 2- and 3-year-olds can and do take account of their listener (Keenan, 1974; Shatz & Gleman, 1973). On the other hand, when children as old as 4 and 5 years are given an experimental task such as describing one picture so that a listener can identify it in an array of pictures, they typically give informationally inadequate messages (e.g., Glucksberg, Krauss, & Higgins, 1975). Furthermore, when 5-year-old listeners are given inadequate information, they are likely to go ahead and act anyway rather than request more information (Flavell, Speer, Green, & August, 1981). These findings raise a question: If even preschoolers can take account of characteristics of their listeners, why do 5-year-old speakers produce such communicatively inadequate messages? Furthermore, why do 5-year-old listeners tolerate them?

***Comprehension monitoring.***   Research on children as message receivers suggests that part of the explanation of 5-year-olds' communicative difficulties is the fact that 5-year-olds do not realize when a message is inadequate. In studies where children are asked to assess the quality of incomplete or ambiguous messages, researchers typically find that children in kindergarten and early elementary grades overestimate the message quality (for example, Markman, 1977; Robinson, 1981). Children tend to think that the messages they were given were fine when, by design, they were not. The process of message evaluation is also referred to as **comprehension monitoring.** When children are given inadequate directions, they act anyway because they don't realize that they don't understand.

In a major investigation of the development of comprehension monitoring, Flavell, Spear, Green, and August (1981) gave kindergartners and second-graders the task of making buildings with blocks according to instructions that they were told had been previously tape-recorded by a 12-year-old named Kiersten. Sometimes the instructions were clear, and sometimes they were contradictory, incomplete, or impossible to execute with the blocks available. Flavell and colleagues (1981) found that second-graders were more likely than kindergartners to express difficulty in following the inadequate instructions, evidenced by producing puzzled facial expressions, replaying the tape, or saying something to the experimenter. In addition, after the children finished each building (following Kiersten's instructions), they were asked two questions: (1) Did they think their building looked exactly like the one that Kiersten built or might it look different? and (2) Did they think that Kiersten had done a good or bad job of telling them how to make a building exactly like hers? The kindergartners were more likely than the second-graders to say that their building looked exactly like Kiersten's (even when the instructions were too inadequate to guarantee that), and they were more likely to say that Kiersten had done a good job even when she hadn't. In another study, Beal and Flavell (1983) found that the ability to evaluate messages improves from preschool through first grade, although even first-graders had difficulty. This inability to evaluate messages may go a long way toward explaining the communication failures children in the early elementary grades experience. If, in the role of listener, you don't know that a message is inadequate, then you don't know to request more information. Similarly, if, in the role of speaker, you don't know that your message is inadequate, then you don't know you need to revise it.

***Message repair.*** Although realizing that a message is inadequate is crucial to the ability to repair it, simply telling children that their messages are inadequate is insufficient to elicit repairs. Several studies using a referential communication task have looked at children's ability to repair messages when either the experimenter or another child asks for more information (Alvy, 1968; Glucksberg & Krauss, 1967; Karabenick & Miller, 1977; Peterson, Danner, & Flavell, 1972). These studies find that children's performance is better when the task is to describe familiar, easily labeled items (Karabenick & Miller, 1977) than when the stimuli are abstract, difficult-to-describe figures (Glucksberg & Krauss, 1967). However, these studies also suggest that children from age 5 to 7 years are successful at providing more information to repair an inadequate message less than half the time, even under the best of circumstances (Karabenick & Miller, 1977).

In contrast, if the children themselves realize that a message is inadequate, they are far more successful at message repair. Beal (1987) gave first- and second-grade children road maps that were drawn with colored felt pens on poster board, and she gave them directions for driving a toy car on the map to particular locations. The messages (like Kiersten's block-building instructions) were sometimes conflicting or ambiguous. In this study, first-graders recognized only half of the inadequate messages, whereas second-graders recognized more than two-thirds. When both first- and second-graders were asked to "fix up" the messages they recognized as inadequate, they were almost always able to do so. In sum, the evidence suggests that comprehension monitoring is a major component of communication skill, which raises the question of what underlies the development of comprehension monitoring. Why can't young children evaluate messages, and what develops during the school years that allows improvement in this ability?

Remember from the discussion of joint attention in infancy that according to some researchers, understanding that others have minds is a prerequisite to intentional communication. The argument holds that communication is the meeting of another mind and that one cannot really intend to do that without understanding that others have minds. However, the intention to communicate does not guarantee that communication will be successfully executed. For that, one needs not only to understand that others have minds, but also to understand something about how those minds work. To be specific, according to Beal (1988), communication depends on understanding (1) that mental entities such as knowledge, thoughts, and beliefs exist; (2) that others may not share your knowledge, thoughts, and beliefs; (3) that the information in one mind can come to be shared if it is transmitted in a message; but (4) that messages have to include all the information to be transferred. What develops in children is the understanding that the message is the vehicle for transmitting information. Preschool children seem not to understand this, instead assuming that "individuals will understand one another as long as a message is produced and received" (Beal, 1988, p. 316). It isn't until children understand that messages don't automatically represent the speaker's intended meaning that children can revise their own messages and request others to revise theirs.

***The course of communicative skill development.***   As was the case for many aspects of later language development, there is no single endpoint that all adults reach in the development of communication skills. As adults we may understand that knowing something and successfully communicating that knowledge are two different things, but we are not always sufficiently attentive to the task of communicating or sufficiently skillful at putting our ideas into words. There is no age at which communication is always successful. Computer programmers write documentation that is indecipherable to the novice. Even college professors are occasionally less than perfectly clear.

On the listener's side, communicative development is also a long process with no single endpoint. As the material presented becomes more complicated, monitoring one's own comprehension becomes more difficult. Markman (1979) asked third- through sixth-graders to read essays that contained inconsistencies such as "There is absolutely no light at the bottom of the ocean. Some fish that live at the bottom of the ocean know their food by its color. They will only eat red fungus." Markman found that a sizable proportion of 12-year-olds judged such essays as comprehensible. The implication of Markman's finding hits very close to home for many college students. In comprehension-monitoring experiments, the messages are deliberately made inadequate to guarantee that comprehension is impossible. However, adult listeners may fail to comprehend an adequate message for a variety of reasons, including inattention, lack of background knowledge, unfamiliarity with the vocabulary used, and so on. College students are often in that position, but if they are adequately monitoring their comprehension of the material they are encountering, they can ask for more information. It's thinking that you understand when you really don't that gets you into trouble. College students are not the only ones who suffer from the problem of fallible comprehension monitoring. Most adults have experiences that force them to realize that even though they thought they understood the laws, the instructions, or the directions they were given, they in fact did not (Markman, 1979).

## Developing nonliteral uses of language

A notable change in children's language that occurs during the school years is in the ability to understand nonliteral uses of language such as metaphor, irony, and idioms (Dews et al., 1996). Of these, the development of metaphoric uses of language has been the most thoroughly investigated.

Spontaneous instances of metaphor use appear in the speech of children as young as 2 years. A charming collection of expressions, such as a child describing her naked state as being "barefoot all over," is in Chukovsky (1963). Adultlike understanding of metaphoric figures of speech is only gradually achieved, and the process continues into late childhood and adolescence. Ellen Winner and colleagues asked children to interpret metaphors such as *After many years of working at the jail, the prison guard had become a hard rock that could not be moved*. Children at 6 and 7 years were able to sometimes provide genuine metaphoric interpretations (*The guard was mean and did not care about the feelings of the prisoners*), but more frequently children this age gave magical or literal interpretations (*The king had a magic rock and he turned the guard into another rock*, or *The guard worked in a prison that had hard rock walls*). By the age of 10 years, genuine metaphoric interpretations were the most frequent sort of interpretation, and performance was almost at ceiling by 14 years (Winner, Rosenstiel, & Gardner, 1976).

## ORAL LANGUAGE AND SCHOOLING

Oral language skills continue to develop during the school years not only because children continue to mature and to accumulate language experience with the passage of time, but also because schooling itself exerts an influence. There are three points to make about the influence of school on oral language development. The first is that, on average, the experience of school promotes more rapid language development and the development of particular school-related language skills more than does experience outside of school. The second point is that some classrooms and teachers promote oral language development more than other classrooms and teachers. The third point is that school does a better job of promoting language development for some children than for others.

***Schooling effects on language development.*** One sort of evidence that schooling promotes oral language development comes from a comparison of children's rate of language growth during different 6-month time periods in which children spend more or less of their time in school. Huttenlocher, Levine, and Vevea (1998) measured children's vocabulary and grammar comprehension at four time points. These measurement points defined three 6-month intervals: (1) the interval between October of the kindergarten year and April of the kindergarten year, (2) the interval between April of the kindergarten year and October of first grade, and (3) the interval between October of first grade and April of first grade. The size of difference in skill between the October and April measurements for both grades was greater than the size of the difference between the April and October measurement. These results are shown in Figure 9.6. The conclusion is that children's language skills advance less during a 6-month period that includes

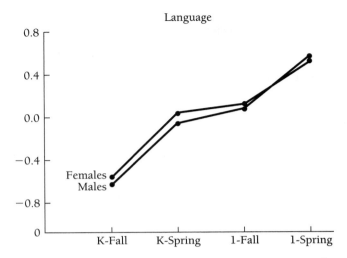

**Figure 9.6**   Growth in children's language skills in 6-month time periods that differ in time spent in school

Source: Huttenlocher, Levine, & Vevea, 1998.

summer vacation than during adjacent 6-month periods with less vacation time. Another method for separating the effects of maturation from the effects of schooling is to compare children who just made the cutoff age for kindergarten entrance to those who just missed it. That is, in a kindergarten class of children who are 5 years old by September 1, some children will be barely 5 years and some will be nearly 6. Using this cutoff method, Morrison and colleagues have found that some syntactic skills and phonological skills develop as a result of schooling, independent of age (Ferreira & Morrison, 1994; Morrison, Smith, & Dow-Ehrensberg, 1995).

Another language skill that seems to particularly depend on school experience is the ability to provide definitions of words (Kurland & Snow, 1997). A definition describes a word in terms of other words. Thus, producing definitions is a completely decontextualized use of language. Beyond skill at decontextualized language use and beyond knowing what the words to be defined mean, producing good definitions (by Western academic standards) also requires knowing the structure of a definition. Formal definitions provide both superordinate category membership and distinguishing features within that category (e.g., a *duck* is an aquatic bird with a flat bill, short legs, and webbed feet). Every year beginning in kindergarten and ending in fourth grade, Kurland and Snow (1997) elicited definitions from 68 children attending a program for low-income children. The researchers also elicited definitions from the children's mothers. They found that definition skill improves throughout this period and that children in fourth grade tend to produce better (formal) definitions than their mothers who are not in school and tend to take a less formal approach. Contrast the definition of diamond provided by a 10-year-old and his mother:

> 10-year-old: Kind of a jewel that women wear and . . . I think that's it.

> Mother: It's supposed to be a girl's best friend, but—um it's a material made of carbon and it's a stone, and often women wear them when they pledge to be married and they get engaged. It's like a promissory of uh future bliss, but let me tell you it's not always that way! (Kurland & Snow, 1997, p. 623).

The notion that this skill at providing definitions is a school-taught skill and somewhat independent of knowing the word meanings also is supported by research on children's abilities to define words in their native and nonnative language. Snow (1990) studied definition skill in children attending the United Nations school in New York City. These children came from all over the world and had many different native languages; the school program was entirely in English. Snow found that the children could perform better on a definitions task in English than they could in their native languages.

***Teacher effects on children's language development.***  The effects of schooling just described are average effects. Classrooms differ in the language environments they provide and in the language outcomes of the children in those classrooms. For example, a study of 3-year-old children in different Head Start classrooms found that the time that the children spent hearing talk about books or book-related activities ranged from 18 percent of classroom time to zero percent, depending on the classroom (Snow & Dickinson, 1990). With respect to language outcomes, studies have found that children in child care centers with high adult to child ratios (and thus more opportunities to hear adult speech) perform better on a variety of language and cognitive outcome measures than do children from centers with lower adult to child ratios (NICHD, 2000, 2002) and that preschool children whose classroom teachers use more complex sentence structures increase the complexity of their own speech more over the course of the school year than do children whose teachers use less complex speech (Huttenlocher, Vasilyeva, Cymerman, & Levine, 2002).

***Effects of cultural mismatches between home and school.***  For all children, classroom language use is different from home language use, but the degree of difference is greater for some children than for others. For example, in classrooms teachers ask children test questions, that is, questions that are asked solely for the purpose of testing the child's knowledge. Normally, if someone asks you a question (e.g., What time is it?), he or she does so in order to get information he or she does not already have. In contrast, teachers ask children questions they do know the answers to (What's your name? What is 4 plus 2?). Not only does the teacher know the answer to these questions, but also the children know that the teacher knows. This sort of questioning for the purpose of eliciting displays of knowledge happens frequently in North American middle-class homes (middle-class mothers frequently ask their children where their noses are), but for children from other backgrounds this manner of language use may be very unfamiliar (Heath, 1983).

As another example, children in classrooms are typically called on and expected to respond individually. Some children are used to individual language performances while others are not. Inuit children (the Inuit are one of the native peoples of northern Canada) are not expected to talk very much and are not expected to show themselves off as individuals at home. As a result, they are frequently uncomfortable and unwilling to stand and answer questions alone in the classroom. Mainstream teachers often mistakenly interpret this lack of response as reflecting either a lack of knowledge or inattention (Crago, Eriks-Brophy, Pesco, & Alpine, 1997; Genesee, Paradis, & Crago, 2004).

Cultural mismatch between teachers and children in the classroom may also affect the degree to which teachers can promote the children's language development. That is, in much the same way that mothers aid their young children's narrative development by asking supportive questions, so teachers can potentially provide scaffolding for children's talk in school. Sarah Michaels (1981; 1983) studied teacher–child interaction during sharing time (also known as circle time or show-and-tell) to find out how teachers help children acquire competence at this particular form of decontextualized language use. She found that when the child's discourse style matched the teacher's discourse style, the teachers were good at asking questions or making comments in the right places to help the child produce a better narrative. However, when the child's narrative style differed from the teacher's, the teachers were not very good at providing scaffolding. White middle-class teachers were not very helpful to African American children who were producing topic-associating rather than topic-centered narratives. As Michaels (1981) points out, the problem is not simply prejudice or failure to accept a different narrative style. If the teacher is unable to follow the story, then the teacher cannot ask appropriately focused questions.

## THE FOUNDATIONS OF LITERACY

For children in literate societies, mastering literacy is a crucial developmental task. Children who are poor readers have difficulty in other areas of school, and they are more likely to drop out of high school than children who do not have reading problems. Some of the statistics on reading are quite dramatic. Only 4 percent of children with serious reading difficulties finish college, and individuals with a history of reading difficulty are over-represented among those who have criminal records (Neuman & Dickinson, 2002). Because literacy is so important and because many children have difficulty achieving literacy, literacy acquisition is a topic of a great deal of research. In this section, we consider the foundations of literacy, including the oral language skills acquired prior to literacy and the literacy-related experiences of the preschool years.

## Oral language and literacy

***Literacy and human nature.***        The first point to make about the relation between oral language development and literacy is that literacy is not a natural next step in the acquisition of human language. In fact, there may be nothing "natural" about literacy at all. Although every human society has language, many human societies, historically and currently, have no written language (Anderson, 1989). Furthermore, the transmission of literacy requires considerably more effort than does the transmission of spoken language. The transmission of oral language from generation to generation requires only normal human interaction, whereas the transmission of literacy is usually the result of formal instruction in school. This is not to deny that there are considerable environmental supports for the acquisition of spoken language. It may well be that instruction in language is embedded in the nature of human interaction. And it is also true that some children figure out how to read on their own, without formal instruction. Still, there is a huge difference between oral language and literacy in the degree of deliberate instruction that cultures provide and in the rate of successful acquisition in the absence of such instruction. Finally, as we saw in Chapter 2, using language to communicate is so much a part of human nature that children who are not exposed to language will invent their own means of communication, and new languages have been created many times in the course of human history when people who shared no common language were placed together. In contrast, writing seems to have been invented only a few times in the course of history, and an alphabetic writing system in which one symbol corresponds to one sound was invented only once (Adams, 1990; Anderson, 1989). In sum, literacy seems less intrinsic to human nature than oral language does. Literacy does build, however, on earlier-acquired oral language skills. Many aspects of children's oral language skill in kindergarten predict the ease with which children will learn to read and, in fact, predict reading skill through the middle school years (Scarborough, 2001; Snow, Tabors, & Dickinson, 2001).

***Phonological skills and reading.***        A very large body of research conducted over the past 20 years has established that children's oral language phonological-processing skills are related to the development of reading skill.

The centrally important skill, among phonological-processing skills, appears to be **phonological awareness,** which is the ability to attend to the sound structure within spoken words (see, for example, Wagner et al., 1997; Snow et al., 1998). One task that measures phonological awareness asks children to say a word such as *cup*, and then to say what word would be left if the examiner said *cup* without saying /k/. Other phonological tasks include finding words that begin with the same sound as a target word or finding words that rhyme with a target word (Wagner et al., 1997). Evidence that phonological awareness is related to reading comes from longitudinal studies that have found that differences among children in phonological awareness before they learn to read predicts their later reading skill—through at least the fourth grade (e.g., Bryant, MacLean, Bradley & Crossland, 1990; Wagner et al., 1997; and see Rayner et al., 2001). Also, children with dyslexia (who have difficulty reading) and children who turn out later to be dyslexic perform less well than typical readers on tasks of phonological awareness (Lyytinen et al., 2001; Manis, Custodio, & Szeszulski, 1993). Finally, training programs that increase children's performance on phonological awareness tasks also benefit reading scores (see Rayner et al., 2001 and references therein).

***Vocabulary, grammar, and reading.*** Children's vocabulary knowledge is also a strong correlate of reading achievement (Chall, Jacobs, & Baldwin, 1990; Snow et al., 1998). Some evidence suggests that whereas phonological awareness is an important predictor early in the course of reading development, vocabulary is most important in the middle elementary years. According to Chall and associates (1990), this change in the oral language correlates of reading is the result of the fact that the process of reading itself changes with development. In the beginning stages, reading is primarily a process of word recognition and decoding—hence the importance of phonological skills. In the middle elementary years, when the mechanics of reading have become automatic for most children, the differences among children have to do with their ability to understand the message. Children who have not acquired the vocabulary used in the material they are assigned at this level will be at a disadvantage. Consistent with this hypothesis, Storch and Whitehurst (2002) found that in third and fourth grades, children's scores on vocabulary tests were related to their reading comprehension scores but not to their reading (out loud) accuracy scores.

Two directions of influence seem to underlie the well-established relation between vocabulary and reading. First, the more words you know, the better able you will be to understand what you read (Stanovich, 1986). In addition, the same skills that got you a big vocabulary in the first place (being able to figure things out from the context) are useful for reading comprehension (Sternberg, 1987). The relation between reading skill and vocabulary size also works in the other direction (Stanovich, 1986). Good readers will have bigger vocabularies because good readers read more, and reading is a major source of exposure to new words. There is strong evidence that the amount of reading children do predicts their vocabulary size (Cunningham & Stanovich, 1991). Consistent with the evidence that exposure to words through reading and the ability to learn new words in context are the crucial influences on vocabulary development after early childhood, Gathercole and associates (1992) found that the influence of phonological memory skills on vocabulary development subsides after the age of 5. Grammar, as measured by tests of children's ability to understand complex syntactic and morphological forms, also predicts success at learning to read (Snow et al., 1998), although it is less strongly related to reading than either phonological skills or vocabulary (Chall et al., 1990), at least among typically developing children.

One final piece of evidence that oral language skills contribute to learning to read is that children with oral language disorders also typically have reading problems (Catts, Fey, Zhang, & Tomblin, 1999; Scarborough, 1990), although the pattern of relations between particular oral language skills and reading skills may be different for children with language impairment than for typically developing children (Bishop, 1991; Storch & Whitehurst, 2002).

***Language use and reading.***    Entering the world of written language requires more than learning how to derive meaning from the printed word. Written language is a style of discourse (Ravid & Tolchinsky, 2002; Watson, 2002). Some children have become quite familiar with that style of discourse well before they begin to read. For example, the 4-year-old who recounted the story of his dog's eating his preschool science project by saying "and Poof!, it was gone in a flash," is a child obviously familiar with a literary style of language use (personal data).

Aside from stylistic aspects, another important feature of written language is that it is decontextualized. In **decontextualized language use,** the words stand on their own. (Other characteristics are summarized in Box 9.3.) In con-

---

**Box 9.3    Characteristics of decontextualized language use**

1. Distance between the sender and receiver
2. Use of complex syntactic structure
3. Permanency of the information
4. Autonomous (rather than interactive) establishment of truth
5. Explicitness of reference
6. High degree of cohesion

Source: From Snow (1983) and Tannen (1982).

trast, in contextualized language use, the nonlinguistic context supports the interpretation of the linguistic message. Spoken language is often contextualized, as in the case of face-to-face conversation about the here and now; or it may be decontextualized, as in the case of narratives. Written language is almost always decontextualized. The relation between the form of language (oral or written) and decontextualized language use is presented in Table 9.2. It has been argued that skill at decontextualized oral language use provides an important bridge from oral language to literacy (Snow, 1983; Watson, 2002). As we discussed earlier, the ability to produce decontextualized speech (as in narrative production) emerges first in conversation and receives significant support from children's conversational partners (see also McNamee, 1987). Because some caregivers have conversational styles that provide better support than others do for the use of decontextualized language, some children will meet the task of acquiring literacy better prepared than others. Parent–child book reading is another important source of exposure to decontextualized oral language, and the frequency with which children are read books as preschoolers is a strong predictor of children's early literacy achievement (Bus et al., 1995; Teale, 1984; Wells, 1985).

Other features of written language may be less unique to written language, but still not equally familiar to all children. Every language has more and less formal forms of use and varieties of language associated with particular ethnic groups or social classes. Typically, only a "standard" variety of the language is used in writing, and some children may be more familiar with that variety than others. The degree to which discontinuity between home and school or literate language makes a difference to children is matter of some controversy (Ravid & Tolchinsky, 2002). The idea that discontinuity makes learning to read difficult has been behind periodic proposals to teach children in their home language, but these proposals have often met with resistance from parents who expect schools to teach their children mainstream forms of language use. (See, for example, the controversy surrounding the Ebonics movement of the 1990s [Fillmore, 1997; Wolfram, 1997].)

**Table 9.2  Types of contextualized and decontextualized oral and written language**

|  | Oral language | Written language |
| --- | --- | --- |
| Contextualized | Face-to-face conversation about the here-and-now | Menus, labels, some signs |
| Decontextualized | Narratives and lectures | Almost all written language |

## Early experience and literacy

The ease with which a child will learn to read depends on skills, knowledge, and attitudes developed years before reading instruction begins. Some of these skills are manifest in oral language, including phonological awareness, vocabulary knowledge, and skill at decontextualized oral language. Other precursors to reading are knowledge about print, about books, and about the functions of literacy. For example, well before they can actually read, many children know how to hold a book and turn the pages, they know that words and stories are contained in the print on the page, they know that the print on signs and labels also contains information. This collection of skills and knowledge about literacy is termed **emergent literacy.** Many studies have found that emergent literacy skills predict later reading and writing skills (e.g., Hecht & Greenfield, 2002; Storch & Whitehurst, 2002; Whitehurst & Lonigan, 1998). A sketch of the developmental accomplishments in the acquisition of literacy is presented in Table 9.3.

Emergent literacy skills, in turn, have their roots in early home and preschool experiences, which both socialize children to be users of literacy and prepare them to acquire the skills that literacy demands (Britto & Brooks-Gunn, 2001; Bus et al., 1995; Dickinson & Tabors, 2001; Senechal & LeFevre, 2002). The term **family literacy** has been coined to refer to the naturally occurring literacy practices in the home and community (Britto & Brooks-Gunn, 2001). Literacy is a tool that can be used for different functions, and the functions served by literacy vary depending on culture and socioeconomic status. Literacy activities in some homes may be minimal—reading labels, signs, and the Bible. In other homes, literacy activities may also include reading newspapers, magazines, and books. In some homes, it is clear that reading and writing are integral to the way the adults earn their livings. Literacy, in this view, is a set of cultural practices that is transmitted from one generation to the next (see, for example, Heath, 1982; Schieffelin & Gilmore, 1986).

Literacy is also a set of skills, and the roots of these skills can be found in properties of children's early language and literacy experiences. One recent study of predictors of literacy measured the home and preschool language and literacy experiences of 85 children from low-income homes. Language experience was assessed at ages 3 and 4; oral language and emergent literacy skills were assessed at age 5, in kindergarten (Dickinson & Tabors, 2001). The study found that children from homes in which there was more extended discourse and in which caregivers used a more advanced vocabulary when the children were 3 and 4 had better skills at age 5 than children who participated in less extended discourse and heard a simpler vocabulary at home (Tabors, Roach, & Snow, 2001). Extended discourse is talk in which multiple utterances build on a common theme—as in establishing pretend play or recounting a past event. Advanced vocabulary is the use of words that the average child at this age would not be expected to know—examples of such words in the speech to 3- and 4-year-olds are *assure, delicious,* and *sparkles.* This study also examined the chil-

**Table 9.3    Developmental accomplishments in the acquisition of literacy**

BIRTH TO 3 YEARS

Recognizes specific books by cover
Pretends to read
Enjoys wordplay, rhyming
Listens to stories
Begins to produce some letter-like forms in own "writing"

3 TO 4 YEARS

Knows that alphabet letters have names and are different from pictures
Recognizes some environmental print (e.g., EXIT signs)
Pays attention to separate sounds in language (e.g., notices rhyming
    words and alliteration, as in Peter, Peter, pumpkin eater)
Shows interest in books and reading
Connects events in stories to life experiences
"Writes" (i.e., scribbles) own messages

KINDERGARTEN (5 YEARS)

Recognizes and can name all uppercase and lowercase letters
Understands that the sequence of letters in a written word
    represents the sequence of sounds in the spoken word (the
    alphabetic principle)
Can name some book titles and authors
Makes predictions based on illustrations or portions of stories
Uses invented spelling to write own messages
Can write own name
Can write most letters and some words when they are dictated

FIRST GRADE (6 YEARS)

Can accurately decode (i.e., sound out) regular single-syllable
    words
Recognizes common, irregularly spelled words by sight (*have,
    said, where, two*)
Predicts and justifies what will happen next in stories
Monitors own comprehension when reading; notices when
    simple texts fail to make sense
Creates own written texts for others to read

Source: Based on Snow, Burns, & Griffin, 1998.

**Figure 9.7**    Early experience of joint book reading supports later literacy development.

dren's language experiences at preschool and found that the same sorts of experiences at school were predictive of language and literacy development. The children who had teachers who participated in more adult–child conversation (as opposed to uninterrupted teacher talk) and who used a more advanced vocabulary performed better on the language and literacy assessments at kindergarten than did children with less such experience at school. Last, this study found that children's literacy experiences at home at ages 3 and 4 years were positive predictors of children's kindergarten language and literacy skills (Tabors et al., 2001).

The finding that early literacy experience predicts later language and literacy skills is consistent with the findings of several other recent studies and one large meta-analysis that have found a more specific relationship: The amount that children are read to as preschoolers is a strong predictor of their later success in learning to read (Bus et al., 1995; Senechal & LeFevre, 2002). It is possible that some of this relationship reflects effects of preschool chil-

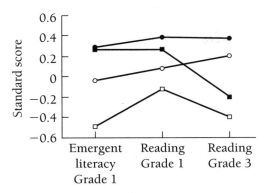

Legend:
- High-teach–high-read
- High-teach–low-read
- Low-teach–high-read
- Low-teach–low-read

**Figure 9.8** Children's emergent literacy and reading skills as a function of literacy teaching and storybook reading
Source: From Senchal and LeFevre (2001).

dren's interest in being read to on both their parents' behavior and their own later interest in reading, but it is likely the experience of joint book reading also has real effects. One reason for thinking this is that the amount of time parents spend reading to their children is related to the parents own level of education—that is not something caused by the children. Another reason for thinking that the relationship between joint book reading experience and learning to read reflects real causation is that longitudinal studies find predictive relationships even when the effects of other properties of children are statistically controlled (Storch & Whitehurst, 2001; Senechal & LeFevre, 2002).

Evidence that early literacy experiences can have both a socialization of literacy effect and a skill-building effect comes from a longitudinal study of parental practices and children's development of emergent literacy and reading skill. Senechal and LeFevre (2001) separately measured how much direct teaching of reading and writing parents did and also how much exposure to books they provided their preschool children. These two behaviors were sufficiently independent that the children could be classified into four groups: (1) high teaching and high reading, (2) high teaching but low reading, (3) low teaching and high reading, and (4) low teaching and low reading. The development of these children in terms of emergent literacy at the beginning of grade 1, reading skill at the end of grade 1, and reading skill at the end of grade 3 is depicted in Figure 9.8. The results suggest that the benefit of teaching shows primarily in grade 1, whereas the benefit of being read to persists. Although it is clear that environmental factors play an important role in preparing children for literacy acquisition, the environment is not the sole influence on the success children experience when they begin to learn to read.

There is also a strong genetic component, as evidenced by studies of the heritability of reading skill and reading disorders (Olson & Gayan, 2002). There is less to say about the genetic than the environmental contribution at this point. Just what it is that is inherited remains to be determined.

## LEARNING TO READ

### The reading process

The process of reading is one of mentally turning written symbols into words with meanings. In **alphabetic systems** such as English (and Russian, Korean, and many more), the symbols (i.e., the letters) correspond to phonemes. This letter–phoneme correspondence is known as the **alphabetic principle**. The process of mentally going from letter through sound to get to meaning is known as **phonological recoding**. This is what children have to learn how to do when they learn to read an alphabetic writing system. (We will focus in this section on learning to read an alphabetic system. There are other sorts of systems. In syllabaries, such as Japanese Kana, the printed symbols correspond to whole syllables. In logographic systems, printed symbols correspond to whole words or morphemes. Chinese is, in some respects, such a system.)

Evidence suggests that in the process of learning to read, children first learn the essence of the alphabetic principle, then apply it to words as they try to read, and this activity in turn leads to increases in alphabetic knowledge and recoding skill. Skilled readers do not sound out the words they read phoneme by phoneme; they recode whole words into their phonological representations. Becoming a skilled reader, then, involves not just learning the letter–sound correspondences of one's language, but also depends on having a large repertoire of spelling–sound correspondences at the level of whole words. The amount of reading children (and adults) do is a strong predictor of their reading skill (Stanovich, 1986). The function of reading practice seems, at least in part, to be the building of a repertoire of words that can be recoded on sight (Rayner et al., 2001).

This effect of practice may be the basis of what has been termed the **Matthew effect,** that is, that individual differences in reading skill increase over time. Children who are initially good readers improve at a faster rate than children who are initially poor readers. It is dubbed the Matthew effect after the passage in the book of Matthew that states that the rich get richer and the poor get poorer. The argument is that good readers like to read, read a great deal, and get better at reading. Poor readers, in contrast, do not like to read, read little, and fall farther and farther behind (Stanovich, 1986). Several studies using data collected in the United States have reported this finding, and one, using data from the Netherlands, found that the effect was carried by a reciprocal relation between phonological skills and the word recognition component of reading (Bast & Reisma, 1998).

Not all studies find this effect, however. A longitudinal study of children in Finland found that during the preschool years, individual differences did, indeed, increase with the rich getting richer, so to speak, but once formal instruction began, in grade 1, individual differences in reading skill diminished. The instruction had the effect of bringing the lower-performing children closer to the level of the better-performing children (Leppanen, Niemi, Aunola, & Nurmi, in press). It is possible that differences in the regularities of spelling–sound correspondences between English and Finnish contribute to the explanation—they are simpler or shallower in Finnish. English has a deeper orthographic in which the spelling–sound correspondences are less transparent. It is also possible that differences between American and Finnish educational practices play a role. In Finland, reading instruction consists of explicit phonics instruction; in the United States, in recent years, it has not. (The Dutch study does not report on instructional method.) **Phonics** instruction, explicit teaching of sound–letter correspondences, has been found to be more helpful to poor readers than to good readers (Connor, Morrison, & Katch, in press). It is consistent with this account that the Matthew effect is observed in Finland before children begin formal instruction. The results suggest that when children are provided phonics instruction, children who do not read catch up to children who do. In the absence of phonics instruction, the readers, who are children who managed to learn to read without phonics instruction, continue to make progress, but the nonreaders, who could not learn to read without phonics instruction, stay nonreaders. We return to the topic of reading instruction in a subsequent section of this chapter.

## Explaining individual differences in reading achievement

Part of the motivation for the scientific study of reading is the goal of helping those children who have difficulty with reading. One area of research concerns the persistent fact that children from higher socioeconomic strata (SES) outperform children from lower socioeconomic strata on measures of reading achievement and seeks to explain this SES-related gap. Another area of research concerns identifying internal characteristics of those children who have difficulty learning to read.

***Explaining SES-related differences in reading achievement.*** The research reviewed earlier on the relation of oral language skills to reading helps to explain the SES-related differences in reading achievement. That is, oral vocabulary size is related to reading, there are SES-associated differences in children's vocabulary, and, in part as a result, there are SES-related differences in reading skill. In fact, SES-associated differences in reading become greater during the middle school years when vocabulary knowledge is most strongly related to reading skill (Chall et al., 1990). Experiences that support reading, such as being read to, also vary as a function of socioeconomic status; thus, differences in early exposure to books and in the skill at decontextualized language use that book reading fosters are likely to explain part of the SES-associated differences in literacy achievement. Also, adults reading books on their own, and thus modeling book reading, occurs more frequently in higher- than in lower-SES homes (Hoff, 2003). Lee and Croninger (1994) found that the difference in literacy achievement between poor and middle-class eighth-graders was partly explained by home environment measures, such as the books in the home and family use of the public library (see also Snow, Burns, & Griffin, 1998). Thus, SES-related differences in the centrality of literacy activities may be a continuing source of SES-related differences in children's literacy achievement. Last, mismatch between the style of language use valued at home and the style of language use expected in school often makes the school environment less supportive of literacy for low-SES minority children than for middle-class children. On the other hand, several sources of evidence suggest that mismatch between home and school language use cannot be the whole explanation for the lower reading and lower general school achievement of low-income children. Working-class, low-income children who come from the same culture and speak the same dialect as their middle-class counterparts still do less well in school (Chandler, Argyris, Barnes, Goodman, & Snow, 1986).

***Developmental dyslexia.***   Although, on average, higher-SES children achieve higher levels of reading skill than lower-SES children, there are children at every level of socioeconomic status that experience difficulty learning to read. **Developmental dyslexia** is the term applied to children whose reading ability is lower than would be expected on the basis of their IQ (Rayner et al., 2001). The category is much like the category of specific language impairment in that it implies that the difficulty is isolated to reading and is a discrete disorder. As is also the case for specific language impairment, there is disagreement about how discrete the disorder is, with some arguing that children labeled dyslexic merely represent the low end of the distribution in reading skill (see Stanovich, 2000). There is evidence that children who are poor readers have the same sorts of reading problems as children labeled dyslexic—just not to the same degree (Rayner et al., 2001). There is also evidence that those with reading difficulties, both the garden-variety poor readers and those with developmental dyslexia, are a heterogeneous group with more than one underlying pathology at work (Stanovich, 2000).

***Theories of dyslexia.***   At one time it was proposed that dyslexia was essentially a visual impairment (Orton, 1925) resulting from a failure to achieve a normal division of labor between the left and right hemisphere. That view

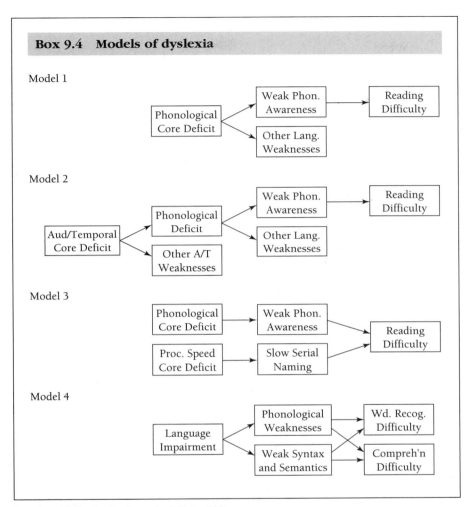

Box 9.4   Models of dyslexia

Based on McCardle, Scarborogh, & Catts, 2001.

still circulates in some quarters, but there is no evidence to support it (Rayner et al., 2001). Although some recent studies have found some kinds of visual-processing deficits in children with reading disabilities, the current evidence suggests that visual impairments are at most a small part of the underlying problem in cases of dyslexia (Rayner et al., 2001).

All current theories include phonological deficits as a central component of the underlying problem in dyslexia (Scarborough, 2002). This view is consistent with the large body of evidence that finds that phonological awareness is the best predictor of reading skill, that phonological training improves reading skills, and that children who are poor readers and children who have dyslexia quite reliably have difficulty reading isolated words and reading pseudo-words (e.g., words like *mard* that are pronounceable and could be English words). There are differences among current theories, however, in just where they place the phonological deficits in a larger theory of what underlies reading difficulties. Box 9.4 depicts the current major theoretical approaches (McCardle, Scarborough, & Catts, 2001).

According to the most widely held view (Model 1), there is a core phonological deficit that results in children having difficulty developing phonological awareness, discovering the alphabetic principle, and learning to decode. Although this model is consistent with a great deal of evidence, it does not really explain why other language measures, such as vocabulary and story recall, are related to reading skill over and above any relation they might have to phonological skills. That is, according to Model 1, every correlate of reading ought to be traceable to a core of phonological skills, and that seems not to be the case. Thus, other models have been proposed which add, in some way, deficits other than solely phonological deficits to the underlying causes of reading difficulty.

It has been proposed that the phonological deficits underlying reading difficulties derive from a more basic deficit in auditory temporal processing (Model 2). This is the same deficit that was central to one theory of specific language impairment (Tallal et al., 1985). A commercial program to help children with reading difficulties has been developed on the basis of this theory (FastForWord), but despite strong claims made for its efficacy, no scientifically acceptable evaluation of the program has been published (McCardle et al., 2001). At present, this model is not endorsed by the community of researchers in the field of reading difficulties (McCardle et al., 2001).

Another type of model allows that there may be two sorts of underlying deficit: a phonological deficit and a processing speed deficit (Model 3). According to this view, there are different subtypes of dyslexia. All children with reading difficulties have phonological deficits, but some also have processing speed deficits (Wolf, Bowers, & Biddle, 2000). A fourth sort of model proposes that the underlying deficit is a general language deficit, of which phonological deficits are one component (Model 4). This model accommodates the findings that other measures of oral language skill besides phonological measures predict reading. These models all describe the deficit underlying reading difficulties at the functional level. A very new area of research uses neuroimaging techniques and finds differences between good readers and individuals with dyslexia in the areas of the brain that are recruited during reading (Shaywitz et al., 2000). This is likely to be a growth area for future research on reading disorders.

## Reading instruction—the reading wars

The best method of teaching children to read has been a matter of considerable controversy in recent years. A little history is necessary as background to this controversy: Going back as far as there exist records of how children were taught to read English, one finds evidence that reading instruction consisted of phonics instruction. In the 1700s, children sat at their desks with their McGuffey's Readers and received explicit instruction in letter names and sounds. Children then progressed to sounding out syllables and then words. In the 1900s, the whole-word approach was introduced, in which children were first taught correspondences between whole printed words and their sounds. The goal was first to build a "sight vocabulary" that enabled children to go straight from print to meaning. Then, this initial vocabulary provided the basis for learning letter–sound correspondences. The difference between the phonics method and the whole-word method was in the order of doing things, but both methods usually involved explicit instruction in the alphabetic principle (based on Rayner et al., 2001).

In the 1970s, these methods of teaching reading were largely supplanted by a new method—the whole-language approach. The basic premises of the **whole-language approach** to reading are (1) that reading is as natural as talking, (2) that the child learns to talk by being surrounded by language, and therefore (3) children will learn to read by being surrounded by print. This reasoning yields the conclusion that phonics instruction is not necessary. However, the whole-language approach goes further and asserts that phonics instruction is harmful and should not be done. What seems to have happened in the history of approaches to teaching reading is that phonics instruction became associated with the rigid classroom structure and rote-drill approach to learning that characterized much of elementary education until the 1970s. The whole-language approach, in contrast, was associated with a new set of beliefs embraced by the educational community. These beliefs included the notion that if you make children's education meaningful and empower children, they will blossom. Thus, the whole-language approach (also termed literature-based instruction) focuses on providing children with interesting materials to read and interesting experiences to pair with literacy experiences. So, for example, children will take a trip to a fire station, read a book about a fire station, and write stories about a fire station.

While no one disputes that it is beneficial for children to read and write about things that are interesting to them, there have been great disputes about the proper role of phonics instruction. The debates between whole-language advocates, who disavow phonics, and proponents of teaching decoding skills have been termed the Reading Wars (see more complete treatments in Rayner et al., 2001; Stanovich, 2000). Because elementary school curricula are selected by state boards of education, the proper method of reading instruction became a political battle in the 1990s. Somehow, the phonics approach became associated with political conservatism and the whole-language approach became associated with more progressive and liberal political views. Scientific evidence sometimes took a back seat to political posturing.

From the point of view of science, there is little controversy about the relation of instructional method to success in learning to read. The findings of several large-scale studies and reviews of the literature converge on the conclusion that phonics instruction produces higher levels of reading achievement than the nonphonics alternative and that the difference in efficacy between methods is greatest for children at risk for reading failure (Adams, 1990; Chall, 1996; National Reading Panel, 2000; Snow et al., 1998). There is a consensus among these reports that in order to read, children must learn how to decode and that decoding does not come naturally to most children—it must be taught. Some children do seem to figure out decoding on their own, and some children receive instruction at home. For these children, who are advantaged by skill or circumstance, the method of reading instruction in the school is less critical than for other children. But for those many children who need instruction and who depend on school to provide it, phonics instruction is essential if they are to learn to read.

## ● SUMMARY

Although children have mastered the essentials of language before schooling begins, language continues to develop during the school years. Children further consolidate their phonological representations, phonological awareness increases (largely as a result of reading), and style of language use—including accent—may change under the influence of peers. In the lexical domain, children continue to learn new words, and they also learn the word formation processes of compounding and derivational morphology. The grammatical complexity of children's language increases further after the age of 5—not so much because children are acquiring new aspects of the grammar, but because they are producing the complex constructions they know with greater frequency. During the school years, children learn to use grammatical devices to link sentences together into connected discourse. Children's ability to sustain and structure discourse also continues to develop—as seen in both their conversations and narrative productions. School itself becomes a new influence on language development, as school makes new linguistic demands on children and provides new sorts of language experience.

For children in most cultures, a central language development of the school years is the attainment of literacy. Literacy skills have their roots in early childhood. Good oral language skills and experience with print material provide the foundations for literacy acquisition. The reading process itself requires that children be able to map letters onto sounds; thus, the quality of children's phonological representations and their phonological awareness are crucial to success in learning to read. Children who have difficulty reading consistently show difficulties with the phonological component of language. Reading an alphabetic language such as English depends on the phonological decoding of the printed word. The best method of teaching reading has been a highly disputed topic for many years, but the evidence clearly demonstrates that effective reading instruction must include instruction in phonics.

# ● KEY TERMS

phonemic awareness

derivational morphology

inflectional morphology

compounding

coherence

cohesion

story grammar

comprehension monitoring

phonological awareness

decontextualized language use

emergent literacy

family literacy

alphabetic systems

alphabetic principle

phonological recoding

Matthew effect

phonics

developmental dyslexia

whole-language approach

# ● REVIEW QUESTIONS

1. What changes in children's oral language knowledge and use occur during the school years? What do we know about sources of influence on these changes?

2. What does individual identity have to do with language use? What's the evidence?

3. Describe and explain examples of the influence of peers on the acquisition of dialect and gender-typed language use.

4. What are family literacy and emergent literacy, and what do they have to do with children's success in learning to read?

5. What is phonological awareness, and why would it be such a strong predictor of reading skill?

6. What is the alphabetic principle, and what does it have to do with the role of phonics in reading instruction?

7. Although there are some differences among current models of developmental dyslexia, they all agree on a central component of the underlying deficit. What is that core deficit, and what is the evidence for it?

8. What is the difference between the phonics and whole-language approach to reading instruction? What does the evidence say with respect to the efficacy of these approaches?

# GLOSSARY

**Adaptation** A characteristic that an organism possesses because the forces of natural selection operating during that organism's evolution made that particular characteristic advantageous. For example, long necks are adaptations that gave giraffes an advantage in reaching food and spotting predators. It has been proposed that the capacity for language is an adaptation that humans have because the ability to communicate gave humans a survival advantage.

**Allophones** Acoustically different speech sounds (phones) that are not functionally different (that is, are the same phoneme) in a particular language. For example, [p] and [pʰ] are allophones of the phoneme /p/ in English.

**Alphabetic principle** The association of letters with phonemes that characterizes English and other alphabetic writing systems.

**Alphabetic systems** Writing systems in which printed symbols correspond to phonemes. Examples include English, Russian, and Korean.

**American Sign Language (ASL)** The manual language used by the deaf in the United States and the English-speaking provinces of Canada. It is not a system of pantomime; rather, it shares the same structural features as other natural languages.

**Analytical approach** An approach to language acquisition that is more characteristic of some children than of others. It involves breaking down the speech stream into its component parts (words and—within words—phonemes) and figuring out the system for productively combining these component parts. (*See also* Holistic approach.)

**Aphasia** Any of a range of language disorders caused by brain damage.

**Articulatory phonetics** The system of describing speech sounds in terms of how they are produced.

**Autism** A disorder, with an onset before the age of 30 months, that involves severe social and communicative impairment and may or may not be accompanied by mental retardation.

**Autonomy (of grammar)** The proposal that the structure of language is separate from and cannot be explained in terms of anything else about language, such as its meaning or communicative function. (*See also* Formalism.)

**Babbling drift** The notion that the sounds in infants' babbling are influenced by the ambient language. Their babbling "drifts in the direction of the speech the infant hears" (Brown, 1958, p.199).

**Behaviorism** The theoretical perspective that seeks to explain behavior in terms of factors external to the mind. (*See also* Cognitivism.)

**Bilingual education** Education in which the curriculum is taught in two languages.

**Bound morpheme** A morpheme that cannot stand alone, but rather is attached to a word stem (such as *-ed* to indicate past tense; *-s* to indicate plural). (*See also* Free morpheme.)

**Brain-imaging technique** A technique that shows the relative levels of activity of different parts of the brain during performance of a particular task. Positron emission tomography (PET) scans and magnetic resonance imaging (MRI) are examples of this technique.

**Broca's aphasia** The condition in which the ability to produce speech is severely impaired because of brain damage.

**Broca's area** An area in the front portion of the left temporal lobe of the brain that is involved in language functioning.

**Canonical babbling** A reduplicated series of the same consonant–vowel combination in clear syllables (such as *da-da*). (*See also* Reduplicated babbling.)

**Canonical form** A whole-word sound pattern that young children sometimes use as a basis for pronouncing new words.

**Categorical perception** The perception of stimuli that vary along a physical continuum as belonging to discrete categories. (*See also* Phoneme boundary effect.)

**Cerebral cortex** The outer layer of the brain that controls higher mental functions such as reasoning and planning.

**Chatterbox syndrome** A disorder characterized by severe mental retardation but remarkable linguistic abilities.

**Child-directed speech** The speech that adults and older children address to younger children. It has certain typical characteristics that distinguish it from adult-directed speech. (Also referred to as infant-directed speech and motherese.)

**CHILDES** Child Language Data Exchange System. A computer program for the analysis of transcripts, and an archive of previously collected transcripts of children's speech.

**Closed-class word** A word from categories such as determiners (for example, *a, the*), auxiliaries (for example, *can, would*), and prepositions (for example, *on, over*). These categories share the characteristics that they serve grammatical functions (for example, determiners mark the beginnings of noun phrases) and that speakers cannot readily invent new words to add to these categories—in contrast to categories such as noun and verb that readily admit newly coined words. (*See also* Functional categories and Open-class word.)

**Cochlear implant** A device surgically implanted in the cochlea that allows a deaf individual to perceive sound by enabling sound to bypass damaged cells in the ear and directly stimulate the auditory nerve.

**Code switching** Changing from one type of language use to another, such as switching from a formal to an informal register when talking to people who differ in status. The term is also used to describe the switching between two languages that is characteristic of bilingual language use.

**Cognitive model of phonological development** The proposal that children try to sound like adults and actively work on figuring out how to do so.

**Cognitive science** An interdisciplinary field including psychology, linguistics, philosophy, computer science, and neuroscience devoted to understanding how the mind works.

**Cognitivism** The theoretical perspective that seeks to explain behavior in terms of processes that occur inside the mind.

**Coherence** The property of story that pertains to how the events of the story are related to each other. In a coherent story, the events in sequence are related to each other in a meaningful way.

**Cohesion** The property of a story that pertains to how the sentences of the story are linked together. In a cohesive story, linguistic devices, for example, pronominal reference, link sentences to each other.

**Collective monologue**   A type of pseudoconversation engaged in by preschool children. The children take turns speaking, but each speaker's contribution to the conversation has little to do with the content of what other speakers are saying.

**Combinatorial speech**   Speech in which words are combined in utterances (in contrast to single-word utterances).

**Communicative competence**   The ability to use language in socially appropriate ways for communicative purposes.

**Complex sentence**   A sentence that contains more than one clause.

**Compounding**   The creation of a single new word by combining two existing words (such as *birdhouse*).

**Comprehension monitoring**   The evaluation of one's own understanding. Young children seem to accept and act on inadequate messages in part because they don't realize that they don't understand.

**Concept**   A mental category that includes individual exemplars of that concept. For example, the concept "dog" includes all examples of things that are dogs. Words with different meanings encode different concepts.

**Connectionism**   A theoretical perspective that holds that thinking consists of activating connections in a network of interconnected nodes and of activation spreading in this network along paths determined by the strengths of the connections among those nodes.

**Connectionist model**   A type of model of how a phenomenon, such as some aspect of language acquisition, could be accomplished by a device that consists of a network of interconnected nodes. Typically such models are implemented as computer programs, and the ability of the computer program to mimic human language development is taken as evidence of the plausibility of a connectionist account of language acquisition. (*See also* Connectionism.)

**Constraints on word learning**   Internal biases that, by hypothesis, limit the number of possible meanings of new words children must consider.

**Constructivism**   A view of development that holds that language (or any form of knowledge) is constructed by the child using inborn mental equipment that operates over information provided by the environment.

**Context-bound word use**   Word use that is tied to particular contexts.

**Contextualized language use**   Language use in which the nonlinguistic context supports interpretation of the language; speech about the here and now.

**Continuity assumption**   The theoretical position that it should be assumed children have the same kind of grammar adults do unless the evidence proves otherwise.

**Continuity hypothesis**   The proposal that the nature of children's linguistic knowledge is not different in kind—although perhaps in degree—from adults' linguistic knowledge.

**Contralateral connections**   A feature of the human nervous system in which the primary connections from the brain to the body extend from each hemisphere of the brain to the opposite side of the body. (*See also* Ipsilateral connections.)

**Conversation**   A stretch of talk that involves two or more people.

**Cooing**   Vowel-like sounds that babies produce when they appear to be happy and contented.

**Corpus callosum**   A band of nerve fibers that connects the right and left hemispheres of the brain.

**Creole**   A language that develops when children acquire a pidgin language as their native language and which is grammatically more complex than a pidgin language.

**Critical period**   A biologically determined window of time during which an organism must have certain experiences in order for development to proceed normally.

**Critical period hypothesis**   The theory that there is a biologically determined period during which language acquisition must occur.

**Decontextualized language use**   Language use in which the words stand on their own without support from the nonlinguistic context.

**Derivational morphology**   The process that creates new words by adding certain suffixes or prefixes (derivational morphemes) to existing words (such as dance + *er* = dancer; sad + *ness* = sadness).

**Descriptive rules**   Rules that describe speakers' linguistic knowledge (in contrast to prescriptive rules).

**Developmental approach**   The approach to research on language development that attempts to answer the question, "What is the course of language development and how can we explain it?" (*See also* Learnability approach.)

**Developmental dyslexia**   The condition in which a child's reading ability is lower than would be expected on the basis of his or her IQ.

**Developmental dysphasia**   *See* Developmental language disorder.

**Developmental language disorder**   A delay in language development in the absence of any clear sensory or cognitive disorder; also referred to as specific language impairment or developmental dysphasia.

**Developmental psycholinguistics**   One term for the modern study of language development.

**Dialects**   Variations within a language that are a function of the speaker, as opposed to being a function of the setting.

**Dichotic listening task**   An experimental procedure in which two auditory stimuli are presented simultaneously (one to each ear). The purpose is to infer which cerebral hemisphere is responsible for processing the stimuli on the basis of which stimulus the listener perceives.

**Discourse knowledge**   The knowledge that underlies the ability to use language in units larger than a sentence (such as conversation and narratives).

**Dishabituation**   Renewed interest in a stimulus. (*See also* Habituation.)

**Dissociable functions**   Mental functions that operate independently, based on separate underlying mental capacities. For example, the evidence that some forms of mental retardation severely affect nonlinguistic cognition yet leave language skills relatively spared is taken as evidence for the dissociability of language and nonlinguistic cognition.

**Distinctive feature**   A phonetic feature (such as voicing) that creates a phonemic distinction between two speech sounds. (*See also* Phonemes.)

**Domain-general capacities**   Mental capacities or abilities that are used for many different tasks and domains. For example, if the ability to detect patterns in input is used for acquiring language and for learning about the physical properties of the world, then pattern detection would be a domain-general capacity.

**Domain-specific capacities**   Mental capacities or abilities that are useful for only one task or domain. For example, if the mental capacity responsible for language acquisition were used only to acquire language and nothing else, it would be a domain-specific capacity.

**Dominant language switch hypothesis**   The hypothesis that children tend to learn a second language more completely than adults do because children, more than adults, tend to switch to the second language as their dominant language and use it more.

**Down syndrome**   A chromosomal abnormality that causes moderate to severe mental retardation and typically affects language development.

**Echolalic speech**   Speech that merely repeats part of what the previous speaker said. Producing echolalic speech is a characteristic of individuals with autism.

**Egocentrism**   A characteristic of preschool children, according to the developmental theory of Jean Piaget, that makes them unable to consider what a situation is like from the point of view of another person.

**Emergent literacy**  Skills and knowledge about literacy that children acquire before they learn to read, such as knowing how to hold a book and turn the pages, knowing that words and stories are contained in the print on the page, and knowing that the print on signs and labels contains information.

**Emergentism**    The view that new knowledge can arise from the interaction of biologically based learning processes and input from the environment. It differs from constructivism in its explicit claim that what emerges from the process of innate structure operating on environmental input can be more than was provided in either the innate structure or the input.

**Empiricism**    A view of development that asserts that the mind at birth is a blank slate and all knowledge and reason come from experience.

**Equipotentiality hypothesis**    The hypothesis that at birth both hemispheres of the brain have equal potential for acquiring language.

**Event-related brain potential (ERP)**    A measure of brain activity. Electrodes placed on the scalp record voltage fluctuations in the brain as the individual perceives or responds to presented stimuli. These voltage fluctuations are electrical potentials associated with the experimenter-controlled events, and the location of the potentials is taken as evidence of where in the brain the processing of that event occurred.

**Evolutionary psychology**    The approach to the study of human mental functioning that attempts to understand human cognitive abilities by considering their adaptive function and evolutionary history.

**Expansion stage**    A stage of prespeech phonological development immediately prior to the emergence of babbling. Infants at this stage, typically between 16 and 30 weeks, produce a variety of speech sounds but no true syllabic babbling.

**Expressive language style**    A style of vocabulary development in which early lexicons contain relatively fewer object labels and relatively more words that serve social functions than do the early lexicons of children with a referential language style. (*See also* Referential language style.)

**Extended optional infinitive hypothesis**    The notion that all children go through a stage in which verbs are produced without inflection, that is, they optionally appear in their infinite form without the endings that mark person, tense, and aspect, and

that in children with specific language impairment, this stage lasts longer than normal.

**Familial concentration**    The rate of occurrence of a particular characteristic (such as specific language impairment) within a family. High familial concentration suggests a genetic basis.

**Family literacy**    Literacy practices that occur in the home, including reading labels, newspapers, magazines, and books, and writing lists, notes, and letters.

**Fast mapping**    The process children engage in when they hypothesize a meaning for a newly heard word on the basis of hearing the word once or at most a few times.

**Formalism**    The view that the structure of language is arbitrary and cannot be explained in terms of the meanings language conveys or the communicative functions language serves.

**Free morpheme**    A morpheme that stands alone as a word. (*See also* Bound morpheme.)

**Fricative**    A category of consonants produced by partially obstructing the flow of air; for example, [f] and [s].

**Functional architecture (of the brain)**    How the brain is organized to serve the functions it performs.

**Functional asymmetry**    The characteristic of the human brain in which each hemisphere serves different functions.

**Functional categories**    The term used in Chomsky's Government and Binding Theory to refer to words such as auxiliaries, prepositions, and determiners (articles) that do not carry thematic content but rather serve primarily grammatical functions. (*See also* Closed-class word and Lexical categories.)

**Functionalism**    The theory that the structure of language has a basis in the communicative functions language serves.

**Functionalist theory of language acquisition** The theory that children can discover the structure of language by virtue of the correspondence between that structure and the communicative functions for which children are trying to use language.

**Genders** Categories of nouns that take different forms of articles and grammatical morphemes, such as the plural marker.

**Gender-typed discourse style** Differences in language use that depend on the sex of the speaker.

**Grammar** The rules that describe the structure of a language.

**Grammatical morphemes** Words and word endings that mark grammatical relations, such as articles, prepositions, auxiliary verbs, and noun and verb endings.

**Grammatical morphology** The structure of words that results from combining word roots with endings that mark grammatical relations, such as the -*s* at the end of verbs to mark agreement with a third person subject ("he runs") or the -*ed* at the end of verbs to mark the past tense. Grammatical morphology is also known as inflectional morphology.

**Habituation** Apparent loss of interest in a repeatedly presented stimulus.

**Head-turn technique** An experimental procedure used to test when infants perceive two sounds as different; the technique relies on conditioning the infant to produce a head turn when a repeatedly presented sound changes. Typically used with infants 5 months and older.

**High-amplitude sucking (HAS) technique** An experimental procedure used to test when infants perceive two sounds as different; the technique relies on the infant's first habituating to one sound and then showing dishabituation when a new sound is presented. Typically used with infants under 5 months old.

**Holistic approach** An approach to language acquisition that is more characteristic of some children than others and which consists of memorizing large, unanalyzed chunks of speech. (*See also* Analytical approach.)

**Home sign** Gestural communication systems that deaf children typically invent to communicate if they are not exposed to a sign language.

**Illocutionary force** The intended function of a speech act (such as to request or promise).

**Immediate echolalia** The meaningless repetition of a word or word group immediately after hearing it produced by another speaker.

**Immersion program** A program that teaches children a second language by providing not only language instruction but also regular classes in that second language. It is a form of bilingual education.

**Infant-directed speech** *See* Motherese.

**Inflectional morphology** *See* Grammatical morphology.

**Instrumental motivation** Interest in learning a second language for utilitarian purposes such as job advancement.

**Integrative motivation** Interest in learning a second language for the purpose of associating with members of the culture in which that language is spoken.

**Intentionality** The purpose or goal in the mind of the speaker.

**Interactionism** A view of development that, although acknowledging there must be some innate characteristics of the mind that allow for language development, places greater emphasis on the nature of the language-learning environment of the child.

**Invariance hypothesis** The theory that holds that the left hemisphere of the brain has the adult specialization for language from birth.

**Ipsilateral connections** The nervous system connections between each hemisphere of the brain and the same side of the body. The primary connections in the nervous system are contralateral. (*See also* Contralateral connections.)

**Jargon** Sequences of variegated babbling that have the intonation contour of sentences.

**Joint attention** The state in which two people, for example the child and a conversational partner, are attending to the same object or event. This skill at coordinating attention with others is related to language development. (*See also* Secondary intersubjectivity.)

**Language bioprogram hypothesis** The hypothesis proposed by Bickerton (1981) that humans possess a biologically based, innate linguistic capacity that includes a skeletal grammar. By hypothesis, this capacity underlies both children's language acquisition and the process of creolization and accounts for similarities between child language and creoles.

**Language differentiation**   The task of children growing up exposed to two (or more) languages to figure out that they are hearing two different languages rather than one language that is some combination of both.

**Language mixing**   The phenomenon, which occurs in bilinguals, of using words from two different languages within a single utterance or conversation, also referred to as code-mixing or code-switching.

**Language play**   Activities such as rhyming, using alliteration, and making puns, which manipulate the sound of language.

**Language socialization**   The process by which children learn the socially appropriate use of language in their communities.

**Language transfer**.   Influences of the native language on second language learning.

**Lateralization of function**   The specialization of each hemisphere of the brain for different functions.

**Learnability approach**   The question of whether language, or some aspect of language, could in fact be learned by children. If language is not learnable, then it must be innate. The learnability approach to the study of language acquisition focuses on explaining how language could be learned, in contrast to the developmental approach, which focuses on explaining the course of language development. (*See also* Developmental approach.)

**Lesion method**   The method of investigating the functions performed by different areas of the brain by correlating impaired function with the location of damage to the brain.

**"Less is more" hypothesis**   The hypothesis (proposed by Newport, 1990) that children's smaller short-term memory span (compared with that of adults) facilitates language acquisition by giving children smaller chunks of language to analyze.

**Lexical categories**   The term in Chomsky's Government and Binding Theory for categories of words (such as noun and verb) that carry thematic content. (*See also* Open-class word and Functional categories.)

**Lexical organization**   The way in which the mental lexicon represents the relation between words and meanings.

**Lexical principles**   Assumptions about how the lexicon works that are attributed to the child in order to explain how word learning is so successful and rapid. Lexical principles guide the child in mapping new words to meaning by constraining the possible interpretations of new words that children must consider. The whole-object assumption and mutual exclusivity are two examples.

**Linguistic competence**   The ability to produce and understand well-formed, meaningful sentences.

**Linguistic perception (receptive phonology)**   The perception of speech sounds in terms of the phonological categories of the language, including the ability to discriminate words based on contrasting sounds.

**Linguistic relativity hypothesis**   *See* Whorfian hypothesis.

***Linguistics and Language Behavior* Abstracts**   An index to articles on language and language-related fields in 1500 journals.

**Locution**   The linguistic form of a speech act (such as declarative or imperative).

**Manner of articulation**   How the airflow is obstructed as a consonant is produced.

**Mapping problem**   The logical problem of learning word meanings that arises because an infinite number of hypotheses about word meaning may be consistent with information in the nonlinguistic context of use.

**Marginal babbling**   The long series of sounds that infants produce just before they begin to produce canonical babbling. This kind of sound production is typical around 5 and 6 months of age.

**Mean length of utterance (MLU)**   A common measure of grammatical development. It is the average length of the utterances in a sample of spontaneous speech, usually counted in terms of the number of morphemes.

**Mental lexicon** The knowledge of words that speakers of a language possess; the dictionary in the head.

**Metalinguistic awareness** The conscious awareness of how language works.

**Modularity** The cognitive theory that holds that the ability to develop language is a self-contained module in the mind, separate from other aspects of mental functioning.

**Morpheme** The smallest element in a language that carries meaning. Free morphemes are words; bound morphemes are prefixes, suffixes, and, in some languages, infixes. (*See also* Word.)

**Morphology** A system of rules for combining the smallest units of language into words.

**Motherese** The kind of speech that mothers (and others) produce when talking to infants and young children. It is characterized by higher pitches, a wider range of pitches, longer pauses, and shorter phrases than speech addressed to adults. (Also referred to as child-directed speech or infant-directed speech.)

**Mutual exclusivity assumption** A word-learning constraint according to which children assume that objects can have only a single name.

**Narrative** A verbal description of past events that is longer than a single utterance.

**Nativism** The view that knowledge is innate, as opposed to being learned from experience.

**Natural partitions hypothesis** The notion that the world makes obvious the things that take nouns as labels, that is, that the meanings that nouns encode are natural chunks of meaning. That makes the task of learning nouns one in which the child must simply find the label—the meaning is provided outside of language. (*See, in contrast,* Relational relativity hypothesis.)

**Nature vs. nurture** Two contrasting views of the determinants of development. According to the nature view, development is biologically determined. According to the nurture view, development is shaped by experience.

**Negative evidence** Evidence that a sentence is ungrammatical—in contrast to positive evidence that a sentence is grammatical. All the sentences that children hear are positive evidence of possible constructions in the language. Negative evidence would be feedback or correction when the child produces an ungrammatical sentence. The availability of negative evidence in children's input is a matter of some controversy.

**Neurolinguistics** The study of the brain and language.

**Nominal** A word that labels things; a common noun.

**Onset** The initial consonant or consonant cluster of a syllable.

**Open-class word** A word from the categories of noun, verb, adjective, adverb; labeled open class because new nouns, verbs, adjectives, and adverbs can readily be coined and added to the language. (*See also* Closed-class word.)

**Oral language development** The development of spoken, as opposed to gestural or written, language.

**Oralist method** An approach to language education for the deaf that focuses on the development of the ability to produce speech and read lips.

**Otitis media** Infection of the middle ear. This is frequently associated with fluid build-up in the middle ear (otitis media with effusion), resulting in temporary hearing impairment.

**Overextension** A type of error in children's early word usage that seems to reflect an overly inclusive meaning in the mind of the child (such as referring to all four-legged animals as "doggie"). (*See also* Underextension.)

**Overgeneralization** An overly general rule that children might infer from the speech they hear.

**Overregularization** An overapplication of rules to irregular parts of the language (such as pluralizing *foot* as *foots*).

**Parameter** A feature of Universal Grammar that handles the variation among languages. For example, some languages are left-branching and some languages are right-branching.

**Parameter setting** The process of determining which set of options, which by hypothesis is specified in Universal Grammar, applies to the target language.

**Perlocution** The effect of a speech act on the listener.

**Phone** A speech sound, such as [p], [ph], and [b], used by any language.

**Phoneme boundary** The location on a continuum of change in some acoustic property of a sound where the listener's perception of the sound changes from one phoneme to another. (*See also* Phoneme boundary effect.)

**Phoneme boundary effect** The phenomenon in which the same acoustic difference (such as a 20 millisecond difference in voice onset time [VOT]) is perceptible if the two stimuli are on opposite sides of a phoneme boundary (as in /b/ versus /p/) but is imperceptible if the two stimuli are within the range of variation perceived as one phoneme. (*See also* Categorical perception.)

**Phonemes** Speech sounds that signal a difference in meaning in a particular language.

**Phonemic awareness** The awareness of phonemes as units of words—a component of phonological awareness.

**Phonetic feature** A characteristic of the way speech sounds are produced that is used to describe differences and similarities among speech sounds. For example, [b] and [p] differ in the feature of voicing.

**Phonics** The method of reading instruction that involves explicit teaching of letter-sound correspondences.

**Phonological awareness** Conscious awareness of the phonological properties of language, such as the ability to count the number of syllables in a word and to identify rhymes.

**Phonological bootstrapping hypothesis** The hypothesis that language-learning children find and use clues to the syntactic structure of language in phonological properties of the speech they hear. (*See also* Prosodic bootstrapping hypothesis.)

**Phonological idiom** A word that children pronounce in a very adultlike manner while still incorrectly producing other words that use the same sounds.

**Phonological knowledge** Knowledge of the sounds and sound patterns of a language.

**Phonological memory** The function of short-term memory responsible for the temporary storage of the sound of a stimulus.

**Phonological processes** Rules that map sounds in the target language to sounds in young children's limited production repertoires. Phonological processes that are common to many children give young children's speech typical features, such as pronouncing *r*'s as *w*.

**Phonological recoding** The process of mentally going through the sound of the word to get from the printed word to the word's meaning.

**Pidgin** A structurally simple language that arises when people who share no common language come into contact.

**Place of articulation** The location where the airflow is obstructed as a consonant is produced.

**Plasticity** The ability of parts of the brain to take over functions they normally would not serve. There is much more plasticity in the child's brain than in the adult's.

**Pragmatic bootstrapping** The hypothesis that when children start speaking, they produce utterances in order to accomplish goals. This pragmatically based system gets children started in using language and is later replaced by a system with word meanings and grammatical structure.

**Pragmatic knowledge** The knowledge that enables speakers to use language for communicative purposes in ways that are socially appropriate in their community.

**Pragmatic principle** A principle about how words are used that, by hypothesis, helps children figure out the meaning of newly encountered words.

**Pragmatics** Language use.

**Prelingually deaf** The characteristic of having become deaf prior to acquiring language.

**Prerepresentational phonology**    The period of phonological development during which children have mental representations for the sounds of whole words but not for individual speech sounds. (*See also* Representational phonology.)

**Prescriptive rules**    Rules of grammar that define how language should be used, as taught in writing classes and specified in style manuals. For example, the rules that prohibit splitting infinitives and ending sentences with prepositions are prescriptive rules. (*See also* Descriptive rules.)

**Primary intersubjectivity**    The ability to relate to an object or to another person but not to both at the same time. (*See also* Secondary intersubjectivity.)

**Principle of contrast**    A pragmatic principle that, by hypothesis, leads children to assume that different words have different meanings.

**Principle of conventionality**    A pragmatic principle that, by hypothesis, leads children to assume that words are used by all speakers to express the same meaning—that is, that word meaning is a convention.

**Principles and parameters theory**    The theory that the child has innate knowledge of Universal Grammar, consisting of principles that hold true for every language, and a set of options, or parameters, that have to be filled in by experience.

**Private speech**    Speech produced for one's self (as opposed to for another listener).

**Productivity or generativity of language**    The characteristic of all human languages by which they make use of a finite repertoire of sounds to produce a potentially infinite number of sentences.

**Prosodic bootstrapping hypothesis**    The hypothesis that language-learning children find and use clues to syntactic structure of language in the prosodic characteristics of the speech they hear. (*See also* Phonological bootstrapping hypothesis.)

**Prosody**    The intonation contour of speech, including pauses and changes in stress and pitch.

**Protoword**    An idiosyncratic sound sequence that children use with consistent meaning but which is not clearly derived from a word in the target language.

*Psychological Abstracts/PsycINFO*    An index to a large number of journals, books, and book chapters in psychology and related fields (*Psychological Abstracts*) and its computer-accessible form (*PsycINFO*).

**Reduplicated babbling**    Babbling that consists of repeating the same syllable over and over (such as *da-da-da-da*). This is characteristic of infant sound production around 8 to 10 months of age. (*See also* Canonical babbling.)

**Reference**    The notion of words as symbols that stand for their referents.

**Referential communication**    A communication task in which the speaker must indicate to a listener which item to select out of an array of items.

**Referential language style**    A style of vocabulary development in which a child's early lexicon is heavily dominated by object labels. (*See also* Expressive language style.)

**Referential word use**    Word use that is not bound to one particular context.

**Register**    The styles of language use associated with a particular social setting.

**Relational meaning**    The relation between the referents of the words in a word combination (for example, possession is indicated by "Daddy's shirt").

**Relational relativity hypothesis**    The notion that verb meanings do not naturally emerge from the structure of the world. This leaves open the possibility that verb meanings will vary from language to language, and thus children will have to figure out verb meanings from hearing the verb in use. (*See, in contrast,* Natural partitions hypothesis.)

**Representational phonology**    The stage of phonological development in which the child first has a mental representation of the phonemes in the target language. Prior to this stage, children represent the sounds of words as whole words or in syllabic units. (*See also* Prerepresentational phonology.)

**Response strategy**    Children's method of falling back on ways of responding that do not depend on understanding, used when they do not fully understand what is said to them. For example, 1-year-old children appear to have a strategy of responding to whatever is said to them by doing something. This has been termed an action strategy.

**Right-ear advantage**    The relatively greater probability that stimuli presented to the right ear in a dichotic listening test will be perceived by the listener. Typically there is a right-ear advantage for linguistic stimuli, which suggests that the left cerebral hemisphere is primarily responsible for processing linguistic stimuli.

**Rime**    The vowel plus any final consonants in a syllable; syllables are composed of an onset and a rime.

**Rule learning**    The learning of relationships among abstract entities for which different items may be substituted, such as learning the pattern $x$ $y$ $x$, where any item can be substituted for $x$ and for $y$. In contrast, statistical learning is learning patterns among the items actually experienced, as opposed to patterns among abstract variables.

**Scaffolding**    A term used to describe the support for children's language use that more-competent speakers sometimes provide. Examples of scaffolding include routinized formats for interaction and leading questions that adults ask, both of which enable children to perform at a more-advanced level than they could on their own.

**Secondary intersubjectivity**    The ability to relate to another person about an object. Infants first appear to be capable of secondary intersubjectivity around the age of 9 or 10 months. (*See also* Primary intersubjectivity and Joint attention.)

**Secondary language activities**    Language activities that involve the manipulation of the sounds of language, such as rhymes and word games.

**Semantic bootstrapping**    The theory that the correspondence between semantic and syntactic categories provides the language-learning child entry into the grammatical system.

**Semantic organization**    The organization of meaning expressed in a language, as distinct from cognitive organization.

**Semantically based grammar**    A grammar in which rules operate over meaning-based categories such as agent, action, location, and so on.

**Sensitive period**    A term sometimes used instead of critical period to indicate that the ability to acquire language may be greatest during a particular period of development but that later language acquisition is not impossible.

**Sequential bilingualism**    Bilingualism that results from a person's learning a second language after acquisition of the first language is well under way.

**Simultaneous bilingualism**    Bilingualism that results from a person's being exposed from birth or shortly after birth to two languages.

**Social interactionism**    A view of development that holds that a crucial aspect of language-learning experience is social interaction with another person.

**Social/cognitive view**    The view that the starting point of language acquisition is provided by general cognition, as are the mechanisms of language development. The requisite experience for language acquisition is social interaction with other speakers.

**Sociolinguistic knowledge**    The knowledge of how language use varies as a function of changes in speaker status, sex, setting, and so on.

**Sociolinguistics**    The study of how language use varies as a function of sociological variables such as status, culture, and gender.

**Sociopragmatic cue**    A cue to the meaning of a new word that children find in the way words are used in social interaction. For example, children take a speaker's eye gaze as a cue to what the speaker is referring to.

**Sparse morphology hypothesis**    The theory that explains specific language impairment by suggesting that the functional role of the morphology of a language is relevant to its ease of acquisition. Languages in which the morphological system does relatively little grammatical work, such as English, will cause particular problems for children with specific language impairment.

**Specific language impairment**    See Developmental language disorder.

**Speech act**    Utterance as behavior; the notion that talking is "doing things with words."

**Speech sample** A video-recorded or tape-recorded record of spontaneous speech used to assess children's language development.

**Speech segmentation** The mental process of separating the speech stream into separate words.

**Split-brain patient** A patient who has had his or her corpus callosum severed (usually to relieve epileptic seizures).

**Stabilization (of function)** The process whereby some neural pathways become permanently committed to serve particular functions while other, unused neural circuits lose their capacity.

**Statistical learning** Learning of the co-occurrence probabilities of experienced stimuli. For example, babies presented with sequences of sounds appear to learn the conditional probability of one sound following another in the sequence they heard. This is one mechanism for learning the patterns in input that could contribute to learning language. (*Compare with* Rule learning.)

**Stop** A consonant sound that is produced by completely closing the vocal tract at some point and then releasing the air to pass through the vocal tract, as in [p] and [k].

**Story grammar** The structure all stories follow. There are different proposals for what this structure is, and this structure varies as a function of culture. For example, Western stories tend to consist of a setting plus one or more episodes. The setting includes the place and the characters; each episode includes an initiating event, a problem or obstacle, and a resolution of the problem.

**Subcortical structure** A structure of the brain beneath the cerebral cortex that controls primitive functions as opposed to higher mental processes.

**Supralaryngeal vocal tract** The vocal tract located above the larynx that is responsible for the production of speech sounds.

**Syntactic bootstrapping hypothesis** The hypothesis that children find and use clues to the meaning of new words in the syntactic structure of the sentences in which new words are encountered.

**Syntactically based grammar** A grammar in which rules operate over formal categories, such as noun and verb. These formal categories are not defined in terms of their meaning or their communicative function.

**Syntax** A system of rules for building phrases out of words (which belong to particular grammatical categories, such as noun and verb) and for building sentences out of these constituent phrases.

**Tadpole–frog problem** The problem of accounting for the change from a semantically based system to a syntactically based system if one describes children's grammars as semantically based. This change is compared to the metamorphosis that tadpoles undergo to become frogs. (*See also* Semantically based grammar and Syntactically based grammar.)

**Taxonomic assumption** The child's assumption that words label categories of things of the same kind (taxonomic categories). This assumption is proposed as one word-learning constraint that helps children learn the meaning of new words.

**Telegraphic speech** Speech, typical of 2-year-old children, that includes primarily content words and omits such grammatical morphemes as determiners and endings on nouns and verbs. So named because the result sounds like sentences adults use in writing telegrams.

**Theory of mind** The theory that other persons have minds and that mental contents such as beliefs and intentions guide their behavior. Adults operate according to this theory; children must develop this theory.

**Topic** What a sentence or longer unit of discourse is about.

**Topic-associating narrative style** A style of describing past events that consists of a related set of personal anecdotes. This style is typical among some African Americans.

**Topic-centered narrative style** A style of describing past events that tends to be tightly organized around a single topic. This style is typical among middle-class European Americans.

**Total communication** An approach to language education for the deaf in which oral language is combined with a signing or gestural system.

**Transitional forms** Utterances such as vertical constructions that children produce between producing single-word and clear two-word utterances.

**Two-way program** A bilingual education program that involves content instruction in both languages.

**Underextension** Using words with a range of meanings narrower than the meaning of the word in the target language (such as using *car* to refer only to cars seen from a window). (*See also* Overextension.)

**Universal Grammar (UG)** The set of principles and parameters that describes the structure of all languages of the world; hypothesized by some to be part of the child's innate knowledge. (*See also* Principles and parameters theory.)

**Variegated babbling** Strings of nonreduplicated syllables.

**Vegetative sounds** Sounds that accompany biological functions, such as breathing, sucking, and burping.

**Vocal play** The activity of producing a variety of different consonant and vowel sounds that is typical of infants between 16 and 30 weeks.

**Voice onset time (VOT)** The time lag in the production of a consonant between the release of air and the beginning of vocal cord vibration. Consonants with a VOT greater than 25 milliseconds are perceived as voiceless (such as [p]), and VOTs less than 25 milliseconds are perceived as voiced (such as [b]).

**Voicing** A feature of sound production in which the vocal cords vibrate as air is released in the production of a consonant. Consonants [b] and [g] are voiced; [p] and [k] are voiceless.

**Wernicke's aphasia** The condition in which patients speak rapidly and fluently but without meaning as a result of damage to part of the left hemisphere of the brain.

**Wernicke's area** An area in the left hemisphere of the brain, located next to the primary auditory cortex, that is responsible for language functions.

**Wh- questions** Questions that begin with *who, what, where, why, when,* or *how.*

**Whole-language approach** The method of reading instruction based on the notions that children do not need explicit phonics instruction to learn to read and that children will learn to read if they are surrounded by interesting print material. Activities focus on reading for meaning rather than instruction in letter–sound correspondences.

**Whole-object assumption** A word-learning constraint according to which children assume that a new word refers to a whole object, not to a part or property of an object.

**Whorfian hypothesis** The hypothesis that language influences thought and, therefore, that differences among languages might cause differences in the cognition of speakers of those languages. (Also known as linguistic relativity hypothesis.)

**Williams syndrome** A rare disorder that produces severe mental retardation but leaves language functions relatively intact.

**Word** A sound sequence that symbolizes meaning and can stand alone. (*See also* Morpheme.)

**Word spurt** The increase in the rate at which children acquire new words; it occurs sometime around the achievement of a 50-word vocabulary, or about 18 months of age.

**Yes/no questions** Questions that can be answered with *yes* or *no.*

# REFERENCES

ABBEDUTO, L., MURPHY, M. M., CAWTHON, S. W., RICHMOND, E. K., WEISSMAN, M. D., KARADOTTIR, S., & O'BRIEN, A. (2003). Receptive language skills of adolescents and young adults with Down or Fragile X syndrome. *American Journal on Mental Retardation, 108,* 149–160.

ACREDOLO, L. P., & GOODWYN, S. W. (1998). *Baby signs: How to talk with your baby before your baby can talk.* Chicago: NTB/Contemporary Publishers.

ADAMS, M. J. (1990). *Beginning to read: Thinking and learning about print.* Cambridge, MA: MIT Press.

AITCHISON, J. (1983). On roots of language. *Language & Communication, 3,* 83–97.

AITCHISON, J. (1987). *Words in the mind.* Oxford: Blackwell.

AITCHISON, J. (1989). *The articulate mammal: An introduction to psycholinguistics, 3rd edition.* London: Routledge.

AITCHINSON, J. (1998). On discontinuing the continuity-discontinuity debate. In J. R. Hurford, M. Studdert-Kennedy, & C. Knight (Eds.), *Approaches to the evolution of language* (pp. 17–29). Cambridge: Cambridge University Press.

AKHTAR, N., CARPENTER, M., & TOMASELLO, M. (1996). The role of discourse novelty in early word learning. *Child Development, 67,* 635–645.

AKHTAR, N., DUNHAM, F., & DUNHAM, P. J. (1991). Directive interactions and early vocabulary development: The role of joint attentional focus. *Journal of Child Language, 18,* 41–50.

AKSU-KOC, A. A., & SLOBIN, D. I. (1985). The acquisition of Turkish. In D. I. Slobin (Ed.), *The crosslinguistic study of language acquisition: Vol. 1. The data* (pp. 839–880). Hillsdale, NJ: Erlbaum.

ALBERT, M., & OBLER, L. K. (1978). *The bilingual brain: Neuropsychological and neurolinguistic aspects of bilingualism.* New York: Academic Press.

ALLEN, R., & SHATZ, M. (1983). "What says meow?" The role of context and linguistic experience in very young children's responses to *what*-questions. *Journal of Child Language, 10,* 321–335.

ALVY, K. T. (1968). Relation of age to children's egocentric and cooperative communication. *Journal of Genetic Psychology, 112,* 275–286.

*American Heritage Dictionary, Second College Edition.* (1985). Boston: Houghton Mifflin Company.

AMERICAN PSYCHIATRIC ASSOCIATION (1994). *Diagnostic and statistical manual of mental disorders (4th ed.)*. Washington, DC: Author.

ANDERSON, J. M. (1989). Writing systems. In W. O'Grady, M. Dobrovolsky, & M. Aronoff (Eds.), *Contemporary linguistics: An introduction* (pp. 358–382). New York: St. Martin's Press.

ANGLIN, J. M. (1993). Vocabulary development: A morphological analysis. *Monographs of the Society for Research in Child Development, 58* (No. 10).

ANSELMI, D., TOMASELLO, M., & ACUNZO, M. (1986). Young children's responses to neutral and specific contingent queries. *Journal of Child Language, 13,* 135–144.

APPEL, R., & MUYSKEN, P. (1987). *Language contact and bilingualism*. London: Arnold.

ARAM, D. M., EKELMAN, B. L., ROSE, D. F., & WHITAKER, H. A. (1985). Verbal and cognitive sequelae following unilateral lesions acquired in early childhood. *Journal of Clinical and Experimental Neuropsychology, 7,* 55–78.

ARDILA, A. (2002). Spanish-English bilingualism in the United States of America. In F. Fabbro (Ed.), *Advances in the neurolinguistics of bilingualism* (pp. 49–67). Udine, Italy: Forum.

ARNBERG, L. (1987). *Raising children bilingually: The preschool years*. Clevedon, Avon: Multilingual Matters.

ASLIN, R. N., JUSCZYK, P. W., & PISONI, D. (1998). Speech and auditory processing during infancy: Constraints on and precursors to language. In W. Damon, Editor in Chief, D. Kuhn & R. S. Siegler, volume editors, *Handbook of child psychology 5th ed., vol 2: Cognition, perception, and language* (pp. 147–198). New York: John Wiley & Sons.

ASLIN, R. N., SAFFRAN, J. R., & NEWPORT, E. L. (1998). Computation of conditional probability statistics by 8-month-old infants. *Psychological Science, 9,* 321–324.

ASLIN, R. N., SAFFRAN, J. R., & NEWPORT, E. L. (1999). Statistical learning in linguistic and nonlinguistic domains. In B. MacWhinney (Ed.), *The emergence of language* (pp. 359–380). Mahwah, NJ: Erlbaum.

ATKINSON, M. (1992). *Children's syntax*. Cambridge, MA: Blackwell.

AU, T.K., & GLUSMAN, M. (1990). The principle of mutual exclusivity in word learning: To honor or not to honor? *Child Development* 61(5), 1474–1490.

AUSTIN, J. L. (1962). *How to do things with words*. Oxford: Oxford University Press.

BABY TALK. (1984).In NOVA. The Open University. Public Broadcasting System.

BACCHINE, S., KUIKEN, F., & SCHOONEN, R. (1995). Generalizability of spontaneous speech data: The effect of occasion and place on the speech production of children. *First Language, 15,* 131–150.

BALABAN, M. T., & WAXMAN, S. R. (1997). Do words facilitate object categorization in 9-month-old infants? *Journal of Experimental Child Psychology, 64,* 3–26.

BALDWIN, D. (1993). Infants' ability to consult the speaker for clues to word reference. *Journal of Child Language, 20,* 395–419.

BAMBERG, M. (1987). *The acquisition of narratives*. Berlin: Mouton de Gruyter.

BARKOW, J. H., COSMIDES, L., & TOOBY, J. (1992). *The adapted mind: Evolutionary psychology and the generation of culture*. New York: Oxford University Press.

BARON-COHEN, S., BALDWIN, D. A. & CROWSON, M. (1997). Do Children with autism use the speaker's direction of gaze strategy to crack the code of language? *Child Development, 68,* 48–57.

BARON-COHEN, S., TAGER-FLUSBERG, H., & COHEN, D. J. (1993). *Understanding other minds: Perspectives from autism*. Oxford: Oxford University Press.

BARRETT, M. (1995). Early lexical development. In P. Fletcher & B. MacWhinney (Eds.), *The handbook of child language* (pp. 362–392). Oxford: Blackwell.

BARRETT, M. D. (1986). Early semantic representations and early word usage. In S. A. Kuczaj & M. D. Barrett (Eds.), *The development of word meaning* (pp. 39–67). New York: Springer-Verlag.

BARTON, M. E., & TOMASELLO, M. (1994). The rest of the family: The role of fathers and siblings in early language development. In C. Gallaway & B. J. Richards (Eds.), *Input and interaction in language acquisition* (pp. 109–134). Cambridge, England: Cambridge University Press.

BAST, J., & REITSMA, P. (1998). Analyzing the development of individual differences in terms of Matthew effect in reading: Results from a Dutch longitudinal study. *Developmental Psychology, 34,* 1373–1399.

BATES, E. (1975). Peer relations and the acquisition of language. In M. Lewis & L. Rosenblum (Eds.), *Friendship and peer relations* (pp. 259–292). New York: Wiley.

BATES, E. (1976). *Language and context: The acquisition of pragmatics.* New York: Academic Press.

BATES, E. (1984). Bioprograms and the innateness hypothesis. *Behavioral and Brain Sciences, 7,* 188–190.

BATES, E. (1993). Comprehension and production in early language development (Commentary on language comprehension in ape and child by Savage-Rumbaugh et al.). *Monographs of the Society for Research in Child Development, 58* (3–4, Serial No. 233).

BATES, E., BENIGNI, L., BRETHERTON, I., CAMIONI, L., & VOLTERRA, V. (1979). *The emergence of symbols: Cognition and communication in infancy.* New York: Academic Press.

BATES, E., BRETHERTON, I., & SNYDER, L. (1988). *From first words to grammar: individual differences and dissociable mechanisms.* Cambridge, England: Cambridge University Press.

BATES, E., CAMIONI, L., & VOLTERRA, V. (1975). The acquisition of performatives prior to speech. *Merrill-Palmer Quarterly, 21,* 205–226.

BATES, E., DALE, P., & THAL, D. (1995). Individual differences and their implications for theories of language development. In P. Fletcher & B. MacWhinney (Eds.), *The handbook of child language* (pp. 96–151). Oxford: Blackwell.

BATES, E., & GOODMAN, J. (1999). On the emergence of grammar from the lexicon. In B. MacWhinney (Ed.), *The emergence of language* (pp. 29–80). Mahwah, NJ: Lawrence Erlbaum Assoc.

BATES, E., & MACWHINNEY, B. (1982). Functionalist approaches to grammar. In L. Gleitman & E. Wanner (Eds.), *Language acquisition: The state of the art* (pp. 173–218). Cambridge, England: Cambridge University Press.

BATES, E., MARCHMAN, V., THAL, D., FENSON, L., DALE, P., REZNICK, J. S., REILLY, J., & HARTUNG, J. (1994). Developmental and stylistic variation in the composition of early vocabulary. *Journal of Child Language, 21,* 85–124.

BATES, E., THAL, D., & MARCHMAN, V. (1991). Symbols and syntax: A Darwinian approach to language development. In N. A. Krasnegor, D. M. Rumbaugh, R. L. Schiefelbusch, & M. Studdert-Kennedy (Eds.), *Biological and behavioral determinants of language development* (pp. 29–66). Hillsdale, NJ: Erlbaum.

BAUER D. J., GOLDFIELD B. A., & REZNICK, J.S. (2002). Alternative approaches to analyzing individual differences in the rate of early vocabulary development. *Applied Psycholinguistics 23,* 313–335. Cambridge: Cambridge University Press.

BAUMAN, M. L. (1999). Autism: Clinical features and neurobiological observations. In H. Tager-Flusberg (Ed.), *Neurodevelopmental disorders* (pp. 383–400). Cambridge, MA: MIT Press.

BAVIN, E. L. (1992). The acquisition of Warlpiri. In D. I. Slobin (Ed.), *The cross linguistic study of language acquisition,* Vol. 3 (pp. 309–372). Hillsdale, NJ: Lawrence Erlbaum Assoc.

BAYNES, K., & GAZZANIGA, M. S. (1988). Right hemisphere language: Insights into normal language mechanisms? In F. Plum (Ed.), *Language, communication, and the brain* (pp. 117–126). New York: Raven.

BEAL, C. R. (1987). Repairing the message: Children's monitoring and revision skills. *Child Development, 58,* 401–408.

BEAL, C. R. (1988). Children's knowledge about representations of intended meaning. In J. W. Astington, P. L. Harris, & D. R. Olson (Eds.), *Developing theories of mind* (pp. 315–325). Cambridge, England: Cambridge University Press.

BEAL, C. R., & FLAVELL, J. H. (1983). Young speakers' evaluations of their listener's comprehension in a referential communication task. *Child Development, 54,* 148–153.

BECHTEL, W., & ABRAHAMSEN, A. (1991). *Connectionism and the mind.* Cambridge, MA: Blackwell.

BECKER, J. A. (1982). Children's strategic use of requests to mark and manipulate social status. In S. Kuczaj (Ed.), *Language development: Language, thought, and culture* (pp. 1–33). Hillsdale, NJ: Erlbaum.

BECKER, J. A. (1990). Processes in the acquisition of pragmatic competence. In G. Conti Ramsden & C. E. Snow (Eds.), *Children's language* (Vol. 7, pp. 7–24). Hillsdale, NJ: Erlbaum.

BECKER, J. A. (1994). "Sneak-shoes," "sworders" and "nose-beards": A case study of lexical innovation. *First Language, 14,* 195–212.

BECKMAN, M. E., & EDWARDS, J. (2000). The ontogeny of phonological categories and the primacy of lexical learning in linguistic development. *Child Development, 71,* 240–249.

BEEGHLY, M. & CHICCHETTI, D. (1987). An organizational approach to symbolic development in children with Down syndrome. In D. Cicchetti & M. Beeghly (Eds.), Symbolic development in atypical children (pp. 5–30). *New Directions for Child Development, No. 36.* San Francisco: Jossey-Bass Inc.

BEHREND, D. A. (1990). Constraints and development: A reply to Nelson (1988). *Cognitive Development, 5,* 313–330.

BEHREND, D. A., ROSENGREN, K. S., & PERLMUTTER, M. (1992). The relation between private speech and parental interactive style. In R. M. Diaz & L. E. Berk (Eds.), *Private speech: From social interaction to self-regulation* (pp. 85–100). Hillsdale, NJ: Erlbaum.

BELL, S., & AINSWORTH, M. (1972). Infant crying and maternal responsiveness. *Child Development, 43,* 1171–1190.

BELLUGI, U., MILLS, D., JERNIGAN, T, HICKOK, G., & GALABURDA, A. (1999). Linking cognition, brain structure, and brain function in Williams syndrome. In H. Tager-Flusberg. (Ed.),

*Neurodevelopmental disorders* (pp. 111–136). Cambridge, MA: MIT Press.

BELLUGI, U., POIZNER, H., & KLIMA, E. (1989). Language, modality and the brain. *Trends in Neurosciences, 12,* 380–388.

BELLUGI, U., VAN HOEK, K., LILLO-MARTIN, D., & O'GRADY, L. (1993). The acquisition of syntax and space in young deaf signers. In D. Bishop & K. Mogford (Eds.), *Language development in exceptional children* (pp. 132–149). Hove, England: Erlbaum.

BELLUGI, U., WANG, P. P., & JERNIGAN, T. L. (1994). Williams syndrome: An unusual neuropsychological profile. In S. H. Froman & J. Grafman (Eds.), *Atypical cognitive deficits in developmental disorders: Implications for brain function* (pp. 23–56). Hillsdale, NJ: Erlbaum.

BENASICH, A. A., & TALLAL, P. (2002). Infant discrimination of rapid auditory cues predicts later language impairment. *Behavioural Brain Research, 136,* 31–49.

BENEDICT, H. (1979). Early lexical development: Comprehension and production. *Journal of Child Language, 6,* 183–200.

BEN-ZEEV, S. (1977). The influence of bilingualism on cognitive strategy and cognitive development. *Child Development, 48,* 1009–1018.

BERKO, J. (1958). The child's learning of English morphology. *Word, 14,* 150–177.

BERKO, J., & BROWN, R. (1960). Psycholinguistic research methods. In P. H. Mussen (Ed.), *Handbook of research methods in child development* (pp. 517–557). New York: Wiley.

BERMAN, R. A. (1986). A crosslinguistic perspective: Morphology and syntax. In P. Fletcher & M. Garman (Eds.), *Language acquisition* (2nd ed., pp. 429–447). Cambridge, England: Cambridge University Press.

BERMAN, R. A. (1988). On the ability to relate events in narrative. *Discourse Processes, 11,* 469–497.

BERMAN, R. A., & SLOBIN, D. I. (1994). *Relating events in narrative: A crosslinguistic developmental study.* Hillsdale, NJ: Erlbaum.

BERNHARDT, B. H. & STEMBERGER, J. P. (1998). *Handbook of phonological development. From the perspective of constraint-based nonlinear phonology.* San Diego: Academic Press.

BERNICOT, J., & ROUX, M. (1998). La structure et l'usage des énoncés: Comparison d'enfants uniques et d'enfants second nés. In J. Bernicot, H. Marcos, C. Day, M. Guidetti, J. Rabain-Jamin, V. Laval, & G. Babelot (Eds.), *De l'usage des gestes et des mots chez les enfants* (pp. 157–178). Paris: Armand Colin.

BERNSTEIN, B. B. (1970). A socio-linguistic approach to social learning. In F. Williams (Ed.), *Language and poverty* (pp. 25–61). Chicago: Markham.

BERNSTEIN, B. B. (1981). Elaborated and restricted codes: Their social origins and some consequences. In K. Danziger (Ed.), *Readings in child socialization* (pp. 165–186). Oxford: Pergamon Press.

BERTENTHAL, B. I., & CAMPOS, J. J. (1987). Commentary—New directions in the study of early experience. *Child Development, 58,* 560–567.

BEST, C. T. (1988). The emergence of cerebral asymmetries in early human development: A literature review and a neuroembryological model. In D. L. Molfese & S. J. Segalowitz (Eds.), *Brain lateralization in children: Developmental implications* (pp. 5–34). New York: Guilford Press.

BEST, C. T. (1994). The emergence of native-language phonological influences in infants: A perceptual assimilation model. In J. C. Goodman & H. C. Nusbaum (Eds.), *The development of speech perception: The transition from speech sounds to spoken words* (pp. 167–224). Cambridge, MA: MIT Press.

BEVER, T. G., & CHIARELLO, R. J. (1974). Cerebral dominance in musicians and nonmusicians. *Science, 185,* 537–539.

BHATIA, T. K., & RITCHIE, W. C. (1999). The bilingual child: Some issues and perspectives. In W. C. Ritchie & T. K. Bhatia (Eds.), *Handbook of child language acquisition* (pp. 569–646). San Diego: Academic Press.

BIALYSTOK, E. (Ed.). (1991). *Language processing in bilingual children.* Cambridge, England: Cambridge University Press.

BIALYSTOK, E. (1991a). Metalinguistic dimensions of bilingual language proficiency. In E. Bialystok (Ed.), *Language processing in bilingual children* (pp. 113–141). Cambridge, England: Cambridge University Press.

BIALYSTOK, E. (1991b). *Language processing in bilingual children.* Cambridge, England: Cambridge University Press.

BIALYSTOK, E. (1999). Cognitive complexity and attentional control in the bilingual mind. *Child Development, 70,* 636–644.

BIALYSTOK, E., & HAKUTA, K. (1994). *In other words.* New York: Basic Books.

BIALYSTOK, E., & MAJUMDER, S. (1998). The relationship between bilingualism and the development of cognitive processes in problem solving. *Applied Psycholinguistics, 19,* 69–85.

BICKERTON, D. (1981). *Roots of language.* Ann Arbor, MI: Karoma.

BICKERTON, D. (1984). The language bioprogram hypothesis. *The Behavioral and Brain Sciences, 7,* 173–221.

BICKERTON, D. (1988). Creole languages and the bioprogram. In F. J. Newmeyer (Ed.), *Linguistics: The Cambridge Survey* (Vol. II, pp. 268–284). Cambridge, England: Cambridge University Press.

BICKERTON, D. (1990). *Language and species.* Chicago: University of Chicago Press.

BIGELOW, A. (1987). Early words of blind children. *Journal of Child Language, 14,* 47–56.

BIJELJAC-BABIC, R. J., BERTONCINI, J., & MEHLER, J. (1993). How do 4-day-old infants categorize multisyllabic utterances? *Development Psychology, 29,* 711–721.

BIKLEN, D. (1990). Communication unbound: Autism and praxis. *Harvard Educational Review, 60,* 291–314.

BIRDSONG, D. (1999). Introduction: Whys and why nots of the critical period hypothesis for second language acquisition. In D. Birdsong (Ed.), *Second language acquisition and the critical period hypothesis* (pp. 1–22). Mahwah, NJ: Erlbaum.

BIRDWHISTELL, R. L. (1970). *Kinesics and context: Essays on body motion communication.* Philadelphia: University of Pennsylvania Press.

BISHOP, D. V. M. (1983). Linguistic impairment after hemidecortication for infantile hemiplegia? A reappraisal. *Quarterly Journal of Experimental Psychology, 35,* 199–207.

BISHOP, D. V. M. (1988). Can the right hemisphere mediate language as well as the left? A critical review of recent research. *Cognitive Neuropsychology, 5,* 353–367.

BISHOP, D. V. M. (1991). Developmental reading disabilities: The role of phonological processing has been overemphasized. *Mind & Language, 6,* 97–101.

BISHOP, D. V. M. (1995). Nonword repetition as a phenotypic marker for inherited language impairment. Paper presented at the 16th Symposium on Research in Child Language Disorders, University of Wisconsin–Madison, June 2–3.

BJORKLUND, D. F., & PELLIGRINI, A. D. (2000). Child development and evolutionary psychology. *Child Development, 71,* 1687–1708.

BLANK, M., & ALLEN, D. A. (1976). Understanding "why": Its significance in early intelligence. In M. Lewis (Ed.), *Origins of Intelligence* (pp. 259–278). New York: Plenum.

BLANK, M., GESSNER, M., & ESPOSITO, A. (1979). Language without communication: A case study. *Journal of Child Language, 6,* 329–352.

BLOOM, L. (1973). *One word at a time*. The Hague, The Netherlands: Mouton.

BLOOM, L. (1991). *Language development from two to three*. Cambridge, England: Cambridge University Press.

BLOOM, L. (1993b). *The transition from infancy to language: Acquiring the power of expression*. Cambridge, England: Cambridge University Press.

BLOOM, L. (1970). Language development: Form and function in emerging grammars. Cambridge, MA: MIT Press.

BLOOM, L. (1998). Language acquisition in its developmental context. In D. Kuhn & R. S. Siegler (Eds.), *Handbook of child psychology, 5th Ed.: Vol. 2. Cognition, perception, and language* (pp. 309–370). New York: Wiley & Sons.

BLOOM, L. & CAPATIDES, J. B. (1987). Expression of affect and the emergence of language. *Child Development, 58,* 1513–1522.

BLOOM, L., LIGHTBOWN, P., & HOOD. L. (1975). Structure and variation in child language. *Monographs of the Society for Research in Child Development, 40* (2, Serial No. 160).

BLOOM, L., ROCISSANO, L., & HOOD, L. (1976). Adult–child discourse: Developmental interaction between information processing and linguistic knowledge. *Cognitive Psychology, 8,* 521–552.

BLOOM, P. (1998). Some issues in the evolution of language and thought. In D. D. Cummins & C. Allen (Eds.), *The evolution of mind* (pp. 204–223). Oxford: Oxford University Press.

BLOOM, P. (2000). How children learn the meanings of words. Cambridge, MA: MIT Press.

BLOOM, P. & MARKSON, L. (1998). Intention and analogy in children's naming of pictorial representations. *Psychological Science, 9,* 200–204.

BLUMSTEIN, S. E. (1988). Linguistic deficits in asphasia. In F. Plum (Ed.), *Language, communication, and the brain* (pp. 199–214). New York: Raven Press.

BOHANNON, J. N., & STANOWICZ, L. (1988). The issue of negative evidence: Adult responses to children's language errors. *Developmental Psychology, 24,* 684–689.

BONVILLIAN, J. D., ORLANSKY, M. D., & NOVACK, L. L. (1983). Developmental milestones: Sign language acquisition and motor development. *Child Development, 54,* 1435–1445.

BONVILLIAN, J. D. (1999). Sign language development. In M. Barrett (Ed.), *The development of language* (pp. 277–311). East Sussex: Psychology Press.

BORNSTEIN, M. H., HAYNES, M. O., & PAINTER, K. M. (1998). Sources of child vocabulary competence: A multivariate model. *Journal of Child Language, 25,* 367–393.

BORNSTEIN, M. H., & TAMIS-LEMONDA, C. S. (1989). Maternal responsiveness and cognitive development in children. In M. H. Bornstein (Ed.), *Maternal responsiveness: Characteristics and consequences* (pp. 49–61). San Francisco: Jossey-Bass.

BOTVIN, G. J., & SUTTON-SMITH, B. (1977). The development of structural complexity in children's fantasy narratives. *Developmental Psychology, 13,* 377–388.

BOWERMAN, M. (1973). Structural relationships in children's utterances: Syntactic or semantic? In T. E. Moore (Ed.), *Cognitive development and the acquisition of language* (pp. 197–214). New York: Academic Press.

BOWERMAN, M. (1976). Semantic factors in the acquisition of rules for word use and sentence construction. In D. M. Morehead & A. E. Morehead (Eds.), *Normal and deficient child language.* Baltimore, MD: University Park Press.

BOWERMAN, M. (1978). The acquisition of word meaning: An investigation into some current conflicts. In N. Waterson & C. Snow (Eds.), *The development of communication* (pp. 263–287). Chichester, England: Wiley.

BOWERMAN, M. (1979). The acquisition of complex sentences. In P. Fletcher & M. Garman (Eds.), *Language acquisition* (pp. 285–306). Cambridge, England: Cambridge University Press.

BOWERMAN, M. (1985). Beyond communicative adequacy: From piecemeal knowledge to an integrated system in the child's acquisition of language. In K.E. Nelson (Ed.), *Children's language* (Vol. 5, pp. 369–398). Hillsdale, NJ: Erlbaum.

BOWERMAN, M. (1988). The "no negative evidence" problem: How do children avoid constructing an overly general grammar? In V.A. Hawkins (Ed.), *Explaining language universals.* Oxford: Blackwell.

BOWERMAN, M. (1990). Mapping thematic roles onto syntactic functions: Are children helped by innate linking rules? *Linguistics, 28,* 1253–1289.

BOWERMAN, M. & CHOI, S. (2001). Saping meanings for language: universal and language-specific in the acquisition of spatial semantic categories. In M. Bowerman & S. C. Levinson (Eds.), *Language acquisition and conceptual development* (pp. 475–511). Cambridge: Cambridge University Press.

BRADSHAW, G. (1993). Beyond animal language. In H. L. Roitblat, L. M. Herman, & P. E. Nachtigall (Eds.), *Language and communication: Comparative perspectives* (pp. 25–44). Hillsdale, NJ: Erlbaum.

BRAINE, M. D. S. (1963). The ontogeny of English phrase structure: The first phase. *Language, 39,* 1–14.

BRAINE, M. D. S. (1976). Children's first word combinations. *Monographs of the Society for Research in Child Development, 41* (1, Serial No. 164).

BRAINE, M. D. S. (1988). Modeling the acquisition of linguistic structure. In Y. Levy, I. M. Schlesinger, & M. D. S. Braine (Eds.), *Categories and processes in language acquisition* (pp. 217–259). Hillsdale, NJ: Erlbaum.

BRAINE, M. D. S. (1992). What sort of innate structure is needed to "bootstrap" into syntax? *Cognition, 45,* 77–100.

BRAINE, M. D. S. (1994). Is nativism sufficient? *Journal of Child Language, 21,* 9–32.

BRETHERTON, I., MCNEW, S., SNYDER, L., & BATES, E. (1983). Individual differences at 20 months: Analytic and holistic strategies in language acquisition. *Journal of Child Language, 10,* 293–320.

BRINTON, B., FUJIKI, M., LOAB, D., & WINKLER, E. (1986). Development of conversational repair strategies in response to requests for clarification. *Journal of Speech and Hearing Research, 29,* 75–81.

BRITTO, P. R. & BROOKS-GUNN, J. (2001). The role of family literacy environments in promoting young children's emerging literacy skills. *New directions for child and adolescent development, 104.* San Francisco: Jossey-Bass.

BROOKS-GUNN, J., & MATTHEWS, W. S. (1979). *He and she: How children develop their sex–role identity.* Englewood Cliffs, NJ: Prentice-Hall.

BROWN, P. (2001). Learning to talk about motion Up and DOWN in Tzeltal: is there a language specific-bias for verb learning? In M. Bowerman & S. Levinson (Eds.), *Language acquisition and conceptual development.* (pp. 512–543). Cambridge: Cambridge University Press.

BROWN, R. (1957). Linguistic determinism and the part of speech. *Journal of Abnormal and Social Psychology, 55,* 1–5.

BROWN, R. (1958a). How shall a thing be called? *Psychological Review, 65,* 14–21.

BROWN, R. (1958b). *Words and things.* New York: Free Press.

BROWN, R. (1973). *A first language: The early stages.* Cambridge, MA: Harvard University Press.

BROWN, R. (1980). The maintenance of conversation. In D. R. Olson (Ed.), *The social foundations of language and thought* (pp. 187–210). New York: Norton.

BROWN, R., & FRASER, C. (1963). The acquisition of syntax. In C. N. Cofer & B. S. Musgrave (Eds.), *Verbal behavior and learning* (pp. 158–196). New York: McGraw-Hill.

BRUNER, J. (1977). Early social interaction and language acquisition. In H. R. Schaffer (Ed.), *Studies in mother-infant interaction* (pp. 271–289). London: Academic Press.

BRUNER, J. (1986). *Actual minds, possible worlds.* Cambridge, MA: Harvard University Press.

BRYANT, P. E., BRADLEY, L., MACLEAN, M., & CROSSLAND, J. (1989). Nursery rhymes, phonological skills and reading. *Journal of Child Language, 16,* 407–428.

BRYANT, P. E., MACLEAN, M., BRADLEY, L. L., & CROSSLAND, J. (1990). Rhyme and alliteration, phoneme detection, and learning to read. *Developmental Psychology, 26,* 429–428.

BRYDEN, M. P., & ALLARD, F. (1978). Dichotic listening and the development of linguistic processes. In M. Kinsbourne (Ed.), *Asymmetrical function of the brain* (pp. 392–404). Cambridge, England: Cambridge University Press.

BRYDEN, M. P., HECAEN, H., & DEAGOSTINI, M. (1983). Patterns of cerebral organization. *Brain and Language, 20,* 249–262.

BUDWIG, N. (1991). Introduction (to special issue on functional approaches to child language). *First Language, 11,* 1–5.

BUDWIG, N. (1995). *A developmental-functionalist approach to child language.* Mahwah, NJ: Erlbaum.

BUDWIG, N. (2001). An exploration into children's use of passives. In M. Tomasello & E. Bates (Eds.), Language development: The es-

sential readings (pp. 227–247). Oxford: Blackwell Publishing.

BULLOCK, D., LIEDERMAN, J., & TODOROVIC, D. (1987). Commentary—Reconciling stable asymmetry with recovery of function: An adaptive systems perspective on functional plasticity. *Child Development, 58,* 689–697.

BURGESS, C. A., KIRSCH, I., SHANE, H., NIEDERAUER, K. L., GRAHAM, S. M., & BACON, A. (1998). Facilitated communication as an ideomotor response. *Psychological Science, 9,* 71–74.

BURLING, R. (1959). Language development of a Garo- and English-speaking child. *Word, 15,* 48–68.

BUS, A. G., VAN IJZENDOORN, M. H., & PELLEGRINI, A. D. (1995). Joint book reading makes for success in learning to read: A meta-analysis on intergenerational transmission of literacy. *Review of Educational Research, 65,* 1–21.

BUS, A. G., & VAN IJZENDOORN, M. H. (1999). Phonological awareness and early reading: A meta-analysis of experimental training studies. *Journal of Education Psychology, 91,* 403–414.

BUTLER, S. (1980). The tum phenomenon. *Journal of Child Language, 7,* 428–429. (Original work published 1920.)

CAMAIONI, L. (1993). The development of intentional communication: A reanalysis. In J. Nadel & L. Camaioni (Eds.), *New perspectives in early communicative development* (pp. 82–96). London: Routledge.

CAMAIONI. L. & PERUCCHINI, P. (2003). Profiles in declarative/imperative pointing and early word production. Paper presented at the European Conference for Developmental Psychology, Milan, Italy.

CAMPBELL, T. F., COLLAGHAN, C. A., ROCKETTE, H. E., PARADISE, J. L., FELDMAN, HE. M., SHRIBERG, L. D., SABO, D. L., & KURS-LASKY, M. (2003). Risk factors for speech delay of unknown origin in 3-year-old children. *Child Development, 74,* 346–357.

CAPLAN, D. (1987). *Neurolinguistics and linguistic aphasiology: An introduction.* Cambridge, England: Cambridge University Press.

CAREY, S. (1978). The child as a word learner. In M. Halle, J. Bresnan, & G. A. Miller (Eds.), *Linguistic theory and psychological reality* (pp. 264–293). Cambridge, MA: MIT Press.

CAREY, S. (1994). Does learning a language require the child to reconceptualize the world? In L. Gleitman & B. Landau (Eds.), *The acquisition of the lexicon* (pp. 143–168). Cambridge, MA: Elsevier/MIT Press.

CARPENTER, M., NAGELL, K., & TOMASELLO, M. (1998). Social cognition, joint attention, and communicative competence from 9 to 15 months of age. *Monographs of the Society for Research in Child Development, 63* (4, Serial No. 255).

CARREL, R. E. (1977). Epidemiology of hearing loss. In S. E. Gerber (Ed.), *Audiometry in infancy* (pp. 3–16). New York: Gruene & Stratten.

CARTER, A. (1978). The development of systematic vocalizations prior to words: A case study. In N. Waterson & C. E. Snow (Eds.), *The development of communication* (pp. 127–138). Chichester, England: Wiley.

CASBY, M. W. (2001). Otitis media and language development: A meta-analysis. *American Journal of Speech-Language Pathology, 10*, 65–80.

CASELLI, M. C., BATES, E., CASADIO, P., FENSON, J., FENSON, L., SANDERS, L., & WEIR, J. (1995). A cross–linguistic study of early lexical development. *Cognitive Development, 10,* 159–199.

CATTS, H. W., FEY, M., ZHANG, X., & TOMBLIN, J. B. (1999). Language basis of reading and reading disabilities: Evidence from a longitudinal study. *Scientific Studies of Reading, 3,* 331–361.

CHAIKA, E. (1989). *Language: The social mirror* (2nd ed.). Cambridge, MA: Newbury House.

CHALL, J. S. (1996). *Learning to read: The great debate* (3rd ed.). Fort Worth, TX: Harcourt Brace.

CHALL, J. S., JACOBS, V. A., & BALDWIN, L. E. (1990). *The reading crisis: Why poor children fall behind.* Cambridge, MA: Harvard University Press.

CHANDLER, J., ARGYRIS, D., BARNES, W. S., GOODMAN, I. F., & SNOW, C. E. (1986). Parents as teachers: Observations of low-income parents and children in a homework-like task. In B. B. Schieffelin & P. Gilmore (Eds.), *The acquisition of literacy: Ethnographic perspectives* (pp. 171–187). Norwood, NJ: Ablex.

CHAPMAN, R. S. (1978). Comprehension strategies in children. In J. F. Kavanaugh & W. Strange (Eds.), *Speech and language in the laboratory, school, and clinic* (pp. 308–327). Cambridge, MA: MIT Press.

CHAPMAN, R. S. (1981). Exploring children's communicative intents. In J. F. Miller (Ed.), *Assessing language production in children* (pp. 111–136). Austin, TX: Pro-Ed.

CHAPMAN, R. S. (1995). Language development in children and adolescents with Down syndrome. In P. Fletcher & B. MacWhinney (Eds.), *The handbook of child language* (pp. 641–663). Oxford: Blackwell.

CHAPMAN, R. S., & THOMPSON, J. (1980). What is the source of overextension errors in comprehension testing of two-year-olds? A response to Fregmen and Fay. *Journal of Child Language, 7,* 575–578.

CHARLES-LUCE, J. & LUCE, P. A. (1990). Similarity neighborhoods of words in young children's lexicons. *Journal of Child Language, 17,* 205–215.

CHENEY, D. L. (1995). Sociality without frills. *Science, 267,* 909–910.

CHERRY, L., & LEWIS, M. (1978). Differential socialization of girls and boys: Implications for sex differences in language development. In N. Waterson & C. Snow (Eds.), *The development of communication* (pp. 189–197). New York: Wiley.

CHOI, S. (1991). Early acquisition of epistemic meanings. *First Language, 11,* 93–120.

CHOI, S., & BOWERMAN, M. (1991). Learning to express motion events in English and Korean: The influence of language-specific lexicalization patterns. *Cognition, 41,* 83–121.

CHOMSKY, C. (1969). *The acquisition of syntax in children from 5 to 10.* Cambridge, MA: MIT Press.

CHOMSKY, N. (1959). A review of B. F. Skinner's Verbal Behavior. *Language, 35,* 26–58.

CHOMSKY, N. (1965). *Aspects of the theory of syntax.* Cambridge, MA: MIT Press.

CHOMSKY, N. (1981). *Lectures on government and binding.* Dordrecht, The Netherlands: Foris.

CHOMSKY, N. (1982). Discussion of Putnam's comments. In M. Piattelli-Palamarini (Ed.), *Language and learning: The debate between Jean Piaget and Noam Chomsky* (pp. 310–324). Cambridge, MA: Harvard University Press.

CHOMSKY, N. (1991). Linguistics and cognitive science: Problems and mysteries. In A. Kasher (Ed.), *The Chomskyan turn* (pp. 26–53). Cambridge, MA: Blackwell.

CHOMSKY, N. (1993). On the nature, use, and acquisition of language. In A. I. Goldman (Ed.), *Readings in philosophy and cognitive science* (Vol. C., pp. 511–534). Cambridge, MA: MIT Press. (Original work published 1987.)

CHOUINARD, M. M. & CLARK, E. V. (2003). Adult reformulations of child errors as negative evidence. *Journal of Child Language, 30,* 637–670.

CHUKOVSKY, K. (1963). *From two to five.* Berkeley, CA: University of California Press.

CLAHSEN, H. (1999). Linguistic perspectives on specific language impairment. In W. C. Ritchie & T. K. Bhatia (Eds.), *Handbook of child language acquisition* (pp. 675–704). New York: Academic Press.

CLANCY, P. (1985). The acquisition of Japanese. In D. I. Slobin (Ed.), *The crosslinguistic study of language acquisition* (pp. 373–524). Hillsdale, NJ: Erlbaum.

CLANCY, P. (1986). The acquisition of communicative style in Japanese. In B. B. Schieffelin & E. Ochs (Eds.), *Language socialization across cultures* (pp. 213–250). Cambridge, England: Cambridge University Press.

CLARK, E. V. (1973). What's in a word? On the child's acquisition of semantics in his first language. In T. E. Moore (Ed.), *Cognitive development and the acquisition of language* (pp. 65–110). New York: Academic Press.

CLARK, E. V. (1979). Building a vocabulary: Words for objects, actions, and relations. In P. Fletcher & M. Garman (Eds.), *Language acquisition* (pp. 149–160). Cambridge, England: Cambridge University Press.

CLARK, E. V. (1993). *The lexicon in acquisition.* Cambridge, England: Cambridge University Press.

CLARK, E. V. (1995). Later lexical development and word formation. In P. Fletcher & B. MacWhinney (Eds.), *The handbook of child language* (pp. 393–412). Oxford: Blackwell.

CLARK, E. V., & HECHT, B. F. (1982). Learning to coin agent and instrument nouns. *Cognition, 12,* 1–24.

COADY, J. A. & ASLIN, R. N. Phonological neighborhoods in the developing lexicon. *Journal of Child Language, 30,* 441–470.

COMEAU, L., & GENESEE, F. (2001). Bilingual children's repair strategies during dyadic communication. In J. Cenoz & F. Genesee (Eds.), *Trends in bilingual acquisition* (pp. 231–256). Amsterdam: John Benjamins Publishing Company.

CONNOR, C. M., MORRISON, F. J., & KATCH, L. E. (in press). Beyond the reading wars: Exploring the effect of child-instruction interactions on growth in early reading. *Scientific Studies of Reading.*

CONTI-RAMSDEN, G. (2003). Processing and linguistic markers in young children with specific language impairment (SLI). *Journal of Speech, Language, and Hearing Research, 46,* 1029–1037.

COOPER, R. P., & ASLIN, R. N. (1990). Preference for infant-directed speech in the first month after birth. *Child Development, 61,* 1584–1595.

COOPER, R. P., & ASLIN, R. N. (1994). Developmental differences in infant attention to the spectral properties of infant-directed speech. *Child Development, 65,* 1663–1677.

COPPIETERS, R. (1987). Competence differences between native and nonnative speakers. *Language, 63,* 544–573.

CORBALLIS, M. C. (1992). On the evolution of language and generativity. *Cognition, 44,* 197–226.

CORNE, C. (1984). On the transmission of substratal features in creolisation. *Behavioral and Brain Sciences, 7,* 191–192.

CORRIGAN, R. (1979). Cognitive correlates of language: Differential criteria yield differential results. *Child Development, 50,* 617–631.

COSMIDES, L. (1989). The logic of social exchange: Has natural selection shaped how humans reason? Studies with the Wason selection task. *Cognition, 31,* 187–276.

COSMIDES, L., & TOOBY, J. (1994). Origins of domain specificity: The evolution of functional organization. In L. A. Hirschfeld & S. A. Gelman (Eds.), *Mapping the mind: Domain specificity in cognition and culture* (pp. 85–116). Cambridge, England: Cambridge University Press.

CRAGO, M. B., & ALLEN, S. E. M. (1994). Morphemes gone askew: Linguistic impairment in Inuktitut. *McGill Working Papers in Linguistics, 10* (Nos. 1 & 2).

CRAGO, M. B., ALLEN, S. E. M., HOUGH-EYAMIE, W. P. (1997). Exploring innateness through cultural and linguistic variation: An Inuit example. In M. Gopnik (Ed.), *The biological basis of language* (pp. 70–90). Oxford: Oxford University Press.

CRAGO, M. B., ERIKS-BROPHY, A., PESCO, D., & MCALPINE, L. (1997). Culturally based miscommunication in classroom interaction. *Language, Speech, and Hearing Services in Schools, 28,* 245–254.

CROMER, R. F. (1994). A case study of dissociations between language and cognition. In H. Tager-Flusberg (Ed.), *Constraints on language acquisition: Studies of atypical children* (pp. 141–153). Hillsdale, NJ: Erlbaum.

CRYSTAL, D. (1986). Prosodic development. In P. Fletcher & M. Garman (Eds.), *Language acquisition* (2nd ed., pp. 174–197). Cambridge, England: Cambridge University Press.

CRYSTAL, D. (1995). The Cambridge encyclopedia of the English language. Cambridge: Cambridge University Press.

CUMMINS, J. (2000). Language, power, and pedagogy: Bilingual children in the crossfire. Clevedon, England: Multilingual Matters.

CUMMINS, J., & CORSON, D. (Eds.). (1997). *Encyclopedia of language and education: Vol 5. Bilingual education.* Dordrecht, The Netherlands: Kluwer Academic Publishers.

CUNNINGHAM, A. E., & STANOVICH, K. E. (1991). Tracking the unique effects of print exposure in children: Associations with vocabulary, general knowledge, and spelling. *Journal of Educational Psychology, 83,* 264–274.

CURTISS, S. (1977). *Genie: A psycholinguistic study of a modern day "wild child."* New York: Academic Press.

CURTISS, S. (1985). The development of human cerebral lateralization. In D. F. Benson & E. Zaidel (Eds.), *The dual brain: Hemispheric specialization in humans* (pp. 97–116). New York: Guilford Press.

CURTISS, S. (1988). Abnormal language acquisition and the modularity of language. In F. Newmeyer (Ed.), *Linguistics: The Cambridge survey: Vol. II. Linguistic theory: Extensions and implications* (pp. 96–116). Cambridge, England: Cambridge University Press.

CURTISS, S. (1989). The independence and task-specificity of language. In M. H. Bornstein & J. S. Bruner (Eds.), *Interaction in human development* (pp. 105–138). Hillsdale, NJ: Erlbaum.

CUTLER, A. (1994). Segmentation problems, rhythmic solutions. In L. Gleitman & B. Landau (Eds.), *The acquisition of the lexicon* (pp. 81–104). Cambridge, MA: Elsevier/MIT Press.

CUTLER, A. (1996). Prosody and the word boundary problem. In J. L. Morgan & K. Demuth (Eds.), *Signal to syntax: Bootstrapping from speech to grammar in early acquisition* (pp. 87–100). Mahwah, NJ: Erlbaum.

CUTLER, A., MEHLER, J. NORRIS, D., & SEGUI, J. (1992). The monolingual nature of speech segmentation by bilinguals. *Cognitive Psychology, 24,* 381–410.

DALE, P. S., DIONNE, G., ELEY, T. C., & PLOMIN, R. (2003). Lexical and grammatical development: a behavioral genetic perspective. *Journal of Child Language, 27,* 619–642.

DAMASIO, A. R. (1988). Concluding remarks: Neuroscience and cognitive science in the study of language and the brain. In F. Plum (Ed.), *Language, communication, and the brain* (pp. 275–282). New York: Raven.

DARWIN, C. (1877). A bibliographical sketch of an infant. *Mind, 2,* 285–294.

DAUGHERTY, K. G., & SEIDENBERG, M. S. (1994). Beyond rules and exceptions: A connectionist approach to inflectional morphology. In S. Lima, R. Corrigan, & G. Iverson (Eds.), *The reality of linguistic rules* (pp. 353–388). Philadelphia: Benjamins.

DE BOYSSON-BARDIES, B., HALLE, P., SAGART, L., & DURAND, C. (1989). A crosslinguistic investigation of vowel formants in babbling. *Journal of Child Language, 16,* 1–17.

DE BOYSSON-BARDIES, B., SAGART, L., & DURAND, C. (1984). Discernable differences in the babbling of infants according to target language. *Journal of Child Language, 8,* 511–524.

DE BOYSSON-BARDIES, B., VIHMAN, M., ROUG-HELLICHIUS, L., DURAND, C., LANDBERG, I., & ARAO, F. (1992). Material evidence of infant selection from target language: A crosslinguistic study. In C. A. Ferguson, L. Menn, & C. Stoel-Gammon (Eds.), *Phonological development* (pp. 369–391). Timonium, MD: York Press.

DECASPER, A. J., & FIFER, W. P. (1980). Of human bonding: Newborns prefer their mothers' voices. *Science, 208,* 1174–1176.

DECASPER, A. J., & SPENCE, M. J. (1986). Prenatal maternal speech influences newborns' perception of speech sounds. *Infant Behavior and Development, 9,* 133–150.

DE HOUWER, A. (1995). Bilingual language acquisition. In P. Fletcher & B. MacWhinney (Eds.), *The handbook of child language* (pp. 219–250). Oxford: Blackwell.

DEMETRAS, M. J., POST, K. N., & SNOW, C. E. (1986). Feedback to first language learners: The role of repetitions and clarification questions. *Journal of Child Language, 13,* 275–292.

DEMUTH, K. (1993). Issues in the acquisition of the Sesotho tonal system. *Journal of Child Language, 20,* 275–302.

DEMUTH, K. (1994). On the underspecification of functional categories in early grammars. In B. Lust, M. Suñer, & J. Whitman (Eds.), *Syntactic theory and first language acquisition: Crosslinguistic perspectives* (pp. 119–134). Hillsdale, NJ: Erlbaum.

DEMUTH, K. (1996). The prosodic structure of early words. In J. L. Morgan & K. Demuth (Eds.), *Signal to syntax: Bootstrapping from speech to grammar in early acquisition* (pp. 171–186). Hillsdale, NJ: Erlbaum.

DENNIS, M. (1980). Capacity and strategy for syntactic comprehension after left and right hemidecortication. *Brain and Language, 7,* 153–169.

DERWING, B. L. (1976). Morpheme recognition and the learning of rules for derivational morphology. *The Canadian Journal of Linguistics, 21,* 38–66.

DERWING, B. L., & BAKER, W. J. (1979). Research on the acquisition of English morphology. In P. Fletcher & M. Garman (Eds.), *Language acquisition* (pp. 209–223). Cambridge, England: Cambridge University Press.

DERWING, B. L., & BAKER, W. J. (1986). Assessing morphological development. In P. Fletcher & M. Garman (Eds.), *Language acquisition* (2nd ed., pp. 326–338). Cambridge, England: Cambridge University Press.

DESCARTES, R. (1911). *Trait de l'homme.* (E. S. Haldane & G. R. T. Ross, Trans.). Cambridge, England: Cambridge University Press. (Original work published 1662.)

DEUCHAR, M. (1989). ESRC report on project "Infant bilingualism: one system or two?" Unpublished manuscript. (Cited in A. De Houwer, 1995, Bilingual language acquisition. In P. Fletcher & B. MacWhinney (Eds.), *The handbook of child language* (pp. 219–250). Oxford, UK: Basil Blackwell, Ltd.

DEUCHAR, M., & QUAY, S. (1999). Language choice in the earliest utterances: a case study with methodological implications. *Journal of Child Language, 26,* 461–476.

DE VILLIERS, J. (1995a). Questioning minds and answering machines. In D. MacLaughlin & S. McEwen (Eds.), *Proceedings of the 19th Annual Boston University Conference on Language Development* (pp. 20–36). Somerville, MA: Cascadilla Press.

DE VILLIERS, J. (1995b). Empty categories and complex sentences: The case of wh- questions. In P. Fletcher & B. MacWhinney (Eds.), *The handbook of child language* (pp. 508–540). Oxford: Blackwell.

DE VILLIERS, J. G., & DE VILLIERS, P. A. (1973). A cross-sectional study of the acquisition of grammatical morphemes in child speech. *Journal of Psycholinguistic Research, 2,* 267–278.

DE VILLIERS, J. G., & DE VILLIERS, P. A. (1978). *Language acquisition.* Cambridge, MA: Harvard University Press.

DE VILLIERS, J., DE VILLIERS, P., & HOBAN, E. (1994). The central problem of functional categories in the English syntax of oral deaf children. In H. Tager-Flusberg (Ed.), *Constraints on language acquisition: Studies of atypical children* (pp. 9–48). Hillsdale, NJ: Erlbaum.

DE VILLIERS, J., & ROEPER, T. (1995). Relative clauses are barriers to wh-movement for young children. *Journal of Child Language, 22,* 389–405.

DEWS, S., WINNER, E., KAPLAN, J., ROSENBLATT, E., HUNT, M., LIM, A., MCGOVERN, A., QUALTER, A., & SMARSH, B. (1996). Children's understanding of the meaning and functions of verbal irony. *Journal of child development. 67,* 3071–3085.

DIAZ, R. M. (1983). Thought and two languages: The impact of bilingualism on cognitive development. *Review of Research in Education, 10,* 23–54.

DICKINSON, D. K., & TABORS, P. O. (Eds.). (2001). *Beginning literacy with language: Young children learning at home and in school.* Baltimore, MD: Paul H. Brookes Publishing Co.

DIESENDRUCK, G. & MARKSON, L. (2001). Children's avoidance of lexical overlap: A pragmatic account. *Developmental Psychology, 37,* 630–641.

DIXON, W. E., JR., & SMITH, P. H. (2000). Links between early temperament and language acquisition. *Merrill-Palmer Quarterly, 46,* 417–440.

DODD, B. (1987). Lip-reading, phonological coding and deafness. In B. Dodd & R. Campbell (Eds.), *Hearing by eye: The psychology of lip-reading* (pp. 177–190). London: Erlbaum.

DOLLAGHAN, C. (1985). Child meets word: "Fast mapping" in preschool children. *Journal of Speech and Hearing Research, 28,* 449–454.

DOLNICK, E. (1993). Deafness as culture. *The Atlantic Monthly, 272,* 37–53.

DONEGAN, P. J., & STAMPE, D. (1979). The study of natural phonology. In D. A. Dinnsen (Ed.), *Current approaches to phonological theory* (pp. 126–173). Bloomington: Indiana University Press.

DORE, J. (1975). Holophrases, speech acts, and language universals. *Journal of Child Language, 2,* 20–40.

DORE, J. (1977). "Oh them sheriff": A pragmatic analysis of children's responses to questions. In S. Ervin-Tripp & C. Mitchell-Kernan (Eds.), *Child Discourse* (pp. 139–164). New York: Academic Press.

DORE, J., FRANKLIN, M. B., MILLER, R., & RAMER, A. L. H. (1976). Transitional phenomena in early language acquisition. *Journal of Child Language, 3,* 13–28.

DORVAL, B., & ECKERMAN, C. O. (1984). Developmental trends in the quality of conversation achieved by small groups of acquainted peers. *Monographs of the Society for Research in Child Development, 49* (Serial No. 206).

DRESHER, B. E. (1996). Introduction to metrical and prosodic phonology. In J. L. Morgan & K. Demuth (Eds.), *Signal to syntax: Bootstrapping from speech to grammar in early acquisition* (pp. 41–54). Hillsdale, NJ: Erlbaum.

DROMI, E. (1987). *Early lexical development.* Cambridge, England: Cambridge University Press.

DUNLEA, A. (1984). The relationship between concept formation and semantic roles: Some evidence from the blind. In L. Feagans, C. Garvey, & R. Golinkoff (Eds.), *The origins and growth of communication* (pp. 224–243). Norwood, NJ: Ablex.

DUNLEA, A. (1989). *Vision and the emergence of meaning: Blind and sighted children's early language.* New York: Cambridge University Press.

DUNN, J., & KENDRICK, C. (1982). The speech of two- and three-year-olds to infant siblings: "Baby talk" and the context of communication. *Journal of Child Language, 9,* 579–595.

DUNN, J., & SHATZ, M. (1989). Becoming a conversationalist despite (or because of) having an older sibling. *Child Development, 60,* 399–410.

ECHOLS, C. H. (1996). A role for stress in early speech segmentat on. In J. L. Morgan & K.

Demuth (Eds.), *Signal to syntax: Bootstrapping from speech to grammar in early acquisition* (pp. 151–170). Mahwah, NJ: Erlbaum.

ECHOLS, C. H., & NEWPORT, E. L. (1992). The role of stress and position in determining first words. *Language Acquisition, 2,* 189–220.

ECKERT, P. (1988). Adolescent social structure and the spread of linguistic change. *Language in Society, 17,* 183–207.

EDER, D., & HALLINAN, M. T. (1978). Sex differences in children's friendships. *American Sociological Review, 43,* 237–250.

EHRI, L. C., NUNES, S. R., WILLOWS, D. M., VALESKA SCHUSTER, B., YAGHOUB-ZADEH, A., & SHANAHAN, T., (2001). Phonemic awareness instruction helps children learn to read: Evidence from the National Reading Panel's meta-analysis. *Reading Research Quarterly, 36,* 250–283.

EILERS, R. E., & OLLER, D. K. (1976). The role of speech discrimination in developmental sound substitutions. *Journal of Child Language, 3,* 319–330.

EILERS, R. E., & OLLER, D. K. (1976). The role of speech discrimination in developmental sound substitutions. *Journal of Child Language, 3,* 319–329.

EIMAS, P. D., SIQUELAND, E. R., JUSCZYK, P., & VIGORITO, J. (1971). Speech perception in infants. *Science, 171,* 303–306.

EISENBERG, A. (1985). Learning to describe past experiences in conversation. *Discourse Processes, 8,* 177–204.

EISENBERG, A. (1986). Teasing: Verbal play in two Mexicano homes. In B. B. Schieffelin & E. Ochs (Eds.), *Language socialization across cultures* (pp. 182–198). Cambridge, England: Cambridge University Press.

ELDREDGE, N. (1995). *Reinventing Darwin: The great debate at the high table of evolutionary theory.* New York: Wiley.

ELEY, T. C., BISHOP, D. V. M., DALE, P. S., OLIVER, B., PETRILL, S. A., PRICE, T. S., PURCELL, S., SAUDINO, K. J., SIMONOFF, E., STEVENSON, J., & PLOMIN, R. (1999). Genetic and environmental origins of verbal and performance

components of cognitive delay in 2-year-olds. *Developmental Psychology, 35,* 1122–1131.

ELMAN, J. L. (1993). Learning and development in neural networks: The importance of starting small. *Cognition, 48,* 71–99.

ELMAN, J. L., BATES, E. A., JOHNSON, M. H., KARMILOFF-SMITH, A., PARISI, D., & PLUNKETT, K. (1996). *Rethinking innateness: A connectionist perspective on development.* Cambridge, MA: MIT Press.

ELMAN, J. L., (2001). Connectionism and language acquisition. In M. Tomasello & E. Bates (Eds.), *Language development: The essential readings* (pp. 295–306). Oxford: Blackwell.

ELY, R., & GLEASON, J. B. (1995). Socialization across contexts. In P. Fletcher & B. MacWhinney (Eds.), *The handbook of child language* (pp. 251–270). Oxford: Blackwell.

ELY, R., & MCCABE, A. (1994). The language play of kindergarten children. *First Language, 14,* 19–36.

ERVIN-TRIPP, S. (1976). Is Sybil there? The structure of some American English directives. *Language in Society, 5,* 25–66.

ERVIN-TRIPP, S. (1977). Wait for me roller skate. In S. Ervin-Tripp & C. Mitchell-Kernan (Eds.), *Child discourse* (pp. 165–188). New York: Academic Press.

ESPOSITO, A. (1979). Sex differences in children's conversations. *Language and Speech, 22,* 213–220.

FALTIS, C. (1997). Bilingual education in the United States. In J. Cummins & D. Corson (Eds.), *Encyclopedia of language and education: Vol. 5. Bilingual education* (pp. 189–198). Dordrecht, The Netherlands: Kluwer Academic Publishers.

FAY, W. H. (1993). Infantile autism. In D. Bishop & K. Mogford (Eds.), *Language development in exceptional circumstances* (pp. 190–202). Hillsdale, NJ: Erlbaum.

FELDMAN, H. H., GOLDIN-MEADOW, S., & GLEITMAN, L. R. (1978). Beyond Herodotus: The creation of language by linguistically deprived deaf children. In A. Locke (Ed.), *Action, gesture, and symbol: The emergence of language* (pp. 351–414). London: Academic Press.

FELDMAN, H. H., HOLLAND, A. L., KEMP. S. S., & JANOSKY, J. E. (1992). Language development after unilateral brain injury. *Brain and Language, 42,* 89–102.

FENSON, L., DALE, P. S., REZNICK, J. S., BATES, E., THAL, D. J., & PETHICK, S. J. (1994). Variability in early communicative development. *Monographs of the Society for Research in Child Development, 59* (Serial No. 242).

FERGUSON, C. A., & FARWELL, C. B. (1975). Words and sounds in early language acquisition. *Language, 51,* 439–491.

FERNALD, A. (1985). Four-month-old infants prefer to listen to motherese. *Infant Behavior and Development, 8,* 181–195.

FERNALD, A. (1989). Intonation and communicative intent in mothers' speech to infants: Is the melody the message? *Child Development, 60,* 1497–1510.

FERNALD, A. (1992). Human maternal vocalizations to infants as biologically relevant signals: An evolutionary perspective. In J. H. Barkow, L. Cosmides, & J. Tooby (Eds.), *The adapted mind: Evolutionary psychology and the generation of culture* (pp. 391–428). New York: Oxford University Press.

FERNALD, A., & KUHL, P. K. (1987). Acoustic determinants of infant preference for motherese speech. *Infant Behavior and Development, 10,* 279–293.

FERNALD, A., & MCROBERTS, G. (1995). Infants' developing sensitivity to language-typical word order patterns. Paper presented at the 20th Annual Boston University Conference on Child Language Development, Boston, MA.

FERNALD, A., & MCROBERTS, G. (1996). Prosodic bootstrapping: A critical analysis of the argument and the evidence. In J. L. Morgan & K. Demuth (Eds.), *Signal to syntax: Bootstrapping from speech to grammar in early acquisition* (pp. 249–262). Mahwah, NJ: Erlbaum.

FERNALD, A., & MORIKAWA, H. (1993). Common themes and cultural variations in Japanese and American mothers' speech to infants. *Child Development, 64,* 637–656.

FERNALD, A., & SIMON, T. (1984). Expanded intonation contours in mothers' speech to newborns. *Developmental Psychology, 20,* 104–113.

FERNALD, A., TAESCHNER, T., DUN, J., PAPOUSEK, M., DE BOYSSON-BARDIES, B., & FUKUI, I. (1989). A cross-language study of prosodic modifications in mothers' and fathers' speech to preverbal infants. *Journal of Child Language, 16,* 477–501.

FERREIRA, F., & MORRISON, F. J. (1994). Children's knowledge of syntactic constituents: Effects of age and schooling. *Developmental Psychology.* 30, 663–678.

FERRIER, L. J. (1978). Some observations of error in context. In N. Waterson & C. Snow (Eds.), *The development of communication* (pp. 301–309). Chichester, England: Wiley.

FEY, M., & GANDOUR, J. (1982). Rule discovery in early phonology acquisition. *Journal of Child Language, 9,* 71–82.

FILLMORE, C. J. (1997). A linguist looks at the Ebonics debate. Center for Applied Linguistics website. www.cal.org/ebonics/ebfillmo.html. Retrieved 3/12/2003.

FISHER, C., HALL, D. G., RAKOWITZ, S., & GLEITMAN, L. (1994). When it is better to receive than to give: Syntactic and conceptual constraints on vocabulary growth. In L. Gleitman & B. Landau (Eds.), *The acquisition of the lexicon* (pp. 333–376). Cambridge, MA: MIT Press/Elsevier.

FISHMAN, P. M. (1978). Interaction: The work women do. *Social Problems, 25,* 397–406.

FIVUSH, R. (1991). The social construction of personal narratives. *Merrill-Palmer Quarterly, 37,* 59–81.

FLAVELL, J. H., SPEER, J. R., GREEN, F. L., & AUGUST, D. L. (1981). The development of comprehension monitoring and knowledge about communication. *Monographs of the Society for Research in Child Development, 46* (Serial No. 5).

FLEGE, J. E. (1987). A critical period for learning to pronounce foreign languages? *Applied Linguistics, 8,* 162–177.

FLEGE, J. E. (1995). Second language speech learning: Theory, findings and problems. In W. Strange (Ed.), *Speech perception and linguistic experience: Issues in cross-language research* (pp. 233–277). Baltimore: York Press.

FLEGE, J. E., & FLETCHER, K. L. (1992). At what age of learning (AOL) do foreign accents first become perceptible? *Journal of the Acoustical Society of America, 91,* 370–389.

FODOR, J. (1997). Do we have it in us? (Review of Elman et al., *Rethinking innateness*). *Times Literary Supplement,* May 16, pp. 3–4.

FODOR, J. A. (1983). *The modularity of mind.* Cambridge, MA: MIT Press.

FODOR, J. A., & PYLYSHYN, Z. (1988). Connectionism and cognitive architecture: A critical analysis. *Cognition, 28,* 3–71.

FOLEY, W., & VAN VALIN, R. (1984). *Functional syntax and universal grammar.* Cambridge, England: Cambridge University Press.

FOLVEN, R. J., & BONVILLIAN, J. D. (1991). The transition from nonreferential to referential language in children acquiring American Sign Language. *Developmental Psychology, 27,* 806–816.

FOSTER, S. H. (1986). Learning discourse topic management in the preschool years. *Journal of Child Language, 13,* 231–250.

FOWLER, A. E. (1988). Determinants of rate of language growth in children with Down syndrome. In L. Nadel (Ed.), *The psychobiology of Down syndrome.* Cambridge, MA: MIT Press.

FOWLER, A. E., GELMAN, R., & GLEITMAN, L. R. (1994). The course of language learning in children with Down syndrome: Longitudinal and language level comparisons with young normally developing children. In H. Tager-Flusberg (Ed.), *Constraints on language acquisition: Studies of atypical children* (pp. 91–140). Hillsdale, NJ: Erlbaum.

FOWLES, B., & GLANZ, M. E. (1977). Competence and talent in verbal riddle comprehension. *Journal of Child Language, 4,* 433–452.

FOY, J. G., & MANN, V. (2001). Does strength of phonological representations predict phonological awareness in preschool children? *Applied Psycholinguistics, 22,* 301–325.

FRAIBERG, S. (1977). *Insights from the blind: Comparative studies of blind and sighted infants.* New York: Basic Books.

FREGMEN, A., & FAY, D. (1980). Overextensions in production and comprehension: A methodological clarification. *Journal of Child Language, 7,* 205–211.

FRENCH, L. A., LUCARIELLO, J., SEIDMAN, S., & NELSON, K. (1985). The influence of discourse content and context on preschoolers' use of language. In L. Galda & A. Pellegrini (Eds.), *Play, language and stories.* Norwood, NJ: Albex.

FRIEL-PATTI, S., & FINITZO, T. (1990). Language learning in a prospective study of otitis media with effusion in the first two years of life. *Journal of Speech and Hearing Research, 33,* 188–194.

FROMKIN, V., & RODMAN, R. (1988). *An introduction to language* (4th ed.). New York: Holt, Rinehart & Winston.

FURROW, D., & LEWIS, S. (1987). The role of the initial utterance in contingent query sequences: Its influence on responses to requests for clarification. *Journal of Child Language, 14,* 467–479.

GALLAGHER, T. M. (1977). Revision behaviors in the speech of normal children developing language. *Journal of Speech and Hearing Research, 20,* 303–318.

GALLAGHER, T. M., & CRAIG, H. K. (1978). Structural characteristics of monologues in the speech of normal children: Semantic and conversational aspects. *Journal of Speech and Hearing Research, 21,* 103–117.

GALLAWAY, C., & RICHARDS, B. J. (1994). *Input and interaction in language acquisition.* Cambridge, England: Cambridge University Press.

GARDNER, H. (1980). Cognition comes of age. In M. Piattelli-Palmarini (Ed.), *Language and learning: The debate between Jean Piaget and Noam Chomsky* (pp. xix–xxxvi). Cambridge, MA: Harvard University Press.

GARDNER, H. (1985). *The mind's new science: A history of the cognitive revolution.* New York: Basic Books.

GARDNER, R. C., & LAMBERT, W. E. (1972). *Attitudes and motivation in second-language learning.* Rowley, MA: Newbury House Publishers.

GARNICA, O. (1973). The development of phonemic speech perception. In T. E. Moore (Ed.), *Cognitive development and the acquisition of language* (pp. 215–222). New York: Academic Press.

GARVEY, C. (1975). Requests and responses in children's speech. *Journal of Child Language, 2,* 41–63.

GARVEY, C., & HOGAN, R. (1973). Social speech and social interaction: Egocentrism revisited. *Child Development, 44,* 562–568.

GATHERCOLE, S. E. (1999). Cognitive approaches to the development of short-term memory. *Trends in Cognitive Science, 3,* 410–418.

GATHERCOLE, S. E., & BADDELEY, A. D. (1989). Evaluation of the role of phonological STM in the development of vocabulary in children: A longitudinal study. *Journal of Memory and Language, 28,* 200–213.

GATHERCOLE, S. E., & BADDELEY, A. D. (1990). Phonological memory deficits in language disordered children: Is there a causal connection? *Journal of Memory and Language, 29,* 336–360.

GATHERCOLE, S. E., WILLIS, C. S., EMSLIE, H., & BADDELEY, A. D. (1992). Phonological memory and vocabulary development during the early school years: A longitudinal study. *Developmental Psychology, 28,* 887–898.

GATHERCOLE, S. E., & ADAMS, A. M. (1994). Children's phonological working memory: Contributions of long-term knowledge and rehearsal. *Journal of Memory and Language, 33,* 672–688.

GATHERCOLE, V. C. (1989). Contrast: A semantic constraint? *Journal of Child Language, 16,* 685–702.

GAZZANIGA, M. S. (1983). Right hemisphere language following brain bisection: A twenty-year perspective. *American Psychologist, 38,* 525–537.

GEARY, D. C., & BJORKLUND, D. F. (2000). Evolutionary developmental psychology. *Child Development, 71,* 57–65.

GEE, J. P. (1993). *An introduction to human language: Fundamental concepts in linguistics.* Englewood Cliffs, NJ: Prentice-Hall.

GELMAN, R., & BAILLARGEON, R. (1983). A review of some Piagetian concepts. In P. Mussen (Ed.), *Handbook of child development: Cognitive development* (Vol. 3, pp. 167–230). New York: Wiley.

GELMAN, S. A., & BLOOM, P. (2000). Young children are sensitive to how an object was created when deciding what to name it. *Cognition, 76,* 91–103.

GELMAN, S. A., COLEY, J. D., ROSENGREN, K. S., HARTMAN, E., & PAPPAS, A. (1998). Beyond labeling: The role of maternal input in the acquisition of richly structured categories. *Monographs of the Society for Research in Child Development, 63,* Serial No. 253.

GELMAN, S. A., & MARKMAN, E. M. (1985). Implicit contrast in adjectives vs. nouns: Implications for word-learning in preschoolers. *Journal of Child Language, 12,* 125–145.

GELMAN, S. A., & TAYLOR, M. (1984). How two-year-old children interpret proper and common names for unfamiliar objects. *Child Development, 55,* 1535–1540.

GENESEE, F. (1983). Bilingual education of majority-language children: The immersion experiments in review. *Applied Psycholinguistics, 4,* 1–46.

GENESEE, F. (1989). Early bilingual development: One language or two? *Journal of Child Language, 16,* 161–180.

GENESEE, F. (2003). Rethinking bilingual acquisition. In J. M. deWaele (Ed.), *Bilingualism: Challenges and directions for future research* (pp. 158–182). Clevedon, England: Multilingual Matters.

GENTNER, D. (1978). On relational meaning: The acquisition of verb meaning. *Child Development, 49,* 988–998.

GENTNER, D. (1982). Why nouns are learned before verbs: Linguistic relativity versus natural partitioning. In S. A. Kuczaj (Ed.), *Language development: Syntax and semantics.* Hillsdale, NJ: Erlbaum.

GENTNER, D., & BORODITSKY, L. (2001). Individuation, relativity, and early word learning. In Bowerman, M., & Levinson, S., *Language acquisition and conceptual development* (pp. 215–256). Cambridge: Cambridge University Press.

GERKEN, L. (1994). Child phonology: Past research, present questions, future directions. In M.A. Gernbacher (Ed.), *Handbook of psy-*

cholinguistics. (pp 781–820). New York: Academic Press.

GERKEN L. (2002). Early sensitivity to linguistic form. In *Annual Review of Language Acquisition 2*, 1–36. John Benjamins Publishing Co.

GERKEN, L., LANDAU, B., & REMEZ, R. E. (1990). Function morphemes in young children's speech perception and production. *Developmental Psychology, 26*, 204–216.

GERKEN, L. A., & MCINTOSH, B. J. (1993). The interplay of function morphemes and prosody in early language. *Developmental Psychology, 29*, 448–457.

GERSHKOFF-STOWE, L., THAL, D. J., SMITH, L. B., & NAMY, L. (1997). Categorization and its developmental relation to early language. *Child Development, 68*, 843–859.

GESCHWIND, N., & LEVITSKY, W. (1968). Human brain: Left–right asymmetries in temporal speech region. *Science, 161*, 186–187.

GILGER, J. W. (1996). How can behavioral genetic research help us understand language development and disorders? In M. L. Rice (Ed.), *Toward a genetics of language* (pp. 77–110). Mahwah, NJ: Lawrence Erlbaum.

GILLETTE, J., GLEITMAN, H., GLEITMAN, L. & LEDERER, A. (1999). Human simulations of vocabulary learning. *Cognition, 73*, 135–176.

GLEASON, J. B. (1973). Code switching in children's language. In T. E. Moore (Ed.), *Cognitive development and the acquisition of language* (pp. 159–168). New York: Academic Press.

GLEASON, J. B. (1992). Language acquisition and socialization. University lecture, Boston University, MA.

GLEASON, J. B., & WEINTRAUB, S. (1976). The acquisition of routines in child language. *Language in Society, 5*, 129–136.

GLEITMAN, H. (1995). *Psychology* (4th ed.). New York: Norton.

GLEITMAN, H., CASSIDY, K., MASSEY, C., & SCHMIDT, H. (1995). Instructors resource manual with classroom demonstrations. *Gleitman's Psychology* (4th ed.). New York: Norton.

GLEITMAN, H., & GLEITMAN, L. R. (1979). Language use and language judgement. In C. Fillmore, D. Kempler, & W. S.-Y. Wang (Eds.),

*Individual differences in language ability and language behavior* (pp. 103–129). New York: Academic Press.

GLEITMAN, L. R. (1981). Maturational determinants of language growth. *Cognition, 10*, 103–114.

GLEITMAN, L. R. (1990). The structural sources of verb meanings. *Language Acquisition, 1*, 3–55.

GLEITMAN, L. R., & GLEITMAN, H. (1991). Language. In H. Gleitman (Ed.), *Psychology* (pp. 333–390). New York: Norton.

GLEITMAN, L. R., NEWPORT, E. L., & GLETIMAN, H. (1984). The current status of the motherese hypothesis. *Journal of Child Language, 11*, 43–79.

GLICK, J. (1987). Bilingualism: cognitive and social aspects. In P. Homel, M. Palij, & D. Aaronson (Eds.), *Childhood bilingualism: Aspects of linguistic, cognitive, and social development* (pp. 171–180). Hillsdale, NJ: Erlbaum.

GLUCKSBERG, S., & KRAUSS, R. M. (1967). What do people say after they have learned how to talk? Studies of the development of referential communication. *Merrill-Palmer Quarterly, 13*, 309–316.

GLUCKSBERG, S., KRAUSS, R. M., & HIGGINS, E. (1975). The development of referential communication skills. In F. Horowitz (Ed.), *Review of child development research*. (Vol. 4, pp. 305–346). Chicago: University of Chicago Press.

GOLDFIELD, B. A., & REZNICK, J. S. (1990). Early lexical acquisition: Rate, content, and the vocabulary spurt. *Journal of Child Language, 17*, 171–184.

GOLDFIELD, B. A., & REZNICK, J. S. (1996). Measuring the vocabulary spurt: A reply to Mervis and Bertrand. *Journal of Child Language, 23*, 241–246.

GOLDIN-MEADOW, S. (1982). The resilience of recursion: A study of a communication system developed without a conventional language model. In E. Wanner & L. R. Gleitman (Eds.), *Language acquisition: The state of the art* (pp. 51–77). Cambridge, England: Cambridge University Press.

GOLDIN-MEADOW, S. (1997). The resilience of language in humans. In C. Snowdon & M. Hausberger (Eds.), *Social influences on vo-*

*cal development* (pp. 293–311). Cambridge, England: Cambridge University Press.

GOLDIN-MEADOW, S. (2003). *The resilience of language: What gesture creation in deaf children can tell us about how all children learn language.* New York: Psychology Press.

GOLDIN-MEADOW, S., & MYLANDER, C. (1984). Gestural communication in deaf children: The effects and noneffects of parental input on early language development. *Monographs of the Society for Research in Child Development, 49* (Nos. 3–4).

GOLDIN-MEADOW, S., SELIGMAN, M. E. P., & GELMAN, R. (1976). Language in the two-year-old. *Cognition, 4,* 189–202.

GOLINKOFF, R. M. (1983). The preverbal negotiation of failed messages: Insights into the transition period. In R. M. Golinkoff (Ed.), *The transition from prelinguistic to linguistic communication.* Hillsdale, NJ: Erlbaum.

GOLINKOFF, R. M. (1986). "I beg your pardon?": The preverbal negotiation of failed messages. *Journal of Child Language, 13,* 455–476.

GOLINKOFF, R. M., & ALIOTO, A. (1995). Infant-directed speech facilitates lexical learning in adults hearing Chinese: Implication for language acquisition. *Journal of Child Language, 22,* 703–726.

GOLINKOFF, R. M., & GORDON, L. (1983). In the beginning was the word: A history of the study of language acquisition. In R. M. Golinkoff (Ed.), *The transition from prelinguistic to linguistic communication* (pp. 1–19). Hillsdale, NJ: Erlbaum.

GOLINKOFF, R. M., MERVIS, C. B., & HIRSH-PASEK, K. (1994). Early object labels: The case for a developmental lexical principles framework. *Journal of Child Language, 21,* 125–156.

GOMEZ, R. L., & GERKEN, L. (1999). Artificial grammar learning by 1-year-olds leads to specific and abstract knowledge. *Cognition, 70,* 109–135.

GOODALL, J. (1986). *The chimpanzees of Gombe: Patterns of behavior.* Cambridge, MA: Harvard University Press.

GOODGLASS, H. (1979). Effect of aphasia on the retrieval of lexicon and syntax. In C. J.

Fillmore, D. Kempler, & W. S.-Y. Wang (Eds.), *Individual differences in language ability and language behavior* (pp. 253–260). New York: Academic Press.

GOODGLASS, H. (1993). *Understanding aphasia.* New York: Academic Press.

GOODLUCK, H. (1991). *Language acquisition: A linguistic introduction.* Cambridge, MA: Blackwell.

GOODMAN, J. C., & NUSBAUM, H. C. (1994). *The development of speech perception: The transition from speech sounds to spoken words.* Cambridge, MA: MIT Press.

GOODMAN, M. (1984). Are creole structures innate? *Behavioral and Brain Sciences, 7,* 193–194.

GOODSITT, J. V., MORSE, P. A., VER HOEVE, J. N., & COWAN, N. (1984). Infant speech recognition in multisyllabic contexts. *Child Development, 55,* 903–910.

GOODWYN, S. W., & ACREDOLO, L. P. (1993). Symbolic gesture versus word: Is there a modality advantage for onset of symbol use? *Child Development, 64,* 688–701.

GOODZ, N. (1989). Parental language mixing in bilingual families. *Infant Mental Health Journal, 10,* 25–44.

GOPNIK, A. (1988). Three types of early word: The emergence of social words, names and cognitive relational words in the one-word stage and their relation cognitive development. *First Language, 8,* 49–70.

GOPNIK, A., & CHOI, S. (1990). Do linguistic differences lead to cognitive differences? A cross-linguistic study of semantic and cognitive development. *First Language, 10,* 199–215.

GOPNIK, A., & CHOI, S. (1995). Names, relational words, and cognitive development in English and Korean speakers: Nouns are not always learned before verbs. In M. Tomasello & W. E. Merriman (Eds.), *Beyond names for things: Young children's acquisition of verbs* (pp. 83–90). Hillsdale, NJ: Erlbaum.

GOPNIK, A., CHOI, S., & BAUMBERGER, T. (1996). Cross-linguistic differences in early semantic and cognitive development. *Cognitive Development,* 11, 197–227.

GOPNIK, A., CHOI, S., & BAUMBERGER, T. (1996). Cross-linguistic differences in early semantic and cognitive development. *Cognitive Development, 11,* 197–227.

GOPNIK, A., & MELTZOFF, A. N. (1984). Semantic and cognitive development in 15- to 21-month-old children. *Journal of Child Language, 11,* 495–513.

GOPNIK, A., & MELTZOFF, A. N. (1986). Relations between semantic and cognitive development in the one-word stage: The specificity hypothesis. *Child Development, 57,* 1040–1053.

GOPNIK, A., & MELTZOFF, A. N. (1987). The development of categorization in the second year and its relation to other cognitive and linguistic developments. *Child Development, 58,* 1523–1531.

GOPNIK, M. (1990). Feature-blind grammar and dysphasia. *Nature, 344,* 715.

GOPNIK, M. (1994). Theoretical implications of inherited dysphasia. In Y. Levy (Ed.), *Other children, other languages* (pp. 331–358). Hillsdale, NJ: Erlbaum.

GOPNIK, M., & CRAGO, M. B. (1991). Familial aggregation of a developmental language disorder. *Cognition, 39,* 1–50.

GORDON, P. (1985). Level-ordering in lexical development. *Cognition, 21,* 73–93.

GOSWAMI, U., & BRYANT, P. (1990). *Phonological skills and learning to read.* Hillsdale, NJ: Erlbaum.

GOULD, S. J., & LEWONTIN, R. C. (1979). The spandrels of San Marco and the Panglossian paradigm: A critique of the adaptationist programme. *Proceedings of the Royal Society of London, 205,* 581–598.

GREENOUGH, W. T., BLACK, J. E., & WALLACE, C. S. (1987). Experience and brain development. *Child Development, 58,* 539–559.

GREGORY, S., & MOGFORD, K. (1981). Early language development in deaf children. In B. Woll, J. Kyle, & M. Deuchar (Eds.), *Perspectives on British sign language and deafness* (pp. 218–237). London: Croom Helm.

GRICE, H. P. (1957). Meaning. *The Philosophical Review, 66,* 377–388.

GRICE, H. P. (1969). Utterer's meaning and intentions. *The Philosophical Review, 78,* 147–177.

GRICE, H. P. (1975). Logic and conversation. In P. Cole & J. Morgan (Eds.), *Speech acts: Syntax and semantics.* (Vol. 3, pp. 41–58). New York: Academic Press.

GRIESER, D. L., & KUHL, P. K. (1988). Maternal speech to infants in a tonal language: Support for the universal prosodic features in motherese. *Developmental Psychology, 24,* 14–20.

GRIESER, D. L., & KUHL, P. K. (1989). Categorization of speech by infants: Support for speech-sound prototypes. *Developmental Psychology, 25,* 577–588.

GRIMM, H. (1993). Patterns of interaction and communication in language development disorders. In G. Blanken, J. Dittmann, H. Grimm, J. D. Marshall, & C.-W. Wallesch (Eds.), *Linguistic disorders and pathologies: An international handbook* (pp. 697–711). Berlin: Walter de Gruyter.

GRIMM, H., & WEINERT, S. (1990). Is the syntax development of dysphasic children deviant and why: New findings to an old question. *Journal of Speech and Hearing Research, 33,* 220–228.

GRIMSHAW, J., & ROSEN, S. (1990). Knowledge and obedience: The developmental status of the binding theory. *Linguistic Inquiry, 21,* 189–222.

GROPEN, J., PINKER, S., HOLLANDER, M., & GOLDBERG, R. (1991). Affectedness and direct objects: The role of lexical semantics in the acquisition of verb argument structure. In B. Levin & S. Pinker (Eds.), *Lexical and conceptual semantics.* Cambridge, MA: Blackwell.

GROSJEAN, F. (1982). *Life with two languages: An introduction to bilingualism.* Cambridge, MA: Harvard University Press.

GRUNWELL, P. (1981). The development of phonology: A descriptive profile. *First Language, 3,* 161–191.

GRUNWELL, P. (1986). Aspects of phonological development in later childhood. In K. Durkin (Ed.), *Language development in the school years* (pp. 34–56). Cambridge, MA: Brookline Books.

GUMPERZ, J. (1976). The sociolinguistic significance of conversational code-switching. In: J. Cook Gumperz and J. Gumperz (Eds.), *Papers on language and context, working paper no. 46.* Berkeley: Language Behavior Research Laboratory, University of California.

HADEN, C. A., HAINE, R. A., & FIVUSH, R. (1997). Developing narrative structure in parent-child reminiscing across the preschool years. *Developmental Psychology 33*, 295–307.

HAKUTA, K. (1986). *Mirror of language: The debate on bilingualism*. New York: Basic Books.

HAKUTA, K., & MCLAUGHLIN, B. (1996). Bilingualism and second language learning: Seven tensions that define the research. In D. Berliner & R.C. Calfee (Eds.), *Handbook of educational psychology* (pp. 603–621). New York: Macmillan Library Reference USA

HAKUTA, K. (2001). A critical period for second language acquisition? In D. B. Bailey Jr., J. T. Bruer, F. J. Symons, & J. W. Lichtman (Eds.) *Critical thinking about critical periods* (pp. 193–205). Baltimore, MD: Paul H. Brookes Publishing Co.

HAKUTA, K., BIALYSTOK, E., & WILEY, E. (2003). Critical evidence: A test of the critical-period hypothesis for second-language acquisition. *Psychological Science, 14,* 31–38.

HALL, D. G., WAXMAN, S. R., & HURWITZ, W. R. (1993). How two- and four-year-old children interpret adjectives and count nouns. *Child Development, 64,* 1651–1664.

HALLIDAY, M. A. K. (1975). *Learning how to mean*. London: Edward Arnold.

HALVORSEN, C. F., & WALDROP, M. F. (1970). Maternal behavior toward own and other preschool children: The problem of "ownness." *Child Development, 41,* 839–845.

HARDING, E., & REILLY, P. (1987). *The bilingual family: A handbook for parents*. Cambridge, England: Cambridge University Press.

HARRIS, M., BARRETT, M., JONES, D., & BROOKES, S. (1988). Linguistic input and early word meaning. *Journal of Child Language, 15,* 77–94.

HART, B., & RISLEY, T. R. (1995). *Meaningful differences in the everyday experience of young American children*. Baltimore: Paul H. Brookes.

HAUSER, M., CHOMSKY, N., & FITCH, T. (2002). The faculty of language: What is it, and how did it evolve? *Science, 298,* 1569–1579.

HAUSER, M., NEWPORT, E., & ASLIN, R. (2000). Segmentation of the speech stream in a non-human primate: Statistical learning in cotton-top tamarins. *Cognition 78,* B53–B64.

HEATH, S. E. (1982). What no bedtime story means: Narrative skills at home and school. *Language in Society,* 11, 29–76.

HEATH, S. E. (1983). *Ways with words*. Cambridge, England: Cambridge University Press.

HECHT, S. A., & GREENFIELD, D. B. (2002). Explaining the predictive accuracy of teacher judgments of their students' reading achievement: The role of gender, classroom behavior, and emergent literacy skills in a longitudinal sample of children exposed to poverty. *Reading and Writing: An Interdisciplinary Journal, 15,* 789–809.

HIRSCHFELD, L. A., & GELMAN, S. A. (1994). *Mapping the mind: Domain specificity in cognition and culture*. Cambridge, England: Cambridge University Press.

HIRSH-PASEK, K., & GOLINKOFF, R. M. (1991). Language comprehension: A new look at some old themes. In N. A. Krasnegor, D. M. Rumbaugh, R. L. Schiefelbusch, & M. Studdert-Kennedy (Eds.), *Biological and behavioral determinants of language development* (pp. 301–320). Hillsdale, NJ: Erlbaum.

HIRSH-PASEK, K., & GOLINKOFF, R. M. (1996). *The origins of grammar: Evidence from early language comprehension*. Cambridge, MA: MIT Press.

HIRSH-PASEK, K., GOLINKOFF, R. M., & NAIGLES, L. (1996). Young children's use of syntactic frames to derive meaning. In K. Hirsh-Pasek & R. M. Golinkoff (Eds.), *The origins of grammar: Evidence from early language comprehension* (pp. 123–159). Cambridge, MA: MIT Press.

HIRSH-PASEK, K., KEMLER NELSON, D. G., JUSCZYK, P. W., WRIGHT CASSIDY, K., DRUSS, B., & KENNEDY, L. (1987). Clauses are perceptual units for young infants. *Cognition, 26,* 269–286.

HISCOCK, M. (1988). Behavioral asymmetries in normal children. In D. L. Molfese & S. J. Segalowitz (Eds.), *Brain lateralization in children: Developmental implications* (pp. 85–170). New York: Guilford Press.

HOCKETT, C. F. (1960). The origin of speech. *Scientific American, 203* (48), pp. 88–96.

HOEK, D., INGRAM, D., & GIBSON, D. (1986). Some possible causes of children's early word overextensions. *Journal of Child Language, 13,* 477–494.

HOFF, E. (2003). The specificity of environmental influence: Socioeconomic status affects early vocabulary development via maternal speech. *Child Development, 74,* 1368–1378.

HOFF, E. (2003). Language development in childhood. In R. M. Lerner, M. A. Easterbrooks, & J. Mistri (Eds.), *Handbook of psychology, Vol. 6. Developmental psychology* (pp. 171–193). New York: Wiley.

HOFF, E., LAURSEN, B. & TARDIF, T. (2002). Socioeconomic status and parenting. In M. H. Bornstein (Ed.), *Handbook of Parenting, Volume II: Ecology and Biology of Parenting* (pp. 161–188). Mahwah, New Jersey: Lawrence Erlbaum Associates.

HOFF, E. & NAIGLES, L. (2002). How children use input to acquire a lexicon. *Child Development, 73,* 418–433.

HOFF-GINSBERG, E. (1985). Some contributions of mothers' speech to their children's syntax growth. *Journal of Child Language, 12,* 367–385.

HOFF-GINSBERG, E. (1986). Function and structure in maternal speech: Their relation to the child's development of syntax. *Developmental Psychology, 22,* 155–163.

HOFF-GINSBERG, E. (1987). Topic relations in mother–child conversation. *First Language, 7,* 145–158.

HOFF-GINSBERG, E. (1990). Maternal speech and the child's development of syntax: A further look. *Journal of Child Language, 17,* 337–346.

HOFF-GINSBERG, E. (1991). Mother–child conversation in different social classes and communicative settings. *Child Development, 62,* 782–796.

HOFF-GINSBERG, E. (1994). Influences of mother and child on maternal talkativeness. *Discourse Processes, 18,* 105–117.

HOFF-GINSBERG, E. (1998a). The relation of birth order and socioeconomic status to children's language experience and language development. *Applied Psycholinguistics, 19,* 603–630.

HOFF-GINSBERG, E. (1998b). What explains the SES-related difference in children's vocabularies and what does that reveal about the process of word learning? Paper presented at the Boston University Conference on Language Development, Boston, MA, November 6–8.

HOFF-GINSBERG, E. (1999). Formalism or functionalism? Evidence from the study of language development. In M. Darnell, E. Moravcsik, F. Newmeyer, M. Noonan, & K. Wheatley (Eds.), *Functionalism and formalism in linguistics: Volume II. Case studies* (pp. 317–340). Amsterdam/Philadelphia: Benjamins.

HOFF-GINSBERG, E., & KRUEGER, W. (1991). Older siblings as conversational partners. *Merrill-Palmer Quarterly, 37,* 465–482.

HOFF-GINSBERG, E., & SHATZ, M. (1982). Linguistic input and the child's acquisition of language. *Psychological Bulletin, 92,* 3–26.

HOFFMAN, C. (1991). *An introduction to bilingualism.* Essex, England: Longman Group.

HSU, J. R., CAIRNS, H. S., & FIENGO, R. W. (1985). The development of grammars underlying children's interpretation of complex sentences. *Cognition, 20,* 25–48.

HUDSON, J. A., & NELSON, K. (1984). Play with language: Overextensions as analogies. *Journal of Child Language, 11,* 337–346.

HUDSON, J. A., & SHAPIRO, L. R. (1991). From knowing to telling: The development of children's scripts, stories, and personal narratives. In A. McCabe & C. Peterson (Eds.), *Developing narrative structure* (pp. 89–136). Hillsdale, NJ: Erlbaum.

HURFORD, J. R., STUDDERT-KENNEDY, M., & KNIGHT, C. (1998). *Approaches to the evolution of language.* Cambridge: Cambridge University Press.

HUTTENLOCHER, J. (1974). The origins of language comprehension. In R. Solso (Ed.), *Theories in cognitive psychology* (pp. 331–368). New York: Erlbaum.

HUTTENLOCHER, J., HAIGHT, W., BRYK, A., SELTZER, M., & LYONS, T. (1991). Early vocabulary growth: Relation to language input and gender. *Developmental Psychology, 27,* 236–248.

HUTTENLOCHER, J., & SMILEY, P. (1987). Early word meanings: The case of object names. *Cognitive Psychology, 19,* 63–89.

HUTTENLOCHER, J., LEVINE, S., & VEVEA, J. (1998). Environmental input and cognitive growth: A study using time-period comparisons. *Child Development, 69,* 1012–1029.

HUTTENLOCHER, J., VASILYEVA, M., CYMERMAN, E. & LEVINE, S. (2002). Language input at home and at school: Relation to child syntax. *Cognitive Psychology, 45,* 337–374.

HUTTENLOCHER, P. R. (1994). Synaptogenesis in human cerebral cortex. In G. Dawson & K. W. Fischer (Eds.), *Human behavior and the developing brain* (pp. 137–152). New York: Guilford Press.

HYMES, D. H. (1961). Functions of speech: An evolutionary approach. In F. C. Gruder (Ed.), *Anthropology and education* (pp. 55–83). Philadelphia: University of Pennsylvania Press.

HYMES, D. H. (1972). Models of the interaction of language and social life. In J. Gumperz & D. Hymes (Eds.), *Directions in sociolinguistics: The ethnography of communication* (pp. 35–71). New York: Holt, Rinehart & Winston.

INGRAM, D. (1981). *Procedures for the phonological analysis of children's language.* Baltimore: University Park Press.

INGRAM, D. (1988). Toward a theory of phonological acquisition. Paper presented at the Symposium on Research in Child Language Disorders, Madison, WI.

INGRAM, D. (1989). *First language acquisition: Method, description, and explanation.* Cambridge, England: Cambridge University Press.

INGRAM, D. (1995). The cultural basis of prosodic modifications to infants and children: A response to Fernald's universalist theory. *Journal of Child Language, 22,* 223–234.

INGRAM, D. (1999). Phonological acquisition. In M. Barrett (Ed.), *The development of language* (pp. 73–98). East Sussex: Psychology Press.

INGVAR, D. H., & SCHWARTZ, M. S. (1974). Blood flow patterns induced in the dominant hemisphere by speech and reading. *Brain, 97,* 273–288.

JAKOBSON, R. (1968). *Child language, aphasia, and phonological universals* (R. Keiler, Trans.). The Hague, The Netherlands: Mouton. (Original German version published 1941.)

JENSEMA, C. J., KARCHMER, M. A., & TRYBUS, R. J. (1978). The rated speech intelligibility of hearing impaired children: Basic relationships and a detailed analysis (Series R., no. 6). Washington, DC: Office of Demographic Studies, Gallaudet College.

JIA, G., & AARONSON, D. (1999). Age differences in second language acquisition: The dominant language switch and maintenance hypothesis. In A. Greenhill, H. Littlefield, & C. Tano, *Proceedings of the 23rd Annual Boston University Conference on Language Development* (pp. 301–312). Somerville, MA: Cascadilla Press.

JIA, G., & AARONSON, D. (2003). A longitudinal study of Chinese children and adolescents learning English in the United States. *Applied Psycholinguistics, 24,* 131–162.

JOHNSON, J., & NEWPORT, E. (1989). Critical period effects in second language learning: The influence of maturational state on the acquisition of English as a second language. *Cognitive Psychology, 21,* 60–99.

JOHNSON, R. E., LIDDELL, S. K., & ERTING, C. J. (1989). Unlocking the curriculum: Principles for achieving access in deaf education. Gallaudet Research Institute Working Paper 89–3. Department of Linguistics and Interpreting and the Gallaudet Research Institute, Gallaudet University, Washington, DC.

JOHNSON, R. E., LIDDELL, S. K., & ERTING, C. J. (1992). Towards theoretically sound practices in deaf education. In *Bilingual considerations in the education of Deaf students: ASL and English.* College for Continuing Education, Gallaudet University, Washington, DC.

JOHN-STEINER, V. (1992). Private speech among adults. In R. M. Diaz & L. E. Berk (Eds.), *Private speech: From social interaction to self-regulation* (pp. 285–296). Hillsdale, NJ: Erlbaum.

JOHNSTON, J. (1997). Specific language impairment, cognition and the biological basis of language. In M. Gopnik (Ed.), *The inheritance and innateness of grammars* (pp. 161–180). New York: Oxford University Press.

JOHNSTON, J. R. (1982). Narratives: A new look at communication problems in older language-disordered children. *Language, Speech, and Hearing Services in Schools, 13,* 145–155.

JOHNSTON, J. R. (1988). Specific language disorders in the child. In N. J. Lass, L. V. McReynolds, J. L. Norther, & D. E. Yoder (Eds.), *Handbook of speech-language pathology and audiology* (pp. 685–715). Toronto: B. C. Decker.

JOHNSTON, J. R. (1992). Cognitive abilities of language-impaired children. In P. Fletcher & D. Hall (Eds.), *Specific speech and language disorders in children: Correlates, characteristics and outcomes* (pp. 105–116). San Diego, CA: Singular Publishing Group, Inc.

JOHNSTON, J. R., & SCHERY, T. (1976). The use of grammatical morphemes by children with communication disorders. In D. Morehead & A. Morehead (Eds.), *Normal and deficient child language* (pp. 239–259). Baltimore: University Park Press.

JOURDAN, C. (1991). Pidgins and creoles: The blurring of categories. *Annual Review of Anthropology, 20,* 187–209.

JUSCZYK, P. W., & DERRAH, C. (1987). Representation of speech sounds by young infants. *Developmental Psychology, 23,* 648–654.

JUSCZYK, P. W., FRIEDERICI, A. D., WESSELS, J. M. I., & SVENKERUD, V. Y. (1993). Infants' sensitivity to the sound patterns of native language words. *Journal of Memory and Language, 32,* 402–420.

KAKO, E. (1999). Elements of syntax in the systems of three language-trained animals. *Animal Learning and Behavior, 27,* 1–14.

KAMHI, A. G. (1993). Children with specific language impairment (developmental dyphasia): Perceptual and cognitive aspects. In G. Blanken, J. Dittmann, H. Grimm, J. D. Marshall, & C.W. Wallesch (Eds.), *Linguistic disorders and pathologies: An international handbook* (pp. 625–640). Berlin: Walter de Gruyter.

KARABENICK, J. D., & MILLER, S. A. (1977). The effects of age, sex, and listener feedback on grade school children's referential communication. *Child Development, 48,* 678–683.

KARMILOFF-SMITH, A. (1986). Some fundamental aspects of language development after age 5. In P. Fletcher & A. M. Garman (Eds.), *Language acquisition* (2nd ed., pp. 455–474). Cambridge, England: Cambridge University Press.

KARMILOFF-SMITH, A. (1992). *Beyond modularity: A developmental perspective on cognitive science.* Cambridge, MA: MIT Press.

KARMILOFF-SMITH, A. (1998). Development itself is the key to understanding developmental disorders. *Trends in Cognitive Sciences, 2,* 389–398.

KARMILOFF-SMITH, A., GRANT, J., BERTHOUD, I, DAVIES, M., HOWLIN, P., & UDWIN, O. (1997). Language and Williams syndrome: How intact is "intact"? *Child Development, 68,* 246–262.

KARMILOFF-SMITH, A., Brown, J. H., Grice, S., & Paterson, S. (2003). Dethroning the myth: Cognitive dissociations and innate modularity in Williams syndrome. *Developmental Neuropsychology, 23(1–2),* 227–242.

KARZON, R. G. (1985). Discrimination of polysyllabic sequences by one- to four-month-old infants. *Journal of Experimental Child Psychology, 39,* 326–342.

KATZ, N., BAKER, E., & MACNAMARA, J. (1974). What's in a name? A study of how children learn common and proper names. *Child Development, 50,* 1–13.

KAY, D. A., & ANGLIN, J. M. (1982). Overextension and underextension in the child's expressive and receptive speech. *Journal of Child Language, 9,* 83–98.

KAYE, K., & CHARNEY, R. (1980). How mothers maintain "dialogue" with two-year-olds. In D. R. Olson (Ed.), *The social foundations of language and thought* (pp. 211–230). New York: Norton.

KEHOE, M. M. & STOEL-GAMMON, C. (2001). Development of syllable structure in English-speaking children with particular reference to rhymes. *Journal of Child Language, 28,* 393–432.

KEENAN, E. O. (1974). Conversational competence in children. *Journal of Child Language, 1,* 163–183.

KEKELIS, L. S., & ANDERSEN, E. S. (1984). Family communication styles and language development. *Journal of Visual Impairment and Blindness, 78,* 54–64.

KELLER-COHEN, D. (personal communication, January, 1978).

KELLERMAN, E. (1986). An eye for an eye: Crosslinguistic constraints on the development of the L2 lexicon. In E. Kellerman & M. Sharwood Smith (Eds.), *Crosslinguistic influences in second language acquisition* (pp. 35–48). Elmsford, NY: Pergamon Press.

KELLY, M. (1996). The role of phonology in grammatical category assignments. In J. L. Morgan & K. Demuth (Eds.), *Signal to syntax: Bootstrapping from speech to grammar in early acquisition* (pp. 249–262). Mahwah, NJ: Erlbaum.

KELLY, M. H. & MARTIN, S. (1997). Domain-general abilities applied to domain-specific tasks: Sensitivity to probabilities in perception, cognition, and language. In L. Gleitman & B. Landau (Eds.), *The acquisition of the lexicon* (pp. 105–140). Cambridge, MA: MIT Press.

KEMLER NELSON, D. G., HIRSH-PASEK, K., JUSCZYK, P. W., & WRIGHT CASSIDY, K. (1989). How the prosodic cues in motherese might assist language learning. *Journal of Child Language, 16,* 55–68.

KHUBCHANDANI, L. M. (1997). Bilingual education for indigenous groups in India. In J. Cummins & D. Corson (Eds.), *Encyclopedia of language and education: Vol. 5. Bilingual education* (pp. 67–76). Dordrecht, The Netherlands: Kluwer Academic Publishers.

KILLEN, M., & NAIGLES, L. R. (1995). Preschool children pay attention to their addressees: Effects of gender composition on peer disputes. *Discourse Processes, 19,* 329–346.

KIM, K. H. S., RELKIN, N. R., LEE, K.-M, & HIRSCH, J. (1997). Distinct cortical areas associated with native and second languages. *Nature, 388,* 171–174.

KIMURA, D. (1967). Functional asymmetry of the brain in dichotic listening. *Cortex, 3,* 163–178.

KINSBOURNE, M. (1993). Neurological aspects of language development disorders. In G. Blanken, J. Dittmann, H. Grimm, J. D. Marshall, & C.-W. Wallesch (Eds.), *Linguistic disorders and pathologies: An international handbook* (pp. 585–594). Berlin: Walter de Gruyter.

KISILEVSKY, B. S., HAINS, S. M. J., LEE, K., XIE, X., HUAN, H. YE, H. H., ZHANG, K, & WANG, Z. (2003). Effects of experience on fetal voice recognition. *Psychological Science, 14,* 220–224.

KLANN-DELIUS, G. (1981). Sex and language acquisition—Is there any influence? *Journal of Pragmatics, 5,* 1–25.

KLEE, T., & FITZGERALD, M. D. (1985). The relation between grammatical development and mean length of utterance in morphemes. *Journal of Child Language, 12,* 251–270.

KLEIN, D., MILNER, B., ZATORRE, R. J., MEYER, E., & EVANS, A. C. (1995). The neural substrates underlying word generation: A bilingual functional-imaging study. *Proceedings of the National Academy of Sciences, 92,* 2899–2903.

KLEIN, D., MILNER, B., ZATORRE, R. J., ZHAO, & NIKELSKI, J. (1999). Cerebral organization in bilinguals: A PET study of Chinese-English verb generation. *NeuroReport, 10,* 2841–2846.

KLIMA, E. S., & BELLUGI, U. (1967). Syntactic regularities. In J. Lyon & R. J. Wales (Eds.), *Psychological Papers*. Edinburgh: University Press.

KLIMA, E. S., & BELLUGI, U. (1979). *The signs of language*. Cambridge, MA: Harvard University Press.

KOHLBERG, L., YEAGER, J., & HJERTHOLM, E. (1968). Private speech: Four studies and a review of theories. *Child Development, 39,* 691–736.

KOHNERT, K. J. (2002). Picture naming in early sequential bilinguals; A 1-year follow-up. *Journal of Speech Language & Hearing Research, 45,* 759–771.

KOHNERT, K. & BATES, E. (2002). Balancing bilinguals II: Lexical comprehension and cognitive processing in children learning Spanish and English. *Journal of Speech Language & Hearing Research, 45,* 347–359.

KOHNERT, K., BATES, E., & HERNANDEZ, A. E. (1999). Balancing bilinguals: Lexical-semantic production and cognitive processing in children learning Spanish and English. *Journal of Speech Language & Hearing Research, 42,* 1400–1413.

KOLB, B. (1989). Brain development, plasticity, and behavior. *American Psychologist, 44,* 1203–1212.

KONSTANTAREAS, M. M. (1993). Language and communicative behavior in autistic disorder. In G. Blanken, J. Dittmann, H. Grimm, J. D. Marshall,

& C.-W. Wallesch (Eds.), *Linguistic disorders and pathologies: An international handbook* (pp. 804–824). Berlin: Walter de Gruyter.

KUHL, P. K. (1976). Speech perception in early infancy: The acquisition of speech-sound categories. In S. K. Hirsh, D. H. Eldredge, I. J. Hirsh, & S. R. Silverman (Eds.), *Hearing and Davis: Essays honoring Hallowell Davis* (pp. 265–280). St. Louis, MO: Washington University Press.

KUHL, P. K. (1980). Perceptual constancy for speech-sound categories in early infancy. In G. H. Yeni-Komshian, J. F. Kavanagh, & C. A. Ferguson (Eds.), *Child Phonology: Vol. 2. Perception* (pp. 41–66). New York: Academic Press.

KUHL, P. K. (1983). Perception of auditory equivalence classes for speech in early infancy. *Infant Behavior and Development, 6,* 263–285.

KUHL, P. K. (1987). Perception of speech and sound in early infancy. In P. Salapatek & L. Cohen (Eds.), *Handbook of Infant Perception* (pp. 275–382). New York: Academic Press.

KUHL, P. K. (1999). The role of experience in early language development: Linguistic experience alters the perception and production of speech. In N. A. Fox, L. A. Leavitt, J. G. Warhol (Eds.), *The role of early experience in infant development*. Johnson & Johnson Pediatric Institute Pediatric Roundtable. Johnson & Johnson, Publishers.

KUHL, P. K., ANDRUSKI, J. E., CHISTOVICH, I. A., CHISTOVICH, L. A., KOZHEVNIKOVA, E. V., RYSKINA, V. L., STOYAROVA, E. I., SUNDBERG, U., & LACERDA, F. (1997). Cross-language analysis of phonetic units in language addressed to infants. *Science, 277,* 684–686.

KUHL, P. K., & MELTZOFF, A. N. (1988). Speech as an intermodal object of perception. In A. Yonas (Ed.), *Perceptual development in infancy: The Minnesota symposia on child psychology*. (Vol. 20, pp. 235–266). Hillsdale, NJ: Erlbaum.

KUHL, P. K., & MELTZOFF, A. N. (1997). Evolution, nativism and learning in the development of language and speech. In M. Gopnik (Ed.), *The inheritance and innateness of grammars* (pp. 7–44). New York: Oxford University Press.

KUHL, P. K., & MILLER, J. D. (1975). Speech perception by the chinchilla: Voiced–voiceless distinction in alveolar plosive consonants. *Science, 190,* 69–72.

KUHL, P. K., WILLIAMS, K. A., LACERDA, F., STEVENS, K. N., & LINDBLOM, B. (1992). Linguistic experience alters phonetic perception in infants by 6 months of age. *Science, 255,* 606–608.

KURLAND, B. F., & SNOW, C.E. (1997). Longitudinal measurement of growth in definitional skill. *Journal of Child Language, 24,* 603–625.

LABOV, W. (1970). Stages in the acquisition of standard English. In H. Hungerford, J. Robinson, & J. Sledd (Eds.), *English linguistics* (pp. 275–302). Glenview, IL: Scott Foresman.

LABOV, W. (1972b). *Sociolinguistic patterns*. Philadelphia: University of Pennsylvania Press.

LAKOFF, R. (1975). *Language and woman's place*. New York: Harper and Row.

LANDAU, B., & GLEITMAN, L. R. (1985). *Language and experience: Evidence from the blind child*. Cambridge, MA: Harvard University Press.

LANE, H. (1976). *The wild boy of Aveyron*. Cambridge, MA: Harvard University Press.

LANE, H. (1984). *When the mind hears*. New York: Random House.

LANZA, E. (1992). Can bilingual two-year-olds code switch? *Journal of Child Language, 19,* 633–658.

LANZA, E. (2001). Bilingual first language acquisition: A discourse perspective on language contact in parent-child interaction. In J. Cenoz & F. Genesee (Eds.), *Trends in bilingual acquisition* (pp. 95–106). Amsterdam: John Benjamins Publishing Company.

LAWRENCE, V., & SHIPLEY, E. F. (1996). Parental speech to middle and working class children from two racial groups in three settings. *Applied Psycholinguistics, 17,* 233–256.

LAWSON, C. (1967). Request patterns in a two-year-old. Unpublished manuscript. Berkeley, CA.

LEADHOLM, B. J., & MILLER, J. F. (1992). *Language sample analysis: The Wisconsin guide*. Madison, WI: Wisconsin Department of Public Instruction.

LEAKEY, R., & LEWIN, R. (1992). *Origins reconsidered: In search of what makes us human.* New York: Doubleday.

LEDERBERG, A. (1980). The language environment of children with language delays. *Journal of Pediatric Psychology, 5,* 141–158.

LEE, V. E. & CRONINGER, R. G. (1994). The relative importance of home and school in the development of literacy skills for middle-grade students. *American Journal of Education, 102,* 286–329.

LENNEBERG, E. H. (1964). The capacity for language acquisition. In J. A. Fodor & J. J. Katz (Eds.), *The structure of language: Readings in the philosophy of language* (pp. 579–603). Englewood Cliffs, NJ: Prentice-Hall.

LENNEBERG, E. H. (1967). *Biological foundations of language.* New York: Wiley.

LEONARD, L. (1996). Characterizing specific language impairment: A crosslinguistic perspective. In M. L. Rice (Ed.), *Toward a genetics of language* (pp. 243–256). Mahway, NJ: Erlbaum.

LEONARD, L. (1998). *Children with specific language impairment.* Cambridge, MA: MIT Press.

LEONARD, L. B. (1979). Language impairment in children. *Merrill-Palmer Quarterly, 25,* 205–232.

LEONARD, L. B. (1987). Is specific language impairment a useful construct? In S. Rosenberg (Ed.), *Advances in applied psycholinguistics: Vol. 1. Disorders of first language development* (pp. 1–39). Cambridge, England: Cambridge University Press.

LEONARD, L. B. (1989). Language learnability and specific language impairment in children. *Applied Psycholinguistics, 10,* 179–202.

LEONARD, L. B. (1991). Specific language impairment as a clinical category. *Language, Speech, and Hearing Services in Schools, 22,* 66–68.

LEONARD, L. B. (2003). Specific language impairment: Characterizing the deficits. In Y. Levy & J. Schaeffer, J. (Eds.) *Language competence across populations: Toward a definition of specific language impairment* (pp. 209–232). Mahwah, NJ: Lawrence Erlbaum, Assoc.

LEONARD, L. B., BORTOLLINI, U., CASELLI, M. C., MCGREGOR, K. K., & SABBADINI, L. (1992). Morphological deficits in children with specific language impairment: The status of features in the underlying grammar. *Language Acquisition, 2,* 151–179.

LEONARD, L. B., MCGREGOR, K. K., & ALLEN, G. D. (1992). Grammatical morphology and speech perception in children with specific language impairment. *Journal of Speech and Hearing Research, 35,* 1076–1085.

LEONARD, L. B., NEWHOFF, M., & MESELAM, L. (1980). Individual differences in early child phonology. *Applied Psycholinguistics, 1,* 7–30.

LEONARD, L. B., SABBADINI, L., VOLTERRA, V., & LEONARD, J. S. (1988). Some influences on the grammar of English- and Italian-speaking children with specific language impairment. *Applied Psycholinguistics, 9,* 39–57.

LEOPOLD, W. F. (1939–1949). *Speech development of a bilingual child: a linguist's record.* (Vols. 1–4). Evanston, IL: Northwestern University Press.

LEPPANEN, U. NIEMI, P., AUNOLA, K., & NURMI, J.-E. (2004). Development of reading skills among preschool and primary school pupils. *Reading Research Quarterly, 39,* 72–93.

LEVER, J. (1976). Sex differences in the games children play. *Social Problems, 23,* 478–487.

LEVY, E. (1989). Monologue as development of the text-forming function of language. In K. Nelson (Ed.), *Narratives from the crib* (pp. 123–170). Cambridge, MA: Harvard University Press.

LEVY, Y. (1983). It's frogs all the way down. *Cognition, 15,* 75–93.

LEVY, Y., AMIR, N., & SHALEV, R. (1992). Linguistic development of a child with a congenital, localised L. H. lesion. *Cognitive Neuropsychology, 9,* 1–32.

LEVY, Y. & SCHAEFFER, J. (2003). *Language competence across populations: Toward a definition of specific language impairment.* Mahwah, NJ: Lawrence Erlbaum, Assoc.

LI, C. N., & THOMPSON, S. A. (1977). The acquisition of tone in Mandarin speaking children. *Journal of Child Language, 4,* 185–201.

LIBERMAN, I. Y., SHANKWEILER, D., FISCHER, F. W., & CARTER, B. (1974). Explicit syllable and phoneme segmentation in the young child. *Journal of Experimental Child Psychology, 18,* 201–212.

LIEBERMAN, D. A. (1993). *Learning: Behavior and cognition.* Pacific Grove, CA: Brooks/Cole.

LIEBERMAN, P. (1984). *The biology and evolution of language.* Cambridge, MA: Harvard University Press.

LIEBERMAN, P. (1991). *Uniquely human: The evolution of speech, thought, and selfless behavior.* Cambridge, MA: Harvard University Press.

LIEVEN, E. V. M. (1994). Crosslinguistic and crosscultural aspects of language addressed to children. In C. Gallaway & B. J. Richards (Eds.), *Input and interaction in language acquisition* (pp. 56–73). Cambridge, England: Cambridge University Press.

LIMBER, J. (1973). The genesis of complex sentences. In T. Moore (Ed.), *Cognitive development and the acquisition of language* (pp. 169–186). New York: Academic Press.

LINDHOLM, K. J. (1980). Bilingual children: Some interpretations of cognitive and linguistic development. In K. E. Nelson (Ed.), *Children's language* (Vol. 2, pp. 215–266). New York: Gardner Press.

LITOWITZ, B. E. (1987). Language and the young deaf. In E. D. Mindel & M. Vernon (Eds.), *They grow in silence: Understanding deaf children and adults* (pp. 111–147). Boston: College Hill Press.

LOCKE, J. (1959). *An essay concerning human understanding.* (A. C. Fraser, Annot.). New York: Dover.

LOCKE, J. L. (1983). *Phonological acquisition and change.* New York: Academic Press.

LOCKE, J. L. (1993). *The child's path to spoken language.* Cambridge, MA: Harvard University Press.

LOCKE, J. L. (1999). Towards a biological science of language development. In M. Barrett (Ed). *The development of language* (pp. 373–396). East Sussex, England: Psychology Press.

LOCKE, J. L., & PEARSON, D. M. (1992). Vocal learning and the emergence of phonological capacity: A neurobiological approach. In C. A. Ferguson, L. Menn, & S. Stoel-Gammon (Eds.),

*Phonological Development* (pp. 91–129). Timonium, MD: York Press.

LONIGAN, C. J., FISCHEL, J. E., WHITEHURST, G. J., ARNOLD, D. S., & VALDEZ-MENCHACA, M. C. (1992). The role of otitis media in the development of expressive language disorder. *Developmental Psychology, 28,* 430–440.

LORD, C., & PAUL, R. (1997). Language and communication in autism. In D. J. Cohen & F. R. Volkmar (Eds.), *Handbook of autism and pervasive developmental disorders* (2nd ed.) (pp. 195–225). New York: John Wiley & Sons.

LOVAAS, O. I. (1987). Behavioral treatment and normal educational and intellectual functioning in young autistic children. *Journal of Consulting and Clinical Psychology, 55,* 3–9.

LOVAAS, O. I., & SMITH, T. (1988). Intensive behavioral treatment for young autistic children. In B. B. Lahey & A. E. Kazdin (Eds.), *Advances in clinical psychology* (Vol. II, pp. 285–324). New York: Plenum.

LOVELAND, K. A., & LANDRY, S. H. (1986). Joint attention and language in autism and developmental language delay. *Journal of Autism and Developmental Disorders, 16,* 335–349.

LUCARIELLO, J. (1987). Concept formation and its relation to word learning and use in the second year. *Journal of Child Language, 14,* 309–332.

LUDLOW, C. L., & DOOMAN, A. G. (1992). Genetic aspects of idiopathic speech and language disorders. *Molecular Biology and Genetics, 25,* 979–994.

LYYTINEN, H., AHONEN, T., EKLUND, K., GUTTORM, T.K., LAAKSO, M.L., LEINONEN, S., LEPPAENEN, P.H.T., LYYTINEN, P., POIKKEUS, A.M., PUOLAKANAHO, A., RICHARDSON, U., & VIHOLAINEN, H. (2001). Developmental pathways of children with and without familial risk for dyslexia during the first years of life. *Developmental Neuropsychology, 20,* 535–554.

MACKEN, M. A., & FERGUSON, C. (1983). Cognitive aspects of phonological development: Model, evidence, and issues. In K. E. Nelson (Ed.), *Children's language.* (Vol. 4, pp. 256–282). Hillsdale, NJ: Erlbaum.

MACLEAN, M., BRYANT, P. E., & BRADLEY, L. (1987). Rhymes, nursery rhymes and reading in early childhood. *Merrill-Palmer Quarterly, 33,* 255–282.

MACWHINNEY, B. (1987). The competition model. In B. MacWhinney (Ed.), *Mechanisms of language acquisition* (pp. 249–308). Hillsdale, NJ: Erlbaum.

MACWHINNEY, B. (1991). *The CHILDES Project: Tools for analyzing talk.* Hillsdale, NJ: Erlbaum.

MACWHINNEY, B. (1999). *The emergence of language.* Mahwah, NJ: Erlbaum.

MACWHINNEY, B., BATES, E., & KLIEGL, R. (1984). Cue validity and sentence interpretation in English, German, and Italian. *Journal of Verbal Learning and Verbal Behavior, 23,* 127–150.

MALTZ, D. N., & BORKER, R. A. (1982). A cultural approach to male–female miscommunication. In J. J. Gumperz (Ed.), *Language and social identity* (pp. 196–216). Cambridge, England: Cambridge University Press.

MANDEL, D. R., JUSCZYK, P. W., & PISONI, D. B. (1995). Infants' recognition of the sound patterns of their own names. *Psychological Science, 6,* 314–317.

MANEVA, B. & GENESEE, F. (2002). Bilingual babbling: Evidence for language differentiation in dual language acquisition. In B. Skarabela, S. Fish, & A. H. J. Do, *Proceedings of the 26th Boston University Conference on Language Development,* (pp. 383–392). Somerville, MA: Cascadilla Press.

MANIS, F. R., CUSTODIO, R., & SZESZULSKI, P. A. (1993). Development of phonological and orthographic skill: A 2-year longitudinal study of dyslexic children. *Journal of Experimental Child Psychology, 56,* 64–86.

MANN, V. A. (1986). Phonological awareness: The role of reading experience. *Cognition, 24,* 65–92.

MANN, V. A. (1991). Phonological abilities: Effective predictors of future reading ability. In L. Rieben & C. A. Perfetti (Eds.), Learning to read: Basic research and its implications (pp. 121–133). Hillsdale, NJ: Erlbaum.

MANNLE, S., & TOMASELLO, M. (1987). Fathers, siblings, and the bridge hypothesis. In K. Nelson & A. Van Kleeck (Eds.), *Children's language.* (Vol. 6, pp. 23–42). Hillsdale, NJ: Erlbaum.

MANUEL-DUPONT, S., ARDILA, A., ROSSELLI, M., & PUENTE, A. E. (1992). Bilingualism. In A.

E. Puente & R. J. McCaffrey, (Eds.), *Handbook of neuropsychological assessment: A biopsychosocial perspective* (pp. 193–209). New York: Plenum Press.

MARATSOS, M. (1983). Some current issues in the study of the acquisition of grammar. In J. Flavell & E. Markman (Eds.), *Carmichael's handbook of child psychology.* (Vol. 3, pp. 709–786). New York: Wiley.

MARATSOS, M. (1988). Cross-linguistic analysis, universals, and language acquisition. In F. S. Kessel (Ed.), *The development of language and language researchers: Essays in honor of Roger Brown* (pp. 121–152). Hillsdale, NJ: Erlbaum.

MARATSOS, M. (1993). Discussion in the symposium "Issues in the acquisition of inflectional processes," presented at the meetings of the Society for Research in Child Development, New Orleans.

MARATSOS, M. (1998). The acquisition of grammar. In D. Kuhn & R. S. Siegler (Eds.), *Handbook of child psychology: Vol. 2. Cognition, perception, and language* (5th ed., pp. 421–466). New York: Wiley.

MARATSOS, M. P., & CHALKLEY, M. A. (1980). The internal language of children's syntax: The ontogenesis and representation of syntactic categories. In K. E. Nelson (Ed.), *Children's language.* (Vol. 2, pp. 127–214). New York: Gardner Press.

MARKUS, J., MUNDY, P., MORALES, M., DELGADO, C. E. F., & YALE M. (2000). Individual differences in infant skills as predictors of child-caregiver joint attention and language. *Social Development, 9,* 301–315.

MARCUS, G. F. (1993). Negative evidence in language acquisition. *Cognition, 46,* 53–85.

MARCUS, G. F. (1995). Children's overregularization of English plurals: A quantitative analysis. *Journal of Child Language, 22,* 447–460.

MARCUS, G. F. (1998). Rethinking eliminative connectionism. *Cognitive Psychology, 37,* 243–282.

MARCUS, G. F., PINKER, S., ULLMAN, M., HOLLANDER, M., ROSEN T. J., & XU, F. (1992). Overregularization in language acquisition. *Monographs of the Society for Research in Child Development, 57* (4, Serial No. 228).

MARCUS, G. F., VIJAYAN, S., BANDI RAO, S., & VISHTON, P. M. (1999). Rule learning by seven-month-old infants. *Science, 283,* 77–80.

MARKMAN, E. M. (1977). Realizing that you don't understand: A preliminary investigation. *Child Development, 48,* 986–992.

MARKMAN, E. M. (1979). Realizing that you don't understand: Elementary school children's awareness of inconsistencies. *Child Development, 50,* 643–655.

MARKMAN, E. M. (1989). *Categorization and naming in children: Problems of induction.* Cambridge, MA: MIT Press.

MARKMAN, E. M. (1991). The whole-object, taxonomic, and mutual exclusivity assumptions as initial constraints on word meanings. In S. A. Gelman & J. P. Byrnes (Eds.), *Perspectives on language and thought: Interrelations in development* (pp. 72–106). Cambridge, England: Cambridge University Press.

MARKMAN, E. M. (1994). Constraints on word meaning in early language acquisition. In L. Gleitman & B. Landau (Eds.), *The acquisition of the lexicon* (pp. 199–229). Cambridge, MA: MIT Press/Elsevier.

MARKMAN, E. M., & HUTCHINSON, J. E. (1984). Children's sensitivity to constraints on word meaning: Taxonomic vs. thematic relations. *Cognitive Psychology, 16,* 1–27.

MARKMAN, E. M., & WACHTEL, G. A. (1988). Children's use of mutual exclusivity to constrain the meanings of words. *Cognitive Psychology, 20,* 121–157.

MARKMAN, E. M., WASOW, J. L., & HANSEN, M. B. (2003). Use of the mutual exclusivity assumption by young word learners. *Cognitive Psychology; 47,* 241–275.

MARKSON, L. & BLOOM, P. (1997). Evidence against a dedicated system for word learning in children. *Nature, 385,* 813–815.

MARLER, P. (1970). Birdsong and speech development: Could there be parallels? *American Scientist, 58,* 669–673.

MARLER, P., & TENAZA, R. (1977). Signalling behavior of apes with special reference to vocalization. In T. A. Sebeok (Ed.), *How animals communicate* (pp. 965–1033). Bloomington, IN: Indiana University Press.

MARTINDALE, C. (1991). *Cognitive psychology.* Pacific Grove, CA: Brooks/Cole.

MARTINEZ, I., SHATZ, M. (1996). Linguistic influences on categorization in preschool children: A cross-linguistic study. *Journal of Child Language, 23,* 529–545.

MARTON, K., & SCHWARTZ, R. G. (2003). Working memory capacity and language processes in children with specific language impairment. *Journal of Speech, Language, and Hearing Research, 46,* 1138–1153.

MAYBERRY, R., & WODLINGER-COHEN, R. (1987). After the revolution: Educational practice and the deaf child's communication skills. In E. D. Mindell & M. Vernon (Eds.), *They grow in silence: Understanding deaf children and adults* (pp. 149–185). Boston: College Hill Publishing.

MAYBERRY, R. I., & EICHEN, E. B. (1991). The long-lasting advantage of learning sign language in childhood: Another look at the critical period for language acquisition. *Journal of Memory and Language, 30,* 486–512.

MAYE, J., WERKER, J. F., & GERKEN, L. (2002). Infant sensitivity to distributional information can affect phonetic discrimination. *Cognition, 82,* 101–111.

MAYER, M. (1969). *Frog, where are you?* NY: Dial Books.

MAZZIOTTA, J. C., & METTER, E. J. (1988). Brain cerebral metabolic mapping of normal and abnormal language and its acquisition during development. In F. Plum (Ed.), *Language, communication, and the brain* (pp. 245–266). New York: Raven Press.

MCCABE, A., & PETERSON, C. (1984). What makes a good story? *Journal of Psycholinguistic Research, 13,* 457–480.

MCCABE, A., & PETERSON, C. (1991). Getting the story: A longitudinal study of parental styles in eliciting narratives and developing narrative skill. In A. McCabe & C. Peterson (Eds.), *Developing narrative structure* (pp. 217–253). Hillsdale, NJ: Erlbaum.

MCCARDLE, P., SCARBOROUGH, H. S., & CATTS, H. W. (2001). Predicting, explaining, and preventing children's reading difficulties. *Learning Disabilities Research & Practice, 16,* 230–239.

MCCARTHY, D. (1930). *The language development of the preschool child.* Institute of Child Welfare Monograph (Serial No. 4). Minneapolis, MN: University of Minnesota Press.

MCCARTHY, D. (1954). Language development in children. In L. Carmichael (Ed.), *Manual of child psychology* (2nd ed., pp. 492–630). New York: Wiley.

MCCARTNEY, K. (1984). Effect of quality of day care environment on children's language development. *Developmental Psychology, 20,* 244–260.

MCGLONE, J. (1980). Sex differences in human brain asymmetry: A critical survey. *Behavioral and Brain Sciences, 3,* 215–263.

MCKEOWN, M. G., & CURTIS, M. E. (Eds.). (1987). *The nature of vocabulary acquisition.* Hillsdale, NJ: Erlbaum.

MCNAMEE, G. D. (1987). The social origins of narrative skills. In M. Hickmann (Ed.), *Social and functional approaches to language and thought* (pp. 287–304). New York: Academic Press.

MCSHANE, J. (1980). *Learning to talk.* Cambridge, England: Cambridge University Press.

MEADOW, K. P. (1980). *Deafness and child development.* Berkeley, CA: University of California Press.

MEHLER, J., DUPOUX, E., NAZZI, T., & DEHAENE-LAMBERTZ, G. (1996). Coping with linguistic diversity: The infant's viewpoint. In J. L. Morgan & K. Demuth (Eds.), *Signal to syntax: Bootstrapping from speech to grammar in early acquisition* (pp. 101–116). Mahwah, NJ: Erlbaum.

MEHLER, J., JUSCZYK, P., LAMBERTZ, G., HALSTED, N., BERTONCINI, J., & AMIEL-TISON, C. (1988). A precursor of language acquisition in young infants. *Cognition, 29,* 143–178.

MEIER, R. P. (1984). Sign as creole. *Behavioral and Brain Sciences, 7,* 201–202.

MEISEL, J. M. (1989). Early differentiation of languages in bilingual children. In K. Hyltenstam & L. K. Obler (Eds.), *Bilingualism across the lifespan: Aspects of acquisition, maturity, and loss* (pp. 13–40). Cambridge, England: Cambridge University Press.

MENKEN, H. L. (1935). The future of English. *Harpers Magazine.* (Reprinted 1999.)

MENN, L., & STOEL-GAMMON, C. (1995). Phonological development. In P. Fletcher & B. MacWhinney (Eds.), *The handbook of child language* (pp. 335–360). Oxford: Blackwell.

MENYUK, P. (1993). Children with specific language impairment (developmental dysphasia): Linguistic aspects. In G. Blanken, J. Dittmann, H. Grimm, J. D. Marshall, & C.-W. Wallesch (Eds.), *Linguistic disorders and pathologies: An international handbook* (pp. 606–624). Berlin: Walter de Gruyter.

MENYUK, P., & MENN, L. (1979). Early strategies for the perception and production of words and sounds. In P. Fletcher & M. Garman (Eds.), *Language acquisition* (pp. 49–70). Cambridge, England: Cambridge University Press.

MENYUK, P., MENN, L., & SILBER, R. (1986). Early strategies for the perception and production of words and sounds. In P. Fletcher & M. Garman (Eds.), *Language acquisition* (2nd ed., pp. 198–222). Cambridge, England: Cambridge University Press.

MERVIS, C. B., & BERTRAND, J. (1994). Acquisition of the novel name–nameless category principle. *Child Development, 65,* 1646–1662.

MERVIS, C. B., & BERTRAND, J. (1995). Early lexical acquisition and the vocabulary spurt: A response to Goldfield & Reznick. *Journal of Child Language, 22,* 461–468.

MERVIS, C. B., & LONG, L. M. (1987). Words refer to whole objects: Young children's interpretation of the referent of a novel word. Paper presented at the biennial meeting of the Society for Research in Child Development, Baltimore, MD.

MERVIS, C. B., & MERVIS, C. A. (1988). Role of adult input in young children's category evolution: An observational study. *Journal of Child Language, 15,* 257–272.

MERVIS, C. B., MERVIS, C. A., JOHNSON, K. E., & BERTRAND, J. (1992). Studying early lexical development: The value of the systematic diary method. In C. Rovee-Collier & L. P. Lipsitt (Eds.), *Advances in infancy research* (Vol. 7, pp. 291–379). Norwood, NJ: Ablex.

MERVIS, C. B., MORRIS, C. A., BERTRAND, J., & ROBINSON, B. F. (1999). Williams syndrome: Findings from an integrated program of research. In H. Tager-Flusberg, (Ed.), *Neurodevelopmental disorders* (pp. 65–110). Cambridge, MA: MIT Press.

MERVIS, C. (2003). Williams syndrome: 15 years of psychological research. *Developmental Neuropsychology, 23,* 1–12.

MICHAELS, S. (1981). "Sharing time": Children's narrative styles and differential access to literacy. *Language in Society, 10,* 423–442.

MICHAELS, S. (1983). The role of adult assistance in children's acquisition of literate discourse strategies. *Volta Review, 85,* 72–85.

MILLER, G. A. (1977). *Spontaneous apprentices: Children and language.* New York: Seabury.

MILLER, G. A. (1981). *Language and speech.* San Francisco: W. H. Freeman.

MILLER, J. D., WIER, C. C., PASTORE, R. E., KELLEY, W. J., & DOOLING, R. J. (1976). Discrimination and labeling of noise-buzz sequences with varying noise-lead times: An example of categorical perception. *Journal of the Acoustic Society of America, 60,* 410–417.

MILLER, J. F. (1992). Development of speech and language in children with Down syndrome. In I. T. Lott & E. E. McCoy (Eds.), *Down syndrome: Advances in medical care* (pp. 39–50). New York: Wiley-Liss.

MILLER, J. F., & CHAPMAN, R. S. (1981). The relation between age and mean length of utterance. *Journal of Speech and Hearing Research, 24,* 154–161.

MILLER, J. F., & CHAPMAN, R. S. (1985). *SALT II: Systematic analysis of language transcripts.* Madison: Language Analysis Laboratory, Waisman Center on Mental Retardation and Human Development, University of Wisconsin–Madison.

MILLER, J. F., & KLEE, T. (1995). Computational approaches to the analysis of language impairment. In P. Fletcher & B. MacWhinney (Eds.), *The handbook of child language* (pp. 454–572). Oxford: Blackwell.

MILLER, J. L., & EIMAS, P. D. (1994). Observations on speech perception, its development, and the search for a mechanism. In J. C. Goodman & H. C. Nusbaum (Eds.), *The development of speech perception: The transition from speech sounds to spoken words* (pp. 37–56). Cambridge, MA: MIT Press.

MILLER, P. (1986). Teasing as language socialization and verbal play in a white working-class community. In B. B. Schieffelin & E. Ochs (Eds.), *Language socialization across cultures* (pp. 199–212). Cambridge, England: Cambridge University Press.

MILLER, P. J., & SPERRY, L. L. (1988). Early talk about the past: The origins of conversational stories of personal experience. *Journal of Child Language, 15,* 293–315.

MILLER, W., & ERVIN, S. (1964). The development of grammar in child language. In U. Bellugi & R. Brown (Eds.), The acquisition of language. *Monographs of the Society for Research in Child Development, 29,* 9–34.

MILLS, A. (1985). The acquisition of German. In D. I. Slobin (Ed.), *The crosslinguistic study of language acquisition: Vol. 1. The data* (pp. 141–254). Hillsdale, NJ: Erlbaum.

MILLS, A. (1987). The development of phonology in the blind child. In B. Dodd & R. Campbell (Eds.), *Hearing by eye: The psychology of lipreading* (pp. 145–162). London: Erlbaum.

MILLS, A. (1993). Visual handicap. In D. Bishop & K. Mogford (Eds.), *Language development in exceptional children* (pp. 150–164). Hove, England: Erlbaum.

MILLS, D., COFFEY, S., & NEVILLE, H. (1993). Language acquisition and cerebral specialization in 20-month-old children. *Journal of Cognitive Neuroscience, 5,* 326–342.

MILLS, D., COFFEY, S., & NEVILLE, H. (1994). Changes in cerebral organization in infancy during primary language acquisition. In G. Dawson & K. Fischer (Eds.), *Human behavior and the developing brain.* New York: Guilford.

MILLS, D. L., COFFEY-CORINA, S., NEVILLE, H. (1997). Language comprehension and cerebral specialization from 13 to 20 months. *Developmental Neuropsychology, 13,* 395–445.

MILNER, B. (1974). Hemispheric specialization: Scope and limits. In F. O. Schmitt & F. G. Worden (Eds.), *The Neurosciences: Third Study Program* (pp. 75–89). Cambridge, MA: MIT Press.

MINAMI, M., & MCCABE, A. (1995). Rice balls and bear hunts: Japanese and North American family narrative patterns. *Journal of Child Language, 22,* 423–446.

MINKOWSI, M., (1927). Klinischer beitrag zur aphasie bei plyglotten speziel im hinblick auf sweizerdeutsch. *Schweizer Archiv fur Neurologie und Psychiatrie, 21,* 43–72.

MINTZ, T. H., NEWPORT, E. L., & BEVER, T. B. (2002). The distributional structure of grammatical categorical in speech to young children. *Cognitive Science, 26,* 393–424.

MOGFORD, K. (1993). Oral language acquisition in the prelinguistically deaf. In D. Bishop & K. Mogford (Eds.), *Language development in exceptional children* (pp. 110–131). Hove, England: Erlbaum.

MOGFORD-BEVAN, K. (1993). Language acquisition and development with sensory impairment: Hearing-impaired children. In G. Blanken, J. Dittmann, H. Grimm, J. D. Marshall, & C.W. Wallesch (Eds.), *Linguistic disorders and pathologies: An international handbook* (pp. 660–679). Berlin: Walter de Gruyter.

MOLFESE, D. L., & BETZ, J. C. (1988). Electrophysiological indices of the early development of lateralization for language and cognition, and their implications for predicting later development. In D. L. Molfese & S. J. Segalowitz (Eds.), *Brain lateralization in children: Developmental implications* (pp. 171–190). New York: Guilford Press.

MOLFESE, D. L., FREEMAN, R. B., & PALERMO, D. S. (1975). The ontogeny of brain lateralization for speech and nonspeech stimuli. *Brain and Language, 2,* 356–368.

MOORE, C., & CORKUM, V. (1994). Social understanding at the end of the first year of life. *Developmental Review, 14,* 349–372.

MOORES, D. F. (1978). Current research and theory with the deaf: Educational implications. In L. Liben (Ed.), *Deaf children: Developmental perspectives* (pp. 173–193). New York: Academic Press.

MORAIS, J., CARY, L., ALEGRIA, J., & BERTELSON, P. (1979). Does awareness of speech as a sequence of phones arise spontaneously? *Cognition, 7,* 323–331.

MORALES, M., MUNDY, P., DELGADO, C, YALE, M., MESSINGER, D., NEAL, R.& SCHWARTZ, H. K. (2000). Responding to joint attention across the 6- through 24-month age period and early language acquisition. *Journal of Applied Developmental Psychology, 21,* 283–198.

MORALES, M., MUNDY, P., & ROJAS, J. (1998). Following the direction of gaze and language development in 6-month-olds. *Infant Behavior & Development, 21,* 373–377.

MORGAN, J. L. (1986). *From simple input to complex grammar.* Cambridge, MA: MIT Press.

MORGAN, J. L. (1990). Input, innateness, and induction in language acquisition. *Developmental Psychobiology, 23,* 661–678.

MORGAN, J. L., & DEMUTH, K. (1996). *Signal to syntax: Bootstrapping from speech to grammar in early acquisition.* Mahwah, NJ: Erlbaum.

MORRISON, F. J., SMITH, L., & DOW-EHRENSBERGER, M. (1995). Education and cognitive development: A natural experiment. *Developmental Psychology, 31,* 789–799.

MOWRER, O. (1960). *Learning theory and symbolic processes.* New York: Wiley.

MULLER, N. & HULK, A. (2001). Crosslinguistic influence in bilingual language acquisition: Italian and French as recipient languages. *Bilingualism: Language and Cognition, 4,* 1–53.

MUNDY, P., & GOMES, A. (1998). Individual differences in joint attention skill development in the second year. *Infant Behavior & Development, 21,* 469–482.

MUNDY, P., FOX, N., & CARD, J. (2003). EEG coherence, joint attention and language development in the second year. *Developmental Science, 6(1),* 48–54.

MUYSKEN, P. (1988). Are creoles a special type of language? In F. J. Newmeyer (Ed.), *Linguistics: The Cambridge survey: Vol. II. Linguistic theory: Extensions and implications* (pp. 285–301). Cambridge, England: Cambridge University Press.

NAGY, W. E. & SCOTT, J. A. (2000). Vocabulary processes. In M. L. Kamil, & P. B. Mosenthal (Ed.), *Handbook of reading research, vol.III* (pp. 269–284). Mahway, NJ: Lawrence Erlbaum Associates.

NAIGLES, L. (1990). Children use syntax to learn verb meanings. *Journal of Child Language, 17,* 357–374.

NAIGLES, L. (1995). The use of multiple frames in verb learning via syntactic bootstrapping. *Cognition, 58,* 221–251.

NAIGLES, L., EISENBERG, A., KAKO, E., HIGHTER, M., & MCGRAW, N. (1998). Speaking of motion: Verb use by English and Spanish speakers. *Language and Cognitive Processes, 13,* 521–549.

NAIGLES, L., & GELMAN, S. (1995). Overextensions in comprehension and production revisited: Preferential-looking in a study of dog, cat, and cow. *Journal of Child Language, 22,* 19–46.

NAIGLES, L. & HOFF, E. (in press). Verbs at the very beginning: Parallels between comprehension and input? In K. Hirsh-Pasek & R. Golinkoff (Eds.), *Action meets word: How children learn verbs.* Oxford University Press.

NAIGLES, L., & HOFF-GINSBERG, E. (1995). Input to verb learning: Evidence for the plausibility of syntactic bootstrapping. *Developmental Psychology, 31,* 827–837.

NAIGLES, L. R., & HOFF-GINSBERG, E. (1998). Why are some verbs learned before other verbs? Effects of input frequency and structure on children's early verb use. *Journal of Child Language, 25,* 95–120.

NAIGLES, L., & TERRAZAS, P. (1998). Motion verb generalizations in English and Spanish: Influences of language and syntax. *Psychological Science, 9,* 363–369.

NATIONAL INSTITUTE OF CHILD HEALTH AND HUMAN DEVELOPMENT EARLY CHILD CARE RESEARCH NETWORK (2000). The relation of child care to cognitive and language development. *Child Development, 71,* 960–980.

NATIONAL READING PANEL. (2000). *Teaching children to read: An evidence-based assessment of the scientific research literature on reading and its implication for reading instruction.* Washington, DC: National Institute of Child Health and Human Development.

NAVARRO, A. M., PEARSON, B. Z., COBO-LEWIS, A., & OLLER, D. K. (1998). Identifying the language spoken by 26-month-old monolingual- and bilingual-learning babies in a no-context situation. In A. Greenhill, M. Hughes, H. Littlefield, & H. Walsh (Eds.), *Proceedings of the 22nd Annual Boston University Conference on Language Development* (Vol. 2, pp. 557–568,). Somerville, MA: Cascadilla Press.

NAZZI, T., BERTONCINI, J., & MEHLER, J. (1998). Language discrimination by newborns: Towards an understanding of the role of rhythm. *Journal of Experimental Psychology, 24(3),* 756–766.

NEILS, J., & ARAM, D. M. (1986). Family history of children with developmental language disorders. *Perceptual and Motor Skills, 63,* 655–658.

NELSON, K. (1973). Structure and strategy in learning to talk. *Monographs of the Society for Research in Child Development, 38* (1 and 2, Serial No. 149).

NELSON, K. (1989). *Narratives from the crib.* Cambridge, MA: Harvard University Press.

NELSON, K., & GRUENDEL, J. M. (1979). At morning it's lunchtime: A scriptal view of children's dialogues. *Discourse Processes, 2,* 73–94.

NELSON, K., & GRUENDEL, J. M. (1981). Generalized event representations: Basic building blocks of cognitive development. In A. L. Brown & M. E. Lamb (Eds.), *Advances in developmental psychology* (Vol. 1, pp. 131–158). Hillsdale, NJ: Erlbaum.

NELSON, K., & LUCARIELLO, J. (1985). The development of meaning in first words. In M. Barrett (Ed.), *Children's single-word speech.* New York: Wiley.

NELSON, K. E., DENNINGER, M. M., BONVILLIAN, J. D., KAPLAN, B. J., & BAKER, N. D. (1984). Maternal input adjustments and nonadjustments as related to children's linguistic advances and to language acquisition theories. In A. D. Pellegrini & T. D. Yawkey (Eds.), *The development of oral and written languages: Readings in developmental and applied linguistics* (pp. 31–56). New York: Ablex.

NELSON, K. E., WELSH, J., CAMARATA, S. M., BUTKOVSKY, L., & CAMARATA, M. (1995). Available input for language-impaired children and younger children of matched language levels. *First Language, 15,* 1–17.

NEUMAN, S. B. & DICKINSON, D. K. (2002). *Handbook of early literacy research.* New York: The Guilford Press.

NEVILLE, H. J. (1991). Neurobiology of cognitive and language processing: Effects of early experience. In K. R. Gibson & A. C. Petersen (Eds.), *Brain maturation and cognitive development: Comparative and cross-cultural perspectives* (pp. 355–380). New York: Aldine de Bruyter.

NEVILLE, H. J. (1995a). Developmental specificity in neurocognitive development in humans. In M. S. Gazzaniga (Ed.), *The cognitive neurosciences* (pp. 219–231). Cambridge, MA: MIT Press.

NEVILLE, H. J. (1995b). Developmental specificity in neurocognitive development in humans. Presentation to the Symposium on Research in Child Language Disorders. Madison, WI.

NEVILLE, H. J., NICOL, J. L., BARSS, A., FORSTER, K. I., & GARRETT, M. (1991). Syntactically based sentence processing classes: Evidence from event-related brain potentials. *Journal of Cognitive Neuroscience, 3,* 151–165.

NEWPORT, E. L. (1982). Task specificity in language learning? Evidence from speech perception and American Sign Language. In E. Wanner & L. R. Gleitman (Eds.), *Language acquisition: The state of the art* (pp. 450–486). Cambridge, England: Cambridge University Press.

NEWPORT, E. L. (1990). Maturational constraints on language learning. *Cognitive Science, 14,* 11–28.

NEWPORT, E. L. (1991). Constraining concepts of the critical period for language. In S. Carey & R. Gelman (Eds.), *The epigenesis of mind: Essays on biology and cognition* (pp. 111–130). Hillsdale, NJ: Erlbaum.

NEWPORT, E. L., & ASLIN, R. N. (2000). Innately constrained learning: Blending old and new approaches to language acquisition. In C. Howell, S. A. Fish, & T. Keith-Lucas (Eds.), Proceedings of the 24th Annual Boston University conference on language development (pp. 1–21). Somerville, MA: Cascadilla Press.

NEWPORT, E. L., GLEITMAN, H., & GLEITMAN, L. (1977). Mother, I'd rather do it myself: Some effects and noneffects of maternal speech style. In C. E. Snow & C. A. Ferguson (Eds.), *Talking to children: Language input and acquisition* (pp. 109–150). Cambridge, England: Cambridge University Press.

NEWPORT, E. L., & MEIER, R. P. (1985). The acquisition of American Sign Language. In D. I. Slobin (Ed.), *The cross-linguistic study of language acquisition: Vol. 1. The data* (pp. 881–938). Hillsdale, NJ: Erlbaum.

NICOLADIS, E., & GENESEE, F. (1996), A longitudinal study of pragmatic differentiation in young bilingual chidren. *Language Learning, 46,* 439–464. NICOLADIS, E. (2002). The cues that children use in acquiring adjectival phrases and compound nouns: Evidence from bilingual children. *Brain & Language, 81(1–3),* 635–648.

NINIO, A. (1995). Expression of communicative intents in the single-word period and the vocabulary spurt. In K. E. Nelson & Z. Reger (Eds.), *Children's language* (Vol. 8, pp.103–124). Mahwah, NJ: Erlbaum.

NINIO, A., & SNOW, C. E. (1999). The development of pragmatics: Learning to use language appropriately. In W. C. Ritchie & T. K. Bhatia (Eds.), *Handbook of child language acquisition* (pp. 347–386). New York: Academic Press.

NOTTEBOHM, F. (1970). Ontogeny of birdsong. *Science, 167,* 950–956.

OBLER, L. K., & GJERLOW, K. (1999). *Language and the brain.* Cambridge, England: Cambridge University Press.

OCHS, E. (1982). Talking to children in Western Samoa. *Language in Society, 11,* 77–104.

OCHS, E. (1988). *Culture and language development.* Cambridge, England: Cambridge University Press.

O'GRADY, W. (1999). The acquisition of syntactic representations: A general nativist approach. In W. C. Ritchie & T. K. Bhatia (Eds.), *Handbook of child language acquisition* (pp. 157–194). New York: Academic Press.

O'GRADY, W., DOBROVOLSKY, M., & ARONOFF, M. (1989). *Contemporary linguistics: An introduction.* New York: St. Martin's Press.

OLGUIN, R., & TOMASELLO, M. (1993). Twenty-five-month-old children do not have a grammatical category of verb. *Cognitive Development, 8,* 245–272.

OLLER, D. K. (1980). The emergence of the sounds of speech in infancy. In G. H. Yeni-Komshian, J. F. Kavanagh, & C. A. Ferguson

(Eds.), *Child phonology* (Vol. 1, pp. 93–112). New York: Academic Press.

OLLER, D. K. (1986). Metaphonology and infant vocalizations. In B. Lindblom & R. Zetterstrom (Eds.), *Precursors of early speech* (pp. 21–35). New York: Stockton Press.

OLLER, D. K. (2000). The emergence of the speech capacity. Mahway, NJ: Erlbaum.

OLLER, D. K. & DELGADO, R. E. (1999). Logical International Phonetics Programs (Version Windows). Miami: Intelligent Hearing Systems Corp.

OLLER, D. K., & EILERS, R. E. (1988). The role of audition in infant babbling. *Child Development, 59,* 441–449.

OLLER, D. K., & EILERS, R. E. (1998). Interpretive and methodological difficulties in evaluating babbling drift. *Parole, 7/8,* 147–164.

OLLER, D. K., EILERS, R. E., BASINGER, D., STEFFENS, M. L., & URBANO, R. (1995). Extreme poverty and the development of precursors to the speech capacity. *First Language, 15,* 167–189.

OLLER, D. K., EILERS, R. E., BULL, D. H., & CARNEY, A. E. (1985). Prespeech vocalizations of a deaf infant: A comparison with normal metaphonological development. *Journal of Speech and Hearing Research, 28,* 47–63.

OLLER, D. K., EILERS, R. E., URBANO, R., & COBO-LEWIS, A. B. (1997). Development of precursors to speech in infants exposed to two languages. *Journal of Child Language, 24,* 407–425.

OLLER, D. K., & LYNCH, M. P. (1992). Infant vocalizations and innovations in infraphonology: Toward a broader theory of development and disorders. In C. A. Ferguson, L. Menn, & C. Stoel-Gammon (Eds.), *Phonological development: Models, research, implications* (pp. 509–538). Timonium, MD: York Press.

OLLER, D. K., & PEARSON, B. Z. (in press). Assessing the effects of bilingual: A background. In D. K. Oller (Ed.), *Language and literacy in bilingual children.* Clevedon, UK: Multilingual Matters.

OLSON, R. K. & GAYAN, J. (2002). Brains, genes, and environment in reading development. In S. B. Neuman & D. K. Dickinson (Eds.), *Handbook of early literacy research* (pp. 43–53). New York: The Guilford Press.

OVIATT, S. L. (1982). Inferring what words mean: Early development in infants' comprehension of common object names. *Child Development, 53,* 274–277.

OWENS, E. (1989). Present status of adults with cochlear implants. In E. Owens & D. K. Kessler (Eds.), *Cochlear implants in young deaf children* (pp. 25–52). Boston: College Hill Publications.

OWENS, E., & Kessler, D. K. (1989). *Cochlear implants in young deaf children.* Boston: College Hill Publications.

OYAMA, S. (1976). A sensitive period in the acquisition of a nonnative phonological system. *Journal of Psycholinguistic Research, 5,* 261–285.

OYAMA, S. (1978). The sensitive period and comprehension of speech. *Working Papers on Bilingualism, 16,* 1–17.

PADDEN, C., & HUMPHRIES, T. (1988). *Deaf in America: Voices from a culture.* Cambridge, MA: Harvard University Press.

PALIJ, M., & HOMEL, P. (1987). The relationship of bilingualism to cognitive development: Historical, methodological and theoretical considerations. In P. Homel, M. Palij, & D. Aaronson (Eds.), *Childhood bilingualism: Aspects of linguistic, cognitive, and social development* (pp. 131–148). Hillsdale, NJ: Erlbaum.

PAN, B. A., IMBENS-BAILEY, A., WINNER, K., & SNOW, C. E. (1996). Communicative intents of parents interacting with their young children. *Merrill-Palmer Quarterly, 42,* 248–266.

PARADIS, M. (1997). The cognitive neuropsychology of bilingualism. In A. M. B. De Groot & J. F. Kroll (Eds.), *Tutorials in bilingualism: Psycholinguistic perspectives* (pp. 331–354). Mahwah, NJ: Erlbaum.

PARADISE, J. L., DOLLAGHAN, C. A., CAMPBELL, T. F., FELDMAN, H. M., BERNARD, B. S., COLBORN, D., K., ROCKETTE, H. E., JONOSKY, J. E., PITCAIRN, D. L., SABO, D. L., KURS-LASKY, M. & SMITH, C. G. (2000). Language, speech sound production, and cognition in three-year-old children in relation to otitis media in their first three years of life. *Pediatrics, 105*, 1119–1130.

PAUL, R. (1987). Communication. In D. J. Cohen, A. M. Donnellan, & R. Paul (Eds.), *Handbook of autism and pervasive developmental disorders* (pp. 61–84). New York: Wiley.

PAUL, R., & COHEN, D. J. (1985). Comprehension of indirect requests in adults with autistic disorders and mental retardation. *Journal of Speech and Hearing Research, 28*, 475–479.

PAYNE, A. (1980). Factors controlling the acquisition of the Philadelphia dialect by out-of-state children. In W. Labov (Ed.), *Locating language in time and space* (pp. 143–177). New York: Academic Press.

PEAL, E., & LAMBERT, W. E. (1962). The relation of bilingualism to intelligence. *Psychological Monographs, 76* (27, Whole No. 546).

PEARSON, B. Z., & FERNANDEZ, S. C. (1994). Patterns of interaction in the lexical growth in two languages of bilingual infants and toddlers. *Language Learning, 44*, 617–653.

PEARSON, B. Z., FERNANDEZ, S. C., LEWEDEG, V., & OLLER, D. K. (1997). The relation of input factors to lexical learning by bilingual infants. *Applied Psycholinguistics, 18*, 41–58.

PEARSON, B. Z., FERNANDEZ, S. C., & OLLER, D. K. (1993). Lexical development in bilingual infants and toddlers: Comparison to monolingual norms. *Language Learning, 43*, 93–120.

PEARSON, B. Z., FERNANDEZ, S. C., & OLLER, D. K. (1995). Cross-language synonyms in the lexicons of bilingual infants: One language or two? *Journal of Child Language, 22*, 345–368.

PERANI, D., PAULESU, E., GALLES, N. S., DUPOUX, E., DEHAENE, S., BETTINARDI, V., CAPPA, S. F., FAZIO, F., & MEHLER, J. (1998). The bilingual brain: Proficiency and age of acquisition of the second language. *Brain, 121*, 1841–1852.

PEREZ-PEREIRA, M., & CASTRO, J. (1992). Pragmatic functions of blind and sighted children's language: A twin case study. *First Language, 12*, 17–37.

PETERS, A. M. (1983). *The units of language acquisition*. Cambridge, England: Cambridge University Press.

PETERS, A. M. (1986). Early syntax. In P. Fletcher & M. Garman (Eds.), *Language acquisition* (2nd ed., pp. 307–325). Cambridge, England: Cambridge University Press.

PETERS, A. M. (1994). The interdependence of social, cognitive, and linguistic development: Evidence from a visually impaired child. In H. Tager-Flusberg (Ed.), *Constraints on language acquisition.* (pp. 195–219). Hillsdale, NJ: Erlbaum.

PETERS, A. M. (1995). Strategies in the acquisition of syntax. In P. Fletcher & B. MacWhinney (Eds.), *The handbook of child language* (pp. 462–483). Oxford: Blackwell.

PETERS, A. M. (1997). Language typology, prosody, and the acquisition of grammatical morphemes. In D. Slobin (Ed.), *The crosslinguistic study of language acquisition: Vol. 5. Expanding the contexts* (pp. 135–198). Mahwah, NJ: Erlbaum.

PETERSON, C. L., DANNER, R. W., & FLAVELL, J. H. (1972). Developmental changes in children's response to three indications of communicative failure. *Child Development, 43*, 1463–1468.

PETERSON, C. L., & MCCABE, A. (1988). The connective *and* as discourse glue. *First Language, 8*, 19–28.

PETITTO, L. (1987). On the autonomy of language and gesture: Evidence from the acquisition of personal pronouns in American Sign Language. *Cognition, 27*, 1–52.

PETITTO, L. (1988). "Language" in the prelinguistic child. In F. S. Kessel (Ed.), *The development of language and language researchers: Essays in honor of Roger Brown* (pp. 187–222). Hillsdale, NJ: Erlbaum.

PETITTO, L. A. (2002). On the biological foundations of human language. In K. Emmorey & H. Lane, (Eds.), *The signs of language revisited: An anthology to honor Ursula Bellugi and Edward Klima*. Mahway, NJ: Erlbaum.

PETITTO, L. A., KATERELOS, M., LEVY, B. G., GAUNA, K., TETREALT, K., & FERRAROI, V. (2001). Bilingual signed and spoken language acquisition from birth: implications for the mechanisms underlying early bilingual language acquisition. *Journal of Child Language, 28,* 453–496.

PETITTO, L. A. (2000).   The acquisition of natural signed languages: Lessons in the nature of human language and its biological foundations. In C. Chamberlain & J. P. Morford (Eds.), *Language acquisition by eye* (pp. 41–50). Mahwah, NJ: Erlbaum.

PHELPS, M. E., & MAZZIOTTA, J. C. (1985).   PET: Human brain function and biochemistry. *Science, 228,* 799–809.

PIAGET, J. (1926).   *The language and thought of the child.* London: Routledge & Kegan Paul.

PINE, J. M. (1994).   Environmental correlates of variation in lexical style: Interactional style and the structure of the input. *Applied Psycholinguistics, 15,* 355–370.

PINE, J. M. (1995).   Variation in vocabulary development as a function of birth order. *Child Development, 66,* 272–281.

PINE, J. M., & LIEVEN, E. V. M. (1990).   Referential style at thirteen months: Why age-defined cross-sectional measures are inappropriate for the study of strategy differences in early language development. *Journal of Child Language, 17,* 625–632.

PINE, J. M., & LIEVEN, E. V. M. (1993).   Re-analysing rote-learned phrases: Individual differences in the transition to multi-word speech. *Journal of Child Language, 20,* 551–573.

PINKER, S. (1984).   *Language learnability and language development.* Cambridge, MA: Harvard University Press.

PINKER, S. (1989).   *Learnability and cognition: The acquisition of argument structure.* Cambridge, MA: MIT Press.

PINKER, S. (1994).   *The language instinct: How the mind creates language.* New York: Morrow.

PINKER, S. (1999).   *Words and rules.* New York: Basic Books.

PINKER, S., & BLOOM, P. (1990).   Natural language and natural selection. *Behavioral and Brain Sciences, 13,* 707–784.

PINKER, S., LEBEAUX, D. S., & FROST, L. A. (1987).   Productivity and constraints in the acquisition of the passive. *Cognition, 26,* 195–267.

PINKER, S., & PRINCE, A. (1994).   Regular and irregular morphology and the psychological status of rules of grammar. In S. Lima, R. Corrigan, & G. Iverson (Eds.), *The reality of linguistic rules* (pp. 321–352). Philadelphia, PA: Benjamins.

PLUNKETT, K. (1995).   Connectionist approaches to language acquisition. In P. Fletcher & B. MacWhinney (Eds.), *The handbook of child language* (pp. 36–72). Cambridge, MA: Blackwell.

PLUNKETT, K. (1998).   Language acquisition and connectionism. *Language and Cognitive Processes, 13,* 97–104.

PLUNKETT, K., & MARCHMAN, V. (1991).   U-shaped learning and frequency effects in a multi-layered perception: Implications for child language acquisition. *Cognition, 38,* 43–102.

PLUNKETT, K., & SCHAFER, G. (1999).   Early speech perception and word learning. In M. Barrett (Ed.), *The development of language* (pp. 51–72). East Sussex, England: Psychology Press.

POULIN-DUBOIS, D., & GOODZ, N. (2001).   Language differentiation in bilingual infants: evidence from babbling. In J. Cenoz & F. Genesee (Eds.), *Trends in bilingual acquisition* (pp. 95–106). Amsterdam: John Benjamins Publishing Company.

PREMACK, D. (1986).   *Gavagai! Or the future history of the animal language controversy.* Cambridge, MA: MIT Press.

PRESSLEY, M., LEVIN, J. R., & MCDANIEL, M. A. (1987).   Remembering versus inferring what a word means: Mnemonic and contextual approaches. In M. G. McKeown & M. E. Curtis (Eds.), *The nature of vocabulary acquisition* (pp. 107–128). Cambridge, MA: MIT Press.

PRINZ, P. M., & PRINZ, E. A. (1979).   Simultaneous acquisition of ASL and spoken English (in a hearing child of a deaf mother and hearing father). Phase I: Early lexical development. *Sign Language Studies, 25,* 283–296.

PRIZANT, B. M. (1983).   Language acquisition and communicative behavior in autism: Toward an understanding of the "whole" of it. *Journal of Speech and Hearing Disorders, 48,* 296–307.

PYE, C. (1986). One lexicon or two? An alternative interpretation of early bilingual speech. *Journal of Child Language, 13,* 591–594.

PYE, C. (1992). The acquisition of K'iche' Maya. In D. I. Slobin (Ed.), *Cross-linguistic studies of language acquisition* (Vol. 3, pp. 221–308). Hillsdale, NJ: Erlbaum.

PYE, C., INGRAM, D., & LIST, H. (1987). A comparison of initial consonant acquisition in English and Quiche. In K. E. Nelson & A. van Kleeck (Eds.), *Children's language* (Vol. 6, pp. 175–190). Hillsdale, NJ: Erlbaum.

QUIGLEY, S. P., & KING, C. M. (1980). Syntactic performance of hearing impaired and normal hearing individuals. *Applied Psycholinguistics, 1,* 329–356.

QUIGLEY, S. P., POWER, D. J., & STEINKAMP, M. W. (1977). The language structure of deaf children. *The Volta Review, 79,* 73–84.

QUINE, W. V. O. (1960). *Word and object.* Cambridge, England: Cambridge University Press.

RADFORD, A. (1990). *Syntactic theory and the acquisition of English syntax: The nature of early child grammars of English.* Oxford: Blackwell.

RADFORD, A. (1995). Phrase structure and functional categories. In P. Fletcher & B. MacWhinney (Eds.), *The handbook of child language* (pp. 483–507). Oxford: Blackwell.

RATNER, N. B. (1996). From "signal to syntax": But what is the nature of the signal? In J. L. Morgan & K. Demuth (Eds.), *Signal to syntax: Bootstrapping from speech to grammar in early acquisition* (pp. 135–150). Mahwah, NJ: Erlbaum.

RATNER, N. B., & Pye, C. (1984). Higher pitch in BT is not universal: Acoustic evidence from Quiche Mayan. *Journal of Child Language, 2,* 515–522.

RAYNER, K., FOORMAN, B. R., PERFETTI, C. A., PESETSKY, D., & SEIDENBERG, M. S. (2001). How psychological science informs the teaching of reading. *Psychological Science in the Public Interest, 2,* No. 2.

READ, C., ZHANG, Y.-F., NIE, H.-Y., & DING, B. Q. (1986). The ability to manipulate speech sounds depends on knowing alphabetic spelling. *Cognition, 24,* 31–44.

REES, N. S. (1978). Pragmatics of language: Applications to normal and disordered language development. In R. L. Schiefelbusch (Ed.), *Bases of language intervention* (Vol. 1, pp. 191–268). Baltimore, MD: University Park Press.

REESE, E., & FIVUSH, R. (1993). Parental styles of talking about the past. *Developmental Psychology, 29,* 596–606.

REGAL, R. A., ROONEY, J. R., & WANDAS, T. (1994). Facilitated communication: An experimental investigation. *Journal of Autism and Developmental Disorders, 24,* 345–355.

REICH, P. A. (1986). *Language development.* Englewood Cliffs, NJ: Prentice-Hall.

REILLY, J., KLIMA, E. S., & BELLUGI, U. (1990). Once more with feeling: Affect and language in atypical populations. *Development and Psychopathology, 2,* 369–391.

RESCORLA, L. A. (1980). Overextension in early language development. *Journal of Child Language, 7,* 321–335.

REZNICK, J.S., CORLEY, R., CARTER, A., ROBINSON, J. (1997). A longitudinal twin study of intelligence in the second year. *Monographs of the Society for Research in Child Development, 62(1),* p. 1–154.

RHEINGOLD, H. L., GEWIRTZ, J. L., & ROSS, H. W. (1959). Social conditioning of vocalizations in the infant. *Journal of Comparative and Physiological Psychology, 52,* 68–73.

RICE, M. L. (1990). Preschooler's QUIL: Quick incidental learning of words. In G. Conti-Ramsden & C. E. Snow (Eds.), *Children's language* (Vol. 7, pp. 171–196). Hillsdale, NJ: Erlbaum.

RICE, M. L., BUHR, J., & NEMETH, M. (1990). Fast mapping word-learning abilities of language-delayed preschoolers. *Journal of Speech and Hearing Disorders, 55,* 33–42.

RICE, M. L., & WOODSMALL, L. (1988). Lessons from television: Children's word learning when viewing. *Child Development, 59,* 420–429.

RICE, M. K. (2003). A unified model of specific and general language delay: Grammatical tense as a clinical marker of unexpected variation. In Y. Levy & J. Schaeffer (Eds.), *Language competence across populations: Toward a definition of specific language impairment* (pp. 63–94). Mahwah, NJ: Erlbaum.

RICE, M. K., WEXLER, K., & CLEAVE, P. L. (1995). Specific language impairment as a period of extended optional infinitive. *Journal of Speech, Language, and Hearing Research, 38,* 850–863.

RICHARDS, B. (1990). *Language development and individual differences: A study of auxiliary verb learning.* Cambridge, England: Cambridge University Press.

RICHARDS, B. J. (1994). Child directed speech and influences on language acquisition: methodology and interpretation. In C. Gallaway & B. J. Richards (Eds.), *Input and interaction in language acquisition* (pp. 74–106). Cambridge, England: Cambridge University Press.

ROBINSON, B. F. & MERVIS, C. B. (1998). Disentangling early language development: Modeling lexical and grammatical acquisition using an extension of case-study methodology. *Developmental Psychology, 34,* 363–375.

ROBINSON, B. F., MERVIS, C. B., & ROBINSON, B. W. (2003). The roles of verbal short-term memory and working memory in the acquisition of grammar by children with Williams syndrome. *Developmental Neuropsychology, 23,* 13–31.

ROBINSON, E. J. (1981). The child's understanding of inadequate messages and communication failure: A problem of ignorance or egocentrism? In W. P. Dickson (Ed.), *Children's oral communication skills* (pp. 167–188). New York: Academic Press.

ROBERTS, J. E., BURCHINAL, M. R., JACKSON, S. C., HOOPER, S. R., ROUSH, J., MUNDY, M., NEEBE, E. C., & ZEISEL, S. A. (2000). Otitis media in early childhood in relation to preschool language and school readiness skills among black children. *Pediatrics, 106,* 725–735.

ROHDE, D. L. T., & PLAUT, D. C. (1999). Language acquisition in the absence of explicit negative evidence: How important is starting small? *Cognition, 72,* 67–109.

ROITBLAT, H. L., HERMAN, L. M., & NACHTIGALL, P. E. (1993). *Language and communication: Comparative perspectives.* Hillsdale, NJ: Erlbaum.

ROLLINS, P. R., SNOW, C. E., & WILLETT, J. B. (1996). Predictors of MLU: Semantic and morphology development. *First Language, 16,* 243–259.

ROMAINE, S. (1984). *The language of children and adolescents: The acquisition of communicative competence.* Oxford: Blackwell.

ROMAINE, S. (1988). *Pidgin and creole languages.* New York: Longman.

RONDAL, J. A. (1993). Down's syndrome. In D. Bishop & K. Mogford (Eds.), *Language development in exceptional children* (pp. 165–176). Hove, England: Erlbaum.

RONDAL, J. A., GHIOTTO, M., BREDART, S., & BACHELET, J. F. (1987). Age relation, reliability and grammatical validity of measures of utterance length. *Journal of Child Language, 14,* 433–446.

RONJAT, J. (1913). *Le developpement du langage observe chez un enfant bilingue.* Paris: Champion.

ROSENBERG, S., & ABBEDUTO, L. (1993). *Language and communication in mental retardation: Development, processes, and intervention.* Hillsdale, NJ: Erlbaum.

ROSENBLUM, T., & PINKER, S. A. (1983). Word magic revisited: Monolingual and bilingual children's understanding of the word-object relationships. *Child Development, 54,* 773–780.

RUHLEN, M. (1976). *A guide to the languages of the world.* Language Universals Project, Stanford University, CA.

RUTTER, M. (1978). Language disorder and infantile autism. In M. Rutter & E. Schopler (Eds.), *Autism: A reappraisal of concepts and treatment* (pp. 85–104). New York: Plenum.

RVACHEW, S., SLAWINSKI, E. B., WILLIAMS, M., & GREEN, C. L. (1996). Formant frequencies of vowels produced by infants with and without early onset otitis media. *Canadian Acoustics, 24,* 19–28.

RVACHEW, S., SLAWINSKI, E. B., WILLIAMS, M., & GREEN, C. L. (1999). The impact of early onset otits media on babbling and early language development. *Journal of the Acoustic Society of America, 105,* 467–475.

RYMER, R. (1993). *Genie: A scientific tragedy.* New York: HarperCollins.

SACHS, J. (1983). Talking about there and then: The emergence of displaced reference in parent–child discourse. In K. E. Nelson (Ed.), *Children's language* (Vol. 4, pp. 1–28). Hillsdale, NJ: Erlbaum.

SACHS, J. (1987). Preschool boys' and girls' language use in pretend play. In S. U. Phillips, S. Steele, & C. Tanz (Eds.), *Language, gender and sex in comparative perspective* (pp. 178–188). Cambridge, England: Cambridge University Press.

SACHS, J., & DEVIN, J. (1976). Young children's use of age appropriate speech styles in social interaction and role-playing. *Journal of Child Language, 3,* 81–98.

SACHS, J., & TRUSWELL, L. (1978). Comprehension of 2-word instructions by children in the 1-word stage. *Journal of Child Language, 5,* 17–24.

SACKS, H., SCHEGLOFF, E. A., & JEFFERSON, G. (1974). A simplest systematics for the organization of turn-taking for conversation. *Language, 50,* 696–735.

SAFFRAN, J. R., ASLIN, R. N., & NEWPORT, E. L. (1996). Statistical learning by 8-month-old infants. *Science, 274,* 1926–1928.

SAFFRAN, E. M., & SCHWARTZ, M. F. (2003). Language. In M. Gallagher & R. J. Neson (volume eds.), *Handbook of psychology, Vol. 3. Biological psychology* (pp. 595–636). NY: John Wiley & Sons.

SAFFRAN, J.R. (2001). The use of predictive dependencies in language learning. *Journal of Memory and Language* 44, 493–515.

SAFFRAN, J. R., & THIESSEN, E. D. (2003). Pattern induction by infant language learners. *Developmental Psychology, 39,* 484–494.

SAMUELSON, L. K., & SMITH, L. B. (1998). Memory and attention make smart word learning: An alternative account of Akhtar, Carpenter, and Tomasello. *Child Development, 69,* 94–104.

SANDER, E. K. (1972). When are speech sounds learned? *Journal of Speech and Hearing Disorders, 37,* 55–63.

SANKOFF, G., & LABERGE, Z. (1973). On the acquisition of native speakers by a language. *Kivung, 6,* 32–47.

SANTELMANN, L., & JUSCZYK, P. (1998). Sensitivity to discontinuous dependencies in language learners: Evidence for limitations in processing space. *Cognition, 69,* 105–134.

SATZ, P., & LEWIS, R. (1993). Acquired aphasia in children. In G. Blanken, J. Dittmann, H. Grimm, J. D. Marshall, & C-W. Wallesch (Eds.), *Linguistic disorders and pathologies: An international handbook* (pp. 646–659). Berlin: Walter de Gruyter.

SATZ, P., STRAUSS, E., & WHITAKER, H. (1990). The ontogeny of hemispheric specialization: Some old hypotheses revisited. *Brain and Language, 38,* 596–614.

SAUNDERS, G. (1988). *Bilingual children: From birth to teens.* Clevedon, Avon: Multilingual Matters.

SAVAGE-RUMBAUGH, E. S., MCDONALD, K., SEVCIK, R., HOPKINS, W., & RUPERT, E. (1986). Spontaneous symbol acquisition and communicative use by pygmy chimpanzees (*Pan paniscus*). *Journal of Experimental Psychology: General, 115,* 211–235.

SAVAGE-RUMBAUGH, E. S., MURPHY, J., SEVCIK, R. A., BRAKKE, K. E., WILLIAMS, S. L., & RUMBAUGH, D. M. (1993). Language comprehension in ape and child. *Monographs of the Society for Research in Child Development, 58* (3–4, Serial No. 233).

SCARBOROUGH, H. S. (1990). Very early language deficits in dyslexic children. *Child Development, 61,* 1728–1734.

SCARBOROUGH, H. S. (2001). Connecting early language and literacy to later reading (dis)abilities: Evidence, theory, and practice. In S. Neuman & D. Dickinson (Eds.), *Handbook for research in early literacy* (pp. 97–110). New York: Guilford Press.

SCHIEFFELIN, B. B. (1979). Getting it together: An ethnographic approach to the study of the development of communicative competence. In E. Ochs & B. B. Schieffelin (Eds.), *Developmental pragmatics* (pp. 73–110). New York: Academic Press.

SCHIEFFELIN, B. B. (1985). The acquisition of Kaluli. In D. I. Slobin (Ed.), *The crosslinguistic study of language acquisition: Vol. 1. The data* (pp. 525–594). Hillsdale, NJ: Erlbaum.

SCHIEFFELIN, B. B., & OCHS, E. (1986). Language socialization. *Annual Review of Anthropology, 15,* 163–191.

SCHLESINGER, H. S., & MEADOW, K. P. (1972). *Sound and sign: Childhood deafness and mental health.* Berkeley: University of California Press.

SCHOEBER-PETERSON, D., & JOHNSON, C. J. (1989). Conversational topics of four-year-olds. *Journal of Speech and Hearing Research, 32,* 857–870.

SCHOEBER-PETERSON, D., & JOHNSON, C. J. (1991). Non-dialogue speech during preschool interactions. *Journal of Child Language, 18,* 153–170.

SCHOPLER, E., SHORT, A., & MESIBOV, G. (1989). Relation of behavioral treatment to "normal functioning": Comment on Lovaas. *Journal of Consulting and Clinical Psychology, 57,* 162–164.

SCHWARTZ, R. (1983). Diagnosis of speech sound disorders in children. In Mertus & Weinberg (Eds.), *Diagnosis in speech-language pathology* (pp. 113–149). Baltimore, MD: University Park Press.

SCHWARTZ, R., & LEONARD, L. (1982). Do children pick and choose? An examination of phonological selection and avoidance in early acquisition. *Journal of Child Language, 9,* 319–336.

SCOLLON, R. (1979). A real early stage: An unzippered condensation of a dissertation on child language. In E. Ochs & B. B. Schieffelin (Eds.), *Developmental pragmatics* (pp. 215–228). New York: Academic Press.

SCOTT, C. M. (1984). Adverbial connectivity in conversations of children 6 to 12. *Journal of Child Language, 11,* 423–452.

SEARLE, J. (1969). *Speech acts.* Cambridge, MA: University Press.

SEGALOWITZ, N. (1997). Individual differences in second language acquisition. In A. M. B. de-Groot & J. F. Kroll (Eds.), *Tutorials in bilingualism: Psycholinguistic perspectives* (pp. 85–112). Mahwah, NJ: Erlbaum.

SEIDENBERG, M. S., & PETITTO, L. A. (1979). Signing behavior in apes: A critical review. *Cognition, 7,* 177–215.

SEIDENBERG, M. S., & PETITTO, L. A. (1987). Communication, symbolic communication, and language: Comment on Savage-Rumbaugh, McDonald, Sevcik, Hopkins, and Rupert (1986). *Journal of Experimental Psychology: General, 116,* 279–287.

SELKIRK, E. (1996). The prosodic structure of function words. In J. L. Morgan & K. Demuth (Eds.), *Signal to syntax: Bootstrapping from speech to grammar in early acquisition* (pp. 187–214). Mahwah, NJ: Erlbaum.

SENECHAL, M. & LEFEVRE, J. (2001). Storybook reading and parent teaching: Links to language and literacy development. In P. R. Britto & J. Brooks-Gunn (Eds.), The role of family literacy environments in promoting young children's emerging literacy skills, *New directions for child and adolescent development, 104* (pp. 39–52). San Francisco: Jossey-Bass.

SENECHAL, M., & LEFEVRE, J. (2002). Parental involvement in the development of children's reading skill: A five-year longitudinal study. *Child Development, 73,* 445–460.

SENGHAS, A. (1995). The development of Nicaraguan Sign Language via the language acquisition process. In D. MacLaughlin & S. McEwen (Eds.), *Proceedings of the 19th Boston University Conference on Language Development* (pp. 543–552). Somerville, MA: Cascadilla Press.

SENGHAS, A., & COPPOLA, M. (2001). Children creating language: How Nicaraguan Sing Language acquired a spatial grammar. *Psychological Science, 12,* 323–328.

SERVICE, E. (1992). Phonology, working memory, and foreign-language learning. *The Quarterly Journal of Experimental Psychology, 45,* 21–50.

SERVICE, E., & KOHONEN, V. (1995). Is the relation between phonological memory and foreign language learning accounted for by vocabulary acquisition? *Applied Psycholinguistics, 16,* 155–172.

SEYFARTH, R. M., & CHENEY, D. L. (1993). Meaning, reference, and intentionality in the natural vocalizations of monkeys. In H. L. Roitblat, L. M. Herman, & P. E. Nachtigall (Eds.), *Language and communication: Comparative perspectives* (pp. 195–220). Hillsdale, NJ: Erlbaum.

SHANE, H. (1993). The dark side of facilitated communication. *Topics in Language Disorders, 13,* ix–xv.

SHAPIRO, L. R., & HUDSON, J. A. (1991). Tell me a make-believe story: Coherence and cohesion in young children's picture-elicited narratives. *Developmental Psychology, 27,* 960–974.

SHATZ, M. (1978a). On the development of communicative understandings: An early strategy for interpreting and responding to messages. *Cognitive Psychology, 10,* 271–301.

SHATZ, M. (1978b). Children's comprehension of their mothers' question-directives. *Journal of Child Language, 5,* 39–46.

SHATZ, M. (1983a). Communication. In P. H. Mussen (Ed.), *Handbook of child psychology* (pp. 841–889). New York: Wiley.

SHATZ, M. (1985). A song without music and other stories: How cognitive process constraints influence children's oral and written narratives. In D. Schiffrin (Ed.), *Georgetown University Round Table on Language and Linguistics 1984* (pp. 313–324). Washington, D. C.: Georgetown University Press.

SHATZ, M. (1992). A forward or backward step in the search for an adequate theory of language acquisition? *Social Development, 1,* 2.

SHATZ, M. (1994a). Review article. (Review of articles *Laura: A case for the modularity of language* by J. E. Yamada and *First verbs: A case study of early grammatical development* by M. Tomasello), *Language, 70,* 789–796.

SHATZ, M. (1994b). *A toddler's life: Becoming a person.* New York: Oxford University Press.

SHATZ, M., DIESENDRUCK, G., MARTINEZ-BECK, I., & AKAR, D. (2003). The influence of language and socioeconomic status on children's understanding of false belief. *Developmental Psychology, 39,* 717–729.

SHATZ, M., & GELMAN, R. (1973). The development of communication skills: Modifications in the speech of young children as a function of listener. *Monographs of the Society for Research in Child Development, 38,* 1–37.

SHATZ, M., & MCCLOSKEY, L. (1984). Answering appropriately: A developmental perspective on conversational knowledge. In S. Kuczaj (Ed.), *Discourse development* (pp. 19–36). New York: Springer-Verlag.

SHATZ, M., & WATSON O'REILLY, A. (1990). Conversational or communicative skill? A reassessment of two-year-olds' behaviour in miscommunication episodes. *Journal of Child Language, 17,* 131–146.

SHELDON, A. (1990). Pickle-fights: Gendered talk in preschool disputes. *Discourse Processes, 13,* 5–31.

SHERMAN, J. C., & LUST, B. (1993). Children are in control. *Cognition, 46,* 1–51.

SHIPLEY, E. F., SMITH, C. S., & GLEITMAN, L. (1969). A study in the acquisition of language: Free responses to commands. *Language, 45,* 322–342.

SHORE, C., O'CONNELL, B., & BATES, E. (1984). First sentences in language and symbolic play. *Developmental Psychology, 20,* 872–880.

SHRIBERG, L. D., FRIEL-PATTI, S., FLIPSEN, P., & BROWN, R. (2000). Otitis media, fluctuant hearing loss, and speech-language outcomes: A preliminary structural equation model. *Journal of Speech, Language, and Hearing Research, 43,* 100–120.

SIGMAN, M., MUNDY, P., SHERMAN, T., & UNGERER, J. (1986). Social interactions of autistic, mentally retarded and normal children and their caregivers. *Journal of Child Psychology and Psychiatry, 27,* 647–656.

SINCLAIR-DE-ZWART, H. (1969). Developmental psycholinguistics. In D. Elkind & J. Flavell (Eds.), *Studies in cognitive development* (pp. 315–336). New York: Oxford University Press.

SINGER HARRIS, N. G., BELLUGI, U., BATES, E., JONES, W., & ROSSEN, M. (1997). Contrasting profiles of language development in children with Williams and Down syndromes. *Developmental Neuropsychology, 13,* 345–370.

SINGLETON, J. L., & NEWPORT, E. L. (1987). When learners surpass their models: The acquisition of American Sign Language from impoverished input. Unpublished manuscript.

SKARAKIS, E. A., & PRUTTING, C. A. (1977). Early communication: Semantic functions and communicative intentions in the communication of the preschool child with impaired hearing. *American Annals of the Deaf, 122,* 382–391.

SKEHAN, P. (1989). *Individual differences in second language learning.* London: Edward Arnold.

SKEHAN, P. (1991). Individual differences in second language learning. *Studies in Second Language Acquisition, 13,* 275–298.

SKINNER, B. F. (1957). *Verbal behavior.* Englewood Cliffs, NJ: Prentice-Hall.

SLOBIN, D. I., GERHARDT, J., KYRATZIS, & GUO, J. (Eds.). (1996). *Social interaction, social context, and language: Essays in honor of Susan Ervin-Tripp.* Mahwah, NJ: Erlbaum.

SLOMKOWSKI, D. L., NELSON, K., DUNN, J., & PLOMIN, R. (1992). Temperament and language: Relations from toddlerhood to middle childhood. *Developmental Psychology, 28,* 1090–1095.

SMITH, L. B. (1995). Self-organizing processes in learning to learn words: Development is not induction. In C. A. Nelson (Ed.), Basic and applied perspectives on learning, cognition, and development. *The Minnesota Symposia on Child Psychology,* (Vol. 28, pp. 1–32). Mahwah, NJ: Erlbaum.

SMITH, L. B. (2001). How domain-general processes may create domain-specific biases. In M. Bowerman & S. Levinson (Eds.), *Language acquisition and conceptual development.* (pp. 101–131). Cambridge: Cambridge University Press.

SMITH, L. B., JONES, S. S., & LANDAU, B. (1992). Count nouns, adjectives, and perceptual properties in children's novel word interpretations. *Developmental Psychology, 28,* 273–289.

SMITH, M. D., HAAS, P. J., & BELCHER, R. G. (1994). Facilitated communication: The effects of facilitator knowledge and level of assistance on output. *Journal of Autism and Developmental Disorders, 24,* 357–367.

SNEDEKER, J. & GLEITMAN, L. (2004). Why it is hard to label our concepts. In G. Hall & S. Waxman (Eds), *Weaving a lexicon.* Cambridge, MA: MIT Press.

SNOW, C. E. (1977). The development of conversation between mothers and babies. *Journal of Child Language, 4,* 1–22.

SNOW, C. E. (1983). Literacy and language: Relationships during the preschool years. *Harvard Educational Review, 53,* 165–189.

SNOW, C. E. (1989). Understanding social interaction and language acquisition: Sentences are not enough. In M. H. Bornstein & J. S. Bruner (Eds.), *Interaction in human development* (pp. 83–104). Hillsdale, NJ: Erlbaum.

SNOW, C. E. (1990). The development of definitional skill. *Journal of Child Language, 17,* 697–710.

SNOW, C. E. (1999). Social perspectives on the emergence of language. In B. MacWhinney (Ed.), *The emergence of language* (pp. 257–276). Mahwah, NJ: Erlbaum.

SNOW, C. E., BURNS, M. S., & GRIFFIN, P. (Eds.). (1998). *Preventing reading difficulties in young children.* Washington, DC: National Academy Press.

SNOW, C. E., BURNS, M. S., & GRIFFIN, P. (Eds.). (1998). *Preventing reading difficulties in young children.* Washington, DC: National Academy Press.

SNOW, C. E., & DICKINSON, D. K. (1990). Social sources of narrative skills at home and at school. *First Language, 10,* 87–103.

SNOW, C. E., & HOEFNAGEL-HÖHLE, M. (1978). The critical period for language acquisition: Evidence from second language learning. *Child Development, 49,* 1114–1128.

SNOW, C. E., PAN, B., IMBENS-BAILEY, A., & HERMAN, J. (1996). Learning how to say what one means: A longitudinal study of children's speech act use. *Social Development, 5,* 56–84.

SNOW, C. E., PERLMANN, R., & NATHAN, D. (1987). Why routines are different: Toward a multiple-factors model of the relation between input and language acquisition. In K. Nelson & A. van Kleeck (Eds.), *Children's language* (Vol. 6, pp. 65–98). Hillsdale, NJ: Erlbaum.

SNOW, C. E., TABORS, P. O., & DICKINSON, D. K. (2001). Language development in the preschool years. In D. K. Dickinson & P. O. Tabors (Eds.). *Beginning literacy with language* (pp. 1–26). Baltimore: Paul H. Brookes, Publishing Co.

SNOWDON, C. T. (1993). Linguistic phenomena in the natural communication of animals. In H. L. Roitblat, L. M. Herman, & P. E. Nachtigall (Eds.), *Language and communication: Comparative perspectives* (pp. 175–194). Hillsdale, NJ: Erlbaum.

SOJA, N. N., CAREY, S., & SPELKE, E. S. (1991). Ontological categories guide young children's inductions of word meaning: Object terms and substance terms. *Cognition, 38,* 179–211.

SPRINGER, A., & DEUTSCH, G. (1981). *Left brain, right brain.* San Francisco: W. H. Freeman.

STAATS, A. W. (1971). Linguistic-mentalistic theory versus an explanatory S-R learning theory of language development. In D. I. Slobin (Ed.), *The ontogenesis of grammar* (pp. 103–152). New York: Academic Press.

STARK, R. E. (1986). Prespeech segmental feature development. In P. Fletcher & M. Garman (Eds.), *Language acquisition* (2nd ed., pp. 149–173). Cambridge, England: Cambridge University Press.

STANOVICH, K. E. (1986). Matthew effects in reading: Some consequences of individual differences in the acquisition of literacy. *Reading Research Quarterly, 21,* 360–406.

STANOVICH, K. E. (2000). In M. L. Kamii, & P. B. Mosenthal (Ed.), *Handbook of reading research, vol. III.* Mahway, NJ: Erlbaum.

STARK, R., & TALLAL, P. (1981). Selection of children with specific language deficits. *Journal of Speech and Hearing Disorders, 46,* 114–122.

STECKOL, K., & LEONARD, L. (1979). The use of grammatical morphemes by normal and language-impaired children. *Journal of Communication Disorders, 12,* 291–301.

STEIN, N. L. (1988). The development of children's storytelling skill. In M. B. Franklin & S. Barten (Eds.), *Child language: A book of readings* (pp. 282–297). New York: Oxford University Press.

STEIN, N. L., & GLENN, C. G. (1979). An analysis of story comprehension in elementary school children. In R. O. Freedle (Ed.), *New directions in discourse processing: Vol. 2. Advances in discourse processes* (pp. 53–120). Norwood, NJ: Ablex.

STEMBERGER, J. P. (1992). A connectionist view of child phonology phonological processing without phonological processes. In C. A. Ferguson, L. Menn, & C. Stoel-Gammon (Eds.), *Phonological development* (pp. 165–189). Timonium, MD: York Press.

STERN, C., & STERN, W. (1907). *Die Kindersprache.* Leipzig, Germany: Barth.

STERNBERG, R. J. (1987). Most vocabulary is learned from context. In M. G. McKeown & M. E. Curtis (Eds.), *The nature of vocabulary acquisition* (pp. 89–106). Hillsdale, NJ: Erlbaum.

STEVENS, G. (2004). Using census data to test the critical-period hypothesis for second-language acquisition. *Psychological Science, 15,* 215–216.

STILES, J., BATES, E. A., THAL, D., TRAUNER, D., & REILLY, J. (1998). Linguistic, cognitive, and affective development in children with pre- and perinatal focal brain injury: A ten-year overview from the San Diego longitudinal project. In C. Rovee-Collier, L. Lipsitt, & H. Hayne (Eds.), *Advances in Infancy Research* (Vol. 12, pp. 131–164). Stamford, CT: Ablex Publishing Corporation.

STILES, J., & THAL, D. (1993). Linguistic and spatial cognitive development following early focal brain injury: Patterns of deficit and recovery. In M. H. Johnson (Ed.), *Brain development and cognition: A reader* (pp. 643–664). Oxford: Blackwell.

STOEL-GAMMON, C., & COOPER, J. (1984). Patterns of early lexical and phonological development. *Journal of Child Language, 11,* 247–271.

STOEL-GAMMON, C., & OTOMO, K. (1986). Babbling development of hearing-impaired and normally hearing subjects. *Journal of Speech and Hearing Disorders, 51,* 33–41.

STOKOE, W. C., CASTERLINE, D. C., & CRONEBERG, C. G. (1965). *A dictionary of*

*American Sign Language on linguistic princi-ples.* Washington, DC: Gallaudet College Press.

STORCH, S. A. & WHITEHURST, G. J. (2001). In P. R. Britto & J. Brooks-Gunn, The role of family literacy environments in promoting young chil-dren's emerging literacy skills. *New directions for child and adolescent development, 104* (pp. 53–71). San Francisco:Jossey-Bass.

STORCH, S. A., & WHITEHURST, G. J. (2002). Oral language and code-related precursors to reading: Evidence from a longitudinal structural model. *Developmental Psychology, 38*, 934–947.

STROMSWOLD, K. (1998). The genetics of spo-ken language disorders. *Human Biology, 70,* 297–324.

STROMSWOLD, K. (2000). The cognitive neuro-science of language acquisition. In M. Gazzaniga (Ed.), *The new cognitive neurosciences* (2nd ed.) (pp. 909–932). Cambridge, MA: MIT Press.

STROMSWOLD, K. (2001). The heritability of language: A review and meta analysis of twin, adoption and linkage studies. *Language, 77,* 647–723.

STROMSWOLD, K., CAPLAN, D., ALPERT, N., & RAUSCH, S. (1996). Localization of syntactic comprehension by positron emission tomogra-phy. *Brain and Language, 52,* 452–473.

SUGARMAN, S. (1984). The development of pre-verbal communication: Its contribution and lim-its in promoting the development of language. In R. L. Schiefelbusch & J. Pickar (Eds.), *The acquisition of communicative competence* (pp. 23–68). Baltimore, MD: University Park Press.

SUGARMAN-BELL, S. (1978). Some organiza-tional aspects of preverbal communication. In I. Markova (Ed.), *The social context of lan-guage* (pp. 49–66). New York: Wiley.

SVIRSKY, M. A., ROBBINS, A. M., KIRK, K. I., PISONI, D., & MIYAMOTO, R. T. (2000). Lan-guage development in profoundly deaf chil-dren with cochlear implants. *Psychological Sci-ence, 11,* 153–158.

SWINGLEY, D., & ASLIN, R. N. (2000). Spoken word recognition and lexical representation in very young children. *Cognition, 76,* 147–166.

SWINGLEY, D., & FERNALD, A. (2002). Recogni-tion of words referring to present and absent objects by 24-month-olds. *Journal of Memory and Language, 461, 39–56.*

SWINGLEY, D., PINTO, J. P., & FERNALD, A. (1999). Continuous processing in word recog-nition at 24 months. *Cognition, 71,* 73–108.

TABORS, P. O. (1997). *One child, two languages: A guide for preschool educators of children learning English as a second language.* Balti-more: Paul H. Brookes.

TABORS, P. O., ROACH, K. A., & SNOW, C. E. (2001). In D. K. Dickinson & P. O. Tabors (Eds.).*Beginning literacy with language* (pp. 111–138). Baltimore: Paul H. Brookes.

TAGER-FLUSBERG, H. (1981). On the nature of linguistic functioning in early infantile autism. *Journal of Autism and Developmental Disor-ders, 11,* 45–56.

TAGER-FLUSBERG, H. (1985). The conceptual ba-sis for referential word meaning in children with autism. *Child Development, 56,* 1167–1178.

TAGER-FLUSBERG, H. (1989). A psycholinguistic perspective on language development in the autistic child. In G. Dawson (Ed.), *Autism: na-ture, diagnosis, and treatment* (pp. 92–115). New York: Guilford Press.

TAGER-FLUSBERG, H. (1993). What language re-veals about the understanding of minds in chil-dren with autism. In S. Baron-Cohen, H. Tager-Flusberg, & D. J. Cohen (Eds.), *Understanding other minds: Perspectives from autism* (pp. 139–157). Oxford: Oxford University Press.

TAGER-FLUSBERG, H. (1994). Dissociations in form and function in the acquisition of lan-guage by autistic children. In H. Tager-Flusberg (Ed.), *Constraints on language acquisition: Studies of atypical children* (pp. 175–194). Hillsdale, NJ: Erlbaum.

TAGER-FLUSBERG, H. (1999). Language acquisi-tion and theory of mind: Contributions from the study of autism. In L. B. Adamson & M. A. Romski (Eds.), *Communication and language acquisition: Discoveries from atypical develop-ment* (pp. 135–160). Baltimore: Brookes.

TAGER-FLUSBERG, H. & ANDERSON, M. (1991). The development of contingent discourse abil-ity in autistic children. *Journal of Child Psy-chology and Psychiatry, 32,* 1123–1134.

TAGER-FLUSBERG, H., CALKINS, S., NOLIN, T., BAUMBERGER, T., ANDERSON, M., & CHADWICK-DIAS, A. (1990). A longitudinal study of language acquisition in autistic and Down syndrome children. *Journal of Autism and Developmental Disorders, 20,* 1–21.

TAGER-FLUSBERG, H., & COOPER, J. (1999). Present and future possibilities for defining a phenotype for special language impairment. *Journal of Speech, Language, and Hearing Research, 42,* 1275–1278.

TAGER-FLUSBERG, H. (2001). Understanding the language and communicative impairments in autism. In L. M. Glidden (Ed.), *International review of research in mental retardation: Autism, vol. 23* (pp. 185–207). Boston: Academic Press.

TALLAL, P. (1978). An experimental investigation of the role of auditory temporal processing in normal and disordered language development. In A. Caramazza & E. B. Zurif (Eds.), *Language acquisition and language breakdown* (pp. 25–61). Baltimore: Johns Hopkins University Press.

TALLAL, P., ROSS, R., & CURTISS, S. (1989). Familial aggregation in specific language impairment. *Journal of Speech and Hearing Disorders, 54,* 167–173.

TALLAL, P., STARK, R. E., & MELLITS, E. D. (1985). Identification of language impaired children on the basis of rapid perception and reproduction skills. *Brain and Language, 25,* 314–322.

TALLAL, P. (2003). Language learning disabilities: Integrating research approaches. *Current Directions in Psychological Science, 12,* 206–212.

TALLAL, P., TOWNSEND, J., CURTISS, S., & WULFECK, B. (1991). Phenotypic profiles of language-impaired children based on genetic/family history. *Brain and Language, 41,* 81–95.

TALMY, L. (1985). Lexicalization patterns: semantic structure in lexical form. In T. Shopen (Ed.), *Language typology and syntactic description, Vol. 3: Grammatical categories and the lexicon* (pp. 57–149). Cambridge: Cambridge University Press.

TAMIS-LEMONDA, C., BORNSTEIN, M. H., KAHANA-KALMAN, R., BUAMWELL, L., & CYPHERS, L. (1998). Predicting variation in the timing of language milestones in the second year: an events history approach. *Journal of Child Language, 25,* 675–700.

TANNEN, D. (1982). *Spoken and written language: Exploring orality and literacy.* Norword, NJ: Ablex.

TANNEN, D. (1990). *You just don't understand: Men and women in conversation.* New York: Morrow.

TARDIF, T., GELMAN, S. A., & XU, F. (1999). Putting the "noun bias" in context: A comparison of Mandarin and English. *Child Development, 70,* 620–635.

TAYLOR, D. M. (1987). Social psychological barriers to effective childhood bilingualism. In P. Homel, M. Palij, & D. Aaronson (Eds.), *Childhood bilingualism: Aspects of linguistic, cognitive, and social development* (pp. 183–196). Hillsdale, NJ: Erlbaum.

TAYLOR, M., & GELMAN, S. A. (1988). Adjectives and nouns: Children's strategies for learning new words. *Child Development, 59,* 411–419.

TEALE, W. H. (1984). Reading to young children: Its significance for literacy development. In H. Goelman, A. Oberg, & F. Smith (Eds.), *Awakening to literacy* (pp. 110–121). Exeter: Heineman Education Books.

TEELE, D. W., KLEIN, J. O., ROSENER, B. A., & THE GREATER BOSTON OTITIS MEDIA STUDY GROUP. Otitis media with effusion during the first three years of life and development of speech and language. *Pediatrics, 74,* 282–287.

TEMPLIN, M. (1957). *Certain language skills in children.* University of Minnesota Institute of Child Welfare Monograph Series 26. Minneapolis: University of Minnesota Press.

TERRACE, H. S. (1979). *Nim.* New York: Knopf.

TERRACE, H. S., PETITTO, L. A., SANDERS, R. J., & BEVER, T. G. (1979). Can an ape create a sentence? *Science, 206,* 891–902.

THAL, D., BATES, E., & BELLUGI, U. (1989). Language and cognition in two children with Williams syndrome. *Journal of Speech and Hearing Research, 32,* 489–500.

THEAKSTON, A., LIEVEN, E., PINE, J., & ROWLAND, C. (2001). The role of performance limitations in the acquisition of verb-argument structure. *Journal of Child Language, 28*, 127–152.

THOMPSON, R. B. (1999). Gender differences in preschoolers' help-eliciting communication. *The Journal of Genetic Psychology, 160*, 357–368.

THIESSEN, E. D. & SAFFRAN, J. R. (2003). When cues collide: Use of stress and statistical cues to word boundaries by 7- to 9-month-old infants. *Developmental Psychology, 39*, 706–716.

TODD, L. (1974). *Pidgins and creoles*. London: Routledge & Kegan Paul.

TOLCHINSKY, L. & RAVID, D. (2002). Developing linguistic literacy: A comprehensive model. *Journal of Child Language, 29*, 417–447.

TOLKIEN, J. R. R. (1966). *The hobbit*. New York: Ballantine Books. (First published 1937.)

TOMASELLO, M. (1992a). Author's response: On defining language: Replies to Shatz and Ninio. *Social Development, 1*, 159–162.

TOMASELLO, M. (1992b). *First verbs: A case study of early grammatical development*. Cambridge, England: Cambridge University Press.

TOMASELLO, M. (1994). Can an ape understand a sentence? A review of *Language comprehension in ape and child* by E. S. Savage-Rumbaugh et al. *Language & Communication, 14*, 377–390.

TOMASELLO, M. (2000). Do young children have adult syntactic competence? *Cognition, 74*, 209–253.

TOMASELLO, M. (2001). Perceiving intentions and learning words in the second year of life. In M. Bowerman & S. C. Levinson (Eds.), *Language acquisition and conceptual development* (pp. 132–158). Cambridge: Cambridge University Press.

TOMASELLO, M. (2003). *Constructing a language*. Cambridge MA: Harvard University Press.

TOMASELLO, M., & BARTON, M. (1994). Learning words in non-ostensive context. *Developmental Psychology, 30*, 639–650.

TOMASELLO, M., CALL, J., NAGELL, K., OLGUIN, R., & CARPENTER, M. (1994). The learning and use of gestural signals by young chimpanzees: A trans-generational study. *Primates, 35*, 137–154.

TOMASELLO, M. & FARRAR, M. J. (1986). Joint attention and early language. *Child Development, 57*, 1454–1463.

TOMASELLO, M., FARRAR, M. J., & DINES, J. (1984). Children's speech revisions for a familiar and an unfamiliar adult. *Journal of Speech and Hearing Research, 27*, 359–363.

TOMASELLO, M., & MANNLE, S. (1985). Pragmatics of sibling speech of one-year-olds. *Child Development, 56*, 911–917.

TOMASELLO, M., MANNLE, S., & KRUGER, A. C. (1986). Linguistic environment of 1- to 2-year-old twins. *Developmental Psychology, 22*, 169–176.

TOMASELLO, M., & TODD, J. (1983). Joint attention and lexical acquisition style. *First Language, 4*, 197–212.

TOMASELLO, M. (2003). *Constructing a language: A usage-based theory of language acquisition*. Cambridge, MA: Harvard University Press.

TOMBLIN, J. B. (1989). Familial concentration of developmental language impairment. *Journal of Speech and Hearing Disorders, 54*, 287–295.

TOMBLIN, J. B., RECORDS, N. L., & ZHANG, X. (1996). A system for the diagnosis of specific language impairment in kindergarten children. *Journal of Speech and Hearing Research, 39*, 1284–1294.

TOUGH, J. (1977). *The development of meaning*. London: Unwin Education Books.

TOUGH, J. (1982). Language, poverty, and disadvantage in school. In L. Feagans & D. C. Farran (Eds.), *The language of children reared in poverty: Implications for evaluation and intervention* (pp. 3–18). New York: Academic Press.

TRAUB, J. (1999). The bilingual barrier. *The New York Times Magazine*. January 31.

TREHUB, S. E. (1973). Infants' sensitivity to vowel and tonal contrasts. *Developmental Psychology, 9*, 91–96.

TREHUB, S. E. (1976). The discrimination of foreign speech contrasts by infants and adults. *Child Development, 47*, 466–472.

TREIMAN, R. (1985). Onsets and rimes as units of spoken syllables: Evidence from children. *Journal of Experimental Child Psychology, 39*, 181–191.

TREMBLAY, P. F., & GARDNER, R. C. (1995). Expanding the motivation construct in language learning. *The Modern Language Journal, 79*, 505–518.

TREVARTHEN, C., & HUBLEY, P. (1978). Secondary intersubjectivity: Confidence, confiding and acts of meaning in the first year. In A. Lock (Ed.), *Action, gesture and symbol: The emergence of language.* New York: Academic Press.

TWENEY, R. D., HOEMAN, H. W., & ANDREWS, C. E. (1975). Semantic organization in deaf and hearing subjects. *Journal of Psycholinguistic Research, 4,* 61–73.

TYLER, A., & NAGY, W. (1989). The acquisition of English derivational morphology. *Journal of Memory and Language, 28,* 649–667.

TYLER, R. S., & SUMMERFIELD, A. Q. (1996). Cochlear implantation: Relationships with research on auditory deprivation and acclimatization. *Ear and Hearing, 17,* 38–50.

ULLMAN, M. T., CORKIN, S., COPPOLA, M., HICKOK, G. GROWDON, J. H., KOROSHETZ, W. J., & PINKER, S. (1997). A neural dissociation within language: Evidence that the mental dictionary is part of declarative memory, and that grammatical rules are processed by the procedural system. *Journal of Cognitive Neuroscience, 9,* 266–276.

ULLMAN, M. T., & GOPNIK, M. (1999). Inflectional morphology in a family in inherited specific language impairment. *Applied Psycholinguistics, 20,* 51–118.

UMBEL, V. M., PEARSON, B. Z., FERNANDEZ, S. C., & OLLER, D. K. (1992). Measuring bilingual children's receptive vocabularies. *Child Development, 63,* 1012–1020.

UMIKER-SEBEOK, D. J. (1979). Preschool children's intraconversational narratives. *Journal of Child Language, 6,* 91–109.

URWIN, C. (1978). The development of communication between blind infants and their parents. In A. Lock (Ed.), *Action, gesture, and symbol: The emergence of language* (pp. 79–108). London: Academic Press.

VAID, J. & HALL, D. G. (1991). Neurpsychological perspectives on bilingualism: Right, left, and center. In A. G. Reynolds (Ed.), *Bilingualism, multiculturalism, and second language learning.* (pp. 81–112). Hillsdale, NJ: Lawrence Erlbaum.

VALIAN, V. (1986). Syntactic categories in the speech of young children. *Developmental Psychology, 22,* 562–579.

VALIAN, V. (1991). Syntactic subjects in the early speech of American and Italian children. *Cognition, 40,* 21–81.

VALIAN, V., & LYMAN, C. (2003). Young children's acquisition of wh-questions: the role of structured input. *Journal of Child Language, 30,* 117–144.

VANDELL, D., & WILSON, K. (1987). Infants' interactions with mother, sibling, and peer: Contrasts and relations between interaction systems. *Child Development, 58,* 176–186.

VAN DER LELY, H. K. J. (1994). Canonical linking rules: Forward vs. reverse linking in normally developing and specifically language impaired children. *Cognition, 51,* 29–72.

VAN DER LELY, H. K. J. (2003). Do heterogeneous deficits require heterogeneous theories? SLI subgroups and RDDR hypothesis. In Y. Levy & J. Schaeffer (Eds.), *Language competence across populations: Toward a definition of specific language impairment* (pp. 109–134). Mahwah, NJ: Erlbaum.

VAN DER LELY, H. K. J., & HOWARD, D. (1993). Children with specific language impairment: Linguistic impairment or short-term memory deficit? *Journal of Speech and Hearing Research, 36,* 1193–1207.

VAN VALIN, R. D. (1991). Functionalist linguistic theory and language acquisition. *First Language, 11,* 7–40.

VARGHA-KHADEM, F., O'GORMAN, A. M., & WATTERS, G. V. (1985). Aphasia and handedness in relation to hemispheric side, age at injury and severity of cerebral lesion during childhood. *Brain, 108,* 677–696.

VARGHA-KHADEM, F., WATKINS, K., ALCOCK, K., FLETCHER, P., & PASSINGHAM, R. (1995). Praxic and nonverbal cognitive deficits in a large family with a genetically transmitted speech and language disorder. *Proceedings of the National Academy of Sciences of the United States, 92,* 930–934.

VELLEMAN, S., MANGIPUDI, L., & LOCKE, J. L. (1989). Prelinguistic phonetic contingency. *First Language, 9,* 169–173.

VIHMAN, M. M. (1988a). Early phonological development. In J. Bernthal & N. Bambson (Eds.), *Articulation and phonological disorders* (2nd ed., pp. 60–109). New York: Prentice-Hall.

VIHMAN, M. M. (1988b). Later phonological development. In J. Bernthal & N. Bambson (Eds.), *Articulation and phonological disorders* (2nd ed., pp. 110–144). New York: Prentice-Hall.

VIHMAN, M. M. (1993). Variable paths to early word production. *Journal of Phonetics, 21,* 61–82.

VIHMAN, M. M. (1996). *Phonological development: The origins of language in the child.* Cambridge, MA: Blackwell.

VOLTERRA, V., & TAESCHNER, T. (1978). The acquisition and development of language by bilingual children. *Journal of Child Language, 5,* 311–326.

VON FRISCH, K. (1962). Dialects in the language of the bees. *Scientific American, 207,* 79–87.

VYGOTSKY, L. (1962). *Thought and language.* Cambridge, MA: MIT Press.

VYGOTSKY, L. (1978). In M. Cole, V. John-Steiner, S. Scribner, & E. Souberman (Eds.), *Mind in society: The development of higher mental processes.* Cambridge, MA: Harvard University Press. (Original work published 1930, 1933, 1935.)

WAGNER, R. K., & TORGESEN, J. K. (1987). The nature of phonological processing and its causal role in the acquisition of reading skills. *Psychological Bulletin, 101,* 192–212.

WAGNER, R. K., TORGESEN, J. K., RASHOTTE, C.A., HECHT, S. A., BARKER, T. A., BURGESS, S. R., DONAHUE, J. & GARON, T. (1997). Changing relations between phonological processing abilities and word-level reading as children develop from beginning to skilled readers: A 5-year longitudinal study. *Developmental Psychology, 33,* 468–479.

WALLACE, I. F., GRAVEL, J. S., MCCARTON, C. M., & RUBEN, R. J. (1988). Otitis media and language development at 1 year of age. *Journal of Speech and Hearing Disorders, 53,* 245–251.

WALLEY, A. C. (1993). The role of vocabulary development in children's spoken word recognition and segmentation ability. *Developmental Review, 13,* 286–350.

WALLMAN, J. (1992). *Aping language.* Cambridge, England: Cambridge University Press.

WARREN, A. R., & TATE, C. S. (1992). Egocentrism in children's telephone conversations. In R. M. Diaz & L. E. Berk (Eds.), *Private speech: From social interaction to self-regulation* (pp. 245–266). Hillsdale, NJ: Erlbaum.

WARREN, S. F., & REICHLE, J. (Eds.). (1992). *Causes and effects in communication and language intervention* (Vol. 1). Baltimore, MD: Paul H. Brookes.

WATKINS, R. (1997). The linguistic profile of SLI: Implications for accounts of language acquisition. In L. Adamson & M. A. Romski (Eds.), *Communication and language acquisition: Discoveries from atypical development* (pp. 161–186). Baltimore, MD: Paul H. Brookes.

WATSON, R. (2002). Literacy and oral language: implications for early literacy acquisition. In S. B. Neuman & D. K. Dickinson (Eds.), *Handbook of early literacy research* (pp. 81–96). New York: The Guilford Press.

WAXMAN, S. R. (1994). The development of an appreciation of specific linkages between linguistic and conceptual organization. In L. Gleitman & B. Landau (Eds.), *The acquisition of the lexicon* (pp. 229–258). Cambridge, MA: MIT Press/Elsevier.

WAXMAN, S. R., & MARKOW, D. B. (1995). Words as invitations to form categories: Evidence from 12- to 13-month-old infants. *Cognitive Psychology, 29,* 257–303.

WAXMAN, S. R. (1994). The development of an appreciation of specific linkages between linguistic and conceptual organization. *Lingua, 92,* 229–257.

WEBER-FOX, C. M., & NEVILLE, H. J. (1996). Maturational constraints on functional specializations for language processing: ERP and behavioral evidence in bilingual speakers. *Journal of Cognitive Neuroscience, 8,* 231–256.

WEINER, P. (1974). A language-delayed child at adolescence. *Journal of Speech and Hearing Disorders, 39,* 202–212.

WEIR, R. H. (1962). *Language in the crib*. The Hague, The Netherlands: Mouton.

WEISMER, S. E. (1985). Constructive comprehension abilities exhibited by language-disordered children. *Journal of Speech and Hearing Research, 28,* 175–184.

WEISMER, S. E., EVANS, J., & HESKETH, L. J. (1999). An examination of verbal working memory capacity in children with specific language impairment. *Journal of Speech, Language, and Hearing Research, 42,* 1249–1260.

WEIZMAN, Z. O. & SNOW, C. E. (2001). Lexical input as related to children's vocabulary acquisition: Effects of sophisticated exposure and support for meaning. *Developmental Psychology, 37,* 265–279.

WELLMAN, H. M., & LEMPERS, J. D. (1977). The naturalistic communicative abilities of two-year-olds. *Child Development, 48,* 1052–1057.

WELLS, G. (1985). Preschool literacy-related activities and success in school. In D. R. Olson, N. Torrance, & A. Hildyard (Eds.), *Literacy, language, and learning* (pp. 229–255). Cambridge, England: Cambridge University Press.

WERKER, J., LLOYD, V., COHEN, B., & CASASOLA, M. (1998). Acquisition of word-object associations by 14-month-old infants. *Developmental Psychology, 34, 6,*1289–1309.

WERKER, J. F., GILBERT, J. H. V., HUMPHREY, K., & TEES, R. C. (1981). Developmental aspects of cross-language speech perception. *Child Development, 52,* 349–355.

WERKER, J. F., & POLKA, L. (1993). Developmental changes in speech perception: New challenges and new directions. *Journal of Phonetics, 21,* 83–101.

WERKER, J. F., & TEES, R. C. (1984). Cross-language speech perception: Evidence for perceptual reorganization during the first year of life. *Infant Behavior and Development, 7,* 49–63.

WERKER, J. F., FENNELL, C. T., CORCORAN, K. M., & STAGER, C. L. (2002). Infants' ability to learn phonetically similar words: Effects of age and vocabulary size. *Infancy, 3,* 1–30.

WERKER, J. F., PEGG, J. E., & MCLEOD, P. J. (1994). A cross-language investigation of infant preference for infant-directed communication. *Infant Behavior & Development 17,* 323–333.

WERTSCH, J. (1985). *Vygotsky and the social formation of mind.* Cambridge, MA: Harvard University Press.

WEST, C., & ZIMMERMAN, D. (1977). Women's place in everyday talk: Reflections on parent–child interaction. *Social Problems, 24,* 521–529.

WEXLER, K. (2003). Lenneberg's dream: learning, normal language development, and specific language impairment. In Y. Levy & J. Schaeffer, J. (Eds.) *Language competence across populations: Toward a definition of specific language impairment* (pp. 11–62). Mahwah, NJ: Erlbaum.

WEYLMAN, S. T., BROWNELL, H. H., & GARDNER, H. (1988). "It's what you mean, not what you say": Pragmatic language use in brain-damaged patients. In F. Plum (Ed.), *Language, communication, and the brain* (pp. 229–244). New York: Raven.

WHITE, L. (1996). The tale of the ugly duckling (or: the coming of age of second language acquisition research). In D. Cahana-Arnitay, L. Hughes, A. Stringfellow, & A. Zukowske (Eds.), *Proceedings of the 20th Boston University Conference on Language Development.* Somerville, MA: Cascadilla Press.

WHITEHURST, G. J., & LONIGAN, C. J. (1998). Child development and emergent literacy. *Child Development, 69,* 848–872.

WILBUR, R. B. (1979). *American Sign Language and sign systems.* Baltimore, MD: University Park Press.

WILCOX, M. J., & WEBSTER, E. J. (1980). Early discourse behavior: An analysis of children's responses to listener feedback. *Child Development, 51,* 1120–1125.

WILSON, S. (2003). Lexically specific constructions in the acquisition of inflection of English. *Journal of Child Language, 30(1), p.* 75–115.

WIMMER, H., LANDERL, K., LINORTNER, R., & HUMMER, P. (1991). The relationship of phonemic awareness to reading acquisition: More consequence than precondition but still important. *Cognition, 40,* 219–249.

WINDSOR, J., & HWANG, M. (1999a). Testing the generalized slowing hypothesis in specific language impairment. *Journal of Speech, Language, and Hearing Research, 42,* 1205–1218.

WINDSOR, J., & HWANG, M. (1999b). Children's auditory lexical decisions: A limited processing capacity account of language impairment. *Journal of Speech, Language, and Hearing Research, 42,* 990–1002.

WINNER, E., ROSENSTIEL, A.,K. & GARDNER, H. (1976). The development of metaphoric understanding. *Developmental Psychology. 12,* 289–297.

WINNER, E., GARDNER, H., SILBERSTEIN, L., & MEYER, C. (1988). Creating a world with words. In F. S. Kessel (Ed.), *The development of language and language researchers: Essays in honor of Roger Brown* (pp. 353–372). Hillsdale, NJ: Erlbaum.

WINSLER, A., CARLTON, M. P., BARRY, M. J. (2000). Age-related changes in preschool children's systematic use of private speech in a natural setting. *Journal of Child Language, 27,* 665–688.

WINSLER, A., DE LEON, J. R., WALLACE, B. A., CARLTON, M. P., & WILLSON-QUAYLE, A. (2003). Private speech in preschool children: developmental stability and change, across-task consistency and relations with classroom behavior. *Journal of Child Language, 30,* 583–609.

WITELSON, S. F. (1977). Early hemisphere specialization and interhemispheric plasticity: An empirical and theoretical review. In S. J. Segalowitz & F. A. Gruber (Eds.), *Language development and neurological theory* (pp. 213–289). New York: Academic Press.

WITELSON, S. F. (1987). Neurobiological aspects of language in children. *Child Development, 58,* 653–688.

WOLF, M., BOWERS, G. B., & BIDDLE, K. (2000). Naming speech processes, timing, and reading: A conceptual overview. *Journal of Learning Disabilities, 33,* 387–407.

WONG FILLMORE, L. (1991). When learning a second language means losing the first. *Early Childhood Research Quarterly, 6,* 323–346.

WOOD, C. C. (1976). Discriminability, response bias, and phoneme categories in discrimination of voice onset time. *Journal of the Acoustical Society of America, 60,* 1381–1389.

WOOD, C. C., GOFF, W., & DAY, R. (1971). Auditory evoked potential during speech perception. *Science, 173,* 1248–1251.

WOOD, D., WOOD, H., & MIDDLETON, D. (1978). An experimental evaluation of four face-to-face teaching strategies. *International Journal of Behavioral Development, 1,* 131–147.

WOOD, H., & WOOD, D. (1992). Signed English in the classroom: IV. Aspects of children's speech and sign. *First Language, 12,* 125–145.

WOODS, B. T., & CAREY, S. (1979). Language deficits after apparent clinical recovery from childhood aphasia. *Annals of Neurology, 6,* 405–409.

WOODS, B. T., & TEUBER, H. L. (1978). Changing patterns of childhood aphasia. *Annals of Neurology, 3,* 273–280.

WOODWARD, A. L., & MARKMAN, E. M. (1998). Early word learning. In D. Kuhn & R. S. Siegler (Eds.), *Handbook of child psychology: Vol. 2. Cognition, perception, and language* (5th ed., pp. 371–420). New York: Wiley.

WOODWARD, A. L., MARKMAN, E. M., & FITZSIMMONS, C. M. (1994). Rapid word learning in 13- and 18-month-olds. *Developmental Psychology, 30,* 553–566.

WORDEN, R. (1998). The evolution of langauge from social intelligence. In J. R. Hurford, M. Studdert-Kennedy, & C. Knight (Eds.), *Approaches to the evolution of language* (pp. 148–168). Cambridge: Cambridge University Press.

WRANGHAM, R. W., MCGREW, W. C., DE WAAL, F. B. M., & HELTNE, P. G. (1994). *Chimpanzee culture.* Cambridge, MA: Harvard University Press.

XU, F., & CAREY, S. (1995). Do children's first object kind names map onto adult-like conceptual representations? In D. MacLaughlin & S. McEwen (Eds.), *Proceedings of the 19th Annual Boston University Conference on Lan-*

*guage Development* (pp. 679–688). Somerville, MA: Cascadilla Press.

XU, F., & CAREY, S. (1996).   Infants' metaphysics: The case of numerical identity. *Cognitive Psychology, 30,* 111–153.

YAMADA, J. E. (1990).   *Laura: A case for the modularity of language.* Cambridge, MA: MIT Press.

YOSHIOKA, J. G. (1929).   A study of bilingualism. *Journal of Genetic Psychology, 36,* 473–479.

ZAIDEL, E. (1985).   Language in the right hemisphere. In D. F. Benson & E. Zaidel (Eds.), *The dual brain: Hemispheric specialization in humans* (pp. 205–232). New York: Guilford Press.

ZIATAS, K., DURKIN, K., & PRATT, C. (2003). Differences in assertive speech acts produced by children with autism, Asperger syndrome, specific language impairment, and normal development. *Development and Psychopathology, 15,* 73–94.

ZUKOW, P. G. (1990).   Socio-perceptual bases for the emergence of language: An alternative to innatist approaches. *Developmental Psychobiology, 23,* 705–726.

ZURIF, E. B. (1995).   Brain regions of relevance to syntactic processing. In L. R. Gleitman & M. Liberman (Eds.), *Language: An invitation to cognitive science* (Vol. 1, 2nd ed., pp. 381–398). Cambridge, MA: MIT Press.

# PHOTO CREDITS

# Name Index

# SUBJECT INDEX

## TO THE OWNER OF THIS BOOK:

I hope that you have found *Language Development*, Third Edition useful. So that this book can be improved in a future edition, would you take the time to complete this sheet and return it? Thank you.

School and address:_____

Department:_____

Instructor's name:_____

1. What I like most about this book is:_____

   _____

   _____

2. What I like least about this book is:

   _____

   _____

3. My general reaction to this book is:

   _____

   _____

4. The name of the course in which I used this book is:

   _____

5. Were all of the chapters of the book assigned for you to read?_____

   If not, which ones weren't?_____

6. In the space below, or on a separate sheet of paper, please write specific suggestions for improving this book and anything else you'd care to share about your experience in using this book.

   _____

   _____

   _____

## BUSINESS REPLY MAIL
FIRST-CLASS MAIL    PERMIT NO. 102    MONTEREY CA

POSTAGE WILL BE PAID BY ADDRESSEE

Attn:  Vicki Knight/Psychology Publisher

Wadsworth/Thomson Learning
60 Garden Ct  Ste 205
Monterey CA  93940-9967

- - - - - - - - - - - - - - - - - - - - - - - - - - - - - - - - -

FOLD HERE

OPTIONAL:

Your name:_____ Date: _____

May we quote you, either in promotion for *Language Development*, Third Edition,
or in future publishing ventures?

Yes: _____   No: _____

Sincerely yours,

Erika Hoff